A Queer Thing Happened to America

A Queer Thing Happened to America

And what a long, strange trip it's been

MICHAEL L. BROWN

EqualTime Books

Concord, North Carolina

A Queer Thing Happened To America
Copyright © by Michael L. Brown, 2011

EqualTime Books
PO Box 5546
Concord, NC 28027

ISBN-10: 0615406092
ISBN-13: 978-0615406091

Printed in the United States of America
2011, First Edition

"The ultimate test of a moral society
is the kind of world that it leaves to its children."

Dietrich Bonhoeffer

CONTENTS

	Preface	**9**
	Introduction	**15**
Chapter 1	A Stealth Agenda	**21**
Chapter 2	Jewish Hitlers, Christian Jihadists, and the Magical Effects of Pushing the "Hate" Button	**53**
Chapter 3	Boys Will Be Girls Will Be Boys: Undoing Gender and Teaching "Gay is Good" in Our Children's Schools	**85**
Chapter 4	Something Queer on Our Campuses: From Traditional Academics and the Arts to GLBTQ and "Ze"	**121**
Chapter 5	Brokeback Mountain, the Fab Five and Hollywood's Celebration of Queer	**153**
Chapter 6	Is Gay the New Black? Analyzing the Argument That "I Was Born That Way"	**197**
Chapter 7	Speaking of the Unspeakable: Some Disturbing Parallels to Pro-Gay Arguments	**227**
Chapter 8	Diversity or Perversity? Corporate America's Embrace of Gay Pride at Its Worst	**273**
Chapter 9	Lavender Language, Gender Speak, and Queer Semantics: Towards an Omnisexual Society?	**309**
Chapter 10	Queer Theology, a Gay/Lesbian Bible, and a Homoerotic Christ	**339**
Chapter 11	So, It's Not About Sex? The Attempt to Separate Behavior from Identity	**373**

Chapter 12   The "Ex-Gay" Movement: Fact or Fiction?   **419**

Chapter 13   The Stifling of Scientific Debate   **455**

Chapter 14   Big Brother is Watching,
and He Really Is Gay   **495**

Chapter 15   GLBT and Beyond: Reflections
on Our Current Trajectory   **549**

Further Resources   **600**
Endnotes   **601**
Note on Bibliography and Index   **691**

PREFACE

An Associated Press article published in October, 2003 noted that the word "queer," which originally was "a synonym for 'odd' or 'unusual' . . . evolved into an anti-gay insult in the last century, only to be reclaimed by defiant gay and lesbian activists who chanted: 'We're here, we're queer, get used to it.'" Today, however, "'queer' is sneaking into the mainstream – and taking on a hipster edge as a way to describe any sexual orientation beyond straight." Indeed, "queer" has become so mainstream that, not only was the *Queer Eye for the Straight Guy* TV show a big hit, but in June, 2005, the gay stars of the show actually threw out the opening pitch of a Boston Red Sox game. Talk about a cultural shift! And it is a shift that is affecting virtually every area of American society.

In October, 2006, New York City's Metropolitan Transit Authority legalized the use of the ladies' bathrooms for men who identified as women (and vice versa), with one article running the headline, "Be careful, ladies – it's his bathroom, too." In San Francisco schools, a boy who identifies as a girl can use the girl's bathroom and locker room, while the *New York Times* reported (December, 2006) that at the Park Day School in Oakland, California, "teachers are taught a gender-neutral vocabulary and are urged to line up students by sneaker color rather than by gender." In Charlotte, North Carolina, a pre-school teacher shared with me that she was not allowed to address the children as "boys and girls," since that would be making a gender distinction. Instead, she had to call them "friends."

On August 16, 2010, *Newsweek* asked the question, "Are We Facing a Genderless Future?" One year earlier, Newsweek featured a major article on "relationships with multiple, mutually consenting partners." The article, entitled, "Polyamory: The Next Sexual Revolution," stated, "It's enough to make any monogamist's head spin. But the traditionalists had better get used to it." Just two years before that (2007), *Time Magazine* raised the question, "Should Incest Be Legal?", and in December, 2010, when Columbia University professor David Epstein was arrested for a three-year, consensual affair with his adult daughter, his attorney noted, "It's OK for homosexuals to do whatever they want in their own home. How is this so different? We have to figure out why some behavior is tolerated and some is not." Not surprisingly, some Columbia students asked why any sexual acts committed by consenting adults should be considered a crime.

In September, 2004, the convocation address for the 150th anniversary of the Chicago Theological Seminary was delivered by a gay professor and focused on a "Queer Reading" of the Bible. In 2006, the 859 page *Queer Bible Commentary* was published, while gay Reform Jews now have a prayer book featuring a blessing to be recited after an anonymous sexual encounter. And the list goes on and on.

It is the purpose of this book to see how we got to this point in history, to examine some of the main lines of pro-gay thought, to consider the impact of gay activism on our society, and to ask the question: Where is the current trajectory taking us?

But to ask that question – even in a respectful, fair-minded way – is to ask for trouble. As a colleague told me a few years ago, to take issue on any level with gay activism is to commit professional suicide. My e-correspondence over the last six years (during which time I have been working on this book in the midst of other writing and speaking responsibilities) only confirms those words.

A conservative pundit wrote: "Book publishing is a difficult business now, and no media is willing to promote a book that opposes homosexuality. . . . Economic self-interest is going to make it very tough for a publisher to say yes." In keeping with this, a conservative publisher explained to me that "there would be a very concrete, though difficult to measure financial penalty to pay for publishing your book. . . . Practically speaking it could actually destroy the firm . . . Of course no library would carry your book." (We shall see if the last statement proves true.)

Similarly, a bestselling conservative author opined: "Honestly, there is no NY publisher . . . who will touch this manuscript." Another insider explained that, if the project was subsidized generously, he wouldn't be afraid to publish it. Otherwise, he said, "I'd be better off burning the money in my fireplace. . . . The economics of publishing a book like this are bleak." At the same time, of course, I was hearing from the GLBT community that there is no gay activist pressure to silence opposing ideas. How ironic!

Although I had never used a literary agent before, despite having written twenty books with solid publishers, I agreed to work with a leading agent who was willing to take on the book. After several months, however, his secretary wrote to me explaining that, of the major publishers to whom they had offered the book, none would take it on: "Most thought the material was too controversial....all felt that the title would need to be changed."

Too controversial? The title needed to be changed? This is the day of TV shows like *Queer Eye for the Straight Guy* and of books like *Queering Elementary Education* and *The Queer Bible Commentary*. This is the day in which major bookstore chains proudly carry volumes featuring what can only be called gay pornography. Yet I was told that the title of my book needed to be changed and the material was too controversial. Amazing! So, after much consideration, we decided to launch our own imprint, EqualTime Books. The name of the company says it all.

When it came to working directly with a publicity firm (also something I had never done before), the story was the same. I was told confidentially by a friend in the business that it would be very costly for him to schedule interviews on this subject, since he would lose clients over it. Another publicity firm (that I did not solicit but rather was introduced to me) was not able to find a single person in their company willing to take the book on. And in all these discussions, not a syllable was ever raised to me disputing the accuracy or quality of the book. It was simply too hot to handle. What happened to "tolerance" and "diversity"?

I'm aware, of course, that I touch on many sensitive, even volatile, issues, and it is easy to pull a quote out of context or to read into my words something that I have not written. May I, then, ask each of you to approach this book with an open heart and mind, reading (and quoting) everything in context? And to my detractors, may I ask you be kind enough to differ with what I actually wrote, not what you might feel I wrote?

One reason for the length of this book is that I was determined to let GLBT advocates and allies speak for themselves, always providing ample reference to sources that would support their views. (Given that my doctoral work was in ancient Near Eastern languages and literatures, it is my habit to be somewhat meticulous in research and documentation, striving for objectivity. Hopefully, the reader will be rewarded by the efforts that have been made.) Those looking for a right-wing diatribe based on unreliable, second-hand sources will have to look elsewhere, as will those looking for an angry, mean-spirited screed. In fact, in the pages that follow, the reason there is no anger or hatred in my words is because there is no anger or hatred in my heart.

That being said, I fully expect to be vilified by many for writing this book, but that can hardly deter someone from honest research and writing. In fact, it was Randy Shilts the late, acclaimed, gay journalist, explaining why a reporter must rise above criticism, who wrote: "I can only answer that I tried to tell the truth and, if not be objective, at least be fair; history is not served when reporters prize trepidation and propriety over the robust journalistic duty to tell the whole story." (Cited in the *Los Angeles Times*, February 18, 1994, A-1.) I too share those sentiments, feeling deeply committed "to tell the whole story," regardless of cost or consequences, ever mindful of the old Russian proverb popularized by Alexander Solzhenitsyn, "One word of truth outweighs the whole world."

* * *

It is my pleasure to express appreciation to Kermit Rainman, Steve Alt, and Donald Enevoldsen, for carefully reading the manuscript, catching many errors, and making many helpful editorial suggestions. And I am indebted to a gentleman with unwanted same-sex attractions for reviewing the manuscript in microscopic detail and sending me (literally) thousands of references to check and sources to examine. My appreciation is also extended to Joseph P. Infranco, Senior VP of Allied Attorney Coordination and Senior Attorney of the Alliance Defense Fund, for carefully reviewing the entire manuscript with special attention to his related areas of expertise, and to Robert Knight, Senior Writer for Coral Ridge Ministries, for reviewing Chapter Five. Other chapters (in whole or in part) were reviewed by philosophers, attorneys, educators, psychologists, activists, and religious leaders who remain nameless. My thanks also go to my close friends and colleagues in the FIRE Church community who have been sources of unflinching support and solidarity. Special appreciation is always reserved for Nancy, my wife and best friend of thirty-five years, an unfailing beacon of truth without compromise and a well of never-ending compassion. I have never known anyone who shed so many tears for hurting souls in this world.

With regard to references and citations, note that I use LGBT and GLBT interchangeably; that I rechecked many of the Internet citations in the final months of editing and proofing so as to provide working web addresses whenever possible; that I did not add sic to the scores of typos and grammatical errors in sources copied from online articles and posts; that I attempted to make uniform the style used when citing academic journal articles (which vary from field to field) but certainly did not attain complete consistency; and that books and articles are cited with full bibliographical data the first time they are introduced in each chapter, after which a short title is used within that chapter. A bibliography is provided on the book's website, AQueerThing.com, and it is possible that we will keep updating it in the future. The website also provides many practical ways in which you can get involved in the important moral, social, and spiritual issues discussed in the book.

For those readers intimidated by the length of the book, fear not. Virtually every chapter can be read on its own, and while I strongly encourage you to work through the contents of the book in order, since the chapters do build on each other, if reading 600 pages is a lot for you, feel free to jump around to points of special interest. As for the endnotes, those who like such things will profit from them; those who don't can safely ignore them.

Finally, a note about the cover: Those are not my legs and those are not my slippers (sorry to disappoint!), but I do think the graphics company, Roark Creative Group, came up with a very catchy design.

Now that you have picked up the book for yourself, whether drawn in by the cover, the title, the content, or the controversy, I hope and pray that it will have a positive and even life-changing impact on you. Feel free to share your thoughts with me at AQueerThing.com or AskDrBrown.org. The phone lines of my daily, talk radio show, the Line of Fire, are always open as well.

Michael L. Brown, January 15, 2011

INTRODUCTION

From Stonewall Inn to the White House: What a Long, Strange Trip It's Been

June 28, 1969, Greenwich Village, New York City, 1:20 AM.
The Stonewall riots begin.

Police had often raided gay bars in the city, including the Stonewall Inn, and it was always without resistance. But on this fateful night, things were different. The clientele fought back, and soon the police were dealing with a full-blown riot.

Interestingly, the primary reason for the police action that night was not the conduct of the homosexual patrons. To be sure, back in 1969, people of the same sex were not allowed to dance together in public and cross-dressing was illegal. But neither of those offenses sparked the Stonewall raid. Instead, the police were cracking down on the Mafia, using the bar's illegal selling of alcohol as the formal pretense for their actions.

Gay author David Eisenbach explains:

> As in most Mafia-run joints, the Stonewall operators exploited the opportunity to blackmail successful older patrons. A staff member would strike up a conversation with a successful-looking man, learning his name and profession. If the mark worked in a law firm or stock brokerage, he was later blackmailed with the threat of being outed to his colleagues. The discovery of this operation led to the famous Stonewall raid on June 28, 1969.
>
> Sometime in early 1969 INTERPOL, the UN-affiliated international police organization, noticed an unusual number of negotiable bonds surfacing in foreign countries and requested that the New York Police Department investigate whether they were counterfeit. Police detectives found

that the Mafia had been acquiring large numbers of bonds by blackmailing gay employees of New York banks. From studying police reports on various gay clubs, investigators concluded that the extortion rings were operating in Greenwich Village. The Stonewall . . . quickly became a prime suspect in a multimillion-dollar international criminal enterprise.[1]

The police were determined to shut the place down, and so during the raid, they actually tore up parts of the bar. In keeping with their customary routine, they also began to arrest the transvestites (who were accustomed to being booked and then released a few hours later) along with the bar staff. But the rest of the patrons, rather than heading over to another gay bar as they typically would have done, lingered outside, watching the events unfold and turning it into a festive event. Soon the crowd had grown to 150 interested onlookers.

But the good humor vanished when a police officer began shoving a transvestite who turned around and slammed the cop with his purse. Another officer rushed over and clubbed him with a nightstick. Moans and furious yells erupted from the crowd. One witness recalled, "People began beating the wagon, booing, trying to see who was being hauled out and off. Several pigs [cops] were on guard and periodically threatened the crowd unless they moved back. Impossible to do." One young man roared, "Nobody's going to f--- around with me. I ain't going to take this s---." Pennies pinged against the side of the paddy wagon punctuated by the loud slam of a beer can.[2]

As the police tried to arrest more patrons and push them into squad cars, "The whole crowd went berserk. 'Police brutality!' 'Pigs!' 'Up against the wall, faggots!' 'Beat it off, pigs!'"[3] Within minutes, the crowd was out of control and the police, fearing for their safety and not wanting to use their guns, retreated into the bar and barricaded themselves in, calling for reinforcements.

Outside, the crowd's frustration turned into rage. They had had it with their bars being raided. They had had it with being mistreated by the cops. Now it was time to fight back.

Someone hurled a garbage can through the bar window; gay patron Morty Manford later likened the shattering of glass to "the lancing of the festering wound of anger at this kind of unfair harassment and prejudice."[4] The cops were now under siege, trying to board up the windows with plywood as they continued to wait for reinforcements to arrive.

The bar door was smashed open, followed by a hail of beer cans and bottles, one of them striking a policeman and opening a bloody gash under his eye. Others in the crowd tried to set the building on fire, while another group ripped a parking meter from the pavement and used it as a battering ram to try and break through the door. Bricks were hurled at the cops and their vehicles. Chaos was erupting in the streets, and the crowd wanted blood.

> The mob became even more frenzied when someone in the crowd lit a trash can full of paper and stuffed it through one of the bar's windows, setting the coatroom ablaze. . . . A short, scrawny kid poured a can of lighter fluid through another broken window, followed by a match.[5]

The flames danced dangerously close to the lead officer, Inspector Pine. People were in a frenzy, and the impassioned, out of control crowd, feeling its power for the first time, was not about to stand down, even when two busloads of riot police arrived.

> Equipped with helmets, shields, and billy clubs, the riot police lined up shoulder to shoulder like Roman legions and pushed their way down Christopher Street. Squaring off against one of their flying wedges was a brave, if foolish, group of street kids who formed a Rockette-style kick line while singing,
>
> > We are the Stonewall girls,
> > We wear our hair in curls.
> > We wear no underwear:
> > We show our pubic hairs.
>
> The riot police charged into the kick line, smacking the singing youths with night sticks. Over the next hour, gay rioters dodged cops in the winding streets of the Village, setting fires in trash cans and breaking windows.[6]

News of the uprising spread rapidly (the media was intrigued by the fact that it was homosexuals – hitherto stereotyped as limp-wristed "fairies" – who were fighting back), and by the evening of the 28th, less than 24 hours after the initial raid, several thousand people had gathered in the Village proclaiming, "Gay Power," "We Want Freedom Now," and "Equality for Homosexuals." And rioting erupted again,[7] with police cars in particular becoming "the targets of the crowd's mounting aggression."[8] Once more, riot police were called in to quell the crowd. But a line had been crossed, and for the homosexual community, there was no turning back.

Thus the spark that ignited the gay liberation movement was lit: Two nights of rioting in response to a police raid; attacks on arresting officers and an attempt to injure them or even burn them alive; vandalizing of police cars; chaos on the streets . . . . This was the Stonewall uprising.

* * *

JUNE 29, 2009, WASHINGTON, DC, 7:00 PM

President Barack Obama welcomes 300 gay activists to the White House to commemorate the 40th anniversary of the Stonewall riots.

Addressing the enthusiastic gathering with the words, "Welcome to your White House," Barack Obama, the 44th president of the United States of America, spoke proudly of

> the story of the Stonewall protests, which took place 40 years ago this week, when a group of citizens – with few options and fewer supporters – decided they'd had enough and refused to accept a policy of wanton discrimination. And two men who were at those protests are here today. Imagine the journey that they've traveled.[9]

Yes, imagine the journey, from the Stonewall Inn, quite literally, to the White House. In the words of a famous Grateful Dead anthem, "Lately it occurs to me, what a long, strange trip it's been."[10]

A long, strange trip indeed. Perhaps even a queer trip. Or how else should we describe it when McDonald's – the ultimate, kids' fast-food chain, the world famous Mickey D's, the home of Ronald McDonald the clown – finds it appropriate to air a TV commercial proclaiming that, "Gay pride month commemorates the June 1969 rebellion of a courageous group of gay, lesbian and transgendered people who took action during a raid on New York City's Stonewall Inn." [11]

McDonald's celebrating the rebellion of a courageous group of gay, lesbian and transgendered people at Stonewall? The president commemorating a violent assault on police officers before a handpicked audience of 300 gay activists in the White House?

During his address, President Obama belittled those who "still hold fast to worn arguments and old attitudes" (like the notion that homosexual practice is wrong according to the Bible, or the idea that marriage is the union of a man and woman). And the president singled out Frank Kameny for special praise and appreciation – Frank Kameny, now in his 80's, a courageous gay rights pioneer[12] and a sexual libertarian of the most extreme kind, a man who wrote in 2008, "Let us have more and better enjoyment of more and better sexual perversions, by whatever definition, by more and more consenting adults"; and, "If bestiality with consenting animals provides happiness to some people, let them pursue their happiness"; and, "Let us have more and better enjoyment of more and better and harder-core pornography by those to whom such viewing provides happiness"; [13] a man who stated that the God of the Bible is a "sinful homophobic bigot" who needs to repent. [14] Of this man President Obama said, "And so we are proud of you, Frank, and we are grateful to you for your leadership"[15] Grateful for your leadership?

Yes, it really has been a long, strange, and, for many, quite unexpected trip thus far. But the story has just begun.

*The "Gay Agenda" is but one of the many lies promulgated
by radical religious political activists.*

The Rainbow Alliance

*The "gay agenda" is a term that has been coined for propaganda purposes
by the forces of religious fundamentalism. To enhance what they would
have others believe is the ominous dimension of this term,
they also refer to "the homosexual agenda."*

Jack Nichols, *The Gay Agenda*

*There is no "Gay Agenda." Stop mentioning this phantom
of the Religious Right. There are those people who care about civil rights
and those who do not. That is all. Nobody is trying to take over the world,
nobody wants "special rights," and nobody is trying to warp Western society
to suit his or her individual needs . . . . This is not a conspiracy.*

Posted by "Mayhemystic" on Plastic.com

THERE IS NO GAY AGENDA
Gays are just as much of a mixed bag as the rest of you nuts.

Posted on the pro gay-marriage website Pryhills: Living in Wholly Matrimony,

*Repeat after me: There is no homosexual agenda. There is no homosexual agenda.
There is no homosexual agenda.*

Posted by "Hadanelith" on Fstdt.com

1

A Stealth Agenda

s there really a homosexual agenda? Is there truly an insidious gay plot to undermine traditional values and subvert the American family? The very idea of it appears to be laughable – especially to the gay and lesbian community.

According to one source, identified only as "L.," this is the menacing and dangerous "gay agenda":

THE GAY AGENDA

7:45 a.m. Alarm rings
8:00 a.m.-8:10 a.m. Take shower
8:15 a.m.-8:30 a.m. Dress and put items

into briefcase
8:35 a.m. Leave house
8:45 a.m. Starbucks
9:00 a.m. Arrive at job
12:00 p.m. Lunch with a co-worker. Perhaps Chili's?
12:45 p.m. Return to job
1:30 p.m. - 2:30 p.m. Meeting
5:00 p.m. Leave work
5:30 p.m. - 6:30 p.m. Work out in gym
7:00 p.m. Return home
7:20 p.m. Prepare and eat dinner
8:00 p.m. Watch Law & Order on TNT
11:00 p.m. Go to sleep[1]

Do you detect just a little sarcasm? Then consider this anonymous, widely-circulated posting:

THE GAY AGENDA
Author Unknown

I know that many of you have heard Pat Robertson, Jerry Falwell and others speak of the "Homosexual Agenda," but no one has ever seen a copy of it. Well, I have finally obtained a copy directly from the Head Homosexual. It follows below:

6:00 am Gym
8:00 am Breakfast (oatmeal and egg whites)
9:00 am Hair appointment
10:00 am Shopping
12:00 pm Brunch
2:00 pm
1) Assume complete control of the U.S. Federal, State and Local Governments as well as all other national governments,
2) Recruit all straight youngsters to our debauched lifestyle,
3) Destroy all healthy heterosexual marriages,
4) Replace all school counselors in grades K-12 with agents of Colombian and Jamaican drug cartels,
5) Establish planetary chain of homo breeding gulags where over-medicated imprisoned straight women are turned into artificially impregnated baby factories to produce prepubescent love slaves for our devotedly pederastic gay leadership,
6) Bulldoze all houses of worship, and
7) Secure total control of the Internet and all mass media for the exclusive use of child pornographers.

2:30 pm Get forty winks of beauty rest to prevent facial wrinkles from stress of world conquest
4:00 pm Cocktails
6:00 pm Light Dinner (soup, salad, with Chardonnay)
8:00 pm Theater
11:00 pm Bed (du jour)[2]

A gay agenda? What a joke! Simply stated, a "gay agenda" does not exist anymore than a "Head Homosexual" exists – at least, that's what many gays and lesbians would surely (and sincerely) say.[3]

An animated cartoon posted Feb. 18, 2004 by gay political illustrator Mark Fiore entitled "Attack of the Gay Agenda" tries to expose the absurdity of this concept in the eyes of the homosexual community. The cleverly conceived cartoon first mocks heterosexuals as mired in their own hypocritical, moral crisis, then former President Bush as a puppet of Karl Rove and the religious right, then Democratic presidential candidates as waffling and indecisive, and then conservatives as trumpeting their same old shallow position, before announcing: "And now, before your very eyes, the AWFUL, TERRIFYING *GAY AGENDA* will be revealed!!!"

The final frame reveals the horrible truth. It is two gay men having a meal together in their home, their wedding picture on the table next to them, making but one request: "Please leave us alone." That's the terrifying gay agenda![4]

According to those allegedly responsible for this plot, the very idea is laughable. A homosexual plan to change America replete with detailed plans and goals? Hardly!

As expressed by the widely-read, lesbian blogger Pam Spaulding, "**The Homosexual Agenda** is an elusive document. We've been looking around for a copy for quite some time; the distribution plan is so secret that it's almost like we need a queer Indiana Jones to hunt the master copy down. The various anti-gay forces are certain that we all have a copy and are coordinating a[n] attack to achieve world domination."[5] Right!

Of course, most gays and lesbians *do* have "an agenda." They want to live productive, happy, fulfilling lives, just like everyone else. Beyond that, they probably want others to accept them as they are. That would be the "agenda" of the majority of homosexual men and women worldwide.[6] As stated (again, with real sarcasm) by a poster on the website of gay activist Wayne Besen, responding to a prior, negative comment by another poster,

> Us faggots DO have a homosexual agenda. I'm risking my life by telling you, and the Council will revoke my license for sure, but I'm going to tell you exactly what it is. You ready? The insidious gay agenda is . . . We want you to leave us the [expletive] alone and to be treated like normal human beings with the same rights that YOU take for granted. THAT'S the gay agenda."[7]

What then are we to make of books written by conservative Christians with titles such as *The Agenda: The Homosexual Plan to Change America*, or *The Homosexual Agenda: The Principle Threat to Religious Freedom Today*, or *The Gay Agenda: It's Dividing the Family, the Church, and a Nation*?[8] Perhaps the authors of these studies are delusional? Perhaps they are displaying symptoms of hysteria? Perhaps they are projecting their own homophobic fears? Maybe *they* are the ones with an agenda, an oppressive campaign to deprive gays and lesbians of their constitutional rights?

In September, 2004, Salon Magazine quoted Sen. Tom Coburn as stating that, "The gay community has infiltrated the very centers of power in every area across this country, and they wield extreme power" and the "[gay] agenda is the greatest threat to our freedom that we face today."[9] Can such sentiments be taken seriously?

This much is sure: Despite the fact that the "homosexual community" is as diverse as the "heterosexual community," there is vast agreement among homosexuals that there is no such thing as a gay agenda. In fact, such terminology is to be studiously avoided, as noted by GLAAD (the Gay & Lesbian Alliance Against Defamation) in its informational posting "Offensive Terminology to Avoid":

> **OFFENSIVE: "gay agenda" or "homosexual agenda"**
> **PREFERRED: "lesbian and gay civil rights movement"**
> **or "lesbian and gay movement"**

> Lesbians and gay men are as diverse in our political beliefs as other communities. Our commitment to equal rights is one we share with civil rights advocates who are not necessarily lesbian or gay. "Lesbian and gay movement" accurately describes the historical effort to achieve understanding and equal treatment for gays and lesbians. Notions of a "homosexual agenda" are rhetorical inventions of anti-gay extremists seeking to portray as sinister the lesbian and gay civil rights movement.[10]

There you have it, straight from an authoritative source: "Notions of a 'homosexual agenda' are rhetorical inventions of anti-gay extremists seeking to portray as sinister the lesbian and gay civil rights movement." Thus, there are no facts behind this claim, only *notions*; there is no substance to this charge only *rhetorical inventions*; those behind these accusations are not balanced, well-meaning people but rather *anti-gay extremists*; the movement in question is nothing less than a civil rights movement, and the only thing *sinister* about this movement is the way it is portrayed by the fanatical opposition.

As explained by the late Jack Nichols, a highly literate, pioneer, gay-rights advocate:

> Propagandistic hate films touting a so-called gay agenda have been produced and circulated widely by the religious right. Each has been carefully edited so as to create false impressions of gay men and lesbians as well as the "evil" social program they are accused, en masse, of desiring. Fund-raising letters, couched in inflammatory language to frighten recipients, are sent out over the signatures of ministers. They promise to use the dollars sent to bring a halt to this imaginary gay agenda, one, they say, that favors a variety of outrageous proposals ranging from the "right" to molest children to a fondness for spreading AIDS.[11]

To restate the prevailing gay consensus: There is no such thing as a gay agenda, a fact underscored time and again by the common practice (especially among gays and lesbians) of putting this term in quotes. It simply doesn't exist. As stated succinctly by the Rainbow Alliance, "The 'Gay Agenda' is but

26

one of the many lies promulgated by radical religious political activists."[12] As expressed by a representative for Soulforce, a leading gay, religious organization, "It is only the extreme religious right who suggest that there is a homosexual agenda."[13] So there you have it!

Charles Karel Bouley II, writing February, 22, 2005 on Advocate.com, a leading gay website, put it like this:

> We've heard about it for years. Many have tried to define it, including 22 organizations that released a combined statement in January 2005 to outlets such as Advocate.com [for this statement, see below]. It's the Gay Agenda, and while many pontificate about it, condemn it, or allegedly try and further it, I as a gay man have yet to figure out what it is.
>
> Actually, let me flat-out say it: There is no gay agenda. I hate to break it to all those antigay organizations out there that have made such a myth the bedrock of their bigotry campaigns, but really, it just doesn't exist.[14]

In a speech on behalf of same-sex marriages delivered to the House of Representatives February 20, 1996, Iowa Republican Ed Fallon stated,

> Heterosexual unions are and will continue to be predominant, regardless of what gay and lesbian couples do. To suggest that homosexual couples in any way, shape or form threaten to undermine the stability of heterosexual unions is patently absurd.
>
> And I know, you'll say: "What about the gay agenda?" Well, just as there turned out to be no Bolsheviks in the bathroom back in the 1950s, there is no gay-agenda in the 1990s. There is, however, a strong, well-funded anti-gay agenda, and we have an example of its efforts here before us today.[15]

So then, the "gay agenda" is a myth?

In response to the proposed ban on gay marriages in her state in 2004, Stacy Fletcher of the gay activist group Arkansans for Human Rights said, "We were not looking for this fight. There is no gay agenda. All our community was doing was working, paying taxes and trying to live our lives."[16] After the November 2004 elections, Rev. Beth Rakestraw, a lesbian minister of the Gospel of Jesus Christ Community Church in Midland, Michigan, stated, "I'm very frightened by the trend in our government that right-wing evangelicals are pursuing their own agenda. They say there's a gay agenda? What about the right-wing agenda? There is no gay agenda."[17]

The testimony is unanimous and unequivocal: There is a right-wing, bigoted, anti-gay agenda, but there is no gay agenda. Case closed. Or is it?

IS THERE MORE TO THE STORY?

Pointing back to the turning point in modern homosexual history, the Stonewall riots in New York City in 1969, gay activist Marc Rubin asked in 1999, "How did that singular event in June 1969 become the fountainhead for so many of the changes that have made the world so different for queers thirty years later?" His answer? "It spawned the Gay Liberation Movement."[18] Rubin continues:

> First there was The Gay Liberation Front proclaiming loudly, clearly, and brilliantly, the truth that gay is good, that queers had embodied within them all of the genius of Humanity, and owned all privileges of that status. . . .
>
> GLF, the Gay Liberation Front, was conceived as being part of the entire Liberation movement, one segment of a worldwide struggle against oppression. . . .

What exactly did this mean?

> The Gay Activists Alliance stood for writing the revolution into law. Although individual members would ally themselves to causes not directly related to the oppression of homosexuals, the organization's single issue focus enabled it direct all of its energies toward working intensively in, on, with, and against "The Establishment" on issues effecting lesbians and gay men.
>
> It said, "We demand our Liberation <u>from</u> repression and <u>to</u> the point where repressive laws are removed from the books and our rights are written into the documents that protect the rights of all people, for without that

writing there can be no guarantees of protection from the larger society."

And how would this be implemented?

The means to achieving these ends included, street actions famously defined as "zaps", marches, picket lines, political lobbying, education, active promotion of the need for lesbians and gay men to come out of their closets, and a constant in-your-face presentation of the fact that gay is good. Its goals were revolutionary in that it sought, through these means, to restructure society.[19]

Yes, society has been greatly restructured by gay "revolutionary" goals, *but there is no gay agenda*.

Carl Wittman's landmark *Refugees from Amerika: Gay Manifesto*, dated Thursday, January 1, 1970, concluded with **AN OUTLINE OF IMPERATIVES FOR GAY LIBERATION**:

1. Free ourselves: come out everywhere; initiate self defense and political activity; initiate counter community institutions.
2. Turn other gay people on: talk all the time; understand, forgive, accept.
3. Free the homosexual in everyone: we'll be getting a good bit of [expletive] from threatened latents: be gentle, and keep talking & acting free.
4. We've been playing an act for a long time, so we're consummate actors. Now we can begin *to be*, and it'll be a good show![20]

But there is no gay agenda, despite a gay manifesto with a call to action for the purpose of gay liberation.

In Chicago, Illinois, the 1972 Gay Rights Platform was formulated, including nine federal goals and eight state goals, some of which called for:

Issuance by the President of an executive order prohibiting the military from excluding for reasons of their sexual orientation, persons who of their own volition desire entrance into the Armed Services; and from issuing less-than-fully-honorable discharges for homosexuality; and the upgrading to fully honorable all such discharges previously issued, with retroactive benefits. (1972 Federal-2)

Federal encouragement and support for sex education courses, prepared and taught by Gay women and men, presenting homosexuality as a valid, healthy preference and lifestyle as a viable alternative to heterosexuality. (1972 Federal-6)

Repeal of all state laws prohibiting private sexual acts involving consenting persons; equalization for homosexuals and heterosexuals for the enforcement of all laws. (1972 State-2)

Repeal of all state laws prohibiting transvestism and cross-dressing. (1972 State-6)

Repeal of all laws governing the age of sexual consent. (1972 State-7)

Repeal of all legislative provisions that restrict the sex or number of persons entering into a marriage unit; and the extension of legal benefits to all persons who cohabit regardless of sex or numbers. (1972 State-8)[21]

But there is no gay agenda, despite a gay rights platform spelling out militant, comprehensive goals, including the repeal "of all laws governing the age of sexual consent" (an endorsement of pederasty!) and governmental recognition of multiple-partner "marriages" (today called "polyamory") at both the national and statewide level.

Literature distributed at the 1987 March on Washington listed seven major demands, including the legal recognition of lesbian and gay relationships and the repeal of all laws that make sodomy between consenting adults a crime, while the 1993 event was billed as the March on Washington for Lesbian, Gay, and Bi Equal Rights and Liberation. The opening item in the Platform Demands stated: "We demand passage of a Lesbian, Gay, Bisexual, and Transgender civil rights bill and an end to discrimination by state and federal governments including the military; repeal of all sodomy laws and other laws that criminalize private sexual expression between consenting adults." The third Platform Demand stated: "We demand legislation to prevent discrimination against Lesbians, Gays, Bisexuals and Transgendered people in the areas of family diversity, custody, adoption and foster care and that the definition of family includes the full diversity of all family structures."[22] *But there is no gay agenda!*

Expressing himself with great vigor – and perhaps an extremist tone even for gay activists – ACT UP leader Steve Warren intoned an ominous sounding alarm for religious Jews and Christians in his September, 1987 "Warning to the Homophobes." (Despite the threatening tone, this *was* published by *The Advocate*, the nation's most prominent gay magazine.)

1. Henceforth, homosexuality will be spoken of in your churches and synagogues as an "honorable estate."
2. You can either let us marry people of the same sex, or better yet abolish marriage altogether. ...
3. You will be expected to offer ceremonies that bless our sexual arrangements. ... You will also instruct your people in homosexual as well as heterosexual behavior, and you will go out of your way to make certain that homosexual youths are allowed to date, attend religious functions together, openly display affection, and enjoy each other's sexuality without embarrassment or guilt.
4. If any of the older people in your midst object, you will deal with them sternly, making certain they renounce their ugly and ignorant homophobia or suffer public humiliation.
5. You will also make certain that ... laws are passed forbidding discrimination against homosexuals and heavy punishments are assessed. ...
6. Finally, we will in all likelihood want to expunge a number of passages from your Scriptures and rewrite others, eliminating preferential treatment of marriage and using words that will allow for homosexual interpretations of passages describing biblical lovers such as Ruth and Boaz or Solomon and the Queen of Sheba. Warning: If all these things do not come to pass quickly, we will subject Orthodox Jews and Christians to the most sustained hatred and vilification in recent

memory. We have captured the liberal establishment
and the press. We have already beaten you on a number
of battlefields. ... You have neither the faith nor the
strength to fight us, so you might as well surrender
now.

Yes, Warren states clearly that gays are taking over and religious people
had better be ready for the radical changes that are coming – *but there is no
gay agenda!*

In their pioneering 1990 volume *After the Ball: How America Will
Conquer Its Fear and Hatred of Gays in the 1990's*, Harvard-trained gay authors
Marshall Kirk and Hunter Madsen offered a brilliant and comprehensive
strategy for changing America's attitudes towards homosexuality, as indicated
by the subtitle, *How America Will Conquer Its Fear and Hatred of Gays in the
'90s.* The book built on the authors' 1987 article, "The Overhauling of Straight
America,"[23] and their six-fold plan has been referred to many times in the last
two decades, especially by conservatives who have noted how successful this
plan has been:

1. Talk about gays and gayness as loudly and often as
   possible.
2. Portray gays as victims, not aggressive challengers.
3. Give homosexual protectors a "just" cause.
4. Make gays look good.
5. Make the victimizers look bad.
6. Solicit funds: the buck stops here (i.e., get corporate
   America and major foundations to financially support
   the homosexual cause).[24]

Kirk and Madsen's strategies have been implemented with tremendous
success, resulting in a major shift in the nation's perception of homosexuals and
an equally major shift in the perception of those who oppose homosexuality
– indeed, these once-radical proposals seem utterly benign today – *but there
is no gay agenda!*

In the Introduction to *After the Ball*, Kirk and Madsen explain:

The gay revolution has failed.
Not completely, and not finally, but it's a failure just

the same. The 1969 Stonewall riot – in which a handful of long-suffering New York drag queens, tired of homophobic police harassment, picked up rocks and bottles and fought back – marked the birth of 'gay liberation.' As we write these lines, twenty years have passed. In those years, the combined efforts of the gay community have won a handful of concessions in a handful of localities. Some of those concessions have been revoked; others may be. We should have done far better.

What has gone wrong? And what can we do about it?

This book is about hope and dread. It explores the dire necessity – and the real possibility – of reconciling America to its large, oppressed, and inescapable minority: gay men and women. *It proposes a practical agenda* for bringing to a close, at long last, the seemingly permanent crisis of American homosexuality. And it aims to launch upon this task in an era of superlative need and supreme difficulty, the frightening era of the 'the gay plague,' AIDS.[25]

So, this national #1 bestselling volume, which candidly speaks of "the gay revolution," actually proposed "*a practical agenda* for bringing to a close, at long last, the seemingly permanent crisis of American homosexuality." In fact, the authors even stated that, "In February 1988 . . . a 'war conference' of 175 leading gay activists, representing organizations from across the land, convened in Warrenton, Virginia, to establish a *four-point agenda* for the gay movement"[26] – *but there is no gay agenda*. In fact, according to gay blogger Jonathan Rowe, "Kirk and Madsen's book has become something of an urban myth among the looney right." He claims that, "the overwhelming majority of 'gay activists' have never read and probably never even heard of the book" and the idea that the book has been widely used by gay leaders is simply the result of "antigay conspiracy mongering." As echoed by gay activist Steve Miller, "To suggest that this book is and has been driving a 'gay agenda' is bizarre to say the least."[27] But of course! There *is* no gay agenda.

In his article "Visibility is Victory" (June, 2005), Wayne Besen, founder of Truth Wins Out, stated:

I am so proud to stand with you as a member of the gay, lesbian, bisexual and transgender community. Just to be here [at South Carolina Pride], out and proud, we have overcome obstacles and persevered against prejudice and persecution. We are robust and resilient; vibrant and vital. And, we will succeed and create a new reality in America.

But first, we must turn our pride into passion, and our passion into action. Our future is in our hands and we must not drop the fragile object of freedom. One person can make a difference. Think of Gandhi, Martin Luther King, Susan B. Anthony and Rosa Parks. Their singular acts of courage liberated the world and unleashed the soaring spirits of millions.

While not everyone can lead a movement, we can all do our small part to move the world forward. Here are five things you can do:

1. If you have straight friends and family ask them to support full equality. You have taken the courageous step to come out. Now it is time your friends and family step-up.
2. If you are a person of faith, don't let counterfeit Christians such as Jerry Falwell, James Dobson and Pat Robertson hijack religion. Jesus never once mentioned homosexuality. Yet, these phoniest of Pharisees are obsessed with the issue. If you are a Christian, whose priorities do you trust? Jerry Falwell's or Jesus Christ's?
3. Look around you and you will see that there is strength in numbers. Join a gay civil rights group today, because they need you and you need them. Together, we can win.
4. Get involved in the political process. I guarantee you that many of your representatives do not think that any GLBT people live in their districts. Come out to politicians in your area.
5. We can create a new reality, but first we must be real. Coming out turns the meek into mighty, and turns the passive minority into the massive movement. Visibility is victory.

6. Be out. Be strong. Be vigilant, Be Proud. And be the best openly gay, lesbian, bisexual or transgender person God intended you to be.
7. Thank You and Happy Pride Month![28]

But there is no gay agenda – despite the call to "create a new reality in America," despite the exhortation to "turn our pride into passion, and our passion into action," despite the references to "Gandhi, Martin Luther King, Susan B. Anthony and Rosa Parks," despite a five-fold strategy, including political activism, despite an inspired vision for a "massive movement."

A major organization pushing for same-sex marriages in the state of New York is Empire State Pride Agenda, and its website is prideagenda. org. Its stated mission is, "Winning Equality and Justice for Lesbian, Gay, Bisexual & Transgender New Yorkers and Our Families"[29] – *but there is no gay agenda*, despite the fact that this focused and determined group calls itself "Empire State Pride Agenda" and runs the PrideAgenda.org website.

On January 13, 2005, twenty-two national gay and lesbian organizations released a joint statement of purpose with eight goals, an article on GayPeoplesChronicle.com noting that, "The 22 organizations signing the document include just about all of the major national LGBT [Lesbian, Gay, Bisexual, Transgender] groups."[30] The statement itself observed that, "The speed with which our movement is advancing on all fronts is absolutely historic. We are born into families as diverse as our nation . . . We, literally, are everywhere." The eight goals were:

- Equal employment opportunity, benefits and protections
- Ending anti-LGBT violence
- HIV and AIDS advocacy, better access to health care, and LGBT-inclusive sex education
- Safe schools
- Family laws that strengthen LGBT families
- Ending the military's gay ban
- Exposing the radical right's anti-LGBT agenda and fighting their attempts to enshrine anti-gay bigotry in state and federal constitutions
- Marriage equality

The article reporting this on GayPeoplesChronicle.com was entitled "The Gay Agenda" – *but there is no gay agenda.*

An August 11th, 2010 article on the National Review Online noted that, "Nine college and university presidents gathered in Chicago over the weekend and decided to form a new organization that will promote the professional development of gay academics as well as work on education and advocacy issues." The meeting was hailed as "the first attempt to gather the growing number of out college presidents (25 were invited)," and, according to the report, "participants said in interviews after the event that they wanted to encourage more gay academics to aspire to leadership positions and wanted to *push higher education to include issues of sexual orientation when talking about diversity.*"[31]

So, openly gay college and university presidents have decided to work together to "promote the professional development of gay academics as well as work on education and advocacy issues," including pushing higher education to make sexual orientation a core part of "diversity" – *but there is no gay agenda.*

The Human Rights Campaign (HRC), founded in 1980 and described on its website as "America's largest gay and lesbian organization," provides "a national voice on gay and lesbian issues. The Human Rights Campaign effectively lobbies Congress; mobilizes grassroots action in diverse communities; invests strategically to elect a fair-minded Congress; and increases public understanding through innovative education and communication strategies."[32] And it does all this with an annual budget of more than $35 million and a staff or more than 110. And for three years, Joe Solmonese, the president of the HRC, hosted a radio show called "The Agenda."[33] *But there is no gay agenda.*

The National Gay and Lesbian Task Force (NGLTF), founded in 1974, and with an annual income in excess of $3.5 million, "works to build the grassroots political power of the LGBT [Lesbian, Gay, Bisexual, Transgender] community to win complete equality. We do this through direct and grassroots lobbying to defeat anti-LGBT ballot initiatives and legislation and pass pro-LGBT legislation and other measures."[34] In addition to this,

> The Task Force's Organizing and Training Program is designed to build a powerful political infrastructure nationally by bringing together the best and most experienced trainers as faculty with local and state activists

and leaders to strengthen the grassroots of the LGBT movement. . . . The Policy Institute of the National Gay and Lesbian Task Force is a think tank that conducts social science research, policy analysis, strategy development, public education and advocacy to advance equality and greater understanding of LGBT people. . . . Creating Change is the premier national grassroots organizing LGBT conference, proven year after year to be a thought provoking and skills building conference with over 2,000 attendees from all over the country. Each year the conference is held in a different region of the United States and is well known for providing a unique environment where activists and leaders come together from diverse places and backgrounds to create a unique community that is both strengthening and inspiring to the participants.[35]

So, there is a national gay, lesbian, bisexual, and transgender task force, an organizing and training program, a policy institute, and an annual "Creating Change" conference. *But there is no gay agenda.*

ILGA (The International Lesbian and Gay Association) "is a world-wide network of national and local groups dedicated to achieving equal rights for lesbian, gay, bisexual and transgendered (LGBT) people everywhere. Founded in 1978, it now has more than 400 member organisations. Every continent and around 90 countries are represented. ILGA member groups range from small collectives to national groups and entire cities."[36] More specifically, "**ILGA is basically a network of activists**, and our success lies to a large extent in the achievements and progress of our many member groups."[37] *But there is no gay agenda.*

The mission statement of Lambda Legal, with an income of better than $10 million annually, explains: "Lambda Legal is a national organization committed to achieving full recognition of the civil rights of lesbians, gay men, bisexuals, transgender people and those with HIV through impact litigation, education, and public policy work."[38] In an oft-quoted statement, Paula Ettelbrick, the former legal director of the Lambda Legal Defense and Education Fund, once said, "Being queer is more than setting up house, sleeping with a person of the same gender, and seeking state approval for doing so. ... Being queer means pushing the parameters of sex, sexuality, and family, and in the process transforming the very fabric of society."[39] *But there is no gay agenda.*

Another major player is PFLAG (Parents, Families & Friends of Lesbians & Gays), with an annual income just under $2.5 million. PFLAG describes itself as "a national non-profit organization with over 200,000 members and supporters and over 500 affiliates in the United States."[40] Its website offers clearly articulated statements of Vision, Mission, and Strategic Goals, including "full civil rights" for GLBT people (which, of course, would include the "right" to same-sex marriage) and the "full inclusion of gay, lesbian, bisexual and transgender persons within their chosen communities of faith" (which would imply some of those communities having to modify their standards and beliefs)[41] – *but there is no gay agenda.*

Working in the educational system is GLSEN (pronounced "glisten"), with an annual budget of almost $6 million. Its mission statement explains: "The Gay, Lesbian and Straight Education Network strives to assure that each member of every school community is valued and respected regardless of sexual orientation or gender identity/expression."[42] This includes training teachers in what is called "gender speak,"[43] recommending textbooks such as the famous (or, infamous) *Heather Has Two Mommies*,[44] encouraging children to question their parents' non-gay-affirming views,[45] and sponsoring an annual "Day of Silence" to draw attention to what is referred to as the widespread oppression and persecution of gays and lesbians[46] – *but there is no gay agenda.*

QueerToday.com bills itself as "THE QUEER VOICE OF THE GAY LIBERATION MOVEMENT," stating,

WE ADVOCATE FOR EQUALITY FOR ALL LGBTQIP...ETC. PEOPLE. WE ACTIVELY SPEAK OUT AGAINST RACISM, SEXISM, HOMOPHOBIA AND OTHER FORMS OF INJUSTICE. WE WILL GET OUR SILENCED OPINIONS HEARD IN THE MAINSTREAM MEDIA AND GAY MEDIA THROUGH DEMONSTRATIONS AND CAMPAIGNS.[47]

So, there is a militant, activist voice representing the Gay Liberation Movement, replete with demonstrations and campaigns – *but there is no gay agenda.*

The gay campus organization Campuspride.net offers specific strategies for events during what has been dubbed "Gaypril," announcing, "If April showers brings May flowers, than GayPril brings campus queers. . . . April is the time to celebrate, educate and stimulate for campus Gay Pride!" The organizers urge student groups to: "Create Visibility," "Create Awareness," and "Foster Community."[48] Under the first category, they suggest:

> Poster Campaigns – get together with other LGBTQIA students [see chapter 000 for explanations of acronyms such as this], faculty and staff and make posters that display positive slogans relating to the LGBTQIA community (i.e. "Gay is Great!" "Trans-Liberation" "Loud and Proud"). Make sure to hang them all over campus (the inside doors of bathroom stalls are a great place to advertise!). Be aware that the posters may get ripped down or defaced. Create a policy where any posters found with graffiti on them are returned to you – use this to show other students and the administration the extent of homophobia on campus.
>
> Fly the Flag – you can't get more visible than flying the rainbow flag from the school's flagpole. Use your faculty and staff allies to help you lobby the administration to make this happen. Give-aways and/or Fundraisers – Condoms/Dental Dams/ Finger Cots – promote safer sex by distributing or selling (at a reasonable price or for donations) materials at your events and information tables. . . .[49]

So, there is a specific plan of attack with targeted goals – indeed, the gay flag should be flown throughout the month of April and the call for "Trans-Liberation" must be loud and clear – *but there is no gay agenda.*

The mission statement of GLAAD, whose own annual budget exceeds $4 million, states: "The Gay & Lesbian Alliance Against Defamation (GLAAD) is dedicated to promoting and ensuring fair, accurate and inclusive representation of people and events in the media as a means of eliminating homophobia and discrimination based on gender identity and sexual orientation."[50] *But there is no gay agenda.*

Upon becoming GLAAD's president in 2005, Neil G. Giuliano, declared in an open letter:

> We must also continue to reach the moveable middle

with our message of non-discrimination based on sexual orientation and gender identity/expression. Make no mistake, those who seek to further deny us full equality are powerful adversaries and we must prepare better, communicate better and go beyond our efforts of the past if we are to succeed and steadily advance. I am genuinely looking forward to working with my colleagues at other LGBT organizations to do just that - succeed and advance. . . .

Our efforts will be the same: neither the first nor the last, yet inspiring and significant because it is our time to march, to make a lasting difference for lesbian, gay, bisexual and transgender Americans. We will because we must.[51]

But there is no gay agenda – despite the impassioned vision to "succeed and advance," despite the call "to march" and "make a lasting difference for lesbian, gay, bisexual and transgender Americans."

When the Human Rights Campaign held its $195-a-plate, fundraising dinner in Charlotte in 2005, gay campus activist and Charlotte resident Shane Windmeyer stated that the event "offers an opportunity for us to come together and look at how we want Charlotte to be in five or 10 years."[52] *But there is no gay agenda.*

So, there are well-funded, highly-motivated, sharply-focused gay activist organizations such as HRC and NGLTF and PFLAG and GLSEN and GLAAD and Lambda Legal – just to mention a few – but there is no gay agenda.

WHY DENY HE EXISTENCE OF A GAY AGENDA?

What is behind this consistent and concerted denial of a gay agenda?

Could it simply be a matter of semantics, since it would be more accurate to speak of a gay and lesbian civil rights movement rather than a gay agenda? Hardly. The civil rights movement, both past and present, has freely and unashamedly spoken of a "civil rights agenda."[53] To give some representative examples, an illustrated, Southern Methodist University presentation of "The Civil Rights Movement, 1954-1963" states:

To pressure the government and Congress to act more quickly on *the civil rights agenda*, a massive march on the nation's capital was planned, scheduled, and carried out on August 28th, 1963. According to estimates, over 250,000 participated in the peaceful demonstration which culminated in the speech given by Reverend Martin Luther King.[54]

The website of the "The Citizens' Commission on Civil Rights" explains:

The Citizens' Commission on Civil Rights is a bipartisan organization established in 1982 to monitor the civil rights policies and practices of the federal government. Its work is grounded in the belief that *the civil rights agenda* benefits the entire country, not just particular interest groups. For the nation to remain strong, we must continue to struggle together to fight bias and invidious discrimination, to promote equality of opportunity in education, employment, and housing, to promote political and economic empowerment and to guarantee equal treatment in the administration of justice. Achieving these goals depends upon vigorous civil rights enforcement as a duty and obligation of the federal government.[55]

Walter Williams wrote an important article in *Capitalism Magazine* (November 12, 2001) entitled "The Unfinished Civil Rights Agenda,"[56] while the USDA 1997 Annual Report of the Secretary of Agriculture spoke clearly about "Setting a Sweeping Civil Rights Agenda."[57] Joyce A. Ladner's 2000 article in the *Brookings Review* (vol. 18, 26-28) was entitled, "A New Civil Rights Agenda: A New Leadership Is Making a Difference," in which she also speaks of the "Unfinished Civil Rights Agenda," stating, "Two issues remain on the civil rights agenda. The first is addressing the persistence of racial disparities. The second is redefining the agenda to fit a vastly changing American demographic profile."[58] It appears that people are not hesitant to speak of a civil rights agenda.

The same can be said of the feminist movement, which freely speaks of a feminist agenda. The phrase "feminist agenda" (in quotes) yielded 84,800 hits on Google (August 2, 2009), including websites such as FeministAgenda. org.au and others which announce, "Welcome to the feminist agenda home page!"[59] The NOW (National Organization for Women) website features articles such as, "NOW's Progressive Feminist Agenda for Peace"[60] and "NOW Vows to Help Address Diversity Issues and To Bring a Feminist Agenda to The Millennium March."[61] The feminists are not hesitant to speak of a feminist agenda! The same can be said of moral conservatives, who also speak freely of an agenda (indeed, as illustrated in some of the citations, above, gays frequently refer to this "conservative" or "right wing" or "radical right" agenda).

There is nothing wrong with having an agenda, as civil rights leaders, feminist leaders, and conservative leaders would readily agree. Why then is it taboo to speak of a gay agenda?

If the goal of this agenda was simply to achieve "civil rights" for gays, lesbians, bisexuals, and transgender people, why refuse to speak of an agenda? That *was* the agenda of the civil rights movement: civil rights! Yet when the gay community strives for what it believes to be these very same rights, it refuses to call this an agenda. Why?

There is a gay revolution, a gay liberation movement, a plethora of gay activist organizations with clearly identified missions and goals, but no gay agenda. There is a civil rights agenda, a feminist agenda, a conservative agenda, but no gay agenda. How can this be?

Why is there such a unified gay denial of such an obvious gay agenda? Why the claim, quoted above, that, "Notions of a 'homosexual agenda' are rhetorical inventions of anti-gay extremists seeking to portray as sinister the lesbian and gay civil rights movement"? Why not state that the so-called gay and lesbian civil rights movement has a definite agenda? Why not articulate what this agenda includes?

Perhaps the answer is provided by gay columnist Charles Bouley:

> Those who think [a gay agenda exists] are giving gays and lesbians too much credit. For there to be a gay agenda, there would have to be immense unity among us, since we would have to agree across the globe on said agenda. It might even have to be put up for a vote. Only then could it be disseminated to community leaders as well as the millions of gays and lesbians scattered across the world.
>
> Frankly, that does not, will not, and cannot happen.
>
> Gays and lesbian are a diverse community, composed of many voices with many ideas on how to achieve goals. We don't all agree on any issue, be it same-sex marriage

or the usefulness of pride festivals. We're not all of the same political ideology (yes, for some reason, there are still gay Republicans—but then again, the world is filled with oxymorons), and many of us still keep our sexuality private or hidden. No, there is no consensus among us, let alone an agenda.[62]

Is this, then, the reason that gays and lesbians insist that there is no gay agenda, namely, the lack of "immense unity" among them on a global level? While Bouley might be quite sincere, his thesis is untenable. Since when does an agenda require "immense unity" on a global level? How many groups have this? Certainly not conservatives, who disagree on a multitude of religious, political, and social issues – yet no one denies that there is a conservative agenda. And there has always been great diversity among leaders in the civil rights movement – think of the differences between Malcolm X and Dr. Martin Luther King, Jr. – yet hardly anyone would deny that there has been a civil rights agenda. And, realistically, no agenda comes from the people as a whole. Rather, it comes from the activists who seek to represent what they believe to be in the best interests of those people. So "immense unity" on a global scale is hardly required.

Ironically, when it comes to *denying* the existence of a gay agenda, there *is* "immense unity" in the gay community. Why? *It is because the denial of that agenda is part of the agenda* (although for some, it might be a sincere, heartfelt denial). That is a necessary piece of the puzzle: It must be a stealth agenda. Otherwise, its progress will be thwarted and its success greatly impeded, because the open, unambiguous, full disclosure of the goals and ramifications of the gay agenda would stop that agenda in its tracks.[63]

Am I claiming that all gay organizations work in unison together? Certainly not. Am I claiming that all gays and lesbians embrace the same societal goals? Not at all. Am I claiming that most major gay organizations agree on certain fundamental goals and that the clear majority of gays and lesbians support those goals? Absolutely.[64]

Just look at the mission statements of the primary gay advocacy and lobbying groups, the primary gay educational groups, the primary gay media-related groups. They are in fundamental harmony, and they are all devoted to bringing about societal change. That constitutes an agenda. Then read the primary gay publications – the leading gay magazines and newspapers, the most visited gay websites, the most respected gay scientific journals – and they too are in fundamental harmony as far as viewpoints, issues of concern, and points of action. That constitutes an agenda. Then look at what is proclaimed loudly and clearly at gay pride events, with clear calls for political action for major gay causes. The message is consistent and the demands are clear. That constitutes an agenda. And then research the writings and messages of gay religious groups, both Jewish and Christian, and they too share a fundamental harmony in their primary theological positions, clearly believing that their fellow-religionists who do *not* share these views are wrong and need to change. That constitutes an agenda.

Do you think I'm taking things too far? Perhaps, some might argue, the real issue is that this so-called agenda is really not an agenda at all. Perhaps the reason for the consistent gay denial of a gay agenda is that the extent of that agenda is simply: Please leave us alone and let us live our lives in peace.[65]

Once again I beg to differ. That is not the only thing all the gay organizations and individuals are fighting for. To the contrary, the *legitimizing* of homosexuality as a perfectly normal alternative to heterosexuality also requires that all opposition to homosexual behavior must be *delegitimized*. At the very least, the gay agenda requires this (and let recognized gay leaders renounce this if it is not so):

- Whereas homosexuality was once considered a pathological disorder, from here on those who do not affirm homosexuality will be deemed homophobic, perhaps themselves suffering from a pathological disorder.[66]
- Whereas gay sexual behavior was once considered morally wrong, from here on public condemnation – or even public criticism – of that behavior will be considered morally wrong.[67]
- Whereas identifying as transgender was once considered abnormal by society, causing one to be marginalized, from here on those who do not accept transgenderism will be considered abnormal and will be marginalized.[68]

IMPLICATIONS OF THE GAY AGENDA

This is all part of the mainstream gay agenda, a necessary corollary to the call for "gay and lesbian civil rights." In keeping with this:

- When the father of a six year-old child in Lexington, Massachusetts, notified his son's school that he wanted prior notification if anything related to homosexuality was to be taught in his son's first-grade class, he was rebuffed by the superintendent of schools who informed him that the court had ruled that it was more important to teach "diversity" – with specific reference to homosexuality – than to honor the requests of the parents.[69] So much for parental rights! As expressed by a concerned San Francisco mother, "My children's teachers say they want students to think for themselves, but when my children say they think they should obey their parents or God, they're ridiculed. What kind of diversity can you have when children are pressured into thinking the same things?"[70]

- A Swedish pastor in his seventies, was given a prison sentence for simply *preaching a sermon in his own church* on sexual ethics in which stated that all non-marital sexual relations (including homosexual acts) were sinful, since his message was said to offend gays. The verdict, which was ultimately overturned by the Swedish Supreme Court, was supported by the Swedish Ambassador, Cecilia Julin, who said, "Swedish law states that public addresses cannot be used to instigate hatred towards a certain group."[71]

- A Christian leader in Pennsylvania was charged with "Disorderly Conduct" and "Disrupting Meetings and Processions" for trying to read a passage from the New Testament that dealt with homosexual practices during his designated speaking time at a city council meeting. (He was actually shut down before he could read the passage.) Assistant District Attorney Alyssa Kunsturiss explained that the borough president, Norman Council, "perceived what he was reading as hate speech. It would be homophobic today. They couldn't let him go on. You can't go up to the podium and start reading from the Bible."[72] Yes, this is an accurate quote from an attorney right here in America, supposedly "one nation under God" and the home of free speech – as long as that speech does not challenge or differ with the gay agenda.[73]

- In Boise, Idaho, an employee of Hewlett Packard was fired for posting Bible verses on his cubicle after a pro-gay poster was placed near his workspace. According to the Ninth Circuit Court of Appeals, "An employer need not accommodate an employee's religious beliefs if doing so would result in discrimination against his co-workers or deprive them of contractual or other statutory rights." In response to this, author Janet Folger (now Porter) asks, "The homosexual agenda trumps an employee's religious beliefs?"[74] But of course! (Note that even if Folger's rhetorical question was rephrased to read, "Gay rights trump religious rights?", the answer would be the same.)

- In England, a bishop in the Anglican Church was "ordered to undergo equal opportunities training and to pay a gay youth worker nearly £50,000 [roughly $80,000] for refusing him a job because of his sexuality." According to a report in the *Telegraph*, the youth worker "took the Hereford Diocesan Board of Finance to an employment tribunal and said today he was 'delighted' with the payout. . . . Ben Summerskill, chief executive of the gay rights pressure group Stonewall, added: 'We're delighted that the tribunal has sent such a robust signal, both to the bishop and other employers. The substantial level of compensation sends out a very clear message. Not even a bishop is above this law.'"[75]

- The Associate Vice President of Human Resources at the University of Toledo, an African American woman, was fired from her job "for stating in a guest column in a local newspaper that choosing homosexual behavior is not the same as being black or handicapped."[76] The university president stood behind the decision to dismiss her.

You can be assured that there has been no widespread gay outcry over these court rulings, arrests, fines, firings, and reprimands, most of which were instigated by offended members of the GLBT community, since full recognition of "gay rights" means limited recognition of the rights of others. That's why these rulings are celebrated as victories among gay activists, since this is all a necessary part of the agenda. The rule of thumb for gay rights can therefore be stated as follows: "We have the right to be ourselves, even it offends you, but you do not have the right to be yourselves or to be offended. And under no circumstances do you have the right to offend us."

Shockingly, the examples just cited are only the tiny tip of a massive iceberg. Here are just a few more. Were you aware of things such as:

- A "reeducation class" to ensure that foster parents embrace the gay agenda (California)?
- Public schools with a mandated pro-homosexual ["antidiscrimination"] policy that sends objecting students to "appropriate counseling" without notifying their parents (California)?
- Being put out of business (with a $150,000 fine) for firing a man in a dress (California)?
- Being told by a judge that you can't teach your daughter anything "homophobic" (Colorado)?[77]

THE INEVITABLE PROGRESSION OF GAY ACTIVISM

All this is part of an inevitable process which can be summarized with this progression:

First, gay activists came out of the closet;
Second, they demanded their "rights";
Third, they demanded that everyone recognize those "rights";
Fourth, they want to strip away the rights of those who oppose them;
Fifth, they want to put those who oppose their "rights" into the closet.[78]

Look again at the statement on the GLSEN website: "The Gay, Lesbian and Straight Education Network strives to assure that each member of every school community is valued and respected regardless of sexual orientation or gender identity/expression." In contrast, it does *not* strive to assure that each member of every school community is valued and respected regardless of religious beliefs, moral convictions, or different views on sexual orientation. In fact, it has vigorously opposed the views and activities of groups that differ with the gay agenda, protesting the presence of such things as ex-gay material (i.e., literature from former homosexuals) in any school discussion of sexual orientation, where GLSEN believes that only the pro-gay position can be represented.

As stated explicitly by GLSEN founder Kevin Jennings, "Ex-gay messages have no place in our nation's public schools. A line has been drawn. There is no 'other side' when you're talking about lesbian, gay and bisexual students."[79] And did I mention that on May 9, 2009, the Department of Education appointed this gay activist leader, Kevin Jennings, to serve as Assistant Deputy Secretary for the Office of Safe & Drug Free Schools?[80]

It would appear, then, that "civil rights" for some means "limited rights" for others, and *that* by specific design. As stated explicitly in a teacher's lesson aid published by the Gay and Lesbian Educators [GALE] of British Columbia: "We must dishonour the prevailing belief that heterosexuality is the only acceptable orientation even though that would mean dishonouring the religious beliefs of Christians, Jews, Muslims, etc."[81] All this is part of the gay agenda.

Does this surprise you? If so, bear in mind that these are *not* predictions. They are statements of fact, a recap of what has already taken place in America and what is currently taking place around the world. Even our vocabulary is being affected,[82] as the gay agenda has produced these new definitions and concepts:

- From here on, embracing *diversity* refers to embracing all kinds of sexual orientation, (homo)sexual expression, and gender identification but rejects every kind of religious or moral conviction that does not embrace these orientations, expressions, and identifications.[83]
- From here on, *tolerance* refers to the complete acceptance of GLBT lifestyles and ideology – in the family, in the work place, in education, in media, in religion – while at the same time refusing to tolerate

any view that is contrary.[84]

- From here on, *inclusion* refers to working with, supporting, sponsoring, and encouraging gay events, gay goals while at the same time systematically refusing to work with and excluding anyone who is not in harmony with these events and goals.

- From here on, *hate* refers to any attitude, thought, or word that differs with the gay agenda, while gays are virtually exempt from the charge of hate speech – no matter how vile and incendiary the rhetoric – since they are always the (perceived) victims and never the victimizers.[85]

And how does this activist, gay agenda work itself out in everyday life? Much of this is already taking place throughout the country.

- Children in elementary schools will be exposed to the rightness and complete normality of homosexuality, bisexuality, and transgender expression – witness highly-praised academic books such as *The Queering of Elementary Education* – and opposing views will be branded as dangerous and homophobic, to be silenced and excluded from the classroom.[86]

- Middle schools, high schools, and colleges will go out of their way to encourage both the celebration of homosexuality and deep solidarity with gay activism – witness The Annual Day of Silence in our schools in recognition of "the oppression and "persecution of homosexuals"[87] and the Lesbian, Gay, Bisexual and Transgender Students' Bill Of Educational Rights in our universities, not to mention Queer Study Programs and the celebration of "Gaypril."[88]

- The federal and state governments will legalize same-sex marriages – as has already been done in Massachusetts, Connecticut, Vermont, and Iowa – along with, currently, ten countries worldwide, including Canada and Spain in the same week in 2005 – meaning that all heterosexuals must accept the

legality of these marriages and that anyone refusing
to do so could be prosecuted for discriminatory
behavior.[89]

- Corporate America will embrace every aspect of non-
heterosexuality (including bisexuality, transgender, and
beyond) – calling for the dismissal of those who refuse
to follow suit – and religious groups will no longer
be allowed to view homosexual practice as immoral,
branding such opposition as "hate speech."[90]

In the last four decades, major changes have taken place in: 1) the public's
perception of homosexuality and same-sex relationships; 2) the educational
system's embrace of homosexuality; 3) legislative decisions recognizing gays
and lesbians as a distinct group of people within our society, equivalent
to other ethnic groups; 4) the media's portrayal of GLBT people; and 5)
corporate America's welcoming of what was once considered unacceptable
behavior. Is this simply one big coincidence? Did all this happen by chance?
Don't these very results – which barely tell the story – give evidence to a
clearly defined gay agenda?

Well, just in case you're not 100% sure, a leading gay activist has helped
remove all doubt. Speaking shortly after the 2006 elections, Matt Foreman,
then the executive director of the National Gay and Lesbian Task Force, had
this to say:

"You want to know the state of our movement on
November 10, 2006? We are strong, unbowed, unbeaten,
vibrant, energized and ready to kick some butt."

And what exactly does this mean?
"The agenda and vision that we must proudly articulate is that yes, indeed,
we intend to change society."[91]

Or, in the words of gay leader (and former seminary professor) Dr. Mel
White,

It is time for a campaign of relentless nonviolent resistance
that will convince our adversaries to do justice at last.
They have assumed that we are infinitely patient or too
comfortable to call for revolution. For their sake, and for

the sake of the nation, we must prove them wrong.[92]

So, the cat is out of the bag and the covert agenda is becoming overt, backed by a movement that proclaims itself "strong, unbowed, unbeaten, vibrant, energized and ready to kick some butt." It is nothing less than a gay revolution – and it is coming to a school or court or business or house of worship near you.

America, are you ready?

Liberty Counsel [an evangelical Christian legal organization] is a distinctly un-Christian, hate-filled intolerant gang of thugs with law degrees.

From an editorial in *Q-Notes*, the gay newspaper of the Carolinas

The homo-hatred of the religious right has driven so many beautifully-gifted women and men into the arms of suicide, alcoholism, promiscuity, and self-destruction.

Pastor Mike Piazza, *Holy Homosexuals*

A garden of homophobia: our black churches are fertile soils for planting and cultivating homo hatred.

Article in the *Advocate* by Irene Monroe

You, just like everyone who is against gay marriage, is a mentally retarded bigot. No exceptions. Now go to hell.

WizzyBoy 520, responding to a YouTube video by a twelve-year old boy who opposed same-sex marriage based on the Bible

. . . the charge of "hate" is not a contribution to argument; it's the recourse of people who would rather not have an argument at all.

Matthew J. Franck, *The Washington Post* December 19, 2010

2

Jewish Hitlers, Christian Jihadists, and the Magical Effects of Pushing the "Hate" Button

N o one likes being manipulated. No one enjoys being used as a pawn. Yet psychological manipulation has taken place on a massive scale in our country, and it's as simple as pushing a one-word button. Yes, the moment the button is pushed, clear-minded, rational thinking virtually ceases and people respond with one accord, as if on cue.

What makes this all the more striking is that it was scripted out twenty years ago when two Harvard-trained, gay authors, Marshall Kirk and Hunter Madsen, published their watershed book *After the Ball: How America Will Conquer Its Fear and Hatred of Gays in the '90s.* Their goal was the "conversion of the average American's emotions, mind, and will, through a planned psychological attack, in the form of propaganda fed to the nation via the media."[1]

One of their strategies was to "jam" people's emotions by associating "homo-hatred" with Nazi horror, bringing to mind images such as "Klansmen demanding that gays be slaughtered," "hysterical backwoods preachers," "menacing punks," and "a tour of Nazi concentration camps where homosexuals were tortured and gassed."

The strategy has worked like a charm, as Jeff Jacoby, a conservative columnist with the *Boston Globe*, noted, "Dare to suggest that homosexuality may not be something to celebrate and you instantly are a Nazi. . . . Offer to share your teachings of Christianity or Judaism with students 'struggling with homosexuality' and you become as vile as a Ku Kluxer . . ."[2] Or, in the words of Dr. Laura Schlessinger, "Simply because I am opposed to legislating homosexual marriage and adoption, I am labeled a Nazi."[3]

So, *two Jews*, Jacoby and Schlessinger, can be called Nazis – without the slightest hint of irony – simply because they expressed their differences with the goals of homosexual activism. Yes, all you have to do is push that "hate button," and the results are utterly predictable.

Not that long ago, "to hate" meant: "to feel hostility or animosity toward; to detest." In recent years, however, the Contemporary Lexicon of Political Correctness and Sensitivity to Sexual Orientation has expanded this definition of "hate" to include: "to hold to Judeo-Christian principles and values; to stand for biblical morality," and, quite specifically, "to take issue with homosexual practice."

Pushing the hate button has proven quite effective, causing levelheaded, reasonable discourse to come to a sudden halt and quickly making the person with whom you differ into a small-minded, mean-spirited bigot. Immediately, the playing field becomes unequal, and your ideological opponent becomes a monster whose ideas are unworthy of serious consideration. And should that opponent happen to be a person with strong religious convictions, then pushing the hate button becomes all the more useful. The conservative Christian or Jew is caricatured as a modern day crusader, witch-hunter, and jihadist rolled into one, a self-righteous, insensitive hypocrite who gleefully consigns all but a few likeminded fanatics to eternity in hell.[4]

To be sure, many homosexual men and women have been subjected to all kinds of abuse and, sadly, they often continue to be the objects of vicious and even violent hatred. Homophobia *does* exist, despite the extreme overuse of that word today, and in the strongest possible terms, I decry hateful acts and words directed against the gay and lesbian community.[5]

But let's be candid here. Things have shifted so dramatically – they have literally been turned upside down – that it now appears that no matter what you say and no matter how carefully and graciously you say it, if you dare to differ with the GLBT agenda, if you believe that it is immoral for a man to have sex with another man, if you do not support same-sex marriage, then you are an extremist, a bigot, a Nazi, and a jihadist.

AN EXAMPLE OF GENUINE HATE SPEECH

This is not the slightest exaggeration. In fact, I can confirm this firsthand. But first, let's take a look at some real, hardcore, unabashed, hate speech by none other than Rev. Fred Phelps, considered by many to be one of the foremost practitioners of hate speech in our day.[6] Consider this representative sampling of his shocking, venomous words:

> **God hates America!**
> Thank God for IEDs killing American soldiers in strange lands every day. WBC [Westboro Baptist Church] rejoices every time the Lord God in His vengeance kills or maims an American soldier with an Improvised Explosive Device (IED). . . . WBC will picket the funerals of these Godless, fag army American soldiers when their pieces return home. WBC will also picket their landing spot, in Dover, Delaware early and often. . . . Face it, America! You have become a fag-filled nation of flag worshipers and necromancers. Your only terrorist is the Lord your God! He fights against you personally. . . . Bloody butcher Bush thinks he can distract from these facts by taking over

Babylon with his fag army. As a result of his foolishness, body bags are coming home by the truckload.[7]

God hates Sweden!
THANK GOD FOR ALL DEAD SWEDES!!! Unconfirmed numbers of Swedes are dead as a result of the tsunamis which ravaged Thailand and the other lush resorts of that region, and thousands more are unaccounted for, either still rotting in the tropical conditions or buried, as they deserve, as asses in mass graves . . . . . Scarcely a family in Sweden has been untouched by the devastation. Bible preachers say, THANK GOD for it all![8]

Are you shocked? Mortified? Read on:

> Reggie White is in hell. . . . Ronald Reagan is in hell. The Church of the LORD Jesus Christ will not sit silently by while you maudlin haters of God try to preach this senile old fool into heaven. Despite what dumbo George W. says, he's *not* in a better place, unless you consider fiery torment better than dribbling his cream of wheat![9]
>
> Pope John Paul II, the Great Pedophile Pope, is in hell. No burning candles, no indulgences, and no prayers to Mary will change that. The new Pope Benedict, Pope of the Great Whore, will burn in hell with him shortly.[10]
>
> WBC [Westboro Baptist Church] to picket the arch-heretic, traitor, and rebel against the great King of Glory – Billy Graham . . . . God hates Billy Graham and will ere long cast him into Hell and torment him with fire and brimstone . . . .[11]

It seems that there is no end to the ire of Rev. Phelps, as he continues to spew bile and launch one hateful website after another, including, godhatesamerica.com, hatemongers.com, and, as expected, godhatesfags.com. Yes, it is homosexuals who are the special target of his wrath, as evidenced in his response to someone who dared question his use of the word "fags":

Answer to a nit-picking freak who pretends

> not to understand why we call fags fags
>
> ...I must say: GET A GRIP! GET A CLUE! These are filthy beasts, no matter what you call them! Those three letters don't change the fact that the Lord will shortly return to execute judgment on this evil, froward world – and you will have to give an accounting for your rebellion against the Lord your God (and your attempt at distracting the saints).
>
> God hates fags. You are going to hell. Have a lovely day.[12]

This is hate speech, plain and simple, and without apology. In fact, it is not only without apology, it is with his explicit justification, since Phelps believes that God's hatred of homosexuals (and other sinners) "goes way past hate if you credit the Bible with full authority. It goes to abhor, and it goes to despise. Worse forms of the attitudinal approach of almighty God to a certain class of people."[13] And, Phelps would surely argue, because God hates, abhors, and despises homosexuals, we should wholeheartedly join Him in this hate-fest.

Sadly, this is the attitude of some misguided people who seek to validate their venom through a bogus use of the Bible, and Phelps has gained national notoriety for his vitriolic campaign, perhaps most famously for his "God hates fags" placards and signs.

"FRED PHELPS MINUS THE COLORFUL SIGNS"?

You can imagine, then, that I was more than a little surprised when a young, Charlotte-based gay activist and newspaper editor, Matt Comer, referred to me and my organization, the Coalition of Conscience, as "Fred Phelps minus the colorful signs."[14] To be sure, I was fully aware of the reflex reaction that immediately associates all opponents of homosexual activism with "hysterical backwoods preachers." But comparing the Coalition of Conscience to "Fred Phelps minus the colorful signs" – wasn't this a little over the top, especially given our track record in our city?

In May, 2006, we had issued a public statement in which we *apologized* to the gay and lesbian community of Charlotte for the shortcomings of the Church, saying in part:

> We recognize that we have sometimes failed to reach out

to you with grace and compassion, that we have often been insensitive to your struggles, that we have driven some of you away rather than drawn you in, that we have added to your sense of rejection. For these failings of ours, we ask you to forgive us. By God's grace, we intend to be models of His love.[15]

And in February, 2007, when we held a five-night lecture series on "Homosexuality, the Church, and Society" at the Booth Playhouse of the Blumenthal Performing Arts Center in Charlotte, we went out of our way to air our differences with gay and lesbian activists respectfully. The *Charlotte Observer* even noted in a supportive editorial that I had stated clearly that the lectures would "not be 'a forum for gay bashing'" and that I would "do nothing that's 'bigoted or mean-spirited.'" All this was known to Matt Comer when he made the Phelps comparison.

In fact, on September 20, 2007, Matt attended a public forum we conducted at our church devoted to the theme, "Can You Be Gay and Christian?" We had invited local gay and gay-affirming clergy to present their views and have a public dialogue with us, assuring them that there would be no gay-bashing or hate speech permitted. Although those invited decided to boycott the event, Matt did come and, with our permission, videotaped the entire presentation for his blog, without restriction. I spent time with him before the meeting and then, later in the evening, after our presentations were over, we gave him the microphone and let him share his own personal story.

In the midst of his "testimony" he said something that was quite striking: "You had some very good points, and they were couched in very compassionate language, but for a person like me, throughout this whole thing, all I'm going to hear is 'the queers need to die.'"[16]

How telling and how sad. To paraphrase: "No matter what you say, and no matter how compassionately you say it, I'm still going to hear hatred coming from your lips."

What an admission, and what a window of understanding into the whole question of "hate speech." Could it be that the "hate" is not so much on the lips of the speakers (with notable exceptions such as Fred Phelps) as much as it is in the ears of the hearers? And, to take this one step further, could it be that the tables have now turned so dramatically that most of the hate speech is coming *from* the lips and pens of those who perpetually push the hate button, namely, the gay and lesbian community?

In an editorial published in *Q-Notes*, the gay newspaper of the Carolinas, Matt wrote that I followed "a carefully plotted and scripted message of 'compassion,' 'love' and 'gentleness'" (in other words, he couldn't find fault with what I actually said in terms of my spirit and attitude), but in reality, I was a "predator," and a "wolf in sheep's clothing," while those who agreed with me were "fanatics."[17] And to cap things off, the editorial featured a ridiculous, doctored photo of me depicted as a Muslim terrorist and meant to be fear-inciting.

There you have it: Michael Brown, Christian Jihadist, aka Fred Phelps minus the signs. It looks like Jeff Jacoby and Laura Schlessinger had it right after all![18]

In late 2007 and early 2008, I got involved in some lengthy online discussions after stories were run about me on two well-read internet sites, Prof. Warren Throckmorton's blog and the Ex-Gay Watch blog.[19] I thought it would be instructive to engage in serious, written discussion with gay activists and others, discussion that could be documented for the sake of future readers, little knowing that the two threads would end up totaling more than 150,000 words (meaning, roughly 500 pages!) in just a matter of weeks.[20] As always, I sought to be respectful, clearly sharing my differences but under no circumstances engaging in anything that an unbiased reader could refer to as hate speech. (For a refresher on real hate speech, just look back at the Fred Phelps' quotes.)

The results? I was likened (albeit with hesitation) to a psychopathic personality, told that I hated gay people in general, labeled a jihadist (this actually preceded the Muslim terrorist picture of me in Q-Notes), compared in detail to Hitler, referred to as a wolf, constantly accused of lying and having ulterior motives, and called, among other things, hostile, self-righteous, and arrogant (the last two epithets coming not long after I had listed, with shame, the miserable sins and hypocrisy of many heterosexual Christians!). And what, according to these bloggers, was my greatest sin? It was that I was guilty of *judging them*.

Yes, they could label me a jihadist and a Hitler and a wolf and a liar for respectfully stating that, after much careful study and reflection, I was convinced that the Bible forbade homosexual practice, yet *I* was the one who was being judgmental. This eventually prompted me to ask: "Is the pot calling the kettle black?" Really now, who was judging whom? Who was doing the name calling? Who was engaging in hate speech?

One commenter even composed this poem (hey, it's not every day that someone writes a poem about you, even a hateful one):

> Brown comes to our turf with nice civil discourse,
> but his goal is to smite us without remorse.
> Concern for all gets a nod,
> while he goes forth in jihad
> as a virulent bigot in a Trojan Horse.[21]

Do you note the recurring pattern? I engaged people with "nice civil discourse" – so *what I actually said* was polite and respectful – but I was in reality a "virulent bigot" going forth "in jihad."

Another wrote, "I see you as a vicious enemy who merits no compassion whatsoever.... You're not just an anti-gay activist, you're an anti-me activist."[22]

Someone posting on a different blog gushed, "The truth is you're full of garbage, a disgrace to the Lord, and your hate group is about as 'Christian' as an Ozzy Osborn CD," while still another compared me to "the sleaziest of . . . bigots," claiming that I was "starting to see dollar signs from the fearful, the wounded, the hurting, the self-righteous."[23]

How fascinating! And what, again, was my crime? Daring to air publicly my differences with gay activists – with respect and without name-calling, anger, or rancor – and daring to come to the conclusion that the Scriptures taught against homosexual practice. And *this* made me "a disgrace to the Lord" and "the sleaziest of . . . bigots," the leader of a "hate group." To repeat: How the tables have turned!

JUST THE WAY IT WAS SCRIPTED

But this was not the first time I experienced this. In fact, it seems to happen like clockwork, just as Kirk and Madsen (and others) scripted it.

At a news conference on February 15th, 2007, as well as in our half-page ad in the *Charlotte Observer* announcing our lecture series at the Booth Playhouse, I explicitly stated to the media that no hate speech would be permitted at the lectures, even encouraging the airing of dissenting viewpoints in the 45 minutes that would be devoted each night to open mike Q & A. To be sure, I was taking strong issue with the Human Rights Campaign, the world's largest GLBT advocacy group, claiming that their name was actually misleading (seeing that they focus only on homosexual rights, not the rights of all citizens). But to repeat: We were determined to state our differences with grace and respect.

Yet no sooner did the word get out concerning these lectures then the hate speech started flying – I mean *against* us, not *from* us. In emails and on blogs, I was referred to as a hell-bound Neo-nazi, a mindless bigot, an ignorant moron, a lunatic, and a frothing nut bar; I was accused of openly touting the Nazi agenda, being part of the KKK in Charlotte, and espousing the American version of Nazism – and all this without any of the accusers attending a single lecture. And in a letter to the editor in the *Observer*, a local college professor chimed in as well, asking, "Can we soon expect Klan Kapers and Holocaust-deniers Hoedowns" at the Booth Playhouse?

What triggered some of the harshest reaction was my statement that the Human Rights Campaign would more accurately be called the "Homosexual Rights Campaign," although I pointed out that they had every legal right to do what they were doing.[24] Almost immediately, however, this was changed by bloggers on DemocraticUndergroud.com into an announcement that I was holding a lecture series, "To explain why homosexuals cannot legitimately call themselves human."

The readers on the website bought this revisionist statement hook, line, and sinker, joining in with passion. (I cite all this to demonstrate a point, not to paint myself as a martyr; getting blasted on the Internet is hardly "suffering.") They wrote:

- Life must really s--k for you when you're filled with that much hate
- Brown will be an inspiration to haters everywhere
- Why doesn't someone silence these 'unintelligently designed', ignorant morons?
- Time for these types to crawl back into the woodwork, where they belong.
- Vomit. Just vomit.
- I hope this gets a huge amount of publicity because this can only backfire in their faces. It will convince even more straight people that we really are facing lunatics, and the struggle for our rights against these lunatics really does need to be taken seriously.
- These people are a cancer on the body politic. The day when they're a forgotten and ignored footnote in our history can't come too soon.
- Membership in the KKK is also on the rise in the

Charlotte area. Unfortunately, that part of NC is full of hate mongers.

- [Expletive] bigots, that's all they are.[25]

And all I did was announce a lecture series on "Homosexuality, the Church, and Society"! Talk about a programmed reaction and the successful "conversion of the average American's emotions, mind, and will, through a planned psychological attack, in the form of propaganda fed to the nation via the media." And note in these posts that simple, ever-recurrent, operative, four-letter word: *hate.* Yes, "Brown will be an inspiration to haters everywhere."

Yet in a laughable twist of irony, one of the guidelines for posting on this website was:

> Do not post messages that are inflammatory, extreme, divisive, incoherent, or otherwise inappropriate. Do not engage in anti-social, disruptive, or trolling behavior. Do not post broad-brush, bigoted statements. The moderators and administrators work very hard to enforce some minimal standards regarding what content is appropriate.[26]

It would appear, then, that these accusatory posts were not "broad-bushed, bigoted, inflammatory, extreme, divisive, or anti-social." Rather, it was my detestable lecture series that was all of the above.

Has the world been turned completely upside down? Has everything gone topsy-turvy? Calling someone a frothing nut bar and a Nazi and a member of the KKK *without a scintilla of supporting evidence* is quite acceptable, but raising a moral objection to homosexual practice or a social objection to gay activism is completely unacceptable and worthy of hate-filled ridicule and expletive-laden loathing. How can this be? What has become of our capacity to think and reason rather than simply react? Have we no resistance to the very obvious strategy of pushing the hate-button?

All this is reminiscent of the sentiments of some Muslim extremists who responded to their critics by saying, "How dare you call us terrorists. We'll kill you for saying that!" Similarly, the moment you claim that some gay activists are guilty of pushing the hate button, they respond by saying, "You bigoted Nazi! You fundamentalist fanatic! You name-calling predator! How dare you accuse us of pushing the hate button!" (Just for the record, and with the slight hope that I will be quoted accurately, I am *not* comparing gay activists to

Muslim terrorists; I am simply comparing the rhetoric of the responses, both of which demonstrate the point that is being denied.)

"FEELING THE LOVE" ON A NATIONAL PLATFORM

This theater of the absurd reached a new height (or, more accurately, new low) on May 12, 2009, when I was interviewed for a second time by Thom Hartmann on his nationally syndicated, decidedly liberal, radio show. The subject of the interview (also for the second time, by Thom's choice) was the Bible and homosexual practice. When Thom asked for my views on homosexual practice, I grouped it together with other practices that the Bible forbade, including adultery and drunkenness and religious hypocrisy. In other words, I was not singling out homosexual practice as the worst of sins. And I specifically told Thom that, only the day before, when a Christian woman asked me how she should treat her twenty year-old son who had just come out as gay, I told her "to show him unconditional love." I also stated that I fully understand that most gays and lesbians feel as if they have been born this way, or, at least, did not consciously choose homosexuality.

How did Thom's listeners respond to this? Some of them wrote to our website with appreciation, one of them wanting me to know "that your composure on the air held grace and compassion. The fires of intolerance and hate come in the opposition of Thom's voice." Another listener was even more positive:

> In every instance you were well prepared with facts, rational logic, and a loving approach that steadfastly rejected the temptation to be petty and hostile. Particularly refreshing was the gentleness with which you corrected his claim that there was no Biblical condemnation of lesbian practice. I don't know why he chose you to represent the Christian viewpoint, but I suppose he must have wished for a narrow-minded bigot to confirm the stereotype he wanted to portray, and must have been disappointed you were so rational, well-prepared, and loving, yet did not fail to assert the truth.

But others saw things quite differently:

Having just heard you on Thom Hartmann, (5/12/09),

all you've done is convey to the public at large that you are an ignoramus, who no more warrants the moniker of "Doctor" than an earthworm.

A homosexual no more chooses to be so than a Heterosexual chooses to be, and no more can a homosexual change into a heterosexual than ..... well, you get the point. We are BORN this way. If we're gay, we can't be straight; if we're straight, we can't be gay! Duuuuh! Very simple and straight-forward. What is it you don't get, you stupid jack---!? Your "Holy Holy Holy" hypocricy doesn't fool me. You're either a very sick individual, or evil to the core. Which is it? . . .

People like you are bigots, hate-mongers, dare I say racist, and more lunatic than lunatic. You are clearly a dangerous, mean-spirited madman - and a CHARLATAN, SNAKE-OIL SALESMAN, and a hypocrite of the first order. If there is a hell - which, of course, there isn't - I hope there's a special place for wicked, nasty people like you.

Another wrote:

I heard you today on the Tom Hartman show. You sir are full of s---. Your "friends" who have changed from being Gay to Stright may be keeping up appearances, but in the end, they are sneaking around doing what comes naturally. I know because I meet these guys on Craigslist all over the US who want to "play" on the down low....and they do. Most are married and are only Stright on the surface. So sir, you don't know what you're talking about and are not good Christians because you have no tolerance for people who God has created differently. You hide behind religion to make yourself feel better about your lack luster life. In listening to you and seeing your picture I would dare to say you probably hang out on Craigslist or other sites yourself. You are a fraud.

Still another opined:

Leviticus 11:9-11
Deuteronomy 21:11
I just heard you on the Thom Hartmann show and was disgusted by your hatred and dubious agenda. I've included these two bible passages that god also gave to the Jews. Why aren't you so passionate about shellfish and clothing? Why do modern religions cherrypick passages to enforce your narrowminded, dogmatic views. If god does exist I think it would be ashamed of what people like you have done with the information. Every time human moratlity makes a step forward it is because we've stopped looking to a divisive, plagarised book called the bible. Ex. Slavery, Civil Rights, Womens Rights, Gay Rights. Shame on you! The policies you advocate are dangerous and scary for America, and I will oppose your ignorance at every juncture.

But there was one email that took the cake, the ultimate example of an unconscious double standard:

Dear Dr Brown:

I just heard you on the Thom Hartmann show. I feel sorry for you! You are a horrendous arrogant bigot. Jesus said, "Judge ye not, lest ye be judged." You are playing God and judging gay people when you should leave that all up to God. Some day soon, all the hateful homophobic bigots like you will shuffle of this mortal [s]oil, just like all of the racist bigots before you and leave the rest of us more tolerant and loving people to march forward into a wonderful future.

How extraordinary! Look at these two sentences side by side: "You are a horrendous arrogant bigot. Jesus said, 'Judge ye not, lest ye be judged.'" Yet I seriously doubt that the author of this email – identified as "A. Everyman" – caught the irony of this absurd juxtaposition. But the *coup de grace* comes in "Everyman's" closing line. He claims that soon the earth will be rid of "hateful homophobic bigots" like me, leaving the planet to "more tolerant and loving people" like him "to march forward into a wonderful future"! The "more tolerant and loving people"? I can really feel the love!

To summarize, "Dr. Brown, since you dare to differ respectfully with our views, you are an ignoramus, a stupid jack---, either very sick or evil to the core, a bigot, a hate-monger, dare I say racist, and more lunatic than lunatic; clearly a dangerous, mean-spirited madman – and a CHARLATAN, SNAKE-OIL SALESMAN; a hypocrite of the first order, wicked, nasty, full of [expletive]; a fraud (who secretly practices homosexuality), holding to dangerous, scary, and narrow-minded and dogmatic views, a horrendous, arrogant, hateful homophobic bigot."

Oh, that the world only had more tolerant and loving people like these kindhearted, peace-loving folks. How beautiful things would be as they "march[ed] forward into a wonderful future." And to think: These non-judgmental, love-filled souls were disgusted by *my* hatred. It really is ironic.

"I WOULD LIKE TO DO A LOT OF VIOLENT THINGS TO HIM TOO"

Even more ironic was the response of some viewers reacting to my appearance on a Tyra Banks program (January 27, 2010) devoted entirely to "transgender children" (referring to children who feel they are trapped in the wrong-sex body). In the few, hotly contested minutes that I had on the air, I emphasized that the most loving and compassionate thing we can do is try to help these children be at home in their own bodies. In other words, let's try to help them from the inside out.

Within a day, the entire show was posted on YouTube, and the brief segment in which I appeared generated a spirited discussion on the YouTube link.[27] (Opposite me in this segment were Kim Pearson, a transgender activist, and Dr. Marci Bowers, a male-to-female surgeon who is called the "rock star of sex change surgery.")[28] Some of those posting comments felt that I was frequently and unfairly interrupted. One person even commented, "wow - I never thought I'd find myself agreeing with a religious guy!!!"

But others were quite hostile, especially an atheistic, Australian, transgender teen, identified as 1993Vanessa2009. Apparently, I was not one of her favorites! She wrote:

> Dr. Brown is completely corrupt.
> That man is a corrupt [expletive].
> Well, that's because Dr. Brown was talking nonsense, and what he was saying was completely false and he knows

it is false, he is simply destroying society, and what makes me absolutely furious is people don't know about this major corrupt behaviour.

Dr. Brown is an [expletive] who isn't worthy of the title 'doctor.'

Don't listen to what Dr. Brown has to say--he is corrupt (and religious (whats the difference?)).

That man is a corrupt [expletive], would you like me to explain why? I'd be more than happy to.[29]

Well, I guess she thought I was corrupt! (Somehow, she never got around to explaining why.) She wasn't too impressed with my line of reasoning either:

Yes, he only got powerful points across to naive people, who'll prefer to listen to a corrupt man than two highly successful and intelligent women.

And moronic deceiving [expletives] are moronic deceiving [expletives]. Fact.

Well that dude is a total [expletive], did you know that? Want me to elaborate on why he is an [expletive]? lol, Dr. Brown is an [expletive]. Want to know why?

I also refuse to acknowledge his Phd.[30]

But there's more. She actually wished for violence against me, the expression of her deep, unmasked hatred:

He deserve to be beaten, just like trans women get beaten world wide, and murdered even. He is the reason why trans women are prevantly murdered each year. He was lucky I wasn't there, I would do a lot more than grap his arm [referring to the fact that Dr. Bowers repeatedly grabbed my arm as I spoke].

I would like to do a lot of violent things to him too.

I would horse kick him in the [expletives] while wearing high heels. I hate that man.

YES!!!!! He is a [EXPLETIVE] IDIOT!!!!! Don't you just hate him??!!

God I [expletive] HATE him!!!!!!

Such is the voice of enlightened tolerance – yet I and people like me are the "haters"! In fact, in another comment in this YouTube discussion I was branded as the "bigot" who "thinks that gays are freaks of nature and thinks that God ordained the gender binary [meaning male-female distinctives] and homophobia." This is more twisted than ironic, and yet it's all too typical these days. In fact, "Vanessa" wasn't the only one wanting to inflict some pain. Shadowcat8 added, "That guy is a moron. I wanna punch him in the face." And XCrystalXClearXLoveX exclaimed, "i really want to punch that man in the face. you dumb [expletive]." To this, "Vanessa" added, "Yes, I feel for you. I would like to do a lot of violent things to him too."[31]

And who is this 1993Vanessa2009? On her YouTube site she writes, "I'm a 16 year old girl, who is fairly intellectually mature; I'm probably the most intellectually mature teenager in my school. I am open minded, and a loving person."[32] Open minded and loving? Really?

To be sure, it appears that this young lady has been hurt by people around her (she was eager to start her hormone therapy leading to sex-change surgery, so she must have been through some internal and external conflicts already in her young life) and obviously, she is deeply pained by the misunderstanding and violence suffered by others who identify as transgender. But all this has apparently blinded her to the fact that her "open minded" and "loving" self-image is the picture of intolerance and hate.[33] And she is not alone in holding to this self-justified double-standard towards those perceived as conservative, religious bigots.

THE HATED DR. DOBSON

Consider one of the most admired men – and hated men – in America today, psychologist, author, radio host, and influential evangelical leader Dr. James Dobson. In his book *Marriage Under Fire*, he wrote:

> At the risk of being misunderstood, let me acknowledge that there is a great reservoir of hatred in the world, and some of it unfortunately gets directed toward homosexuals. It is wrong and hurtful, but it does happen. Every human being is precious to God and is entitled to acceptance and respect. Each of us has a right to be treated with the dignity that comes from being created in the image of God. I have no desire to add to the suffering that homosexuals are already experiencing. In fact, it has been my intention to

help relieve suffering by clarifying its causes and pointing to a way out.[34]

How would you characterize those words? Compassionate? Concerned? Caring? Without question, Dobson seems to go out of his way to express his love for gay men and women. Yet he is consistently charged with being hateful and homophobic. Why? Because he dares to suggest that homosexual practice is wrong and that homosexuals can potentially change, and therefore he is hateful. Are you surprised?

Here is another statement from *Marriage Under Fire*:

> I am especially sympathetic to homosexual men who, as effeminate boys, were routinely called "fag" and "queer" and "homo" by their peers. The scars left by those incidents can last a lifetime. In fact, I'm convinced that some of the anger in the homosexual community can be traced to the cruel treatment these boys were subjected to at the hands of other children.
>
> As Christians, we must never do anything to cause hurt and rejection, *especially* to those with whom we disagree emphatically. We certainly cannot introduce homosexuals to Jesus Christ if we are calling them names and driving them away. Believers are called to show compassion and love to those who would be our enemies. These people, some of whom seem hateful themselves, need to be welcomed into the church and made to feel accepted and appreciated.[35]

Hate speech? Certainly not by any rational criteria. Yet as quickly as Dobson's name is mentioned in the context of homosexuality, the hate button will be pushed.

Here are a couple of representative quotes from one online bulletin board:

> Mr. Dobson is just like the rest of the religious fanatics out there. He's been raised and educated in an environment that promotes ignorance and stupidity. An environment that bases their faith upon a book that is up to 85% incomplete and inaccurate (as do the large majority of Americans.)
> That Dobson is a manic homophobe is no surprise.[36]

A student editor for a Decatur, Illinois college newspaper expressed similar sentiments:

> Hey conservative Christians! Why do so many of you hate Americans and other people and the entire world? Why do you pass judgment as though that's what you were put on earth to do? And why have you let Dr. James Dobson be a "moral leader" for the last twenty-seven years when he is clearly an irrational, insane homophobe on a quest from his hateful god to divide and destroy instead of unite and love? Come on, you can do better than that. You can have minds of your own![37]

Now, stop for a moment and ask yourself a question: Who here is guilty of hate speech, Dr. Dobson or his critics? Whose rhetoric more closely resembles that of the aforementioned Fred Phelps? Who is guilty of name-calling? Who is guilty of crass speech? Who is guilty of character defamation? Surely it is Dobson's critics.

In these few quotes alone, he was grouped with "religious fanatics," said to have "been raised and educated in an environment that promotes ignorance and stupidity" – does that include his post-graduate studies at UCLA? – called a "manic homophobe" and an "irrational, insane homophobe on a quest from his hateful god." (For far uglier quotes, see below, Chapter Twelve.) Yet it is Dobson and his ideological colleagues who are labeled hate-filled. How utterly incongruous – and yet how marvelously effective. Pushing the hate button works wonders!

What was the cardinal sin committed by Dobson? Could it be that he stated that, "These people, some of whom seem hateful themselves, need to be welcomed into the church and made to feel accepted and appreciated." Honestly, it would be challenging for even the most ardent Dobson critic to cite this as a prime example of hate speech. Rather, it is the very next sentence, which I intentionally left out the first time I cited this paragraph, which causes such outrage: "At the same time," he writes, "we must oppose their agenda, which is harmful to society, to families, and ultimately to homosexuals themselves."

That's it! There it is! Hate speech, plain and simple. Dobson not only dares to suggest that there is actually a homosexual agenda,[38] but he goes one step further: He calls it harmful and encourages people to oppose it. Hatred!

Homophobia! Bigotry! Intolerance! Shades of Nazi eugenics!

In the words of AIDS activist Larry Kramer, speaking to a gay audience shortly after the 2004 elections,

> They have not exactly been making a secret of their hate. This last campaign has seen examples of daily hate on TV and in the media that I do not believe the world has witnessed since Nazi Germany. I have been reading Ambassador Dodd's Diary; he was Roosevelt's ambassador to Germany in the 30's, and people are always popping in and out of his office proclaiming the most awful things out loud about Jews. It has been like that. . . .[39]

So, opposition to same-sex marriage (and related homosexual causes) is similar to Nazism, just another form of pure and unadulterated hatred, and today's homosexuals are the moral equivalent of the Jews slaughtered in the Holocaust. I wish I was only making this up.[40]

For Kramer, the emphasis on "moral values" in the 2004 elections was merely a cover-up for hate:

> "Moral values." In case you need a translation that means us. It is hard to stand up to so much hate. Which of course is just the way they want it.
>
> Please know that a huge portion of the population of the United States hates us.
>
> I don't mean dislike. I mean hate. You may not choose to call it hate, but I do. Not only because they refuse us certain marital rights but because they have also elected a congress that is overflowing with men and women who refuse us just about every other right to exist as well. "Moral values" is really a misnomer; it means just the reverse. It means they think we are immoral. And that we're dangerous and contaminated. How do you like being called immoral by some 60 million people? This is not just anti-gay. This is what Doug Ireland calls "homo hate" on the grandest scale.[41]

There is no misunderstanding of Kramer's position, which represents the perspective of many (or most?) gays and lesbians. If you do not agree with same-sex marriages, you are hateful. If you say that gays can potentially change, you are hateful. If you believe that homosexual behavior is wrong, you are hateful. Yes, any form of disagreement, any form of disapproval, any form of dissent is labeled "hate speech," indeed, "'homo hate' on the grandest scale."

And what of the flaming rhetoric directed by some gays against moral conservatives? *That* is a subject not to be touched. After all, how can the *victims* of hatred, oppression, persecution, and unending scorn be criticized for "hate"? As gay activist Evan Hurst stated on a post on my website, "I just explained to you why 'tolerance' doesn't include tolerance for bigotry. You all are bigots. . . . The blood is on your hands."[42] Or, as articulated by lesbian blogger Melanie Nathan, people like me are "sick and depraved bigot[s] who clothe themselves in hate and greed."[43] She even encouraged her readers to "join the WAR and visit the criminal abuserers [sic] directly" by going to my website.[44]

This is the lens through which everything is filtered, and the perception in the LGBT community runs very deep that any restriction of their "rights" can be motivated by nothing but hate. And God forbid you ever suggest that homosexuality can be unhealthy, be it emotionally or physically. That is raw hatred going off the charts!

AN ANGRY LITTLE BOOK?

Psychiatrist and professor Jeffrey Satinover penned a very compassionate and yet forthright book called *Homosexuality and the Politics of Truth*.[45] In the Introduction, he described in vivid detail how the subject of homosexuality first became a major focus in his life back in 1981. It was when he encountered his first AIDS victim (although the disease was not yet known by that acronym), a young man named Paul. Satinonver spoke tenderly of him and "of his all-too-brief life and painful, wasting death,"[46] also stating that "AIDS was certainly unexpected and more horrifying than anyone could have imagined."[47] And while he clearly expressed his opposition to certain aspects of gay activism, he also wrote, "How can our hearts not go out to the young, prehomosexual boy or girl who is already shy, lonely, sensitive, and who surely suffers taunting rejection and maybe even beatings by the very peers he or she envies and most longs to be with?"[48]

Some reviewers on Amazon, however, were not impressed with Satinover's tone:

An angry little book full of error and distortion, June 3, 2005

This book is quite ridiculous. My ex-boyfriend's mother gave it to him to read when he came out, thinking it might set him on the path to a "cure." Well, with the inexorable march of time, it was she who was "cured" of her misconceptions, prejudice etc. We can all look back and laugh at it now. So if anyone out there is having difficulty accepting the social fact of homosexuality, I would say to you- there is a better way forward. In involves accepting people's basic humanity, and the diversity of human experience. The alternative is the vile hatred espoused in a book like this. I think the world has well and truly moved on since it was published.

Why can't we give 0 stars!!, July 20, 2003

. . . I would suggest reading this book if you are a strict fundamentalist christian or have some particular hatred of gay people. If that describes you this book will make you feel more justified in your opinion and as long as you don't act on that opinion it's good to at least feel good about yourself, just be sure not to read any modern scientific studies on the subject because any study done in the last several decades by any of the most respected names in mental health easily crush this book's weak evidence and show it to be nothing more than an attempt to justify hatred.[49]

Angry little book? Vile hatred? Some particular hatred of gay people? An attempt to justify hatred? One reviewer, whose language was fairly moderate – aside from calling the book "horrifying" – wrote, "Although Satinover goes out of his way to present himself as someone who genuinely cares about gay people and wants to help them, he does not seem to acknowledge their role in their own lives, preferring instead to see them as victims of their own nature."[50]

Is it possible that he does, in fact, genuinely care, and it is that care that motivated him to write the book? Is it so hateful to believe that homosexual practice is harmful and that change is possible? (If a doctor takes issue with you or me being overweight, do we brand him or her an anti-fat, hate-filled bigot, or do we recognize that the doctor is expressing concern for our well-being? Isn't the doctor trying to be helpful rather than hateful?)

It is one thing to disagree with Satinover's findings from a scientific viewpoint or from personal experience to deny that change is possible. But why must the hate button be pushed incessantly? Are the only two options "embracing homosexuality" or "hatred"?

In 2008, McDonald's found itself in the middle of controversy when it joined the National Gay and Lesbian Chamber of Commerce, placing an executive on the group's board of directors and making a $20,000 donation to the chamber. When McDonald's initially declined the request of the American Family Association (AFA) to resign from the chamber, the AFA called for a boycott of McDonald's. As explained by AFA president Tim Wildmon, "We're saying that there are people who support AFA who don't appreciate their dollars from the hamburgers they bought being put into an organization that's going to fight against the values they believe in."[51]

In response, McDonald's USA spokesman Bill Whitman said, "Hatred has no place in our culture. That includes McDonald's, and we stand by and support our people to live and work in a society free of discrimination and harassment."[52]

Hatred? What hatred? The AFA was simply asking McDonald's to remain neutral in today's culture wars. Why the perpetual "hatred" accusation?

On February 14th, 2008, I held a public dialogue with Mr. Harry Knox, director of Religion and Faith for the Human Rights Campaign (HRC) and now a member of President Obama's Faith Advisory Council, part of a sequel to my lecture series from 2007.[53] Our subject was, "A Christian Response to Homosexuality," and within the first minute of my opening comments, I stated:

> I'm not speaking from the vantage point of moral superiority as a heterosexual to a homosexual but as someone fully dependent on the mercy and grace of God, believing with all my heart that Jesus shed His blood for heterosexual and homosexual alike. I also believe that heterosexuals have done more to destroy the family than have any gay activists, and I'm ashamed of the rampant pornography, divorce, and scandals that have plagued the heterosexual church in recent years. So, there's no self-righteousness here! Let me also say that there will be no gay bashing on my lips

because there is no homo-hatred in my heart. What you see is what you get.

Then, several minutes later, I made a candid apology:

> . . . I'm sad to say that in many respects, the Church has fallen very short here, treating gays and lesbians as the worst of sinners, demonizing a whole group of people because of the words and actions of a segment, not providing an environment where they can work through their struggles, proclaiming God's judgment more loudly than his love. For this, I offer my heartfelt apologies as a Christian leader and follower of Jesus, and by His grace, I pledge to do better and to help others to do better as well.[54]

And so, in a widely-publicized, well-attended forum, I explained that "in some profound ways, we have sinned against you in the gay and lesbian community," before stating "I will not add to this the sin of being dishonest. Truth is beautiful – especially when contrasted with lies and deception. Don't we thank those who are truthful – like doctors and colleagues and friends – since their words which, for the moment seem hurtful, can bring healing and help in the end?"

So, in the most gracious, respectful terms– and spoken from the heart – I laid out my honest differences with Harry Knox. How were these comments viewed?

The HRC issued an official report the day after the dialogue, accusing me of abusive behavior one year earlier. It began:

> Last year, Dr. Michael Brown, director of the conservative Charlotte-based Coalition of Conscience, picketed the HRC Carolinas Gala dinner and insulted attendees arriving at the Charlotte Convention Center with incendiary hate speech. The bullying presence of Brown and a small group of his supporters has been a disruptive and dispiriting presence in Charlotte for a number of years. Last year, Joe Solmonese decided enough was enough and that the people of North Carolina deserved better. He made it clear to Brown that his anti-GLBT hate rhetoric would

not go unanswered. And he kept his word![55]

For the record, the HRC report, written by Chris Johnson, only got a few minor details wrong here in the opening paragraph (sarcasm intended), such as 1) accusing me of picketing their 2007 gala dinner when, in reality, I was nowhere near their event; 2) stating that I had "insulted attendees arriving at the Charlotte Convention Center [in 2007] with incendiary hate speech," which is a real trick since I wasn't at the Charlotte Convention Center; 3) making reference to my "bullying presence," although it's quite difficult to have a bullying presence when you're not even present; 4) making reference to my "anti-GLBT hate rhetoric," although the entire account was imaginary and, having been nowhere near the Convention Center at that time, I could not have uttered any words, let alone the kind of words alleged here. (In addition, everyone had heard my words the previous night at the Harry Knox dialogue, and those words were anything but "anti-GLBT hate rhetoric"). Well, you can't expect a reporter to get *everything* right, can you?[56]

But this much is sure: The moment I took issue with gay activism in any shape, size, or form, regardless of the graciousness of my speech, I was deemed guilty of "incendiary hate speech" and "anti-GLBT hate rhetoric." What else could we expect? And remember: This report was written immediately after the dialogue from which I just quoted, above. You might want to read the quotes again and then ask yourself where the incendiary, anti-GLBT hate rhetoric is to be found.

But the lesson has been learned: If you define marriage as the union of a man and woman, as every dictionary in our history has, you are full of hate; if you say that you don't think men were designed to have sex with men or women were designed to have sex with women, you are full of hate; if you say that you know people who were formerly homosexual, you are full of hate; if you say, from a biblical point of view, that you believe that the Scriptures speak against homosexual practice, you are full of hate – indeed, anti-gay hate of the highest order.

"PROPOSITION HATE!"

The examples I have just cited, however, pale in comparison with the gay reaction to the passage of Proposition 8 on November 4, 2008, thereby amending the California constitution to limit marriage to the union of a man and a woman, overturning the 4-3 ruling of the California Supreme Court just six months earlier.[57] The sound of "Prop 8 = Hate!" was heard across the land, with gay protests taking place on November 15, 2008, in as many as 300 American cities. In fact, a Google search on December 19, 2008, yielded almost 1.5 million hits for the words, "Prop 8" and "hate" (1,490,000, to be precise). The message certainly got out!

This sampling of headlines says it all:

- Keith Olbermann Eloquently Breaks Down Prop 8 Hate
- Prop 8 = Hate
- Californians Against Hate – Fighting for Marriage Equality.

The origins of the "Prop 8 = Hate" slogan are traced back to a gay blogger:

NBC Blogger: 'Prop 8 = Hate. Repeat'
Comedian ANT, who blogs for NBC on an almost daily basis, is entering the gay marriage debate. The actor and co-median, whose material has included homophobia ("Ho-mophobic means fear of gays. Uhhhh...what are they afraid of? Afraid that we're going to beat them up... and then [expletive] 'em?") began a blog entry early this morning with what will probably be No on Prop 8's unofficial cam-paign slogan: "Prop 8 equals hate." Don't be surprised to see more and more buttons and bumper stickers saying just that this election season. T-shirts are already being sold.[58]

And what about the "Proposition Hate" musical? Dennis Prager explains:

Marc Shaiman, the Tony Award-winning composer of the film and stage musical "Hairspray," has done the country a major, if inadvertent, service. He has composed a brief musical piece against California Proposition 8 that takes only three minutes to reveal the ignorance and hate that pervades so much anti-Proposition 8 activism.

This short musical, viewed more than 2 million times on the Internet, features major Hollywood talents playing (through song) two groups on a beach -- gay men and women in beach clothes and a stuffy formally dressed church group composed of whites and blacks.

Its message begins with a religious man and woman reacting to the cheerful gay group (celebrating the Barack Obama victory) by singing these words:

"Look! Nobody's watching
It's time to spread some hate
And put it in the constitution
Now, how? Proposition Hate!
Great!"

Shaiman puts hateful words in the mouths of the religious proponents of the man-woman definition of marriage: "It's time to spread some hate and put it in the constitution." But no one put hate in the constitution. The only words Proposition 8 added to the California Constitution were: "Only marriage between a man and a woman is valid or recognized in California." What is hateful about that?[59]

Proposition Hate? Spreading hate and putting it in the constitution? Who can believe this kind of rhetoric?[60]

Of course, I understand the heartfelt belief of many in the GLBT community (along with their straight sympathizers) that they are being deprived of one of the most fundamental human rights, finding Prop 8 supporters to be bigots of the worst kind. And I'm sure there are many devoted, same-sex couples among them who are absolutely heartbroken. But is it impossible for them to see that people can differ with their quite novel view that people of the same sex can marry – something utterly foreign to virtually all world cultures for all time – without being filled with hate? Why must the hate button always be pushed?

I once asked some gays and lesbians with whom I was in dialogue why a blood brother and sister couldn't marry, making reference to a famous case in Germany.[61] In response to my question, I was told that there were potential health issues with children born to siblings, among other issues.[62]

Of course, I agreed with their points, but my question back to my gay and lesbian interlocutors was: Why isn't your position hateful? Why aren't you rightly called bigots? Why couldn't this couple, deeply in love, look at you and say, "You are spewing hate towards us! And rather than telling us about the potential health risks to our offspring, you should be advocating research to help find cures for our children."

Opponents of same-sex marriage, some of whom are liberal, non-religious people, have put forth many sound reasons why male-female union alone can be called "marriage," just as opponents of incestuous marriage have put forth many sound reasons for their position.[63] To suggest that it is unwise to tamper with the foundations of human society is hardly "hate," but with the "Prop 8 = Hate" mantra being so effective, it's doubtful that any kind of civil dialogue can take place.

And in another ironic twist – a repeat of "the victim can't be guilty" syndrome (otherwise known as "the object of hate cannot be accused of hate") – some of the Prop 8 protestors spewed some venom of their own. One of the uglier scenes took place in Sacramento, CA, where demonstrators held signs reading:

- Prop 8=American Taliban
- Ban Bigots
- Majority Vote Doesn't Matter
- 52%=Nazi [this referred to the 52-48% vote in favor of Prop 8]
- Don't Silence the Christians, Feed Them 2 the Lions
- Your Rights Are Next[64]

And all this was part of a protest *against* hate![65]

Predictably, all the standard rhetoric was there, including the all-too common epithets of Taliban, bigots, and Nazi (of course!), but this time, a few more threatening touches were added, such as the exhortation to feed Christians to the lions and the (perhaps more realistic) threat, "Your Rights Are Next."

May I ask again, which side is guilty of hate, the side that says, "Marriage is the union of a man and woman," or the side that says, "Feed them to the lions"? Does anyone else see the (very pink) elephant in the room?[66]

Maggie Gallagher is the president of the National Organization for Marriage and is a persistent and clear opponent of same-sex marriage, often appearing as a talking head on TV news. But is she a gay-bashing, hate-filled woman? There is no lack of love, however, on the lips of her critics, some of whom find joy in calling for her death. On Nov. 9, 2009, the Queerty.com website reported that, "Fresh off its victory in Maine, where it helped rape away the marriage rights of gays and lesbians there, the National Organization for Marriage confirms what we all expected: It's taking its Church-backed dollars to New Jersey."[67]

The report elicited some choice responses:

No. 1 · Mark
jersey queers
Gallagher = Hoffa
you know the routine

No. 2 · terrwill
MARK: Where do we send contribtions for to pay for that "assginment"????
No. 3 · terrwill
What a vile, hateful, nasty, old sexually repressed [expletive] Maggie Gallager is..........Can someone please hire a private investigator to dig up dirt on this vile witch?

What is so damm frustrating is that her traveling band of hate is so gladly funded by the rightwing-nutbag zealots. This [expletive] reportedly made something like $250,000.00 the last few years.

When is karma gonna catch up with her fat, disgusting, cottage cheesed filled celluite ridden [expletive]????

No. 4 · YellowRanger
She'd look lovely in a pair of solid cement loafers.

No. 5 · vernonvanderbilt
@YellowRanger
She'd still float. She's extra-buoyant.

No. 6 · terrwill
Hmmm last time they were building a stadium in NJ, they found "preferred seating" for Jimmmy Hoffa...............
Seems to be a new stadium being constructed now............

just sayin……

So, some of those who are protesting against hate are (playfully or otherwise) wishing that Maggie Gallagher would be killed just as Jimmy Hoffa was years ago. How delightful!

But it is not just bloggers who are making their hostile feelings known. Even major gay activist organizations, like the Gill Action Fund, the political arm of multi-millionaire Tim Gill, sounding dire warnings to politicians who dare to stand for male-female marriage. As deputy executive director Bill Smith, stated in December, 2010:

> This is the first time we're going to name names and say, "We're coming to get you because you're against marriage equality. The point is, when you vote against marriage equality, there are consequences."[68]

Consequences indeed.

Even racial hatred can be spewed in the name of gay-rights, as Pastor D. L. Foster, an African American former homosexual (now married with children) learned a few years back. When Pastor Foster responded clearly to a man who accused him of narcissism – he is not one to pull punches in his posts – he received this response:

> I hope someone kills you soon you piece of NIGGER [expletive]. I certainly hope someday you [expletive] off the wrong person and you get killed as a result, you ugly NIGGER, Thats RIght Big fat ugly NIGGER You were never gay to begin with you can never provide incontrovertible proof that you ever were which means you are a liar, a liar and a NIGGER. I hope that person kills you in the most painful manner imaginable.[69]

The irony of these interactions was not lost on Dr. Mike Adams, the UNC Wilmington criminology professor and acerbic columnist, who described an incident that took place at one of his speeches at UMASS-Amherst.

> When protestors showed up at my UMASS speech with a giant "F*** Mike Adamz" sign I asked them two questions:

1) "Did you know that you spelled Mike Adams wrong?" and 2) "What group do you guys represent?" When the protestors told me they represented the "UMASS Coalition Against Hate" I laughed heartily. Should the "Coalition against Hate" be holding a giant sign with the F-word? Or should they instead be holding a giant sign saying "F*** Irony"?[70]

Need I say more?

At the end of a June 24, 2005 editorial in the *Charlotte Observer*, I wrote: "If some still choose to push this emotionally charged button, others can choose to make it ineffective by determining instead to seek out and hear the truth, recognizing that whoever uses the rhetoric of 'hate' is most likely deflecting discussion from the real issues at hand. And it is only through bringing the real issues into the light that we can render the hate button obsolete. Isn't it time?"[71]

I have made the personal determination never to push the hate button but rather to hear out those who differ with me? Will you join me?

It is particularly important to begin to make
three to five-year-olds aware of the range of families that exist in the
UK today; families with one mum, one mum and dad, two mums,
two dads, grandparents, adoptive parents, guardians etc.

Recommendation from the UK's National Union of Teachers (NUT),
July, 2006

Restroom Accessibility: Students shall have access to the restroom
that corresponds to their gender identity exclusively and consistently at school.

Official Policy of the San Francisco Unified School District School Board
(SFUSD)

"Gender identity" refers to one's understanding, interests,
outlook, and feelings about whether one is female or male, or both,
or neither, regardless of one's biological sex.

From the Los Angeles Unified School District Reference Guide

Heterosexism: An overt or tacit bias against homosexuality
rooted in the belief that heterosexuality is superior or the norm.

Common Vocabulary Regarding Sexual Orientation/Gender Identity
(for the SFUSD)

Whoever captures the kids owns the future.

Patricia Nell Warren, "Future Shock," *The Advocate*, Oct 3, 1995.

3

Boys Will Be Girls
Will Be Boys:
Undoing Gender and
Teaching "Gay is Good" in
Our Children's Schools

oms and dads, boys and girls, it's time to read a special poem that I wrote just for you. It's called "Here at School the Slant Is Gay." Let's read out loud together on the count of three!

HERE AT SCHOOL THE SLANT IS GAY

Little Johnny went to school
There to learn a brand new rule;

No longer could the boys be boys
Or have their special trucks and toys;

Only six, so young and tender
It's time for him to unlearn gender

And break the binding two-sex mold
That hurtful thinking that's so old.

Parents at home can have their say
But here at school, the slant is gay.

In other words, to make this clear
There's nothing wrong with being queer.

Having two moms is mighty fine;
To disagree is out of line.

We'll deconstruct the family
And smash religious bigotry

And keep the church out of the state
By saying faith is really hate.

Free speech can only go one way,

Since here at school, the slant is gay.

So little ones, it's time to learn
'bout famous queers, each one in turn;

Lesbian greats long neglected
Well-known gays just now detected.

Some, perhaps, were man-boy lovers;
We'll keep that stuff under the covers.

GLSEN will fill in for Granny
And help kids find their inner-trannie.

Those born in a body that's wrong
Will hear of sex-change before long.

And through the years as Johnny grows
He will learn that anything goes.

With Bill, who's trans and Joe, who's bi-,
And Sue, who thinks that she's a guy.

United in the Day of Silence,
Joining the Gay Straight Alliance –

A queer new system rules the day,
Since here at school, the slant is gay.

Does this poem seem farfetched or exaggerated? Or does it strike you as a complete fabrication? If so, then you're in for a rude awakening. Welcome to the contemporary American school system. This is the day of the "queering of elementary education" – to quote the title of a highly-praised book – and much of this is due to the influence of GLSEN, the Gay, Lesbian, and

Straight Educational Network.

MOMS AND DADS, MEET GLSEN

Celebrating their tenth anniversary in 2005, Kevin Jennings, GLSEN's founder and, at that time, Executive Director, was effusive:

> **One Decade Ago...**
> The education community was in profound denial about the very existence of LGBT students.
> Fewer than a hundred gay-straight alliances existed.
> Fewer than 2 million students attended schools where harassment based on sexual orientation was prohibited.
> In short, just about nobody cared. . . .
> Today, ten years after we began our mission, more than 12 million students are protected by state laws. Nearly 3,000 schools have GSA's [Gay Student Alliances] or other student clubs that deal with LGBT issues. Over fifty national education and social justice organizations, including the National Education Association (NEA) have joined GLSEN in its work to create safe schools for our nation's children through projects like "No Name-Calling Week".

Then, after pointing out how much more work needed to be done, Jennings wrote:

> GLSEN's tenth anniversary is a cause for celebration. It is a milestone for the organization, for the movement, and most importantly, for America's students. Let us take this joyous occasion to rededicate ourselves to the work of making our nation's schools places where young people learn to value and respect everyone, regardless of sexual orientation or gender identity/expression. The next generation deserves nothing less.[1]

To be sure, some of GLSEN's goals are praiseworthy, and it's important for all families and educators to understand the struggles and, at times, severe trauma that many children experience while growing up. I wholeheartedly agree with GLSEN that kids shouldn't pick on other kids because they seem to be different. I absolutely affirm that it's very harmful and dead wrong for children to call their classmates "faggots" or "sissies."[2] And without a doubt, kids struggling with Gender Identity Disorder (for more on this, see below) deserve our compassion, not our criticism. But GLSEN's agenda goes far beyond this. GLSEN wants homosexuality and transgenderism completely normalized – and even encouraged, celebrated, and nurtured – in the educational system.

To put Jennings' ten-year statement in context, consider that by 1995, which was ground zero for GLSEN, dramatic changes had already taken place in our schools. In his book *School's Out: The Impact of Gay and Lesbian Issues on America's Schools*, Dan Woog expressed the seismic shift that had taken place from 1985 to 1995. For the sake of emphasis, I have inserted my comments in brackets:

> A decade ago, who would have thought that an entire book could be written on the subject of homosexuality and education – written, in fact, using real names, real schools, and real incidents, many of them not only positive but spectacularly so? [Today, you could fill a small library with books like this.] Who would have thought that in so many buildings throughout the United States, in large cities, medium-sized suburbs, and tiny towns, there would be not only openly gay teachers, administrators, coaches, and students, but also gay-straight alliances, gay-themed curricula, and gay topics discussed honestly and intelligently in workshops, classes, and the pages of school newspapers? [And who would have thought that, from 1995 to 2010, these gay straight alliances would grow by more than 3000%?] It would have seemed like a fairy tale.[3]

Today, in 2010, this hardly sounds like a fairy tale at all. In fact, it sounds rather ho-hum and commonplace. Gay-inspired curricula and gay-affirming educational programs are everywhere today, and according to GLSEN, from 1999-2007, Gay Straight Alliances in our schools have grown from 100 to 3,000.

What *does* seem like a fairy tale is that this scenario would have been unimaginable back in 1985. Today, *that* seems unthinkable. For gay educational activists, however, this is just the beginning, as expressed so clearly by Jennings.

THE GLSEN LUNCHBOX

What exactly, then, does this mean? And what precisely does GLSEN want to teach our children? Let's start with the GLSEN Lunchbox, an attractively packaged training tool for teachers beginning at *kindergarten* level, described as "A Comprehensive Training Program for Ending Anti-LGBT Bias in Schools." The GLSEN website states:

> *The GLSEN Lunchbox 2* is a comprehensive training program aimed at providing educators and community members with the background knowledge, skills, and tools necessary to make schools safer and more affirming places for lesbian, gay, bisexual, and transgender (LGBT) students.[4]

Does this sound innocent? Let's take a look inside.

The Lunchbox (which literally is a blue lunchbox), contains, among other items, a one hour video, a "How to Use the GLSEN Lunchbox" manual, and a set of large cards outlining the format for each of the exercises, some of which address educators only, and some of which are for students of different ages. Outside of the lunchbox is a 141 page notebook binder, "The GLSEN Lunchbox Trainer's Manual."[5]

Some of the activities include "North American History Game Cards," listing twenty-eight North Americans, most of whom are fairly well known and all of whom, according to GLSEN, are (or were) gay or transgender. (Among the better known names are Sara Josephine Baker, James Baldwin, Leonard Bernstein, George Washington Carver, Babe Didrickson, Allen Ginsberg, Barbara Jordan, Margaret Mead, Harvey Milk, Bayard Rustin, Renee Richards, Andy Warhol, Walt Whitman, and Tennessee Williams.)

A similar game card activity is provided for World History, listing luminaries such as Alexander the Great, Hans Christian Anderson, Pope John XII, King Edward II, Noel Coward, Hadrian, Dag Hammserskjold, Joan of Arc, Elton John, Juvenal, Leonardo da Vinci, Michelangelo, Rudolph Nureyev, Pyotr Tchaikovsky, and Oscar Wilde. According to GLSEN, all of them were gay (or bisexual?).

The object of these activities is to help children and teachers recognize that many outstanding personalities in world and national history, including musicians, artists, statesmen, religious leaders, authors, and others, were gay. Therefore, being gay is neither negative nor bad nor degrading nor harmful nor dangerous.

Of course, a different set of conclusions could have been reached, namely, that until recently, these alleged homosexuals (or bisexuals) were content to function effectively and creatively in society without making a major issue of their sexuality – indeed, in a number of cases, the sexual orientation of these individuals is a matter of debate *because* they did not make an issue of their sexuality – and they were able to make important contributions to their generations and beyond without drawing attention to their sexual orientation.[6]

There's also a dirty little secret that GLSEN will never mention, namely, that some of the men on this list were not just alleged homosexuals but alleged *pederasts*. As noted by Jim Kepner, formerly curator of the International Gay and Lesbian Archives in Los Angeles,

> if we reject the boylovers in our midst today we'd better stop waving the banner of the Ancient Greeks, of Michelangelo, Leonardo da Vinci, Oscar Wilde, Walt Whitman, Horatio Alger, and Shakespeare. We'd better stop claiming them as part of our heritage unless we are broadening our concept of what it means to be gay today.[7]

I guess as far as famous pedophiles are concerned, GLSEN has adopted a "Don't ask, don't tell" policy. As we said in the poem, "We'll keep that stuff under the covers." Thus the NAMBLA website boasts in its article "History of Man/Boy Love":

> From famous couples such as Oscar Wilde and Lord Alfred Douglas, to cultural institutions such as that of ancient Greek pederasty, to cultural concepts such as China's "passion of the cut sleeve", to iconic figures such as Francis Bacon or Walt Whitman. From the earliest known homoerotic couple, Smenkhkare and Akhenaten, to medieval Andelusian troubadors, to 20th century figures such as Allen Ginsburg and Arthur C. Clark, man/boy love spans every dimension of history, both Western and

non-Western.[8]

So, some of these men cited in GLSEN's Lunchbox as being gay are cited by NAMBLA as being pedophiles. In fact, according to NAMBLA, among the famous men listed in GLSEN's North American and World History Game Cards, Alexander the Great, Leonard Da Vinci, Michelangelo, and Oscar Wilde, were all "man-boy lovers."[9] Thus, much of the alleged evidence for their homosexuality points specifically to pederasty. So, if they were practicing homosexuals, they were practicing pederasts. Should this be celebrated?

But there's more to the GLSEN lunchbox than queer history. It also seeks to strike at the very root of male-female distinctives. Thus, the activity called "Getting in Touch with Your Inner Trannie" (i.e., inner transgender identity) has as its stated purpose, "To help participants better understand and personally relate to the breadth of issues around gender identity and expression," asking the children questions such as: "Have you ever been told, 'Act like a lady/woman/girl,' or 'Act like a man?' What was the situation? How did it make you feel and why?" And, "If you see someone on the street whose gender is unclear to you, how do you react – both internally and externally?"[10]

THE ANTITHESIS OF "DICK AND JANE"

While these questions might seem benign in another context, in the world of GLSEN they are certainly not benign, since many gay educators are eager to remove the assumption that there is such a thing as "masculinity" and "femininity." Rather, these should be viewed as antiquated constructs that hold countless children in bondage to the false expectations of society. We need a new set of more fluid, enlightened definitions.

Maybe the *Girls Will Be Boys Will Be Girls* coloring book will help. The book's write-up states,

> *The antithesis of the "Dick and Jane" coloring book, this is a funny, playful and provocative deconstruction of traditional gender roles. The activist authors use drawings as well as images taken from old children's books to show how completely silly and unnecessary most common gender assumptions are. Covering topics such as clothing, assumptions about bodies, toys, intimacy and education, this entertaining book affirms our right to be ourselves. Ages 12 and up.* [11]

The opening page lists these thought-provoking questions:

- How do you define gender?
- How many genders are there?
- What would the world look like without gender?
- In what ways do you feel confined or restricted by your assigned gender?
- Was the gender assigned to you the one you feel most comfortable with?
- What privileges do you or don't you have due to the gender you have been labeled?
- Do you feel forced to act in certain ways because of your assigned gender?
- What happens when you don't act these ways?
- How do you unlearn gender?

And I remind you: This book is for kids as young as twelve.

One of the illustrations features two kids of undetermined sex standing in front of the school bathrooms, with one of them commenting, "I should have worn a skirt. The pants bathroom is full." Another picture shows three kids, at least one of whom appears to be a cross-dresser, standing in front of four "Gender Menus." The caption reads, "I never knew we had so much to choose from!" There's even a page featuring four girls holding the GAGA sign – standing for "Girls against Gender Assignment." GAGA? Seriously?

And while the kids are coloring, maybe mom and dad (or, mom and mom, or dad and dad) can read Judith Butler's book, *Undoing Gender*. That way the entire family can be deconstructed together.

For those who like posters they can hang on the wall, there is always Mollie Biewald's "How to Eradicate Gender or Multiply it Exponentially," available from the Syracuse Cultural Worker's Catalog.[12] (Neither Butler's book nor this poster are part of the GLSEN Lunchbox.)

This poster, which is also available in postcard size, features novel suggestions like:

- Spend a day in drag
- Write to organizations that call themselves "gay and lesbian" and ask them to change it to "Queer."
- Think twice before you ask people if their child is a

boy or a girl.
- Join the transsexual menace.
- Refer to everyone by the incorrect pronoun.
- Challenge the binary gender paradigm over Thanksgiving dinner.
- Refuse to check off your sex when filling out forms.
- Hang out with children and teach them how to cross dress Barbie and GI Joe.
- Experiment with new ways to accentuate your queerness using language, dress, movement and, of course, accessories.[13]

Not to be outdone, the GLSEN lunchbox has an activity called "Deconstructing Definitions of Family." Yes, the lunchbox is chock full of wonderful educational tools designed to recreate the family in a queer new way.

Especially helpful are the "Terminology Game Cards," which quiz students and teachers on terms such as: Biological Sex, Gender Identity, Gender Role, Transgender, Gender Expression, Sexual Orientation, Heterosexism, Transphobia, Asexual, Bisexual, Lesbian, Gay, Transsexual, Intersexual, Androgyny, Cross Dresser, Genderqueer, Gender Non-Conforming, Queer, LGBTQ, Sexual Reassignment Surgery, D/L (Down Low), MSM. The matching answers to the game cards include these definitions:

Biological Sex: Our "packaging" determined by our chromosomes, hormones, and internal and external genitalia.[14]

Gender Identity: One's innermost concept of self as "male," "female," or "intersexual."[15]

Gender Role: The socially constructed and culturally specific behavior and appearance expectations imposed on females ("femininity") and males ("masculinity").

Transgender: A broad term for all gender-variant people, including transsexuals, cross-dressers, and people who choose to identify as neither of the two sexes as they are currently defined.

Cross Dresser: People who regularly or occasionally wear the clothing socially assigned to the other sex, but are usually comfortable with their birth-assigned sex and do not wish to change it.

Genderqueer: People who do not identify, or who do not express themselves as completely male or female; may or may not identify as transgender.

Gender Non-Conforming: Perceived to have gender characteristics and/or behaviors that do not conform to traditional or societal expectations; may not identify as lesbian, gay, bisexual, transgender, or queer.

In short, say goodbye to male and female, to masculinity and femininity, to "biological sex," and say hello to genderqueer, gender non-conforming, transgender, and transsexual.

We certainly have come a long way from Dick and Jane story books, and if the categories of male and female are up for grabs in kindergarten, can you imagine what's coming next? And you thought my poem was exaggerated?

DISCOVERING YOUR INNER TRANNIE

Moms and dads, consider this scenario, which is anything but farfetched. Your six year-old son Johnny comes home from the school, and when you ask him what he learned today, he tells you that he played a fun game in the morning called "discovering your inner trannie," in which he tried to see if he had a little girl hiding inside his body. Then, after lunch he learned that sometimes it's better to have two daddies than just one daddy and one mommy (better known as "deconstructing definitions of family"), and then, before going home, he learned some fun sounding terms like Genderqueer and Crossdresser. And when you ask him if he's been working on his ABC's, he might just tell you, "Yes, and my LGBTQ's too!"

Of course, Johnny might also ask if he can invite his friend Sally over to play, and when you tell him you don't remember him having a friend named Sally, he tells you, "Well, Sally used to be Billy, but now Billy wears a dress to school and his new name is Sally!"

Outrageous, you say? Impossible? Then consider this Dec. 2, 2006, *New York Times* report by Patricia Leigh Brown, entitled "Supporting Boys or Girls When the Line Isn't Clear."

Until recently, many children who did not conform

to gender norms in their clothing or behavior and identified intensely with the opposite sex were steered to psychoanalysis or behavior modification.

But as advocates gain ground for what they call gender-identity rights . . . a major change is taking place among schools and families. Children as young as 5 who display predispositions to dress like the opposite sex are being supported by a growing number of young parents, educators and mental health professionals.[16]

Of course, not everyone is ready for this new approach, and "Cassandra Reese, a first-grade teacher outside Boston, recalled that fellow teachers were unnerved when a young boy showed up in a skirt."[17] More and more, however, little kids are going to school dressed as the opposite sex, and often, the media portrays them, along with their parents, as heroes (see below). Shocking headlines like this are losing some of their shock value: "3rd-graders asked to help classmate in gender change. Parents given 1-day notice of presentation explaining boy would now wear girl clothes."[18] Third-graders!

And what happens as these young children start to get older? The *NY Times* reports, "As their children head into adolescence, some parents are choosing to block puberty medically to buy time for them to figure out who they are, raising a host of ethical questions." Not surprisingly, "some schools are engaged in a steep learning curve to dismantle gender stereotypes."[19]

What exactly does this mean?

At the Park Day School in Oakland, teachers are taught a gender-neutral vocabulary and are urged to line up students by sneaker color rather than by gender. "We are careful not to create a situation where students are being boxed in," said Tom Little, the school's director. "We allow them to move back and forth until something feels right."[20]

Yes, they don't want their students, some of them as young as five, to feel "boxed in" – meaning, "boxed in" to being a boy or a girl. Not surprisingly, "The prospect of *cross-dressing kindergartners* has sparked a deep philosophical divide among professionals over how best to counsel families."[21] Yes, you read that correctly: *cross-dressing kindergartners.*

"WHAT'S WITH THE DRESS, JACK?"

The rest of us, of course, need to accept this development and become sensitized to it, otherwise we're being hateful and bigoted and intolerant. How our sense of right and wrong has shifted! Already in 2004, GLSEN offered a lesson plan that included a section on "cross dressing and non-gender conforming clothing," with the cross dressing lesson entitled, "What's With the Dress, Jack?"[22]

Yet it gets worse. According to a March 30, 2008 article in the *Boston Globe* by Pagan Kennedy, the renowned Boston Children's Hospital has been offering full transgender service for prepubescent children, beginning with hormone-blocking treatments and then sex-change surgery.[23] The article points to the real pain experienced by kids who think they have been born in the wrong body, and it is a pain we must take seriously:

> CHILDREN HAVE CUT themselves. In some cases, 9- or 10-year-old kids have staged suicide attempts. The little boys sob unless they're allowed to wear dresses. The girls want to be called Luke, Ted, or James.
>
> Their parents, desperate to know what is wrong, go online and type "gender disorder."[24]

The medical alternatives, however, have been few and far between: "Until recently, children with cross-gender feelings rarely received modern medical care – and certainly not hormone shots. After all, who would allow a child to redesign his or her body?"[25]

Recently, though, things have been changing:

> ...in the past few years, some doctors have come to believe that kids should be allowed to have some control over how they grow up. Dr. Norman Spack, 64, argues that transgender kids tend to be much happier - and less likely to harm themselves - when they're able to live in their preferred gender role.[26]

So, the medical profession – for ostensibly compassionate reasons – along with the educational system – ostensibly for similar reasons – is helping to reorder the lives of children who are not at home with the "gender they were assigned at birth," to use the popular-but-mind-boggling terminology of the day.[27] And in just a few years, these kids can move from being cross-dressing kindergarteners to body-mutilating young adults (pardon the bluntness).[28] Or put another way, instead of cutting themselves – and I'm not for a moment making light of the children's emotional pain– they can have paid professionals hack off their breasts or mutilate their penises, with the active support of the school system until they are of age. (For more on the question of sex change surgery, see below, Chapter Fifteen.)

To put this in the context of today's popular media, when I was asked to appear on the Tyra Banks show January 27th, 2010 to discuss the issue of transgender children, I was the only voice in a sixty-minute program raising any question about the rightness of sending seven-year-old boys to school dressed as girls, or putting older kids on hormone blockers to delay the onset of puberty, or advocating sex-change surgery as the best, long-term solution. The whole program, from beginning to end (aside from the five-minute segment in which I appeared, opposite two transgender advocates, plus Tyra), celebrated the boldness of these cross-dressing kids and their families, bringing them onstage as very persuasive, emotionally compelling guests.[29] Even to raise a question about this was considered fringe.

What makes this all the more striking is that, as of this writing, Gender Identity Disorder (GID) is still recognized as a diagnosable mental illness by psychologists and psychiatrists. In other words, the major mental health organizations, which tend to be quite gay-affirming, still recognize GID as a real mental disorder, as the name implies.[30] Yet this aberrant behavior is now being codified as fully acceptable in our schools, protected by the GLSEN-inspired "anti-bullying" policies which seek to ensure all students are "valued and respected regardless of sexual orientation or *gender identity/expression*" (my emphasis).[31] So seven year-old Mark, who in his genetics and body is a boy, can decide that he is "Mary" and come to first grade wearing a dress, and students will be taught and expected to "respect" his cross-dressing behavior by requiring little girls to share their bathroom and locker room facilities with him as well as requiring all students and teachers to refer to him as "her" – despite the fact that none of this comports with objective reality.

Little Mark and his family certainly deserve care and compassion and help. But he needs a counselor or a doctor (not Dr. Spack!) rather than a dress, yet in today's queer new world, we who see Mark as needing help are told that *we* need to see a doctor. In fact, in Maryland, the Montgomery County School District has written cross-dressing "Portia" into its elementary school curriculum, despite strong protests from a number of family-based organizations.

As noted by John Garza in a dissenting editorial, "The curriculum presents the story of 'Portia' the boy who becomes a girl. When Portia finally becomes a girl, 'she' gets a key to the teachers' unisex bathroom." Garza is therefore quite right to ask, "When our children follow the curriculum and chop off body parts, take hormones and 'reassign their gender,' won't they expect the key to the bathroom like Portia?"[32] So there is even a reward for being transgender.

At the risk of overkill, I repeat: This is not fantasy, this is reality – and it could be coming to (or already in) a school near you. One pre-school teacher in Charlotte, North Carolina reported to me that she was not allowed to address the *four year-old children* as "boys and girls" – I kid you not – since that would be making a gender distinction. Rather, she had to call them "friends."[33] And we wonder why so many more kids these days are confused about their gender identity? Our schools are contributing to the problem, and if GLSEN has its way, that contribution will be active, rather than passive, the rule rather than the exception.[34]

STRAIGHT FROM THE PAGES OF GAY ACTIVIST MANUALS

GLSEN's "Safe Space Kit," which includes a forty-two page manual, was released in 2009, with the goal of being used in all of America's more than 100,000 middle and high schools. The manual offers this advice for those wanting to be "allies" of GLBT kids (and adults):

> **Make no assumptions**. When engaging with students, or even other staff and parents, do not assume you know their sexual orientation or gender identity. Don't assume that everyone is heterosexual or fits into your idea of gender roles – be open to the variety of identities and expressions. In our society, students constantly receive the message that everyone is supposed to be straight. Show students that you understand there is no one way a person "should" be.[35]

Did you catch that? Yes, we must "be open to the variety of identities and expressions" since "there is no one way a person 'should' be," meaning that the sky is really the limit, and however a kid wants to express his or her gender identity or sexual orientation at school – regardless of age or maturity – we must accept that, embrace that, and nurture that. And anyone thinking that, perhaps, a fifteen-year-old boy "shouldn't" come to school wearing a dress, high-heels and make-up, or that, perhaps, an eleven-year-old girl "shouldn't" be coming out as a genderqueer dyke (without her parents knowledge, no less) – well such a person needs to be reeducated and delivered from their bias. And be sure not to assume that the boy you're talking to is actually a male or that his mom is really a woman!

Who can tell me with a straight face that this will *not* lead to greater gender identity confusion (not to mention overall social confusion) and greater blurring of distinctions between male and female, or that this will *not* lead to an assault on "heteronormativity?" But what else could we expect from a manual that includes a terminology test with definitions like this: "Queer: An umbrella term used to describe a sexual orientation, gender identity or gender expression that does not conform to heteronormative society."[36] This is what is included in the innocuous sounding "Safe School Kit."

Practically speaking, GLBT allies in the school system are encouraged to "Use inclusive language," meaning:

> Through casual conversation and during classroom time, make sure the language you are using is inclusive of all people. When referring to people in general, try using words like "partner" instead of "boyfriend/girlfriend" or "husband/wife," and avoid gendered pronouns, using "they" instead of "he/she." Using inclusive language will help LGBT students feel more comfortable being themselves and coming to you for support.[37]

In other words, goodbye, "husbands and wives"; hello "partners" (and, since "partner" becomes interchangeable with both "husband/wife" *and* "boyfriend/girlfriend," goodbye to marital distinctives too!). Goodbye "boys and girls"; hello "friends." Goodbye "he and she"; hello "they" (or who knows what). Yes, this is what GLSEN is aggressively and actively advocating in your children's schools, with the warm support of Hollywood and beyond.[38] (Bear in mind that I haven't even quoted from other GLSEN publications like, *Bending the Mold: An Action Kit for Transgender Youth*; or, *Beyond the Binary: A Tool Kit for Gender Identity Activism in Schools*. The titles say it all.)[39]

And I remind you: This is not just theory. In many school districts, it is already reality. To quote Patrick Leigh Brown again,

The Los Angeles Unified School District, for instance, requires that students be addressed with a name and pronoun that corresponds to the gender identity. It also asks schools to provide a locker room or changing area that corresponds to a student's chosen gender.[40]

So then, if "he" decides that he is now "she," it is school policy in Los Angeles to address him as her, and to allow this boy to change in the girls' changing area. Yes, this is school policy! As stated in the San Francisco Unified School Policy, "Transgender students shall not be forced to use the locker room corresponding to their gender assigned at birth."[41] Not surprisingly, I read a report about an eight year-old boy who came home from his California school crying, traumatized after having to undress in his locker room in the presence of a girl who considered herself to be a boy.[42] If this were fiction, it would be very bad fiction; as reality, it is tragic.[43]

More shocking still is that, according to some school policies, parents do not have to be informed about changes in their child's gender self-identification (if Ben identifies as Betty at school) or declaration of their perceived sexual orientation (if Jane comes out as a lesbian), since they may not "react well."[44] The National Education Association even "issued standards for multisexual issues several years ago, which instruct school employees to 'respect confidentiality.'"[45]

All that, however, was not enough. There must be changes in school textbooks as well, and thus California bill SB 777, which was introduced by openly lesbian Senator Sheila Kuehl and passed in 2007, bans the use of textbooks or any classroom instruction that is considered to be discriminatory against gays, lesbians, transgenders, bisexuals or those with perceived gender issues. (As first crafted, the bill spoke of "any matter reflecting adversely upon" such persons).[46] In other words, as explained by Meredith Turney, the legislative liaison for Capitol Resource Institute, "The terms 'mom and dad' or 'husband and wife' could promote discrimination against homosexuals if a same-sex couple is not also featured."[47]

Conservative columnist Peter LaBarbera explains further what this bill involves:

> SB 777 incorporates the strange Penal Code definition of "gender" and places it into the Education Code, reading: "Gender" means sex, and includes a person's gender identity

and gender related appearance and behavior whether or not stereotypically associated with the person's assigned sex at birth." This means boys becoming girls and girls becoming boys would have to be positively portrayed in health textbooks, sex education classes and school assemblies.[48]

To repeat: This is now California law. But none of this should surprise us. The handwriting has been on the wall for some time, not to mention that the media has also been fully compliant (see below, Chapter Five, for more on this).

GAY RULES THE DAY IN MASSACHUSETTS SCHOOLS

Consider these examples from Massachusetts schools compiled by John Haskins in his 2001 article, "It's 1984 in Massachusetts, and Big Brother Is Gay."

- In Brookline, a transsexual told first-graders how his penis was cut off and he became a woman. With no sense of irony, the [Boston] Globe called it "sex-change counseling." Parents, never notified, had to comfort their terrified children.
- Newton North High School. Pupils learned in an R-rated film how "Ludo enjoys being a girl. Borrowing mommy's red high heels, her lipstick, her earrings … yummy!" Trouble is, 7-year-old Ludo is a boy, even if he is pretty in pink.
- Ashland children were instructed to play homosexuals in a skit. As reported in the Middlesex News on April 1, 1994, one boy's line was: "It's natural to be attracted to the same sex." Girls were told to hold hands and pretend they were lesbians.
- Framingham pupils found themselves answering this Orwellian questionnaire: "1. What do you think caused your heterosexuality? 2. When did you first decide you were heterosexual? 3. Is it possible heterosexuality is a phase you will grow out of? 4. Is it possible you are heterosexual because you fear the same sex? 5. If you have never slept with anyone of the same sex, how do

you know you wouldn't prefer it? Is it possible you merely need a good gay experience? 6. To whom have you disclosed your heterosexuality? How did they react? 7. Why are heterosexuals so blatant, always making a spectacle of their heterosexuality? Why can't they just be who they are and not flaunt their sexuality by kissing in public, wearing wedding rings, etc.?"[49]

But the Haskins article was written back in 2001. Those were the good old days! A lot has happened since then, beginning with a widely-reported case involving David and Tonia Parker of Lexington, Massachusetts.

The Parkers were shocked when their son Jacob came home from *kindergarten* with a bag of books promoting "diversity," including Robert Skutch's book *Who's In a Family?*, "which depicts different kinds of families, including same-sex couples raising children."[50] David Parker complained to his school district, insisting that the school notify him and his wife "about classroom discussions about same-sex marriage and what they called other adult themes. They also wanted the option to exclude their boy, now 6, from those talks."[51]

When the Parkers' request was declined by the school, leading to other conflicts between the Parkers and the school system, they took their case to court, ultimately making it to the US Court of Appeals. There, a deeply disturbing ruling was rendered against the Parkers, with Judge Mark Wolf writing the decision with a decided focus on "diversity," that special code word for homosexual causes.

> *Diversity* is a hallmark of our nation. It is increasingly evident that our *diversity* includes differences in sexual orientation. . . .
>
> As increasingly recognized, one dimension of our nation's *diversity* is differences in sexual orientation. In Massachusetts, at least, those differences may result in same-sex marriages.
>
> In addition . . . Massachusetts law prohibits discrimination based on sexual orientation . . . . Consistent with this, the Department of Education requires that all public schools teach respect for all individuals regardless of, among other things, sexual orientation. . . . It also encourages

instruction concerning different types of families. . . . Some families are headed by same-sex couples.[52]

So, the schools have a greater responsibility to teach "diversity" than to honor the parents of the students. And because the state is committed to teaching children "diversity," and because same-sex marriage is legal in Massachusetts, the school has no responsibility to notify parents when such issues are being taught.

The court was almost saying, "We couldn't care less about traditional family values and faith-based moral convictions. It's more important to teach kids about two-dad and two-mom families, about homosexuality as a healthy alternative to heterosexuality, and about the ins and outs of transgenderism. As for you parents, you have no right to be informed, let alone to interfere. The courts and the school system, not you, know what's best for your kids."

That, in effect, was the ruling of the US Court of Appeals, and the decision was made right here in America, not some totalitarian, communist regime. The state now knows best![53]

And this ruling is already having its effect. In March, 2008, Dr. Paul Ash, the superintendent of this same Lexington School District announced that,

> On March 18, we presented to the School Committee this new, formalized diversity curriculum in preparation for next year, when we plan to pilot four to five short units in each elementary grade. Some units will focus on families, including families with single parents, foster parents, and gay and lesbian parents.

After all, with a federal court ruling in their favor, why not?

After hearing of the new curriculum, Shawn Landon, whose son attended Estabrook Elementary School with Jacob Parker, sent this email to Martha Batten, the school's principal.

> It seems awful soon to be discussing next year, but since you guys started it.
>
> I will absolutely require prior notification to any discussion, education, training, reading or anything at all related (even remotely) to homosexuality. It is quite clear

by the email I just received that you have a very specific agenda and my family will be exercising our rights to be notified and not to participate. This goes against everything we believe and practice. Thank you in advance for your expected cooperation.

Shawn Landon

His email was then passed on to Superintendent Ash, who replied on April 3, 2008. (I encourage you to read this carefully, especially if you are a parent of school-aged children.)

Dear Mr. Landon:

Ms. Batten has forwarded to me your recent email. Ms. Batten told me that you are new to town and perhaps you are not aware of the lawsuit decided by the United States Court of Appeals (Parker vs. Hurley). This case established Lexington's right to teach diversity units, including stories that show same gender parents. The court decided we are not required to inform parents in advance of teaching units that include same gender parents or required to release students when such topics are discussed.

The Appeals Court dismissed the claim that parents have a right to require the school provide advance notice or the right to remove their children. In addition, the School Committee has decided that teachers must be able to teach topics they feel are appropriate without the requirement parents be notified in advance.

Based on your email, I know you strongly disagree with this policy. I can, however, offer you the opportunity to examine the curriculum. I invite you to visit the Estabrook School to look at the materials before they are piloted next year. If your child happens to be placed in a class with a teacher who will be teaching the four of five diversity units, you will then know what will be taught and will be able to talk to your son or daughter about the topics at home.

Our goal is to develop a curriculum that includes the many faces and backgrounds of all students in our community.

Sincerely,
Dr. Ash[54]

This is an outrage, pure and simple. (Really, it's hard to find a less extreme word to describe it.) There used to be a time when the school system served the families and was sensitive to the religious and moral views of the parents. Not any more, at least not in Massachusetts. Now the schools are serving the interests of a tiny but influential minority, at the complete expense of the religious and moral views of countless thousands of families. Those views have now been effectively trashed.

As cited in chapter one, according to the Gay and Lesbian Educators [GALE] of British Columbia, "We must dishonour the prevailing belief that heterosexuality is the only acceptable orientation even though that would mean dishonouring the religious beliefs of Christians, Jews, Muslims, etc."[55]

"THIS IS THE GENERATION THAT GETS IT"

Is it any wonder that GLSEN's Kevin Jennings, speaking of the wider goals of gay activism, told *Time Magazine*, "We're gonna win because of what's happening in high schools right now ... this is the generation that gets it."[56] And GLSEN and its allies are quite committed to being sure that today's school kids "get it." As expressed in "A Call to Action," issued in conjunction with the film, *It's Elementary: Talking about Gay Issues in School*:

> All teachers have the right, and the responsibility, to weave respectful, age-appropriate messages about LGBT people and issues into their lessons and classrooms. Educators should not need to seek approval or have parental consent to discuss LGBT people and issues in the classroom in age-appropriate ways, unless the discussion involves actual sexual practices.[57]

In light of all this, it is not surprising that the average age of kids "coming out" as homosexual has "dropped to 10 for gays and 12 for lesbians," according to the chair of Cornell University's human-development program – as if children of that age group have full clarity about their sexuality and the long-term consequences of the decisions they are making in this regard.[58] But they are "coming out" earlier because: 1) clear gender definitions and distinctions are being "undone" and "deconstructed"; 2) they are getting indoctrinated about homosexuality and transgenderism; 3) they are being encouraged to "come out." And I remind you: This is happening in our public schools, supported by our tax dollars. How can this be?

Consider some of the teaching material that is now available.

In 2003, Haworth Press began publishing the *Journal for Gay and Lesbian Issues in Education*. Articles in the first two year's issues included:

- The Angel's Playground: Same-Sex Desires of Physical Education Teachers
- Serving the Needs of Transgender College Students
- Queering School Communities: Ethical Curiosity and Gay-Straight Alliances
- A Queer Chaos of Meanings: Coming out of Conundrums in Globalised Classrooms
- Outing the Teacher, Outing the Power: Principle and Pedagogy
- Reconciling Christianity and Positive Non-Heterosexual Identity in Adolescence, with Implications for Psychological Well-Being.

In 1999, the respected publishing house of Rowman & Littlefield released the critically acclaimed volume *Queering Elementary Education: Advancing the Dialogue about Sexualities and Schooling*, edited by William J. Letts IV and James T. Sears.[59] According to Prof. Debra Epstein of the Institute of Education, University of London, "Together and individually, the chapters of this book make a compelling case for queering elementary education, to the benefit of all children in all their diversity." Or, in the words of Prof. Peter McLaren, University of California-Los Angeles, "This volume marks the beginning of the queering of critical pedagogy and is long overdue."[60]

So, the publication of this volume is a cause for celebration in the academic world. The time has arrived for the *queering of elementary education*.

Really now, who would have thought we would live to see the day when the words "queering" and "elementary education" would be joined together? And who would have thought that the joining of these words would produce jubilation among educators?

Chapters in this volume include:

- Teaching Queerly: Some Elementary Propositions

- Why Discuss Sexuality in Elementary School?
- Pestalozzi, Perversity, and the Pedagogy of Love[61]
- Stonewall in the Housekeeping Area: Gay and Lesbian Issues in the Early Childhood Classroom
- Reading Queer Asian American Masculinities and Sexualities in Elementary School
- Using Music to Teach Against Homophobia
- "It's Okay to Be Gay": Interrupting Straight Thinking in the English Classroom
- Children of the Future Age: Lesbian and Gay Parents Talk about School
- Lesbian Mother and Lesbian Educator: An Integrative View of Affirming Sexual Diversity
- When *Queer* and *Teacher* Meet

Among scores of other books that could be mentioned are Arthur Lipkin's, *Understanding Homosexuality, Changing Schools: A Text for Teachers, Counselors, and Administrators*, which includes a chapter lauding "The Massachusetts Model" of LGBT education,[62] and *Queer Theory in Education*, edited by William F. Pinar, with some of the most way-out and bizarre "educational" contributions imaginable.[63]

NOT YOUR GRANDPARENTS' BEDTIME BOOKS

Dear parents, books like this are being used to train your children's educators, with many of these volumes serving as textbooks in colleges and universities. And what shall we say about the books that are being written *for* your children – or perhaps even being read *to* your children as early as pre-school? I'm talking about books like:

- *One Dad, Two Dads, Brown Dad, Blue Dads*, by Johnny Valentine. There is a special dedication at the beginning of the book, "To Jacob, who has only one mom and one dad. But don't feel sorry for him. They're both great parents." So, two dads are not just acceptable; two dads are now *better* than one dad and one mom. Extraordinary!
- Even more overt in its message is *Oh the Things Mommies Do! What Could Be Better Than Having Two?*,

written by Crystal Tomkins with illustrations by "her wife" Lindsey Evans. The *Boston Spirit* magazine writes, "Given the physical and mental capacity available to one mom, it's hard to imagine that of two. Imagine even more phone calls 'to say Hi,' and exponentially more when you've got a cold or vocational hiccup."[64] This is so much better than having one mom and one dad. (Really, what kind of physical and mental capacity does a dad have?)

- *Emma and Meesha My Boy: A Two Mom Story*, by Kaitlyn Considine, recommended for ages three-six.
- *Two Daddies and Me* by Robbie Ann Packard, who, "already a mother herself, had the amazing and joyous opportunity to become a surrogate for a gay couple."
- *The Sissy Duckling*, by gay activist Harvey Fierstein, and dedicated to "proud sissies everywhere."
- *A Family Alphabet Book*, by Bobbie Combs, depicting a two-dad household on the cover, and with lines like, "**C is for cookies.** Both of my dads know how to make great chocolate chip **cookies.**"
- *Molly's Family*, by Nancy Garden, with the cover depicting two sweet moms taking happy Molly for a walk in the woods
- *Felicia's Favorite Story*, by Lesléa Newman, with another two-mom cover and this description on the back: "It's bedtime, but before Felicia goes to sleep she wants to hear her favorite story, the story of how she was adopted by Mama Nessa and Mama Linda."
- Newman has also written *Daddy, Papa, and Me* and *Mommy, Mama, and Me*.
- *And Tango Makes Three*, by Justin Richardson and Peter Parnell, based on the true story of the so-called gay penguins in a New York City zoo and the baby penguin they "adopted." (In a fascinating sequel to the book, but a sequel that has certainly *not* been added to this reader, one of the supposedly "gay" penguins ended up leaving his partner and taking up with a hot new female penguin – and fathering a chick.)[65]

- *King and King*, by Linda de Haan and Stern Nijland. This tells the story of Prince Bertie, who, when informed by his mother, the queen, that he must get married, meets all the lovely princesses who "come from far and wide hoping to catch his eye" but in the end chooses to "simply follow his heart" – and marries Prince Lee. ("Prince" is *not* a typo for Princess. The prince marries another prince, and the last page shows them kissing.) There are now widely-circulated reports of outraged parents who reacted with shock when their first-graders came home to talk with them after reading this book in school.[66]

Following on the heels of *King and King* came *King and King and Family*, celebrating the honeymoon of the two kings and the beginning of their new "family." The book is recommended for children aged four to eight.

Of course, there are the older "classics," like Michael Willhoite's *Daddy's Roommate*, first published in 1990, featuring the typical two-dad cover picture and lines like, "My Mommy and Daddy got a divorce last year. Now there's somebody new at Daddy's house. Daddy and his roommate Frank live together, work together, eat together, sleep together, shave together, and sometimes fight together, but they always make up."[67]

Perhaps the mother of them all (or should I say the "double mother" of them all?) is Lesléa Newman's *Heather Has Two Mommies*, first published in 1989. Not that long ago, this book was hard to come by. Since 2000, however, it has been available in a special Tenth Anniversary Edition and referred to as a "classic."[68]

For the older readers, ages ten and up, there is Robie H. Harris's *It's Perfectly Normal: Changing Bodies, Growing Up, Sex and Sexual Health*, replete with cartoon-like, but fully-graphic, naked illustrations of adolescent boys and girls. (We're talking about full frontal nudity of young teenagers on the inside cover page and full frontal nudity of all ages groups on pages 20-21, along with detailed illustrations of the private parts of young adolescent girls and boys, to the point that the boys are pictured both circumcised and uncircumcised). One of the book's chapters is entitled, "Perfectly Normal: Masturbation," and it not only supplies "how to" details but also notes, "After having an orgasm, a person usually feels quite content and relaxed" (49). (Remember: This book is recommended for kids aged *ten* and up, and it's partly intended to answer the questions parents have a hard time answering.) Of course, there is the requisite chapter on "Straight and Gay: Heterosexuality and Homosexuality," which notes that, "There have been gay relationships all through history, even before ancient Greece," explaining:

> Some people disapprove of gay men and lesbian women. Some even hate homosexuals only because they are homosexual. People may feel this way toward homosexuals because they think homosexuals are different from them or that gay relationships are wrong. Usually these people know little or nothing about homosexuals, and their views are often based on fears and misinformation, not on facts. People are often afraid of things they know little or nothing about (17-18).

There you have it, and that should settle it. After all, the book says so!

If you disagree with homosexual practice, you are either ignorant, fearful, misinformed, hateful, or all of the above. In any case, you have no right to differ with *It's Perfectly Normal* – you *can't* differ with something that is "perfectly normal" – since the glowing endorsements for this award-winning book take up two full pages, including such prestigious honors as being named: an American Library Association's Notable Children's Book; a *Booklist* Editors' Choice; a New York Public Library Best Children's Book; a *New York Times* Notable Book of the Year; a *Parenting* Reading Magic Award Winner; a *Publisher's Weekly* Best Book of the Year; and a *School Library Journal* Best Book of the Year. In keeping with this, the *Los Angeles Times Book Review* called the book "Utterly contemporary and comprehensive," while *USA Today* stated that, "The book, for ages 10 and up, is sophisticated, comprehensive, reassuring."

May I ask you, current and prospective moms and dads, along with grandmas and grandpas, do you find books like this "reassuring"? Does it give you comfort to know that your kids might be reading through this book in school without your knowledge?

Yet the disturbing news doesn't stop with books. When everyone is tired of reading, there are always videos the children can watch, like *Oliver Button Is a Star*, produced by Dan Hunt and featuring the Twin Cities Gay Men's Chorus. It is recommended for ages five to adult. As described in the Syracuse Cultural Worker's Catalog:

Based on Tomie dePaola's classic children's book Oliver Button is a Sissy, this video uses a variety of media to tell the story of a boy who is ridiculed by his parents and peers simply because he'd rather sing and dance than play sports or engage in activities "normal" boys enjoy.[69]

To repeat what I said at the beginning of this chapter, I stand with the gay and lesbian community in opposing all bullying and harassment in schools, and I believe fully in teaching kids to be kind and gracious to their classmates, even if some classmates are "different." But it is profoundly painful to me to think of a five-year-old boy viewing a video (presumably in pre-school or kindergarten) that suggests that he may be gay because he likes to sing and dance rather than play sports – and I write this as a father, grandfather, and educator. And notice that this video is designed to make Oliver Button's parents look bad too.

MAKING A LASTING IMPRESSION ON IMPRESSIONABLE KIDS

Children, especially little children, are so impressionable, so easily influenced, so readily molded. And while it is good that some of our schools have become more sensitive to issues like name-calling and bullying and harassing, it is absolutely unconscionable that our schools have also become bastions of homosexual and transgender activism, places where captive kindergarteners learn about transgender behavior and kids just removed from their toddler years are taught about same-sex households.

According to a May 10, 2008 report:

> A Pennsylvania elementary school has angered parents by giving them one-day's notice of planned counseling sessions with 100 third-grade students to explain that one of their male classmates would soon begin wearing girls' clothing and taking a female name and to ask that they accept him as a girl and not make unkind remarks.
>
> The exercise in "social transition" was initiated by the boy's parents who approached the administration at Chatham Park Elementary School in Haverford Township asking that the school help in having their child's female identity find acceptance among his peers. After consulting

experts on transgender children, the Haverford School District sent letters to parents advising them the school guidance counselor would meet with their children, reported the *Philadelphia Inquirer*.

. . . In the letter to parents, Chatham Park principal Daniel Marsella assured parents the counseling would use "developmentally appropriate language" to explain "how we need to help this student make a social transition in school."

"This is something that was going to come out," said Mary Beth Lauer, district director of community relations. "Isn't it better to be proactive, and let people know what is happening and how we're dealing with it?"[70]

Yes, this happened in a *third-grade* class.

"But," you might protest, "the fact is that there are hundreds of thousands of same-sex households, and you just can't stick your head in the sand and deny that they exist. Kids need to be taught about this when they're little so they can be introduced to these new social realities."

What about polyamorous households, then, where kids are being raised by a mix of several different parents? (See, further, below, Chapter Nine, where a *Newsweek* article is cited claiming that there are half-a-million such households in America today.) Shouldn't children be introduced to these realities too while still in elementary school?

Interestingly, when I asked this question to a local lesbian leader with whom I was in friendly dialogue – a woman who in many ways held to high moral standards – she was repulsed by the thought of teaching kids about multi-parented homes. Might there be a double standard here?

The queering of elementary school education, however, is just the prequel to the full-blown, unapologetic gay and transgender activism that is found with increasing frequency in our middle schools and high schools. It is fueled by special events like the "Queer Youth Advocacy Day," which was described in 2008 on its website as "a youth-led day of lobbying, advocacy training, and educational workshops that took place at the [California] Capitol in Sacramento on May 5, 2008."[71]

The event provided "a super opportunity for hundreds of CA youth activists . . . to unite and educate lawmakers on the needs of LGBTQ youth and what is needed to end harassment and discrimination in school."[72] Or, put more simply, this event stands for the complete legitimization in the classroom of everything that can be called "queer." The very name "the Queer Youth Advocacy Day" says it all.

Also helping to fuel the fires of school-based GLBT activism are special GLSEN events like the conference held at English High School in Boston, Mar. 29, 2008. (This was GLSEN's eighteenth annual conference for their Boston network.) The conference featured addresses by Boston Mayor Thomas M. Menino and Gunner Scott, the female-looking but actually male "queer/transgender social justice activist,"[73] along with entertainment by Kit Yan, "who wants people to realize that being queer is more than okay."[74]

Featured workshops in the conference were devoted to topics such as:

- GSA's [Gay Straight Alliances] in Middle Schools!?!?
- Supporting Gender Variant Youth and Their Families: Consider Adding a "T" to Your GSA
- Beyond Binaries: Identity and the Sexuality Spectrum
- Queerspawn – Children of LGBT Parents in Schools
- Empowering Middle School LGBTQ Students
- Exploring Gender Non-conformity, Identity and the Power of Language[75]

Another major thrust of the conference was the promotion of bisexuality, including handouts like, Bisexuality 101, Bisexual Activism, Embracing Your Bisexuality, and Bisexuality Is the Wild Card of Your Exotic Life.[76] How wonderful! This is just what our schools need. (Dripping sarcasm fully intended.)

To be perfectly candid, I'm no longer shocked when middle school and high school teachers around the country come up to me after a lecture and say, "You have no idea what's happening in our schools." (And remember: They're saying this to me immediately after hearing me lecture about some of the topics found in this book.) "The latest thing," they consistently tell me, "is bisexuality among the girls. It's everywhere! In fact, the majority of the girls in our school are into it." (According to some of the teachers, it's the large majority.[77])

One pastor in rural North Carolina informed me in May, 2010 that a young lady in his daughter's high school had just quit playing on the girls' softball team, despite her love of the game. Her reason for quitting? She was the only non-lesbian on the team.

A middle school teacher from Milton, Florida moved to Orlando, Florida to take a job teaching seventh graders there but returned distraught after just one year. Half of the girls in her class – meaning, girls between twelve and thirteen years old – claimed to be lesbians.[78] This was more than she could handle.

And FoxNews.com reported on October 15, 2010, that many parents of seventh-grade children in a Washington, DC school were upset when they learned that their kids had been asked to fill out a sexual survey form (without the parents' prior consent or knowledge). "The students were asked their genders -- whether male, female or transgender. And they were asked to identify themselves as straight, bisexual, gay or lesbian or 'not sure.'" These were questions for *twelve year-old* children?

> Other questions included: How sure are you that you know the difference between oral, vaginal, and anal sex? Would know where to get condoms if/when you or a friend needed them? Can you correctly put a condom on yourself or your partner?[79]

Open sexual discussion like this is often aided and abetted by the aforementioned, GLSEN-sponsored, rapidly-growing, Gay Straight Alliances (GSA's), which are more than just "safe places" for gay and lesbian students to gather. They too advocate for the full acceptance of homosexuality, bisexuality, and transgenderism in our schools, encouraging children as young as eleven years old to declare themselves gay in the "safety" of the GSA (and without parental knowledge, at that). As explained in the resource paper "School Districts, Children and Gay Straight Alliances: Protecting Children Empowering Parents,"

> A Gay Straight Alliance (GSA) is not merely another club. A newly established GSA often becomes a springboard for pro-homosexual advocacy seeking to alter curriculum and silence dissent through restrictive student speech and conduct codes. An overview of the purpose of a GSA as described by the Gay Straight Alliance Network describes them as an activist club seeking to, "get Lesbian, Gay, Bisexual, Transgender and Questioning (LGBTQ) issues

in the curriculum, LGBTQ related books in the library, and progressive non-discrimination policies implemented at a district level." GSAs may "organize a Pride Week or LGBTQ Awareness Event" or "participate in the Day of Silence" remaining silent as a means of protesting "homophobia." According to the Gay Straight Alliance Network, "GSAs organize a 'Teach the Teachers' staff development day which focuses on teaching school staff how to be better allies for LGBTQ students."

Through GSAs, students are encouraged to freely access a multitude of resources online through websites such as GLSEN.org which are designed to aid them in their efforts to establish an on-campus organization and begin to transform their school's curriculum and environment. . . .[80]

And I remind you that GSA's are now increasingly common in middle schools, influencing kids as young as eleven.

Strikingly, when serious allegations of sexual abuse were lodged against Bishop Eddie Long, a gay watchdog site was quick to point out that, if the charges were true, they would "involve not just homosexual activity and hypocrisy, but abuse of power and assault of *vulnerable adolescents*."[81] Yet these are the very adolescents – vulnerable indeed – that GLSEN is so eager to influence (but not assault, of course), encouraging them in their same-sex attractions rather than telling them that a large percentage of adolescents who initially find themselves attracted to the same sex lose those attractions as they get older.[82]

But it is not just GLSEN that is promoting these causes in our children's schools. The National Education Association (NEA), is an active, open, and proud co-conspirator. In 2009, the NEA released an official statement supporting same-sex marriage[83] (which begs the question of why the *National Education Association* would be involved in this divisive political and moral issue at all). And in 2010, the NEA recognized a new caucus: the NEA Drag Queen Caucus.[84]

Pause for a moment and wrap your mind around *that*: The National Education Association, which is the largest professional organization and labor union in the U.S., has recognized a *drag queen caucus* – and this is in addition to the already extant Gay & Lesbian, Bisexual and Transgender Caucus.[85]

According to the NEAExposed website,

> So far, the purpose of the Drag Queen Caucus has been
> limited to raising scholarship money for gay, lesbian,
> bisexual, and transgender students. To that end, the
> group's founder, Peter J. Konrath, organizes drag shows
> and karaoke sing-offs at some of Wisconsin's finest gay
> bars .... Nevertheless, America's drag queen public school
> teachers now have a voice in the NEA's big tent, which
> increasingly resembles a traveling sideshow.[86]

In 2003, Bob Chase, former president of the NEA, gave a glowing
endorsement of GLSEN's *It's Elementary* training material, stating:

> Schools cannot be neutral when dealing with issues of
> human dignity and human rights [meaning, in particular,
> GLBT "dignity" and "rights"]. I'm not talking about
> tolerance; I'm talking about acceptance.[87]

But now "acceptance" is not enough. Homosexuality and other variant
sexual orientations must be celebrated, as demonstrated by the Riddle
Homophobia Scale, named after Dr. Dorothy Riddle and distributed and
promoted by GLSEN for use in our schools. The scale lists four "Homophobic
Levels of Attitude" and four "Positive Levels of Attitude."

Listed under the Homophobic category are: 1) Repulsion; 2) Pity; 3)
Tolerance; and 4) Acceptance. That's correct: "Tolerance" and "Acceptance"
are now considered homophobic! Listed under the Positive category are: 5)
Support; 6) Admiration; 7) Appreciation; and 8) Nurturance.[88]

Can you believe how much the tables have turned? For gay activists, it
is not enough for our kids to tolerate or accept homosexuality. They must
support and admire and appreciate and nurture it. (Shades of the children's
books that presented same-sex households as superior to mom-and-dad
households.)

As observed by Robert Weissberg, emeritus professor of political science
at the University of Illinois-Urbana,

> Make no mistake, this is not just telling youngsters to ignore
> "odd" classmates, the traditional tolerance-based solution.

. . . Rather, this is a drive to legitimize homosexuality, swathed in the rhetoric of tolerance, by portraying this sexual predilection as "normal" at a time when youngsters barely grasp sexuality of any variety. This quarrel is hardly an academic one: confrontations are real, and, ironically as so often is the case, their tumultuousness undermines the very social tranquility tolerance instruction is supposed to bring.[89]

GLSEN also introduced the annual Day of Silence in 1996. According to the 2008 description, the Day of Silence "brings attention to anti-LGBT name-calling, bullying and harassment in schools. . . . Hundreds of thousands of students will come together on April 25 to encourage schools and classmates to address the problem of anti-LGBT behavior."[90] And these students – often with the support of administration and faculty – will put tape on their mouths or simply refuse to speak or participate in class the entire day, in solidarity with the mistreatment of gays and lesbians worldwide.[91]

But not only do hundreds of thousands of students participate, many thousands of others can testify to the fact that the Day of Silence (indeed, many times the entire week) is devoted to the dissemination of LGBT propaganda in the schools, with opposing views often strongly suppressed. It is frequently those who differ with the Day of Silence who are being silenced.[92]

HAPPY MEALS = BAD;
GAY ACTIVIST SCHOOLTEACHERS = GOOD

Recently, McDonald's was sued "by a group of consumers and nutrition advocates who want to force the fast food chain to stop using toys to entice children to buy meals they say are unhealthy." A mother of two who brought the suit said, "I object to the fact that McDonald's *is getting into my kids' heads without my permission*" while the attorney for the case, Steve Gardner, said: "Every time McDonald's markets a Happy Meal directly to a young child, it *exploits a child's developmental vulnerability . . . .*"[93]

Yet as patently absurd as this lawsuit is (after all, kids cannot magically transport themselves to McDonald's to buy Happy Meals without their parents knowledge, and even when families are at McDonald's, parents can simply say, "No"), there is something far more absurd: Educators *are* getting into our kids' heads without our permission and they *are* exploiting our children's developmental vulnerability, yet hardly anyone raises an objection.

In fact, on October 21, 2010, seven teachers at Concord-Carlisle High School in Massachusetts participated in a school assembly sponsored by the GSA (Gay Straight Alliance) and told students how they came out as gays and lesbians, encouraging students to do the same, and all this took place without parental notification or approval.[94] Talk about getting into our kids' heads without our permission and exploiting our children's developmental vulnerability! And remember: These are the respected role models, the ones whom the kids are encouraged to listen to, learn from, and emulate.

> Several of the teachers described what they portrayed as the irrational fear, "homophobia," and *general backwardness of their parents*, relatives, and others who first reacted negatively to their coming out. But afterwards, they assured the students, their relatives accepted them as gay, so students shouldn't be worried about that.[95]

How twisted that it is the parents who are considered backwards if they are not encouraging their kids to discover their homosexuality, even though a gay math teacher at the assembly "began his talk by saying that **all his college friends have died of AIDS**."[96] And to think: Parents are suing McDonald's over toys in a Happy Meal while at the same time, the courts are protecting the "rights" of teachers to indoctrinate our kids with gay propaganda. What kind of world are we living in?

Even this, however, is child's play – literally – compared to what's happening on our college campuses, where the seeds of gay radicalism planted in the elementary schools have fully blossomed.[97] Are you ready to hear more? Then, keep reading!

So . . . Little Johnny went to school, there to learn that queer was cool. Mom and Dad, what do you think of that?

Yale, and most of American higher education,
has moved from recognizing the worth and value of each student to a
wholesale endorsement of anything gay. It is hard to imagine any school being
more generously supportive than Yale, with its Gay Alliance at Yale, its Gay
Student Center, its Gay and Lesbian Co-operative, a Gay Rights Week, an entire
Pride Month at Yale (BGLAD) each April, gay dances, a Lesbian and Gay
Studies Center, Transgender Awareness Week, and a new Office of LGBTQ
resources. No wonder Yale is the "Gay Ivy." Surely, Yale wins the award for
devoting the most resources and expending the most energy to proclaim the
wonders of any and all sexual practices that 2% of the population prefer.
Anything and everything categorized as "homosexual" goes unquestioned.
However, it clearly does not go unfunded or unstaffed.

Alan Ivy, Ph.D., "Yale's Coveted Title: Gay Ivy,"
Townhall.com, July 20, 2009

Female, Male, Undisclosed (specify below)

Gender choices on Harvard University's
Business School Profile online application

Yale is . . . really, really gay. Like, totally gay.

Sam Heller, writing in the *Yale Daily News*, October 27, 2006

"Why They Call Yale the 'Gay Ivy,"

Cover story and focus of the *Yale Alumni Magazine*, July/August 2009

4

Something Queer on Our Campuses: From Traditional Academics and the Arts to GLBTQ and "Ze"

W ell, little Johnny (and his twin sister Jane) have made their way through elementary school, middle school, and high school, and they're on their way to college now. What's awaiting them there?

They have already been liberated from the terribly confining, "binary constriction" of the male-female paradigm. They've said goodbye to "heteronormativity," that outmoded, discriminatory view that heterosexuality is the norm for society or, perish the thought, in any way superior to homosexuality. They have been thoroughly disengaged from all homophobia, having learned to celebrate "diversity" in all its varied, sexual forms. In fact, thanks to his school's Gay Straight Alliance, Johnny now considers himself "questioning." At college, he might quickly move from questioning to queer!

Gay campus activist Shane Windmyer provides some valuable insights into the contemporary campus scene in his 389-page book, *The Advocate College Guide for LGBT Students*,[1] which documents the most gay-friendly campuses in America. Note carefully how these young people describe themselves. Some of them are your classmates. Some of them are your sons and daughters. Some of them are you!

Answers to the question: **How do you feel about coming out on your campus?**

- I've been out the entire time I've been at AU [American University], and I have had a considerable number of other students come out to me because they see me as a visible part of the campus LGBT community. It's a fantastic thought that my comfort with *my identities* [my emphasis] can help others develop confidence in their own. – *21-year-old genderqueer lesbian, senior* (p. 23)[2]
- I was supported through the process of changing my identity while I was here. Antioch [College] allows for changes in identity. . . . I can attend the Tran Support Group here on campus, which is student-run. There is a doctor in town [who] can write prescriptions for hormones and provides letters in support of having surgery. – *22-year-old queer F-M dyke, senior* (p. 26; F-M stands for Female to Male)

Answers to the question: **How would you describe the social scene for LGBT students?**

- Oh my gosh . . . queer prom! So fun. – *19-year-old lesbian, sophomore* (Bowling Green State University, p. 30; there is also a blurb there from a self-described *21-year-old bisexual queer female, junior*)
- The social scene is best in downtown Center City Philadelphia, where there are several "Gayborhood" clubs dedicated to LGBT-themed events and interests – *20-year-old bi-curious questioning female, senior* (Temple University, p. 189)
- Lots of drama, gay boys and some lezzies. Facebook is huge! There are tons of hotties. – *19-year-old gay, male freshman* (Pennsylvania State University; p. 159)

Answers to the question: **What annual social event should an LGBT student not miss?**

- The Drag Show in October. The DC Kings, some queens, and Queers and Allies put together an awesome show that fills the Tavern to capacity to raise money for a different local DC charity event every year that does work to improve the lives of LGBT people. – *21-year-old genderqueer lesbian, senior* (Speaking of American University; p. 24)
- GenderF—k dance by far! – *21-year-old bisexual female, junior* (Antioch College, p. 27)
- Drag ball, of course. – *22-year-old queer female, senior* (Bryn Mawr College, p. 33)
- This year the Pride Center hosted a drag show on campus. This was a great event that brought together both the LGBT community and allies on campus. – *20 year-old gay male, junior* (California State Polytechnic University, p. 36)
- The Glam Jam, which was held during National Coming Out Week. . . . *18-year-old transgender gay male, freshman* (Carleton College, p. 39; cf. also the

blurb from a *19-year-old genderqueer dyke, sophomore*)
- The Drag Show! Performing Arts hires drag queens from a local bar to perform at school. It gets bigger every year. It is amazing! – *22-year-old gay male, senior* (Suffolk University, p. 183)

Annual LGBT Event Highlights include:

- Lavender Language and Linguistics Conference (American University)
- Queer Take Over Week (Antioch College)
- Queer Film Festival... "It's a three-day film fest full of awesome queer movies ..." (Sarah Lawrence College; p. 171)

And remember that these selections represent just a tiny, typical sampling from a 389-page book.

Johnny and Jane, welcome to college in 21st century America! There you'll meet (or, perhaps, soon identify as) a 21-year-old genderqueer lesbian (with self-described multiple identities), a 22-year-old queer female to male dyke, a 21-year-old bisexual queer female, a 21-year-old bisexual female, a 22-year-old queer female, an 18-year-old transgender gay male, a 19-year-old genderqueer dyke, and many others in the ever-widening spectrum of the LGBTQIPA rainbow (see Chapter Nine for more this).

Conservative columnist Matt Barber drew attention to the sad case of a clearly-confused, 20-year-old, female college student, who identified as a "transgender gay male. His designation means he has a female body, but identifies as a male and is sexually attracted to men."[3] And she claimed that she was the "victim of discrimination at a small Massachusetts community college because *he is biologically female" and she could not use the men's locker room to shower and undress.*[4]

Perhaps this study by a sociology professor in Canada would help?[5]

Or perhaps this book, penned by a number of respected American academics, would be more relevant?[6]

HARVARD UNIVERSITY THEN AND NOW

What makes this scenario all the more striking is that many of our nation's finest colleges and universities were founded by Christian leaders and/

or denominations with the express purpose of training men for the ministry. And the moral requirements for all students, including those who were not training for the ministry, were incredibly high. Consider this sampling from Harvard when it was founded in 1636:

> No student of any class, shall visit any shop or tavern, to eat and drink, unless invited by a parent, guardian, stepparent, or some such relative;
>
> No student shall buy, sell or exchange any thing without the approval of his parents, guardians, or tutors;
>
> No one must, under any pretext, be found in the society of any depraved or dissolute person;
>
> If any student shall, either through willfulness or negligence, violate any law of God or of this college, after being twice admonished, he shall suffer severe punishment, at the discretion of the President or his tutor. But in high-handed offences, no such modified forms of punishment need be expected.[7]

You can be sure that if the students had Spring Break, they did not have the 17th century equivalent of "Girls Gone Wild" (or, in those days of male-only students, "Boys Gone Wild"). In fact, in order to graduate from Harvard with the most basic degree in Arts (not Theology—that came later!), the student had to be able "logically to explain the Holy Scriptures, both of the Old and New Testaments…and…be blameless in life and character."[8] How many students today in our promiscuity-filled campuses, make it through one week "blameless in life and character"?[9]

In their wildest dreams, Harvard students in the 17th, 18th, 19th, and even most of the 20th century, could never have imagined a report from the *Harvard Crimson* like this one, published April 6, 2004:

> About 30 students gathered in [Harvard University's] Boylston Hall last night to kick off "Gaypril," a month set to include gay pride celebrations, a day of silence to raise awareness about the prevalance [sic] of homophobia, and a panel of sadomasochism experts....
>
> In an event unique to this year's Gaypril, BGLTSA will present a screening on April 26 of "Toilet Training,"

a documentary about discrimination linked to gender-segregated bathrooms, accompanied by findings from a study on bathroom access on and near campus.[10]

"A panel of sadomasochism experts" convening at Harvard University? Is this some kind of sadistic joke? If only it were!

In 2005, the online application for the Harvard Business School (HBS) Profile listed *three* choices for gender, namely, Male, Female, and Transgender; by 2010 (if not earlier), it had expanded to, "Female, Male, Undisclosed (specify below)," since, it would appear, more categories than Female, Male, and Transgender were necessary.

Under the heading "Your Interests," the application asks, "Would you be interested in learning more about the following HBS communities and initiatives (check all that apply)?," giving the following options: African-American, International, Latino, Lesbian/Gay/Bisexual/Transgender (LGBT), Women.[11] So, there are special categories for race and ethnicity; a special category for women, but not men; a special category for LGBT (as if it belonged in the same class as either ethnicity or gender) and *not a single religious category of any kind.* What an extraordinary shift from the Harvard of old (and even the Harvard of the not so distant past).

THE CHRISTIAN ORIGINS OF OUR AMERICAN UNIVERSITIES

To put this in context, consider the origins of several of our nation's most prestigious schools, beginning with Harvard.

- **Harvard University** was founded in 1636 as Harvard College with the motto "Truth" (Veritas). Its purpose was, "To train a literate clergy." Among the "Rules and Precepts" to be observed by the students were these: "Let every Student be plainly instructed, and earnestly pressed to consider well, the main end of his life and studies is, to know God and Jesus Christ which is eternal life"; and, "Every one shall so exercise himself in reading the Scriptures twice a day, that he shall be ready to give such an account of his proficiency therein, both in Theoretical observations of Language and Logic, and in practical and spiritual truths . . . ."[12]

- **Princeton University** was founded in 1746 as the College of New Jersey. The school's motto was "Under God's Power She Flourishes,"[13] and until 1902, every president of Princeton was a minister. Although seminary training was the school's first goal, its founding purpose went beyond that: "Though our great Intention was to erect a seminary for educating Ministers of the Gospel, yet we hope it will be useful in other learned professions -- Ornaments of the State as Well as the Church."[14]
- **Columbia University**, which was founded as King's College in 1754 by a royal charter of King George II, had as its goals to "enlarge the Mind, improve the Understanding, polish the whole Man, and qualify them to support the brightest Characters in all the elevated stations in life."[15] The college was distinctly non-denominational and, "The first advertisement of the college disclaims any intention of imposing 'on the scholars the peculiar Tenants of any particular Sect of Christians; but to inculcate upon their tender minds, the great Principles of Christianity and Morality, in which true Christians of each Denomination are generally agreed.'"[16]
- The motto of **Boston University**, was "Learning, Virtue, and Piety." It was founded as a Methodist seminary in Vermont in 1839 before its eventual transfer to Boston in 1867. Until 1967 – meaning just two years before Woodstock! – all of its presidents were Methodist ministers. (The university's first non-Methodist minister president, Arland F. Christ-Janer, was still a graduate of Yale Divinity School.)[17]
- The motto of the **University of Pennsylvania**, founded 1740 but only opened in 1751, was: "Laws without morals are useless" (*Leges sine Moribus vanae*).[18] The motto of **Brown University**, founded in 1764 as Rhode Island College, was: "In God we hope" (*In Deo speramus*).[19] **Rutgers University**, founded in 1766 as Queen's College, had as its motto: "Sun of

righteousness, shine upon the West also" (*Sol iustitiae et occidentem illustra*).[20] Its founding purpose was: "For the education of the youth of the said province and the neighboring colonies in true religion and useful learning and particularly for providing an able and learned protestant ministry."[21]

Needless to say, it was inevitable that these schools would quickly expand their programs, given the broad-based needs of a rapidly growing country and given the strong Christian emphasis on education. Still, it is striking to realize that, "Explicitly Christian higher education was virtually the only form of American collegiate instruction until the years following the Civil War,"[22] while high morals were even more highly prized than academic excellence, as reflected in some of the school mottos just cited, like Boston University's "Learning, Virtue, and Piety" and the University of Pennsylvania's "Laws without morals are useless."

Contrast the scene at Oberlin College in April, 2004:

> Carmen Vazquez, a self-avowed butch lesbian socialist, gave a lecture in which she reproached the queer movement for avoiding larger public policy issues. She enjoined queer activists to battle neo-conservative American leaders in a quest to prevent a new fascist American state. Then she encouraged students to have sex.[23]

At this same college,

> the school's president, has vocally supported students' efforts to officially charter a BDSM (Bondage, Discipline and Sadomasochism) Club at the school, which would qualify the group to receive school funds like other campus clubs. [She] considered chartering the club to be a "free speech" issue.[24]

How our campuses have changed! From an emphasis on purity to an atmosphere of partying, from biblical morality to sexual anarchy, some of our nation's finest schools have undergone a dramatic shift. And part of that shift includes becoming centers for gay activism and "queer studies" – with much pride, at that. Both the rapidity and scope of some of the changes is breathtaking.

YALE UNIVERSITY THEN AND NOW

To get some perspective on this, let's focus on one of the oldest institutions in our nation, Yale University, a school that for many years stood out as one of the most deeply religious schools in the land. Today, Yale remains one of the finest institutions of higher learning in the world, an elite school among elite schools. Among its illustrious list of alumni are presidents of the United States, Supreme Court Justices, and Nobel Prize Winners, to name just a few. Yale's prestigious accomplishments were showcased in the 2004 elections, in which both presidential candidates (George W. Bush and John Kerry), along with one of the two vice-presidential candidates (John Edwards), were Yale graduates. How many other schools can boast of this?

Founded in 1701, Yale's purpose was, "To plant and under ye Divine blessing to propagate in this Wilderness, the blessed Reformed, Protestant Religion, in ye purity of its Order and Worship." In keeping with this, until the turn of the 20th century, every president of Yale was also a Christian minister, and during the tenures of several presidents in the 1700's and 1800's, Yale experienced a series of spiritual revivals, bringing revitalization and renewal to the student body. To this day, Timothy Dwight Chapel stands as a memorial of Yale's rich spiritual history. Inscribed in front of the chapel are the words: "Christ is the only, the true, the living way of access to God. Give up yourselves therefore to him, with a cordial confidence, and the great work of life is done."[25] (Yes, this inscription is still at Yale!)

One of Yale's precepts was,

> All scholars [i.e., students] shall live religious, godly and blameless lives according to the rules of God's Word, diligently reading the Holy Scriptures, the fountain of light and truth; and constantly attend upon all the duties of religion, both in public and secret. Seeing God is the giver of all wisdom, every scholar, besides private or secret prayer, where all we are bound to ask wisdom shall be present morning and evening at public prayer in the hall at the accustomed hour.[26]

(Did you catch that? All students were required to attend public prayer meetings every morning and every evening.) *Compulsory chapel attendance at Yale was not abolished until 1928.*[27]

Yale, however, has undergone quite a radical transformation, and today, not only has a new vision been birthed for part of the school, but a new perspective has also been put on the school's past. Three hundred years ago, the primary goal of Yale's founders was that, "Every student shall consider the main end of his study to wit to know God in Jesus Christ and answerable to lead a Godly, sober life." In 2006, a Yale webpage proudly announced:

> In the over three hundred years since its founding, Yale has educated and been home to some of the most prominent queer scholars, activists, and artists in the nation's history. In the past half-century, we have become a nationally known center for LGBT [Lesbian, Gay, Bisexual, and Transgender] activism and scholarship.[28]

The founding fathers, not to mention its presidents for more than two centuries, would be mortified. Who could imagine that Yale 100 or 200 or 300 years ago would have knowingly educated and accommodated "some of the most prominent queer scholars, activists, and artists in the nation's history"? How can such a revisionist statement be made, in the name of Yale, no less? Who can even identify some of America's "most prominent queer scholars, activists, and artists" in the 1700's or 1800's or even the first two-thirds of the 1900's?[29] Such categories didn't even exist. (It appears that more sober minds have since prevailed, and as of 2009, under the heading, "The History of LGBTS at Yale," a more modest boast is made: "Yale has played a leading role in the development of LGBT and queer studies for almost thirty years."[30] That's quite a change!)

Yes something very odd – "queer" in the words of its proponents – has happened at Yale, and it has long since been out of the closet. In fact, "LGBT" life at Yale is thriving, as outlined in "Queer Life at Yale: A Guide for Students":

> On any given Thursday, Friday, or Saturday night at Yale, you can see a play with queer characters, actors, directors and stagehands, or all of the above. This same weekend, there will be a party thrown by LGBT students: a Co-op dance attended by 700+ undergrads and adventurous

grads, followed by a smaller after-party; a house party publicized on the YaLesbians and PRISM lists; a cast party for the show you just saw.[31] This week, you may have been to a meeting of one of Yale's 10+ discussion/support/action groups for queer students and their allies. You may also have been to a meeting of a women's center, sports, a cappella, or ethnic student group whose membership is predominantly queer. You will probably have seen a film with queer characters and content, whether in a Co-op, T-GAY, or Outlaws film festival; with friends; or in your film, history, or queer studies course. You have also had coffee or a meeting or dinner with a(nother) queer person: your roommate, your professor, or your crush.[32]

Contrast this with the atmosphere at Yale during one of its seasons of spiritual awakening about 200 years ago as described by Benjamin Silliman, an American chemist, science educator and editor, who served on the Yale faculty during the presidency of President Timothy Dwight (1795-1817). Silliman wrote, "Yale College is a little temple: prayer and praise seem to be the delight of the greater part of the students."[33]

Can you picture it? Yale College a little temple? The campus so infused with a heavenly atmosphere that most of the students spent much of their time in prayer meetings and chapel services, walking around the campus with praise to God on their lips? Remember: We're talking about Yale, not a religious summer camp.

Only a few years prior to this season of revival, Yale had been in a state of spiritual and moral decline, similar to many of the American colleges after the Revolutionary War. In fact, when Lyman Beecher entered Yale in 1796, he claimed to be the only professing Christian out of a student body of 200! Revival historian James Edwin Orr describes the post-Revolutionary War scene in America:

> In 1790 America had won its independence, but it had lost something as well. In the wake of the Revolutionary War, French infidelity, deism, and the generally unsettled condition of society had driven the moral and spiritual climate of the colonies to an all-time low. Drunkenness was epidemic; profanity was of the most shocking kind;

bank robberies were a daily occurrence; and for the first time in the history of the American settlement women were afraid to go out at night for fear of being assaulted.

Conditions on campus were no better. A poll taken at Harvard revealed not one believer in the whole student body. At Princeton, where a similar survey showed there to be only two Christians on campus, when the dean opened the Chapel Bible to read, a pack of playing cards fell out, someone having cut a rectangle from each page to fit the deck. Conditions on campus had degenerated to the point that all but five at Princeton were part of the "filthy speech" movement of that day. While students there developed the art of obscene conversation, at Williams College they held a mock communion, and at Dartmouth students put on an "anti-church" play. In New Jersey the radical leader of the deist students led a mob to the Raritan Valley Presbyterian Church where they burned the Bible in a public bonfire. Christians were so few on the average campus and were so intimidated by the non-Christians that they met in secret. They even kept their minutes in code so no one could find out about their clandestine fellowship.[34]

It was Timothy Dwight who helped bring Yale back to its earlier state of faith and spirituality. Before his tenure, many of the faculty had become skeptical and the student body completely lax in its morals. Along with debating students about the inspiration and reliability of the Scriptures, Dwight preached on this theme for six months in chapel, also firing all professors who had embraced the deistic rationalism of the French Revolution. (Whether you agree with this action or not, it does point to the radically different climate that existed then at Yale, and let's not forget that Dwight is hailed as one of Yale's greatest presidents.)

The most famous of his messages was the 1796 sermon, "The Nature and Danger of Infidel Philosophy," and it had an immediate effect. As one student wrote, "From that moment infidelity was not only without a stronghold, but without a lurking place. To espouse her cause was now as unpopular as it had been before to profess a belief in Christianity."[35] That same year, 26 students "founded the Moral Society of Yale College. It discouraged profanity, immorality, and intemperance. By 1800, it included 'between one-third and one-half of all the students in its membership.'"[36]

Yale students today, both heterosexual and homosexual, would be shocked to encounter an atmosphere like *that* on their campus. (In reality, they would probably be far less shocked than would the Yale students from the early 1800's if *they* were suddenly transported to the campus today.) Without question, things have changed greatly at Yale University, from a time in the early 1800's when one-third to one-half of the students pledged to refrain from profanity, immorality, and drunkenness, to the open embrace of queer activism in the late 1900's. The transformation is absolutely stunning.

As Dr. Allen Hunt rightly noted,

> One can only imagine what would happen if any passionate Christians still remaining at Yale demanded a Christ Month, with full staffing and funding from the university? What would the campus look like with crucifixes, crosses, and chalices hanging from trees like the pink and lavender streamers that presently cover the campus each April during the BGLAD Pride Month celebrations? Such an image of Christian images and icons at an Ivy League school founded 300 years ago by a Christian church is unimaginable, isn't it? The answer to that question provides a snapshot of the intellectual and moral deterioration of Yale, in particular, and American higher education, in general, where tolerance is one-way, and morality is in the eyes of the beholder.[37]

LARRY KRAMER INITIATIVE FOR LESBIAN AND GAY STUDIES

In 2001, the Yale LGBT program received a shot in the arm when Arthur Kramer, brother of gay leader and AIDS activist Larry Kramer, donated one million dollars to Yale to fund The Larry Kramer Initiative for Lesbian and Gay Studies at Yale (abbreviated as LKI), which lasted from 2001-2006, greatly expanding LGBT studies at Yale.[38]

Heading up the Larry Kramer Initiative was Professor Jonathan David Katz. According to the Yale write up,

Former chair of the Department of Lesbian and Gay

Studies at City College of San Francisco, Katz was the first tenured faculty in gay and lesbian studies in the US. Katz was an Associate Professor in the Art History Department at the State University of New York at Stony Brook, where he also taught queer studies. Founder of the Harvey Milk Institute, the largest queer studies institute in the world, and the Queer Caucus for Art of the College Art Association, Katz is a committed community activist, who also co-founded Queer Nation San Francisco, in addition to other grass roots activist organizations.

Katz has made the scholarly and institutional development of queer studies the focus of his professional career, as the first artistic director of the National Queer Art Festival in San Francisco and through a wide range of publications in the US and Europe....[39]

Other professors who served in the Larry Kramer Initiative were David Agruss, who expressed his excitement about "being a part of such a vibrant and daring community of scholars working in queer theory, feminism, and gender and sexuality studies." Alongside Prof. Agruss was Megan Sinnott who noted that, "My main area of research is female transgenderism and same-sex sexuality in Thailand." Among her courses were, "Cross Cultural Sex, Anthropology of Sexuality, Women's Sexuality, and Theory and Method in the Study of Sex" – all part of a major degree program at Yale.[40] (One can only wonder into which program these courses would have fit just fifty years ago at Yale, let alone 250 years ago.)

Faculty involved in the LGBT Studies department at Yale as of 2010 include Jafari Sinclaire Allen, who "teaches courses on Black feminist and queer theory," among other subjects; Ron Gregg, who organized a 2009 conference at Yale entitled "Postwar Queer Underground Cinema, 1950-1968"; Siobhán Garrigan, who is a "theologian, teacher, and artist" and the author of a new article entitled "Queer Worship." (She serves at Yale as Associate Professor of Liturgical Studies and Associate Dean at the Institute of Sacred Music. Although I am not an expert on the history of Church liturgy, I am fairly confident that the category of "Queer Worship" is quite new!)[41]

But to mention these things is to quibble. After all, what else could be expected as an outgrowth of initiative founded in the name of Larry Kramer?

(I do not say this as Larry Kramer's personal judge and jury. I simply want to underscore how dramatically – indeed, diametrically – things have changed at Yale. And I do not question the scholarly credentials of the professors just mentioned. It is the *subject matter* that is questionable.)

Larry Kramer became nationally known for his dark, controversial, 1978 novel about gay life in America, entitled, quite bluntly, *Faggots*. Adding to his stature was his groundbreaking and award-winning play on AIDS, *Normal Heart*, which has been produced and performed hundreds of times around the world. As someone who suffers from AIDS himself, he has given more than twenty-five years of his life to raising consciousness about this terrible sickness, fighting on behalf of greater government and medical intervention to help cure and stop AIDS.

Kramer's own connection with Yale dates back to 1953, when as a freshman in October, 1953, he tried to kill himself, thinking he was the only gay student there. In 1997, he offered Yale four million dollars with specific guidelines for gay (male) studies or a gay student center, but Yale declined his offer, leading to a public confrontation with Yale by Kramer. As reported by the *Yale Alumni Magazine*,

> The media dustup went on for weeks, and Kramer was outspoken in his attacks on Yale, calling the University homophobic, President [Richard C.] Levin "spineless," and [Provost Alison] Richard "that termagant woman."
>
> Kramer says that as a result of the media attention, "I had letters from more than 100 institutions of higher learning begging me to consider them," he remembers. "USC sent me a set of blueprints for the building they would put up."[42]

How remarkable would it be if, in fact, "more than 100 institutions of higher learning [were] begging [Kramer] to consider them" for his multi-million dollar donation for queer campus studies – but I have no reason to believe he was lying.

Getting back to Larry Kramer himself, after the 2004 elections, he felt that he needed to speak out, bringing a very pessimistic word to the homosexual community in New York City. (According to reports, 900 attended, 400 were turned away, and no one left during his 90 minute speech.)[43]

His impassioned remarks, which were quite candid, not to mention profanity laden, included these comments about his own sex life:

> I have recently gone through my diaries of the worst of
> the [AIDS] plague years. I saw day after day a notation of
> another friend's death. I listed all the ones I'd slept with.
> There were a couple hundred. Was it my sperm that killed
> them, that did the trick? It is no longer possible for me
> to avoid this question of myself. Have you ever wondered
> how many men you killed? I know I murdered some of
> them. I just know. You know how you sometimes know
> things? I know. Several hundred over a bunch of years, I
> have to have murdered some of them, planting in him the
> original seed. I have put this to several doctors. Mostly they
> refuse to discuss it, even if they are gay. Most doctors do
> not like to discuss sex or what we do or did. (I still have
> not heard a consensus on the true dangers of oral sex, for
> instance.) They play blind. God knows what they must be
> thinking when they examine us. Particularly if they aren't
> gay. One doctor answered me, it takes two to tango so you
> cannot take the responsibility alone. But in some cases it
> isn't so easy to answer so flippantly. The sweet young boy
> who didn't know anything and was in awe of me. I was
> the first man who f----d him. I think I murdered him. The
> old boyfriend who did not want to go to bed with me and
> I made him. The man I let f--- me because I was trying to
> make my then boyfriend, now lover, jealous. I know, by the
> way, that that other one is the one who infected me. You
> know how you sometime know things? I know he infected
> me. I tried to murder myself on that one.

What a terribly tragic confession, and how casually he mentions the
"several hundred" men with whom he slept "over a bunch of years," convinced
that by infecting them with the AIDS virus, he has "murdered some of them,"
including, "The sweet young boy who didn't know anything and was in awe of
me." Kramer admits to being the first to have had anal intercourse with him.[44]
Yet it is in this man's name that Yale launched a special program. What an
extraordinary turn of events from Yale's first centuries![45]

From Timothy Dwight as president of Yale to an initiative in gay and lesbian studies in the name of Larry Kramer. Who would have imagined this? Dwight's impact on Yale was so great that his name has been memorialized in both the Yale Chapel as well as one of the men's dorms. Now Kramer's name has been memorialized in a special gay studies initiative.

At a Sept. 30, 2003 speech at Harvard's Center for Public Leadership at the Kennedy School of Government, Kramer said, "If I were to teach anything here it would be how to confront the system, not work within it. Hit it over the head with a bat and take no prisoners." And to a student "who asked how to address the overwhelming AIDS epidemic in her native Kenya," Kramer answered (after letting her know that she wouldn't like his response): "There's remarkably little activism of a confrontational nature in these countries. Your people have to be made to shove it in their faces. Tie up governments, tie up industry, tie up traffic. Pour fake blood in department stores."[46] Perhaps this too will be taught one day at Yale.

Or maybe one day Yale will offer a course entitled, "New Perspectives on Pederasty," echoing Kramer's comments, cited on the NAMBLA website, that:

> In those cases where children do have sex with their homosexual elders... I submit that often, very often, the child desires the activity, and perhaps even solicits it, either because of a natural curiosity... or because he or she is homosexual and innately knows it. ... And unlike girls or women forced into rape or traumatized, most gay men have warm memories of their earliest and early sexual encounters; when we share these stories with each other, they are invariably positive ones.[47]

I imagine that this is news to thousands of men who were molested as boys, for whom their first sexual encounter carries anything but "warm" and "positive" memories. So much for the name behind the Larry Kramer Initiative at Yale!

QUEER CAMPUS LIFE: COMING TO A SCHOOL NEAR YOU

Unfortunately, the LGBQT emphasis at Yale is not unique these days. In fact, scores of colleges in America now have gay, lesbian, or queer study programs[48] – or, at the least, LGBQT student centers – while it is increasingly common for schools to have a Gay and Lesbian Bill of Rights or the like. Many campuses even designate April as "Gaypril," devoting the whole month to highlighting gay issues and flying the gay flag all thirty days, and things like this happen on large campuses and small campuses throughout America.

How many of you have heard of Gustavus Adolphus College, located in St. Peter, Minnesota? Until October of 2010, I had never heard of this small, Lutheran school, which, according to its website, is:

> a church-related, residential liberal arts college firmly rooted in its Swedish and Lutheran heritage. . . . It is a community where a mature understanding of the Christian faith and lives of service are nurtured and students are encouraged to work toward a just and peaceful world.[49]

Despite this description, freshmen at the school's orientation in 2010 watched vulgar, live skits, including one that jokingly described ways to have sex in your dorm room without being disturbed (sound effects and all) and included notable characters like "Bondage Bob" who says, "Tie me down, gets me up" and "Porno Paul" who says, "Surfin' the net, gets my undies wet." (What a delightful way for the upperclassmen to introduce the incoming students to their campus!)

A second skit was devoted to explaining the meaning and importance of "LGPBBTTQ&A." It began with this little rhyme: "Follow along and listen quite clear to learn of the wonderful world of the queer." Yes, this presentation was part of a freshman orientation at an allegedly Christian campus.

As noted by family activist Laurie Higgins, the mother of an alumnus of the school:

> [The skit] features ignorant, irresponsible upperclassmen, this time defining the terms lesbian, gay, pansexual, bi-curious, bisexual, transgender and transsexual for freshmen, explaining, for example, that lesbian women "make love quite beautifully," and that the term "bi-curious" refers to "testin' the waters, seein' what's attractive." . . .
>
> Next a boy waxes romantic about his male lover and a girl proclaims, "I happen to be a lesbian -- a big one. And my, oh my, I love it. All the women, the flowy hair, the sweet perfume, mmm, mmm. I like sex. I love sex."[50]

According to Higgins' daugther, Easten, who graduated from Gustavus in 2004,

> I suppose this should come as no surprise from a college that invited a transgender speaker to give the daily chapel message during National Coming Out Week over six years ago and that celebrates and affirms such behavior without even an acknowledgment that they are departing from a biblical understanding of sexuality.[51]

Yes, even a small-town, "Christian" college in Minnesota is celebrating "the wonderful world of the queer."

And what kind of effect does this have on some of the young people exposed to these kinds of ideas? A concerned mother sent this email to a colleague of mine on March 8, 2010:

> My daughter started UNC Chapel Hill this past fall. We thought they were placing her in a learning community for diversity-meaning different cultures. She is on a floor that is made up of primarily gay and lesbian. They have a diversity class which has, in my opinion, some assignments and readings that border on pornography.
>
> When I complained to the director last semester, she said that she had noticed the grad students focusing on the topic of gays and lesbians more than needed to be and that she would make sure it changed this semester. About 11 out of 15 readings have something to do with sexuality in the areas. One reading talks about how one culture encourages sexual acts at the age of 7 and it goes into details. ... The diversity class has required students to attend gay pride parades, drag contests, etc She went to a counselor there without my consent who encouraged all types of "lifestyles" as long as one is happy. ...

You can be sure that this is hardly an isolated incident.

OBERLIN COLLEGE THEN AND NOW

Let's take a close up look at one more prominent college to flesh out (double entendre intended) exactly what is happening in the name of gay and lesbian studies and gender sensitivity. The school in question is Oberlin College, founded in 1833 by two Presbyterian ministers and famous in the 19th century for the presence of Charles Grandison Finney, first as a faculty member and then as president. Finney (1792-1875), known as America's greatest revivalist, was also an influential social reformer as well as the namesake of the Finney Chapel at Oberlin.[52]

Shortly after Finney joined the faculty as Professor of Theology in 1835, Oberlin became one of the nation's first colleges to admit women, and soon after that, the campus joined in the fight against slavery, another one of Finney's major life emphases. In fact, Oberlin became part of an underground escape route for slaves, all part of Finney's program of moral reformation.

For Finney, however, the basis of moral reformation was spiritual transformation, and it was this emphasis that lay at the foundation of his work, even during his presidency at Oberlin. Speaking of his time there in the 1850's and 1860's, he wrote:

> ... I had come to Oberlin, and resided here, for the sake of the students, to secure their conversion and sanctification .... Our fall term is properly our harvest here [meaning, spiritual harvest]. It begins about the first of September, when we have a large number of new students, and many of these unconverted ones. I have always felt, as a good many others have, and I believe the faculty generally, that during that term was the time to secure the conversion of our new students. . . . Our general population is a changing one, and we very frequently need a sweeping revival through the whole town, among the householders as well as the students, to keep up a healthy tone of piety. A goodly number of our students learn to work themselves in promoting revivals, and are very efficient in laboring for the conversion of their fellow students. The young men's prayer meetings have been greatly blessed.[53]

Oberlin was a Christian school!

Finney's chapel sermons can still be read today, stored in the Oberlin archives and available electronically as well.[54] The standards he set for all students during his tenure were extremely high, as seen, for example, by his chapel sermon, "On Moral Depravity," preached March 26, 1862, toward the end of which he commented:

> You can see from this subject why men need regeneration, and also what regeneration is. It is the giving up of the carnal mind, a ceasing to mind the flesh, and giving up the whole mind to obey God. *It is a change from being committed to self-gratification, to the committal of the whole soul to obedience to God.*[55]

This sermon, among many others by President Finney, was printed and distributed in *The Oberlin Evangelist*, an official school publication.

Contrast that with a description of Oberlin's commitment to self-gratification today:

> Some 800 to 1,000 students typically attended an annual college-sponsored, administration-approved "Safer Sex Night," an orgy held on campus. The *Oberlin Review*, the student newspaper, described the scene: "Educational, sexually explicit videos played on TV screens, and students sat in booths in g-strings and halter tops." Other students, the paper reported, simply go naked. Students can enter something called the "Tent of Consent" to, shall we say, interact sexually.[56]

How would Finney feel about such a scene at his old school? Would he be turning over in his grave? I don't think so! I think he would be tempted to get out of his grave and make a personal visit to his old campus.

From an emphasis on "committal of the whole soul to obedience to God" to an annual "Safer Sex Night," Oberlin too has been transformed. One century ago – or even fifty years ago – who could have predicted, even in their wildest dreams, that there would be a student-run, Oberlin Sexual Information Center offering the following services to the student body?

- Free, confidential counseling and a space to talk about any sexual issue.
- Safer sex products at wholesale prices including condoms (6-60 cents), lubricants, dental dams,

spermicides, gloves, and more.
- Other products including pregnancy tests (50 cents), alternative menstrual products, specula, sex toys, and much more.
- A lending library including books on sexual health, contraception, pregnancy, HIV/AIDS, sexually transmitted infections, queer issues, safer sex, BDSM, erotica, and more.[57]

When such "services" are offered on our campuses – sex toys for sale and a lending library including books on Bondage, Discipline, and Sadomasochism – things have certainly run amuck.

Of course, it would be terribly misleading to give the impression that the only thing – or the primary thing – that Oberlin students do is party and have sex. Obviously not! Oberlin offers a rich assortment of programs and has a highly-qualified faculty.[58] It is a serious school for serious students, despite the loose morals – loose morals which, generally speaking, have been the norm on our college campuses for the last few decades.

What has remained constant at Oberlin is its activist mentality, from the days of Finney until now, only today's activism has taken on a very different tone.[59] Words like "transgender" and "multicultural" are now front and center, as illustrated by this sampling of some of the sights, sounds, activities, and emphases at the school:

- Every spring, Oberlin sponsors a "Transgender Awareness Week," an event created to "celebrate Oberlin College's queer community," culminating with the annual Drag Ball. This is the conclusion of a week of "talks and film screenings to celebrate the experiences of transgender, transsexual, intersex and other gender-variant people. . . . As Drag Ball nears, students prepare costumes, planning to attend as dominatrixes, thugs and celebrities. Others will attend simply baring their Birthday Suit."[60] Cross-dressing, of course, is normal attire for the Drag Ball.
- Lynn Hickman, a coordinator for Transgender Awareness Week in 2001, said, "The basic assumption of transgenderism is the transgressing of gender norms.

Whether that means completely passing from one end to the other, or finding a space that combines or defies the binary [meaning, the categories of male-female] in our society, it comes down to exploring outside of the norm you were assigned because of the discomfort that you feel in it. . . . Standing in between genders, or completely rejecting the notion of a fixed gender really asks people to question what is considered status quo from day one. You are completely removing yourself from the gender binary, and that's a radical act in and of itself."[61] This, of course, is said with the utmost seriousness.

- As a result of Transgender Awareness Week in 2002, the College and the Oberlin Student Cooperative Association (OSCA) decided to improve their campus housing. A report stated that, "Last month the housing and dining committee approved two policy changes. First, all residence halls with three or more bathrooms would have bathrooms designated specifically for male, female, and non-gender specific. . . . OSCA has voted this week to give singles [meaning single rooms] priority to transgender students who feel uncomfortable living with a roommate. Also, all housing and dining co-ops with bathrooms must maintain at least one gender neutral bathroom at all times.[62] (Before you write this off as completely fringe, you might want to read the *forty-eighty* page resource published in 2005 by the Transgender Law Center and entitled, "Peeing in Peace: A Resource Guide for Transgender Activists and Allies.")[63]

- OSCA will also be abandoning all references to biological sex and instead will use self-identified categories of gender in all internal and external paperwork."[64] (You might want to rub your eyes and read that last sentence again. "Male" and "female" are no longer acceptable categories; instead, "self-identified" sexual categories – of which, presumably, there is no limit – will now be the norm.)

- Oberlin's "Multicultural Resource Center" exists "to serve people who have historically faced oppression on college campuses--low-income and first-generation students, people of color, and people who identify as lesbian, gay, bisexual, or transgender (LGBT)," says the center's director, Rachel Beverly.[65] (And note carefully the diverse groups just lumped together.) Already in 1997, the *Oberlin Review* reported that, "The Multicultural Resource Center's (MRC) new Queer Peer program has more than a catchy name: it also has a mission to mentor students in need of support and education about sexual orientation. . . . MRC intern Cara Wick, the community coordinator for Lesbian, Gay, Bisexual and Transgender (LGBT) students, heads the new program. It currently has 47 members and is, according to its mission statement, 'A gay and lesbian education program to high schools in Lorain County.'"[66] (In other words, the Queer Peers reach out to gay and lesbian high school students near Oberlin, helping them deal with "homophobia.")
- In April of 2002, 1973 Oberlin grad David Halperin, "a noted gay activist and scholar, presented a free, public talk titled, 'Mommie Queerest: Joan Crawford and Gay Male Subjectivity,'"[67] while an exhibit entitled "Queering the Museum" was held in the spring of 2004. Another lecture of note took place on October 4, 2000, when Kevin Jennings "one of the country's leading activists working in the fight for equality for gay and lesbian youth" came to the campus to discuss "The American Dream" in a free, public talk. The Oberlin website notes that, 'Jennings' talk is part of Oberlin's 'Common Ground: Education for Democracy' initiative funded by a grant from the William and Flora Hewlett Foundation to enhance campus community dialogue about pluralism and multicultural issues."[68] There's that word "multicultural" once again!

And what does a weekend day look like for an Oberlin student?

Consider this partial list of activities for Sunday, April 25, 2004 (this overlapped with Oberlin's "Queer Faith Week"), including location and time:

March: Pro-choice march. Washington, D.C. 8 a.m.

Workshop: "Looking Beyond the Single-Issue Lens: Understanding the Intersection of Oppressions," Multicultural Resource Center. Open to all. Advance registration required. King TBA, 9 a.m.

Conference: Beltane workshops on paganism and magic. Wilder TBA, 11 a.m.

Discussion: Queer Faith Week ECO Dinner. "How does your faith tradition address GLBTQ issues?" Lewis House (Center for Service and Learning), 5:30 p.m.

Testing: Peer HIV testing. Wilder 314, 5-11 p.m.

Lecture: "Ritual, Magic and How Pagans Will Save the World," Sam Webster. Science Center: West Lecture Hall, 7:30 p.m.[69]

Of course, these are just some of the weekly, annual, or periodic *events* taking place at Oberlin. As stunning as some of them are – I remind you once more that this is a major institution of higher learning – some of the courses taught are equally stunning, primarily in the department of Comparative American Studies. (This department is not to be confused with the department of Gender and Women's Studies. Courses in that department include Feminist Political Theory; Global Feminisms; Black Feminist Thought: Historical Perspective.)

Consider this sampling of courses and professors in Oberlin's Comparative American Studies department, offered already in 2005. Jane Cooper, then the department director, listed her first research and teaching interest as, "Queer Studies (especially film and television studies)." Another professor, Daphne John, listed as one of her primary interests, "Gender Stratification," while professor Meredith Raimondo taught courses such as "Lesbian, Gay, Bisexual, Transgender, Queer Identities," and "Transnational Sexualities." (Somehow I don't recall any of those courses being offered back when I was in college – but that was in the pristine 1970's, after all.)

What kind of textbooks are required for a course focusing on "Queer

Identities"? This was Prof. Raimondo's list:

- *Queer Families, Queer Politics: Challenging Culture and the State*
- *Selling Out: The Gay and Lesbian Movement Goes to the Market*
- *Exile and Pride: Disability, Queerness, and Liberation*
- *In a Queer Time and Place: Transgender Bodies, Subcultural Lives*
- *Disidentifications: Queers of Color and the Performance of Politics*

The textbooks for the "Transnational Sexualities" course were no less interesting, including books like *Global Divas: Filipino Gay Men in the Diaspora* and *The Night is Young: Sexuality in Mexico in the Time of AIDS.*[70] Prof. Raimondo has also offered a seminar called "Queer Geographies," with an equally fascinating assortment of required texts such as: *Bisexual Spaces: A Geography of Sexuality and Gender; Mapping Gay L.A.: The Intersection of Place and Politics;* and *Men Like That: A Southern Queer History.*[71]

In 2005, visiting professor Jordana Rosenberg offered the course, "Reading Queer Futures." What exactly does this mean? The course description states, in part,

What kind of a future is queer? This course asks us to imagine questions of sexuality as, also, questions of temporality. Queerness, after all, is a way for subjects to imagine themselves by terms other than the ones that they have been given, and so queerness engages futures that exceed familiar progress narratives. But identifying as 'queer' also might be a way of claiming an identity that is as-yet unknown to the subject who claims it. Is queerness, then, a way of casting into a future or a way of suspending presumptions about what that future might consist? Does queerness consolidate new futures or put the category of 'the future' itself under critical scrutiny? In this course, we will read queer fiction and theories that push us to reconceive the relation between sexuality and time."[72]

Yes, these are all serious academic classes taught by serious academicians at a serious academic institution, all part of the queering of our campuses.[73] William Norris, a sociology professor at Oberlin, has taught a course on "Sexualities and Society," with required and/or recommended books for the class including *Queer Theory: An Introduction*; *Gay Macho: The Life and Death of a Homosexual Clone*; *Sex and Sensibility: Stories of a Lesbian Generation*; and *Can Homophobia Be Cured?* One of the videos shown in the class was entitled *Lesbian Avengers*[74] -- and I repeat, these are college classes, not courses taught at the local LGBT community center. Yes, "queer studies" have found a home in many of our college and university campuses.

QUEER STUDIES MEANS QUEER ACTIVISM

The all-female Smith College, perhaps America's most lesbian-friendly campus, offers a Queer Studies emphasis within its Study of Women and Gender program. According to the official website:

> Queer Studies is an emerging interdisciplinary field whose goal is to analyze antinormative sexual identities, performances, discourses and representations in order ultimately to destabilize the notion of normative sexuality and gender. Queer studies comes out of a critique of identity politics. It rejects essentialized conceptualization[s] of sexuality, gender, and sexual identity as innate or fixed. It represents a deconstruction of hegemonic conceptions of sexual and gender categories within straight, gay and lesbian communities.[75]

Clearly, then, this department is not just devoted to education and information. It is devoted to activism – queer activism.

The same can be said of the Williams Institute of the UCLA School of Law, devoted to "advancing critical thought in the field of sexual orientation and public policy,"[76] and underwritten, to date, by more than $12 million from Charles R. Williams. The website states:

> The Williams Institute advances sexual orientation law and public policy through rigorous, independent research and scholarship, and disseminates it to judges, legislators, policymakers, media and the public. A national think

tank at UCLA Law, the Williams Institute produces high quality research with real-world relevance.

Experts at the Williams Institute have authored dozens of public policy studies and law review articles, filed amicus briefs in key court cases, provided expert testimony at legislative hearings, been widely cited in the national media, and trained thousands of lawyers, judges and members of the public. By providing new ideas and reliable information, the Williams Institute makes a difference.[77]

Back in the Ivy League, a June 3, 2009 article in the *New York Times* announced:

Harvard University will endow a visiting professorship in lesbian, gay, bisexual and transgender studies, a position that, it believes, will be the first endowed, named chair in the subject at an American college.

The visiting professorship was made possible by a gift of $1.5 million from the Harvard Gay and Lesbian Caucus, which will formally announce it at a dinner on Thursday, after Harvard's commencement exercises.[78]

But even this does not tell the story adequately. The fact that some very unique speakers are in special demand on the campuses helps fill the picture out. One example will suffice.

THE "TRANSGENDER WARRIOR"

According to her website (actually "hir" is the preferred spelling, as will be explained shortly), this passionate individual has spoken at scores of colleges, including schools like Harvard, Yale, and Johns Hopkins.[79] This impressive résumé belongs to none other than Leslie Feinberg (born 1949), the "transgender warrior" who dresses and looks like a man and prefers to be called "ze."[80]

According to an online GLBTQ encyclopedia entry,

Political organizer, grassroots historian, and writer Leslie Feinberg is a pioneer of transgender activism and culture.

Long a part of the struggle for queer liberation, Feinberg
openly identifies as transgendered and has been outspoken
about "hir" experiences living outside of the gender binary.
("Ze" has expressed the need for our language to incorporate
alternate pronouns such as "hir" rather than "her" or "his,"
and "ze" or "sie" as opposed to "he" or "she.")

Feinberg is perhaps best known as the author of the
widely acclaimed novel *Stone Butch Blues* (Firebrand Books,
1993). . . . Feinberg and hir wife, poet Minnie Bruce Pratt,
live outside of New York City.[81]

Now, it would appear that Feinberg is a woman of courage and conviction,
but "ze" and "hir"? Really, now! Are we supposed to change the most basic
elements of the English language to accommodate someone's personal, sexual
confusion? Yet Feinberg is a highly-sought after campus speaker. It would
appear that "ze" is making quite an impact!

Holly Boswell, a 1972 Oberlin grad and leading transgender activist, had
this to say at the April 2001, Transgender Awareness Week, expanding on
this new vocabulary. As reported by the *Oberlin Review:*

"There is no natural sex. Who owns the meanings of the
category?" Boswell . . . has actively worked in the transgender
movement since the '80s. Hir, which is the preferred
pronoun for transgender persons that identify with neither
sex, talk was entitled "The Spirit of Transgender." Ze
(again: preferred pronoun) said ze began to understand the
spirit of hir sexuality through a circle of theater friends in
hir 30s. "Community means strength, to meet our strength,
to do the [activist] work that needs to be done," ze said.[82]

Yes, this is meant as serious reporting of a serious speech, featuring mind-
numbing lines like, "There is no natural sex. Who owns the meanings of the
category?" Yet, as bizarre as this sounds, there's no doubt that many college
students are taking it to heart. In fact, in 2004, Wesleyan College "eliminated
the word women's from the female rugby team. Why? Because several of the
girls have chosen to be identified as males. One of the girls said, 'We don't
want people yelling, "Go girls."'"[83]

It would not be an exaggeration, then, to say that our campuses have come full circle, from God to gay and from theological acumen to transgender awareness. Put another way, they have now run the gamut from A to "Ze." I can hardly imagine – nor do I care to imagine – where they are going next. And while no one is suggesting for a moment that our universities should be turned back into seminaries, how about a return to sanity? Is this too much to ask? Stranger things have happened, have they not?

A Martian gathering evidence about American society, simply by monitoring our television, would certainly assume that there were more gay people in America than there are evangelical Christians.

Film critic Michael Medved

Hollywood always rewards young actors for taking risks in the service of homosexual values.

Yale Kramer, writing in the American Spectator

If it weren't for gays, honey, there wouldn't be a Hollywood.

Elizabeth Taylor

The debate of 14 years ago about gays in the military seems almost quaint. Kids grow up today with gay friends, gay parents, gay parents of friends and gay friends of parents. . . . Kids are also exposed constantly to an entertainment culture in which gays are not merely accepted but in some ways dominant. You rarely see a reality show without a gay cast member, while Rosie O'Donnell is a coveted free agent and Ellen DeGeneres is America's sweetheart.

Michael Kinsley, "The Quiet Gay Revolution"
Time Magazine, June 14, 2007

For a while now, kissing has been a popular pastime, but over the last few years a particular sub-genre has emerged as perhaps the hottest gimmick in Hollywood: girl on girl.

Scott Harris, "Amanda Seyfried, Julianne Moore Share Steamy Lesbian Scene in 'Chloe'," InsideMovies.Moviefone.Com, January 12, 2010

It's not enough to be "Will and Grace" any more. The benchmark is higher.

Jarrett Barrios, president of GLAAD, January 19, 2010
(quoted on CNN.com)

5

Brokeback Mountain, the Fab Five and Hollywood's Celebration of Queer

T he year was 1976, and some significant changes had already taken place in TV's depiction of gay men. The *Washington Post* was quick to take notice, pointing out that homosexuals were now presented "as squeaky clean and wholesome as was the image of blacks during the sensitive years of the civil rights struggle." The article continued:

> In those days stereotypes were avoided so scrupulously that from TV you got the impression blacks were just like whites, except they didn't have any flaws. From TV today [meaning, 1976], the impression given of homosexuals is that they're just like heterosexuals except they have no hang-ups.[1]

Not that long before, in the 1950's and 1960's, "the stereotypical media images of homosexuals as effeminate fops and insane deviants were so pervasive that few successful gays and lesbians openly associated themselves with homosexuality or gay rights."[2] By the mid-1970's, things had changed dramatically.

What caused such a media transformation in the course of just two decades? According to gay historian Prof. David Eisenbach, there were two primary factors. The first was simply cultural change, specifically "a greater acceptance of homosexuality among a younger generation of media executives and screenwriters who matured in a more tolerant, sexually relaxed society." The second was gay activism. Yes, according to Eisenbach,

> the more positive presentations of homosexuals were also the achievements of organizations like the Gay Activists Alliance and the National Gay Task Force, which monitored portrayals of homosexuals in the media. TV executives discovered they could avoid zaps and bad publicity by having gay activists review scripts that dealt with homosexuality before they were aired.[3] ["Zaps" were the strategically-timed, carefully-staged, gay hit-and-run protests widely used in the 1970's.]

Indeed,

> One of the great achievements of the gay liberation

movement was the display of the nonstereotypical, well-adjusted homosexual on the televisions in millions of American living rooms. More than any other medium, TV had the power to shape and manipulate the conscious and subconscious prejudices of the American public. . . .

Gay activists in the 1960s and 1970s understood that only after the public saw that homosexuals were not threats to society could gay rights make any political and legal progress. By manipulating the media and forcing more sympathetic characterizations of homosexuals on television shows, the gay rights movement offered powerful challenges to common stereotypes.[4]

This gay manipulation of the media, coupled with ongoing cultural changes, has produced absolutely startling results in much the same way that well-executed gay activism in the schools has produced such dramatic results (see above, Chapter Three). In fact, back in 1976, it would have been hard to imagine how far things would have come in little more than thirty years.

THE MAINSTREAMING OF QUEER MEDIA

Who would have predicted popular TV shows with names like *Queer Eye for the Straight Guy*? And who would have imagined that the stars of this show, affectionately known as the "Fab Five" – as if their influence could be compared to that of the Fab Four, the Beatles – would actually throw out a baseball at a Boston Red Sox game? Really now, five gay guys, famous for their queerly-named TV show, throwing the ceremonial opening pitch in front of 30,000 hardcore, sports fans? This could never happen in America – but it did!

On a Sunday afternoon in June 2005, fans in Boston's Fenway Park witnessed a scene that was unimaginable just a few years earlier. With the Green Monster looming in the background [speaking of the large, green wall in left field in Fenway], the cast of television's *Queer Eye for the Straight Guy* threw out the first pitch before a World Champion Red Sox game. In honor of Gay Pride Week, the *Queer Eye* cast had been invited to Fenway to promote their show's season premier, which featured the Fab Five giving style make-overs to a few Boston Red Sox stars.[5]

And the cast received a very warm reception from the crowd. According to the *Boston Globe*,

> The arrival of the "Queer Eye" crew, down one because of a scheduling conflict, was a milestone of sorts for Fenway, where one season ticket holder remarked that 15 years ago it would have been unthinkable for a gay man to run out to the mound in a pink shirt to throw out the opening pitch.
>
> And while the appearance of the "Fab Five" had sparked criticism from some commentators and fans, for many yesterday the occasion was just another example of a changing culture, in which Ellen DeGeneres and the characters from "Will & Grace" are household names, gay people can marry in Massachusetts, and "Take Me Out," a play about a homosexual baseball player, is a Tony winner.
>
> "The Red Sox embraced it," said Kevin Herschen, 26, who came to the game from Rhode Island with his father, Paul. "I don't mind."[6]

Just six months later, "Americans flocked to movie theaters throughout the United States to see *Brokeback Mountain*, a major motion picture about a love affair between two ranch hands in Wyoming,"[7] – and a motion picture with explicit, homosexual love scenes at that (resulting in the desensitizing of countless thousands of viewers). Three years later, gay-themed movies hardly raise an eyebrow.

Who, after all, protested the release of *Breakfast with Scot*? This was a 2008 comedy which told the story of two gay men, Eric and Sam, who had been in a committed relationship for four years when they have to take in an eleven-year-old boy, who turns out to be more openly gay than they are.[8] And how many concerned conservatives even took notice of the July, 2010 release of *The Kids Are Alright*, which tells the story of two lesbian women who are "comfortably raising their two teenage children" when these children decide to "track down the anonymous sperm donor partly responsible for their existence."[9] (For the scathing, anti-conservative, comments of actor Mark Ruffalo, the "donor dad" in the story, see below.)

The review in *USA Today* didn't mention that the subject matter was controversial in the least, giving it three-and-a-half stars out of four, saying that the movie "approaches perfection," and calling it "probing, poignant and, above all, highly entertaining."[10] And certainly, there was not a hint in the review of the trauma that many kids go through because they do not know who their (donor) father is.[11] In this climate, it is no surprise that in July, 2010, it was announced that, "After a meeting with gay and lesbian activists . . . NBC's 'Today' show said it is changing the rules for its annual wedding contest to allow same-sex couples to apply for a ceremony conducted on morning TV."[12]

Yes, things have changed dramatically in the media's presentation of queer, to the point that a PR firm for a gay activist organization could hardly have scripted things any better.[13] In fact, such organizations are hardly needed to manipulate the media anymore, since Hollywood today is not just gay friendly but downright gay activist.

GAY ACTIVISM AND HOLLYWOOD: LIKE A HAND IN A GLOVE

Is bisexuality the desired emphasis of the hour? No problem! Motion pictures and TV have had that covered for some time now. Yes, bisexuality is cool, giving you the best of both worlds.

Is it time to bash the claim that homosexuals can change? Consider it done! Plenty of shows have trashed "ex-gays," and in the most stereotyped, exaggerated terms possible.

Is the latest fad transgender ("the T word")? No problem there either! Both the movies and TV shows are hitting that from every angle, to the point that the media is now normalizing conditions that even the pro-gay psychiatric industry has yet to accept.

Is there a need for gay-slanted talk shows and news programs? Already taken care of! From out and proud lesbians like Ellen and Rosie and Suze Orman and Rachel Maddox to men like Anderson Cooper (who, if not gay, is totally gay-slanted in his perspectives),[14] there seems to be no shortage of popular gay and lesbian hosts to set the tone for deciding what topics are newsworthy and then covering them from a decidedly one-sided, gay activist perspective.

But this is just the tip of the iceberg. How about the shows celebrating the supposedly risk-free wonders of sex change surgery, or the programs presenting the poignant, tear-jerking stories of gay adoption, or the series glorifying the sensual seductions of lesbian love?[15] TV is feasting on this, promoting it all with vigor and passion – and for the most part, in the most biased, one-sided ways imaginable.

To repeat Prof. Eisenbach's observation, "More than any other medium, TV [has] the power to shape and manipulate the conscious and subconscious prejudices of the American public," and those conscious and subconscious prejudices have certainly been altered. It's an open secret!

This was expressed clearly on a December 16, 2007 episode of *Sixty Minutes* dealing with the military's "Don't Ask, Don't Tell" policy regarding homosexuals. According to Army Sgt. Darren Manzella, he "disclosed his sexuality to his superiors, even offering graphic proof, and was neither discharged nor reprimanded,"[16] despite the military's long-standing policy prohibiting open homosexuality and despite the fact that he showed his superiors videos of him making out with his male lover. He was simply told he was not gay and sent back to work as a medic.

In the *Sixty Minutes* report, interviewer Lesley Stahl "spoke with several gay former military members who say they were also out openly in their units, known to be gay by as many as a hundred other service members," none of whom were put off by their homosexuality.[17] Why this enlightened attitude towards gays in the military? Former Marine Corps avionics technician Brian Fricke explained: "They don't care ... .these are our peers ... the 'Will and Grace' generation. They grew up with it in the media ... .They see gay people as people ... Americans. They don't see gay people as people with a disability. . . ."[18]

Yes, this is "the *Will and Grace* generation" who "grew up with it in the media," the generation of *Queer Eye for the Straight Guy*, the generation of shamelessly sexual shows like *Queer as Folk* and *The L[esbian] Word*, the generation of *A Shot at Love with [Bisexual] Tila Tequila*, the generation of *Gay, Straight, or Taken* – and so much more. The generation in which, it seems that every season of *American Idol*, *Saturday Night Live*, *Survivor*, *Amazing Race*, or *Dancing With the Stars* features openly gay participants.

Listen to Leslie Jordan, the openly gay actor who starred on *Will and Grace*, speaking at the Carolina's Banquet of the Human Rights Campaign in Charlotte on February 24, 2006. He stated his belief that there were "two ways that combat homophobia. One is through humor ... and the other is to put a face on it. And I think that America welcomed the characters from *Will and Grace* . . . into their homes. We laughed, we loved, progress was made." And so, our opinions were shaped and our sensitivities dulled without us even realizing.

To be sure, some positive progress has been made through the media's portrayal of gays and lesbians. It is good that gays are no longer caricatured as "effeminate fops and insane deviants." Instead, they are primarily viewed simply as fellow-Americans and fellow-human beings. But it is not good that homosexual behavior is presented as just another alternative to heterosexual behavior, that bisexuality is celebrated, that transgenderism is normalized, that sex-change surgery is presented as the thing to do, that ex-gays are ridiculed and their very existence denied.

IS YOUR TV SCREEN TURNING PINK?

And let's not underestimate how pervasive the gay influence is on TV, from gay themes to gay characters – especially when you consider that roughly 3% of the population claims to be gay or lesbian[19] in contrast with more than 35% of the population that claims to be evangelical Christian,[20] to give just one example. As Robert Knight observed on October 8, 2008, "If you're noticing your TV screen turning pink, it's not just your imagination." Just how pink has TV become?

> The new broadcast TV season includes 22 series featuring a total of 35 openly gay characters, according to the Gay and Lesbian Alliance Against Defamation (GLAAD). GLAAD, which rides herd over all Hollywood scripts dealing with homosexuality, says the number of series with homosexual characters is a record. These series are on ABC, NBC, CBS, Fox and the CW networks. The total figure does not include shows on cable, like *The L Word* on Showtime, or MTV's all-gay LOGO network.[21]

A very limited sampling of prominent shows on the different networks regularly featuring overtly gay characters and/or themes includes:

- ABC: *Grey's Anatomy*; *Desperate Housewives*; *Ugly Betty*; *Brothers and Sisters*
- NBC: *Law & Order: SVU*; *ER*; *The Office*
- CBS: *Survivor China*; *Two and a Half Men*
- Fox: *House*; *American Dad*; *The Simpsons*; *Bones*
- FX: *Nip/Tuck*; *The Shield*; *Rescue Me*
- The CW: *Girlfriends*

- TBS: *Friends; Sex and the City*
- MTV: *The Real World; Road Rules; Next*
- Bravo: *Workout; Project Runway; Queer Eye for the Straight Guy*
- Lifetime (Television for Women): *Gay, Straight, or Taken*
- HBO: *Oz; The Wire; Six Feet Under*
- Showtime: *Queer as Folk; The L Word.*

(Note that I have not listed soap operas here or mentioned any of the shows that air on gay channels, like MTV's Logo Network, nor have I mentioned gay-themed movies, for which see below.)[22] And, with approximately 3% of America's population identifying as gay or lesbian,[23] what should we make of the fact that, according to a July 25, 2009 story,

> In its third annual Network Responsibility Index, the Gay & Lesbian Alliance Against Defamation found that of HBO's 14 original prime-time series, 10 included content reflecting the lives of homosexual, bisexual, and transgender people. That totaled 42 percent of the network's programming hours, in series such as True Blood, Entourage and The No. 1 Ladies' Detective Agency. By contrast, on NBC and CBS only 8 percent and 5 percent, respectively, of prime-time hours included them, the report said.[24]

How enlightening! HBO's gay-themed, original programming represented "42 percent of the network's programming hours" – more than ten times the amount of gays and lesbians in America. And no program, it seems, is off limits: In October, 2010, GLAAD called on the children's puppet show, *Sesame Street*, to begin to depict families headed up by same-sex couples.[25]

GLAAD also has a special web feature called **TV GAYED. GLAAD's Weekly Guide to What's LGBT on TV.**[26] Here are some of the listings for the first week of January, 2009:

Thursday, January 1
> 8:00 PM World Magic Awards, MyNetworkTV (2 hrs) NEW
Believe it or not, **Neil Patrick Harris** [an openly gay actor] is a huge fan of magic, so it's only fitting he's hosting this annual awards show, honoring the best illusionists working today.

> 9:00 PM Grey's Anatomy, ABC (1 hr) REPEAT
"You are glasses." Relive the magic of Erica coming out in this very special episode.

> 10:00 PM The Office, NBC (1 hr) REPEAT
Coming out scenes not your bag? How about the traumatic Season Four finale, in which Toby quits his job at Dunder Mifflin, leaving the rest of the employees to haze the new HR rep, Holly.

Sunday, January 4
> 8:00 PM Extreme Makeover: Home Edition, ABC (1 hr) NEW
Gay designer **Eduardo Xol** helps the crew make a family's dreams come true.

> 9:00 PM Desperate Housewives, ABC (1 hr, 1 min) NEW
Andrew [a gay character on the show] introduces his mom to his future mother-in-law. Something tells me this ain't gonna be pretty.

> 10:01 PM Brothers & Sisters, ABC (59 min) NEW
Love is in the air! Saul finally introduces his secret boyfriend to the family. Turns out Roger Grant (guest star **Nigel Havers**) was actually Saul's high school crush!

Monday, January 5
> 8:00 PM Gossip Girl, The CW (1 hr) NEW
Jenny returns to school, but immediately does her best to

usurp Blair's place as Queen Bee by adopting a bevy of mean girls. Nice try, Little J, but we know B. will never let that happen.

Tuesday, January 6
> 8:00 PM House, Fox (1 hr) REPEAT
Bisexual doctor Thirteen regularly endures the wrath of House.

> 9:00 PM Food Detectives, Food Network (30 min) NEW
Queer Eye's Ted Allen hosts a series looking at common food myths.

> 9:00 PM Privileged, The CW (1 hr) REPEAT
A live-in tutor deals with two spoiled twin sisters in Palm Beach. Their personal chef, Marco, is gay.

> 10:00 PM A Double Shot at Love, MTV (1 hr) NEW
Bisexual identical twins Rikki and Vikki continue to test the endurance of a group of straight guys and lesbian girls participating in ridiculous challenges to win their hearts. Seriously, people, this show is golden.

Wednesday, January 7
> 8:00 PM Bones, Fox (1 hr) REPEAT
Angela is a bisexual lab worker in this forensics drama.

>10:00 PM The Real World: Brooklyn, MTV (1 hr) SEASON PREMIERE
The 21st season (!) brings a record three LGBT housemates! JD is gay, Sarah is bi and Katelynn is *The Real World*'s first transgender cast member. Tune in to watch history unfold!

History is indeed unfolding before our eyes.

Of course, all this makes for a greatly exaggerated picture, very different from the social realities experienced by most Americans. But whoever said that TV was trying to be balanced?[27] As gay writer David Ehrenstein boasted in the *Los Angeles Magazine* back in 1996, "There are openly gay writers on almost every major prime-time situation comedy you can think of ... In short, when it comes to sitcoms, gays rule."[28]

TV: BRINGING GAY ACTIVISM INTO EVERY HOME

So it's not just the gay presence on TV, it's the gay message that's getting out on the airways loud and clear. Consider these prominent examples, beginning with some favorite, long-playing shows.

The "Bad Blood" episode of *Law & Order SVU* followed the standard gay lines to a tee:

- It is stated as a known fact that, "One in ten men is gay"
- It is stated as a known fact that homosexuals are wired that way
- Homosexuality is referred to as a "natural sexual orientation," and certainly not something that anyone would willfully choose, given the abuse attached to being gay
- The idea that homosexuality can be cured or changed is ridiculed
- The prominent moral leader who preaches against homosexuality is labeled a "conservative bigot" and is portrayed as a hypocritHis "camp" for reparative therapy is derogatorily referred to as "Camp Wild Bunch"
- We are told that reparative therapy features practices such as electro-shock therapy to the groin
- It is alleged that the right hand man of the conservative leader is gay himself, but he denies it, of course
- In the end, we learn that the leader's son, whose murder was being investigated, was gay.[29]

Yes, a PR firm for a gay activist organization could not have scripted it any better. But this was hardly an isolated incident. Consider the *Law & Order SVU* episode called "Abomination." According to the official website description:

Don't Ask Don't Tell ... Ever...

When the homosexual poster-boy for a sexual re-education group is found murdered in his bed, Detectives Benson and Stabler suspect an outspoken Midwestern Reverend who was in the process of flooding the victim with hate mail and death threats, to be their killer. However, when the activist's alibi checks out, the detectives turn their investigation towards a paper the victim was working on regarding the failure of sexual re-education groups and a professor who personally objects to the thesis, making him a prime suspect for the murder.[30]

This is classic!

- The murder victim, a former homosexual was, in reality, *not* a former homosexual, since no one can change their sexual orientation
- His return to homosexuality, after being hailed as the poster boy for sexual change, is an indictment of all sexual reorientation groups and ministries (not to mention an indictment of all poster boys for these groups and ministries)
- The Christian leader who opposes homosexuality is a hate-filled religious bigot
- A professor who endorses reparative therapy becomes the prime murder suspect.

Talk about a stereotyped story! To say it once more: A PR firm for a gay activist organization could not have scripted it any better. In fact, the "Abomination" episode was so extreme that it drew a response from Exodus International, the world's largest network of Christian ministries helping those with unwanted same-sex attractions:

Law & Order SVU did a disservice to those of us seeking freedom from a life defined by homosexuality; those pursuing sexual reorientation. We are not simpleton homophobes who can only marry other "ex-gay or ex-lesbian" people. This show also did harm to well respected, educated reparative therapists by portraying them as bigoted, murderous and void of any conclusive research data and results. There are tens of thousands of well adjusted former homosexuals and thousands of credible reparative therapists.[31]

Not according to TV and Hollywood!

The popular series *Boston Legal* also ridiculed the notion that change is possible, but in the "Selling Sickness" episode, the ante is upped, since it is attorney Alan Shore (played by James Spader) who claims in an impassioned closing statement that gays can't change, that it is only religious, hypocritical, money-hungry bigots who perpetuate the "ex-gay" lie, and that all gays are simply born that way. Shades of *Law & Order*! Shades of the GLBT lobby! Shades of virtually every anti-ex-gay organization and website!

Here is a transcript of some of the closing moments of the show, as Judge Judy Weldon asks Alan Shore what he is doing:

Alan Shore: Climbing on my soapbox, Judge. I do it once a week.
Judge Gloria Weldon: Get off that thing now, Mr. Shore!
Alan Shore: You sure? This is vintage soapbox stuff. You've got God, money [steps off soapbox], politics, homosexuality.

Shore then proceeds to describe a number of different illnesses that have recently been diagnosed, including restless leg syndrome, attention deficit disorder, social anxiety disorder, and irritable bowel syndrome, noting that, "You people have all kinds of ailments you don't know about. Luckily, we've got drugs for every one of them." When Judge Weldon asks what he is talking about, he gets to his point:

Alan Shore: Same-sex Attraction Disorder. And what troubles me is why the folks in Big Pharmaceutical haven't invented a pill for this disease. Clearly, they're in the business of selling sickness. If there was a profit to be made, they would make it. And with an estimated gay population of over 10 million in the U.S. alone, there's certainly a big enough market. Could it be that they can't cure it?
Well, not to worry. If Big Pharmaceutical can't do it, maybe Big Religion can. And they are. They're the ones

who coined the term, "Same-Sex Attraction Disorder." It's a very good name. Very important, a good name. It's a crucial first step in disqualifying homosexuals as a segment of the population and categorizing them as a disease. Makes homosexuals seem less like people and more like the flu. And with terrible, awful symptoms [makes a face] but curable, and therefore less concerning when it comes to things like an individual's rights: freedom, privacy, marriage.

But Shore is just getting started. Now he focuses in on his target:

Big Religion is very concerned with marriage. Big Religion is the one filling the pockets of Congress. It actually got them to propose a Constitutional ban on gay marriage. Think about that. A governmentally imposed, systematic prejudice against a class based on their sexual orientation.

Never mind that one of the most trusted evangelical advisors to the President was himself having a homosexual affair on the side [Ted Haggard!]. Never mind that one of our Congressmen was writing naughty e-mails to his teenage male pages [Mark Foley!]. Isn't it just a disease? And I thought it was curable. That's what they told me down at the church.

At this point Shore skeptically casts doubt and begins to call for sympathy:

Well, you can legislate against it. You can give it a clever name and treat people for it. You can shut your eyes, have sex with your wife, and pretend it all feels right. You can join the church and swear to be celibate. You can drive around on a Saturday night with a baseball bat and try to beat it out of some poor soul you happen to meet. You can even come to this courtroom and testify as to your new leaf and how well it's all working. What a miracle! My only response is: Give it time. We'll see.

Meanwhile, this company took $40,000 from my client, promising to cure him of his gayness. Only in

America! Only in a country that overtly and notoriously celebrates its prejudice against a class of people by proposing Constitutional amendments. God bless us all! Home of the brave! Shame on you. Couldn't you have at least offered a money-back guarantee, and thrown in a blender?[32]

Talk about getting the message out!

I said earlier that a gay activist PR firm couldn't have scripted things any better, but that statement appears almost redundant at this point. Who needs a PR firm when you not only have openly gay, gay activist, and or pro-gay writers, but you have scripts being reviewed by a gay anti-defamation organization? As Robert Knight pointed out,

> the Gay and Lesbian Alliance Against Defamation now routinely vets all TV scripts dealing with homosexuality to make sure that the public sees only what the activists want. That means, among other things, no programs showing 'ex-gays, people who have overcome homosexual temptations, unless it is to mock them."[33]

Do you need any further proof?

NO MISTAKING THIS MESSAGE

This one speech on *Boston Legal* contains: 1) the systematic mockery of religious faith ("Big Religion" categorizes gays "as a disease," making "homosexuals seem less like people and more like the flu"; it fills the pockets of Congress, trying to influence legislators to pass a Constitutional ban on gay marriage, which is defined as, "A governmentally imposed, systematic prejudice against a class based on their sexual orientation"; and Big Religion is hopelessly hypocritical, as demonstrated by the failures of Ted Haggard, who is all but mentioned by name); and 2) the vilification of organizations that help people deal with unwanted same-sex attractions (they are greedy – to the tune of charging Shore's client $40,000 – and they do not work). What more can be said than, "Shame on you"?

Actually, *Boston Legal* did have more to say, and the last episode of the five-year series (aired December 8, 2008) had a surprise ending that featured – are you ready? – the same-sex "marriage" of William Shatner (who played attorney Denny Crane) and James Spader (Alan Shore). That's right, the "marriage" of two men who weren't even portrayed as gay.

To be sure, major network TV has had its share of same-sex "marriages." According to an MSN.com report which claimed that 2008 was "The Gayest Year Ever" in pop culture,[34] "GLAAD has compiled a list of same-sex marriages on broadcast television, including 'Roc' (1991), 'Northern Exposure' (1994), 'Roseanne' (1995), 'Friends' (1996), 'Felicity' (2000), 'Will & Grace' (2001), 'Whoopi' (2004) and 'The Simpsons' (2005)."[35] Yes, two same-sex *cartoon characters* even got "married" on TV.[36]

In 2008, the show *Brothers & Sisters* featured the "marriage" of two men, the significance of which was not missed by MSN.com:

> The May 11 wedding of characters Kevin Walker (Matthew Rhys) and Scotty Wandell (Luke Macfarlane) was a first -- two series regulars on prime-time, broadcast TV, getting married, without one of them secretly a woman, or a man pretending to be a woman, or maybe falling off a cliff during the vows.[37]

MSN.com also reported that in 2008, Wanda Sykes got "Same-Sex Married on 'The New Adventures of Old Christine,' and in Real Life," noting that, "The first high-profile black American woman to announce her gayness made worldwide headlines."[38] The *Boston Legal* episode, however, added one more element to the mix, since it portrayed the same-sex "marriage" of opposite-sex-attracted men!

According to Mandi Bierly, writing on EW.com,

> Five years from now, when you're asked the trivia question, "What was the final line spoken on *Boston Legal*?," smile when you answer that it was Denny Crane (William Shatner) saying "It's our wedding night" to Alan Shore (James Spader) as they slowdanced on the balcony of the Chinese-acquired Chang Poole & Schmidt. I know I will. That was the most satisfying series finale I've seen in years.[39]

Perhaps a more apt description than "satisfying" would be "bizarro," to quote gay reporter Greg Hernandez?[40] Or perhaps "beyond queer"? Or maybe just "beyond belief"?

Are you already feeling a little disoriented as you begin to recognize how quickly, dramatically, and comprehensively things have changed in American media and television? Well brace yourself: The worst is still to come. And before we leave *Boston Legal*, allow me to mention the episode that attacked "Don't Ask, Don't Tell" in the military? As advertised on a legal site for gay servicemen, **"Emmy-Winning Series *Boston Legal* Tackles "Don't Ask, Don't Tell" Tonight on ABC."**[41] Quite fittingly, the episode was entitled "Do Tell." *Boston Legal* was certainly not hiding its agenda.

In keeping with this is the consistent, unrelenting assault by the media on "ex-gay" ministries and organizations. As summarized in the article, "The Ignored and Discounted"

> ... when former homosexuals are depicted on the networks, they are typically unhappy or anxious to return to their former lives. On NBC's "Law and Order: SVU," an ex-gay man returns to his former lifestyles but murders another gay man to hide his backslide. On NBC's "Will & Grace," a meeting of former homosexuals ends with everyone present running off with a same-sex member of the group.[42]

This is hardly coincidental.[43]

PROMOTING GAY ACTIVISM MAKES GLAAD GLAD

There *is* something to the fact that scripts are vetted by The Gay & Lesbian Alliance Against Defamation (GLAAD), given their website statement that GLAAD "is dedicated to promoting and ensuring fair, accurate and inclusive representation of people and events in the media as a means of eliminating homophobia and discrimination based on gender identity and sexual orientation."[44] It appears that what is "fair" and "accurate" is actually in the eyes of the beholder, while "inclusive," in keeping with its new meaning, actively *excludes* all ideology and viewpoints that differ with gay activist goals. (See above, Chapter One, and below, Chapter Nine.) The same pro-gay, anti-ex-gay bias pervades the talk shows too, from *Montel Williams* to ABC's 20/20 to *Good Morning America* and beyond.[45]

Think back to Michael Medved's words cited at the beginning of this chapter: "A Martian gathering evidence about American society, simply by monitoring our television, would certainly assume that there were more gay people in America than there are evangelical Christians." We could easily take this one step further. The Martian would also conclude that gay people were, with rare or no exception, incredibly nice, family-oriented, creative, and considerate, while evangelical Christians were all mean-spirited, judgmental, dull, greedy, and hypocritical. How interesting! (Do you remember the gay activist strategy, cited in Chapter One, to "1. Talk about gays and gayness as loudly and often as possible. 2. Portray gays as victims, not aggressive challengers. . . . 4. Make gays look good. 5. Make the victimizers look bad." Well, there you have it!)[46]

Writing for the Culture and Media Institute on April 25, 2007, Colleen Raezler focused on *Good Morning America*'s biased reporting in her article, "ABC Attacks Reparative Therapy for Homosexuals: Diane Sawyer delivers hit piece based on the story of one disappointed lesbian."[47] She noted:

> Diane Sawyer spent nearly seven minutes of Good Morning America's April 23 broadcast attacking religious-based reparative therapy for people struggling with homosexual desires.
>
> Sawyer devoted most of the segment to an interview with Christine Bakke, a 35-year-old lesbian who tried reparative therapy and now claims it doesn't work. According to Sawyer, "Growing up, Christine Bakke struggled to make sense of what she says were homosexual impulses confused by a sheltered Christian perspective."
>
> Sawyer lobbed slanted softballs to Bakke, such as, "What would you say to that girl now, about the whole notion, curing, this is in quotes, curing homosexuality, what would you say to her?" Later in the interview she repeated her verbal scare quotes, saying "the so-called, this is quotes again, 'cures.'"
>
> Sawyer employed a mocking tone, attempting to paint reparative therapy as ridiculous, when she asked Bakke whether "somebody gathered around you and they prayed that you'd be a girl, you'd like accessories."

How about the other side of the story? Was *Good Morning America* eager to hear from those who say they *did* change? Was there an attempt by Diane Sawyer to be balanced in her reporting? Are you kidding me? Raezler continued:

In contrast, Sawyer permitted Alan Chambers, president of Exodus International, an umbrella group for more than 85 ex-gay ministries in the United States and 125 globally, to appear for a total of *4 seconds*, saying, "It's not an easy process, but people can choose not to be a homosexual." Sawyer never asked Chambers, an ex-gay who is now married with children, to explain what is involved in reparative therapy or to relate any of the many accounts of people who have overcome homosexual temptation.

Sawyer provided no statistics about the success and failure rates of ex-gay ministries. Instead, she relied on what she called "informal, unscientific research" performed by Bakke as evidence of the programs' ineffectiveness.

Ironically, given the lack of factual evidence presented, Sawyer ended the segment by saying, "even as the programs are increasing, a reality check from a woman who came forward."[48]

Thank you, *Good Morning America*, for this "reality check" – but certainly not in the sense intended by Sawyer. Yet what else can you say when a show devotes roughly *420 seconds* (seven minutes) to one side of a story and only *four seconds* to the other side? The bias is literally stacked 100 to one – and most viewers probably didn't even recognize it.

Even this, however, is not enough for GLAAD. As a New Year's Resolution for 2011, GLAAD called on its supporters to mount a petition drive *against* CNN (which is already unashamedly gay-slanted in its reporting), urging CNN no longer to allow any counterpoint discussion from "the anti-gay industry." In short, "There is only one side to these issues: Our side! All opposing views must be censored."

According to the petition

> . . . the media needs to do a little housecleaning. Namely, it's time for outlets to finally drop several hundred pounds of *unhealthy weight*, which they've been carrying around for years, in the form of *anti-gay activists*.
>
> . . . The media is elevating their *hurtful messages and attitudes* [meaning, the messages and attitudes of those who do not embrace gay activism] to the level of *rational*

discourse. ...
CNN and the rest of the media are doing nothing but exposing their viewers to *dangerous anti-gay rhetoric* when they invite members of these anti-gay groups onto their programming. Starting in 2011, this needs to stop.[49]

In truth, it appears that GLAAD doesn't stand for the Gay and Lesbian Alliance Against Defamation. It stands for the Gay and Lesbian Alliance Against Disagreement. Networks, beware! The gay censor is near.

THE METEORIC SUCCESS OF THE GAY PROPAGANDA CAMPAIGN

It was barely twenty years ago that gay strategists Kirk and Madsen called for the "conversion of the average American's emotions, mind, and will, through a planned psychological attack, in the form of propaganda fed to the nation via the media" (see above, Chapter Two). The propaganda campaign has succeeded with flying colors. A reality check is just what we need.

In December, 2003, Bill Bennett wrote:

If the "coming out" of Ellen [DeGeneres] was a first for prime-time television [April, 1997], things have since moved very fast. A scant three and a half years later, in December 2000, the cable network Showtime began airing a new drama series, *Queer as Folk*, based on a popular British miniseries and featuring the lives of five young homosexual men and a lesbian couple. Described as an "edgy" and "groundbreaking" new program, *Queer as Folk* lived up to its advance billing. Here is a scene from its opening episode as described by Barbara Phillips in the *Wall Street Journal*:

They all know that Brian is a heartbreaker, and when a sexually inexperienced, blond, and handsome seventeen-year-old, Justin, turns up in the opening minutes of the series, it is Brian who takes the fresh-faced preppie home to his brick-and-steel loft and introduces him to anal and oral sex. (He attempts to introduce him to drugs, too, but is rebuffed.) After their encounter, Justin thinks he's in love. But

Brian has trouble even remembering the boy's name. Heck, Brian is so wasted on illicit substances he can't remember that he just became a father [via a lesbian who had been inseminated with his sperm.]

According to Caryn James of *The New York Times*, the purpose of *Queer as Folk* was to "reverse society's heterosexual assumptions." And in that respect, testified Tom Shales, *The Washington Post*'s media critic, it got off to a "triumphantly provocative start."[50]

And so the message on TV goes beyond bashing the notion that homosexuals can change (or, at least, choose to steward their sexuality in a manner that comports with their ethical and moral convictions). It sends out a positive message as well, accurately described as the "conversion of the average American's emotions, mind, and will . . . through the media," thereby reversing "society's heterosexual assumptions." Thus:

- *Queer Eye for the Straight Guy* tells us that queer is no longer strange, weird, or undesirable; queer is now hipster (see Chapter Nine, below, and remember, we're talking about the transforming of the word *queer*)
- *Queer as Folk* and *The "L" Word* tells us that gays and lesbians are virtually everywhere, almost a hidden majority
- *Gay, Straight, or Taken* conveys the notion to a woman that there is an equal chance that the dream guy she's about to meet is either gay, straight, or already taken
- MTV's *Next* tells young people that all varieties of dating are perfectly fine, be they straight, bisexual, or gay, completely normalizing homosexuality in the process
- MTV's *A Double Shot of Love*, which tells the story of bisexual, bachelorette twins, lets young people know that every kind of sexual mix is not just acceptable, it's desirable and it's hot
- *Will and Grace* puts a normal, likable face on the gay and lesbian who lives next door
- Shows like VH1's *Women Seeking Women: A Bicurious*

Journey, encourage married women to experiment with sex with other women – with their husbands' encouragement and consent

- No sooner does "transgender" become a major focus of gay activism than the networks begin broadcasting emotionally touching stories about transgender children and teens, people who have been, quite tragically, "born in the wrong body"
- Documentaries on Discovery Health tell us that mutilating sex-change surgery is the blissful path to personal liberation and happiness
- Another documentary celebrates the joy of a cute gay couple who find a surrogate lesbian woman willing to help them "create" a baby

And make no mistake about it. These shows are having an impact on their viewers.[51] As explained by gay writer John Cloud in his cover-story article on gay teens for *Time Magazine*, "Because he routinely sees young gays on MTV or even at school, a 14-year-old may now feel comfortable telling friends that he likes other boys, but that doesn't mean he is ready to enfold himself in a gay identity."[52]

So, MTV is helping "out" kids in school, despite the fact that they are not necessarily ready for all that "coming out" entails.[53] (Let's not forget that MTV's viewing audience is primarily 12 to 34-years-old, with roughly 40% being under 18. According to a very sobering 2001 report, "MTV is watched by 73% of boys and 78% of girls in the 12 to 19 years of age group. Boys watch for an average of 6.6 hours per week and girls watch for an average of 6.2 hours per week.")[54]

Cloud continues:

Gay kids can now watch fictional and real teens who are out on shows like *Desperate Housewives*, the dating show *Next* on MTV and *Degrassi* (a high school drama on the N network whose wild popularity among adolescents is assured by the fact that few adults watch). Publishers like Arthur A. Levine Books (of Harry Potter fame) and the children's division of Simon & Schuster have released something like a dozen novels about gay adolescents in the past two years....Gay kids can now subscribe to the 10-month-old glossy *YGA Magazine* (YGA stands for 'young, gay America') and meet thousands of other little gays via young gay america. com (sic) or outproud.org.[55]

Is this news to you? Had you heard of the N network before? Were you aware of the gay adolescent-themed books put out by major publishers? Did you know about the *YGA Magazine* or the gay youth websites?[56] Maybe this is new information to you, but it may not be so new to your kids. And how far do some of these TV shows go?

The VH1 website offers this provocative description of *Women Seeking Women: A Bicurious Journey*:

From the Madonna / Britney kiss to same-sex sizzle on the OC [referring to the 2003-2007 TV series *The O.C.*],[57] there's no denying that women exploring bi-sexuality has become a pop culture phenomenon. But what's surprising is that the trend is also playing out on main street USA.

In a 2005 government survey of American sexual practices, 14 percent of the women surveyed aged 18 to 29 reported at least one homosexual experience -- more than twice the proportion for young men. It reflected a marked increase in female "bi-curiosity" compared to a similar survey conducted in the early 90's.

In spring, 2006, VH1 News accompanied four women (along with their husbands) to the Hedonism resort in Jamaica. While there, they made a bold step in transforming their bi-curious fantasies into bi-sexual reality.

The one-hour cinema vérité-style documentary follows the story of Tammy, a 37-year-old dedicated wife and mom from rural Necedah, Wisconsin -- population 888. Tammy has always fantasized about women, but she never acted on her urge. Now she and husband Mike are traveling to Hedonism, where she plans to have her first same-sex encounter with another vacationer in the group. Will it spice up her 15-year marriage, or lead to its downfall?

Women Seeking Women: A Bi-Curious Journey

explores a sexual trend that's captivated, not only saucy celebs, but soccer moms as well.[58]

Is it just me, or is there something devastatingly incongruous about putting the words "dedicated wife and mom" in the same sentence that says she will "now act on her urge to have sex with another woman"?

Yes, this was all captured on a reality TV show, but what else should we expect, since this trend has now "captivated, not only saucy celebs, but soccer moms as well."

I wonder how Tammy's kids enjoyed watching their mom have a sexual encounter with another woman (a stranger at that), with their dad's explicit encouragement. Come to think of it, I wonder how they felt about (potentially) millions of people watching it?

There was a day not too long ago when someone stating that perversity like this would have been aired on a major, cable TV network would have been deemed out of his or her mind. Today, we're told it's just another slice of "mainstream USA."

BACK IN THE DAY: WHEN HOLLYWOOD HAD A STRONG MORAL CODE

There was a day when Hollywood operated under a strict code of ethics, called the Production Code (or, Hays Code), summarized in three major principles:

1. No picture shall be produced that will lower the moral standards of those who see it. Hence the sympathy of the audience should never be thrown to the side of crime, wrongdoing, evil or sin.
2. Correct standards of life, subject only to the requirements of drama and entertainment, shall be presented.
3. Law, natural or human, shall not be ridiculed, nor shall sympathy be created for its violation.

This code was pretty much in force from the mid-1930's until the late 1960's. I'm not making this up. As noted by Yale history professor George Chauncey (writing in 2004),

Fifty years ago, there was no *Will & Grace* or *Ellen*, no *Queer Eye for the Straight Guy*, no *Philadelphia* or *The Hours*, no annual Lesbian, Gay, Bisexual, and Transgender (LGBT) film festival. In fact, Hollywood films were *prohibited* from including lesbian or gay characters, discussing gay themes, or even inferring the existence of homosexuality.[59]

Now, look again at the first principle of the Hays Code (read it out loud for good measure) and ask yourself if most movies today (really, for several decades now) don't have the exact *opposite* effect and/or goals. (Maybe you'd like to read it once more so it can sink in? I was so stunned the first time I saw that I had to re-read it a few times to take in what I was reading.)

Then look at the "Particular Applications" of the three guiding principles:

- [N]akedness and suggestive dances were prohibited.
- The ridicule of religion was forbidden, and ministers of religion were not to be represented as comic characters or villains.
- The depiction of illegal drug use was forbidden, as well as the use of liquor, "when not required by the plot or for proper characterization."
- Methods of crime (e.g. safe-cracking, arson, smuggling) were not to be explicitly presented.
- References to alleged sex perversion (such as homosexuality) and venereal disease were forbidden, as were depictions of childbirth.
- The language section banned various words and phrases that were considered to be offensive.
- Murder scenes had to be filmed in a way that would discourage imitations in real life, and brutal killings could not be shown in detail. "Revenge in modern times" was not to be justified.
- The sanctity of marriage and the home had to be upheld. "Pictures shall not imply that low forms of sex relationship are the accepted or common thing." Adultery and illicit sex, although recognized as sometimes necessary to the plot, could not be explicit or justified and were not supposed to be presented as

an attractive option.

- Portrayals of miscegenation [black-white romantic/sexual relationships] were forbidden.

- "Scenes of Passion" were not to be introduced when not essential to the plot. "Excessive and lustful kissing" was to be avoided, along with any other treatment that might "stimulate the lower and baser element."

- The flag of the United States was to be treated respectfully, and the people and history of other nations were to be presented "fairly."

- The treatment of "Vulgarity," defined as "low, disgusting, unpleasant, though not necessarily evil, subjects" must be "subject to the dictates of good taste." Capital punishment, "third-degree methods," cruelty to children and animals, prostitution and surgical operations were to be handled with similar sensitivity.[60]

Aside from the prohibition against the "portrayals of miscegenation,"[61] these principles are morally commendable – contrast them with the descriptions of the "Bicurious Women" documentary, or the "A Shot at Love" show, above – but things have changed so dramatically that these principles seem to come from some mythical world that never really existed – yet exist it did. How on earth did we get from there to here? If these principles were followed today, not one in 100 movies would see the light of day in their current form.

To be sure, Hollywood's glorifying of sex and violence and drugs and crime is hardly limited to gay-themed movies and TV, and not everything that comes out of Hollywood is morally corrupt. But in terms of conveying a specific, socially-impacting message, queer Hollywood has excelled.

STOP DR. LAURA!

A few years ago, an anonymous author (later identified as J. Kent Ashcraft)[62] penned a very clever letter to Dr. Laura, asking for her help in sorting out some issues of biblical interpretation:

Dear Dr. Laura,
Thank you for doing so much to educate people regarding God's law. I have learned a great deal from you,

and I try to share that knowledge with as many people as I can. When someone tries to defend homosexuality, for example, I will simply remind him or her that Leviticus 18:22 clearly states it to be an abomination. End of debate.

I do need some advice from you, however, regarding some of the other laws in Leviticus and Exodus and how to best follow them.

1. When I burn a bull on the altar as a sacrifice, I know it creates a pleasing odor for the Lord (Leviticus 1:9). The problem is my neighbors. They claim the odor is not pleasing to them. How should I deal with this?

2. I would like to sell my daughter into slavery, as stated in Exodus 21:7. In this day and age, what do you think would be a fair price for her?

3. I know that I am allowed no contact with a woman while she is in her period of menstrual uncleanliness (Leviticus 15:19-24). The problem is, how can I tell? I have tried asking, but most women take offense.

4. Leviticus 25:44 states that I may buy slaves from the nations that are around us. A friend of mine claims that this applies to Mexicans, but not Canadians. Can you clarify?

5. I have a neighbor who insists on working on the Sabbath. Exodus 35:2 clearly states he should be put to death. Am I morally obligated to kill him myself?

6. A friend of mine says that even though eating shellfish is an abomination (Leviticus 10:10), it is a lesser abomination than homosexuality. I don't agree. Can you settle this?

7. Leviticus 20:20 states that I may not approach the altar of God if I have a defect in my sight. I have to admit that I wear reading glasses. Does my vision have to be 20/20, or is there some wiggle room here?

I know you have studied these things extensively, so I

am confident you can help. Thank you again for reminding us that God's Word is eternal and unchanging.[63]

The letter was certainly well-conceived and humorous, and for those without any foundation in the Bible, maybe even convincing (although, to be sure, any serious student of the Scriptures could easily refute the facile, misleading comparisons).[64] But however widely it was circulated, it achieved much more fame when some of its content was repeated on TV's award-winning *West Wing*, with a "Dr. Laura" figure (named Dr. Jenna Jacobs) appearing as well.[65]

Here is a transcript from the show which aired October 18, 2000. The dialogue began after Dr. Jacobs refused to stand when President Josiah Bartlet (played by Martin Sheen) stood:

President Bartlet: Forgive me Dr. Jacobs, are you an M.D.?
Jacobs: A Ph.D.
Bartlet: A Ph.D.?
Jacobs: Yes, sir.
Bartlet: Psychology?
Jacobs: No sir.
Bartlet: Theology?
Jacobs: No.
Bartlet: Social work?
Jacobs: No. I have a Ph.D. in English literature.
Bartlet: I'm asking 'cause on your show, people call in for advice, and you go by the name of "Dr." Jacobs on your show, and I didn't know if maybe your listeners were confused by that and assumed you had advanced training in psychology, theology or health care.
Jacobs: I don't believe they are confused, no, sir.
Bartlet: Good. I like your show. I like how you call homosexuality an abomination.
Jacobs: I don't say homosexuality is an abomination, Mr. President, the Bible does.
Bartlet: Yes, it does, Leviticus.
Jacobs: 18.22
Bartlet: Chapter and verse. I wanted to ask you a couple of questions while I had you here. I'm interested in selling

my youngest daughter into slavery as sanctioned in Exodus 21:7. She's a Georgetown sophomore, speaks fluent Italian, always cleared the table when it was her turn. What would a good price for her be?

While thinking about that, can I ask another? My chief of staff, Leo McGarry, insists on working on the sabbath. Exodus 35:2 clearly says he should be put to death. Am I morally obligated to kill him myself, or is it OK to call the police?

Here's one that's really important 'cause we've got a lot of sports fans in this town. Touching the skin of a dead pig makes one unclean. Leviticus 11:7. If they promise to wear gloves, can the Washington Redskins still play football? Can Notre Dame? Can West Point?

Does the whole town have to be together to stone my brother John for planting different crops side-by-side? Can I burn my mother in a small family gathering for wearing garments made from two different threads? Think about those questions, would you?[66]

What makes this mockery of a script all the more disturbing is that, at the very same time this episode aired, gay activists were in the midst of a full-scale attack intended to stop the new Dr. Laura TV show from airing, an attack that began in March 2000 and reached its successful conclusion in March 2001. As the StopDrLaura.com website boasted:

The year-long campaign against Dr. Laura — coordinated via this Web site and all done on an $18,000 budget, most of it raised from the online sale of t-shirts — so exposed Dr. Laura's anti-gay rhetoric to the world, that she could not even sneeze without the major national media, and thousands of individual activists like yourselves, watching, recording her every word, and pouncing when action was needed. As a result of the 50+ million hits this pro bono site received in just 10 months, and the 300,000 visitors per month that we continued to get throughout the campaign, protests were organized in 34 cities across the country and Canada, over 170 advertisers dropped Dr. Laura's TV show (including some 70 or so advertisers that Canadian activists got to drop her in that country alone!), and over 30 advertisers dropped her radio show, reportedly costing her over $30 million in advertising.[67]

So, a dialogue for *West Wing* is virtually lifted from a letter written by a Dr. Laura-mocking, gay author, and then the episode airs during the very season that Dr. Laura is under unrelenting, media-related harassment from gay activists. If you want to call this coincidental, I've got a bridge for you to buy in Brooklyn.[68]

With amazing consistency (not to mention with much creativity and passion), Hollywood normalizes and even glorifies homosexuality, bisexuality, and transexuality; it mocks the idea that gays can change; it ridicules "Big Religion" as hypocritical and greedy; it puts forth a tainted (or, should I say, "tinted," as in "pink"?) reading of the Bible; it vilifies those who feel there is a better way than homosexuality; and it uncritically regurgitates the latest findings of gay-biased, pseudo-science.

It's really quite simple: Just look at the latest goals of gay activism, then sit back and turn on the TV or visit your local movie theater, and there you have it. Hollywood and homosexual activism fit together like a hand in a glove. As noted by professor Matthew Franck, director of the William E. and Carol G. Simon Center on Religion and the Constitution of the Witherspoon Institute in Princeton, N.J.

> ... on "$#*! My Dad Says," a CBS sitcom watched by more than 10 million weekly viewers, an entire half-hour episode is devoted to a depiction of the disapproval of homosexuality as bigotry, a form of unreasoning intolerance that clings to the past with a coarse and mean-spirited judgmentalism. And this on a show whose title character is famously irascible and politically incorrect, but who in this instance turns out to be fashionably cuddly and up-to-date.
>
> What's going on here? Clearly a determined effort is afoot, in cultural bastions controlled by the left, to anathematize traditional views of sexual morality, particularly opposition to same-sex marriage, as the expression of "hate" that cannot be tolerated in a decent civil society.[69]

TIME FOR THE "T" WORD

Consider one of the major themes of gay activists today, namely, acceptance of the "T" word, transgender, or, in some aspects of transgenderism, the idea that some people are born in the wrong body. How has this been portrayed by the media? Do you care to take an educated guess?

There was the episode on *ER*, called "Next of Kin," where a man and his twelve-year-old daughter Morgan are rushed to the emergency room after a car accident. When Morgan is asked about her favorite color – for the cast on her ankle – she says, "I like pink," and throughout the dialogue, Morgan is consistently represented as a "she." It is only when one of the doctors is checking on Morgan while "she" tries to use a bed pan that the shocked doctor exclaims, "My God! You're a boy!"[70]

This leads to an exchange between two of the doctors:

Pratt: A twelve year-old crossdresser?
Harkins: All I know is that anatomically she's a he.
Pratt: And you're sure about that?
Harkins: I've seen my fair share of penises. Anyway, she's, he's pretty upset and I think you should speak with him.

Dr. Pratt then sits down to talk with Morgan:

Pratt: So what's the deal? Why are you going around dressed like a girl?
Morgan: Because I am one! I have the wrong body.
Pratt: You're a bit young to be thinking that way, aren't you?
Morgan: No, I always have.
Pratt: Is your dad in on this too?
Morgan: He moved us so that I can start over at a new school. Nobody knows.
Pratt: Well, they're going to find out eventually, don't you think?
Morgan: Not if we keep moving. And when I'm old enough I'll get the operation.
Pratt: What's your Mom have to say about that?
Morgan: She has a different family now.

Pratt: Look... erm... Your Dad's going to be a while, and we
need someone to come and
get you.
Morgan: My Dad's friend lives near us.
Pratt: No, I think your Mom would be more appropriate.
Morgan: She thinks I'm a freak! Just like you do! Please!

When Morgan's father dies in surgery, the operating surgeon
gets the news about her/him:

Corday: Well the girl's father just died.
Harkins: Boy.
Carter: What?
Harkins: Boy. Morgan's a boy. I guess the proper term is
transsexual.
Corday: Wait, I'm sorry? His daughter is actually his son?

Morgan's estranged mother is then called to the hospital (by error, it
turns out, since one of the doctors wanted to wait before calling her, since
the mother and her new husband were not happy with Morgan dressing like
a girl). And true to form, there is a clear hint that the mother is a strong
Christian. (She exclaims "Thank you Jesus" when informed that Morgan's
injury was mild, before she learned of her ex-husband's death).

Now, at this point, Morgan has been referred to as "he" once the doctors
learned his real gender, so it would seem that the episode has been impartial.
But we haven't reached the climax of the story – really, the point of the story
– and when Morgan is placed in his mom's care, after comforting her son,
whom she hasn't seen in three years, the first thing she does is take out scissors
and cut Morgan's hair as Morgan sits and cries. What an uncaring monster
she is!

Dr. Pratt tries to stop her, but the mother is firm: "It's my right. He's my
little boy. I'm doing this for him. It's the best thing."

Two of the doctors then get into a serious discussion about what
happened, one arguing that social services should have been called, rather
than the mother:

Carter: To do what, remove him from the home? Hey, I
feel bad about what happened too. Like it or not, she's his

only family.
Pratt: Define family.

So, anyone who would not let their twelve-year-old boy dress like a girl and be moved from school to school to protect his/her true identity is not worthy of being called family.

The ending is absolutely classic:

> *Pratt emerges into corridor to see Morgan being pushed in wheelchair by mother, with step-father and step-brother dourly at her side, leaving, with cropped hair, dressed in boys' clothes. A blue flannel shirt and dark blue bodywarmer so different to the cerise and flowered jacket, and lavender tops in which she arrived only hours before.*
>
> *The reception staff watch, clearly aware of everything that has happened.*
>
> *Pratt stands, hands in pockets, deeply contemplative.*
>
> *Morgan's eyes follow Pratt as they pass. The look is of infinite sadness, emptiness, hopelessness.*

ER certainly hit a home run with this show. To quote Prof. Eisenbach yet again, "More than any other medium, TV [has] the power to shape and manipulate the conscious and subconscious prejudices of the American public."

Where would your prejudices be after watching this episode? With broken-hearted, sweet little Morgan, who has lost his/her father and his/her true identity in a matter of minutes – not only trapped in the wrong body but about to be trapped in the wrong home? Or would you would side with the "dour" and apparently stiffly-religious mother and family? And, as a caring person, who would you immediately identify with, Dr. Pratt, or Morgan's mother?

I'm sure that painful situations like this (involving gender identity confusion) play out in America all the time – not necessarily in such dramatic fashion, but certainly, in terms of the pain of the child and the differences between the parents – and it's good for us to be aware of this. But if *ER* wanted to be helpful, it could have drawn attention to the problem of Gender Identity Disorder, portraying both parents as caring (that means the Christian parent too!). It could have emphasized the internal confusion reflected in this boy's choice to cross-dress, not to mention the biological disconnect, discouraging him from even thinking about sex-change surgery, and telling him that there are people that understand his situation and could truly help him

But really now, what I am thinking? This is Hollywood! This is TV! I started dreaming there for a moment and lost touch with "reality" – that is, the pink-colored reality of prime time television.

"BORN IN THE WRONG BODY"

Not unexpectedly, Oprah Winfrey has also focused on the "born in the wrong body" syndrome – with much sympathy and pathos[71] – as has *Sixty Minutes*,[72] while Barbara Walters did an up close and personal story for 20-20, interviewing Riley Grant, referred to as "she" throughout, despite the fact that "Riley" (born Richard) is a boy.[73]

This is how the show begins (with my emphasis in bold):

> This past Christmas, **Riley** Grant received a present that can be described as bittersweet -- a video game that allowed **her** to morph a digital body into anything **she** wanted. Almost immediately, Riley, **a 10-year-old transgender girl who is biologically a boy**, adopted a virtual female persona. If only life were so easy, that **she** could punch a button and turn into a girl.
>
> "**She** has a birth defect, and we call it that. I can't think of a worse birth defect, as a woman to have, than to have a penis," Riley's mother, Stephanie, told Barbara Walters. "**She** talks about the day she'll have a baby. That's not in **her** future. But **she** sees **herself** as growing up to be a woman."

A birth defect of the worst kind? A girl being born with a male organ?

In no way do I want to minimize the psychological trauma that Richard/Riley has experienced or the challenges that his parents have faced, but to refer to his being male as a birth defect (when, apparently, there is no congenital intersex condition present) is outrageous. The effect, however, of this mother's comments is quite clear: The viewer is drawn into deep sympathy with poor "Riley" and his caring mom.

It turns out that Richard/Riley has a twin sister Allie, but Richard/Riley is sure that he is a girl too. Truly, the story is painful:

Richard refused to swim topless, always wearing a shirt in the pool. By age two, he became clearly jealous of his sister's "girl" things -- her toys, her pink drinking cups, and especially her clothing.

"We were getting dressed, and he wanted to wear a dress. He wanted to be pretty like his sister," said Stephanie [his mom]. "He was saying, 'I want a dress. I'm a girl, Mommy, I'm a girl.' And I'd say, 'No, honey, you're a boy. You have a penis, you're a boy. Allie's a girl.'"

Then, when the twins were only two and a half, an incident after a bath convinced the Grants just how seriously confused their son was about his gender identity. Stephanie found Richard holding a nail clipper against his penis, saying that "it doesn't go there."

The counsel of their pediatrician, namely to get Richard interested in boy things, failed miserably, and so,

Finally, when Richard was just three years old, Stephanie made the drastic decision to let her son start dressing as a girl. They called it "girl time." Richard could dress up in his sister's clothes but only when his father Neil was out of sight. The secret between mother and son went on for months.

"I took him shopping by himself and we bought his own skirt and his own little tank top because…that little girl trapped inside was so happy when this would happen. But we knew we had to hide it, and we hid them in the back of the closet," she said.

When Neil finally found out that his wife was allowing their son to dress as a girl, he became upset. "I said, 'I didn't believe in it, and I didn't know where this was going to lead to.'"

Richard's double life put a strain on the Grant's marriage, and they almost separated. Richard, now four, was going to school as a boy but wanted to be a girl full time. Stephanie knew about Richard's heart-wrenching prayers in the middle of the night.

"He said, 'Mom, I'm so mad at God, because God made a mistake. He made me a boy, and I'm not a boy, I'm a girl, Mom. Every night I pray that God gives me a girl body but when I wake up I'm still a boy. God won't take back his mistake, he won't make it right,'" Stephanie recalled.

When Richard's parents feared that he would try to harm himself, and when he had an especially severe panic attack, the parents finally shared everything with the school principal, who, to their surprise, suggested that Richard (who by then was going by the name Reggie before changing his name legally to Riley) start to wear a dress to school – at the age of seven! (This, of course, created an environment where Richard/Reggie/Riley was mocked and teased by the other children.) And when a gender specialist diagnosed him with Gender Identity Disorder, the parents were relieved. They were not making this whole thing up.

The problems, however, continue: "Riley" is terribly jealous of his sister and has to hate her to survive; and with the onset of puberty, specialists are divided over what treatment is best: Let it take its natural course or delay it. The Grants were leaning to expensive hormonal treatments (so that Riley would develop breasts and a feminine figure), despite potential health risks (such as breast cancer), with sex-change surgery to follow as soon as possible.

What is so striking in all this – and, once again, in no way do I want to minimize the traumatic situation this family has lived through – is that this child was diagnosed as having a *disorder*, yet rather than looking for comprehensive ways to treat the disorder, they were encouraged to indulge it. Why not interview other parents whose children actually outgrew Gender Identity Disorder?[74] Why not talk with people who suffered from this condition – whether the cause of it is mental, emotional, spiritual, or other – and who no longer do? (Yes, they do exist!)[75] Why only present the problem, with deep and understandable sympathy for "Riley," rather than probe solutions to the problem?

It is unthinkable that the best course of action was for "Riley" to become a cross-dressing seven-year-old boy, then to interfere with his body's natural development through hormonal intervention, then to look forward to sex-change surgery at the earliest possible age (and remember that this surgery entails the mutilation of perfectly healthy, functioning body parts), an age in which we make almost no other major, life decisions. (Picture deciding who you will marry at the age of fourteen or fifteen – with no way to reverse your decision ever – or getting locked into a career for life at that tender, formative age. Yet kids are being allowed to make a more dramatic decision with their bodies – for the rest of their lives! – as young teenagers.)[76]

Of course, TV has much more to say about different aspects of the transgender experience, including shows like "Cruel and Unusual: Transgender Women in Prison," which aired on WE TV in 2006.[77]

> Making its major festival premier at South by Southwest, Cruel and Unusual (2006, 66 minutes) is an unflinching documentary on the lives of transgender women in men's prisons. Shot over three years, *this high-definition documentary film challenges the viewer's basic ideas about gender and justice* through braids of poignantly graphic stories, vibrant landscape portraits and stark prison footage.
>
> *Prisons decide where to place inmates based on their genitalia, not their gender identity.* Ophelia, *who has lived in the prison of a man's body for all of her 46 years*, now resides in a correctional facility in Virginia, having been sentenced to 67 years for bank robbery with an unloaded gun. Denied female hormone treatment, Ophelia felt she had no choice but to mutilate her genitals to force the system "to finish what she started."[78]

So, to recap, "Riley" is suffering from the terrible "birth defect" of being born with male genitalia, while Ophelia "has lived in the prison of a man's body for all of her 46 years." I think we're getting the point – and it is coming across with consistency and clarity. Should we be surprised?

ONE SIDE OF THE STORY IS ENOUGH

And how did CNN report on the story of an eight-year-old boy who was returning to his school as a girl?[79] CNN brought on a woman who knew the family, Kim Pearson, the mother of a cross-dressing daughter who believes that children as young as five are "realizing their true gender identity."[80] During the interview, Pearson referred to her daughter as "he" and explained how good things have been since "he" told her that "he" wanted to live as a boy. (This happened when the daughter was fourteen.) And Pearson commends the school for doing "a fabulous job," since they have decided to call the boy by his new female name, along with provide two unisex bathrooms for him/her to use.

True to form, the segment runs close to five-and-a-half minutes, with no one else called on to comment aside from Pearson. And the only information posted for those wanting help is the website of TransYouth Family Allies (www.imatyfa.org).[81] Yet this is supposed to be a news story, not a gay activist propaganda piece – although the line between the two gets quite blurry at times.[82]

Let's remember that we're talking about a cross-dressing eight-year-old, and yet CNN didn't find it important enough to bring on an expert who would point out the potential dangers of this boy's choice, not to mention the effect it would have on other children in the school.

Yet there is something that is fascinating to observe. We have been told how "silly and unnecessary most common gender assumptions are" (see above, Chapter Three), and so, the idea that boys like sports and girls like dolls is viewed as stereotypical nonsense. We have also been informed that gender cannot be defined by anatomy. But now we are informed that "he" is really a girl in a boy's body, since "he" like dolls and girlie things. So, gender distinctions *do* matter, but only when separated from anatomy and only when in harmony with gay ideology. How then *do* we define male and female, or masculinity and femininity? And what exactly *is* gender?

We'll come back to this subject later in the book (the whole thing actually gets much more convoluted), but suffice it to say for now that both TV and the movies have joined together in a masterful way to shape and change (and twist!) public perceptions, with notable Hollywood flicks including *Brokeback Mountain*, the first major picture featuring sex-scenes with two men; *Capote*, the story of one of America's most famous gays, and *Transamerica*, a movie about a woman undergoing a sex-change, all of which enjoyed their night of fame in the Oscar spotlights in 2006.

GAY TRIUMPHALISM RAISES ITS VOICE AT THE OSCARS

As noted by Alonso Duralde in his "Gay guide to the Oscars: Brokeback Mountain. Capote. Transamerica," "No matter who wins—sorry, no matter who the Oscar goes to—this year's Academy Awards promises to be the gayest in its 78-year history."[83] Why such attention on these three movies? Did it all come down to good film making? Was there no pro-gay Hollywood bias involved – or is off limits even to ask this question?

According to a GLAAD news release,

"Brokeback Mountain, Capote and Transamerica are films that, in many ways, capture an important moment in history and the questions we face today," said GLAAD President Neil G. Giuliano, who celebrated the occasion at an official Oscar Night® America party benefitting the Miami Beach Cinematheque. "Will we fight for a world where all people are able to live and love honestly? Or will we allow hatred and bigotry to force us to hide in the closet, deny our love and deny who we are? Tonight's ceremony was an important tribute to films that have invited audiences to open their hearts to our love and our relationships like never before."[84]

Hollywood was making a statement!
As explained by gay author David Moore,

If cultural change can't be achieved through political means — it's time to do it by sending a message to the country's heart. What better way to do it than by creating thought provoking and emotionally evocative art? "Brokeback Mountain" winner of the best adapted screenplay, best motion picture soundtrack and best director, and "Capote," which captured the award for best actor, are films that have changed [our] worldview. Thanks for getting in touch, Hollywood.[85]

Yes, these are "films that have changed [our] worldview" for sure.
I understand, of course, the positive light in which these movies are seen by many in the gay and lesbian community, but that doesn't change the point I'm making here: Hollywood is sending a message.[86]
As articulated by *Brokeback Mountain* director Ang Lee in his Oscar acceptance speech:

First of all, I want to thank two people who don't even exist - or I should say they do exist because of the imagination of Annie Proulx and the artistry of Larry McMurtry and Diana Ossana. Their names are Ennis and Jack [the two stars of the movie]. And they taught all of us who made

Brokeback Mountain so much about not just all the gay men and women whose love is denied by society, but just as important, the greatness of love itself.

Yes, these gay lovers "taught all of us" about "all the gay men and women whose love is denied by society" – presumably because society as a whole believes that marriage is only for a man and a woman. We're hearing you loud and clear, Ang Lee! And should we be surprised that the number one item on MSN.com's article on 2008 being the "gayest year ever in pop culture" was the amount of money donated to fight against Proposition 8 in California by major celebrities?

> **Same-Sex Marriage Support With Star Power**: Proposition 8 in California was a ballot amendment this November calling a halt to same-sex marriage, and it was a call to action for some big Hollywood names. Brad Pitt publicly donated $100,000 to fight the California ballot initiative, and other well-known contributors included Mary McCormack, Ellen DeGeneres, Bridget Fonda, Gus Van Sant, "The Real World" co-producer Jonathan Murray and George Takei. A pre-election, Beverly Hills fundraiser to defeat 8 that included performances by Mary J. Blige and Melissa Etheridge quickly sold out, and was attended by Barbra Streisand, Rob Reiner and others. And when they weren't donating their time or their performances, celebrities were talking to the media.. . .
>
> And on December 3, a three-minute video, "Prop 8: The Musical," was posted on FunnyOrDie.com. The mock community-theater production included singing and dancing by Neil Patrick Harris, John C. Reilly, Maya Rudolph, Margaret Cho, Rashida Jones and Andy Richter, with Jack Black as Jesus, espousing the concept of gay marriage as the cure for the US's economic woes. Within 24-hours, the clip hit bona fide viral status, with more than 1.1 million views on FunnyOrDie.com.[87]

Do these celebrities have every right to donate and speak out and use their creative gifts and influence on behalf of gay activist issues? Absolutely.

And we have every right to point out the obvious: Hollywood is, by and large, in bed with homosexual activism, and quite comfortably, at that.

The final exclamation point came at the Academy Awards on February 22, 2009, when Sean Penn received the Oscar for Best Actor in his portrayal of the murdered gay activist Harvey Milk and Dustin Lance Black (of the same movie, *Milk*) won the Oscar for best screenwriter, both using their acceptance speeches to bash those of opposing views – especially those who supported Proposition 8. And not to miss the moment, host Hugh Jackman described the message of *Milk* as, "It's okay to be gay."

We're hearing you, Hollywood, loud and clear!

According to Black,

> If Harvey had not been taken from us 30 years ago, I think he would want me to say to all the gay and lesbian kids out there tonight who have been told they are less than by the churches, by the government, by their families, that you are beautiful, wonderful creatures of value, and that no matter what anyone tells you, God does love you and that very soon, I promise you, you will have equal rights, federally, across this great nation of ours. Thank you, God, for Harvey Milk![88]

Penn was more confrontational. After his opening comments, "You Commie, homo-loving sons of guns!," Penn let it fly: "I think it's a good time for those who voted for the ban against gay marriage to sit and reflect on their great shame, and their shame in their grandchildren's eyes if they continue that support. We've got to have equal rights for everyone."[89] Yes, shame on you voters for saying that marriage should be the union of a man and woman. What a bigoted, ugly position!

Actor Mark Ruffalo, who plays the sperm donor for a lesbian couple in the 2010 movie *The Kids Are Alright* (discussed above) was even more blunt, having this to say about those who opposed same-sex marriage:

> It's the last dying, kicking, screaming, caged animal response to a world that is changing, a world that's leaving a lot of those old, bigoted, un-accepting views behind. It's over. Those against it are very tricky and they're using really dark ways to promote their ideas.[90]

How ironic that Hollywood claims the moral higher ground, especially when Kate Winslet received the 2009 Oscar for Best Actress for her role in *The Reader*, where she played a former Auschwitz guard (now thirty-six) who seduces a fifteen-year-old boy – with gratuitous sex and nudity scenes. In the words of a *New York Post* reviewer – and a self-described fan of Winslet – in the movie she is a "pedophile Nazi hottie."[91]

To be sure, none of this should surprise us by now, and to go on any further would be redundant, so we'll have to pass by the many movies containing gay characters or themes.[92] But as we step back and look and gain perspective, there's something very sad about all this as well. Ang Lee claimed that the two gay lovers in *Brokeback Mountain* taught us about "the greatness of love itself." Film critic and radio talk-show host Michael Medved had a different take. On December 20, 2005, he wrote:

> The front runner in this year's Oscar race is "Brokeback Mountain," about two Wyoming cowboys conducting a homosexual affair in the '60's and '70's.
>
> Gay activists embrace the movie, hailing it as a "timeless love story" showing the joys of male-on-male passion, but they ignore one key factor in the plot: both men are married, with children, and their long-standing relationship ultimately destroys both marriages.
>
> Would commentators similarly applaud a story of cheating, if the adultery involved a married man and a married woman?
>
> Political correctness justifies a gay affair for allowing the participant to express his "true self," but a husband involved with a much younger woman could similarly claim that only with his fresh, new love could his real nature come out.
>
> The main problem with "Brokeback Mountain" isn't that it's pro-gay; it's that the emphasis on following your urges rather than honoring your responsibilities is, at its heart, anti-marriage.[93]

And that is truly a shame.

Hollywood and the TV industry really are sending out a powerful message. It is the message that a five-year-old is ready to make a massively complex life decision and begin to cross-dress; the message that you can have sex with the person or persons of your choosing, regardless of your marital status and regardless of the gender of the other person; the message that sex-change surgery is the blissful path to inner peace; the message that anyone who comes out of the closet deserves our sympathy and support while anyone claiming to come of out of homosexuality deserves only mockery and scorn; the message that virtually all queers are cool and open-minded and altruistic while virtually all religious people are greedy, small-minded, hypocritical bigots.[94]

It is a message, as Medved explains, that repeatedly encourages us to follow our urges rather than honor our responsibilities, and the end results are tragic, just like the ending of *Brokeback Mountain*: two broken men, two broken families, many broken lives. . . . Thanks for nothing, Hollywood.

The evidence for the biological basis for homosexuality is very, very strong. It's coming from a lot of different areas. The religious right has been very, very successful at creating controversy where there is none. The scientists who study in this area, it's not a question that there's a biological component, it's just how that biological component is working.

Prof. R. Elizabeth Cornwall, University of Colorado, Colorado Springs, cited in *The (Colorado Springs) Gazette*, July 26, 2007

The scientific argument for a biological basis for sexual orientation remains weak. The political argument that it will bolster gay pride or prevent homophobic bigotry runs counter to experience. The lesbian, gay, and bisexual community does not need to have its "deviance" tolerated because its members were born "that way" and "cannot help it." Rather, society must recognize the validity of lesbian and gay lifestyles. We need an end to discrimination, an acceptance of all human beings, and a celebration of diversity, whatever its origins.

Council for Genetic Research

The current consensus in the scientific community is that there is absolutely no proof that people are born gay. . . . Contrary to what many Americans believe, there are no replicated scientific studies demonstrating that homosexuality is determined by biological or genetic factors.

Glenn T. Stanton and Dr. Bill Maier, *Marriage on Trial*

No one is born gay. The idea is ridiculous.

Lesbian author Camille Paglia, *Vamps and Tramps*

...show me your proof that people aren't born gay. (And don't give me that unscientific c--- about how no "gay gene" has been found yet. A first year student of genetics, even from a Christian school, could explain how stupid that argument is.)

Gay activist Evan Hurst, on TruthWinsOut.org (quoted on CNN.com)

6

Is Gay the New Black? Analyzing the Argument That "I Was Born That Way"

he gay (and also white) author of the December 16, 2008, cover story of the *Advocate* (entitled "Gay Is the New Black"), Michael Joseph Campbell, noted that in the aftermath of the 2008 presidential elections, there was euphoria in the LGBT community because of the election of pro-gay candidate Barack Obama. But there was also stinging pain because same-sex marriage and/or gay adoption was voted down in California, Florida, Arizona, and Arkansas. The passage of Proposition 8 in California was particularly galling to GLBT activists and their allies.

Campbell wrote that gays and lesbians gave into a "post-election temptation," explaining that, "Many drew a simple parallel between our struggle and the black civil rights movement. Signs at protests said, 'I have a dream too,' 'Welcome to Selma,' and 'Gay is the new black.'"[1] But according to Campbell, the idea that gay is the new black is true "in only one meaningful way. At present we are the most socially acceptable targets for the kind of casual hatred that American society once approved for habitual use against black people. Gay is the dark pit where our society lets people throw their fears about what's wrong with the world."[2]

So then, "gay is the new black" in the sense that gays and lesbians are the objects of people's irrational hatred and fear, subject to all kinds of verbal and emotional and even physical abuse (although Campbell is careful to point out that black suffering has been far more severe in America than the suffering of gays).

For many others, however, the equation goes much deeper: Gay is also the new black in that both skin color and homosexuality are said to be genetically determined and therefore immutable. And, just as no one chooses whether they are born black or white or yellow, so also no one chooses to be born gay or straight or transgender. This is simply the card that some people have been dealt – whether we are tall or short or left-handed or right-handed or dark skinned or light skinned or male or female or heterosexual or homosexual is not up to us – and it is unconscionable to think that anyone would be discriminated against because of their genetics.

Really now, haven't we come out of the (all too recent) stone age of slavery and segregation? Haven't we moved beyond the days of treating blacks or women or certain ethnic groups as if they were less than fully human? Don't we all agree today that it is cruel to torment and ridicule someone for the way they were born? And so, the argument goes, just as it was (and is) immoral to stigmatize and demean people for their skin color or gender or physical appearance or ethnicity, so also it is immoral to stigmatize and demean people because of their sexual orientation.

Yet with the LGBT community, the perceived injustice goes even deeper, since they are told that they are *sinful* for being who they were designed to be, that they must repress their God-given desires in order to be accepted, that the only way they can enjoy "the benefits of lifelong marital commitment – and experience a fundamental human right, the right to love" – is if they masquerade as heterosexuals (and deny their true, same-sex love). How utterly cruel! And then, to add agonizing insult to devastating injury, they are subjected to all kinds of "treatments" to cure them of their biological constitution and then told that there's something wrong with them if they fail to change.

Against this backdrop, a gay person could say to a straight person, "I didn't choose to be homosexual anymore than you chose to be heterosexual. My behavior is not 'unnatural,' and being homosexual is neither a sin nor a sickness. In fact, it's as natural for me to be homosexual as it is for a black man to be black or a white woman to be white. It's who I am, and there's nothing I can do to change that. Isn't it about time that people like me received fair and equal treatment under the law? Isn't it time for the public to abandon the horrific prejudices and cruel practices that have tormented so many gay men and women for so many years?"

Put another way, "Since science has demonstrated that homosexuality is genetic and we are hardwired to be gay, we now understand that homosexuality is an inborn trait just as having blue eyes is an inborn trait. And so, no moral distinction can be made between being homosexual and being heterosexual anymore than a moral distinction can be made between having brown eyes or blue eyes or between being black or white."

According to Prof. Timothy F. Murphy, writing for the Council for Responsible Genetics,

> some gay men and lesbians welcome [biogenetic] explanations precisely because they shore up their identities. Homosexuality that is hard-wired - that is a genetic effect, for example - is homosexuality that doesn't lend itself to labels of psychological maladaptation or moral lapse. Genetic and other biological theories seem to read homosexuality into nature alongside heterosexuality, and some gay men and lesbians embrace those biogenetic accounts for that protective effect. They understand biological explanations

as sympathetic to their own 'creation narratives' of who they are and how they come to be.[3]

As summed up by a reviewer of the book *Gay Spirituality* on Amazon. com:

On a daily basis, gay people are inundated with negative messages in every realm: social, political, cultural, and religious-especially religious. Many, if not most, mainstream churches have deliberate proscriptions against homosexuality, and with all that we've seen lately in the news, there seems to be no end in sight to the strife. Despite the fact that each year scientists offer more proof that sexual orientation is genetic (i.e. that's the way God made us), many churchgoers and clergy discriminate against gay people."[4]

These arguments certainly carry emotional weight, and if you're a thoughtful person, they force you to ask some questions. Do I want to be a source of affirmation and support to these fellow-human beings, people who are also created in the image of God, or do I want to add to their pain? Do I want to stand for justice for those who are oppressed, or do I want to be an oppressor? To be sure, I want to be a source of healing and a voice for justice, and to the extent that I can stand with those who are insulted and ridiculed and cast out, I am committed to do so.

SO THEN, IS GAY REALLY THE NEW BLACK?

At the same time, I cannot buy into this line of argument for at least four reasons. First, as Campbell correctly points out in his article, here in the United States, the discriminatory treatment of gays and lesbians cannot fairly be compared with the monstrous suffering endured by the African American community.[5] Today, we have openly gay members of Congress (like Barney Frank), openly gay celebrities (like Ellen Degeneres), openly gay CEO's (like the multimillionaire Tim Gill), openly gay financial gurus (like Suze Orman), openly gay sports stars (like Martina Navratilova), openly gay Hollywood moguls (like David Geffen), and openly gay college professors and bestselling authors and scientists – just to name a few. In the days of segregation in America, there were few, if any, black equivalents to any of these, not to mention the fact that in many cities in America, even the lynching and beating of blacks was accepted. Where in America is such treatment of gays and lesbians accepted today? And what is the LGBT equivalent to the American slave trade?

As noted by conservative gay journalist Charles Winecoff,

> Newsflash: blacks in America didn't start out as hip-hop fashion designers; they were slaves. There's a big difference between being able to enjoy a civil union with the same sex partner of your choice - and not being able to drink out of a water fountain, eat at a lunch counter, or use a rest room because you don't have the right skin color.[6]

Second, there is, to date, no solid evidence that supports the concept that people are born gay or lesbian. Even the unabashedly pro-gay American Psychological Association, the largest association of psychologists worldwide, stated in 2009:

> There are numerous theories about the origins of a person's sexual orientation; most scientists today agree that sexual orientation is most likely the result of a complex interaction of environmental, cognitive and biological factors. In most people, sexual orientation is shaped at an early age. There is also considerable recent evidence to suggest that biology, including genetic or inborn hormonal factors, play a significant role in a person's sexuality. In summary, it is important to recognize that there are probably many reasons for a person's sexual orientation and the reasons may be different for different people.[7]

Yes, "sexual orientation is most likely the result of a complex interaction of environmental, cognitive and biological factors." This echoes the position statement of the (also strongly pro-gay) American Psychiatric Association that, "... to date there are no replicated scientific studies supporting any specific biological etiology for homosexuality."[8]

This means that, despite the many reports of the discovery of a gay gene (or whatever the latest "discovery" may be),[9] people are simply not born homosexual. (We will discuss the difference between a possible genetic contribution to homosexuality and a genetic causation for homosexuality, below.)

As noted by research scientist Neil Whitehead (Ph.D., Biochemistry) after examining more than 10,000 scholarly papers and publications on the subject,

> Geneticists, anthropologists, sociologists, endocrinologists, neuroanatomists, medical researchers into gender, and twin study researchers are in broad agreement about the role of genetics in homosexuality. Genes don't make you do it. There is no genetic determinism, and genetic influence at most is minor.[10]

This conclusion was echoed by Prof. Douglas Abbot, who wrote,

> I believe that the genetic evidence for homosexuality is just not there. It's the values and politics of homosexuals and their supporters that is driving the gay gene agenda, not good science.[11]

As expressed by John D'Emilio, a well-known gay activist and a professor of history and of gender and women's studies at the University of Illinois,

> "Born gay" is an idea with a large constituency, LGBT and otherwise. It's an idea designed to allay the ingrained fears of a homophobic society and the internalized fears of gays, lesbians, and bisexuals. What's most amazing to me about the "born gay" phenomenon is that the scientific evidence for it is thin as a reed, yet it doesn't matter. It's an idea with such social utility that one doesn't need much evidence in order to make it attractive and credible.[12]

Third, it is inaccurate to compare skin color to sexual orientation, since skin color cannot be hidden, whereas a person's sexual orientation is, generally speaking, not outwardly recognizable (and thus not immediately subject to potential harassment or discrimination). In other words, it's one thing for a restaurant to say, "We refuse to serve blacks" (a sad reality in our not too distant past); it's another thing for a restaurant to say "We refuse to serve gays and lesbians" (this, of course, would also be illegal and ugly). Both scenarios reflect bigotry and bias, but my point here is simply that gay cannot truly be called "the new black," since it's one thing for the restaurant to refuse to serve blacks, but how would the restaurant know that a person was gay? Based on what outward (or, even clearly defined, legal) criteria?

Fourth, it is wrong to argue that just because someone may be born with certain desires (or, with a natural propensity to behave a certain way) those desires or behaviors are therefore justifiable and morally acceptable, let alone deserving protection as a "right." The truth be told, there are many behaviors and tendencies that are genetically influenced, yet we have laws against some of those behaviors and we make moral judgments about some of those tendencies. Since when has the claim that "I was born this way" held up in a court of law? Try telling the judge, "But your honor, I couldn't help myself. This is who I am!"[13]

This fourth point is the one we'll focus on for the rest of the chapter, but first, let's briefly review the question of gays being "born that way" before discussing, "Even if you are born that way, what does that prove?"

ARE PEOPLE REALLY BORN GAY?
MOST SAY THE ANSWER IS "NO"

Now, what is immediately apparent is that the general public increasingly believes that sexual orientation is, in fact, inborn. As noted in a June, 2007 article in the *LA Times*, ". . . a Gallup Poll last month [May, 2007] found that 42% of adults believe sexual orientation is present at birth. (Three decades ago, when Gallup first asked the question, just 13% held that view.)"[14] What is that figure today?

Hollywood and the media have certainly done a good job of propagating this notion (see above, Chapter Five), and large segments of the population seem to be buying into it hook, line and sinker. Reinforcing the "born that way" idea is the fact that many more people today have openly gay family members and friends and co-workers, most of whom feel as if they have always been homosexual (or transgender, as the case may be). We are also hearing more and more about people "being born in the wrong body," and in the case of little children going through this terrible trauma (which is also traumatizing to the parents), the emotional appeal is very strong. Despite this anecdotal evidence, however, the scientific data to support the "born that way" theory is sadly lacking.[15]

But scientific accuracy is not always important. Good strategy is often what carries the day. As Marshall Kirk and Hunter Madsen wrote in 1989:

> We argue that, for all practical purposes, gays should be considered to have been *born gay* – even though sexual orientation, for most humans, seems to be the product of a complex interaction between innate predispositions and environmental factors during childhood and early adolescence. *And since no choice is involved, gayness can be no more blameworthy than straightness.*[16]

Who cares about facts when you've got a good angle! And so, gay *is* the new black – especially among influential liberals.

In April, 2009, I wrote an article entitled, "Gays Out, Conservatives In – the Closet," which contained the following line: "Simply stated, if homosexuality is legitimate in every respect, then any opposition to homosexuality is illegitimate." That article was then posted on the ultra-liberal Daily Kos website, and a blogger called PerfectStormer replied, "Let's make a substitution, shall we?" My sentence was then changed to read, "Simply stated, if marriage between black and whites is legitimate in every respect, then any opposition to marriage between black and whites is illegitimate."[17] There you have it! Gay is the new black.

Of course, there are some obvious problems with this "gay is the new black" analogy, in particular, as it applies to attempts to redefine marriage. To begin with, the marriage between a black person and a white person always included the two essential elements of marriage – namely a man and a woman (as opposed to just two people) – and, by design, the marriage could normally produce children and then provide those children with a mother and father. Moreover, laws against interracial marriage were clearly based on bigotry rather than family structure and questions of procreations, as evidenced by their inconsistency (e.g., a white man could not marry a black woman, but, for the most part, he could marry a Native American). But the bigger problem with the analogy is that skin color is 100% genetically predetermined and completely unchangeable (attempts by the late Michael Jackson notwithstanding) while homosexuality is neither totally predetermined nor completely unchangeable. (For more on the question of the possibility of change, see below, Chapters Twelve and Thirteen.)

According to psychiatrist Nathaniel S. Lehrman, former chairperson of the Task Force on Religion and Mental Health (writing in 2005),

It was pointed out 11 years ago how time and again "scientists have claimed that particular genes or chromosomal regions are associated with behavioral traits, only to withdraw their findings when they were not replicated. Findings linking specific genes to complex human behaviors all were announced with great fanfare; all were greeted without skepticism in the popular press; all are now in disrepute."[18] Nevertheless, considerable grant money has been available in this country for research seeking to show a genetic basis for homosexuality. Researchers now openly admit that after searching for more than 20 years, they are still unable to find the "gay gene."[19]

Christl Ruth Vonholdt, a pediatrician and the Director of the German Institute for Youth and Society, summed up the evidence as follows:[20]

There is only one point on which today's scientists agree: homosexuality is not simply innate. It is true that scientists who are close to the homosexual movement have been trying hard to identify a special gene,[21] specific brain structures[22] and a modified hormone balance[23] as possible causes of homosexuality, but none of these attempts have so far been successful.[24] The claim that homosexuality is innate is scientifically not tenable.[25]

Psychologist Louis A. Berman wrote,

Inborn, irreversible, natural; like left-handedness. Predictable in its onset and chronic in its duration, like male pattern baldness or adult diabetes. Surprisingly, this "conventional wisdom" survives despite the abundance of evidence that in fact homosexual behavior comes and goes in the widest variety of ways. It may emerge at 14, or not until well into middle age, or may exist side-by-side an appetite for heterosexual gratification.[26]

And an April 8, 2008 statement by the American College of Pediatricians stated bluntly,

During the last 40 years the majority of SSA [same-sex attraction] studies have been conducted, reviewed and/or published by homosexuality affirming researchers, many of whom are also openly homosexual. Virtually all of the studies were touted by the media as proving that SSA is inborn. In reality, however, every one of them, from gene analysis, to brain structure, fingerprint styles, handedness, finger lengths, eye blinking, ear characteristics, verbal skills and prenatal hormones, have failed to be replicated, were criticized for research limitations, and/or were outright debunked.[27]

With regard to lesbianism in particular, Prof. Robert Alan Brookey, himself a strong proponent of gay rights, noted that "[Gay scientist Dean] Hamer has gone on record as saying that lesbianism is not genetic but socially and culturally produced."[28]

Professor of psychology Mark Yarhouse, after a careful and non-polemical review of many recent studies, opined: "The statement, 'We don't know what causes homosexuality,' sounds like a reasonable conclusion."[29]

ARE PEOPLE REALLY BORN GAY? SOME SAY THE ANSWER IS "YES"

"But," you reply, "aren't there are other researchers who claim that the evidence for a primary biological or genetic cause for homosexuality is undeniable?"

To be sure, many researchers – especially gay researchers – would agree with you. This is the conclusion of professors Qazi Rahman and Glenn Wilson in their book *Born Gay: The Psychology of Sexual Orientation*, in which they argue that, "Sexual orientation is something we are born with and not 'acquired' from our social environment."[30] This is also the basic conclusion of journalist Chandler Burr in his 1996 book *A Separate Creation*. Popular articles reflect this position as well, such as Neil Swidey's, "What Makes People Gay?" published in the *Boston Globe*, August 14, 2005.[31]

There Swidey wrote:

In recent years, researchers who suspect that homosexuality is inborn - whether because of genetics or events happening in the womb - have looked everywhere for clues: Prenatal hormones. Birth order. Finger length. Fingerprints. Stress. Sweat. Eye blinks. Spatial relations. Hearing. Handedness. Even "gay" sheep. . . .

This accumulating biological evidence, combined with the prospect of more on the horizon, is having an effect. Last month, the Rev. Rob Schenck, a prominent Washington, D.C., evangelical leader, told a large gathering of young evangelicals that he believes homosexuality is not a choice but rather a predisposition, something "deeply rooted" in people. Schenck told me that his conversion came about after he'd spoken extensively with genetic researchers and psychologists. He argues that evangelicals should continue to oppose homosexual behavior, but that "many evangelicals are living in a sort of state of denial about the advance of this conversation." His message: "If it's inevitable that this scientific evidence is coming, we have to be prepared with a loving response. If we don't have one, we won't have any credibility."

After noting how scattered and underfunded these studies have been to date, Swidey opines, "Still, no matter how imperfect these studies are, when you put them all together and examine them closely, the message is clear: While post-birth development may well play a supporting role, the roots of homosexuality, at least in men, appear to be in place by the time a child is born."

To date, my own research does not confirm this conclusion, and colleagues who have spent years examining the evidence are not convinced either. In fact, the wide variety of alleged genetic or biological causes for homosexuality actually argues *against* a genetic or biological cause – unless we argue that homosexuality is caused by numerous different factors in numerous different individuals. In that case, it is quite mistaken to treat homosexuality in a monolithic way, as if all forms and manifestations of homosexuality were cut out of the same cloth. (Swidey himself experienced considerable "whiplash" in researching his article, as each new theory moved in a radically new direction, with contrary arguments arising for each one.)

As for Swidey's claim that, "By now, there is substantial evidence showing correlation - though not causation - between sexual orientation and traits that are set when a baby is in the womb," similar sentiments have been echoed by many researchers for years. They have emphasized that correlation is not causation, that predisposition is not predetermination, and that influence is not destiny. Having certain tendencies is not the same as having no choice, and having leanings towards certain behaviors does not mean that one is locked into acting out those behaviors.[32]

And this is where I think we need to step back and look at the larger question of being "born that way" – whether "that way" means gay or straight, passive or violent, athletic or contemplative, obese or thin. What is the genetic contribution to our personalities and traits and tendencies and temptations? To what extent are we hardwired and to what extent are we free moral beings?

HUMAN BEHAVIOR, BIOLOGY, AND GENETICS

For argument's sake, let's say that there is a strong biological or genetic component to homosexual desires and attractions. What then does this prove? Does it prove that homosexual practice is therefore morally acceptable? Does it prove that a homosexual (or, bisexual or transgender) orientation should be embraced and that all those with same-sex attractions should celebrate those attractions and build a life identity based upon them? Does it really say anything as to how society should view same-sex marriage or give any guidance as to what should be taught in our schools regarding homosexuality?

Actually, it does not, since virtually all behaviors or orientations or tendencies have at least some biological or genetic component (or, aspect of hereditability), and yet this does not justify or normalize these behaviors or orientations or tendencies, nor does it mean that people with these behaviors or orientations or tendencies or temptations should not try to change. As noted by openly gay (and/or gay-affirming) psychologists J. Michael Bailey of Northwestern University and Brian Mustanski of Indiana University:

> Despite common assertions to the contrary, evidence for biological causation does not have clear moral, legal, or policy consequences. To assume that it does logically requires the belief that some behaviour is non-biologically caused. We believe that this assumption is irrational because the most proximal cause of behaviour is neurophysiological, and thus all behavioural differences will on some level be attributable to differences in brain structure or process. Thus, no clear conclusions about the morality of a behaviour can be made from the mere fact of biological causation, because all

behaviour is biologically caused.[33]

On April 4, 2008, there was a striking headline on Nature.com announcing, "'Ruthlessness gene' discovered. Dictatorial behaviour may be partly genetic, study suggests."[34] For emphasis, the article featured pictures of truly ruthless dictators like Stalin, Hitler and Saddam Hussein. In the article, Michael Hopkins asked: "Could a gene be partly responsible for the behaviour of some of the world's most infamous dictators?" Absolutely!

Yes,

> Selfish dictators may owe their behaviour partly to their genes, according to a study that claims to have found a genetic link to ruthlessness. The study might help to explain the money-grabbing tendencies of those with a Machiavellian streak — from national dictators down to 'little Hitlers' found in workplaces the world over.
>
> Researchers at the Hebrew University in Jerusalem found a link between a gene called AVPR1a and ruthless behaviour in an economic exercise called the 'Dictator Game'. The exercise allows players to behave selflessly, or like money-grabbing dictators such as former Zaire President Mobutu, who plundered the mineral wealth of his country to become one of the world's richest men while its citizens suffered in poverty.
>
> The researchers don't know the mechanism by which the gene influences behaviour. It may mean that for some, the old adage that "it is better to give than to receive" simply isn't true, says team leader Richard Ebstein. The reward centres in those brains may derive less pleasure from altruistic acts, he suggests, perhaps causing them to behave more selfishly.[35]

To this you might respond, "Very interesting, but who cares? Regardless of the alleged genetic component to their behavior, what these dictators did was criminal and immoral and unjustifiable."[36]

Agreed! And, on another level, no parent would let their kid off the hook because he or she allegedly had a "ruthless gene," as if this genetic component would justify their selfishness or dictatorial behavior.

How about a violent, delinquent gene? As reported by Reuters on July 14, 2008, "Study finds genetic link to violence, delinquency." According to Health and Science editor Maggie Fox:

> Three genes may play a strong role in determining why some young men raised in rough neighborhoods or deprived families become violent criminals, while others do not, U.S. researchers reported on Monday. . . .
>
> People with a particular variation of the MAOA gene called 2R were very prone to criminal and delinquent behavior, said sociology professor Guang Guo, who led the study.
>
> "I don't want to say it is a crime gene, but 1 percent of people have it and scored very high in violence and delinquency," Guo said in a telephone interview. . . .[37]

A "crime gene," leading to violence and delinquency? It is certainly possible that such a gene exists, but again, what does that prove? Do we excuse violent behavior if we find that the violent person has this alleged gene? Does the judge dismiss the charges against a criminal if he has this supposed genetic component? Don't we rather work harder with such an individual to help him change his destructive behavior?

Remarkably, Prof. Guo noted that:

> . . . a certain mutation in [the gene called] DRD2 seemed to set off a young man if he did not have regular meals with his family.
>
> "But if people with the same gene have a parent who has regular meals with them, then the risk is gone," Guo said.
>
> "Having a family meal is probably a proxy for parental involvement," he added. "It suggests that parenting is very important.". . .

How remarkable! Even though there is a genetic predisposition to violent and delinquent behavior, eating together as a family removed the risk entirely. Incredible! Environmental factors certainly do play a major role in determining the decisions we make and the desires we experience, regardless of our genetic or biological predisposition – the very argument constantly raised by those who advocate that homosexuality can be changed.

But even without Prof. Guo's observation about social factors, let's think some more about the weakness of the argument that, "I couldn't help myself," or, "This is the way I was born," or, "My genes made me do it."

Please allow me to wax sarcastic for a moment. Perhaps a violent man who beats up a gay man is only being himself. Perhaps he is only doing what he is genetically predisposed to do. (What folly!) Perhaps he should no more be faulted for his behavior than a gay person should be faulted for engaging in same-sex relationships. After all, if homosexual activity is a matter of *sexual orientation* rather than *sexual preference*, perhaps violent behavior is a matter of *aggressive, angry orientation* rather than *aggressive, angry preference*.

There is, to date, more evidence for a genetic predisposition to violence than there is for a genetic predisposition to homosexuality,[38] yet we criminalize violent behavior and incarcerate violent criminals rather than celebrating their own particular type of "diversity." Perhaps defense lawyers could learn something from gay activists and plead, "Not guilty by means of violent orientation!", or, "Not guilty by genetic predisposition!" And perhaps, rather than incarcerating the violent man for his criminal acts, we should be congratulating him for being himself! (Again, I am being completely sarcastic here, but I trust you get the point.)

To be sure, I do not mean to minimize the conflicts and heartache endured by those in the GLBT community who have desired to become heterosexual for religious or moral or social reasons and have failed in their attempts to change. In no way do I want to be cavalier about this whole subject of being "born that way." I simply want to point out that people are really barking up the wrong tree with this argument and that, quite simply, we cannot determine the morality or acceptability of a habit or orientation or behavior or tendency based on how someone may or may not be born. Rather, the habit or orientation or behavior or tendency must be evaluated on other grounds.

MY GENES MADE ME DO IT?

Let's consider a few more examples. On September 2, 2008, a provocative headline flashed across the internet, proclaiming, "Scientists identify 'unfaithful' gene in men."[39] There you have it! "Honey, it's not my fault I committed adultery. It's not my fault that I broke our marriage vows. I have an unfaithful gene. That explains it all." Right!

Robert Walz, reporting from Stockholm, Sweden, wrote:

> Men who cheat on their wives might be able to blame it on their DNA, according to a study released on Tuesday that indicated that men with a high amount of a gene that influences brain activity are twice as likely to experience marital dysfunction.[40]

(I think I hear the lyrics for a hot new song entitled, "Blame It on My DNA"!)
The article explains that:

> …genetic research at the Karolinska institute in Stockholm shows a direct link between a man's genes and his aptitude for monogamy. Behavioral geneticist Hasse Walum and a team of scientists studied the brains of one-thousand heterosexual couples. 40 percent of men have one or two copies of the allele. "Men with two copies of the allele had twice the risk of experiencing marital dysfunction, with a threat of divorce during the last year, compared to man carrying one or no copies," said Walum in a news release issued on Tuesday.[41]

And what did the ladies think about this new revelation that men with a certain genetic makeup "have a difficult time committing to and maintaining a monogamous relationship"?[42]

> "I think that is a lame excuse for being unfaithful," said Megan Warner as she walked with her son at Salt Lake's Gateway shopping center. "We make choices every day for good and bad and I think it is a matter of choice. "So you won't give men a break on this?" "No way, not at my house!"[43]

(I assume that all you ladies reading this book would also say "Not at my house!")
In a December 12, 2004 column in the Sunday Mirror, a situation was presented to the "Sex Doctor," Dr. Catherine Hood:

I AM having an affair with one of my husband's friends - and I don't feel guilty. Since I had children my life has been one big chore, cleaning up for them and cooking for my husband. It has been wonderful for a man to notice me for the woman I am - my husband never does. I'm told being unfaithful is to do with the genes.[44]

Dr. Hood responded, "It's been suggested that 22% of women are genetically programmed to be unfaithful. You may have the unfaithful gene but you can choose not to act on it!"[45] Well said! Yes, whatever gene you or I may have, we can choose not to act on it. As noted by Tara Parker-Pope in a *New York Times* article on "The Science of a Happy Marriage," a growing body of research indicates that, "while some people may be naturally more resistant to temptation, men and women can also train themselves to protect their relationships and raise their feelings of commitment."[46] Perhaps people can even resist the power of the "rape gene"? I would hope so! (See Nicholas D. Kristof's June 11, 2009 article in the *New York Times*, "Do We Have a Rape Gene?"[47])

How about the "liberal gene?" I kid you not. On October 27, 2010, news services were abuzz with the headline that, "Scientists Find 'Liberal Gene'." One story reported that:

Researchers have determined that genetics could matter when it comes to some adults' political leanings.

According to scientists at UC San Diego and Harvard University, "ideology is affected not just by social factors, but also by a dopamine receptor gene called DRD4." That and how many friends you had during high school. . . .

"It is the crucial interaction of two factors – the genetic predisposition and the environmental condition of having many friends in adolescence – that is associated with being more liberal," according to the study.[48]

Perhaps you disagree with some of the contents of this book because you have a liberal gene and were socially active as an adolescent? (OK. Smile. I was just kidding.)

What about something more serious, like the alleged obesity gene? An April 13, 2006 article reported, "Common genetic change linked to obesity."[49] Roxanne Khamsi noted that "The first common genetic variant that substantially increases a person's risk of obesity has been identified, researchers claim. They hope that their discovery will open doors to new treatments for the condition." Did you catch that? This discovery "will open doors to new treatments for the condition" – not justification for obesity, but rather insights that will help combat obesity, since obesity is harmful to our health.

Based on gay activist logic, however, this discovery should lead to the *embracing* of obesity and even the public *celebration* of obesity. Perhaps we should now hold Fat Pride events in our cities? After all, most name-calling in our schools has to do with appearance,[50] and so kids who are overweight are subject to all kinds of cruel taunts from their classmates, not to mention their inability to compete well in sports, leading to further ostracization.

This, of course, underscores why all name-calling and bullying is wrong, while the discovery of this "obesity gene" should produce greater sympathy for those who struggle with their weight. But does this cause us to embrace and celebrate obesity or to downplay its harmful effects? Absolutely not! Why should it? Obesity remains a dangerous condition.[51]

Interestingly, the article also stressed the importance of "environmental factors," noting that, "More than one-third of people in the US are obese and other countries' populations are increasingly facing similar weight issues. Scientists predict that genes may contribute anywhere from 30% to 70% of the risk of obesity, but they stress that environmental factors, like diet, play a crucial role."[52] So, even when there is a strong genetic component, personal choices "play a crucial role."

And let's not miss a repeated phrase in the article, namely, "the risk of obesity." A similar phrase could be used for same-sex attractions – but not without howls of angry protests, since gay is OK but obesity is not.

In reality, however, we *could* say today that, "Children with thus and such biological or genetic factors at work in their lives have a higher *risk* for homosexuality, yet thus and such environmental factors may militate against it."[53] I can feel the heat already. Just writing these words would spark a furious reaction. In fact, I can hear that "Hitler" charge being raised again! (See above, Chapter Two.)

THE TRUTH ABOUT GENETIC INFLUENCES

On the home page of openly gay scientist Dean Hamer it is noted that, "Many aspects of human personality and behavior are genetically influenced.

. . . Behavioral genetic studies have shown that cigarette smoking is 53% heritable and that there are different genes for starting and continuing to smoke."[54] The same can be said for alcoholism and other harmful traits and habits,[55] all of which brings us back to the question, "What does this prove?" Does it prove that cigarette smoking or alcoholism or violence or unfaithfulness or obesity are therefore acceptable or commendable or helpful because they have an alleged genetic component?

Neil Swidey noted that "[gay scientist Simon Levay] says the hunt for a biological basis for homosexuality, which involves many researchers who are themselves gay or lesbian, 'has contributed to the status of gay people in society."[56] But why should this be? Is it now an *a priori* assumption that any behavior or desire or tendency that has a biological base is therefore morally acceptable? Certainly not.

Let's look at this from yet another angle. Dr. Neil Whitehead estimates the genetic contribution to homosexuality to be roughly 10%; on the other side of the spectrum, some have put the figure as high as 50-60%.[57] But what exactly does that mean? As explained by Prof. Warren Throckmorton,

> Putting the questionable figure in perspective lets [sic] look at other traits and the estimated percent of difference attributable to genetic factors according to existing research found on the American Psychological Association web site.
>
> * Attitudes toward reading books - 55%
> * Feelings about abortion on demand - 54%
> * Feelings about roller coaster rides - 50%
> * Attitudes towards the death penalty for murder - 50%
> * Humility - 58%
> * Likelihood to engage in casual sex - 49%
> * Attitudes toward equality - 55%[58]

So, even if the genetic contribution to homosexuality was 50% -- which is an *extremely* high estimate – that would no more prove that homosexuality was inborn and unchangeable than it would prove that any of these other behaviors and attitudes were inborn and unchangeable. Otherwise, to be consistent, you would have to argue that some people are born to be proud and therefore should not try to cultivate humility, or that other people are bound to engage in casual sex and therefore should not learn to curb their sexual appetites. Is that where you (referring in particular to gay activists and their allies) want to go?

To explain this further, Dr. A. Dean Byrd, professor at the University of Utah School of Medicine, notes that:

> Dr. Francis S. Collins, one of the world's leading scientists who works at the cutting edge of DNA, concluded that "there is an inescapable component of heritability to many human behavioral traits. For virtually none of them is heredity ever close to predictive."
>
> In reviewing the heritability (influence of genetic factors) of personality traits, Dr. Collins referenced the estimates of the percentage of various human personality traits that can be ascribed to heredity from the Bochard and McGue research.
>
> The heritability estimates for personality traits were varied: General Cognitive Ability (50%), Extroversion (54%), Agreeableness (42%), Conscientiousness (49%), Neuroticism (48%), Openness (57%), Aggression (38%) and Traditionalism (54%).[59]

To be sure, there are some neurologists and ethicists and scientists who believe that *all* human behavior is hardwired – in other words, "My brain made me do it!"[60] – but that being the case, homosexuality is just one of many hardwired behaviors, making all moral judgments virtually meaningless. After all, "I" am not responsible, my brain is. (This also begs the question as to who "I" am, but that is a subject for another book, one that neither I nor my brain plan to write.) In fact, a recent study posted on the 365Gay.com website argued that *homophobia* was hardwired into the brain![61] Does this, then, excuse or justify irrational prejudice against gays?

According to Steven Neuberg, professor of social psychology at Arizona State University and one of the authors of the study,

> People sometimes assume that because we say prejudice has evolved roots we are saying that specific prejudices can't be changed. That's simply not the case. What we think and feel and how we behave is typically the result of complex interactions between biological tendencies and learning

experiences. Evolution may have prepared our minds to be prejudiced, but our environment influences the specific targets of those prejudices and how we act on them.[62]

Suffice it to say that most of us recognize that we are ultimately responsible for the choices we make, even if we were predisposed to a certain kind of negative behavior either because of biological tendencies, learning experiences, or both.

Think for a moment about the children of alcoholic parents. According to the National Association of Children of Alcoholics,

- Children of addicted parents are the highest risk group of children to become alcohol and drug abusers due to both genetic and family environment factors.
- Biological children of alcohol dependent parents who have been adopted continue to have an increased risk (2-9 fold) of developing alcoholism.
- Recent studies suggest a strong genetic component, particularly for early onset of alcoholism in males. Sons of alcoholic fathers are at fourfold risk compared with the male offspring of non-alcoholic fathers.[63]

So, both genetic and environmental factors are stacked against these children, making it very likely that they too will become alcoholics – yet it is *not* a given that they will and they *do* have the power to choose a different lifestyle, which is why so many of them do.[64]

As for the children of alcoholics who follow in their parents footsteps, as much as we show them compassion and understanding, we still do not condone their drinking, we still recognize the harmful effects of alcohol addiction, we don't excuse them if they kill someone in a drunk driving accident, and without a doubt, we don't hold Alcoholic Pride events in their honor.

If you say to me, "How dare you compare alcoholism with homosexuality!", I say in reply, I'm making the argument that being genetically or biologically predisposed to do something does not make it right.[65] And, to go one step further, being genetically predisposed to do something that is hardly ideal, to put it mildly, is certainly not something to celebrate (or legislate into protected class status). After all, think of all the challenges that GLBT folks face in this world, and think of their inability to reproduce children of their own, and think of the health risks which they face (especially males; see below, Chapters Eleven and Thirteen for more on this).[66] To be "born that way," or, more realistically, born with a predisposition to go in that direction, should produce pity and heartfelt concern rather than adulation. And in no way should it affect our moral evaluation of that behavior.

And what about the influence of environmental factors – meaning, upbringing, social experiences, or early sexual abuse – on the development of homosexuality? I know it's taboo to talk about this these days (what *isn't* taboo to talk about with regard to the causes of homosexuality, except that it is innate and immutable?), but if environmental factors play a role in the development of alcoholics, and if the failure to eat family meals together can trigger someone's predisposition to violence (see above), then why can't environmental factors play a role in the development of homosexuality? Why should the stories of countless thousands of gays and lesbians be disregarded (including many former gays and lesbians)? Why should we disregard the disproportionately high number of lesbian women who earlier in life suffered sexual abuse at the hands of a man?[67] Why should this be factored out? And why should we ignore the stories of early same-sex encounters in the lives of many gay men? Just because this was not the experience of some gays and lesbians does not mean that we should discount the stories of others. To do so would be intolerant and bigoted. (My apologies for this momentary lapse; I forgot that only my opinions are intolerant and bigoted.)

BORN GAY? REALLY?

Of course, the whole idea that people are "born gay" is absurd, just as it is absurd to think that someone predisposed to obesity is born obese (how many twenty-pound newborns have you heard of?) or someone predisposed to violence is born violent (how many infants have attacked the midwife or doctor who assisted in their births?). In fact, being "gay" implies much more than having homosexual desires. Indeed, gay psychologist Richard Isay wrote a book entitled *Becoming Gay*, in which he purports to help homosexual men embrace their "gay" identity – which could be part of the reason that Camile Paglia exclaimed that, "No one is 'born gay.' The idea is ridiculous."[68]

Consider the following statements from both gay and straight authors, all of which question the simple "born gay" equation:

- Gay professor David Greenberg: "For every lesbian

separatist arguing that lesbianism is a political choice that carries feminism to its logical conclusion, there is someone else saying, 'I was born that way.' Short of definitive evidence, which no theory has thus far received, the disagreement is likely to continue.[69]

- Straight psychiatrist and physicist Jeffrey Satinover: "Because all human behavior is related in some way to genes, we can nonetheless guess that one day higher quality of research will find genetic factors that correlate to homosexuality. But remember, one of the fundamental principles of research is that correlation does not necessarily imply causation."[70]

- Gay researcher, John DeCecco, editor of the *Journal of Homosexuality*: ". . . the sexual act shapes erotic desire as much as desire precedes it."[71]

- Straight researchers Martin Rovers and Ray A. Seutter: "More and more, however, it seems that theorists and critics on both sides of the debate are leaning towards some middle ground, talking about complexity (Byne & Parsons, 1993), multiple pathways (Byne, 1997), multiple factors (LeVay, 1996), and "a mixture of both genes and environment" (Hamer & Copeland, 1994). Sexual orientation seems to be shaped through complex interactions of biological, psychological, and social factors."[72]

According to one prominent theory, a person with a genetic or biological predisposition to homosexuality would be born with certain tendencies that would not be typical for their sex (such as a boy with extreme sensitivities and artistic flair), which could easily lead to a lack of bonding with his father (especially if the dad is a "macho" type), rejection by other boys, a self-identification with girls, and then an attraction to the opposite of that identification, meaning an attraction to boys, who are now the perceived as the opposite sex.[73] This describes the situation of many gay men today – is it any surprise that homosexual men are so creatively gifted? – although it is hardly true for all of them. Again, however, this hardly proves the "born gay" theory; to the contrary, it underscores the fact that predisposition is not predestination.

And what if the genetic or biological component to homosexuality is deeper than this? One prominent pro-homosexual scholar minces no words in sharing his opinion about the search for a "gay gene." I'm referring to none other than the Harvard population geneticist Dr. Richard Lewontin. He wonders aloud: "What happens when we find a difference on a chromosome whose variation between individuals has some effect on a behavioral – or for that matter any – trait? What do I do with information?"[74] This was a question he put to his colleague Dr. Dean Hamer:

> Now, Dean gave a partial answer to that. Politics. "What do I do about it," is *always* political. People think that if they find the gene for a trait, it'll affect people's lives. And he gave an example, he said here's this guy, this right-wing nut [referring to a columnist with the *Washington Times*] who is antigay, and the moment this guy hears homosexuality is biological he stops being antigay. Now that is the political point of view Dr. Hamer has, but I disagree. I'd ask *why* is knowing how sexual orientation is created biologically a good thing to know?[75]

And what does Lewontin think of this? Get ready for a blunt answer! (According to author Chandler Burr, who interviewed Lewontin, "He scowls" here.)

> It's irrelevant! I don't care! What difference does it make to me which genes affect sexual orientation? None whatsoever. That's what I say to my gay friends, that's what they say to me. You get this right-wing guy who thinks a particular sexual orientation is bad, but now that he knows it's genetic, he thinks it's okay. So he's reached the right conclusion. Good for him. But it's stupid! He must be one of the very few people in the world who's become convinced that something is not a defect for the reason that it's biological. The response to that is so simple it's mind-boggling: cancer is biological. Does that make cancer good? There are a million biological defects. It's not even logical."[76]

For Lewontin, looking for a "gay gene" plays into the idea that homosexuality is wrong:

> In that case, [Hamer's] only reinforcing that view that being gay is bad, he's saying okay, I'll show you it's biological so you can't blame me, whereas the right answer is that the issue of blame is not there in the first place. You're going along with the game, "Yeah, I'm bad, but I can't help myself." The proper struggle for gay people is to say, "Why the hell are you blaming me?" Don't blame me at all. Why do you care about the gene? I mean, if God appeared to me in a dream and told me which genes they were, what would I *do* with it?[77]

And this leads to Lewontin's other issue with research into the possible genetic origins of homosexuality:

> But the second thing that's implied is that just because you have the gene, you can't change the trait. Excuse me, everyone's looking for the genes for diabetes. Are they doing this for *fun*? The equation of genetic is unchangeable is absolute garbage! You find a gene that makes some difference in your physiology, but nobody ever said you couldn't change people's physiology, they've been doing it with diabetes for seventy years now by giving people insulin. Is this not obvious? ... So people think that if they find the gene everyone will accept that they can't change it – that's bull----! My genes gave me nose shape but I can get an operation any day of the week.[78]

So, even if it a genetic component to homosexuality *could* be identified with certainty, that would *not* mean that homosexuality could not be altered. After all, other genetically-based "defects" can now be surgically or medically corrected. In fact, the chapter in Burr's *Separate Creation* from which I'm now quoting is entitled, "How Genetic Surgery Can Change Homosexuality to Heterosexuality." Here Burr details the work of molecular biologist Charles J. (Chuck) Link, Jr., and his Human Gene Therapy Research Institute which has "treated" people for homosexuality using their own DNA.[79] Hey, if there's a genetic *cause* for homosexuality, then there could be a genetic *cure* for it, right?

A GENETIC CAUSE AND A GENETIC CURE?

There is, of course, the concern that the discovery of biological or genetic causes for homosexuality might lead to some kind of witch hunt to try to identify those traits in babies in the womb, giving parents the choice to abort a child potentially predisposed to homosexuality, much like older women who are pregnant are offered an amniocentesis in order to determine if the fetus has any genetic abnormalities.[80] How would gay activists welcome *this*? Talk about eugenics with a cruel twist!

And so, in many ways, the "born that way" argument is a (potentially dangerous) dead end since: 1) Genetic predisposition (or even causation) does not determine the morality or desirability of a trait; 2) finding a genetic component for homosexuality doesn't mean there isn't a genetic cure for homosexuality; 3) finding a genetic component for homosexuality doesn't mean that environmental or cognitive factors have no role; 4) finding a genetic component to homosexuality could lead to the abortion of many homosexual fetuses. (Note that this last phrase should underscore the absurdity of being "born gay," since homosexual babies would presuppose homosexual fetuses.)[81]

In 2008, Southern Baptist leader Al Mohler created a firestorm of controversy when he suggested that if it was determined that people were born homosexual, then perhaps a treatment for homosexuality could be found.[82] Gay activists were outraged by his comments (is anyone surprised?), and he even came under attack from conservatives who felt he had capitulated to the "born that way" theory.

But let's think about this for a moment: If it is OK to put a girl with gender identity disorder on medication to delay the onset of puberty, then, as a teenager, to offer her sex-change surgery, then to put her on hormonal medication the rest of her life, why would it be wrong to look for a medical "treatment" for homosexuality? And why would it be wrong to begin such treatment in the womb?

Why is one treatment – a far more radical one! – fully acceptable while another one – far less radical and invasive – unacceptable? Why is one, which involves genital mutilation of perfectly healthy organs and tissues, applauded as progressive while the other, which does not affect the physical body at all, considered regressive? We deplore the nations that still practice female circumcision, yet we applaud those doctors who perform sex-change operations.

If a gay person could be saved the stigma of rejection in a heterosexual world and could have new desires that would allow him or her to have love, partner, and have offspring with a person of the opposite sex simply by getting a series of injections, wouldn't it be worth it? Or if a child (or adult) tormented by GID could now be at home in his or her body by some simple medical treatment, rather than undergoing sex-change surgery and hormonal therapy, not to mention suffering the trauma of telling all their friends and families that they had now become the opposite sex, wouldn't they do it in a heartbeat?[83] (This would be akin to asking a severely overweight person if their appetite could be massively reduced by taking a pill rather than having dangerous gastric bypass surgery, which would they choose?)

According to an August 7, 2009, Reuters story from London, "Psychopaths who kill and rape have faulty connections between the part of the brain dealing with emotions and that which handles impulses and decision-making, scientists have found."[84] (I am *not* equating homosexuals with murderers or rapists, nor am I calling them psychopaths, so stay with me for a moment, OK?)

The report by Kate Kelland continued:

> In a study of psychopaths who had committed murder, manslaughter, multiple rape, strangulation and false imprisonment, the British scientists found that roads linking the two crucial brain areas had "potholes," while those of non-psychopaths were in good shape.
>
> The study opens up the possibility of developing treatments for dangerous psychopaths in the future, said Dr Michael Craig of the Institute of Psychiatry at London's King's College Hospital, and may have profound implications for doctors, researchers and the criminal justice system.[85]

What's the point in citing this story, since I'm *not* equating homosexuality with murder and rape? Certainly, all of us agree that murder and rape are heinous and unjustifiable acts, yet that doesn't stop scientists from asking if there is a genetic or biological or developmental contribution to these criminal behaviors. Why, the scientists ask, do these people do what they do? Is there something different in their brains that contributes to their deplorable actions? Those are important questions, but if there *is* something different in their brains, does that make their actions any less criminal? Certainly not!

So then, the morality (or, immorality) of the act stands apart from the question, "Was I born with a predisposition to a certain behavior? Or did the circuitry in my brain make it easier for me to act a certain way?" The same can be said for homosexual practice: Its rightness or wrongness must be judged in and of itself. The argument that "I was born that way" is irrelevant, not to mention false. As noted by Dean Hamer and Peter Copeland, "In short, biology is amoral; it offers no help distinguishing between right and wrong. Only people, guided by their values and beliefs, can decide what is moral and what is not."[86]

Interestingly, the study about the "faulty connections" in the brains of certain psychopaths also stated this:

> The scientists cautioned against suggestions the study could lead to screening of potential psychopathic criminals before they are able to commit crimes, saying their findings had not established how, when or why the brain links were damaged.
>
> "The most exciting question now...is when do the potholes come -- are people born with them, do they develop early in life, or are they a consequence of something else?"[87]

In other words, our brains develop extensively over the course of our lifetimes, and so, even if it could be demonstrated that there were some differences in the brains of gay and straight men (or women) – and this has *not* been demonstrated to date – those differences could have been the *result* of homosexual practice rather than a *contributing factor* to homosexual practice. Conversely, those differences could have been due to early life development rather than to biology.[88] In either case, we're back to where we started: The sexual act and the sexual orientation must be evaluated independent of any alleged cause. And, therefore, the salient question remains, "Is homosexual practice right or wrong, good or bad?", rather than, "Are people born gay?"

I know that some of you are absolutely furious with me for this discussion, perhaps saying out loud as you read, "But homosexuality is not wrong!" or, "How dare you call homosexuality a defect!"

But your response begs the question, since I can say to you, "Look, men and women complement each other emotionally and are biologically made for each other, whereas homosexuals are not. And all good research to date indicates that kids do best when raised by their mom and dad as opposed to being raised by a single parent or by two moms or two dads,[89] and there are considerably fewer health risks for heterosexuals than for homosexuals,[90] so heterosexuality is clearly preferable to homosexuality. And being at home in your own body is clearly preferable to being tormented by your own body, so being heterosexual is clearly preferable to transgender."

Will you dare say in response, "But I was born this way?" I think not.

*Richard Green was very actively involved thirty years ago
in the removal of homosexuality from the DSM [Diagnostic and Statistical
Manual] list of mental disorders. As is known, homosexuality was successfully
removed in the early seventies. Now he argues for the removal
of pedophilia from the same list.*

Abstract of article by Dr. Richard Green in *Archives of Sexual Behavior* 31 (2002)
(the special issue devoted to pedophilia)

*Freedom is indivisible.
The liberation of children, women, boy-lovers, and homosexuals in general,
can occur only as complementary facets of the same dream.*

David Thorstad, "Pederasty and Homosexuality,"
Speech given at the Semana Cultural Lesbica-Gay,
Mexico City, June 26, 1998

*If paedophiles are no longer forced to live underground and to be
secretive about their relationships, but instead their desires are recognized
as legitimate, and they are guided towards a responsible expression of their desires,
we might prevent some cases of genuine sexual abuse.*

Dr. Theo Sandfort, "Constructive Questions Regarding Paedophilia"
(Sandfort was a member of the Gay and Lesbian Studies Department,
State University of Utrecht, the Netherlands;
he is now a professor at Columbia University)

*[I]f the parents and friends of gays are truly friends of gays,
they would know from their gay kids that the relationship with an older man is
precisely what thirteen-, fourteen-, and fifteen-year-old kids
need more than anything else in the world.*

Harry Hay (American gay rights movement founder), cited in Jeffrey Lloyd,
"When Nancy Met Harry," *The American Spectator*, October 5, 2006

7

Speaking of the Unspeakable: Some Disturbing Parallels to Pro-Gay Arguments

I f there is one thing that galls gay men, it is mentioning homosexuality in the same breath with pedophilia, as if all (or most, or even a sizable minority of) gay men are attracted to boys. I can understand how galling this must be. First, gays would point out that there are both heterosexual and homosexual pedophiles, so pedophilia is hardly a same-sex issue. Second, they would stress that same-sex relationships between consenting adults cannot possibly be compared to exploitative relationships between an adult and a child. Third, the great majority of gay men find the thought of "man-boy" love repulsive.

So, to be perfectly clear, and so as not to elicit a typical (and understandable) knee-jerk response of, "How dare you compare homosexuality to pedophilia! You're the one who's perverted!", I kindly request that you say the following sentences slowly and out loud. (You might want to repeat these lines every few paragraphs, just in case you find yourself getting upset.)

- **MICHAEL BROWN IS NOT EQUATING HOMOSEXUAL PRACTICE WITH PEDOPHILIA.**
- **MICHAEL BROWN IS NOT CALLING ALL HOMOSEXUALS PEDOPHILES.**[1]

Then why bring up the subject at all? It is for three principle reasons: 1) Many of the same arguments that are raised in favor of homosexuality are also raised in favor of pedophilia (it's genetic; it's not a choice; it has a rich history; it has social precedents,; it's about love and liberation, etc.); 2) Many of the same arguments that were raised to remove homosexuality from the APA's Diagnostic and Statistical Manual (DSM) in 1973 are being raised today in an attempt to remove pedophilia from the latest edition of the DSM; 3) Homosexual practice in history (in particular, male homosexuality) was often intertwined with pedophilia, and many of the pioneer gay activists were proponents of "man-boy love."

The offshoot of all this is simple: Before you condone homosexuality and condemn pedophilia, you might want to think again. Perhaps neither should be condoned? (Please note: Throughout this chapter, the terms pedophilia and pederasty will be used in their broad, non-technical sense, referring to "man-boy love" in general. Technically, however, the terms are distinct, with pedophilia referring to attraction to pre-pubescent children and pederasty referring to post-pubescent children. For ephebophilia, referring to attraction to pubescent children, see below.)

Let's try a little exercise. Read this statement and see if you concur:

Homosexuality is no more a matter of voluntary choice than are left-handedness or color blindness. There is no known method of treatment by which it may be effectively and permanently altered, suppressed, or replaced. Punishment is useless. There is no satisfactory hypothesis, evolutionary or otherwise, as to why this exists in nature's overall scheme of things. One must simply accept the fact that this does exist, and then, with optimum enlightenment, formulate a policy of what to do about it.

Those were the words of the famous John Hopkins University professor John Dollar, and they reflect the sentiments of many open-minded people today: Homosexuality is not a matter of voluntary choice any more than being left-handed is a matter of voluntary choice; there is no known treatment that can "cure" it or reverse it; we don't know exactly why the phenomenon exists, but since it does exist, let's make the best of it!

Does that sound reasonable? Well, I have an admission to make. Professor John Dollar does not exist. The words I quoted came from the (truly) famous (or, to many, infamous) Professor John Money of Johns Hopkins, and what he actually wrote was this (my emphasis):

Pedophilia and *ephebophilia* [referring to sexual attraction felt by an adult toward an adolescent] are no more a matter of voluntary choice than are left-handedness or color blindness. There is no known method of treatment by which they may be effectively and permanently altered, suppressed, or replaced. Punishment is useless. There is no satisfactory hypothesis, evolutionary or otherwise, as to why they exist in nature's overall scheme of things. One must simply accept the fact that they do exist, and then, with optimum enlightenment, formulate a policy of what to do about it.[2]

Yes, Dr. Money was speaking about pedophilia and ephebophilia, not homosexuality. And these words were taken from his Introduction to Theo

229

Sandfordt's pro-pedophilia book, *Boys on Their Contacts with Men: A Study of Sexually Expressed Friendships*.[3] (As repulsive as this title is to the vast majority of readers, it's important to understand that these pederasts and pederasty advocates make a distinction between consensual sexual relationships and what they would consider coercive or abusive ones – like the kidnapping and rape of a child. So, in their eyes, there is quite a difference between the two, and they believe that an adolescent boy can intelligently consent to have sex with a man.)

COMPARING THE ARGUMENTS NOT THE ACTS

Now, before you throw the book down and accuse me again of comparing homosexuality to pedophilia, may I request that you simply re-read John Money's quote? What I was comparing was the *arguments* that are used to support both sexual orientations, and the parallels between the arguments are striking indeed. Thus, Dr. Peter J. Fagan (and others), writing in the *Journal of the American Medical Association* in 2002, stated that,

> During psychosexual development, no one decides whether to be attracted to women, men, girls, or boys. Rather, individuals discover the types of persons they are sexually attracted to, i.e., their sexual orientation.[4]

Prof. Fred Berlin, founder of the Johns Hopkins Sexual Disorders Clinic, was even more explicit:

> It is likely that no one would choose voluntarily to develop a pedophilic sexual orientation. Those with such an orientation have no more decided to have it than have any of us decided as children to be either heterosexual or homosexual. Men with pedophilia get erections when fantasizing about children. Heterosexual men get erections when fantasizing about women. In neither case is that so because the individual in question has somehow decided ahead of time to program his mind to work in such a fashion. Persons with pedophilia have simply not chosen to experience an alternative state of mind.[5]

You might say, "I don't care how 'natural' it is for someone to get aroused when fantasizing about children. That's just wrong! And I don't care if they were born like that. It is just plain perverted."

Then, why, pray tell, is it wrong to use that same line of argument against homosexual practice – the very argument we are told we *cannot* use since gays find same-sex attraction to be "natural" and since they believe they were born that way. (For an analysis of the "born that way" argument, see above, Chapter Six.) There are many heterosexuals who find same-sex attraction to be dead wrong and even perverted, yet they are told that there's something wrong with them for feeling that way, since homosexuality is natural and inborn. Do you see the double standard here?

Someone might say to me, "For a guy with a Ph.D., you're obviously not that bright. (Really, you're pretty dense, not to mention quite homophobic.) The difference between adult homosexuality and pedophilia is the difference between night and day. One is consensual and non-abusive, the other is not; one is a relationship between equals; the other is not."

To tell you the truth, I was fully aware of those differences. But that was not the point I was making. Rather, the point was this: If homosexuality should be accepted because it claims to be "natural" and "inborn," then why shouldn't pedophilia be accepted, since it also claims to be "natural" and "inborn"? The question here is not whether the sexual acts (or attractions) are consensual but whether they are "natural" and "inborn." Why, then, should homosexuality be accepted *for these very reasons* when these same reasons are not sufficient to argue for the acceptance of pedophilia? (Please note that in the discussion that follows, when I speak of pedophilia or pederasty, I'll be referring to allegedly "consensual" relationships between adults and children ranging from, say, twelve to sixteen years old.)

Consider these typical arguments raised by a gay person when speaking to a straight person who has a problem with homosexual practice:

1) My homosexuality is not a sexual preference but a sexual orientation, just as much as your heterosexuality is not a sexual preference but a sexual orientation.
2) My homosexuality is just as normal as your heterosexuality.
3) Since my behavior is genetically determined and is not a choice, it is intolerant and hateful to suggest that it is wrong. And to call my sexual behavior illegal or immoral, or to refuse to legitimize same-sex relationships, is to be a moral bigot of the highest order.

4) I deeply resent your attempts to identify areas of my upbringing and environment as alleged causes for my homosexuality.

5) I categorically reject the myth that someone can change his or her sexual orientation. Rather, such statements only add to the anguish and suffering of gays and lesbians, and attempts to change us often lead to catastrophic consequences, including depression and suicide.

Now, let's make a slight adjustment in this polemic and put it on the lips of a pederast speaking to a homosexual:

1) My pederasty is not a sexual preference but a sexual orientation, just as much as your homosexuality is not a sexual preference but a sexual orientation.

2) My pederasty is just as normal as your homosexuality.

3) Since my behavior is genetically determined and is not a choice, it is intolerant and hateful to suggest that it is wrong. And to call my sexual behavior illegal or immoral, or to refuse to legitimize adult-child relationships, is to be a moral bigot of the highest order.

4) I deeply resent your attempts to identify areas of my upbringing and environment as alleged causes for my pederasty.

5) I categorically reject the myth that someone can change his or her sexual orientation. Rather, such statements only add to the anguish and suffering of pederasts, and attempts to change us often lead to catastrophic consequences, including depression and suicide.

It will not work for a homosexual to respond with, "Yes, pederasty is also genetic, but it's wrong, and those people will just have to control themselves," since that is the very position so vehemently rejected by gays and lesbians when applied to them. Nor will it work to simply say, "But you're comparing apples with oranges, since the issue is not the legitimacy of adult-child sex but of adult-adult sex," since gays and lesbians know only too well that heterosexuals would say the very same thing to them. (In other words, using marriage as an example, gays would say, "We're not advocating incest or polygamy or the like. We're advocating the covenantal bond between two, non-related adults," while heterosexuals would immediately reply, "But the very definition of marriage is for a man and woman to be joined together, not two people of the same sex to be joined together. And men are biologically designed to have sex with women, not with men.")

The fact is, there was a time when the vast majority of Americans, along with the mental health profession, thought that homosexuality was a mental disorder and/or sexual perversion, something that was utterly shameful, something to be kept in the closet. Did that mean that the majority view was right? Conversely, does the fact that many Americans today, especially in the younger generation, believe that homosexuality is normal and acceptable mean that it is, in fact, normal and acceptable? In the same way, does society's condemnation of pedophilia mean that it should be condemned? What if people's views changed on this too? Would that make pedophilia acceptable?

"But," you say, "what about the fact that all pedophilic relationships are abusive and coercive and destructive?"

Well, that's not what pedophiles – and some non-pedophile researchers – have to say, and so, as unpleasant as it is to reproduce stuff like this, it's important that we hear the arguments *for* pedophilia (or – gag! – "intergenerational intimacy," as some call it). In our day, few have been as eloquent in support of "man-boy" love as David Thorstad.

A PEDERAST ARGUES HIS CASE

Here are some excerpts from Thorstad's speech on "Pederasty and Homosexuality," delivered at the *Semana Cultural Lesbica-Gay*, Mexico City, June 26, 1998. (According to the report, "More than 600 people showed up for the talk: standing room only, and many had to be turned away." This is an English translation of the speech, which was given in Spanish.)[6]

First, he argues that pederasty, which he defines as "love between a man and a youth of 12 to 18 years of age," is liberating and empowering:

> Our movement today stresses the liberation and empowerment of young people. Instead of pedagogy, democracy. Rather than a Greek love mentor-relationship, the companionship of independent and autonomous individuals. In place of male supremacy, a vision of sexual, economic, and political liberation for all. Freedom is indivisible. The liberation of children, women, boy-

lovers, and homosexuals in general, can occur only as complementary facets of the same dream.[7]

Second, he argues that it is impossible to separate the quest for gay rights from the quest for pederastic rights. In fact, he claims that pederasty and homosexuality have always been inseparable:

The issue of love between men and boys has intersected the gay movement since the late nineteenth century, with the rise of the first gay rights movement in Germany. In the United States, as the gay movement has retreated from its vision of sexual liberation, in favor of integration and assimilation into existing social and political structures, it has increasingly sought to marginalize even demonize cross-generational love. Pederasty - that is, love between a man and a youth of 12 to 18 years of age - say middle-class homosexuals, lesbians, and feminists, has nothing to do with gay liberation. Some go so far as to claim, absurdly, that it is a heterosexual phenomenon, or even "sexual abuse." What a travesty![8]

Isn't it ironic that, just as gay activists accuse the non-affirming society of seeking to marginalize or demonize "same-sex love," so Thorstad accuses today's gay activists of seeking to marginalize or demonize "cross-generational love."

He continues:

Pederasty is the main form that male homosexuality has acquired throughout Western civilization - and not only in the West! Pederasty is inseparable from the high points of Western culture - ancient Greece and the Renaissance (my emphasis).

In Germany, in the late nineteenth century, pederasty was an integral part of the new gay movement. The first gay journal in the world - *Der Eigene*, published beginning in 1896 (one year before the formation of the first homosexual rights group, the Scientific Humanitarian Committee of Magnus Hirschfeld) - was a pederast and anarchist journal "for male culture" . . . .[9]

SPEAKING OF THE UNSPEAKABLE

Third, he argues that it is somewhat hypocritical to claim that homosexuality is inborn (or, at the least, formed in a child before the age of six) while at the same time restricting that child's sexual freedom and expression:

> One obvious contradiction in [this] position is that if homosexual identity is inborn, as they say, then why do they oppose freedom of sexual expression for minors? [They] argue that sexual identity is fixed by age six, but they deny young people the right to enjoy sexual pleasure with the person of their own choice. For them, "protection" is the key word, not "liberation"; they call on the state to "protect" young people from expressing and exploring their own sexual behavior. They want to "protect" young people from "dirty old men" (I, incidentally, am speaking as a "dirty [gay] old man" - something I take as a positive goal), but in reality are protecting them from themselves. They support criminalization of young people's sexuality, especially if it involves sex with an adult man. They condemn any adult who helps a young person to explore his or her sexuality. They are like parents - only worse, because they pretend to offer a guide to the gay future.[10]

Fourth, Thorstad claims that today's gay activism has severed its pederastic heritage for the sake of social acceptance:

> As middle-class gays become increasingly part of the mainstream, and turn their backs on the ideas that gave rise to and inspired their movement - and even on comrades who fought the heterosexual dictatorship before they themselves had come out - and as the ruling class steps up its efforts to control, police, and instill fear in the population, and as it passes laws criminalizing more and more things, and builds prisons at a breakneck pace to hold the millions it has criminalized (huge numbers of whom are imprisoned for consensual and harmless activity, such as possession of marijuana), life and survival for men and boys who love each other is becoming extremely dangerous. To

235

be an active pederast in the United States today is like being a Jew in Nazi Germany. The United States is becoming - perhaps already has become - a police state. The backlash against the increased visibility of homosexuality since the Stonewall Riots in 1969 is striking pederasts most severely. Thousands are currently in jail in the United States for purely consensual relationships, and the gay movement will not lift a finger or a voice in protest. . . .[11]

Did you catch that? "To be an active pederast in the United States today is like being a Jew in Nazi Germany." Really? I thought being an active *homosexual* in the United States today was like being a Jew in Nazi Germany? (For the record, both statements are immoral exaggerations, but once again, the irony of Thorstad's critique of today's politically correct gay activism can't be missed – or easily dismissed.)

Thus Thorstad says:

It is difficult to identify with a movement whose primary goals are to win official approval for gay marriage, gay families, and acceptance in the imperialist military. Homosexuals in the United States seem intent on demonstrating that they can be as conventional as heterosexuals. These days, I have to struggle with myself not to be antigay. . . .

In Minnesota, a highly respected and prominent gay man who has worked with youth for years in state-funded agencies was recently forced to leave his position when parents discovered that he had an 18-year-old boyfriend (hence, not even a minor). The gay movement has maintained a deafening silence about this.

. . . Ten or twenty years ago, the gay movement would have been a source of support for such relationships. Today, it is virtually indistinguishable from the heterosexist dictatorship itself.[12]

Finally, he argues that "Pederasty, like homosexuality, has existed, and exists, in all societies that have ever been studied." It cannot be stamped out, he claims, because it is based on irrepressible love:

Homoeroticism is a ubiquitous feature of human experience, as even efforts to repress it confirm. Men and youths have always been attracted to each other, and, like homosexuality in general, their love is irrepressible. Even if it is far from triumphing, or flowering with the freedom it merits and has enjoyed in some other cultures (for example, Siwa oasis in Egypt), still, it can never be repressed. It will continue to find its way to expression despite all the efforts to suppress and demonize it. As John Henry Mackay wrote in 1924 in *The Books of the Nameless Love*:

They murder our love and yet it lives.
They throttle our cry and it echoes back from the future.[13]

As repulsive as this stuff is, we have all heard similar arguments for homosexuality, including the calls for equality and justice, along with the mantra, "I have the right to marry the one I love!" In fact, the phrase "the love that dare not speak its name," which is commonly taken to refer to homosexuality, may have originally referred to pederasty (see below). And isn't it revealing that virtually all of the examples generally cited to support the existence of same-sex marriage in past and present cultures are actually examples of man-boy "marriages"?[14]

EIGHT PRIMARY ARGUMENTS FOR PEDERASTY (AND PEDOPHILIA)

Let's look at eight primary arguments for pederasty (and/or pedophilia), all from the pens or lips of trained academics:

1) Pedophilia is innate and immutable.
2) Pederasty is richly attested in many different cultures throughout history.
3) The claim that adult-child sexual relationships cause harm is greatly overstated and often completely inaccurate.
4) Consensual adult-child sex can actually be beneficial to the child.
5) Pederasty should not be classified as a mental disorder, since it does not cause distress to the pederast to have these desires and since the pederast can function as a normal,

contributing member of society.

6) Many of the illustrious homosexuals of the past were actually pedophiles.

7) People are against intergenerational intimacy because of antiquated social standards and puritanical sexual phobias.

8) This is all about love and equality and liberation.

1. Pedophilia is innate and immutable.

According to Prof. Gunter Schmidt in his article "The Dilemma of the Male Pedophile," published in *Archives of Sexual Behavior* 31 (2002),

> The [pedophile's] dilemma is tragic because the pedophile's sexual orientation is deeply rooted in the basic structure of his identity. Pedophilia is as much a part of him as is love for the same or opposite sex for the homosexual or heterosexual man or woman, the difference being that the one is accepted, while the other is categorically forbidden and virtually impossible to realize. In view of the pedophile's burden, the necessity of denying himself the experience of love and sexuality, he deserves respect, rather than contempt.[15]

Note carefully Prof. Schmidt's statement: "Pedophilia is as much a part of him as is love for the same or opposite sex for the homosexual or heterosexual man or woman." Now, let's substitute the word *homosexuality* for the word *pedophilia* and adjust this statement accordingly: "Homosexuality is as much a part of him as is love for the opposite sex for the heterosexual man or woman." Once again we must ask, What does this argument prove? The fact that Schmidt can argue that pedophilia is as ingrained and natural as heterosexuality or homosexuality underscores how weak the "born that way" argument is in terms of making a moral assessment of a sexual orientation or behavior. (See above, Chapter Six.)

As for the possibility of "curing" pedophilia, psychiatrist Fred Berlin explained:

> At one time, the majority of people you would ask would have felt it might be possible to cure pedophilia. Now, we look at it more the way we learned to look at alcoholism. We

can teach them ways not to succumb to these temptations. It's a very different view than a cure. This is an enduring vulnerability.[16]

Berlin also wrote that, "It may be no easier for a person with pedophilia to change his or her sexual orientation than it is for a homosexual or heterosexual individual to do so."[17] Similarly, Dr. Michael Seto opined that,

There is no evidence to suggest that pedophilia can be changed. Instead, interventions are designed to increase voluntary control over sexual arousal, reduce sex drive, or teach self-management skills to individuals who are motivated to avoid acting upon their sexual interests.[18]

Writing in the *Boston Globe* on the difficulty of finding a cure for pedophilia, Ellen Barry noted that

. . . the American Psychiatric Association warns that "unlike the successful treatment outcomes for other mental illnesses, the outlook for successful treatment of individuals with pedophilia is guarded." And when the clinical psychologist Maurice Yaffe sat down in 1981 to write about his experience treating pedophiles, he listed the cutting-edge approaches he and his colleagues were using, and then he added, with apparent despair, one "last consideration."

He said doctors could "recommend those whose motivation for change is minimal to move to an environment, e.g. parts of Morocco or Turkey, where legal and social constraints against non-coercive pedophiliac practices are less extreme than in our own society."[19]

How pathetic: The best advice that Dr. Yaffe could offer was to go to a country where pedophilia is accepted!

If you have read much literature on the alleged biological basis for homosexuality, then you have probably heard it mentioned that there is a clear connection between left-handedness and male homosexuality (in other words, there is a higher percentage of left-handed homosexuals than right-handed homosexuals).[20] A similar correlation has been found between left-

handedness and pedophilia:
Reporting on a 2005 study published in *Archives of Sexual Behavior*, Tom
Blackwell explained:

> A new Canadian study that found pedophiles have a strong
> tendency to be left-handed could help change decades of
> thinking about such sexual deviants -- and lead to new
> ways of combating the problem, says one of the researchers
> behind it.
> Most experts have theorized that pedophiles are
> motivated by psycho-social factors such as their early
> upbringing or sexual history, and treatment has responded
> accordingly.
> But the study published this month in *Archives of
> Sexual Behaviour* indicates there is a strong neurological
> factor, perhaps triggered by birth defects, that one day
> might be prevented.[21]

What is the offshoot of this discovery?

> The researchers at Toronto's Centre for Addiction and
> Mental Health now plan to peruse MRI images of
> pedophiles for signs of brain abnormalities.
> "For more than a century, we've been putting a great
> deal of energy and effort into one class of theories about
> pedophilia and essentially ignoring biological components,"
> said Dr. James Cantor, the study's lead author. "This is the
> first evidence that those theories can't be the whole story."
> Pedophiles present a formidable challenge to
> therapists, scientists and correctional authorities, with no
> evidence to date that their penchant for sex with children
> can ever be cured.[22]

Now, however, researchers are hopeful there could be some kind of cure –
but it would be medical, seeking to correct abnormalities in the brain:

> The latest findings suggest there is a neurological component
> in pedophiles that may interact with psycho-social factors

to distort their sexual behaviour, the study says.
The brain problem may have occurred while their mothers were pregnant, Dr. Cantor said.
"This is going to give us a clue as to what, in utero, went wrong. And this might be very helpful in preventing it in the first place," he said.[23]

What is remarkable is that when similar research on the possible biological causes of homosexuality has indicated that there could be *in utero* developments that contributed to one's homosexual orientation,[24] this is *not* viewed as a potential solution to a problem, since homosexuality is something to be celebrated and nurtured, not pitied or rejected. As for speaking of a "cure" for homosexuality, that is absolutely forbidden, even if it could be traced back to developmental abnormalities in the womb. After all, since homosexuality is deemed to be positive, nothing "in utero, went wrong."
Many other studies pointing to the alleged biological or genetic explanation for pedophilia could be cited,[25] but enough has been said to convey the point, and the double standard is stunning. As the line of reasoning goes:

- Homosexuality is right *because* it is innate; pedophilia is wrong *even if* it is innate.
- Homosexuality is right *because* it is immutable; pedophilia is wrong *even if* it is immutable.
- If would be *immoral* to look for a cure for homosexuality should a genetic or biological cause be found; it would be *moral* to look for a cure for pedophilia should a genetic or biological cause be found.
- It is *wrong* for society to judge homosexuals for following their natural, loving desires; it is *right* for society to judge pedophiles for following their natural, loving desires.

Ironically, when French Prime Minister Nicolas Sarkozy suggested that pedophilia might be genetic (while he was a candidate, in April 2007), there was an outcry:

Sarkozy made his comments in an issue of *Philosophie* magazine, where he said he was inclined to "think that people are born pedophiles, and that it is also a problem that we do not know how to manage." . . .

Bernard Golse, a child psychiatrist at Paris' Neckar hospital, said his comments reflected "a very linear, productive and falsely predictable way of using genetics" and it would be "scientifically baseless to launch a crusade based on the genetic aspects of pedophilia."

Archbishop of Paris, Andre Vingt-Trois said that his remarks were "purely ideological nonsense and completely out of touch with current scientific and genetic knowledge."

Gerard Schmidt, of the French College of Child psychiatry, warned against making predictions based upon an individual is genetic makeup same human brain continues to mature through to adolescence.[26]

So, in some circles, suggesting that pedophilia might be genetic is taboo (since, theoretically, it would remove moral responsibility?), while, on the other hand, when it comes to homosexuality, seeking to prove that it is genetic has been trendy for decades now. Fascinating!

2. Pederasty is richly attested in many different cultures throughout history

As summarized by psychiatrist Dr. Richard Green in his much-discussed article in *Archives of Sexual Behavior*,

Intimacy between generations is spread worldwide among so many cultures and in so many eras, that one cannot reasonably argue that all those people have a mental disorder. They may have different cultural customs and opinions. Additionally many primates have these kinds of customs.[27]

(Before getting into this point further, note that this was one of Green's arguments as to why pedophilia should not be classified as a mental disorder; see below, for more on this. Note also Green's statement that "many primates have these kinds of customs," once more providing a parallel for the gay argument that homosexuality is "natural" since it is common in the animal world.[28] So is pedophilia, says Dr. Green!)

Let's consider some additional quotes on the widespread, cross-cultural existence of pedophilia:

> The diversity of sexual behavior in a cross-cultural perspective is amazing to those who assume that their own society's moral standards are somehow laws of nature. Yet it is a fact that almost every sort of sexual activity ... has been considered normal and acceptable in some society at some time.... Man-boy relationships are no exception to this rule of diversity.... Although they are roundly condemned by many segments of Western society as inherently abusive and exploitive, there have been (and still are) many societies that do not share this viewpoint. (Bauserman, 1997, p. 120)[29]

Would you like to hear more? Then consider this:

> Ford and Beach (1951) described cross-cultural examples of child-adult sex from the Human Relation Area files at Yale University. Among the Siwans (Siwa Valley, North Africa), "All men and boys engage in anal intercourse. Males are singled out as peculiar if they did not do so. Prominent Siwan men lend their sons to each other for this purpose" (pp. 131-132). Among the Aranda aborigines (Central Australia), "Pederasty is a recognized custom.... Commonly a man, who is fully initiated but not yet married, takes a boy ten or twelve years old, who lives with him as his wife for several years, until the older man marries" (p. 132).[30]

Still not convinced? Well there's plenty more:

> Suggs (1966) studying Marquesan society, reported considerable childhood sexual behavior with adults (cited in Diamond, 1990). He reported many examples of heterosexual intercourse in public between adults and prepubertal children in Polynesia. The crews of visiting ships were typically involved and assisted by adult natives. Occasions were recorded of elders assisting youngsters in

having sex with other elders. In many cultures of Oceania, prepubertal females were publicly sexually active with adults (Oliver, 1974). In Tahiti, in 1832, the missionary Orsmond observed that "in all Tahitians as well as officers who come in ships there is a cry for little girls" (Oliver, 1974, pp. 458-459, cited in Diamond, 1990).[31]

And still more (all this is only a tiny sampling):

Among the Etoro of New Guinea, from about age 10 years, boys would have regular oral sex with older men, swallowing their semen to facilitate growth (Bauserman, 1997). Among the neighboring Kaluli, when a boy reached age 10 or 11, his father would select a man to inseminate him for a period of months to years. In addition, ceremonial hunting lodges would be organized where boys could voluntarily form relationships with men who would have sexual relations with them (Bauserman, 1997).[32]

Are you willing to accept pederasty because it is found in many cultures around the world? I don't think so! Then why should you accept homosexual practice because it is found in many cultures around the world?

3. The claim that adult-child sexual relationships cause harm is greatly overstated and often completely inaccurate.

This was the conclusion of a meta-analytical study of the APA in 1998, a study that was deemed to be so off-base that it drew a sharp rebuke from Congress (to the astonishment of many APA leaders, showing just how out of touch they were with societal mores).

Matthew Cullinan Hoffman tells the story:

In 1998, the APA released a study by three psychological researchers from Temple University, the University of Pennsylvania, and the University of Michigan, claiming that the "negative potential" of adult sex with children was "overstated" and that "the vast majority of both men and women reported no negative sexual effects from their child sexual abuse experiences." It even claimed that large numbers of the victims reported that their experiences were "positive," and suggested that the phrase "child sex abuse" be replaced with "adult-child sex."[33]

So, university-based psychological researchers concluded that adult-child sex was often positive for the children involved. What did their peers in the APA think of the results of their research? They approved it and defended it!

The APA not only passed the paper through its peer review process where it was approved by multiple psychologists associated with the organization, but actually published it in one of its journals, Psychological Bulletin. Moreover, when objections were raised by radio talk show host Dr. Laura Schlessinger and various pro-family groups, the organization defended the article for an entire year. It was also defended by the American Association for the Advancement of Science, which chillingly stated that it "saw no clear evidence of improper application of methodology or other questionable practices on the part of the article's authors."[34]

Psychologists defending pedophilia? Absolutely. Hoffman continues:

Although the sheer insanity and destructiveness of the content should have prevented the APA from publishing the article in the first place, the sexual libertines in charge of the organization only issued a muted retraction after the U.S. Congress joined the fray, passing an unprecedented resolution condemning the study.[35]

But there's more:

The publication of the paper was only one example of such lunacy by mental health professionals in peer-reviewed journals. One of the three authors of the study, Robert Bauserman, has a history of publishing pedophilia-advocacy "studies," including one for the now-defunct journal *Paidika, The Journal of Paedophilia,* whose editors admitted to being pedophiles.

Since the 1998 article, Bauserman and fellow author Bruce Rind have gone on to write more articles defending child sex abuse, which have appeared in such mainstream journals as the *Archives of Sexual Behavior* (2001) and *Clinical Psychology* (2003). Apparently, the psychology profession is comfortable with Bauserman and Rind's work, and intends to continue publishing it.[36]

Is it so far-fetched to imagine that one day, just as homosexuality is becoming increasingly accepted in America, the same could happen with pedophilia? Why not? After all, it was accepted in ancient cultures like Greece, and it is accepted in some cultures today (see above, #2). And, just as psychologists and psychiatrists argued for the normalization of homosexuality more than thirty-five years ago, some are arguing for the normalization of pedophilia today. Stranger – or should I say queerer? – things have happened, have they not?

Some researchers even argue that consensual pedophilia is not only *not* harmful, it is actually highly *beneficial* to the child or adolescent involved, which leads us to the next point.

4. Consensual adult-child sex can actually be beneficial to the child.

Louis Berman, Emeritus Professor of Psychology at the University of Illinois at Chicago, writes:

It is not unusual for a pedophile to claim that his boy has benefited from their relationship. . . . When man-boy love advocates claim that their boy lovers enjoy a net benefit from their relationship, in some cases they are probably correct.

Homosexual pedophiles probably depend significantly on neglected boys, delinquents and runaways. The Dutch lawyer Edward Brongersma wrote an article sympathetic to man-boy love. He cites (page 160) a report (Rossman, 1976) that "gives several examples of social workers achieving miracles with apparently incorrigible young delinquents – not by preaching to them, but by sleeping with them. Affection demonstrated by sexual arousal upon contact with the boy's body, by obvious pleasure taken in giving pleasure to the boy, did far more good than years in reformatories." Brongersma (page 160) tells of an Amsterdam juvenile judge who in a public speech "openly advocated this form of social therapy." This is a sample of the persuasive case that man-boy lovers make to support their position.[37]

The claim has even been made that, "Only he who is a good pederast can be a perfect pedagogue."[38]

Richard Green also noted that:

> Diamond (1990) reviewed child-adult sex in Hawaiian history and Polynesia. In the eighteenth century, Cook (1773) reported copulation in public in Hawaii between an adult male and a female estimated to be 11 or 12 "without the least sense of it being indecent or improper" (cited in Diamond, 1990). *Sexual interactions between adult and child were seen as benefitting the child, rather than as gratifying the adult* [my emphasis]. The sexual desire by an adult for a nonadult, heterosexual or homosexual, was accepted (Pukui, Haertig, & Lee, 1972, cited in Diamond, 1990).[39]

Psychology professor Bruce Rind (Temple University) provided five case studies that, he asserted, supported this claim (I'll cite just two here, as terribly distasteful as this is):

> Case 2. James, a 23-year-old Canadian, first felt sexually aroused by other males at age 6 and had his first sex at 8 with a peer. At 11, he befriended a neighbor man, to whom he gave many signals, hoping for sex to occur. Eventually, it did, which made him feel proud and closer to the man. Over the next 3 years, he visited the man regularly, often secretly to avoid the possibility of his parents ending the relationship. He saw the relationship as very positive and said it built his personality (e.g., greater self-confidence)

and influenced many of his tastes (e.g., an appreciation for literature).

Case 3. Daniel, a 33-year-old Frenchman, was physically affectionate with his father starting at age 6. By 8, he became sexually attracted to him. At 10, he initiated sexual fondling with him, which the father accepted. In the sexual relationship, which lasted 4 years, Daniel always initiated the sex. In retrospect, he cherished the intimacy and described the relationship as "beautiful, pure, security, confidence, and love." He said it built his sexual self-confidence.[40]

So, the advocate of pederasty turns to the advocate of homosexuality and says, "Not only are both sexual practices innate and immutable, but in the right setting (including an incestual setting!), both are beautiful, beneficial, and non-abusive."[41] (The pederast would also be quick to point out that there are plenty of abusive homosexual relationships, just as there are plenty of abusive pederastic relationships.) Enough said. It's painful enough just to read this, let alone to realize that some people actually believe this, and, worse still, practice it.

5. Pederasty should not be classified as a mental disorder, since it does not cause distress to the pederast to have these desires and since the pederast can function as a normal, contributing member of society.

Three of the main reasons that the APA declassified homosexuality as a mental disorder in 1973 were: 1) Homosexuals were, in other respects, mentally normal; 2) they were able to function normally in society; and 3) they were not internally troubled by their same-sex attraction. Since that time, some of the same psychiatric leaders who raised these arguments in favor of normalizing homosexuality have raised them in favor of normalizing pederasty. The same logic holds true in both cases, not to mention the argument that the pervasive, cross-cultural existence of pedophilia is also raised frequently as a proof against pederasty being considered a mental disorder. (Remember: The issue here is *not* whether man-boy "love" should be accepted by society; the issue is whether it is right to classify pedophilia as a mental illness.)

After citing a number of examples of pedophile practice in other cultures, Richard Green stated:

> These cross-cultural examples are not cited to argue for similar practices in Los Angeles or London. But are we to conclude that all the adults engaged in these practices were mentally ill? If arguably they were not pedophiles, but following cultural or religious tradition, why is frequent sex with a child not a mental illness under those circumstances?
>
> For skeptics of the relevance of these cited exotic examples, for three centuries the age of sexual consent in England was 10. This was not in some loin cloth clad tribe living on the side of a volcano, but the nation that for six centuries was already graduating students from Oxford and Cambridge. Further, the time when age of consent was 10 was not in a period contemporaneous with Cromagnon Man, but continued to within 38 years of World War I. The impetus to raise the age of sexual consent in England from 10 years was fueled not by an outrage over pedophilia per se but concerns over child prostitution. Changes in employment law during the nineteenth century were protecting children from long hours of factory labor, leaving them more accessible for sexual service as the only means of support. Child prostitution was rampant (Bullough, 1990). Were all customers pedophiles? Were they all mentally ill? . . .[42]

Speaking of the treatment of pedophilia in the APA's DSM (Diagnostic and Statistical Manual, the "Bible" of psychiatry; see below, Chapter Thirteen), Green claimed that:

> The evolution of pedophilia in the different editions of DSM is a trip through Alice's Wonderland. . . .
>
> The APA position with its DSM catalogue is logically incoherent. Confronted with the paradox that in contrast to other conditions designated a mental disorder, such as with persons who hand wash to the point of bleeding and can't touch a door knob, or who are harassed by voices

threatening their personal destruction, many pedophiles are not distressed by their erotic interest, aside from the fear of incarceration. Some celebrate their interests, organize politically, and publish magazines or books. So to deal with this paradox, DSM dug itself deep into a logical ditch. If a person's erotic fantasies are primarily of children and masturbatory imagined partners are children, that person does not have a mental illness, without more. Never mind these mental processes, those readers of DSM who are psychiatrists and treaters of the disordered mind. These people with these fantasies do not have a mental disease unless that person translates thought into action. This turns psychiatry on its head. Certainly a society can set rules on sexual conduct and proscribe child-adult sex and invoke sanctions for transgressors. But that is the province of the law and the penal system. The DSM should not provide psychiatry with jurisdiction over an act any more than it should provide the law with jurisdiction over a thought.[43]

Writing in 1983, G. D. Wilson and D. N. Cox concluded that:

... the most striking thing about these results is how normal the paedophiles appear to be according to their scores on these major personality dimensions - particularly the two that are clinically relevant [neuroticism and psychoticism]. ... introversion ... in itself is not usually thought of as pathological.[44]

Writing in 1998, D. Howitt, reached a similar conclusion:

The possibility of finding a simple personality profile that differentiates pedophiles from other men has appeared increasingly unrealistic as the research and clinical base has widened. Simplistic notions such as social inadequacy driving men to sex with children become unviable as highly socially skilled pedophiles are found.[45]

Or, put another way:

Another argument for the normality of pedophilic feelings are the percentages of 'normal people' who are said to feel attracted to children (about 20 to 25%), and who react with penile erection to 'pedophilic' stimuli: more then [sic] 25%. One cannot reasonably argue that about one quarter of the population is mentally ill.[46]

As summed up by Green:

Sexual arousal patterns to children are subjectively reported and physiologically demonstrable in a substantial minority of "normal" people. Historically, they have been common and accepted in varying cultures at varying times.

This does not mean that they must be accepted culturally and legally today. The question is: Do they constitute a mental illness? Not unless we declare a lot of people in many cultures and in much of the past to be mentally ill. And certainly not by the criteria of DSM.[47]

There you have it. Pedophilia should no more be classified as a mental illness than should homosexuality – and this, according to some of the same people who advocated for the removal of homosexuality as a mental illness almost forty years ago. As Green noted (in 2002):

Nearly 30 years ago, I was embroiled in the historic battle within the American Psychiatric Association (APA) over whether homosexuality per se was rightfully deemed a mental illness, as included in the second edition of the Diagnostic and Statistical Manual of Mental Disorders (DSM-II; American Psychiatric Association, 1968). During the controversy, several topics were examined: historical and cross-cultural groundings in homosexual expression, associated psychiatric features accompanying a homosexual orientation, the emotional consequences to the homosexual of societal condemnation, and behaviors of other species. I argued vigorously for removal of homosexuality from the DSM (Green, 1972; see also Stoller, 1973). The Task Force on Nomenclature and Statistics voted to delete homosexuality. . .

For years now, Green and others have been arguing vigorously for the removal of pedophilia (and other "paraphilias") from the DSM. (Paraphilias refer to "referring to "complex psychiatric disorders that are manifested as deviant sexual behavior.")[48] And what happens if they succeed? One of the biggest arguments used by gay activists since 1973, namely, that the APA (and others following in their footsteps) declassified homosexuality as a mental illness, thereby legitimizing homosexual practice, will become virtually meaningless. Perhaps it could even open the door to groups like pederasts claiming legal status as a protected class.[49]

How revealing it is that Dr. Robert Spitzer, famed as one of the key men involved in the removal of homosexuality from the DSM in 1973, observed that a major reason that these paraphilias are not removed from the DSM is because "it would be a public relations disaster for psychiatry."[50] Perhaps it would simply underscore how little stock should be put into the APA's removal of homosexuality from the DSM in 1973.

Gay psychiatrist and activist Dr. Jack Drescher related that:

Following the 1973 decision, cultural attitudes about homosexuality shifted slowly in the US and elsewhere. A new perspective emerged in western societies: (1) if homosexuality is not an illness, and (2) if one does not literally accept biblical prohibitions against homosexuality, and (3) if gay people are able and prepared to function as productive citizens, what is wrong with being gay? Gradually, what had once been a secular view of homosexuality as pathological was replaced by the belief that it was a normal variant of sexual expression.[51]

Defenders of pedophilia are hoping that the same societal shifts and the same "scientific" arguments will hold sway for them too. (Why not repeat the same exercise we tried earlier in the chapter and substitute "pedophilia" for "homosexuality" and "pedophiles" for "gay people" in Drescher's comments? To restate Drescher's rhetorical question, "What is wrong with being a pedophile?" Isn't it just a "normal variant of sexual expression"?)[52]

Writing in support of Richard Green's arguments, cited above, Charles Moser (Ph.D., M.D.) of the Institute for Advanced Study of Human

SPEAKING OF THE UNSPEAKABLE

Sexuality stated:

> The assumption that certain strong, sexual interests are
> mental disorders has pervaded the DSM since its inception
> and has been promulgated from edition to edition without
> serious review. I ask the obvious questions: Are any of the
> paraphilias mental disorders? Do the paraphilias meet the
> DSM definition of a mental disorder? Are there data to
> support the inclusion of any paraphilia diagnosis in the
> DSM? Do we need to argue separately about the removal
> of each paraphilia from the DSM? I believe the answers to
> all these questions is "No!"[53]

Although many more similar statements could be cited,[54] enough has
been said to make the point, namely, that "The situation of the paraphilias
at present" – meaning, the attempt to remove all paraphilias from the DSM
as mental disorders – "parallels that of homosexuality in the early 1970's."[55]

6. Many of the illustrious homosexuals of the past were actually pedophiles.

We saw in Chapter Three, above, that one of the educational strategies
of GLSEN (the Gay, Lesbian, and Straight Educational Network) was to
have children learn that many famous people from the past were actually
gay or lesbian. This would further remove the stigma of being gay. After
all, if powerful leaders like Alexander the Great or influential artists like
Michelangelo were gay, then obviously there's nothing wrong with being gay.
In fact, being gay may be part of someone's greatness!

As advocated in 1987 by Marshall Kirk and Erastes Pill (the pseudonym
for Hunter Madsen), in their oft-quoted article "The Overhauling of Straight
America,"

> In order to make a Gay Victim sympathetic to straights you
> have to portray him as Everyman. But an additional theme
> of the campaign should be more aggressive and upbeat:
> to offset the increasingly bad press that these times have
> brought to homosexual men and women, the campaign
> should paint gays as superior pillars of society. Yes, yes, we
> know--this trick is so old it creaks. Other minorities use it

all the time in ads that announce proudly, "Did you know that this Great Man (or Woman) was _____?" But the message is vital for all those straights who still picture gays as "queer" people-- shadowy, lonesome, fail, drunken, suicidal, child- snatching misfits.

The honor roll of prominent gay or bisexual men and women is truly eyepopping. From Socrates to Shakespeare, from Alexander the Great to Alexander Hamilton, from Michelangelo to Walt Whitman, from Sappho to Gertrude Stein, the list is old hat to us but shocking news to heterosexual America. In no time, a skillful and clever media campaign could have the gay community looking like the veritable fairy godmother to Western Civilization.[56]

Aside from the fact that it is highly dubious to make the claim that, e.g., Abraham Lincoln was gay, as GLSEN and other gay activists do,[57] there is actually evidence that some of these famous people who were gay were also (or, primarily) pederasts. That is something you will *not* learn at school (at least, not yet).

In Chapter Three, I cited Jim Kepner, formerly curator of the International Gay and Lesbian Archives in Los Angeles, who wrote:

> if we reject the boylovers in our midst today we'd better stop waving the banner of the Ancient Greeks, of Michelangelo, Leonardo da Vinci, Oscar Wilde, Walt Whitman, Horatio Alger, and Shakespeare. We'd better stop claiming them as part of our heritage unless we are broadening our concept of what it means to be gay today.[58]

Although it's convenient to sweep these words under the rug, they won't go away that easily, since some the stories are quite well known.

The case of Oscar Wilde is especially relevant, since it was he who explained that "the love that dare not speak its name" was not specifically homosexuality – although that is what the phrase is normally taken to mean – but rather pederasty:

> In April 1895 Wilde was brought to court charged with indecency and sodomy. Charles Gill, a schoolmate of

Wilde's and the prosecutor in the case, asked him "What is the love that dare not speak its name?" Wilde's impromptu response was:

> "The Love that dare not speak its name" in this century is such a great affection of an elder for a younger man as there was between David and Jonathan, such as Plato made the very basis of his philosophy, and such as you find in the sonnets of Michelangelo and Shakespeare. It is that deep, spiritual affection that is as pure as it is perfect. It dictates and pervades great works of art like those of Shakespeare and Michelangelo, and those two letters of mine, such as they are. It is in this century misunderstood, so much misunderstood that it may be described as the "Love that dare not speak its name," and on account of it I am placed where I am now. It is beautiful, it is fine, it is the noblest form of affection. There is nothing unnatural about it. It is intellectual, and it repeatedly exists between an elder and a younger man, when the elder man has intellect, and the younger man has all the joy, hope and glamour of life before him. That it should be so, the world does not understand. The world mocks at it and sometimes puts one in the pillory for it."[59]

Accounts of Wilde's sexual preferences and promiscuity are quite disturbing (including his claim that he had sex with five different boys in one night),[60] yet he and other "man-boy lovers" are hailed by gay activists who point to them as stellar examples of famous gays.[61] This exposes yet again the hypocrisy and double standard of gay activism which distances itself from its often-pederastic past while at the same time claiming these pederastic practitioners to buttress their cause.

The notorious NAMBLA's of this world (NAMBLA stands for the North American Man Boy Love Association) have a stronger claim to some of these past pederastic luminaries than do the "mainstream" gay activist organizations.[62] And this reveals another, sad reality: In both the distant and recent past, homosexual practice often included (or even prominently featured) "man-boy love." And while the vast majority of homosexuals would renounce pedophilia today, finding the practice just as repulsive and abusive as the vast majority of heterosexuals do, in some gay circles, it remains as prominent as ever.

In any case, I don't see gay activists lining up to disassociate themselves from some of their favorite gays of the past, despite their troublesome orientation. Why not? And why is an open pedophile like Allen Ginsberg – a member and defender of NAMBLA – hailed as an icon in GLBT circles to this day?[63] And why did gay activists lobby successfully for an annual Harvey Milk Day to be instituted in California schools, in memory of the now almost-sainted, murdered gay political pioneer, despite the fact that his well-documented homosexual encounters with older men began when he was just eleven years-old?

As noted by gay author Randy Shilts, at age eleven, Milk began attending performances of the New York Metropolitan Opera where he met with "wandering hands," and soon was engaged in "brief trysts [with grown men] after the performances." While still in junior high, he "dove headfirst into the newly discovered subculture," and by the age of fourteen, Milk was "leading an active homosexual life." And as he grew older, the pattern reversed itself to the point that, at age thirty-three, Milk hooked up with a sixteen-year-old named Jack McKinley, one of a number of younger men with whom he was intimate.[64] Why then is there only gay praise for Harvey Milk? Where is the denunciation of his pederasty?

And where is the gay denunciation of Harry Hay, widely considered to be the founder of America's gay liberation movement, when Hay's defense of NAMBLA is well known? Most famously, when a gay pride parade in Los Angeles banned NAMBLA from participating (one major reason being that it was politically incorrect to associate with them), Hay decided to march in the parade carrying a sign that said, "NAMBLA walks with me."[65] Do I need to connect all the dots?

The bottom line is this: If we agree that the pederasty of men like Oscar Wilde or Walt Whitman in no way validates or legitimizes pederasty then we should recognize that the homosexuality of other past luminaries in no way validates or legitimizes homosexuality. Gay activists can't have it both ways.

7. People are against intergenerational intimacy because of antiquated social standards and puritanical sexual phobias.

The late Vern L. Bullough was the SUNY Distinguished Professor and

Dean of Natural and Social Sciences at SUNY College at Buffalo and the recipient of many academic awards. A married heterosexual with children, he fought for civil and sexual liberties, including consensual pedophilia. Not surprisingly, he commended *Paidikia: The Journal of Paedophilia* when it came out in 1987, stating that "underlying the editorial policy of the Journal is an emphasis on the helpful rather than the harmful aspects of what the editors define as consensual intergenerational sexual relationships."[66] When reviewing *Paidikia*, he made special mention of an article entitled, "The Hysteria over Child Pornography and Paedophilia," written by Lawrence A. Stanley, a New York attorney. Bullough claimed that the article served as "an effective antidote to much of the hysteria about child pornography that still prevails in the United States."[67]

Put another way, we Americans would not be so "hysterical" over child pornography and pedophilia if we weren't so embarrassingly puritanical. If only we could outgrow our outdated moral strictures and our primitive prudishness! How desperately we need to be enlightened. (I remind you that I'm simply echoing the sentiments of a distinguished university professor who was upset over American attitudes.)

Bullough also wrote an introduction to *Loving Boys: A Multidisciplinary Study of Sexual Relations Between Adult and Minor Males*, by Dr. Edward Brongersma, who died in 1998. Remarkably, Brongersma was both a Dutch parliamentarian and a pedophile – by which I mean he was an *open* pedophile. For sexual libertarians, this was a tribute to the enlightened condition of the Netherlands. Where else could a known pedophile be knighted? (Brongersma was knighted into the Order of the Dutch Lion in 1975.)[68]

Professor Ken Plummer (University of Essex, England) wrote a positive review of *Loving Boys*, calling it an "extremely valuable source book." He relates:

I first became aware of [Brongersma] when the (now defunct) English paedophile group Paedophile Information Exchange tried to arrange a meeting at which this senior Dutch parliamentarian . . . was to speak. The meeting was boycotted by the media, and ultimately cancelled. Brongersma could not speak and was shocked by the puritanical moralism of the British.

Those dastardly Brits! What were they thinking? Plummer, himself a

British professor, continues:

> In Holland the climate seems much freer – free enough for
> a senior and respected figure to be an 'out' paedophile. With
> his extensive knowledge, he makes an ideal advocate.[69]

So that is what we need: a "freer" climate that would enable a man to
be both a highly esteemed public figure and an out-of-the-closet pedophile.

And let there be no doubt about some of the contents of *Loving Boys*.
According to Brongersma:

> . . . a boy is mature for lust, for hedonistic sex, from his
> birth on; sex as an expression of love becomes a possibility
> from about five years of age; puberty is the best time for
> "oceanic," the mystic experience and for using sex to unite
> one with nature. Procreation should be the privilege of the
> adult man.[70]

If reading this trash makes you want to vomit, it's obvious that you too are
a puritanical prune, a sexually-repressed, morally-backward, unenlightened
troll, unable to move beyond the limitations of your fundamentalist culture.
At least that's what the Edward Brongersmas of this world would say.

But this kind of moral indignation – *by* pedophiles and their defenders,
not *against* them – is quite common. In his introduction to Dr. Theo Sandfort's
book, *Boys on Their Contacts with Men*, Prof. John Money wrote:

> For those born and educated after the year 2000, we will
> be their history, and they will be mystified by our self-
> imposed, moralistic ignorance of the principles of sexual
> and erotic development in childhood. We who are today
> presiding over the demise of the twentieth century are
> defiantly proud of our ability to deny that sexual health
> has a developmental history that, like every other aspect
> of healthy functioning in adolescence and maturity, begins
> in childhood. We safeguard ourselves against evidence to
> the contrary by failing to fund basic pediatric sexological
> research, and by repudiating the findings of those who fund
> themselves.[71]

So, we who reject "man-boy love" are simply safeguarding ourselves against the evidence that challenges our worldviews. Why else would sensible people object to "sexually expressed friendships" between boys and men? Surely we could learn a lesson from the Netherlands here, since it was the Dutch government that largely funded the study of Dr. Sandfort. (He was at that time a professor at the University of Utrecht.)

The bottom line is that, according to Drs. Bullough and Brongersma and Money and Sandfort, it is our puritanical biases that are stopping us from appreciating and embracing consensual "intergenerational intimacy." We have been blinded by our bigotry! (Does this sound familiar?)

Sandfort wrote approvingly of the attitudes toward pedophilia in Holland in the late 1970's (before the country took a step back in the 1980's):

> Toward the end of the 1970s many Dutch newspapers, news and family magazines carried relatively positive articles about "pedophilia"--positive in the sense that an attempt was made in them to understand how both partners involved in pedophile relationships felt. At the same time, however, they invariably stressed the adverse judgement of society at large. During those years even incest received attention which was not altogether critical: in 1969 the magazine of the national homophile organization COC1 carried an article entitled *Why not go to bed with your son?* (Andriesse 1969).[72]

He adds:

> The so-called sexual revolution was a phenomenon of the late 1960s. Influenced by the democratization process, a great deal of stress was then placed upon human self-fulfillment, and the positive view of pedophilia at the end of the 1970s can be seen as a by-product. Why, it was then asked, should pedophiles, just as other humans with deviant sexual preferences, not have the right to express their sexual desires? The real culprit was the social system which stood in the way of sexual fulfillment. Children, too, had to suffer under social repression. Marcuse the philosopher was an important source of such ideas.[73]

Sandfort, who is now a professor at New York's Columbia University, has made himself absolutely clear. On the heels of the sexual revolution of the late 1960's, this question was quite logical: "Why . . . should pedophiles, just as other humans with deviant sexual preferences, not have the right to express their sexual desires?" There was only one thing that prevented the full expression of this liberated sexuality. "The real culprit was the social system which stood in the way of sexual fulfillment."

And nowhere was this antiquated social system more prevalent than in the United States. To Sandfort's dismay, this moralistic American mindset made its way to the Netherlands in 1985. It was at that time that the accusation was made by the American government that most child pornography was exported from the Netherlands and Denmark. According to Sandfort, this accusation was

> born out of a religious/ethical revival movement in North America which has attracted a great deal of attention. It holds that the traditional family must be restored to its dominating position of honor and young people should be protected through censorship of books and pictures from everything that might corrupt them. Abortion is unacceptable and homosexuality can only be viewed as a sickness which is not without many social dangers. The actual "victims" of child pornography, then, were not the only concerns of United States religious fundamentalists and social workers.[74]

There you have it. American opposition to abortion, homosexuality, and child pornography is based on a terribly archaic notion that "the traditional family must be restored to its dominating position of honor." In reality, the only thing that makes pedophilia repulsive is our American puritanical hang-ups.

But haven't we been told the exact same thing when it comes to our attitude towards homosexual practice? If we find ourselves repulsed by the idea of a man having sex with another man we are scolded for being backwards and unenlightened and told that we really don't understand. After all, it's all about love, and it's all quite "natural" too. (To repeat the common mantras yet again: I was born this way; I can't change my orientation; homosexuality is found in the animal kingdom too; homosexuality is found across cultures;

many great figures of the past and present have been gay; homosexual love is beautiful – in other words, the exact same arguments used by pedophiles!)

And those of us who, for many strong and logically rational reasons, affirm that marriage is the union of a man and a woman have been likened by gay activists to Adolph Hitler, labeled Nazis, Jihadists, Taliban, homophobic hate mongers, and the worst kind of bigots, with some gay extremists even calling for our deaths.[75]

Just a few years ago, the idea of same-sex "marriage" was as farfetched (even among most gays) as the idea of human-alien marriage, and the fact that marriage referred to the union of a man and a woman was taken for granted as much as the fact that babies were not delivered on doorsteps by storks. Today, however, you will become the target of all kinds of harassment just for affirming natural (meaning, male-female) marriage.

The parallels here are quite disturbing, and it is not a big stretch at all to say that a society that could celebrate homosexuality after centuries of rejecting it could one day embrace consensual pedophilia as well. After all, it's just a matter of enlightenment and social progress, right? We must move beyond our hopeless provincialism and embrace true sexual liberation in all its many and diverse forms. Isn't that the case? According to Dr. Richard Gardner, who served as the Clinical Professor of Psychiatry at Columbia University for forty years (1963-2003), the answer is emphatically yes, even offering this counsel:

> Older children may be helped to appreciate that sexual encounters between an adult and a child are not universally considered to be reprehensible acts. The child might be told about other societies in which such behavior was and is considered normal. In such discussions the child has to be helped to appreciate that we have in our society an exaggeratedly punitive and moralistic attitude about adult-child sexual encounters.[76]

In other words, "Hey kids, don't feel bad about that sexual encounter with an adult. Not everyone is as hung up as these old-fashioned Americans, and in lots of other cultures, man-boy love is perfectly acceptable." In point of fact, "Gardner blamed the oppressive morality of the Bible for the American view of pedophilia,"[77] even claiming that, "It is of interest that of all the ancient peoples it may very well be that the Jews were the only ones who were punitive toward pedophiles."[78] It's those Jews again!

At this point, let me offer a word of free (and unsolicited) advice: The next time you feel societal pressure to compromise your moral convictions and embrace homosexual practice lest you be branded a bigot and a homophobe, remember the enlightened Netherlands, the country that knighted and elected to parliament an openly practicing pedophile.[79]

8. This is all about love and equality and liberation.

On February 29th, 2008, Dave Rattigan posted an article on ExGayWatch. com entitled, "On Pedophilia, Hedonism & Impending Confusion: Revisiting the Anti-Gay Rhetoric of Michael Brown."[80] According to Rattigan:

> Pentecostal leader Michael Brown continues to throw homosexuality into the mix with an array of exotic sexual fetishes, including pedophilia, zoophilia and coprophilia, sexual arousal from human feces. . . .
>
> His contention amounts to the claim that nothing distinguishes homosexuality morally from any other sexual practice, no matter how bizarre or offensive.[81]

Rattigan was referring to comments I had made in a radio interview with Concerned Women for America, namely, that just because someone has a certain sexual orientation, it does not therefore follow that the particular orientation is right or wholesome or morally acceptable. (I have made this argument elsewhere in this book, especially Chapter Six, above, as well as in this chapter.) Thus, in Rattigan's mind, I am saying that there is "**No moral line between homosexuality and pedophilia.**"

> Broadening the definition of "orientation" as widely as possible, Brown asks:
> Are all sexual orientations gifts from God? Zoophilia, or coprophilia, the sexual stimulation by faeces, or bestiality, I mean things that everyone would be repulsed by, or paedophilia. Are those gifts from God? ... How do you distinguish which sexual orientation is a gift from God and which is not?[82]

To be sure, I was not attempting to broaden "the definition of 'orientation' as widely as possible." I was simply pointing out that "sexual orientation" can refer to more than heterosexuality, homosexuality, or bisexuality.[83] But that is to quibble. Rattigan's issue with my position was much deeper.

He quoted another excerpt from the interview in which I said:

> Really, there's no line between saying this is a gift from God and saying pedophilia's a gift from God. Not to put the two in the same class, but to say, how do you reject anything morally any more? If I like it, if I feel good about it, it's all about me.

In response, Rattigan wrote:

> Love? Respect? Fulfilment? Capacity to help and not harm? Abuse? Consent or lack of it? Ultimately, however, maybe these things are side issues to those whose morality is tied only to the authority of a single interpretation of a single holy book.

My position was then encapsulated in this quote under the heading "Misrepresenting gay morality."

> If I like it, if I feel good about it, it's all about me. … [It's the] Will and Grace culture and the culture of If-I-feel-good-about-it-then-it's-good.

To this Rattigan opined:

> And there you have Brown's slanderous assessment of the morality of gays and lesbians: If it feels good, do it. In other words, gays are hedonists: they have no moral compass other than their own sense of pleasure. This is an outrageous accusation, but unfortunately a ubiquitous one.[84]

Of course, the attitude of "If-I-feel-good-about-it-then-it's-good" is pervasive in our culture among straights and gays alike, a subject I have often addressed in heterosexual circles.[85] Hedonism is alive and well in America today! For Rattigan, however, my claim that homosexuality says, "If I feel good, I'll do it" was "an outrageous accusation."

To be sure, I understand that issues like "love" and "respect" and "fulfillment" are relevant in many gay relationships just as they are in many straight relationships, but the reason that a homosexual person is *not* heterosexual is because to the core of that person's being, he or she feels homosexual. "*I* have these feelings. *I* find fulfillment in this relationship. *I* cannot be true to *myself* in a heterosexual relationship." And that was my whole point: It's all about me – my feelings; my desires; my orientation – to the point that when someone brings a moral or social objection to homosexuality, the response is: "But what about *my* feelings? What about *my* right to be with the one *I* love?"

Rattigan writes:

> In the discussions here and elsewhere, Brown continually argued that we as gays had no moral basis for distinguishing between homosexuality and other (supposedly) non-traditional sexual practices. On the contrary, how about the following as a list of questions I, as a gay person with a moral compass, might ask about my own sexual behaviour:
>
> - Is it loving?
> - Is it consensual?
> - Is it respectful?
> - Is it giving or selfish?
> - Is it mutually beneficial and fulfilling or abusive and unequal?
> - Does it dignify or degrade me and others as human beings?
> - Does it help or hinder me in becoming a better person?
>
> Is there something immoral in that preliminary list of criteria? Is there something lacking (other than that it might not match up to a particular religious viewpoint)? Is it any more or less moral than any other set of criteria? Does it have *anything* to do with Brown's woeful caricature of gay morality as "if it feels good do it"? (If that were really the basis of my morality, at this moment I'd be out doing a hundred more exciting things than sitting here writing this

article, believe me!)[86]

To be candid, I'm not convinced that a lot of gay male activity fulfills this criteria (think of anonymous sexual encounters in bathhouses as one glaring example, a phenomenon virtually unknown in the heterosexual world).[87] But let's just say that the bulk of gay sexuality does fulfill this list. That only illustrates the point I am making: The pedophile involved in consensual relationships with a young person affirms this exact same list. Not only so, but pedophiles will approvingly cite many testimonies from their consensual child/adolescent partners, with the young people affirming this same list too, not only as children, but later, looking back, as adults.

I cited some examples of positive adult reflections on previous childhood sexual experiences above. These adults recall their childhood relationships with older men as liberating and beneficial. Pedophile literature also cites the testimonies of children – while still children – who share these same perspectives.

NAMBLA published a book entitled *Boys Speak Out on Man/Boy Love*.[88] A sampling of the Table of Contents says it all:

Love & Loyalty

The Best Thing That Ever Happened to Me	Greg, age 16
I Love Him, and I Know That He Loves Me	Darrel, age 16
It Shouldn't Be a Crime to Make Love	Bryan, age 12 1/2
Boys Help Men, Too	"College Boy", age 19
I'm Not Going To Be Kept Away from Him	Thijs, age 11

Friendship & Fun

He Listens to Me, Unlike Most People	Robert, age 16
Sex Is Really Beautiful with My Friend	Dennis, age 13
The Beach	Luis Miguelito, age 13
Such a Relationship Is Very Beneficial	Dan, age 19
Man, What a Feeling!	Eric, age 14
Because I Enjoy It (An Interview)	Theo, age 13

Respect & Support
If It Wasn't for Mark I'd Probably
Be Dead Today   Carl, age 14

Loneliness   Mark, age 13
He Makes Me Glad I'm Gay   Ed, age 14
I've Learned So Much from Barend
(An Interview)   Gerrit, age 16

Consent
Thank God for Boy-Lovers   Victor, age 14
For The First Time in My Life I Felt Wanted   Gabriel, age 16

Gay Consciousness
I Need My Lovers   Tyrone, age 16
He Was Very Special and Kind   Barry, age 17
Column No. 8   "The Unicorn", age 12

Body Politics
We Should Be Able to Have the
Relationships We Want   George, age 17
It Was Me Who Started It   Frank, age 15
Column No. 1   "The Unicorn", age 11
Four Resolutions   Second International Gay Youth Congress
It's Adults Who Are
Screwed Up about Sex   (from Lesbian Gay Youth Magazine)

How does this line up with Rattigan's categories? He listed, in part:

- Is it loving?
- Is it consensual?
- Is it respectful?
- Is it giving or selfish?
- Is it mutually beneficial and fulfilling or abusive and unequal?

In *Boys Speak Out on Man/Boy Love* we have claims of:

- Love
- Loyalty
- Friendship
- Fun
- Respect
- Support
- Consent

Doesn't that meet the criteria?
Rattigan asked:

- Does it dignify or degrade me and others as human beings?
- Does it help or hinder me in becoming a better person?

Some of these young people – as young as eleven – explained that their relationships with older men were: "The Best Thing That Ever Happened to Me" or "Really Beautiful" or "The First Time in My Life I Felt Wanted" or "Very Beneficial," with some describing the relationships as the antidote to loneliness or death. What would Rattigan say to this?

As to the matter of the "rights" of these young people, Bryan, aged twelve-and-a-half, summed it up by stating: "It Shouldn't Be a Crime to Make Love."[89] Where, pray tell, have we heard this before?

In retrospect, once you buy into the prevalent gay argument that this is all about "the right to be with/marry the one I love," David Thorstad's comment is not that farfetched: "Freedom is indivisible. The liberation of children, women, boy-lovers, and homosexuals in general, can occur only as complementary facets of the same dream."

In keeping with this mindset, from July 7-12, 1985, about "50 young gay men and lesbians participated in the Second International Gay Youth Congress in Dublin," with ten nations represented among the delegates. These were two of the thirteen resolutions they adopted:

- As young people, we must be free to choose our own identities and lifestyles. We oppose ages of consent and all laws which restrict consensual sexual activity because, as young people, they limit our sexual freedom and deny us the right to choose who we relate to sexually.

- We call for the abolition of all ages of consent and demand that young people's and women's complaints of sexual assault be taken seriously and that positive discrimination be applied to counter existing power imbalances. Youth must be made less dependent on older people, materially and emotionally.[90]

So, according to these young people, this is all a matter of liberation and equality. It is a matter of the right to self-determination. It is a matter of casting off the oppressive shackles of a backwards society.

And this leads to some straightforward questions that must be posed to my GLBT readers and their allies: What moral objection can you raise against the cries of an oppressed and misunderstood people group – young people! – who are simply asking for the right to love and be loved? And how do you respond to a twelve-year old who says, "Who are you to impose your morality on me? Who are you to tell me what's best for me?"

Will you simply tell these people that traditional morality is best? If so, then why are you so upset with me for saying the same thing to you? Or will you say to them, "You're absolutely right. We've been using a double standard. If we want our freedom, you should have yours too." If that is your answer, you have just proved that the "slippery slope" argument is true.[91]

Of course, a pederast reading this chapter would say, "Wonderful! You've just made the case for pederasty." God forbid. To the contrary, what I demonstrated was that none of these arguments can be used to advocate for homosexuality (or pederasty), since none of these arguments prove that homosexuality (or pederasty) are good, positive, beneficial, or even neutral.

Thankfully, on a societal level, and despite the hopes of members of NAMBLA,[92] the vast majority of us have an extreme revulsion towards pederasty and pedophilia, as evidenced by the outrage of Amazon customers when they learned that the giant online company was selling Philip R. Greavy II's e-book entitled *The Pedophile's Guide to Love and Pleasure*. In a matter of days, and aided by websites like FoxNews.com and CNN.com,[93] more than 1,500 one-star reviews of the book had appeared (surely an unprecedented phenomenon), with many customers calling for a boycott of Amazon.[94]

WHERE ARE THE PRO-GAY ARGUMENTS WITH SUBSTANCE?

The real offshoot of this chapter, then, is not that it provides a justification for pederasty (obviously!) but that, to the contrary, it challenges the gay and lesbian community to provide real arguments, arguments of substance, to support their contentions. After all, it is because of our traditional moral values that we have this extreme revulsion towards pederasty and pedophilia – that undeniable "ick factor" that we feel – yet it is those very same traditional moral values that gay activists want us to abandon when it comes to our attitudes towards homosexual practice.

In other words, gay leaders want us to *embrace* our traditional moral values when it comes to our attitude towards pederasty -- we *should* have that "ick" feeling – but they want us to *reject* those values when it comes to our attitude towards homosexuality – we should *not* have that "ick" feeling. Yet, as has been carefully documented in this chapter, gay activists use the exact same arguments as do advocates of pederasty. They cannot have it both ways.

The fact is, just one generation ago, a strong revulsion towards homosexual practice was felt throughout our society, based on our traditional moral values, values which gays and lesbians now tell us are bigoted and backwards. Thus, in June, 2010, when political leader Mike Huckabee made reference to the "ick factor" in terms of same-sex relationships, he was blasted by Fred Sainz, Vice President of the Human Rights Campaign, as being "consistently wrong and uninformed." Sainz even claimed that "ick is certainly an appropriate way to describe Mr. Huckabee's mind going to sex when all that we are asking for is our equality. Ick, indeed."[95]

So, gay leaders, calling for equality and speaking in the name of love – shades of the advocates of "man-boy love"! – want us to abandon the "ick factor" when it comes to our feelings towards homosexuality (because our sexual values are allegedly antiquated and backwards), yet, when it comes to our feelings towards pederasty, these leaders want us to hold on to the "ick factor," *based on the same values that it wants us to reject when it comes to homosexual practice.* What this means is that the same arguments a gay leader would raise against pederasty today are the ones made fifty years ago against homosexuality by those holding to the traditional sexual morals that the gay community so utterly rejects. How enlightening!

And so I challenge my GLBT friends: Give me good reasons to consider the redefinition of marriage, the most foundational and ancient institution in the human race. And while you're at it, please tell me why marriage must be limited to just two people, since you advocate for the removal of the male-female marital foundation.

Why not follow the logic of a recent children's reader which exclaims, *Oh the Things Mommies Do! What Could Be Better Than Having Two?*[96] and why not go one, very natural step further: *My Mommies Bring Me So Much Glee! What Could Be Better Than Having Three?* After all, what's so sacred about the number two, if marriage is not defined as the union of a man and a woman? And if everyone should have the "right" to marry the one they love, shouldn't they be able to marry more than one person if they love more than one?

Show me why it's in the best interest of a child to deprive that child of either a mother or a father for life. (That really is something to think about.) Show me why it is best for that child to be raised in an environment in which they will never see the proper adult interaction between sexes, never see how a husband should treat his wife (or vice versa), never learn the distinctive role of a mom and a dad.[97] (As stated in Chapter Six, above, this cannot be compared to a single-parent household, since the possibility exists that another parent could be added to the equation, whereas that possibility does not exist in the case of a same-sex household. Also, by definition, in a single-parent household, there is a recognition that someone or something is missing, whereas a same-sex household claims to be just as good – in every way – as a male-female household.)

Tell me why gender distinctions are bad while blurring of gender is good, and why it's best to traumatize (or, reeducate) little children in elementary school because of one child's gender confusion (because of which he or she is allowed to "change" gender identity and use bathrooms or locker rooms that do not correspond to his or her biological sex). And tell me why sexual and romantic attraction should be put in the same category as skin color or ethnicity without using the same, tired arguments that are so easily refuted.

Show me why homosexuality should be celebrated proudly, with little or no room for criticism, when there are so many serious health risks associated with homosexual acts (particularly among gay men). On September 27, 2010, the Centers for Disease Control and Prevention reported that nearly 1 out of 5 MSM [men who have sex with men] studied was infected with HIV,"[98] prompting one of my colleagues to exclaim, "Can you imagine what the reaction would be to any other transmittable, infectious disease in which 20% of a given population suffered from it?! The media and governmental medical authorities would launch into full bore quarantine mode and do everything possible to eliminate further spread of the pathogen."[99] Not so when it comes to homosexual acts. Why?

The US Food and Drug Administration reported that "Men who have had sex with men since 1977 have an HIV prevalence . . . 60 times higher than the general population, 800 times higher than first time blood donors and 8000 times higher than repeat blood donors (American Red Cross)."[100] Please show me why pointing this out is an act of hatred rather than love and please demonstrate logically and rationally why homosexual acts can only be considered immoral or harmful or unacceptable because of religious bigotry and intolerance.

Whatever you do, just don't use the same shelf-worn, ineffective arguments anymore, since they just as easily make the case for pederasty (how dreadful), and, in reality, they do not prove the morality or rightness of homosexual practice, nor do they give us a single good reason to queer our educational system, redefine marriage, create special categories of protected peoples, or undermine gender.

SUMMING IT UP

The conclusion is unavoidable: Even if people claim that they have been born a certain way and cannot change; even if their sexual orientation is seen across cultures, both past and present; even if similar sexual activity is present in the animal kingdom; even if many psychologists do not consider their orientation to be pathological; even if they can point to the beneficial, consensual, and loving nature of their relationships; and even if they cry out for liberation and equality, there can still be strong moral and societal objections to their behavior. That goes for homosexuality just as much as pederasty.

*Starbucks is deeply committed to our Mission Statement
and Guiding Principles. One of our six principles is "embracing diversity as
an essential component to the way we do business." This includes the gay and
lesbian community. Supporting local events like the Gay Pride Festival in
Charlotte, NC, gives us the opportunity to live by
the values we have set.*

Letter to the author from Kevin Carothers, Public Affairs, Starbucks,
April 11, 2005, after concerns were raised to Starbucks, a past sponsor
of Charlotte Pride, about lewd public displays at the event in the presence
of toddlers and little children

*As we discussed, Starbucks is a company committed
to its guiding principles, which includes embracing diversity. It is an essential
component of the way we do business and is important to our many partners
(employees) and customers in the 36 countries we serve. While we welcome
differing points of view and respect your opinion, we remain committed
to supporting events that promote diversity and inclusion,
such as the Gay Pride Parade.*

Letter to the author from Kevin Carothers, September 2, 2005,
after he received a packet containing sexually explicit photos from material
fully accessible to children at previous Charlotte Pride events

8

Diversity or Perversity? Corporate America's Embrace of Gay Pride at its Worst

F or some years now, "diversity" has been a buzzword in corporate American culture, to the point that "embracing diversity" is high on the list of many a company's business priorities. Accordingly, the second of six guiding principles for Starbucks is: "Embrace diversity as an essential component in the way we do business."[1] What exactly does this mean?

On the one hand, Starbucks states that, "By actively seeking out women- and minority-owned businesses to purchase from, we help build prosperity and community in diverse neighborhoods."[2] That is certainly commendable, and Starbucks has sought to model this internationally. But "embracing diversity" means more than this in corporate America today. Specifically, it includes embracing homosexuality, bisexuality, and transgenderism, while also showing solidarity with gay and transgender activism. This helps explain why Starbucks, along with many other major companies, is an active and enthusiastic supporter of gay pride events across the nation.[3] Diversity, in this sense, serves as a useful, non-offensive term that, quite frequently, stands as a codeword for "embracing the goals and values of the gay agenda." And in the world of doublespeak, in which language is "deliberately constructed to disguise or distort its actual meaning," the word "diversity" works quite well.[4]

What kind of person would not embrace "diversity"? Only someone who was bigoted, small-minded, and hateful, since all people of good will "embrace diversity," correct? As noted by George Orwell in his prescient volume *1984*, "Newspeak" – a specifically Orwellian term which is quite similar to "Doublespeak" – is "deliberately constructed for political purposes: words, that is to say, which not only had in every case a political implication, but were intended to impose a desirable mental attitude upon the person using them."[5] Such is the case with "diversity." What kind of person would oppose it? Human civility requires that we embrace it.

If phrased differently, however, the question could yield a very different response. What kind of person would not embrace homosexual practice or agree with gay activism? Potentially, a loving, broad-minded, kind-hearted individual who simply believed that homosexuality was either unhealthy or immoral or unnatural or religiously unacceptable, while at the same time believing that gay men and women were entitled to equal protection under the law.[6] In contrast, using the terminology of "embracing diversity," anyone who opposed it could not possibly be loving, broad-minded, or kind-hearted. Hardly!

DIVERSITY AS A CODEWORD FOR GAY AND TRANSGENDER ACTIVISM

Diversity is the codeword for gay and transgender activism, while "embracing diversity" is another way of saying "endorsing homosexuality and supporting the goals of the gay and transgender agenda." To give just a few representative examples out of an almost endless number of possible citations from the worlds of education, business, and beyond:

- A gay and lesbian high-school student group bears the acronym P.R.I.D.E, standing for Peers Rising in Diverse Education,[7] while it is now common for schools to sponsor a gay-focused Diversity Week.[8] Similarly, the University of Denver's "Pride Portal" features this announcement: "The University of Denver welcomes and encourages applications from LGBTIQ identified students, faculty, and staff. We believe that one mark of a leading university is its commitment to *diversity* . . . ."[9]
- The official bio of Mary Ann Horton, Ph.D., a founding member of the gay activist group "It's Time America," reads: "Champion for diversity in the workplace, leading gay, lesbian, bisexual and transgender rights groups and pioneering equal rights for transgendered workers."[10] Diversity is the word![11]
- When British soldiers marched in a gay pride parade for the first time (on August 27, 2005, in Manchester), it demonstrated "that the Army accepts change and is very progressive, open-minded, embracing diversity, showing a higher degree of tolerance."[12]
- A gay-affirming church in Toledo, Ohio states that it is "An *inclusive* and *diverse* church that welcomes and accepts everyone, regardless of race, color, sex, age, national origin, sexual orientation, or disability."[13]
- A September 12, 2010, report from England noted that, "Council bosses are being asked to imagine they are English economic migrants in the fictitious region of Sindia, or go on an 'adventure in Lesbian-andgayland' as part of publicly-funded training sessions on *equality* and *diversity*. More than 30 managers from Brighton and Hove City Council have been on the two-day '*Leading on Diversity*' course in the past year – at a cost of several thousand pounds."[14]
- The large law firm of Hutton & Williams speaks proudly of "A Commitment toDiversity: Supporting Our Lesbian, Gay, Bisexual and Transgender Lawyers." Timothy Toohey, Partner, Los Angeles

Office, and Chair of the LGBT Initiatives Task Force, writes, "I am proud of the firm's continuing commitment to recruiting, retaining and promoting gay, lesbian, bisexual and transgender lawyers as part of the firm's diversity initiative."[15] (Note that on this single web page, the words "diversity" or "diverse" occur seventeen times.) In corporate America today, this is something to boast about.

In the words of IBM's Chairman and CEO, Sam Palmisano:

Diversity policies lie as close to IBM's core as they have throughout our heritage. Today, we're building a workforce in keeping with the global, diverse marketplace, to better serve our customers and capture a greater share of the on demand opportunity.

The lesson to draw from 50 years of leadership in diversity issues: we must stay true to our shared values. The marketplace demands it, and it's what we believe -- and have always believed -- is the right thing to do.[16]

What exactly does this mean? According to J. T. (Ted) Childs, Jr., IBM's Vice President of Global Workforce Diversity:

Our long-standing commitment to workforce diversity — equal opportunity, affirmative action, cultural awareness and work/life balance — has evolved into a legacy of leading social change and setting trends before they became fashionable, politically correct or, more importantly, mandated by law. . . .

Today, the Corporation's definition of diversity includes global cultures. For example, in EMEA [Europe, Middle East, and Africa], IBM is mindful of gender, people with disabilities and the growing number of ethnic minorities. In AP, we need to focus on gender, disability and respecting and valuing the differences between countries and regions. When it comes to business, the once formal global boundaries of the marketplace are evaporating.[17]

This certainly sounds commendable – in fact, it is commendable – and

IBM *should* be mindful of "gender, people with disabilities and the growing number of ethnic minorities." By all means! But it doesn't stop there. An IBM diversity website proclaims,

> IBM's leadership underscores its commitment to an inclusive work environment where people's ideas and contributions are welcome through eight Executive Task Forces - Asian, Black, Gay/Lesbian/Bisexual/Transgender, Hispanic, Men, Native American, People with Disabilities, and Women - established in 1995.[18]

Did you catch that? There are executive task forces for ethnic minorities – Asian, Black, Hispanic, and Native American – for Men and Women as distinct categories, for People with Disabilities, *and for Gay/Lesbian/Bisexual/ Transgender*. How in the world did sexual orientation and one's personal preference for gender expression get included here? IBM would be proud to say, ". . . it's what we believe -- and have always believed -- is the right thing to do."

It is now being touted as good business too. In a 2002 article entitled, "Big Blue Wants You: IBM looks to make an eightfold boost in the number of gay businesses it buys supplies from," *The Advocate* reported that,

> A longtime leader when it comes to diversity, IBM is now making another bold move. The Armonk, N.Y.-based computer giant has announced that it is *actively seeking gay-, lesbian-, bisexual-, and transgender-owned businesses* as part of its effort to diversify the companies it purchases from. It currently uses 30 GLBT-owned businesses as vendors and says it hopes to increase that number to 250 by the end of the year.[19]

Yes, it's all about "diversity" and "diversifying."

ENCOURAGING AND ENFORCING "DIVERSITY" IN THE WORKPLACE

Under the heading of "Supplier Diversity and Inclusion," mortgage giant Fannie Mae states that its company is dedicated to *promoting* and *increasing procurement opportunities* for Minorities and Women, Minority-Owned and Women-Owned Businesses, Small Businesses, Disabled Business Enterprises, Veteran-Owned Businesses, HUBZone (Historically Underutilized Business Zone) Businesses, 8(a) Businesses, and *Gay, Lesbian, Bi-Sexual and Transgender-Owned Businesses* in its procurement process. We take *diversity* into account as we make decisions in our evaluation process.[20]

So, GLBT companies are not just accepted in the name of diversity; they are now specially favored, and just as in the school system (see above, Chapter Three), this kind of "diversity" must now be celebrated, not merely tolerated. As expressed by Cynthia Neff, Director of Global Human Resources Public Policy for IBM:

I would say that there's been an evolution on this whole subject of transgender people, and gender rights is something that we've made an effort over the past several years to really understand more about. We really have migrated ... to including transgender as part of the core work that we do ....*We value these kinds of differences, not just tolerate them.*[21]

According to Debra Capolarello, senior vice president and chief talent officer of Met Life, with explicit reference to gay and lesbian issues, "Our corporate vision to build financial freedom for everyone is all-inclusive for a reason. We recognize that our employees have *diverse* strengths, our customers have *diverse* financial needs, and we are committed to ensuring that respect for *diversity* remains ingrained in our culture."[22]

Reflecting this same attitude, Arthur Ryan, the CEO of Prudential Financial commented, "*Diversity* continues to be key to the ongoing success of our company, and we remain committed to ensuring an *inclusive* and supportive work environment for all people."[23] Similarly, Kodak's Essie Calhoun, Chief Diversity Officer & Director, Community Affairsv and Vice President, stated, "In the long run, *diversity* and *inclusion* are about getting the best ideas from our employees, and empowering them as leaders."[24] Clearly, "diversity" and "inclusion" have become part of the stock vocabulary of gay-friendly political correctness.

Is it any wonder that these four companies – IBM, Met Life, Prudential Financial, and Eastman Kodak – have received perfect scores on the Human Rights Campaign's Corporate Equality Index for most of the last decade, an index measuring corporate policies beneficial to gays, lesbians, bisexuals, and transgenders? (For more on the Corporate Equality Index, see below.) Based on the HRC criteria, MBNA received a rating in 2005 of only 43% since it "has given money to anti-gay organizations."[25] How interesting! It appears that talk about "diversity" and "inclusion" only goes so far – in reality, in one direction only.

THE PERILS OF FAILING TO SUPPORT "DIVERSITY"

In fact, in 2010, the historically gay-friendly Target Corp. found itself targeted for a boycott by gay activists who were upset with a political contribution made by the company to MN Forward, the ad group for Minnesota gubernatorial candidate Tom Emmer. The HRC took out a full page ad in the *Star Tribune*, calling on Target (and Best Buy, which also contributed to MN Forward) to "make it right" for "supporting an extremist," stating plainly that, "Nobody associated with a group that calls for death and violence toward any group of people belongs in a governor's mansion, and yet that's exactly what Tom Emmer is."[26] An extremist? Associating with a group calling for death and violence? Really?

The results of this bad press (and boycott) were dramatic:

> Target [found] itself in political hot water in early August when it was revealed that it donated $150,000 to MN Forward, a group that supports [Minnesota] gubernatorial candidate Tom Emmer, who has aligned himself with radical anti-gay groups. Despite CEO Gregg Steinhafel's Aug. 5 apology on the company's site, Target lost one-third of its buzz score in the course of 10 days.
>
> Although Target's score recovered modestly from Aug. 12 through Aug. 24, it sunk again due to a rash of major newspaper op-eds, blog posts and publicity surrounding televised boycott ads from MoveOn PAC.[27]

And what, exactly, was the "radical anti-gay" stand that "extremist" Tom Emmer had taken? "I believe marriage is the union between one man and one woman," he stated on his website. "As a legislator, I have consistently supported the constitutional marriage amendment that protects traditional marriage."[28] So, simply supporting marriage as it has always been defined -- - and is presently defined in the Minnesota constitution – now makes one a radical anti-gay extremist, and contributing to the campaign of someone who says that marriage is the union of a man and a woman is cause for a boycott. (What truly *is* "radical" is redefining marriage as the union of two people, as opposed to supporting normal, biologically-based, male-female marriage. As for Emmer's alleged connection to a group calling for death and violence to gays and lesbians, see the article cited in n. 36, here.)[29]

"Target's support of the GLBT community is unwavering, and inclusiveness remains a core value of our company," Chief Executive Officer Gregg Steinhafel said, in response to the boycott – unless, of course, "inclusiveness" means supporting anyone who differs with gay activism.[30] According to Monica Meyer, interim head of the gay rights group OutFront Minnesota, "A lot of people feel betrayed by this place where everybody goes to shop and you get to see them at Pride and you feel good that youre supporting a corporation that's giving back to the community."[31] So, "diversity" and "inclusion" mean that Target should support local, gay pride events and get behind GLBT causes while at the same time refusing to stand with a candidate who seeks to uphold male-female marriage (even though Target claimed it was backing Emmer for his non-social stands). All clear!

In a telling remark, Emmer commented, "The sad part to me is, I thought we were supposed to be able to exercise our rights of free speech. We're supposed to celebrate the fact that we have different perspectives."[32] Not quite! Such perspectives are *excluded* by corporate America's current definitions of diversity and inclusion (not to mention tolerance), as Joe Solmonese, president of the HRC, made perfectly clear in response to the apology of Target's CEO:

The fact that their political contribution was used to advance an anti-equality candidate was extremely hurtful to all fair-minded Americans. Target's apology is welcomed but without tangible action behind it, the LGBT community and our allies will continue to question the company's commitment to equality. . . . . Target can still make it right by making equivalent contributions to equality-minded organizations and by making clear the procedure by which they will evaluate potential contributions in the future to include issues of LGBT-equality.[33]

We can safely assume that Solmonese doesn't recognize either the irony, hyperbole, or even hypocrisy of his statement, despite the overloaded rhetoric ("anti-equality candidate," "extremely hurtful to all fair-minded Americans," questioning Target's "commitment to equality," and calling for pro-gay contributions to "equality-minded organizations" supporting "issues of LGBT-equality.")

As far back as 2002, Verizon Communications distributed a handout entitled "101 Ways to Make Your Workplace More Inclusive" at the Gender Public Advocacy Coalition (GenderPAC) annual conference. Among the suggestions were:

- Link being inclusive to being productive;
- Use examples of same-sex couples in business exercises and training role-plays;
- Make gay and lesbian employees visible in your organization's newsletter and other communications;
- Order and display gay publications, like *10 Percent, The Advocate, Out,* or *Victory* where other magazines are displayed;
- Bring gay, lesbian and bisexual speakers into the workplace;
- Seek out opportunities to learn from transgender people;
- On Gay Pride Day and National Coming Out Day, fly the rainbow flag at work locations;
- Sponsor a booth at gay pride events;
- Give your gay employees time off to attend funerals of close friends;
- When putting together information packets for out-of-town guests, include information on gay, lesbian or bisexual places of interest. Include a copy of your local gay paper;
- Encourage your gay, lesbian or bisexual employees to recommend other sexual minorities for jobs within the organization;
- Include openly lesbian, gay and bisexual individuals on company boards and task forces.[34]

Yet in 2010, Verizon scored only a 70 on HRC's Corporate Equality

Index.[35] How the bar has been raised!

THE HRC'S CORPORATE EQUALITY INDEX

It appears that one of Verizon's biggest transgressions fell under the category of "Prohibits Discrimination Based on Gender Identity or Expression" (again meaning transgenderism, transsexuality, cross-dressing, and the like). The company is obviously out of step with corporate America, since, the HRC boasts, "In 2002, the year it was first published, the CEI [Corporate Equality Index] noted just 5 percent of businesses banned discrimination based on gender identity or expression. The 2010 report shows that figure has increased exponentially, now standing at 72 percent."[36]

Yes, corporate America's embrace of the goals of gay activism truly has been exponential. Thus, while "Just 13 businesses received perfect ratings in that first year [2002] . . . by 2005, more than 100 businesses had achieved perfect ratings,"[37] and by 2010, the number had reached 305 – despite the fact that every year, the HRC seems to raise the bar of criteria required for a perfect score. Yet the higher the bar is raised, the higher these companies jump (and the more their numbers multiply). And every year, the release of the HRC's annual report is greeted with great media fanfare.

A review of some of the questions asked as far back as 2005 on the HRC's Corporate Equality Index Survey is enlightening.[38] This is how companies are being evaluated:

Does your company bar employment discrimination based on gender identity or gender expression by including the words "gender identity" or "gender identity or expression" in its primary non-discrimination or EEO policy?

Does your company offer health insurance coverage to your employees' same-sex partners?

What other benefits do you offer, company-wide, to opposite-sex spouses of U.S. employees? Are those benefits also offered, company-wide, to same-sex partners of U.S. employees?

Does your company recognize legal marriages for same-sex couples when deciding eligibility for health insurance coverage of your U.S. employees partners? [Bear in mind that in 2005, same-sex "marriage" was legally recognized in the United States only in Massachusetts.]

Does your company have written Gender Transition [meaning sex-change surgery!] guidelines documenting supportive company policy on issues pertinent to a workplace gender transition such as name change policy, bathroom accommodations, dress codes and harassment?

Some employee health insurance policies exclude coverage for commonplace treatments and procedures for transgender employees, through what is commonly referred to as a "transgender exclusion" clause. Many of these procedures/treatments are available and covered for nontransgender diagnoses. For health care benefits available to your general work force, is there at least one company-sponsored plan where these benefits are also available to transgender employees as part of their medically supervised treatment?

So, in order for an American company to qualify as "working for equality" the company cannot "discriminate" against a man who chooses to wear a dress to work (that's part of what is meant by "gender expression"); it must offer comprehensive insurance benefits to same-sex partners; it must recognize the legality of same-sex marriages performed in America and abroad; it must have a policy for employees who choose to have a sex-change operation ("Gender Transition"!), including special bathroom accommodations; and it must not exclude insurance coverage "for commonplace treatments and procedures for transgender employees" (meaning treatments pertaining to sex-change surgery and lifelong maintenance of one's new gender). This is remarkable.

And let's remember that these guidelines are produced by an organization that calls itself the "Human Rights Campaign," not the "Homosexual Rights Campaign," as if their efforts were also aimed at helping impoverished day laborers, or starving children, or women sold into sex-trafficking, or any other number of needy people groups. No, their focus – which is perfectly understandable and quite legal – is on one segment of the population only, yet they are misleadingly called the *Human Rights* Campaign, as if anyone who differed with them was fighting against universal human rights. Yet they claim to "Focus on Diversity," stating, "In a world defined by difference, our strength depends on our common humanity."[39]

Getting back to the Corporate Equality Index, there must be "Diversity Management and Training," clarified by questions such as:

How many reporting levels are there between your company's CEO and the individual whose primary job function is work force diversity that includes lesbian, gay, bisexual or transgender diversity?

Does your company have an officially recognized LGBT employee affinity group?

Does your company have a company-wide diversity council or working group with a mission that specifically includes LGBT diversity?

If your company provides diversity awareness or employee training, what topics are covered and who is required to attend?

Yes, mandatory training in "diversity awareness" must be part of the package, with required employee attendance the expected norm. Companies are also expected to engage in direct marketing to the LGBT community, to sponsor "a LGBT health, educational, political or community event" and to fund "LGBT health, educational, political or community-related organizations."[40] Without question, gay activists insist that corporate America must wholeheartedly embrace the gay agenda, with all its political and cultural implications, and employees that don't toe the line could risk termination,[41] while offices that don't satisfy the "diversity" quota could lose business.[42]

And the pro-gay-activist momentum is growing at an exponential pace. To repeat: In 2002, the first year that the HRC issued its Corporate Equality Index, only *thirteen* major companies scored a perfect 100 (and remember that the HRC's guidelines were not as stringent back in 2002). By 2010, the number had risen to *305* – an increase of better than 2300% in just eight years.

Just let your eyes scan this list of some of the best-known companies that scored 100% in 2010: 3M Co. * Abercrombie & Fitch * Aetna * Alaska Airlines * Alcoa * Allstate Corp. * American Express * American Airlines * Anheuser-Busch Companies * Apple * AT&T * Bank of America * Barnes & Noble * Bausch & Lomb * Best Buy * Boeing * Borders * Bristol-Myers Squibb Co. * Campbell Soup Co. * Capital One * Charles Schwab * Chevron * Chrysler * Cisco Systems * Citigroup * Clear Channel Communications * Clorox * Coca-Cola * Continental Airlines * Corning * Costco * Cox Enterprises * Dell * Deloitte & Touche * Delta Air Lines * Deutsche Bank

* Dow Chemical * DuPont * Eastman Kodak * eBay Inc. * Ernst & Young * Estee Lauder * Esurance * Freddie Mac * Fannie Mae * Food Lion * Ford * Gap * General Mills * General Motors * Goldman Sachs * Google * Hallmark Cards * Harrah's * Hartford Financial Services * Health Care Service Corp. * Hewlett-Packard * Honeywell International * HSBC USA * Hyatt * ING North America Insurance * Intel * IBM * Intuit * J.P. Morgan Chase & Co. * JetBlue Airways * Johnson & Johnson * Kaiser Permanente * KeyCorp * Levi Strauss * LexisNexis * Liz Claiborne * Lockheed Martin Corp. * Macy * Marriott International * MasterCard * MetLife * Microsoft * MillerCoors * Monsanto * Morgan Stanley * Motorola * Nationwide * NCR * New York Life Insurance Co. * New York Times Co. * Newell Rubbermaid * Nielsen Co. * Nike * Nordstrom * Oracle * Orbitz * Owens Corning * Pacific Life Insurance * PepsiCo * Pfizer * PG&E * Pillsbury Winthrop Shaw Pittman * Procter & Gamble * Progressive Corp. * Prudential Financial * Raytheon * Sears * Shell Oil * Sprint Nextel * Starbucks * Starwood Hotels & Resorts Worldwide * Subaru of America * Sun Life Financial Inc. * Sun Microsystems * SunTrust Banks * Symantec Corp. * Target * Texas Instruments * Time Warner * Toyota Motor Sales USA * Travelport * United Parcel Service * US Airways Group * Viacom * Visa * Volkswagen of America * Walgreen * Walt Disney * Wells Fargo & Co. * Whirlpool * Wynn Resorts * Xerox * Yahoo![43] (Good luck trying to boycott all these companies!)[44]

CORPORATE AMERICA'S OVERT SUPPORT OF GLBT ACTIVISM

Many of these companies also sponsor the HRC with significant financial gifts (as in multiplied hundreds of thousands of dollars), and many are quite "out and proud" about it. For example, in 2006, the HRC's Carolina's fundraising dinner held in Charlotte was sponsored by the city's twin monetary titans, Bank of America and Wachovia (the latter also featuring a video on how to "come out" at work so as to put your company under pressure); Duke Energy (the local power company); and the insurance giant Blue Cross and Blue Shield. Advertisers for the 2006 dinner (which was held in Charlotte from 2005-2009) included the *Charlotte Observer*, noting that it featured 187 articles on LGBT issues the previous year, and Hotels.com, which boasted

THOUSANDS OF GAY-FRIENDLY HOTEL
ROOMS AND NOT A CLOSET TO BE FOUND
AMONG THEM.

*hotels.com is the ultimate source for gay-friendly hotels and is
once again a proud sponsor of HRC.*[45]

And what does corporate sponsorship of the HRC actually mean? It
means that many of the biggest, brightest, and most influential companies
in America are underwriting: GLBT community activism, GLBT-affirming
(and conservative-bashing) educational and media "outreach," the electing
of aggressively pro-GLBT candidates (and the opposing of candidates
with traditional values), the publishing of GLBT activist literature, and the
developing "gay Christian" theology. (Just read the "What We Do" page on
the HRC's website, and then dig in and explore.)[46]

But it's not only the HRC that receives boatloads of money from
corporate America. Other major gay activist organizations receive similar
funding. Thus, to give just two out of many potential examples, the NGLTF
(National Gay and Lesbian Task Force) lists American Airlines, Chili's,
Showtime, and Wells Fargo among their National Corporate Partners[47] (to
grasp just what this means, see the details of the NGLTF 2009 Creating
Change Conference, described in Chapter Eleven, below), while Lamda
Legal, working tirelessly in the courts and the educational system for activist
gay and transgender goals, can boast of sponsors and partners including
Microsoft, Levi Strauss, Pillsbury, and Merrill Lynch.[48]

FROM DIVERSITY TO PERVERSITY

It's also important to understand that the contemporary concept of
"embracing diversity" has opened up a Pandora's box of sexual perversity, to
the point that even the most offensive public displays are included under
the heading of "diversity." This too is sponsored by corporate America.
(Please note that throughout this chapter, I am using the word "perversity"
to describe the more extreme sexual practices of the LGBT community, with
the assumption that many gays and lesbians will also judge these practices to
be perverse.)

To offer a case in point, on April 6th, 2005, I had the pleasure of speaking at length with Mr. Kevin Carothers of the Public Affairs division of Starbucks, sharing my concerns about his company's sponsorship of the annual Charlotte Pride event, an event that at that time was marked by open, vulgar, and even pornographic sexual displays in a public park, in full view of little children.[49] I explained to him that the mayor had publicly voiced his disapproval of this kind of behavior, refusing to write a welcome letter for the event. And I explained to him that this was a highly divisive issue in our city, offending tens of thousands of concerned citizens – again, the issue was Starbucks sponsorship of a well-promoted, sexually explicit event taking place in a public park – and that it would be best for Starbucks to withdraw its frontline, highly-visible support from the event.

In response to our conversation, which was cordial and mutually respectful, he wrote me a gracious letter dated April 11th, 2005, explaining that,

> Starbucks is deeply committed to our Mission Statement and Guiding Principles. One of our six principles is "embracing diversity as an essential component to the way we do business." This includes the gay and lesbian community. Supporting local events like the Gay Pride Festival in Charlotte, NC, gives us the opportunity to live by the values we have set.

So, embracing diversity includes embracing perversity – really, how else could you describe a drag queen, wearing a tutu, gyrating his pelvis in the presence of little kids who were putting money in his panties, or having a Hot Nudist Camp booth with open pornography in full view of young children? Sadly, this sort of perversity – and worse – has often been front and center in gay pride events worldwide, especially at the larger events.

Consider, as just one example among many, Wells Fargo Bank's repeated direct support – actually hosting – of the "Leather Alley" section of San Francisco's Gay Pride festivity in *the company's own parking lot*. As reported on June 22, 2005, by Joe Garafoli,

> This Sunday in a Wells Fargo bank parking lot near San Francisco's City Hall, August Knight will demonstrate for

any adult who cares to stop by what it's like to be flogged -- and enjoy it.

An Oakland hairstylist by day and co-owner of a South of Market dungeon popular with the whip-cracking crowd by night, Knight, 46, is an ambassador of kink. She and about 70 other volunteers will staff Leather Alley, one of the fastest-growing niches at the annual San Francisco Gay, Lesbian, Bisexual, Transgender Pride Parade and Celebration.[50]

And what happens to those who openly speak about what happens at these events? Just ask conservative Canadian politician Doug Elniski. After accepting an invitation to march in a gay pride parade in Edmonton in June 2009, he came under heavy criticism for sending out lighthearted messages from his Twitter account, like these: "I am surrounded by bumping and grinding lesbians waiit [sic] 20 then send help" and "that guy has size 14 stilettos."[51] He was immediately called to task by the local GLBT community, who branded him "insensitive, ignorant and homo/transphobic."[52] Not surprisingly, he was quick to offer a full apology to the offended community, calling his text-messages "inappropriate."[53] Perhaps, instead, it was the behavior of some of those in the parade that was inappropriate?

PERVERSITY AND "GAY PRIDE"

But being "surrounded by bumping and grinding lesbians" is nothing. Consider this representative sampling from some major gay pride events held in the last decade. (In recent years, many of the smaller gay pride events have become more tame, but the biggest events – like those in San Francisco and Atlanta – are still marked by this kind public vulgarity.)

- June 29, 2003, the 33rd annual Gay Pride parade in San Francisco. "A float from the anti-Catholic group Sisters of Perpetual Indulgence took political crassness to a new level. The 'Sisters'— men in drag who dress like nuns, with some sporting perverted names — paraded with their float titled 'Weapons of A-- Destruction [mocking "Mass Destruction"].' It contained a rocket with a phallic tip and the name

'Cheney' painted on the side, pointing at the bulging rear end of a bent-over figure. A man sat astride the rocket simulating sex acts. . . . At [one] booth featuring 'leather' (S&M) implements, a woman wacked a series of other women on the behind with a paddle, after first putting a dog leash on each of the 'wackees.'"[54]

- At this same event, "Hundreds of 'Dykes on Bikes' led off the parade, which consisted of more than 180 contingents and lasted nearly four hours (there was a delay due to a fire incident in a building along the parade route). Some of the women celebrated 'nipple freedom' by riding completely topless. Other marchers included men wearing nothing but shoes. . . ."[55] The police, of course, did nothing to interfere with this celebration, which drew between 150,000 and 750,000 participants, according to unofficial and official estimates. Corporate America did not seem put off by these displays either: "Principal sponsors were Anheuser Busch's 'Bud Light' beer, whose trademark red, white and blue logo was changed to rainbow hues for the occasion, and *The San Francisco Chronicle*, which had this parade slogan: 'We come out every day.' Other sponsors and advertisers included MasterCard, Wells Fargo Bank, Bank of America, Earthlink, Verizon, IBM, United Airlines, Enterprise Rent-a-Car, AAA Travel, Travelocity, and several liquor brands and HIV/AIDS drug manufacturers."[56]

- Videographer Eric Holmberg, an eyewitness to the 2010 San Francisco Gay Pride parade (marking its 40th anniversary), reported that with the mainstreaming of the gay rights movement in America and with politicians like Speaker of the House Nancy Pelosi addressing the crowds by Jumbo-tron, the parade itself had become much more docile, although hardly chaste. What followed the parade, noted Holmberg, "was the big party . . . that sprawled over I don't know how many city blocks -- including the area surrounding and including the city offices for the government of the city (comparable to the capitol building for a medium-sized state). There had to be a couple (or more) hundred thousand people milling about drinking, eating, and partying. I saw dozens of people completely nude -- all men -- though quite a few women with breast nudity. The stench of sin and degradation -- complete moral anarchy -- was overwhelming."

- As a case in point, Holmberg describes "a performance by an openly gay two-women rap/R&B group called God-dess and She. Keep in mind that the concert stage was framed by two very large Jumbo-tron TV screens on both sides -- and all this was right off the south wall of the statehouse building with the capitol-dome-like edifice spiraling over the stage. In other words, this was very much a state-sanctioned and sponsored event. . . . So picture this large, impressive government edifice and an openly girl group standing in its afternoon shadows, flanked by huge TVs, singing (forgive me) 'Lick it' while multiple thousands of people jump, gyrate, fist-pump, shout and sing along to" lyrics about female, oral sex that are unprintable. Sponsors of the event included Bank of America, Home Depot, Kaiser Permanente, and many others.[57]

- In a blatant example of corporate obtuseness, McDonald's, the pioneer of kiddy-based, fast-food restaurants, released a San Francisco TV ad in 2008, proudly proclaiming, "Since 1970, San Francisco has celebrated gay pride, and its annual parade is one of the best-known pride events anywhere in the world." Yes, it is one of the best known gay pride events and one of the most perversity riddled gay pride events, yet McDonald's, the über-family food chain, somehow found it worthy of celebration. This, of course, was all part of diversity, as the ad continued with, "McDonald's is proud of our commitment to a *diverse* workforce . . . ."[58] Equal employment for all is one thing; corporate celebration of perversity is another – at least, it used to be.

- The annual (and appropriately named) Southern Decadence event draws as many as 125,000 GLBT participants to New Orleans and culminates with a massive drag queen parade. The 2004 event was led by grand marshal drag queen Donnie "Jager" Jay James with the theme "DAYDREAMS AND FANTASIES: Welcome to My Harem." Previous themes included: "Carnaval Decadence" (2003); "Menage a trios" (2001); "Taboo X 2: The Forbidden Pleasures Tour" (2000); and "Dark Lady Tour: Dissidents of Decadence" (2000). As is common with major gay events (especially because of their economic impact), the mayor of New Orleans writes a warm letter of welcome to the participants each year. Prominent links featured on SouthernDecadence.com include: BadPuppy.com, boasting more than one million sexual images, and ManHunt.net, featuring sensual ads and images for men looking for men, while special events for the 2010 event included a Big D—k contest and a Hot-ss night.
- The event's official website (SouthernDecadence.com) has reminded those attending that, although they will certainly get an eyeful while there, city laws prohibit not only public urinating but also public sex. (How many events need to *remind* those attending that *public sex* is against the law?) The men are encouraged to keep the sex inside and to keep it safe – something that countless eyewitnesses and lots of video-taped footage will testify is frequently *not* done, as all kinds of perverse sexual acts are flaunted in very public view. In fact, according to the "Southern Decadence 2005: How to Guide," posted on FrenchQuarter.com, "Parades and non-stop parties aside, Southern Decadence may be most famous (or infamous) for the displays of naked flesh which characterize the event – which is only fitting, since New Orleans in early September is generally the closest thing you'll ever experience to walking around in a steambath outside of

a health spa. While police have started to crack down on public lewdness and pressure from a local crackpot conservative religious organization has caused the five-day festival to become a little more sedate than it was in years past, the atmosphere of Southern Decadence has stayed true to its name and public displays of sexuality are pretty much everywhere you look."⁵⁹ Corporate sponsors of recent Southern Decadence events have included Sir Speedy Press, Bud Light, and Harrah's New Orleans, the event's official casino.

- The 2007, San Diego Gay Pride Parade and Festival drew national attention when four San Diego firemen filed a lawsuit against the city after being ordered by their superiors to participate in the event against their will, being required to ride on the fire department's float. According to the complaint, which was settled in their favor, at this event some of the spectators "wear sexually suggestive clothing, expose themselves, engage in lewd displays of sexualized conduct and simulated sex acts, use profanity, and yell vulgar and obscene catcalls. In this way, the Gay Pride Parade is unlike any other parade sanctioned by the City or in which City officials and employees participate." During the parade, the men were "subjected to crude and obscene comments by Parade spectators, such as . . . 'Show me your fire hose!' 'I can't breathe, give me mouth to mouth!' 'Pull out your hose!' . . . In addition to the sexual taunts and catcalls, Parade spectators directed lewd and lascivious gestures at plaintiffs," including exposing their genitalia and making overt sexual contact with each other.⁶⁰ Corporate sponsors of recent San Diego Pride events have included Hewlett Packard, Aetna, Orbitz, Wells Fargo, and Cox.

- According to a conservative watchdog report, at the 2010 Boston Pride event, "There were more BDSM (bondage, discipline, sado-masochism) activists officially participating than ever before, and more open behavior. The literature they were handing out was explicit and, frankly, pretty sick. . . . Transgenderism was a major theme of this year's 'Pride'. Three of the five 'grand marshals' were men dressed as women (including 'Grace' Sterling Stowell, who works with public schoolchildren with state funding). . . . Some of the signs that were carried in parades were so vulgar that we're reluctant to include them in our reports . . . . And the level of weirdness and general dysfunction was beyond past years. The term 'freak show' came to mind a lot. . . . There were far more kids -- from elementary school through high school -- included in events than in past years. In the Pride Parade in particular there were waves of schoolchildren marching, obviously well organized, holding banners from their various schools.. . . Google, Microsoft, Bank of America, Massachusetts General Hospital, Children's Hospital, Beth Israel Hospital, and many, many more marched in the parade, supported it financially, and otherwise participated. . . . Despite all of this, there was a complete news blackout regarding anything unflattering about Gay Pride Week. Only positive, celebratory things were reported throughout the Boston media."[61]

All these events pail, however, in comparison to the annual Folsom Street Fair in San Francisco, the classic example of perversity on display – and in the name of diversity at that. According to a conservative Christian report of the 2007 event,

The Fair is an annual street party for BDSM enthusiasts (meaning bondage, discipline, sadism, masochism — or domination/submission) held on several blocked-off city streets . . . that reportedly draws hundreds of thousands of 'leather' practitioners and curious spectators every year. . . . In addition to the nudity and public sex acts, there were public whippings and spankings. Some were held at booths: the AIDS Emergency Fund was hawking charity spankings for $5 each — and others apparently occurring spontaneously, if you can say that about an act of consensual, 'erotic' violence. We witnessed one man whipping his 'partner' on a sidewalk, the 'whippee's' back becoming a brighter red with each round of punishment — done out of love, we are told by the sadists. . . . And we witnessed many 'master-slave' 'couples,' one leading the other around with a dog collar, of both the homosexual and heterosexual variety. The Folsom Street Fair began as an event mainly for homosexual sadomasochists, but it now attracts many straights, as evidenced by the thousands of women visible at this year's event. . . . So pervasive was the public (mostly male) nudity that it seemed the more 'modest' homosexuals were the ones wearing only underwear or leather chaps exposing their behind.[62]

WELCOMING PERVERSITY IN THE NAME OF DIVERSITY

What does this have to do with "diversity"? We'll let San Francisco mayor Gavin Newsom answer that question. He welcomed the Folsom Street Fair to his city with open arms, and he did it in the name of "diversity."

I am proud to be Mayor of a city that has a long-standing history of being on the forefront of extending civil rights for all citizens. San Francisco is a city that takes pride in its *diverse* communities and neighborhoods. The commitment to *inclusion* and ensuring *diversity* makes this a thriving city and a popular destination for many visitors from around the world. My office is committed to supporting and recognizing the exceptional contributions of all our *diverse* communities. . . .

To all organizers and attendees of the Folsom Street Fair, their families, friends, colleagues, and visitors from home and around the world, have a great day and enjoy the event."[63]

Diversity is the operative word in the mayor's endorsement for something that can only be called perversity. And Miller Beer was a proud sponsor of that 2007 event, running a full page ad in the Folsom Street Fair program.[64]

Of course, plenty of gay men and women disapprove strongly of such behavior – especially in public – and, quite obviously, plenty of them are not involved in these kinds of activities.[65] But the question that must be asked is this: Why have gay pride events been famous for such displays? And why, through the years, has little or no action been taken against these displays by the gay community itself? Why is it that, until recently, these events were toned down when pressure was applied from *outside* the gay community? Why is such perversity paraded and flaunted and championed and celebrated? And why has corporate America been so eager to sponsor these events?

Gay activists are so careful to utilize carefully crafted language to communicate their points, using "gay" rather than "homosexual," speaking of "gay and lesbian civil rights" rather than a "gay agenda," and referring to "sexual orientation" rather than "sexual preference," just to name a few.[66] This makes it all the more ironic that such public, self-exposing, and self-denigrating displays have been standard fare in major gay pride events.[67]

As noted by lesbian, feminist activist, Tammy Bruce:

> . . . if there is suddenly such a concern within the gay community about appearing "normal," perhaps men in suits should replace men in G-strings at gay-pride parades.
>
> I was at an organizing meeting for a gay-pride group that shall remain nameless. One of the bigger arguments at the meeting involved whether or not to have a giant penis on a float, á la the Rose Parade. After a contentious debate, the Giant Penis Float lost out, but just barely. The women in the room were not amused, and a discussion ensued about how negatively the gay community appears to the rest of the country when our ambassadors are men dressed as female high school cheerleaders.[68]

Just think for a moment about how extreme this really is. If traditional couples came together for a "Celebration of Marriage" day in a public park, little children from the community would feel welcome, and people would not have to close their eyes and cover their ears to avoid contact with vulgar and obscene images, gestures, and words.[69] Yet large gay celebrations worldwide are commonly marked by nude or semi-nude parades, simulated sex acts, and floats with massive, protruding phalluses. Isn't this perversity rather than diversity? Shouldn't this be a source of shame rather than "pride"? And shouldn't corporate America distance itself from such displays?

What would have happened to the civil rights movement if Black Pride rallies in the 1960's were marked by lewd public displays and a fixation on male genitalia? Wouldn't this have discredited the whole movement, not to mention the people themselves, in a moment? And what if the immigration rallies of 2006 and 2010 were marked by nudity and gyrating drag queens? Wouldn't this have severely damaged the cause of illegal immigrants?

Could anyone imagine lewd public acts being associated with "Asian Pride" or "White Pride" or "Jewish Pride" or "Muslim Pride"? Yet gay pride events – especially the larger ones – are commonly marked by public lewdness, forming an integral part of gay *pride*, all part of "coming out" and being unashamed. And all this, of course, is to be celebrated under the heading of "diversity" – and eagerly embraced by corporate America. (In a related context, Michael Medved noted, "The raging controversy over an exhibition of 'gay art' at the taxpayer-funded National Portrait Gallery raises an uncomfortable but unavoidable question: *must all celebrations of homosexual history and identity feature disturbing and pornographic content?*")[70]

ARE DIVERSITY AND INCLUSION REALLY DIVERSE AND INCLUSIVE?

There's something else peculiar about the contemporary use of the word "diversity." One would think that "diversity" would be "inclusive," not wanting to cause any one group to feel alienated or put out. Indeed, such language is commonly used to explain the very essence of diversity. But that is hardly the case. Do companies like Starbucks sponsor pro-life celebrations in solidarity with the preborn? Do they sponsor teen abstinence drives? Do they sponsor events honoring the traditional family? The record speaks for itself: The answer is no.

The interaction that I had with US Airways in July-August, 2007, is all too typical. On July 27, 2006, I wrote to the US Airways Customer Relations Department on behalf of the Coalition of Conscience, sharing my concerns about their sponsorship of the Pride Charlotte event:

> This is a highly divisive issue, and one which US Airways should steer clear of, lest you offend a large part of your constituency. I too stand against discriminatory treatment of gays and lesbians, and I'm sure that on many flights, I have been served by gay and lesbian employees of US Airways. Equal opportunity and fairness is not the issue here. Rather, the issue here is one of US Airways making

a public statement that it supports a particular sexual expression, one that is considered immoral by a large part of your constituency, and that it supports an activist gay agenda, one that is sounded loudly and clearly at every Pride Charlotte event....

I received a response from Evelyn Miller, Manager, Diversity & Compliance with US Airways, on July 31, 2007, addressing my concerns

Our overall goal is to recognize, support, and celebrate all of our employees in an effort to create a workplace that fosters inclusion and open communication. US Airways sponsor a number of different activities throughout the year in support of our employees and feel that it would create a difference in treatment if we were to deny this group of employees our support.

I wrote back to her on the same day, noting that:

It would . . . be very helpful to the Coalition members if you could supply me with a list of pro-life and pro-family events that US Airways has sponsored, since there are doubtless thousands of conservatively-oriented US Airways employees who are strongly pro-life and pro-traditional family. So, supplying me with that information would be very helpful as well. Otherwise, the message US Airways would be sending to your constituents would be one of bias, exclusivity, and intolerance. That is to say, US Airways is happy to support gay, lesbian, and transgender employees but not pro-life, pro-traditional family employees.

When I received no direct response to this and other requests I had made (although I did receive permission from Ms. Miller to share her email with my constituents), I asked her on August 8th if I was correct in understanding that US Airways, "Chooses not to offer me a list of pro-life, pro-traditional-family events that US Airways has sponsored," to which she replied on August 9th, "Thank you for your email, but please do not make assumptions." I responded on the same day:

I am making no assumptions. . . . In my previous email to you, I made three specific requests, to which I received no response. I then sent the email again, making the same requests. Your reply was to refer my constituents to your previous email. Therefore, so there was no ambiguity, I restated what you chose not to reply to. Please help me to see where I have made assumptions.

So then, so that we have complete clarity, please respond directly to the following: . . .

I am requesting a list of pro-life, pro-traditional-family events that US Airways has sponsored. Are you willing to supply that? . . .

I look forward to your specific response to these requests. If I do not receive a response, I will understand that the answer to each of the above is "no," but I certainly hope that that is not the case.

And the response from US Airways? You guessed it: I received no response. (My other requests, which also met with no response, were for a face to face meeting and for an address and person to whom I could send pictures documenting what happened at a previous gay pride event in the city.)

A similar exchange of emails (albeit with a more ironic ending!) took place in 2008 when another coffee chain, Caribou Coffee, sponsored the Pride Charlotte event. In response to my concerns, Lauren Mihhajlov, Director of Brand Marketing, wrote back to me and explained that Caribou would "continue our sponsorship as we know it is important to the communities in which we operate." She also noted that "we strive to be a part of our neighborhoods and communities, as this is one of our core values. In being good community members, we also endeavor to be inclusive of all members of our community."

I wrote back to Ms. Mihhajlov and stated that, while I was disappointed with the response, in keeping "with this clearly stated core value of your company, we want to officially invite you to be a sponsor at our second 'Not Ashamed Charlotte' event planned for this coming May." I explained that,

This is a wonderful, positive, wholesome event, reflective of the values of tens of thousands of citizens here, an event in which we celebrate the family (highlighting the importance of male-female marriage and of teen sexual purity) and underscore the sanctity of human rights, beginning in the womb.

I informed her that we already had sponsorship commitments from some fine local companies,

> and we would love to include you in our list of sponsors. Our previous event in 2006 drew positive coverage from the local media along with the participation of a diverse cross-section of the greater Charlotte community.
>
> Your participation in the event would send a great signal to our constituency that you do, in fact, mean what you say when you write that "we strive to be a part of our neighborhoods and communities, as this is one of our core values."

And how did Caribou respond? They would not sponsor our event because they were "inclusive." I kid you not![71] And I imagine they said it with a straight face too.

How then can Starbucks, along with other like-minded companies, possibly claim to embrace diversity if their alleged inclusiveness explicitly *excludes* certain groups? Starbucks plainly states that they say, "**No thank you** . . . to any proposals [for sponsorship] regarding . . . political or religious activities."[72] So, diversity has its limitations!

Companies like Starbucks can hardly claim to be *inclusive* and embracing of *diversity* when they are decidedly *exclusive* in who or what they include and embrace. More importantly, it is downright hypocritical for these companies to consistently sponsor gay pride events when they refuse other activities that are "political or religious" in nature, since a strong political agenda is often at the forefront of the gay pride events, all the more so in the last few years.

To give just a few examples out of hundreds that could be cited, beginning at the 2003 San Francisco gay pride parade, a reporter noted that,

> Hundreds of marchers carried signs that said, "We All Deserve the Freedom to Marry" and "Support AB 205 Domestic Partner Rights" referring to California's "gay marriage" equivalent bill . . . . Other signs said, "We had

sodomy for breakfast" and "Sodomize me, it's legal!" Many waved Texas state flags.[73]

At the June 2004 Stonewall Festival in Miami it was reported that,

> Everywhere there were Jim Stork stickers, hats, posters, and pins. [Stork is a gay political candidate.] Wilton Manner's gay mayor's bid for Congress had the annual Stonewall Festival focusing on politics as much as partying," in particular, since "this year, the party comes three weeks shy of a July U.S. Senate debate over President Bush's proposed ban on gay marriage, which will force Democratic presidential candidate John Kerry to state clearly where he stands on the issue.[74]

Over the years, the promotion of a specific political agenda has become a staple item at gay pride events. Indeed, a gay participant of the 2010 San Francisco Gay Pride parade noted, "It's part political, it's part a party,"[75] while at 2010 Boston Pride, "Repeal of 'Don't Ask Don't Tell' was nearly everywhere, as was support for the Transgender Rights Bill, and also anti-Israel/pro-Palestine messages" (note also that both the governor of Massachusetts and the mayor of Boston participated in the event).[76] And in a city like Charlotte, which is representative of the more church-going South, gay pastors and gay churches are vocal participants in the day's events. (2010 Pride Charlotte included public prayer and worship by local "gay Christian" leaders.) Yet Starbucks, which refuses to sponsor "political or religious activities" actively sponsors gay events which are charged with political – and sometimes religious – content. On what basis?

In 2005, Starbucks chose to refrain from distributing a new CD by Bruce Springsteen, apparently because of the sexually graphic lyrics on the track entitled "Reno," which mention his hiring a prostitute for anal sex. This was certainly a commendable decision, and one that sent out a positive message as well, as I noted in a letter to Starbucks written on June 17th, 2005. Once again, however, the decision only highlighted Starbucks' double standard, one in which "diversity" *includes* perversity but *excludes* any moral objection to such behavior. As I explained in my June, 2005 letter:

> I applaud the decision of Starbucks to refrain from

distributing the new CD of Bruce Springsteen, apparently because of the sexually graphic lyrics on the track entitled "Reno".…

This decision certainly sends out a positive message. Unfortunately, your sponsorship of the gay pride events sends out the exact opposite message, since these events are well-known for their open celebration and endorsement of all kinds of similar sexual behavior.…

Has Starbucks then decided to ban sexually explicit, heterosexual material from its stores while actively sponsoring sexually explicit, homosexual events with the money earned from those stores? [Enclosed with the letter were pictures graphically illustrating some of the public displays that had taken place at Charlotte Pride in 2004 and 2005.][77]

The official response from Starbucks was polite, respectful, but firm: The position of Starbucks remains the same. Their sponsoring of the Charlotte Pride event, including its sexually perverse and explicitly political sides (these are my words, not theirs), was definitely part of their core principle of embracing diversity. (I was told by phone on June 30, 2005, that they understood that I would still be calling them if they had been sponsoring open *heterosexual* displays in the park. Their position, nonetheless, remained the same.) As Kevin Carothers reiterated in his letter dated September 2, 2005:

> As we discussed, Starbucks is a company committed to its guiding principles, which includes embracing diversity. It is an essential component of the way we do business and is important to our many partners (employees) and customers in the 36 countries we serve. While we welcome differing points of view and respect your opinion, we remain committed to supporting events that promote diversity and inclusion, such as the Gay Pride Parade.

The letter also stated, "While we understand you disagree with our perspective, we hope that you will consider taking a look at us from another view. You might find that, like you, we are committed to making a positive impact in the communities we serve," after which Mr. Carothers listed a number of humanitarian works which they help underwrite. To be sure, the endeavors he described are certainly highly commendable, but all of them could continue unabated *without* Starbucks' sponsorship of gay pride events. And it is difficult to see how the sponsoring of these events which flaunt public perversity make a *positive impact* on the local communities. To the contrary, choosing *not* to sponsor these events could make a very positive impact on these communities, but Starbucks is clearly committed to "diversity."

This is evidenced in its conversation-sparking coffee cups called, "The Way I See It." As their website explains,

> **Sparking conversation** In the tradition of coffee houses everywhere, Starbucks has always supported a good, healthy discussion. To get people talking, "The Way I See It" is a collection of thoughts, opinions and expressions provided by notable figures that now appear on our widely shared cups.
>
> **A range of voices** We invited a group of people who brought both diversity and life experiences to the mix. Those who accepted, offered pearls of their life experiences to entertain, engage and hopefully get us all thinking.[78]

And what might that "diversity" include? Consider this quote from Armistead Maupin, author of the well-known chronicle of gay life, *Tales of the City*.[79] Maupin contributed "The Way I See It," #43: "My only regret about being gay is that I repressed it for so long. I surrendered my youth to the people I feared when I could have been out there loving someone. Don't make that mistake yourself. Life's too damn short."

And you thought Starbucks was just another, specialty coffee company? Hardly. As a company committed to "embracing diversity," they are committed to supporting homosexual, bisexual, and transgender expression and activism. Perhaps some of you might be losing your taste for Starbucks just about now?

To be sure, the coffee cups also contained quotes from men like Michael Medved, the Orthodox Jewish, strongly conservative, Hollywood film critic, John Wooden, the legendary UCLA basketball coach, known for his strong moral convictions, and Rick Warren, the internationally-known pastor. But you can be sure that not a single quote uttered by any of these men could be considered "anti-gay" in any way, while an encouragement to young people to embrace their homosexuality was quite OK.[80]

KRAFT FOODS, THE GAY GAMES, AND "DIVERSITY"

During the first half of 2005, Kraft Foods, manufacturers of everything from Ritz Crackers to Oreo Cookies, came under criticism for its major sponsorship of the 2006 Gay Games in Chicago. (These games are held every four years and bring together 10,000-15,000 GLBT athletes from around the world. Cities bid for the right to hold the games.) Responding to this criticism in a May 23rd, 2005 email sent to all Kraft employees, Marc Firestone, Executive Vice President, Corporate Counsel and Corporate Secretary of Kraft Foods Inc., had this to say:

> While Kraft certainly doesn't go looking for controversy, we have long been dedicated to support the concept and the reality of *diversity*. It's the right thing to do and it's good for our business and our work environment.
>
> *Diversity* makes us a stronger company and connects us with the *diversity* that exists among the consumers who buy our products.[81]

So then, diversity, used here with explicit reference to a major gay event, is something to be celebrated. It's "right" and it's "good"; it makes for "a stronger company" and connects that company with "the diversity that exists among the consumers who buy [Kraft's] products" – with the notable exception, however, of the multiplied thousands of customers who complained to Kraft about their involvement in the gay games. Diversity, it would appear, does not extend that far.

Mr. Firestone continues in his email:

> *Diversity* is more than a word many people like to say. At Kraft we truly respect all kinds of differences. And *diversity* is not a selective concept. By definition, it's nothing if not inclusive. We respect *diversity* of ethnicity, gender, experience, background, personal style and yes, sexual orientation and gender identity. Recognizing, respecting and valuing these differences helps us be a more successful business and a workplace where all employees can realize

their full potential.[82]

Really? How can he state that Kraft truly respects "all kinds of differences" when the convictions of millions of conservative Christians, Jews, Muslims, Hindus, and others are disrespected or ignored? (It is no small matter that the sacred, holy books of most of the world's population speak against homosexual practice.) How can he say that diversity is "nothing if not inclusive" when the whole purpose of his communiqué was to explain why Kraft was choosing to *exclude* the views being expressed by a large volume of e-mailers, the majority of whom opposed Kraft's sponsorship of the Gay Games?

Under the rubric of "diversity," Mr. Firestone lists respect for "ethnicity, gender, experience, background, personal style and yes, sexual orientation and gender identity" but does *not* list "religious beliefs" or "personal convictions." Was this merely an oversight, or is "gender identity" protected by diversity – this, of course, would include such personal preferences as cross-dressing and transgenderism – while religious beliefs and personal convictions (as opposed to "personal style") are not? Moreover, since no one has questioned Kraft's respect for heterosexuality, respect for "sexual orientation" can only mean respect for non-heterosexual orientations. Why not state this plainly?

Why don't Starbucks and Kraft and others simply say, "We embrace homosexuality (even in its most base, perverse forms, well illustrated by some of the gay events we sponsor) and we enthusiastically support the gay social and political agenda"? Why not put the cards on the table? Could it be that to do so would cost these companies business? Could it be that to do so would bring about an adverse moral reaction? Could it be that do so would expose the *lack* of diversity actually embraced? (To be candid, ten to fifteen years ago, articulating these views publicly would have cost these companies dearly; twenty-five to thirty years ago, it would have been unthinkable even to have mentioned corporate sponsorship of gay activism; today, the answer is not as clear in terms of adverse reaction.)

HOW LOW CAN "DIVERSITY" GO?

As noted in Chapter Four, for several years, on the campus of Oberlin College, there was a running debate over whether the school should officially charter a student club devoted to Bondage, Discipline, and Sadomasochism (BDSM). Some of the faculty endorsed the concept in the name of promoting diversity. Physics Professor John Scofield demurred, stating, "This just demonstrates the silliness with which we toss around the word 'diversity.'

We can also become more diverse by recruiting more pedophiles and necrophiliacs."[83] Or, put this another way, On what basis should pedophilia and necrophilia *not* be included under the rubric of "diversity"?

On May 31, 2006, a new political party was launched in the Netherlands called "Naastenliefde, Vrijheid & Diversiteit" (abbreviated NVD), which literally means, "Neighborly Love (or, Charity), Freedom, and Diversity." According to their official platform, they want to "maximize diversity and liberty," which means:

> allowing individuals, from the age of 12, to vote, have sex, gamble, choose their place of residence, and use soft drugs. Hard drugs would be legal at 16. They also intend to eliminate marriage in the law, permit public nudity anywhere in the country, make railway travel free [I'm not sure how this fits into their platform!], and institute a comprehensive animal rights platform.[84]

In addition, the NVD

> also wants to legalize private use of child pornography and allow non-violent pornography to be screened on daytime television. They are against laws that would explicitly outlaw sexual contact between animals and humans (which is not illegal in Holland now), and support laws criminalizing the 'sexual maltreatment' of animals."[85]

As reported by Reuters, "The party said it wanted to cut the legal age for sexual relations to 12 and eventually scrap the limit altogether. 'A ban just makes children curious,' Ad van den Berg, one of the party's founders, told the Algemeen Dagblad (AD) newspaper."[86]

So, "diversity" in the Netherlands now includes the legalization of child pornography, the legalization of sex with minors beginning at the age of twelve, and the legalization of bestiality, as long as it does not include the "sexual maltreatment" of animals. Isn't this perversity rather than diversity? And isn't this in the normal progression when "diversity" becomes the codeword – without qualification – for homosexuality and homosexual activism?

Not surprisingly, news of this political party's platform was greeted with shock and outrage in Holland, despite the country's already liberal policies:

"The Netherlands, which already has liberal policies on soft drugs, prostitution and gay marriage, was shocked by the plan."[87] But why should the nation be shocked? Isn't it inevitable that the same nation that was among the first to legalize soft drug use, prostitution, and gay marriage would be among the first to entertain the possibility of legalizing consensual sex with minors and the social acceptance of bestiality – and in the name of diversity at that?

Think about it for a moment. In the past, "diversity" referred to things like ethnic and cultural and religious diversity, but then it became a codeword for homosexuality (then bisexuality, then transgenderism), *without prescribed limits or boundaries.* After all, if it's gay, it's good, and it should be embraced in the name of diversity. Why then should it surprise us that some people would take the concept of "diversity" even further? On what basis should pedophilia and bestiality *not* be included under the rubric of "diversity"? (Again, I'm not equating homosexuality with pedophilia or bestiality; I'm asking on what basis these things should not be included under the heading of "diversity.") And if the public perversity often paraded at gay pride events is protected under the heading of diversity, why shouldn't pedophilia – especially, the allegedly "consensual" sex acts between a minor and his boy "lover" – be protected under that same heading? And why not bestiality? Isn't this all part of sexual "diversity"?

This will obviously sound extreme to many, but I ask you: On what basis is it extreme? To many Americans, the idea of men having sex with men and women having sex with women is morally wrong, yet it is becoming taboo even to suggest such a thing. A good dose of diversity training at work will cure this "homophobic" condition! (For more on this, see below, Chapter Fourteen.)

To many Americans, the idea of topless "Dikes on Bikes" publicly proclaiming nipple freedom or drag queens performing vulgar dances in the presence of little children is perverse, yet acts such as these are not only tolerated in the name of diversity, they are actually *celebrated* under the name of diversity, often with the full sponsorship of corporate America. What's coming next?

The real shock about the recent developments in the Netherlands was not that this new political party was formed (can you imagine proudly and publicly campaigning for such a platform?). The real shock was that, "An opinion poll published Tuesday [May 30th, 2006] showed that 82 percent wanted the government to do something to stop the new party, while 67 percent said promoting pedophilia should be illegal."[88] So, fully 1/3 of Dutch people surveyed thought that the promotion of pedophilia should be legal (or, at least, did not feel it should be illegal).

This too is a natural progression of the concept of "diversity," and I ask once more: Why not? To be sure, I recognize that the "diversity" party in Holland represented an extreme, but it is the inevitable result of the unqualified use of "diversity" in gay activism today.

RECLAIMING PRINCIPLED AMERICAN DIVERSITY

Historically, one of America's greatest strengths has been its embrace of diversity in the wider, less politically-charged, sense of the word. Our nation has been a great melting pot, ethnically, culturally, and religiously, and by design, America embraces diversity of culture, creed, and color. In fact, in 1790, President George Washington received a letter from Moses Seixas, the warden of Touro Synagogue, seeking assurance that the Jewish people would have religious freedom in this newly formed nation. Washington famously replied that his government would "give to bigotry no sanction, to persecution no assistance." Bigotry has no place in our land!

This, indeed, is the American way, and so our past treatment of Native Americans and African Americans is something that every fair-minded American rejects and regrets. To the contrary, we understand that diversity, in its ethnic and cultural sense, is part of what makes us great. Let all peoples of all backgrounds be embraced and loved and honored and esteemed.[89] But let perversity be called for what it is, and let it be renounced rather than respected. And let the businesses of America reconsider their embrace of GLBT activism in the workplace (and beyond) in the name of "diversity," and let them be ashamed rather than proud of their sponsorship of public displays of perversity. Is this too much to ask?

*I have to admit that I enjoy watching Queer Eye for the Straight Guy,
even more than other "regular" makeover shows. Knowing that these guys
are queer -- meaning openly gay men -- makes it more fun.*

Jaap Kooijman, "They're Here, They're Queer, and Straight America Loves It,"
GLQ: A Journal of Lesbian and Gay Studies Number 11 (2005)

Queer is hip, salsa is happening, and rap is here to stay.

Gloria Anzaldúa and AnaLouise Keating
This Bridge We Call Home: Radical Visions for Transformation

*Now that "queer" is hip and studios are making the foray into films
with queer- content, are they really ready to market their films as "gay?"*

Posted in qlounge2004.queerlounge.org

Queer is Hip, Queer is Cool -- Dogmas in the Queer Scene

Posted in queeruption.tribe.net

9

Lavender Language, Gender Speak, and Queer Semantics: Towards an Omnisexual Society?

S*omething queer is happening to the word "queer."* That was the title of a November 5, 2003 Associated Press article.[1] The article explains:

> Originally a synonym for "odd" or "unusual," the word evolved into an anti-gay insult in the last century, only to be reclaimed by defiant gay and lesbian activists who chanted: "We're here, we're queer, get used to it."
>
> Now "queer" is sneaking into the mainstream – and taking on a hipster edge as a way to describe any sexual orientation beyond straight.[2]

Queer as mainstream? Queer as hipster? Without a doubt.

> It's the kind of exchange that still makes many -- gay or straight -- wince. That's because, in the 1920s and '30s the word "queer" became synonymous with "pansy," "sissy" and even "pervert," says Gregory Ward, a Northwestern University linguist who teaches a course on language and sexuality.
>
> Now, Ward says, the increasing use of "queer" -- as in the prime-time TV show titles "Queer Eye for the Straight Guy" and "Queer as Folk" -- is changing the word's image.
>
> "It's really losing the hurtful and quasi-violent nature it had," Ward says.
>
> Trish McDermott, vice president of "romance" at the Match.com online dating service, says she's seeing the word appear more often in personal ads.
>
> The title of one current ad: "Nice Guy for the Queer Guy."
>
> Meanwhile, a recent review in the Chicago Tribune's Metromix entertainment guide defined the crowd in a new upscale bar as "model-types and young clubbers amid dressy Trixies, middle-aged Gold Coast cigar-chompers and queer-eyed straight guys" (the latter term referring to straight men who've spiffed themselves up).[3]

So, it's no longer queer to be queer! Yes, queer has been reclaimed – even redeemed – and quite successfully recycled.[4]

For years, queer meant, "(1) Deviating from the expected or normal; strange; (2) Odd or unconventional, as in behavior; eccentric; (3) Of a questionable nature or character; suspicious."[5] And when used by heterosexuals to describe homosexuals, it was one of the uglier, baser insults. "There's something the matter with you! You're not normal! You're deviant, weird, despicable. Stay away from me! You're queer." Now, universities boast of their Queer Studies programs, the media celebrates queer, and theologians write queer Bible commentaries.[6] Do you think this happened by accident?

DESENSITIZE, JAM AND CONVERT

The oft-cited, threefold strategy of gay social scientists Marshall Kirk and Hunter Madsen – "Desensitize, Jam and Convert" – tells us that this semantic transformation was not the result of chance.[7] Rather, it was part of a well-conceived (even if occasionally subconscious) plan to win the battle of words, since *whoever wins the battle of words wins the war of ideas.*[8]

The strategy is simple: Take the offensiveness out of the offense. Normalize the abnormal. Make the unacceptable acceptable. Legitimize the illegitimate. Remove the outrage from the outrageous. Take the sense of urgency out of the alarm. This way, when the alarm is sounded, people will not even hear it. Their ears will have become so accustomed to its tone that it no longer startles them, no longer alerts them, no longer wakes them up. As Prof. Ward said, above, with respect to "queer," it no longer has "the hurtful and quasi-violent nature it had." Desensitize, jam, and convert.

According to Kirk and Madsen,

> If gays present themselves – or allow themselves to be presented – as overwhelmingly different and threatening, they will put straights on a triple-red alert, driving them to overt acts of political oppression or physical violence.
>
> …to desensitize straights to gays and gayness, inundate them in a continuous flood of gay-related advertising, presented in the least offensive fashion possible. If straights can't shut off the shower, they may at least eventually get used to being wet.[9]

In short,

... The main thing is to talk about gayness until the issue becomes thoroughly tiresome. . . . If you can get [straights] to think homosexuality is just another thing - meriting no more than a shrug of the shoulders - then your battle for legal and social rights is virtually won.[10]

Yes, homosexuality "is just another thing." No big deal. Nothing out of the ordinary. Certainly nothing to get excited about. It's just another variation of sexuality, just everyday, ho-hum, kind of stuff, "meriting no more than a shrug of the shoulders" – if even that.

But that's just the start. Next is "jamming," which amounts to smearing anyone who disagrees with the homosexual agenda. As Kirk and Madsen explain:

> As the name implies, Jamming involves the insertion into the engine of a pre-existing, *incompatible* emotional response, gridlocking its mechanism as thoroughly as though one had sprinkled fine sand into the workings of an old-fashioned pocket watch. . . .
>
> The trick is to get the bigot into the position of feeling a conflicting twinge of shame, along with his reward, whenever his homohatred surfaces, so that his reward will be diluted or spoiled. . . . Thus, propagandistic advertisements can depict homophobic and homohating bigots as crude loudmouths and a—holes – people who say not only 'faggot' but 'nigger,' kike,' and other shameful epithets – who are 'not Christian. . . . In short, it can link homohating bigotry with all sorts of attributes the bigot would be ashamed to possess, and with social consequences he would find unpleasant and scary.[11]

"Jam homo-hatred by linking it to Nazi horror," urge Kirk and Madsen; associate all who oppose homosexuality with images like "Klansmen demanding that gays be slaughtered," "hysterical backwoods preachers," "menacing punks," and a "tour of Nazi concentration camps where homosexuals were tortured and gassed."[12] Yet that is only the second of three steps:

Put briefly, if Desensitization lets the watch run down, and Jamming throws sand in the works, Conversion reverses the spring so that the hands run backward. . . .

In Conversion, the bigot, who holds a very negative stereotypic picture, is repeatedly exposed to literal picture/ label pairs, in magazines, and on billboards and TV, of gays – explicitly labeled as such! – who not only don't look like his picture of a homosexual, but are carefully selected to look either like the bigot and his friends, or like any one of his other stereotypes of all-right guys – the kind of people he already likes and admires. This image must, of necessity, be carefully tailored to be free of absolutely every element of the widely held stereotype of how 'faggots' look, dress, and sound.[13]

Thus, conversion refers to the "conversion of the average American's emotions, mind, and will, through a planned psychological attack, in the form of propaganda fed to the nation via the media."[14]

To the gay objection that such ads would "Uncle Tommify" gays, since the ads are lies – in other words, "that is *not* how *all* gays actually look" and "gays know it and bigots know it," the authors reply,

Yes, of course, we know it, too. But it makes no difference that the ads are lies; not to us, because we're using them to ethically good effect, to counter negative stereotypes that are every bit as much lies, and far more wicked ones; not to bigots, because the ads will have their effect on them whether they believe them or not.[15]

The strategy has worked brilliantly, and many Americans have been "converted" in a very short time span. With respect to "queer," the sting has been largely removed and now queer is cool, even creative. Queer is something to be admired rather than abhorred, even for the straight guy. Is that queer guy giving you the queer eye? How cool! Maybe he'll give you a makeover too, just like on the TV show. Yet as startling as the image makeovers are on the Queer Eye TV show, the complete *semantic makeover* of the concept of queer is even more startling.

IF IT COULD HAPPEN TO "QUEER" . . .

Let me illustrate this for you by using some other words with very negative connotations in the gay and straight world. (I don't engage in this exercise to be offensive or to trivialize the issues involved but rather to drive home the point of just how drastically things have changed with respect to the use of the word "queer." That is to say, at one time "queer" was as offensive as some of the words I'll use as examples, although I fully understand the GLBT community has not chosen to "rehabilitate" them, as it has the word "queer.")

What if the word had been "faggot" instead of "queer"? Could you picture Faggot Studies being taught at Harvard University? How about a professor of Faggot Literature or a Faggot emphasis in the Master's degree program? What about "faggot" making its way into the media with a brand new show, "Faggot Eye for the Frumpy Guy?" Or maybe, "Faggots as Folk"? Is this any more absurd than the reclaiming of "queer"?

What if the word had been "sodomite" or "sodomy" instead of "queer"? Just think of it: "I'm majoring in Sodomite Studies at my college." Or, "He's one of the top Sodomy scholars in the world today." Or, "Did you see the latest episode of Sodomite Eye for the Simple Guy?" What's the difference between this and "queer" in terms of a very ugly word losing its ugliness?

What about substituting the word "pervert"? Can you picture people watching, "Pervert Eye for the Plain Guy"? How about students signing up for classes in the Pervert Studies Department, maybe even taught by a Distinguished Pervert Professor? If it could happen to the word queer, it could happen to faggot or sodomite or pervert – or "dyke" for that matter, instead of lesbian, thus, "The Larry Kramer Initiative for Faggot and Dyke Studies at Yale."[16] Why not?

With respect to "queer," the offense has lost its offensiveness and the outrageous has been robbed of its outrage. The transformation has been complete. As noted by Ramon Johnson on Gaylife.com,

Is "Queer" a Derogatory Word?

Did you know that today, the word "queer" is most often used in a non-derogatory way?

Once used by homophobes to negatively describe a gay man or woman, the term is now being used by the gay community itself as a positive or neutral descriptive of each other. By embracing a word that was used to attack or degrade, the gay community has demagnetized the strength of the word, making it a common everyday term. This lessens the effect of the word when used against them.

This process by which a word meaning changes from negative or neutral to more positive is called amelioration. The word "fag" has also been ameliorated by gays themselves.

Other communities embrace words used to degrade them as well, such as women using the "B" word to describe each other or African-Americans using the "N" word to describe themselves.

Nonetheless, much care should be taken when using an ameliorated word as some may take offense. For instance, just because gays have embraced the word "queer" does not mean it cannot be used as a term of hate by a homophobe.[17]

The remaking of "queer" is reminiscent of the conversation between Humpty Dumpty and Alice in Lewis Carroll's *Through the Looking-Glass*:

"I don't know what you mean by 'glory,'" Alice said.

Humpty Dumpty smiled contemptuously. "Of course you don't—till I tell you. I meant 'there's a nice knock-down argument for you!'"

"But 'glory' doesn't mean 'a nice knock-down argument'," Alice objected.

"When *I* use a word," Humpty Dumpty said, in rather a scornful tone, "it means just what I choose it to mean—neither more nor less."

"The question is," said Alice, "whether you *can* make words mean so many different things."

"The question is," said Humpty Dumpty, "which is to be master – that's all."[18]

Indeed, the one who defines the meaning of words really is "master." Humpty Dumpty was right!

DEFINING HOMOPHOBIA

With respect, to the meaning of "queer," amelioration has certainly worked wonders. But this was only the first step. The next step was to demonize the opposition. So, not only are homosexuals no longer called homosexuals – instead they are gay[19] – but those who do not affirm them or who differ with their agenda are homophobes – not happy, not healthy, not wholesome, but homophobes – suffering from a psychological disorder called homophobia. Yes, if you do not celebrate and embrace homosexuality you are a homophobe, plain and simple.[20]

What exactly is homophobia?[21] Let's break the word down into its two components, *homo* and *phobia* and see what we can figure out.

According to Dictionary.com, a phobia is "a persistent, irrational fear of a specific object, activity, or situation that leads to a compelling desire to avoid it." There are *lots* of phobias out there today. In fact, The Phobia List claims that there are sixty-eight phobias starting with the letter A alone![22] The first ten on the list are:

- Ablutophobia- Fear of washing or bathing.
- Acarophobia- Fear of itching or of the insects that cause itching
- Acerophobia- Fear of sourness
- Achluophobia- Fear of darkness
- Acousticophobia- Fear of noise
- Acrophobia- Fear of heights
- Aerophobia- Fear of drafts, air swallowing, or airborne noxious substances
- Aeroacrophobia- Fear of open high places
- Aeronausiphobia- Fear of vomiting secondary to airsickness
- Agateophobia- Fear of insanity

How about these?
- Ailurophobia- Fear of cats
- Albuminurophobia- Fear of kidney disease
- Alektorophobia- Fear of chickens
- Algophobia- Fear of pain
- Alliumphobia- Fear of garlic
- Allodoxaphobia- Fear of opinions
- Altophobia- Fear of heights
- Amathophobia- Fear of dust
- Amaxophobia- Fear of riding in a car

- Ambulophobia- Fear of walking
- Amnesiphobia- Fear of amnesia

I don't know about you, but I don't want to have any phobias. I want to be a mentally healthy person. Therefore, logic would argue that all phobias must go, and that means getting rid of homophobia, which, presumably would mean "a persistent, irrational fear of homosexuals, homosexual activity, or homosexual situations that leads to a compelling desire to avoid homosexuals and homosexuality."

What exactly would this look like? Well, the person afflicted with alektorophobia suffers from a persistent, irrational fear of chickens, and the person afflicted with alliumphobia suffers from a persistent, irrational fear of garlic. So, if someone suffered from alektorophobia and alliumphobia and homophobia, they would have irrational fears that would sound something like this: "Keep those chickens and that garlic away from me! And don't let those homosexuals come within a mile of my house. I don't want to get infected!" *That* would be homophobia, *that* would be irrational and ugly, and *that* would be something to get rid of.

But that's not what homophobia means. If you don't affirm same-sex marriage and teaching about same-sex households in elementary schools and embracing "diversity" in the workplace, you're a homophobe, an intolerant bigot. Some would even say you're sick, as reflected in this comment from a listener to my interview on the Thom Hartmann show: "You're either a very sick individual, or evil to the core."[23]

As noted by philosophy professor Gary Colwell, "The argument, when unpacked, amounts to this:

> 1 All critics of homosexual practice are homophobic.
> 2 Being homophobic is bad.
> [Thus]
> 3 All critics of homosexual practice are bad, *or*
> 3' What the critics are is bad, *or*
> 3" What the critics have (a phobia) is bad."[24]

And what about those who stand *for* "gay rights"? They are champions and heroes, models of tolerance and acceptance. They are well-adjusted and secure, concerned for justice and equality, proponents of this generation's civil rights battle, and not afraid to stand up to the violent, angry homophobes and religious crazies. At least that's how the picture has been painted.

So, not only have homosexuals been recast as gays (or even queers) but those who do not embrace homosexuality have been recast as homophobes – and this is only the beginning. There is a new term for a heterosexual: nongay.[25] Yes, if you are a heterosexual, you are now defined as *not* being part of a tiny minority – roughly 3% – of our nation's population.[26] You are herewith classified as nongay, leading to an obvious question: Why should our heterosexual identity be defined and described by the fact that we are not homosexuals?

Speaking as a white American man, I'm not non-black or non-Asian or non-Canadian or non-female anymore than a black Jamaican woman is non-white or non-Portuguese or non-Chinese or non-male. Why then should I – or anyone else – be identified as "nongay"? Since when did everything revolve around one's relationship to gay?

Asian Americans number about 4% of our nation's population, so calling all heterosexuals nongay would be roughly equivalent to calling 96% of our population non-Asian. Now, writing from Asia, the home of almost three billion Asians, it would be logical to say that 96% of all Americans are non-Asian – but not writing from America! Yet "gay" has somehow become the dominant position and things are defined in relationship to gay.

If you have been involved in *pro-family* work for decades, you are now dubbed *anti-gay* (more precisely, an anti-gay extremist).[27] On the flip side, if you endorse homosexual practice you embrace *diversity*, even if, in the process, you marginalize and exclude a diverse group of people holding to many different beliefs and convictions.[28] And if you are fiercely opposed to traditional, biblical values but in favor of same-sex marriage, you are *tolerant*. In fact, you have the right to call anyone who does not agree with you *intolerant*. You even have the right to advocate that their freedom of speech be taken away.[29] How dare they not embrace the gay rights movement!

Gay is now the arbiter, the measuring rod, the great divide. How far will this go? Where, exactly, will this semantic and ideological shift take us? Let's look at some more examples.

FROM POLYGAMY TO POLYAMORY TO "INTERGENERATIONAL INTIMACY"

The word *polygamy*, filled with negative connotations in our culture, is now being replaced by *polyamory*, defined as:

the practice of having more than one loving relationship at the same time, with the full knowledge and consent of all partners involved. The relationships are long-term, intimate, and usually (but not necessarily) sexual. Persons who consider themselves emotionally suited to such relationships may define themselves as polyamorous, often abbreviated to *poly*.[30]

Until recently, polyamory had a different name: adultery. Not anymore! Just get all the parties involved to agree to the new relationships (really now, that jealousy stuff is so outmoded) and be poly – which rhymes with jolly – instead.

Not surprisingly, polyamory groups sometimes march in gay pride events, part and parcel of the sexual liberation vanguard.[31] In fact, in 2004, polyamory advocate Jasmine Walston stated, "We're where the gay rights movement was 30 years ago." Five years later, in 2009, *Newsweek* featured an article by Jessica Bennett entitled, "Polyamory: The Next Sexual Revolution"[32] with this bold, provocative beginning: "Only You. And You. And You. Polyamory— relationships with multiple, mutually consenting partners—has a coming-out party."

The article continued:

It's enough to make any monogamist's head spin. But the traditionalists had better get used to it.

Researchers are just beginning to study the phenomenon, but the few who do estimate that openly polyamorous families in the United States number more than half a million, with thriving contingents in nearly every major city.[33]

So, this is not group sex or adultery or even polygamy. It is polyamory – and *Newsweek* warns that "traditionalists had better get used to it." There is even an argument now that polyamory should be classified as a sexual orientation for the purposes of protection against discrimination.[34] Some polyamorists actually claim they were "born that way"![35]

This provides another example of semantic shifting and twisting: Rather than saying, "All those who oppose open adultery have a right to be shocked over these latest developments," the article tells us that polyamory is all about love and expanded families, while those who oppose this lifestyle are old-fashioned, puritanical, stuck-in-the-mud "traditionalists." How remarkable! But the semantic shifts have gone even further. There's not a single gay or straight person I've ever talked with who thought there was anything positive in the term "pedophile." Yet advocates of consensual man-boy relationships (including some leading psychologists), have come up with a new term for pedophilia, namely, "intergenerational intimacy."[36] As wryly observed by John Leo in his online article "Tongue Violence":

> To the amazement of all, pedophiles and some sex researchers now refer to adult sex with children as "intergenerational intimacy." ("Officer, one of these children has just been groped by this intergenerational intimate, formerly a child molester.") It would be interesting to speculate how the rest of the perversions could be brightened up with spiffy new language. Perhaps necrophilia would emerge as "post-terminal intimacy."[37]

You never know! The *Koinos Magazine* website[38] offers an overview of a 2000/2001 volume which states, "In *Koinos* 25, psychiatrist Frank van Ree examines the taboo which applies to intergenerational intimate contacts . . . ."[39] Maybe "post-terminal intimacy" *is* next.

Now, to be perfectly clear, I am not comparing all homosexual practice with pedophilia or necrophilia. But I *am* saying that if queer can become quaint and the world can be divided into gay and nongay, and if sex researchers can invent terms like "intergenerational intimacy," then *anything* is possible in the realm of amelioration and queer semantics. And so, the gay lexicon continues to expand.

LEARNING THE GLBT LEXICON

Here are some examples. How would you define "biphobia"? Is it a fear of bifocals? Maybe a fear of bicycles? Perhaps a fear of biology or a fear of two things? Not even close.

How about "transphobia"? Is it a fear of transition? Maybe a fear of trans-Atlantic flights or a fear of translating? Wrong again.

Let's try one more: Can you define "pomosexual"? Yes, this is a tough one. Perhaps it refers to a sexually active person from Pomona? Or maybe it's a typo for "promosexual," meaning someone who is into promoting sexuality?

Hardly!

The correct answers are as follows: *Biphobia* is "the fear of, discrimination against, or hatred of bisexuals" while *transphobia*, "refers to discrimination against transsexuality and transsexual or transgender people, based on the expression of their internal gender identity."[40]

As for *pomosexual*, it refers to "A person who shuns labels such as *heterosexual* and *homosexual* that define individuals by their sexual preferences."[41] This, of course, is to be distinguished from *pansexual*, which means, "a person who participates in (or is open to) sexual activities of many kinds."[42] This, in turn, is to not to be confused with *heteroflexible*, which describes "A heterosexual person who is open to relationships with people of the same sex."[43]

What about the word "genderqueer"? This is a term "for people who feel that their gender identities [sic] or gender expression do not correspond to the gender assigned to them at birth, but who do not want to transition to the 'opposite' gender."[44]

Let's consider this carefully. First, the concept of having multiple "gender identities" is now acceptable (which means that you might consider yourself male and female and even something else, not biologically but psychologically).[45] Second, it is now widely accepted in many GLBT circles that you are not *born* male or female but you are *assigned a gender* at birth (by society, through the medium of your parents and the doctors).[46] There is even a regulation concerning this in the San Francisco Unified School Policy: "Transgender students shall not be forced to use the locker room corresponding to their gender assigned at birth."[47]

As explained in a GLSEN (Gay, Lesbian, and Straight Educational Network) manual for public schools:

> **Gender** is traditionally thought to be a set of two binary categories: male and female. An individual's gender is also traditionally determined by their body. However, many people are identifying, expressing, and understanding their gender in a broad spectrum of ways that this traditional binary system does not include. Thinking about gender assignment, identity, and expression are three ways to begin to understand how gender may be determined for us by others, and how we experience and express gender as individuals:
> **Assignment:** Gender is usually *assigned* at birth and

determined by our physical body-type to be male or female. This assignment is decided by doctors and parents (not the individual) and is the very first classification that an individual receives. Corresponding gender-roles (behavior, dress, activities that one may participate in, etc.) are usually enforced based on the individual's gender assignment at birth.[48]

To be sure, I am acutely aware that many children and adults suffer terrible emotional distress over their biological sex, convinced that they are trapped in the wrong body, and in some tragic cases, this trauma leads to suicide. I want to repeat that I do not minimize the struggles experienced by those who self-identify as transgender, and the more I interact with them, the more I am pained for them. At the same time, I am convinced that the best solution is to help these individuals from the inside out – in other words, helping them be at home in their bodies – rather than sending a little boy to school dressed as a girl or performing sex-change surgery (coupled with a lifelong hormone regimen) on a teenager or even an adult.[49]

THE IMPLICATIONS OF "TRANSGENDER"

The reality is that once "transgender" is accepted as normal, then everything else has to change, as seen in the just-cited GLSEN definitions. "Traditionally" gender referred to male and female; "traditionally" it was determined by one's body – apparently an outmoded, primitive concept. Worse still, it is doctors and parents who *assign* one's gender at birth based on one's "physical body-type." (In other words, "It's a boy!") These new concepts are being taught to our kids, from elementary school and up, and the conclusion is unavoidable: Accepting homosexuality as a normal variant of sexuality opens up a whole Pandora's box of other "sexualities" that must be accepted. And accepting transgenderism as a normal variant within gender opens up a whole Pandora's box of other "genders" that must be accepted. It can be no other way.

Listen again to the explanations provided in the GLSEN guide:

> **Gender Identity:** This is the individual's internal, deeply felt sense of being either male, female, or something other or in-between. Everyone has a gender identity. . . . For some, however, their gender identity is different from their

biological sex.

Gender Expression: This refers to an individual's characteristics and behaviors such as appearance, dress, mannerisms, speech patterns, and social interactions that are perceived as masculine or feminine. . . . Often, transgender people seek to make their gender expression match their gender identity rather than their birth assigned gender.[50]

So, one's "gender identity" may not match one's biological sex, while one's "gender expression" might not match their "birth assigned gender" – and this is supposedly very important for our educators to grasp. In keeping with this, the "Bi-Gender" website defines "birth gender" as "Gender assigned at birth based on the Doctor's best guess at the time. Usually based on the visible plumbing."[51] Yes,

This site is based on a few beliefs and here is one of the most important.

We believe that the plumbing that one is born with is secondary to the person you want to be.

Birth Gender may well govern what is put on your drivers license...but it is your spiritual gender that governs how you express your life.[52]

Spiritual gender? In the words of Chaz Bono, "Gender is between your ears, not between your legs."[53] Such is the thinking of this postmodern, relativistic generation – a very gender-confused generation – and we seem to have forgotten that, "Each cell of a person's body contains chromosomes which identify that individual as either male or female. It is not simply a question of different genitals. Before birth prenatal hormones shape the brains of boys to be different than those of girls."[54]

GLSEN, of course, would differ with this, providing a glossary of "Gender Speak" for educators and school children, including definitions for: Gender Assignment (Birth Sex); Gender Identity; Gender Equity; Gender Expression; Gender Non-Conforming; Gender Queer; Homophobia; Sexual Orientation; Transgender; Transphobia; and Transsexual.[55]

As bizarre and even twisted as some of this may sound to many of you, we've barely scratched the surface of this queer new lexicon. Consider the word "transcendgender" (I'm not making this up) as defined by the Sex-lexis. com website: "A contraction of transcend + transgender meaning a person who transcends gender."[56]

What exactly does this mean? The definition includes

> pre-operative and post-operative-transsexuals, transgenderists, transvestites, crossdressers, female and male impersonators, drag queens/kings, intersexuals, gender dysphorics, gender-outlaws, transnaturals, variant-expressives, butch-lesbians, boss girls, drag-queens, transitions and everyone in-between. *There is no correlation between sexual-orientation and gender-identity*; some transgendered people prefer members of their own sex , others prefer members of the opposite-sex.
>
> SYNONYMS: gender-variant ; transgendered ; transgressively-gendered.[57]

Additional terms defined on Sex-lexis.com's Translesbigay page include:

> transdetector, transdike, transdyke, transexion, transsexual, transexualism, transfan, transfashion, transgender community, transgendered, transgenderism, transgenderist, transgressively gendered, transhomosexuality, transie, transindividual, transition, transitional bisexuality, transmale, transman, transnatural, transparent, transpeople, transphobia, transrectal, transsectional, transsex procedures, transsexual, transsexualism, transsexuality, transurethal resection of the prostate, transurethral prostatectomy, transvaginal, transversity, transvest, transvestic fetishism, transvestism, transvestite.[58]

Other, related pages on Sex-lexis.com also list: trans fag drag, trans-fag, trans-hag, trans-sex surgery, trans-testicles, and transactivist.[59] And these concepts do not simply represent the most extreme fringe of gay life. Many of them are considered part of the normal gay lexicon, part of the ever growing list of abbreviated, gay-related terms that some have called "alphabet soup."[60] The homepage of the Oberlin Multicultural Resource Center, which is billed as "A Guide to Lesbian, Gay, Bisexual, Transgender, and Queer/Questioning

Resources at Oberlin College," says it all.[61]

So you're queer . . . or transgender . . .
or genderqueer . . .or questioning . . .
or interested in being an ally . . .

The Oberlin Multicultural Resource
Center presents . . .

lesbian gay bisexual
transgender down low
queer grrl questioning
genderqueer in the life

QUEER
@ Oberlin!

asexual ag. transsexual
same gender loving butch
fairy polyamorous
androgynous gender
variant wsw fellagirly
boidyke fluid femme
two spirit mtf allied
transwoman transman
pansexual ftm bi-gender
msm cross-dresser drag
king drag queen gender
bender soffa omnisexual
gender outlow birl
stone butch zami dyke . . .

It began with the *gay* pride movement, and then was expanded to *gay* and *lesbian*, and from there, to *gay*, *lesbian*, and *bisexual*, then to *gay*, *lesbian*, *bisexual*, and *transgender*, abbreviated as GLBT (or, LGBT).[62] But did things stop with GLBT? Of course not. Others felt constricted by these definitions and wanted to add the term *questioning* or *queer*, hence, GLBTQ.[63] Other groups, however, still felt left out, which is understandable, since there really cannot be a limit to self-defined sexual categories.

Now, there is GLBTQI, the "I" standing for "intersexed/intersexual," meaning, "Having both male and female characteristics, including in varying degrees reproductive organs, secondary sexual characteristics, and sexual behavior, as a result of an abnormality of the sex chromosomes or a hormonal imbalance during embryogenesis."[64] In this case, there is a very real, physical condition called intersexed, but once again, within the GLBTQI community, the term has taken on an expanded, quite fluid meaning.[65]

But the gay rights movement *must* include all kinds of sexual orientations and identities – meaning GLBTQI and ??? – otherwise it disqualifies itself. In keeping with this, the letter "P" has been added to the list, as in QueerToday's statement, "We advocate for equality for all LGBTQIP . . . etc. people."[66] And note that even LGBTQIP is not enough (with P apparently standing for pansexual or polysexual); the word "etc." must be added.

Consider this statement from the National Gay and Lesbian Task Force, which, as its name clearly states, originally fought for only gay and lesbian rights. (Actually, it began as the National Gay Task Force, without even mentioning lesbians by name).[67] Things, however, have changed:

> In the 1990s, organizations - including the National Gay and Lesbian Task Force - broadened their scope to include the issues and concerns of bisexual and transgender people, hence the acronym "LGBT" for lesbian, gay, bisexual and transgender people.
>
> The inclusion of bisexual people reflects the broadening recognition of the diversity and range of human sexuality, and the growing community of people dedicated to fighting oppression and discrimination around same sex relationships.[68]
>
> Over the past few years, most gay, lesbian and bisexual (GLB) organizations - including the National Gay and Lesbian Task Force - have broadened the scope of their

work to include the issues and concerns of transgender people, hence the acronym "LGBT" for lesbian, gay, bisexual and transgender people. This change reflects an acknowledgment that sexism and gender stereotyping have a powerful effect on the social and legal treatment of GLB as well as transgender people. It also reflects the growing strength and maturity of the GLBT civil rights movement, which has expanded its self-understanding to include heterosexual family members and friends, allies who have endured similar oppressions, and others who share a broader vision of human rights and social justice than a narrowly defined "gay identity politics" could hope to achieve.[69]

So, G and L have been expanded to GLB and then GLBT, and this represents part of the ongoing "civil rights" battle:

The struggle to establish civil rights protections for transgender people cannot be separated from the struggle to win freedom and equality for gay, lesbian, and bisexual people.

- Many transgender people are gay, lesbian or bisexual.
- Many gay, lesbian, and bisexual people are also transgender.
- Trans people have always been present in the GLB community. Drag and butch/femme culture, as well as androgyny and gender-bending, are hallmarks of transgender influence.
- Gay, lesbian, and bisexual people frequently break gender boundaries in their social (in addition to sexual) behavior, and are often victims of hate crimes because of their gender characteristics, which their attacker has assumed are equal to evidence of particular sexual behavior.
- Breaking gender boundaries is not uniquely the province of bisexual, lesbian, or gay people, and the right to be safe in society should belong to everyone, regardless of sexual orientation.[70]

In conclusion, then:

> The National Gay and Lesbian Task Force leads national efforts to broaden the definition of our communities to include bisexual people in the public policy debates on civil rights, hate crimes and health.[71]

Do you understand the implications of this? It is one thing to argue that homosexuals should be entitled to marry, since, it is claimed, homosexuality is innate and is therefore not a choice, in which case, it is only through same-sex unions that intimacy can be achieved. By very definition, however, the bisexual person is fully capable of being intimate with a member of the opposite sex – at least at some point in his or her life – which potentially includes having children. And a bisexual person can choose not to yield to same-sex attractions, just as a married heterosexual can choose to abstain from extra-marital, opposite-sex attractions. Why then should the bisexual be entitled to special "civil rights"? Why not simply encourage bisexuals, upon recognizing their bisexuality, to enjoy opposite-sex relations and restrain themselves from same-sex relations?

That, however, is not even a topic for discussion among gay leaders, since, if homosexuals are entitled to distinct civil rights recognition, the same must apply to bisexuals. And, since it is taboo to suggest that homosexuals should say "No" to their same-sex attractions, the same must apply to bisexuals. Put another way, if heterosexuality is not the only "normal" sexual expression, there can be no such thing as normal.

The inclusion of "transgender people in the public policy debates on civil rights, hate crimes and health" is merely the natural – and inevitable – extension of the gay rights movement. And remember: The National Gay and Lesbian Task Force is not a fringe group on the wild extremes of gay activism. It is one of the standard bearers, one of the flagship organizations (dating back to 1973), one of the more sober exponents of homosexual activism.[72] And in its championing of the special, civil rights of bisexuals and transgender people, the Task Force represents mainstream thought in the gay community, as seen in the ubiquitous nature of "GLBT." As noted by Canadian gay activist Gilles Marchildon, executive director of Egale Canada, "Trans people are where the gay and lesbian rights movement was a couple decades ago"[73] – by which he means that they are beginning to be recognized and to make progress with their agenda. (This is obviously reminiscent of the statement regarding polyamory, cited above.)

IF QUEER IS NO LONGER QUEER . . .

And yet there is more. If queer is no longer queer and heterosexuals are now nongay; if the categories of gay and lesbian are not enough and now bisexual and transgender must also be included (not to mention transsexual and others); if there is now gender speak, genderqueer, and gender atypicality, then there is no longer a line to be drawn. There cannot be one.

Once homosexuality is legitimized and normalized, so also must other sexual identities be legitimized and normalized. (This is not so much a prediction as a statement of fact.) The National Gay and Lesbian Task Force confirms it; GLSEN confirms it; other gay activist groups confirm it; college courses confirm it; anti-discrimination laws confirm it. All of which means: Get ready for transmen and transwomen, for shemales, birls, fellagirlies, third gender, and gender fluid people.[74] Get ready for heteroflexibles and pomosexuals.[75] Get ready for an omnisexual society.

And what exactly is omnisexual? It is a synonym for pansexual, which, you will recall, means, "A person who is attracted to all genders and all forms of sex."[76] In other words, anything goes and everything goes!

I ask you again: Why should we expect anything less? This is the inevitable conclusion of where gay activism will ultimately take us. As noted by blogger Larry Richman (with credit to Coach Dave Daubenmire):

> It used to be easy when there was just gay and straight. But now, sexual identity is a very a complex continuum of heterosexual, homosexual (gay and lesbian), bisexual, pansexual, polysexual, asexual, transgendered (transwomen and transmen), transsexual, cross-dresser, transvestite, drag king/queen, genderqueer, cross-gender, androgyne, pangender, bigender, ambigender, non-gender, agender, gender fluid, intergender, and autogynephilic.[77]

Is it wrong to ask what's next? Should we be surprised when a young man posting on YouTube describes himself as "polysexual," explaining that he doesn't "believe in male or female"?[78] Should this surprise us? According to Susan Ryker,

> The term transgender dates from the 1980s. Its coinage

is usually attributed to Virginia Prince, the Southern Californian advocate for heterosexual male transvestites, who in the 1960s wrote such pioneering self-help books as *The Transvestite and His Wife* and *How To Be a Woman though Male.*[79]

Since then, authors like Leslie Feinberg (for whom see above, Chapter Four) have written books like *Transgender Warriors* (1997) and *Trans Liberation: Beyond Pink or Blue* (1999). Put another way, it's not enough to have "heterosexual male transvestites." We must move "beyond pink and blue."

Consider the writings of Dr. Virginia Ramey Mollenkott, one of the coauthors of the influential book, *Is the Homosexual My Neighbor? A Positive Christian Response.*[80] Since writing that volume, she coauthored *Transgender Journeys* (with Virginia Sheridan, described as "a male cross-dresser")[81] and also wrote *Omnigender: A Trans-Religious Approach*, among other books.[82] A reader of the *Omnigender* book commented:

In a nutshell, Mollenkott examines the "binary gender construct" that holds us all hostage. In a world centered around the binary gender construct, we are all pigeon-holded [sic] into one of two sexes from birth -- male or female -- and from there, we hammered by social pressure to conform to the associated culturally-defined gender roles. That is, men must be "masculine" men and women must be "feminine" women.

Mollenkott debunks the validity of the binary gender construct by first questioning the biological reality of the two sexes -- male, female. Through an exploration of hermaphroditism or intersexuality and other reasoning, Mollenkott shows that our insistence on two, and only two, sexes is erroneous.

Next, Mollenkott shows how the binary gender construct has been harmful to individuals and to society. When people are forced into one of only two gender slots, that labeling has far-reaching ramifications for the kind of life the individual may lead within the good graces of society. The result is personal limitations on choices and behavior, bigotry and hatred toward those who can't or won't fit into one of the two designated boxes, and a perpetuation of patriarchal oppression.[83]

Yes, it's time to be liberated from the miserably constricting, male-female construct that "holds us all hostage." As stated on the Fellagirly page on Facebook, "Not exactly butch, but not terribly femme either? Sorta in-betweeny? Fellagirly is you. Way to [expletive] the gender binary, kids!"[84]

To repeat yet again: Liberation from male-female, heterosexual categories leads to liberation from all sexual categories. In other words, get ready for the "O" word (and maybe for "omniphobia" too). And while you're at it, be sure to brush up on your "gayspeak."[85]

You should know that "Gaydar" refers to a gay man's ability to discern who is homosexual, while "Gaypril" is a common college campus term for April (since that month is often marked by the celebration of special gay events).[86] And you should know that "yestergay" refers to a homosexual who is now heterosexual (or, at the least, who was once into men and is now married to a woman),[87] while a "hasbian" is a former lesbian (or, at the least, a lesbian who now engages in heterosexual sex),[88] and, more specifically, a SLUG is a "selective lesbian until [college] graduation."[89]

MEET THE BRIDE AND BROOM

This is just the tip of a very big iceberg – but it is an iceberg that continues to grow. And so, when Kirsten Ott and Maria Palladino were "married" in August, 2010, Kirsten was dubbed the broom." (This is not a typo.) As she explained, "Broom is a combination of bride and groom."[90] But of course.

On a more practical level, if you live in Massachusetts, you should be aware that driver's license renewal forms now include a check-off box if your sex has changed.[91] And be sure to learn your transgender etiquette, especially in religious meetings. For this, you'll get help from the "Transgender Resource Page" on Congregation Beth Simchat Torah's website, billed as the world's largest gay and lesbian synagogue. (At the risk of overstating myself, I know there are people who are deeply troubled by issues surrounding gender identity, but rather than catering to their confusion – which is what, I'm convinced, these attempts at "transgender etiquette" actually do – let's find ways to help them find wholeness.)

Beth Simchat Torah's website explains:

Transgender people understand that gender can be complicated and confusing and that most people do not know very much about these issues. The important thing is that people be respectful, and it is generally appreciated when people want to learn. There are ways to ask questions that are respectful and other ways that are not. . . .

Instead of asking "What are you?" or "Are you a man or a woman?", try: "What is the respectful pronoun to use for you?" or "I'm interested in hearing about your gender identity if you are comfortable telling me" or "Is there anything I/we/the community can do to make this a more comfortable place?" . . .

Don't insist that someone must be either a man or a woman. Some people identify themselves as neither gender, as both genders, or as a third gender. This may seem confusing, but this is a legitimate choice. Some people are in a process of discovering their identity or deciding how they wish to live. People may be in various stages of a gender transition. If you need clarification on which pronoun to use, ask. . . .

Do respect a person's choice of name/gender/pronoun. If a person expresses that they prefer a certain name or pronoun, take care to use only the name/gender/pronoun that they prefer, and strongly encourage others in the community to do the same. This can take time to get used to, and most people do make mistakes--don't worry. The person is almost certainly used to mistakes. The important thing is that he or she knows that you respect their preference and are trying. . . .[92]

Remember: This is information on a *synagogue* website. Further practical pointers include:

Language
Language is very important. People pick up on small cues. The following changes may seem minor, but they are among the most important ways to indicate that a community is making an effort to be trans-friendly. It often makes the

difference in whether a transgender person will approach a community and whether they will choose to stay.

    - On flyers, in newsletters, event announcements, etc.: Instead of writing "men and women welcome" or "for both men and women," try "all genders welcome" or "for all genders."

    - In articles, drashot [sermons], essays etc.: Rather than "both genders" or "men and women," refer to "all genders" or "people of any gender."

    - If events, groups or programs (event, social group, chavurah [fellowship gathering], etc.) are advertised or indicated as "gay and lesbian," consider whether it really is only for gay and lesbian people or whether a transgender (or bisexual person, for that matter) would be welcomed. If the latter is true, change the language.[93]

Recent laws in Colorado (the Employment Nondiscrimination Act, passed in 2007, and the Anti-Discrimination Act, or Senate Bill 200, passed in 2008) require workers to refer to their transgender colleagues by the latter's preferred pronoun, meaning, addressing "him" as "her" (or perhaps something else) if so desired.[94]

And lest you feel constricted by all this, you should realize that, to the contrary, these concepts supposedly open up tremendous realms for personal exploration. As noted by Lynn Hickman, a coordinator for Oberlin College's annual Transgender Awareness week (for which see above, Chapter Four):

> *The basic assumption of transgenderism is the transgressing of gender norms.* Whether that means completely passing from one end to the other, or finding a space that combines or defies the binary in our society, it comes down to exploring outside of the norm you were assigned because of the discomfort that you feel in it.[95]

But why stop here, with combining or defying *sexual* categories? Why not go one step further (if, in fact, it is actually further) and create self-identified categories of race or color or nationality? How about, "Even though I was assigned the ethnic identity of a white male at birth, I identify myself as a black female." Why not? Or what if I sense that, despite my American pedigree, I am actually a Viking? What if I was sure I was actually a black Viking and wanted to identify as such? Are ridiculous concepts such as these all that different from "the transgressing of gender norms" and "def[ying] the binary in our society"? Is my (sarcastic) statement about identifying as, say, a black female Viking less absurd than a (seriously intended) statement like this, penned by a man who had sex change surgery?

> Women couldn't be oppressed if there was no such thing as "women." . . . . doing away with gender is key to the doing away with patriarchy . . . Gender fluidity is the ability to freely and knowingly become one or many of a limitless number of genders, for any length of time, at any rate of change. Gender fluidity recognizes no borders or rules of gender [96]

In saying this, I am not making light of the sexual-psychological issues faced by some individuals, and, on another front, I'm fully aware that others are born with indefinite (or dual) genitalia, leading to a host of emotional and physical challenges. To repeat what I wrote earlier: *In no way do I minimize those challenges.* But as I also have stated repeatedly, to embrace the philosophy behind this transgender, genderqueer, omnisexual rhetoric is to play into the problems rather than to help solve the problems, and given the choice of embracing this rhetoric or of raising my voice to saying that something is seriously amiss, I take the latter choice.

Isn't it really one or the other? If you accept homosexuality as positive and normal, then you must follow through to the logical conclusion and open the door to omnisexuality and to a world defined by one's relationship to "gay." And in virtually all the gay literature I have read, there is not one hint of a concerted effort to shut that door. Once it is open, the sky is the limit.

To give you one last example of just where this open door leads, consider a paper that was delivered at the 2005, annual, gay linguistic conference called Lavender Language. (According to the *Washington Blade*, "The conference, which usually draws about 100 scholars, is the longest-running queer theory conference in North America."[97]) The paper, examining covert gay imagery in children's cartoons, was presented by Prof. Richard Reitsma of the University of Mary Washington. It was entitled, *"A Queen's Tale: E"race"ing Queer Sexuality in The Lion King 1.5 and A Shark's Tale."* Reitsma's thesis was this:

Recent animated features such as The Lion King 1.5 and A Shark's Tale deal with issues of difference and acceptance by negotiating the territory of race, masquerading in the drag of vegetarianism. In the case of The Lion King 1.5, the race issue is essentialized by its locale in the Dark Continent, and the very "africanness" of the animated creatures who inhabit the landscape. A Shark's Tale, on the other hand, takes place underwater, but is no less racialized: The reef inhabitants are essentially black, as opposed to the sharks who are godfather mafia types (undeniably white, predatory, and carnivorous).

I doubt that the vast majority of those who saw either of these animated children's movies noticed that any of the characters were "masquerading in the drag of vegetarianism." But vegetarianism was not the main focus of Prof. Reitsma's paper, since, after all, this was the Lavender Language conference. He continues:

> However, if one is attuned to gay themes, one can see that race and vegetarianism are merely covers for a different kind of difference. What is the message when obviously gay images are incorporated into a film supposedly about accepting racial difference, manifested as a difference in "taste" (not eating meat)? This point is explored through characters who find their identity in exile, and whose different "tastes" (not for females) are explored in a racial context ("black culture"), but whose behavior is stereotypically gay, yet utterly asexual.
> I will examine clips from the two movies, showing similarities between these films and other gay films. I argue that the rejection of carnivore behavior in a racially charged environment might be read as a trope for gay identity and a pitch for tolerance (just so long as things remain asexual --buddies, but never lovers). In the end, one wonders what the message is for children?[98]

That, indeed, is the question: What *is* the message for children watching these cartoons? A "trope for gay identity and a pitch for tolerance"? Really?

Yes, it's a queer new world, and the possibilities are limitless: hidden gay meanings in children's movies masquerading under the guise of vegetarianism, and transgender etiquette in the synagogue. Are you ready for this bizarre new world?

Perhaps I am not alone in saying: Not yet! I'll stick with those old fashioned, gender binary distinctions. "Male" and "female" have worked well enough for the last few thousand years.[99]

Mary, Queer of Heaven and Mother of Faggots
Mary the drag queen (or is it Jesus cross-dressing?)

Two of the chapter titles in Marcella Althaus-Reid's book *Indecent Theology*
(Althaus-Reid was Professor of Contextual Theology at the New College,
University of Edinburgh, Scotland)

"Do Not Be Conformed to This World":
Queer Reading and the Task of the Preacher

Title of the convocation address at the Chicago Theological Seminary,
Dr. Ken Stone, September 15, 2004, the 150th anniversary of the seminary
(Stone is the editor of *Queer Commentary and the Hebrew Bible*)

Jesus is a boundary-breaker, transgressing the purity codes
of fundamentalists and challenging proto-heterosexual hegemony.

Rev. Robert E. Goss,
Writing in the *Queer Bible Commentary*

The Queer God is a call to 'disaffiliation' processes in theology.
To be unfaithful to sexual ideological constructions of God in order to
liberate God – a Queer God who also needs to come out of the closet
of theologians of the status quo.

Description of Marcella Althaus-Reid's book *The Queer God*,
posted on www.althaus-reid.com/QGodbook.html

10

Queer Theology, a Gay/Lesbian Bible, and a Homoerotic Christ

Rev. Prof. Peter J. Gomes is considered by many to be one of the foremost leaders in the African American Church, hailed also as one of the nation's most eloquent preachers. His resume is quite impressive, having served as the minister of Harvard University's Memorial Church and as Plummer Professor of Christian Morals at Harvard since 1974.

He is the recipient of thirty honorary degrees, and, according to the Memorial Church website, these are just a few of his accomplishments:

- In 2005 [Prof. Gomes] presented a series of sermons in St. Edmundsbury Cathedral, England, in the presence of Their Royal Highnesses The Prince of Wales and The Duchess of Cornwall.
- In 2001 he was Missioner to Oxford University, preaching in the University Church.
- In 2000 he delivered The University Sermon before The University of Cambridge, England
- Named Clergy of the Year in 1998 by Religion in American Life, Professor Gomes participated in the presidential inaugurations of Ronald Wilson Reagan and of George Herbert Walker Bush.[1]

When he speaks, people listen, and so it is not surprising that he "was included in the summer 1999 premiere issue of *Talk Magazine* as part of its feature article, 'The Best Talkers in America: Fifty Big Mouths We Hope Will Never Shut Up.'"[2]

Without a doubt, Rev. Prof. Gomes is a man of exceptional passion and dedication, and he is also an out of the closet, "gay Christian."[3] Yes, the minister of Harvard's Memorial Church and the long-tenured Harvard professor of *Christian morals* is a homosexual, having come out in 1992 with his now famous statement, "I am a Christian who happens as well to be gay."[4]

In his 1996 bestseller, *The Good Book: Reading the Bible with Heart and Mind*, Gomes devotes a whole chapter to "The Bible and Homosexuality," referring to the moral rejection of homosexual practice as a "biblically sanctioned prejudice."[5] He writes:

> The legitimization of violence against homosexuals and Jews and women and blacks . . . comes from the view that

the Bible stigmatizes these people, thereby making them fair game. If the Bible expresses such a prejudice, then it certainly cannot be wrong to act on that prejudice. This, of course, is the argument every anti-Semite and racist has used with demonstrably devastating consequences, as our social history all too vividly shows.[6]

According to Gomes, it is fear that is "at the heart of homophobia, as it was at the heart of racism, and as with racism, religion – particularly the Protestant evangelical kind that had nourished me – [is] the moral fig leaf that covered prejudice."[7] And it is this kind of prejudice, as Gomes and many other "homosexual Christians" argue, that has driven gays and lesbians out of the Church. This reflects a common theme in "gay Christian" literature: God loves us and accepts us as we are, but the Church closes it doors to us, judging us, rejecting us, and damning us to hell. Jesus takes us in, but the Church puts us out![8]

To be sure, many gays and lesbians have *not* been treated with grace by the Church, as if, in Christian eyes, homosexual acts were worse than all other acts and as if homosexuals were lepers not to be touched. The common attitude of all too many Christians seems to be: "Don't go near them or you'll get the cooties, and don't dare confess that you're struggling with same-sex desires. If you do, you'll be disqualified for life from any meaningful position or place of service in the Church. Stay away from those gays!"

Certainly, in many ways, the Church has failed to reach out to the homosexual community, and, speaking personally as a leader in the Church, I am ashamed at the way we have often treated LGBT men and women. Many times, when reading their stories, especially those who experienced rejection and shunning by the Church, my heart has broken for them. Their pain is palpable, and their hurt anything but silent.[9]

But does that mean it is time to rewrite the Bible? Because gays and lesbians have been hurt by the Church, must we now embrace queer theology? Must we create a homoerotic Christ and a gay God? Must we justify "gay Christianity"?

"But," you ask, "aren't there lots of different interpretations of the Bible? And isn't it true that even scholars disagree on what the Bible says about homosexuality?"

341

WHAT THE BIBLE REALLY SAYS ABOUT HOMOSEXUAL PRACTICE

As a biblical scholar, I'm sorely tempted to weigh in on these questions here and now, since the scriptural witness stands clearly and consistently against homosexual practice. As noted by Pim Pronk, a gay biologist, theologian, and philosopher:

> To sum up: wherever homosexual intercourse is mentioned in Scripture, it is condemned. With reference to it the New Testament adds no arguments to those of the Old. Rejection is a foregone conclusion; the assessment of it nowhere constitutes a problem. It obviously has to be repeated from time to time, but the phenomenon as such nowhere becomes the focus of moral attention. It is never condemned in isolation but always in association with other major sins: unchastity, violence, moral corruption, and idolatry.[10]

So clear is the biblical testimony that even the online GLBTQ encyclopedia stated,

> The bad news from the Christian Bible is that it condemns same-sex desire and same-sex acts without qualification of age, gender, role, status, consent, or membership in an ethnic community.[11]

As stated positively by Prof. Robert Gagnon, rightly regarded by many as today's foremost academic authority on the Bible and homosexual practice,

> Indeed, every narrative, law, proverb, exhortation, poetry, and metaphor in the pages of Scripture that has anything to do with sexual relations presupposes a male-female prerequisite for sexual relations and marriage."[12]

The Bible really is quite clear about all this.

But this is not the time or place to discuss these questions, and there are a number of excellent books that address the issues in depth.[13] Instead, let me share with you the inevitable direction in which "gay Christianity" develops.

Even for readers with little familiarity with the Bible – including readers who embrace other faiths – this will be of interest. Allow me, then, to introduce you to a brave, new – and increasingly queer – world, one that is sure to offend many a sensible reader.

Jesus taught that we could judge a tree by the fruit it produces.[14] What kind of fruit does this "gay Christian" tree produce? In some respects, it resembles the traditional, biblical faith; in other respects, it is shockingly – and tellingly – different. Let's take an up close and personal look.[15]

FROM JESUIT PRIEST TO QUEER THEOLOGIAN

Robert E. Goss is a former Jesuit priest who left the priesthood in order to give himself fully to a homosexual relationship. He earned a Th.D. in Comparative Religion from Harvard University and has become a well-known voice in "gay Christian" circles, even considered a prophetic leader of sorts, also serving as professor and chair of religious studies at Webster University in St. Louis. He followed up his influential 1993 book, *Jesus Acted Up: A Gay and Lesbian Manifesto*, with his 2002 volume, *Queering Christ: Beyond Jesus Acted Up*. Praise for this book – and for Robert Goss himself – has been high.

According to the Reverend Edward Ingebretsen, Director of American Studies, Georgetown University:

> Robert Goss calls his church – indeed all of Christianity – to its prophetic role. . . . Without question Robert Goss is one of the preeminent names helping to break up the ice encasing the practice of Christian theology. This is an important book, and Goss is an important voice for the Catholic Resistance.[16]

In the words of professor Marcella Althaus-Reid of the University of Edinburgh, Scotland:

> A long-standing and committed liberation theologian, Goss offers us a christology grounded in translesbigay experience, taking a clear option for those who have been marginalized by the heterosexual ideology that has regrettably perverted Christianity. The outcome is an insightful, passionate, and original christology for the

21st century, expounded with pastoral compassion and intellectual sophistication. *Queering Christ* is a deeply moving book that will change people's lives.[17]

This is high praise indeed, with some very bold claims: Goss is calling "all of Christianity . . . to its prophetic role." It is "heterosexual ideology that has . . . perverted Christianity," and Goss has written "an insightful, passionate, and original christology for the 21st century." (In this context, Christology, which is normally capitalized, refers to a theological study of the person of Jesus or the words and deeds of Jesus. Thus, Goss is being credited with contributing an important study on the person of Jesus Christ.) Yes, this book "will change people's lives." Echoing this, Mary E. Hunt, Ph.D., the co-director of Women's Alliance for Theology, Ethics, and Ritual (Water) writes, "This is a book that will generate rich, necessary conversations. Read it and talk!"[18]

Of his earlier volume, *Jesus Acted Up*, author Robert Williams exclaimed, "Goss has written a bold, brilliant, in-your-face manifesto calling queer Christians to stop begging for acceptance and start demanding justice. This is clearly a work inspired by the Holy Spirit, the Liberator."[19] Indeed, Dr. Anthony Saldarini, a respected professor in the Department of Theology in Boston College, stated that the book had "a directness, clarity, and power that is appealing to the non-gay reader who is well-disposed to listen. . . . The major impact of the book on me was to make gay life more immediate, real, and authentic."[20]

It would seem, then, that Goss cannot be dismissed as an extremist. Rather, he is a major voice in contemporary gay theology, a recognized leader in the Metropolitan Community Churches (the primary "gay Christian" denomination), a man often quoted by his peers and frequently looked to for his activist leadership. What exactly does he have to say? What kind of ideas is he putting forth that have garnered such praise?

Of his own personal experience, Goss writes: "Jesus evolved from a friend in childhood, to lover, and to the Queer Christ calling me out of the closet into the streets as an activist priest."[21] What exactly does he mean by this? I will quote him at length, but let the reader be forewarned: This is offensive in the extreme. He writes:

I trace my first unspoken words of physical attraction to the crucified Jesus, wanting to strip off his loincloth to gaze at his genitals. As a young prepubescent child, I remember trying to take off the loincloth of a crucified Jesus. As I reached puberty, I gazed erotically at Michelangelo's Risen Christ, a nude sculpture in an art book in the library. I lusted after the figure of Christ, imagining him as the bearded hunk depicted by Michelangelo. Christ was an utterly desirable, bearded hunk, naked on the cross, and I entered the seminary to find union with him and make love with him.[22]

Can you imagine this? A major reason that Goss entered seminary was to have erotic union with Jesus. This is nothing less than perverse: A young Catholic boy gazing at the crucifix, wishing he could pull off Jesus' loincloth so as to stare at his genitals, then, some years later, going into seminary, in part, to pursue an imagined sexual, erotic relationship with Jesus. And Goss claims that such desires are commonplace among gay Christians:

Many gay Christians have imaginatively constructed a Jesus whom they found attractive. In the essay "Tongues United: Memoirs of a Pentecostal Boyhood," queer cultural critic Michael Warner writes, "Jesus was my first boyfriend. He loved me, personally, and told me I was his own." Many Catholic gay youth have grown up on their knees, gazing erotically at the crucified Jesus with his genitals covered and secretly wanting to lift the loincloth and gaze erotically at those genitals.[23]

Yet there is more. Goss offers this reflection on Jesus: "He was penetrated by a Roman centurion, fueling taboo Catholic fantasies for a boy coming to grips with his sexual feelings about men,"[24] referring to the fact that Jesus, after his death but while still hanging on the cross, was pierced in his side by a Roman centurion's spear (see John 19:34). Somehow, for Goss, Jesus being speared by a Roman soldier becomes an erotic image of *sexual penetration*. What kind of mind conceives of such things?

According to Goss, these too are the views of many "gay Christians," for whom Jesus "is claimed as a penetrated male, a bottom [referring to the receptive partner in anal sex] violating the masculine code of penetration and phallic domination."[25] Jesus as a penetrated male, a bottom in anal sex? Even irreligious people would rightly cringe at this, no matter what symbolic or spiritual import it was purported to have. Yet, as quoted above, a minister and scholar at Georgetown University, having read these same words, could write, "Robert Goss calls his church – indeed all of Christianity – to its prophetic role"!

And what does Goss say of those Christians who would call such erotic descriptions of Jesus "perverse or obscene"? They are guilty of making "homophobic judgments," failing to recognize that for "two millennia, many Christian men have read the story of Jesus with a homoerotic gaze and devotion."[26] Yes, "I and many other Catholic men, priests and laymen, have found the naked Jesus utterly sexually desirable, calling us to pursue a relationship, and many of us have discovered that we were utterly desirable to Jesus," presumably in a sexual and erotic way as well.[27]

Tragically, it is rubbish like this – what else should it be called? – that is being hailed as a prophetic corrective for a perverted Christianity. In reality, spiritual eroticism like this is perverted, just as it would be perverted for a heterosexual Christian woman to mingle her spiritual devotion to Jesus with all kinds of erotic fantasies about him, including explicit sexual role playing. Such things are unheard of in normative Christian literature,[28] yet they are part of the spiritual-sexual world of Robert Goss – and he is not alone among gay theologians. Indeed, his musings, which could be cited at length, are warmly welcomed by many "gay and lesbian Christians."[29] In fact, Goss "won the 2000 Templeton Course Prize in Religion and Science."[30]

Of course, there are conservative "gay Christians" who would be appalled by such sexual depictions, yet the sad fact is that "gay Christian" literature has a strong sexual fixation that is marked by extremely frequent references to sexual orientation and sexual issues. Indeed, as we shall see shortly, all of Scripture, not to mention God Himself, is interpreted against the grid of homosexuality, which is one of the reasons that "gay Christians" are not lining up to denounce the writings of Goss and to express their revulsion at his words. Instead, many are lining up to praise his moral courage and spiritual sensitivity.[31]

Yes, while a large proportion of readers, religious and non-religious alike, would find descriptions of a "homo-erotic Christ" terribly offensive, for large segments of the "gay Christian" world, a "queer Christ" is normal and acceptable, part of a larger attempt to turn the Bible and its moral teachings upside down.

As Goss loudly proclaimed:

Easter becomes the hope of queer sexual liberation. The queer struggle for sexual liberation will triumph; this is the promise of Easter.... On Easter, God made Jesus queer in his solidarity with us. In other words, Jesus "came out of the closet" and became the "queer" Christ....

If Jesus the Christ is not queer, then his *basileia* [kingdom] message of solidarity and justice is irrelevant. If the Christ is not queer, then the gospel is no longer good news but oppressive news for queers. If the Christ is not queer, then the incarnation [God becoming flesh in the person of Jesus] has no meaning for our sexuality.[32]

In keeping with this, Goss and others have written on topics such as "Re-Visioning God as Erotic Power,"[33] explaining that:

God is reconceptualized and experienced as the shared erotic power that liberates lesbians and gay men from sexual alienation, homophobic oppression, gender domination, closetedness, oppression[,] sickness, and abusive violence.

God's erotic power bursts forth on Easter into connectedness or solidarity with the once-dead and now risen Jesus. God's erotic power is revealed as a shared power with Jesus. In turn, Jesus the Christ becomes the sign of God's erotic power, breaking the linkages of erotic desire and inequality ... Jesus becomes the Christa for feminist Christians and the Queer Christ for queer Christians.

. . . For queer Christians, erotic power is God's empowering way of acting in the world.... Sexuality is the practice in which God's erotic power may be embodied, in which queer Christians find connectedness with each other, the oppressed, nature, and God.[34]

WHEN RELIGION BECOMES QUEER

Similar concepts are found in the volume of collected essays entitled *Religion is a Queer Thing: A Guide to the Christian Faith for Lesbian, Gay, Bisexual and Transgendered People*, considered a mainstream book in "gay Christian" circles.[35] Thus, Elizabeth Stuart contributes a group lesson-guide and article on "The queer Christ," the aims of which are:

- to explore how traditional Christology was developed out of and reflects a context which has had negative repercussions for queer Christians;
- to explore some queer Christologies
- to encourage participants to reflect on their own understanding of Christ and bring it into critical dialogue with that of queer theologians and others in the group[36]

More practical still are the prayers and liturgies collected by Stuart, including "A Rite of Repentance," in which the only sin that is addressed refers to "those times when we have denied God and the divine gift of our sexuality by pretending to know or understand nothing about homosexuality, bisexuality or transgender issues."[37] Yes, repentance is offered for: "The times when we have smiled at and even joined in the anti-queer jokes for fear of being exposed as 'one of them.' The times when we have betrayed God our creator, ourselves, and our queer brothers and sisters by denying implicitly or explicitly that we are 'one of them.'"[38]

There is also "A Liturgy for Coming Out":

> *The room should be darkened.*
> **The person coming out:** As Eve came out of Adam, as the people of Israel came out of slavery into freedom, as the exiled Israelites came out of Babylon back to their home, as Lazarus came out of the tomb to continue his life, as Jesus came out of death into new life I come out – out of the desert into the garden, out of the darkness into the light, out of exile into my home, out of lies into the truth, out of denial into affirmation. I name myself lesbian/gay/bisexual/transgendered. Blessed be God who has made me so.
> **All:** Blessed be God who made you so.
> *The person coming out lights a candle and all present light their candles from it. Flowers are brought in. Music is played. The whole room is gradually filled with light, colour and music. Bread and wine are then shared.*[39]

So, Eve "coming out" of Adam, the Israelites "coming out" of Egypt and

Babylon, and Jesus and Lazarus "coming out" of the grave serve as prototypes for gays and lesbians coming out of the closet? Indeed, some of these themes are repeated in the writings of other queer theologians.

More striking still is a "Prayer of Thanks for our Bodies" written by Chris Glaser. The first two stanzas read:

Thank you for the body that loves me.

My own body:
it tingles with pleasure
and sends me pain as a warning;
it takes in food and air
and transforms them to life;
it reaches orgasmic bliss
and reveals depths of peace.

Thank you for the body that loves me.

My lover's body [referring to a gay lover, of course]:
it surrounds me with safe arms,
and senses my needs and joys;
it allows me vulnerability,
and enables my ecstasy;
it teaches me how to love
and touches me with love.[40]

Is it any wonder that a liturgical prayer celebrating "orgasmic bliss" is found in a book entitled, *Coming out to God: Prayers for Lesbians and Gay Men, Their Families and Friends*? Have you found prayers like this in the prayer book used by your religious tradition?

How about this stanza from a lesbian rendition of the Christmas carol "Silent Night," written in the midst of great spiritual and social struggles by Lucia Chappelle:

Silent night, raging night,
Ne'er before, such a sight.
Christian lesbians hand in hand.
Many theories, one mighty band.

Christ's new Body is born,
Christ's new Body is born.

Have you found this in any church hymnbook? It's found in the Metropolitan Community Church hymnal![41]

In the New Testament, Jesus told his followers that "where two or three come together in my name, there am I with them" (Matt 18:20). This statement seems to be fairly straightforward in meaning,[42] unless, of course, you are reading the Bible through queer eyes, as is Prof. Kathy Rudy. In her article, "Where Two or More Are Gathered: Using Gay Communities as a Model for Christian Sexual Ethics," she applies the words of Jesus to *random sexual encounters* between gays:

> Each sexual encounter after that [in a bathroom or bar] shores up his membership in the community he finds there; and his participation and contribution subsequently makes the community he finds stronger for others. His identity begins to be defined by the people he meets in those spaces. Although he may not know the names of each of his sex partners, each encounter resignifies his belonging. And although no two members of the community make steadfast promises to any one person in the community, each in his own way promises himself as part of this world. Intimacy and faithfulness in sex are played out on the community rather than the individual level.[43]

So, even anonymous sexual encounters with multiple partners, which reinforce the gay man's belonging to his community (and which, supposedly, and without a hint of irony, reflect "faithfulness in sex"), serve to exemplify what Jesus meant when he said, "where two or three come together in my name, there am I with them." This is put forth as serious theology.

REWRITING THE BIBLE IN THE IMAGE OF HOMOSEXUALITY

Yet a queer reading of the Bible goes farther still. It's as if everything is stood on its head and normal becomes abnormal. Indeed, the Bible is often understood and evaluated in light of homosexuality rather than homosexuality being understood and evaluated in light of the Bible. In other words, rather than asking, "What does the Bible teach us about homosexuality?" the question is, "What does homosexuality teach us about the Bible?"

In the section of *Religion Is a Queer Thing* entitled "Queer living: Ethics for ourselves, our societies and our world," John McMahon cites a 1991 article written by gay liberation theologian Rev. Dr. Robin H. Gorsline, "Let Us Bless Our Angels: A Feminist-Gay-Male-Liberation View of Sodom," in which Gorsline stated:

> Gay liberation is deeply suspicious of attempts, however well intentioned, to address the issue of homosexuality in the Bible. The issue is not of homosexuality and whether the Bible sustains, condemns, or is neutral about it. *Neither canonical testament* [i.e., neither the Old Testament nor the New Testament] *carries any authority for gay liberation on the subject of homosexuality.* Gay liberation interprets scripture, not the other way around.[44]

Significantly, McMahon does not criticize this view, a view that for most Christians would be abhorrent. Instead, he simply raises a question for group discussion: "Do you think that the Bible has any place in discerning queer ethics? What do you make of Robin Gorsline's view that we enlighten scripture, rather than the other way around?"[45]

What if a promiscuous heterosexual used this same approach, "enlightening" Scripture based on his sexual ethics? What if a sado-masochist did the same? (Again, I am not here equating homosexuals with sado-masochists or promiscuous heterosexuals; I am simply demonstrating the folly of claiming that we have the right to interpret the Bible based on our sexual orientation, choices, or behavior.)

And yet there is more: The Bible is actually reinterpreted – and sometimes even rewritten – in queer terms. Consider this example, also taken from McMahon's article. According to Mark 4:21-23, Jesus encouraged his followers to be unashamed of their faith, reminding them that, ultimately, everything would come to light:

> Is a lamp brought in to be put under the bushel basket, or under the bed, and not on the lampstand? For there is nothing hidden, except to be disclosed; nor is anything secret, except to come to light. Let anyone with ears to

hear listen!

McMahon quotes this same text, adding the words in brackets. What a massive change a few words can make!

> Is a [queer] lamp brought in to be put under the bushel basket, or under the bed, and not on the lampstand? For there is nothing hidden [in the closet], except to be disclosed; nor is anything secret, except to come [out] to light. Let anyone with ears to hear listen!

According to McMahon's reinventing of the text, Jesus is now encouraging homosexuals to come out of the closet, reminding them that they have a queer lamp. So then, if the Bible doesn't say what you want it to, just add a few extra words, and *voilá*, there you have it.

This reflects common gay theological practice, as seen by the title of another book edited by Goss, *Take Back the Word: A Queer Reading of the Bible*,[46] and as reflected by a joint presentation Goss gave with Rev. Jim Mitulski at the Metropolitan Community Churches' 2005 annual conference. As described in the program brochure:

> **Queering Luke-Acts**
> This workshop presents queer theory (queer theology) in its practical application to interpreting Biblical texts. How it can be used to understand the scriptural writings of Luke-Acts and preaching the texts to congregations. There will be opportunity for hands on practice in queering particular texts in Luke-Acts and the highlighting of themes for prayer and preaching.[47]

Care to hear more? Then let's look at the "queering" of some familiar biblical stories.

THE JESUS OF QUEER THEOLOGY

Matthew 8 contains the account of Jesus healing the paralyzed servant of a Roman soldier. It is simple and straightforward:

> When Jesus had entered Capernaum, a centurion came to

him, asking for help. "Lord," he said, "my servant lies at home paralyzed and in terrible suffering."

Jesus said to him, "I will go and heal him."

The centurion replied, "Lord, I do not deserve to have you come under my roof. But just say the word, and my servant will be healed. For I myself am a man under authority, with soldiers under me. I tell this one, 'Go,' and he goes; and that one, 'Come,' and he comes. I say to my servant, 'Do this,' and he does it."

When Jesus heard this, he was astonished and said to those following him, "I tell you the truth, I have not found anyone in Israel with such great faith. I say to you that many will come from the east and the west, and will take their places at the feast with Abraham, Isaac and Jacob in the kingdom of heaven. But the subjects of the kingdom will be thrown outside, into the darkness, where there will be weeping and gnashing of teeth."

Then Jesus said to the centurion, "Go! It will be done just as you believed it would." And his servant was healed at that very hour (Matt 8:5-13).

There is nothing mysterious in this account, and any reference to sex in general – let alone to homosexual practice – is nowhere to be found. All the more, then, it is surprising to find this account used by gay authors Rev. Jeff Miner and John Tyler Connoley. (This is actually a common, "gay Christian" interpretation.) They write:

Just another miracle story, right? Not on your life!

In the original language, the importance of this story for gay, lesbian, and bisexual Christians is much clearer. The Greek word used in Matthew's account to refer to the servant of the centurion is *pais*. In the language of the time, *pais* had three possible meanings, depending upon the context in which it was used. It could mean "son or boy"; it could mean "servant," or it could mean a particular type of servant – one who was "his master's male lover." Often these lovers were younger than their masters, even teenagers.

... In that culture, if you were a gay man who wanted a male "spouse," you achieved this, like your heterosexual counterparts, through a commercial transaction – purchasing someone to serve that purpose.[48]

The authors then proceed to "prove" that, in this context, the word *pais* must mean the centurion's purchased, young male lover – although such "proofs" would be considered utterly laughable in serious biblical scholarship, despite the authors' great sincerity – stating, "For objective observers, the conclusion is inescapable: In this story Jesus healed a man's male lover. When understood this way, the story takes on a whole new dimension."[49] A whole new dimension indeed! In fact, a positively queer dimension, to say the least.

Miner and Connoley proceed to reenact the centurion's encounter with Jesus:

> ... the centurion approaches Jesus and bows before him. "Rabbi, my ...," the word gets caught in his throat. This is it – the moment of truth. Either Jesus will turn away in disgust, or something wonderful will happen. So, the centurion clears his throat and speaks again, "Rabbi, my *pais* – yes my *pais* lies at home sick unto death." Then he pauses and waits for a second that must have seemed like an eternity. The crowd of good, God-fearing people surrounding Jesus became tense. This was a gay man asking a televangelist to heal his lover. What would Jesus do?
>
> Without hesitation, "Jesus says, "Then I'll come and heal him."
>
> It's that simple! Jesus didn't say, "Are you kidding? I'm not going to heal your *pais* so you can go on living in sin!" Nor did he say, "Well, it shouldn't surprise you that your *pais* is sick; this is God's judgment on your relationship."
>
> Instead, Jesus' words are simple, clear, and liberating for all who have worried about what God thinks of gay relationships. "I will come and heal him."[50]

Talk about rewriting the Bible! Talk about reading one's own ideas into the text and about understanding the Bible based on homosexuality rather than understanding homosexuality based on the Bible. This is absolutely classic – and really, very sad.

So then, from this simple account of healing, and based on an inexcusably gratuitous interpretation of the word *pais* (after all, in Matthew's Gospel Jesus is called the *pais* of God, his Father!), we now "know" that: 1) The Roman soldier was gay; 2) his servant functioned as his gay lover (more specifically, a purchased teen lover); 3) Jesus knew all this; 4) and rather than rebuking him or refusing to heal the man's slave-lover, he worked a miracle and made him whole.

Jesus, therefore, according to this "interpretation" – really, it is pure fabrication rather than true interpretation – set an example by accepting homosexuals without condemnation and by fully condoning homosexual practice. How striking that the same Jesus who forgave the woman caught in adultery but said to her, "Go and sin no more" (see John 8:11) said no such thing to the Roman soldier and his (bought and owned) boy sex toy.[51] Instead, according to the queer version of the story, he basically said, "Be healed and keep up the pederastic love-fest!"

It would appear then, that, according to gay biblical interpretation, Jesus disapproved of adultery but sanctioned the practice of purchasing a young slave for same-sex intercourse. Can moral evaluations like this be called anything less than queer – and in the most negative sense of the word?

On a personal level, Miner and Connoley seem quite likable, and their own life stories are certainly touching. But their rewriting of the Scriptures and their recreating Jesus in the image of homosexual thought and gay theology are completely without foundation, not to mention dangerous, misleading, and even perverted.[52] In fact, the interpretation is so baseless that it's not even mentioned in the *Study New Testament for Lesbians, Gays, Bi, and Transgender*.[53] And, for the record, the Greek word *pais* is found in the Greek Scriptures (the Septuagint and the New Testament) approximately 90x, and *never once* does it have any sexual overtones. In every single case, it simply means "son" or "servant," and thus, not a single scholarly Greek lexicon recognizes the sexual meaning of *pais* in the Bible at all.[54]

All this, however, didn't stop gay activists from launching a billboard campaign in Dallas-Fort Worth in 2009, featuring this very scriptural account and making the claim that "Jesus affirmed a gay couple."[55]

Yes, according to this invented interpretation of the Gospels, "In this story, Jesus restores a gay relationship by a miracle of healing and then holds up a gay man as an example of faith for all to follow," despite the fact that, "To our modern minds, the idea of buying a teen lover seems repugnant."[56] In reality, what is repugnant is the attempt to make Jesus complicit in an alleged man-boy tryst.

GAYS AND LESBIANS EVERYWHERE

Here are some further examples of a "translesbigay" Bible. David and Jonathan are commonly depicted as homosexual lovers, despite the fact that David himself had numerous wives and concubines (see 2 Samuel 5:13), and despite the fact that his great, personal fall came as a result of his adulterous lust for Bathsheba, whose husband David killed so he could have her for himself (see 2 Samuel 11). So much for a gay David!

Sadly, the homosexual reading of Scripture seems unable to understand the extraordinarily close, non-sexual relationship that can exist between two men (or two women), a type of relationship that was more common and culturally accepted in many ancient cultures and a relationship that remains common and culturally accepted in certain parts of the world today – again, in totally non-sexual terms. Instead, the gay reading of Scripture insists that these words of David, eulogizing Jonathan, must be interpreted in sexual terms:

> I grieve for you, Jonathan my brother;
> you were very dear to me.
> Your love for me was wonderful,
> more wonderful than that of women (2 Sam 1:26).

So, Jonathan's love for David had to be sexual, despite the fact that David, whom, I reiterate, was anything but gay according to the Scriptures, referred to Jonathan as his brother, not his lover.[57] Similarly, because Naomi and her daughter-in-law Ruth were very close, they must have been lesbian lovers (I kid you not!), despite the fact that the Bible does not even give the slightest hint of this, and despite the fact that both of them married and had children (Ruth even remarried after she was widowed).[58] So also Mary and Martha, the sisters of Lazarus, whom Jesus raised from the dead, must also have been lesbian spinsters. Otherwise, why were they not married and out of the house? Come to think of it, why was Lazarus living at home too? He must have been gay! Yes, all this has been put forth in "gay Christian" writing.[59]

Even Perpetua and Felicity, martyred by the Romans in 203 and known for their unshakable love for Jesus and their great devotion for each other, must have been lesbian lovers – despite the fact that Perpetua had a child and was married, and despite the fact that there is not a single syllable in any ancient Christian literature that suggested any same-sex interest between them – since the only deep love that can exist between people of the same-sex must be sexual in nature. Thus the martyrs Perpetua and Felicity have been called "Queer saints."[60]

Not surprisingly, whole books have been written on the alleged erotic relationship between Jesus and his disciple John, the one often called "the beloved disciple" because John spoke of Jesus' special love for him (see, e.g., John 21:20; for a representative study, see Theodore W. Jennings, Jr., *The Man Jesus Loved: Homoerotic Narratives from the New Testament*.)[61] In this case too, however, the Bible makes no reference of any kind to any form of sexual or "homoerotic" relationship between Jesus and John, and so the question must be asked: Is it that hard to conceive that Jesus, the Son of God, especially cared for one of his disciples without that care having to be sexual? Must queer theology insist on "queering Christ"?[62]

According to biblical teaching, God created man and woman in His image, and since then, people have been creating gods in their own images (see Psalm 115:1-8; Romans 1:20-25). That is exactly what has happened in "queer theology" – and quite unashamedly, at that. Thus, Toby Johnson has written a *Gay Perspective: Things Our Homosexuality Tells Us About the Nature of God and the Universe* (Alyson Books, 2003)[63] – interpreting God and the universe through the lens of homosexuality, rather than the reverse – while Donald L. Boisvert, a professor and Dean of Students at Concordia University (Canada), has written, *Sanctity And Male Desire: A Gay Reading Of Saints* (Pilgrim Press, 2004).[64]

Further examples can be found in the volume of collected essays edited by Robert E. Goss and Mona West, *Take Back the Word: A Queer Reading of the Bible*,[65] a book that is certainly "mainstream" in terms of gay biblical interpretation. Chapters in this book, which were written by prominent gay and lesbian scholars and religious leaders, include:

- "Reading the Bible from Low and Outside: Lesbitransgay People as God's Tricksters," by Virgina Ramey Mollenkot, professor emeritus of English language and literature at William Patterson University, Wayne, New Jersey. (For more on Prof. Mollenkot, see Chapter Nine, above.)
- "Outsiders, Aliens, and Boundary Crossers: A Queer

Reading of the Hebrew Exodus," by Mona West, Pastor of Spiritual Life at the Cathedral of Hope in Dallas, Texas, billed as the largest gay and lesbian church in the world. (This congregation was originally part of the Metropolitan Community Churches but is now part of the United Church of Christ denomination.). She holds a Ph.D. in Old Testament studies from Southern Baptist Theological Seminary. For Dr. West, the Israelites "coming out" of Egypt serves as a pattern for the coming out of gays and lesbians.

- "Coming Out, Lazarus's and Ours: Queer Reflections of a Psychospiritual, Political Journey," by Benjamin Perkins, a Harvard graduate and a Unitarian Universalist, who sees the story of the death and resurrection of Lazarus "as a starting point for exploring the sacramental elements of coming out and the psychospiritual, political journey of the queer person" (196). So, both the exodus of the Israelites from Egypt and the resurrection of Lazarus serve as patterns for gays and lesbians coming out of the closet.

- "Insider Out: Unmasking the Abusing God," by Rabbi Dawn Robinson Rose, the director of the Center for Jewish Ethics at the Reconstructionist Rabbinical College and a graduate of the University of Berkeley and the Jewish Theological Seminary. As the chapter description explains, "Dawn Robinson Rose wrestles with the Hebrew images of an abusive God who pornographically punishes the whore. She reads the pornographic texts of terror [i.e., the Old Testament!] against a backdrop of her own familial experience." How tragic.

- "'And Then He Kissed Me': An Easter Love Story," by James Martin, a Metropolitan Community Church pastor. In harmony with the statement of Robert Goss, quoted above, Martin claims that, "Throughout Christian history there has been an underground of Christian men sexually attracted to men, and they intuited that Jesus was one of them" (219). Based on this, Martin creates a new version of Luke 24:13-32, where Jesus, after his resurrection, appeared to two disciples and spoke with them. In Martin's version, a disciple named Joseph, with whom Jesus had previously been sexually involved – the kisses between them are described with wonderment by Joseph – meets Jesus again after his resurrection. Talk about reading one's own ideas into the Bible!

Yet this is "mainstream," gay biblical interpretation, with well-known leaders from the "gay Christian" community contributing, and with the now familiar gay emphases, which include a fixation on sexual issues and the creation of a queer Christ.

"CRUISING" THE SCRIPTURES?

And yet there is more. Gay pastor Timothy R. Koch, in his article "Cruising as Methodology: Homoeroticism and the Scriptures," published in *Queer Commentary and the Hebrew Bible*, proposed a method of biblical interpretation "for gay men that moves 'from within outward, in touch with the power of the erotic within ourselves'." This he called "Cruising the Scriptures, for cruising *is* the name gay men give to using our own ways of knowing, our own desire for connection, our own savvy and instinct, our own response to what compels us." As a result of "cruising the Scriptures" – in other words, searching the Bible for allegedly gay characters – Koch, who holds a Ph.D. from Boston University, expected to find "some friends, some enemies, a lot who don't care one way or the other (or else don't really 'do anything' for us!) – and a few really hot numbers!"[66] (I remind you that Koch currently serves as a *pastor*.)

What did Dr. Koch discover? Well, since the Bible describes the prophet Elijah as a hairy man who wore a leather belt (see 2 Kin 1:8), that means that he is now "the Hairy Leather-Man," also deducing through a bizarre reading of the Hebrew that Elijah may not only been thought of as a hairy man but also as "Lord of the Goats." He writes:

At this point in my cruising, I felt suddenly as if bells and whistles were going off all over the place. Elijah as a goat god, wrapped in goat skins?! Judy Grahn, in *Another Mother Tongue: Gay Words, Gay Worlds*, devotes an *entire section* to detailing holy homosexuals who, through history, dressed up in goat skins, channeling goat gods (gods who were often thunder gods as well) . . . .[67]

So, Elijah the prophet, one of the most extraordinary figures in both Jewish and Christian tradition, now becomes a gay leather man, perhaps even clad in goat skins and channeling goat gods!

Koch makes other, remarkable "discoveries," such as: Jehu, the zealous king of Israel who slaughtered the idol-worshipers, was an "ancient Lawrence of Arabia" (famous, of course, for his homosexuality). Koch bases this on 2 Kings 10:12-17 (you'll be amazed at his deductions when you read the verses), where Jehu took the hand of a man named Jehonadab and helped him into his chariot after questioning his loyalty and devotion. Through Koch's interpretive method, Jehu's question to Jehonadab becomes, "'Are you thinking what I'm thinking?!' The answer is YES! and suddenly these men are holding hands and riding together in the chariot."[68]

More bizarre is his reading of Judges 3:12-26, where Ehud, a left-handed Israelite, hid an 18" sword on his right thigh then gained a private audience with the Moabite king Eglon before plunging the knife all the way into the obese king's stomach. For Koch, it is significant that Ehud was left-handed, while the 18" knife "would certainly be an impressive measurement for *anything* found snaking down (okay, okay, 'fastened' to) a young man's right thigh!" (Did I say already that the author of these words is a pastor?) And, having gained a private audience with the king, Koch comments, "What, may I ask, do you actually think that the king believes Ehud to be removing at this point from the folds of his garment, that cubit along his thigh?!"

He concludes, "There are dozen [sic] of these gems scattered and buried in the pages of the Bible."[69] Gems? What kind of biblical interpretation is this? A long knife on a man's thigh – used to kill his enemy – becomes an 18" phallus, and this is an interpretive gem?

Not to be outdone, in the same volume Lori Rowlett writes on "Violent Femmes and S/M [Sadomasochism]: Queering Samson and Delilah," asking the question of what happens when the biblical story of Samson and Delilah (see Judges 14-16) "is read through a glass queerly?"

The pattern of domination by the exotic Other emerges as a stock S/M scenario. Delilah is the femme dominatrix, teasing and tormenting Samson, who has all the characteristics of a 'butch bottom'. . . . The constant give and take between the two lovers resembles S/M role play, complete with ritual questions, hair fetishism and other power games. . . . The story therefore can be read in terms of the ritual codes of S/M games. Other codes come into play as well: issues of gender, political identity and power are interwoven with a deeper question of divine control and relinquishment of control, raising the possibility that the structure of the book of Judges places Yahweh in a rotating game of S/M.[70]

So, not only are Samson and Delilah into sadomasochism, God himself is too!

Such interpretations are not limited to "gay Christian" literature either. They can be found in "gay Jewish" literature as well, witnessed recently in the *Torah Queeries* volume, containing "Weekly Commentaries on the Hebrew Bible," some of which are more bizarre than others – and I mean bizarre.

PERVERSE READINGS OF SACRED JEWISH TEXTS

Here are just three examples. Amichai Lau-Lavie, likens his dancing in a gay bar in Tel Aviv one night as a conflicted, gay, Orthodox teenager to the biblical account of the children of Israel dancing around the golden calf at Mount Sinai, an act for which God sternly judged them for their idolatry. In fact, as the Book of Exodus relates, Moses was so angry with the people for worshiping the image of a calf rather than the Lord that he shattered the two stone tablets which were in his hands, the tablets of the Ten Commandments (see Exodus 32).

Yet for Lau-Lavie, this biblical narrative of divine punishment brings him liberation and not condemnation, and rather than being judged for his sin (as the Israelites were in the biblical story), he fashions himself to be dancing with God (in the gay bar), his homosexual impulses even sanctioned by God.

This is his account: He had run outside the bar in tears, not knowing how to reconcile his feelings and his faith. Then something happened:

> I experienced my own private shattering of the law, reenacting, unconsciously, the central mythic battle of my inherited legacy. My sexual urges crashed against the voice

of the law – and something did die inside of me: an old fear of disobedience. After I was done crying, I went back inside and kept on dancing. A voice, clear inside my head, was saying, "You are made in the image of God – and this too [meaning, your homosexuality and your dancing in a gay bar] is sacred."...

Dancing with my shirt off, I had a revelation – suddenly knowing, deeply, that my body was holy and my sexuality sacred – owning it, for the very first time [with explicit reference again to Exodus 32, which he takes, not as the Torah intends, as a lesson against idol worship, but rather as a "courageous act of dancing with God"].[71]

In another article, Noach Dzmura offers reflections on the eternal flame that was to burn on the Temple altar (and which became a symbol of the endurance and preservation of the Jewish people),[72] asking, "How can queer Jews fan the flame of eternity that resides within?" He answers, "One way might be to recognize that 'flaming queen' is not a pejorative but an indicator of one's spiritual health," adding that, "all queer Jews, no doubt, feel that they have an inner flame that animates them not only as Jews but as queers."[73]

So, we move from the eternal flame burning on the Temple altar to a "flaming [homosexual] queen." This is extraordinary – but it is hardly surprising in a queer Torah commentary.

The last example is more extreme still. Tamar Kamionkowski discusses a sobering account in the book of Leviticus that describes the death of the high priest's oldest sons for an act of presumption on their part. (The high priest was named Aaron, the brother of Moses; the sons were Nadab and Abihu.) The text in Leviticus 10:1-3 reads:

Now Aaron's sons Nadab and Abihu each took his fire pan, put fire in it, and laid incense on it; and they offered before the LORD alien fire, which He had not enjoined upon them. And fire came forth from the LORD and consumed them; thus they died at the instance of the LORD. Then Moses said to Aaron, "This is what the LORD meant when He said: Through those near to Me I show Myself holy, And gain glory before all the people." And Aaron was silent. (New Jewish Version)

Their presumptuous act took place during a sacred time when they were being consecrated as priests, hence the severity of the judgment. For Kamionkowski, however, this becomes a homoerotic act between God and the sons of Aaron, whom Kamionkowski depicts as standing naked as they offer the alien fire to the Lord:

> God accepts the men and takes them into his innermost sanctum, and he consumes them in an act of burning passion. . . . This text offers an example of homoerotic attraction between human males and the male God of the Bible. Each desires to come closer to the other. Nadav and Avihu strip themselves literally and figuratively – they strip themselves of their clothing, their societal expectations, of confining rules – and they come forward. God meets them in a passion of fire, taking them in completely.[74]

How twisted! A presumptuous act by two Israelite priests which brought about their fiery deaths at the hand of God becomes a homoerotic scene where two naked men are so desired by the Lord that he "meets them in a passion of fire, taking them in completely." Kamionkowski even claims that "God's holiness" was "enhanced and supported by the acts of Nadab and Abihu."

How does one describe such warped thinking? Yet the contributors to this volume were Jewish professors and rabbis and academics and community leaders, and the book was published by the highly respected New York University Press (the publishing house of my alma mater). And I am hardly "cherry picking" in terms of the contents of the book.

THE EVER-PRESENT SEXUAL FIXATION

In keeping with the sexual fixation of queer theology – how can it be "queer" and *not* sexually fixated, since sexuality and sexual orientation form a key component of the theology? – Stephen D. Moore wrote *God's Beauty Parlor: And Other Queer Spaces in and Around the Bible* (Stanford University Press, 2001), described on Amazon as opening "the Bible to the contested body of critical commentary on sex and sexuality known as queer theory and to masculinity studies. The author pursues the themes of homoeroticism, masculinity, beauty, and violence through such texts as the Song of Songs, the Gospels, the Letter to the Romans, and the Book of Revelation."

Perhaps even more explicit – if a book is to be judged by its cover (I mean that literally; the cover is quite vulgar) – is Will Roscoe's *Jesus and the Shamanic Tradition of Same-Sex Love* (Suspect Thoughts Press, 2004). According to a reviewer on Amazon,

> In "Jesus and the Shamanic Tradition of Same-Sex Love", Will Roscoe suggests that baptism is a Christian adaptation of some shamanic rituals in which a spirit passes from one person to another. There are cults in which the two individuals, one with a spirit, are nude and touch, with or without sex, to become one flesh with one spirit, before separating into two bodies with two spirits.
>
> [As for his arrest] Jesus would be taken in for some sodomy- or pedophilia-related charge, in addition to those for overturning the tables at the Temple and harrassing the authorities.[75]

This is absolutely outrageous: The baptisms of Jesus were homosexual happenings, ultimately leading to Jesus' arrest on charges of sodomy or pedophilia?[76] Little wonder, then, that this book was published by Suspect Thoughts, which is advertised as a "press for connoisseurs of transgressive, intelligent literature."[77] Transgressive, yes, but in this case, hardly intelligent, despite the author's erudition.

And what shall we make of the new volume of collected essays entitled *Queer Theology: Rethinking the Western Body?* The book is described on Amazon as making

> an important contribution to public debate about Christianity and sex. This remarkable collection reconceptualizes the body and its desires, enlarging the meaningfulness of Christian sexuality for the good of the Church. By divinizing desire, it radicalizes "queer theory" and its deconstruction of sexual and gender identities; and it invokes a complex social space in which transcendent Eros frees us from the fear of our differences. Written by some of the brightest and best of Anglo-American scholars, established and up-coming, from a variety of academic and religious backgrounds, the book shows us how western

bodies and their desires are queerer than often thought. Our bodies are, the contributors propose, the mobile products of ever changing discourses and regimes of power; and God, they help us to understand, is indeed a bodily god.[78]

Yet this is written by "some of the brightest and best of Anglo-American scholars" – and it is just a representative sampling from a large body of queer theological writings.[79]

This, however, should come as no surprise, especially since some *theology schools* and *seminaries* now offer courses in Queer Theology. Thus, the Pacific School of Religion held a series of lectures from January 25-27, 2005 entitled "Sex and the City of God: Intimacy and Wholeness," attracting "one of the largest audiences in the event's 104-year history" (speaking of the annual Earl Lectures) and featuring as one of the lecturers the Right Rev. V. Gene Robinson, bishop of the Episcopal Diocese of New Hampshire and celebrated as the first openly gay Episcopal bishop.[80]

The school website also noted that:

In addition, the 31 workshops of the Pastoral Conference enabled participants to delve deeper into specific issues, such as sex in the Bible, queer theology, pastoral care responses to sex, coming out, youth ministry and sexuality, sexual ethics, issues in Asian/Pacific Islander and African American families and congregations, and HIV/AIDS ministry.[81]

Sounds like quite a pastoral conference!

In similar fashion, the Convocation Address at the Chicago Theological Seminary by Dr. Ken Stone, on September 15, 2004 called for a queer reading of the Scriptures.[82] Here is an excerpt from his message, followed by the conclusion (remember, this was the convocation address at the beginning of the school year at a *theological seminary*):

Consider, for example, the frequent addition of the word "transgendered" to the phrase, "lesbians, gay men, and bisexuals." Queer theory pushes us to consider quite broadly the possible implications of this term, "transgendered."

For is it not the case, queer theorists ask, that the

existence of people and practices we call "transgendered" casts doubt on the firm boundary that we often construct between male and female? . . .

Queer reading asks us to take the realities of male and female seriously, while living our way into a world in which the boxes of sex and gender would no longer normalize us in just the ways that they currently do. Queer reading therefore gives us tools, even for understanding the message of Paul, who after all incorporates assumptions about male and female (sometimes with very problematic consequences) and yet who preaches that for the Christian there is no longer Jew or Greek, slave or free, or male and female. Queer reading therefore gives good practice, and necessary resources, to those of us who, in the best traditions of CTS, wish to practice ministry for the real world, while refusing to allow ourselves to be conformed to it.[83]

In reality, what is happening is that the Bible is being conformed – really, deformed – into a very queer image, and the end results are troubling indeed.

ALL THEOLOGY IS SEXUAL THEOLOGY?

Consider these statements from the back cover of Prof. Marcella Althaus-Reid's *Indecent Theology*:

All theology is sexual theology.

Indecent Theology is sexier than most.

What can sexual stories of fetishism and sadomasochism tell us about our relationship with God, Jesus and Mary?

Isn't it time the Christian heterosexuals came out of their closet too?

By examining the dialectics of decency and indecency and exploring a theology of sexual stories from the margins, this books brings together for the first time Liberation Theology, Queer Theory, post-Marxism and Postcolonial analysis in an explosive mixture. **Indecent Theology** is an out-of-the-closet style of doing theology and shows how we can reflect on the Virgin Mary and on Christology from sexual stories taken from fetishism, leather lifestyles and transvestism.[84]

I am not making this up.

Section One of the book is entitled, "Indecent proposals for women who would like to do theology without using underwear," while Section Two is entitled, "The Indecent Virgin," featuring chapters such as: Sexual positions: locating the G(od) spot of virginal reflections; Making theological violence sexy; What does the Guadalupana have under her skirts; Mary as a historical figure? Now that is Queer; The popular theology of tranvestism.[85]

Other chapters in the book include: French kissing God: the sexual hermeneutic circle of interpretation; Black leather: doing theology in corsetlaced boots; A story of fetishism and salvation; Theological misfortunes: from bottoms to tops; On mediation: does Messianism submit to sexual desires? On Queers, revolutionaries and theologians.

The late Althaus-Reid was also the author of *The Queer God* (Routledge, 2003), described on Amazon as follows:

The Queer God introduces a new theology from the margins of sexual deviance and economic exclusion. Its chapters on bisexual theology, Sadean holiness, gay worship in Brazil and queer sainthood mark the search for a different face of God--the Queer God who challenges the oppressive powers of heterosexual orthodoxy, whiteness, and global capitalism. Inspired by the transgressive spaces of Latin American spirituality, where the experiences of slum children merge with queer interpretations of grace and holiness, *The Queer God* seeks to liberate God from the closet of traditional Christian thought, and to embrace God's part in the lives of gays, lesbians, and the poor. Only a theology that dares to be radical can show us the presence of God in our times. *The Queer God* creates a concept of holiness that overcomes sexual and colonial prejudices and shows how queer theology is ultimately the search for God's own deliverance. Using liberation theology and queer theory, it exposes the sexual roots that underlie all theology, and takes the search for God to new depths of social and sexual exclusion.

The Queer God? The search for God's own deliverance? A new theology from the margins of sexual deviance? Just how far does this go?

A BLASPHEMOUS READING OF THE BIBLE

I hesitate to answer, since the end is not in sight and some of the things that have already been written are nothing less than blasphemous. How else should we describe the thirty-eight page study of Theodore W. Jennings, Jr. entitled "YHWH as Erastes," in which Yahweh – speaking of the Lord God Himself – was depicted as being erotically involved with king David, described as a perennial "bottom."[86] And the fact that David danced before the Lord wearing a linen ephod (see 2 Samuel 6:12-16) – which the priests also wore – is highly suggestive:

> The ephod, we have noticed, is ambiguous: it both hides and focuses attention upon the genitals of the wearer. Here we may think of something like a loincloth or breechcloth, a g-string or jockstrap. [I should point out that nowhere in any biblical or Hebrew dictionary or encyclopedia will you find any such notion.] Such a piece of apparel may serve to decently cover as well as indecently draw attention to the male genitalia. In the case of YHWH's 'jockstrap', what happens when it serves not as a piece of apparel but as an item that represents its wearer? What happens when it becomes a fetish in other words? And as such is cast in hard and shiny metal like the ephods made by Gideon and Micah. How does the carrying around of a large metallic jockstrap represent YHWH?[87]

The priestly ephod is now Yahweh's jockstrap, a fetish? Again we can only ask, What kind of mind reads the Scriptures like this?

Jennings goes on to speak of an "erotic, even sexual" consummation of the relationship between David and the Lord although the biblical text does not describe this consummation in "specifically sexual terms."[88] That, however, does not stop Jennings from putting his own explicit spin on things: "For if in this tale Adonai [the Lord] is the top and David (as usual) plays the role of the bottom, it is by no means the case that the top is always in control or that the bottom is simply dominated. This is not, after all, rape. It is love."[89] God as the "top" and David as the "bottom" in a sexual relationship? To repeat: I am not making this up!

And yet there is more – although once again, I'm reluctant even to quote these words, words which can only be described as so sick that they are sickening. Yet they have been written in a well-received academic volume and they are considered part of the cutting edge of queer theology and "gay Christian" scholarship. I leave you then with the article of Roland Boer, "A Lost Targum [speaking of an ancient Jewish paraphrase of different books of the Bible]: Yahweh as Top [meaning again the male who is on top of the other male in homosexual, anal sex]."[90]

Boer, who is Associate Professor in Comparative Literature and Cultural Studies at Monash University in Australia, with a Ph.D. from McGill University, creates a fictitious dialogue, depicting Moses meeting with the Lord on Mount Sinai along with other notables, including Leopold von Sacher-Masoch, Jacques Lacan, Sigmund Freud, Gilles Deleuze, and the Marquis de Sade. After climbing the mountain, Moses meets an elderly, long-bearded gay man who is none other than Yahweh himself, saying to him, "Big f---ing mountain you've got here, Yahweh." This is how Moses talks to God!

The Lord, who addresses Moses as "Dear," is depicted quite graphically, a sadomasochist, also into fetishes: "A few heads now turn in Yahweh's direction, looking upon his furs, fantastic calf-length boots, manicured hands, beautifully done hair, the whips hanging from his chair . . . ." (104). He is speaking about God here! But it gets worse.

As the Lord gives Moses instructions on how to build his tabernacle, also describing the garments that Moses' brother Aaron will wear – with a special robe made with "pomegranates of blue, purple and scarlet yarn around the hem of the robe, with gold bells between them" (see Exodus 28:33), Moses gets sexually aroused:

> All this talk of tingling clothing, pomegranates and bells and hems, has made Moses horny; he is already at the half husky, dying for a look beneath those furs that Yahweh insists on wearing on this unbearably hot mountain. I'm sure he's got a great, pert upright butt, he asserts. But Yahweh remains seated, for now. . .[91]

As I asked earlier, what kind of mind conceives of such things? It is nothing less than perverse. And yet there is more still.

The Bible often speaks of God's glory and splendor in terms of great,

369

transcendent radiance, to the point that no one can see His face and live. It would be the spiritual equivalent of looking into a star ten million times brighter than the sun. The gaze would be utterly blinding. And so, biblical authors who had visions of God wrote things like this: "Under his feet was something like a pavement made of sapphire, clear as the sky itself" (Exodus 24:10); or, "To the Israelites the glory of the LORD looked like a consuming fire on top of the mountain" (Exodus 24:17); or, "I saw that from what appeared to be his waist up he looked like glowing metal, as if full of fire, and that from there down he looked like fire; and brilliant light surrounded him. Like the appearance of a rainbow in the clouds on a rainy day, so was the radiance around him" (Ezekiel 1:27-28). As Paul wrote, God is the one who "lives in unapproachable light, whom no one has seen or can see" (1 Timothy 6:16).

And so, when Moses, meeting with the Lord on Mount Sinai, pleaded that he could see his glory, God said to him, "There is a place near me where you may stand on a rock. When my glory passes by, I will put you in a cleft in the rock and cover you with my hand until I have passed by. Then I will remove my hand and you will see my back; but my face must not be seen" (Exodus 33:21-23). The Bible then records that God passed by, proclaiming his goodness to Moses and giving him his holy laws, and when Moses came down from Mount Sinai "he was not aware that his face was radiant because he had spoken with the LORD" (Exodus 34:29). Moses was literally glowing after coming out of God's majestic presence and hearing his holy words.

As for God's "passing by" Moses – as he promised he would – this is what the book of Exodus recounts:

> Then the LORD came down in the cloud and stood there with him and proclaimed his name, the LORD [i.e., Yahweh]. And he passed in front of Moses, proclaiming, "The LORD, the LORD, the compassionate and gracious God, slow to anger, abounding in love and faithfulness, maintaining love to thousands, and forgiving wickedness, rebellion and sin. Yet he does not leave the guilty unpunished; he punishes the children and their children for the sin of the fathers to the third and fourth generation." (Exod 34:6-7)

How, then, is this beautiful, highly-ethical portion of Scripture rewritten by queer theology in Prof. Boer's made-up "Targum"? It is actually too vulgar and blasphemous to cite, crossing a line that goes too far, and it is so crassly written that I can not, in good conscience, quote Boer directly, instead providing a summary of his words. In short, Yahweh, who is now male and female, staggers as he/she walks away, his/her fur coat slipping for a moment and revealing the most splendid derriere that Moses, Freud and the others have ever seen – one of them also spotting a phallus and another spotting a female breast – making "their own faces shine for days afterward."[92]

So, Moses did not see the Lord's *back* (which the Bible itself explains in terms of spiritual revelation) but his *backside*, causing Moses' face to glisten with erotic excitement – a total and absolute perversion of a precious biblical text, not to mention a tragically outrageous depiction of the glorious heavenly Father. Is it wrong to call this blasphemous? Is it wrong to call this sick?

But this is the inevitable path down which queer theology leads, the unavoidable fruit that grows from the roots of "gay Christianity" (or, "gay Judaism"). As the Scriptures warned more than nineteen centuries ago, "But there were also false prophets among the people, even as there will be false teachers among you" (2 Peter 2:1). Need I say more?

We always feel like we are fighting against people who deny publicly, who say privately, that being queer is not at all about sex. . . . We believe otherwise. We think that sex is central to every single one of us and particularly queer youth.

Margot E. Abels, Coordinator, HIV/AIDS Program,
Massachusetts Dept. of Education

Religious fundamentalists . . . as a matter of strategy, still define homosexuality in terms of sex acts alone. We who are gay-identified reject this approach, knowing that all-around affection is, as among opposite-sex lovers, the major focus of our self-definition.

Jack Nichols, *The Gay Agenda*

The Gay and Lesbian Alliance against Defamation (GLAAD) led two media-oriented workshops at the "True Spirit 2000 Conference" held in Alexandria, Virginia during February 18-20, 2000. The discussions included breast surgery for female-to-male transsexuals, genital piercing, bisexuality, pansexuality, and polyamory. Sadomasochist workshops discussed SM singletail whipping, sensory deprivation, immobilizing bondage, edge play, piercing, cutting, branding, bloodsports, and consensual-non-consensuality, among 201 sadomasochistic practices.

Erik Holland, *The Nature of Homosexuality*

The personal is still political. Come to this workshop and find out how to connect the dots between claiming your power in the bedroom and seizing power in the streets or the halls of justice.

From the Sexual Liberation Institute workshop
at the NGLTF's annual Creating Change Conference, Feb. 3-7, 2010

11

So, It's Not About Sex? The Attempt to Separate Behavior from Identity

O ne of the strategies laid out in Kirk and Madsen's *After the Ball* was to counteract the common belief that "Gays are kinky sex addicts" with the counter statement, "The sex and love lives of most gays and straights today are both similar and conventional."[1] In other words, "Even with respect to their sex lives, gays are just are like everybody else." This perception, namely, that "gays are kinky sex addicts," is one of the main obstacles that gays have had to overcome, since, in other respects, most people probably recognize that in many areas of life, homosexuals are no different than anyone else. Thus, it has also been a major gay strategy, traced back to the 1980's, to shift the emphasis from *behavior* to *identity*, emphasizing the "rights" of gays *as people* and deemphasizing their sexual behavior.

As explained by conservative journalist David Kupelian:

> Simple case in point: homosexual activists call their movement "gay rights." This accomplishes two major objectives: (1) Use of the word gay rather than homosexual masks the controversial sexual behavior involved and accentuates instead a vague but positive-sounding cultural identity – gay, which, after all, once meant "happy"; and (2) describing their battle from the get-go as one over "rights" implies homosexuals are being denied the basic freedoms of citizenship that others enjoy.
>
> So merely by using the term gay rights, and persuading politicians and the media to adopt this terminology, activists seeking to transform America have framed the terms of the debate in their favor almost before the contest begins. (And in public relations warfare, he who frames the terms of the debate almost always wins. . . .)[2]

Put in more sympathetic terms, Prof. David M. Halperin explains:

> In the wake of more than a century of medical and forensic treatment of homosexuality as a psychiatric pathology or aberration, lesbians and gay men of the post-Stonewall era directed much political effort to undoing the presumption that there was something fundamentally wrong with us. In this context, it seemed necessary to close off the entire topic of gay subjectivity to respectable inquiry, so as to prevent

gayness from ever again being understood as a sickness.

In pursuit of that goal, the lesbian and gay movement has produced a remarkably plausible and persuasive new definition of homosexuality in political rather than psychological terms. To be gay, according to this new definition, is not to exhibit a queer subjectivity, but to belong to a social group. Homosexuality refers not to an individual abnormality but to a collective *identity*. . . . What gay people have in common, then, is not a psychological disorder but a social disqualification. We also share a long history of savage, even genocidal oppression, which gives us an immediate claim to social tolerance, freedom from discrimination, and overall improvement in our life chances[3]

What this ultimately means is that, rather than seeing the LGBT movement as part of the sexual revolution of the 60's (which is associated with promiscuity and the casting off of moral restraints) or, worse still, as reflecting an aberrant, disordered condition, it is seen as part of the Civil Rights movement, thereby being identified as a struggle for equality and justice.[4] Thus LGBT issues are framed in terms of civil rights rather than being associated with a sexual behavior or sexual focus.[5]

A MATTER OF CIVIL RIGHTS ALONE?

Now, to be quite clear, for the gay and lesbian community, this *is* perceived as a matter of civil rights and as a struggle for equality and justice. In other words, this is not merely a matter of rhetoric or good PR strategy. Gays would emphasize that they are regular people who live their lives like everyone else, going to school, working jobs, paying their taxes, falling in love, having families. Why stigmatize them because of their sexual orientation or sexual behavior?

That's why more and more Americans seem to believe that the battle for gay rights *is* a battle for social justice. As reported in a January 30, 2010 story in the *Salt Lake Tribune*, over the previous twelve months, polls indicated that there had been a "dramatic jump" among "Utahns for gay rights."[6] According to Brandie Balken, Executive Director of Equality Utah (a gay rights organization), it is critically important to continue "to educate people about how happy and healthy our families are and how happy and healthy our kids are." She also noted that "Once you know someone who is gay or transgender, you're much less likely to have a negative opinion of them. People have started to recognize that this really is a basic issue of fairness."

The article confirmed this observation:

> Poll respondent Jania Evans, a 69-year-old Mormon who lives in Draper, says knowing people who are gay has changed her opinions over time. She supports basic protections for same-sex couples, anti-discrimination measures and -- having worked with a gay man parenting two children with his partner -- adoption rights for unmarried couples. Because of her religious beliefs, she says, she does not support civil unions or gay marriage.
>
> "They have as much love and affection for their soul mates as heterosexuals who are married," Evans says. "I see no reason why they should be denied [basic rights]."[7]

But is this line of thinking entirely correct? Can the battle for GLBT equality be boiled down to a matter of civil rights alone? Or, put another way, should the issue of gay sexuality (i.e., homo*sexuality* or same-sex sexual behavior) be totally ignored?[8] After all, it is a person's sexual attractions, behavior, and orientation that identifies him or her as gay, lesbian, or bisexual, so it is certainly possible that sexual issues receive more focus among gays than straights. All the more reason, then, that GLBT leaders and activists would want to shift the focus from gay behavior to gay identity: "This is about equality and justice, not about sex!"

To be sure, it is not only gay leaders and activists who have sought to remove the "sex-crazed" stigma from the homosexual community. Left-leaning, evangelical professor Tony Campolo expressed his displeasure with the typical depiction of the sex lives of homosexuals by Christian preachers:

> Antigay rhetoric has long been a part of what people hear from evangelical pulpits. At a "Jesus festival" that had brought together more than twenty-thousand young people, I once had to follow a speaker who created a sensation as he whipped up animosity against homosexuals. He sent shivers of revulsion through the crowd with his vivid descriptions of what he claimed were common homosexual acts. His

explicit details of sadomasochistic body mutilations and his generalizations about how homosexuals defecate on each other to get perverted thrills achieved the desired ends. Out of the crowd of young Christians, someone yelled, "Kill the fags!" The evangelist stopped and piously responded, "Oh no! We should love them! We must hate the sin, but we must love the sinner."

As I stood backstage, waiting to speak, I wondered how that man would explain that he *loved* homosexuals. Was it love to exaggerate the facts and create a frenzy of hate among young people? Was it love to aggrandize his image as a sensational preacher at the expense of the homosexual teenagers who silently suffered as they listened to his tirade? . . . . One gay man said, "To be told you are loved by somebody like that is like being kissed by somebody with bad breath."[9]

Ex-gay leader Joe Dallas writes,

I remember sitting in a gay bar in 1978, where someone had brought in some literature put out by Christians on homosexuality. The pamphlets and fliers, detailing all the elaborate sexual things we allegedly did to each other, were being passed from barstool to barstool. You could tell another man was reading it by the fresh eruption of laughter. *We found these Christian materials hilarious!* They were largely untrue, and obviously designed to incite revulsion toward homosexuals by accusing us of practices most of us had never heard of, much less indulged in.[10]

More scorchingly, the very liberal, *New York Times* columnist Frank Rich had nothing but disdain for right-wing fundamentalist rhetoric about gay sex in his May 15, 2005 editorial, "How Gay is the Right?"

The American Family Association, whose leader, the Rev. Donald Wildmon . . . had been whipping up homophobia long before anyone suspected SpongeBob SquarePants of being a stalking horse (or at least a stalking sea sponge) for same-sex marriage. So-called research available on the Wildmon Web site for years - and still there as of last week - asserts that 17 percent of gay men "report eating and/or rubbing themselves with the feces of their partners" and 15 percent "report sex with animals."[11]

GAYS AND LESBIANS: "JUST NORMAL FOLK"?

Most gay men would state emphatically that such claims are gross, misleading exaggerations, to say the least. As Dr. Mel White explained in an open letter to his former employer, Rev. Jerry Falwell,

> . . . we are your fellow pastors, deacons, church musicians, and people in the pew. We write and arrange the songs you sing. We are your studio technicians and members of your staff. We are doctors and scientists, secretaries and clerks. We even write your books.
> We are not a threat to the American family, either. We are committed to the family. Millions of us have raised wonderful families of our own. We have adopted the unwanted and the unloved and proved to be faithful, loving parents by anyone's standards. . . .
> Most of us gay and lesbian people are just normal folk who try our best to live respectable, productive lives in spite of the hatred and the condemnation heaped upon us.[12]

Naturally, there is some degree of hyperbole here – certainly, it is only a small minority of active homosexuals who are involved in ministry in heterosexual churches, while a much smaller percentage are actually ghost writers for Christian authors (obviously!). And the statement that, "We are not a threat to the American family" will draw nods of agreement from some circles and raised eyebrows from others. In general, however, White presents an accurate description of many gays and lesbians: We "are just normal folk who try our best to live respectable, productive lives in spite of the hatred and the condemnation heaped upon us." This sentiment, among others, is reflected in the title of "conservative" gay author Andrew Sullivan's well-known volume, *Virtually Normal.*[13]

Approaching this from another angle, Letha Dawson Scanzoni and Virginia Mollenkott asked the question, "Is the homosexual my neighbor?"

That was the title of their influential 1978 book, appealing to Christians to "love your neighbor as yourself" (see also Luke 10:25-29).[14] Is the homosexual *your* neighbor? (I'm asking this question specifically to heterosexual readers.) It's possible that the answer is yes, especially if you live in a major city.[15] And it's also possible that the gay man or lesbian woman who lives next door to you is the best neighbor you've ever had, very kind, helpful, and courteous. It's also possible that you have a lesbian coworker or boss or employee, or a gay teammate or colleague or fellow-student, and it's possible that each of these people is hardworking, honest, and ethical. I have no doubt that in countless thousands of cases, this is true.[16]

GAYS AND LESBIANS: "KINKY SEX ADDICTS"?

But what about the sex lives of gays and lesbians? Aren't all homosexuals really kinky sex addicts? Aren't some of the wild charges denounced by Campolo and Rich actually true? So strong is this stigma that Kevin Naff, editor of the gay newspaper the *Washington Blade*, wrote, "The two greatest weapons that opponents of gay rights wield against us are charges that gay men are pedophiles and that homosexuality is a choice. Overcoming those two obstacles would mean instant victory for the movement."[17]

Of course, he has overstated his point, both in terms of pedophilia and of potential "instant victory." If restated, however, he could have said with little exaggeration: "Two of the greatest weapons that opponents of gay rights wield against us are charges that gay men are terribly and carelessly promiscuous and that homosexuality is a choice. Overcoming those two obstacles would mean great progress for the movement." It is understandable, then, that gay leaders, in the words of, Kirk and Madsen want people to believe that, "The sex and love lives of most gays and straights today are both similar and conventional."[18]

In keeping with this philosophy, popular gay author Eric Marcus states that homosexuals are no different than heterosexuals when it comes to sexual activity, noting that, "Just like heterosexual couples, most gay and lesbian couples have less sex with each other over time," which is presumably true. He also states that, "There's no mystery about what gay and lesbian people do to stimulate each other sexually, because what gay and lesbian people do is essentially what heterosexuals do."[19]

As to the question, "Are gay men promiscuous?" he replies:

If you believe what some people say about gay men, you

would think that all gay men have had a thousand or more sexual partners by the time they're thirty. Some very sexually active men – gay and nongay – *have* had a thousand or more sexual partners by the time they're thirty, but most single gay men feel lucky if they can get a date on Saturday night.[20]

So, Marcus wants to downplay the notion that gay men are especially promiscuous, but in doing so, he raises some questions. Before we tackle those questions, however, let's ask some questions of our own.

SOME IMPORTANT DIFFERENCES BETWEEN MALES AND FEMALES

First, is it true that men, in general, are more focused on sex than women? I think there is widespread agreement that this is true.[21] Second, do women have a domesticating, tempering effect on men when they are in a committed relationship together? Again, I think this is generally recognized to be true as well.[22] As Christian apologist Frank Turek asks, "How many married men do you know who rove neighborhoods in street gangs?"[23]

So, putting these two questions together, if men are more overly focused on sex than women, and if gay men do not experience the tempering effects of a long-term, committed relationship with a woman, isn't it likely that gay men will be especially promiscuous? This is not because they are especially evil; it is simply a logical corollary of being a gay male, as noted boastfully by gay sex columnist Dan Savage, "Gay people know more about sex than straight people do, have more sex than straight people do, and are better at it than straight people are."[24]

Let's take this a little further. Heterosexual sex is inherently procreative in nature, even if every instance of sex doesn't result in children, so there is a major procreative side to sex for heterosexuals, in addition to the intimate and sensual side. In contrast, the procreative dimension of sex is inherently absent in homosexual relationships, in every instance, without exception. Thus, along with the intimate side of a sexual and romantic relationship, sex itself can easily take on a more dominant role in gay relationships. Wouldn't this aspect of sexuality within homosexual relationships naturally lead to more promiscuity and to a broader emphasis on sex itself?

And as far as gay men are concerned, they don't have partners who have to deal with various aspects of womanhood and motherhood, both of which also have a tempering effect on married, heterosexual relationships. This too places the emphasis more squarely on sex itself, as explained by gay activist and author Michael Bronski, who stated approvingly that "homosexuality offers a vision of sexual pleasure completely divorced from the burden of reproduction: sex for its own sake, a distillation of the pleasure principle."[25]

Finally, since heterosexuality is the assumed norm for the vast majority of people, "being gay" (in terms of embracing a homosexual orientation and lifestyle) means swimming against the tide of a heterosexual society. Thus, one's homosexuality can easily become the major focus of life (often by necessity, in order to survive and maintain sanity, or, at the least, in order to keep intact one's sexual – meaning, gay – identity). Moreover, because most gays and lesbians do not raise children and are not in committed, long-term relationships (especially the men), multiple relationships and an identity wrapped up in sex become the norm for many. Some gay men have also explained how their sexualized attraction toward other males was driven by a sense of inadequacy in their own masculinity, fueling a desire to "acquire masculinity" and self-confidence through sexual intimacy with other masculine males.[26] Whatever the factors may be, these observations help us to understand better Marcus's comments that, "Some very sexually active men – gay and nongay – have had a thousand or more sexual partners by the time they're thirty."

Really now, how common is it for a heterosexual man to have had *one thousand* sexual partners by the time he's thirty years old – or even fifty years old? To answer with, "Uncommon to the point of being *extremely* rare," would be accurate.[27] Truthfully and sadly, the same cannot be said for a significant minority of gay men. In fact, according to a 1978 survey – and thus before the AIDS epidemic began – 28% of white homosexual men in America claimed more than 1,000 lifetime partners while 43% claimed more than 500.[28] "Seventy-nine percent said that more than half of these partners were strangers and 70 percent said that more than half were men with whom they had sex only once."[29] Initial interviews with gay AIDS victims conducted by the Center of Disease Control indicated that these men *averaged* 1,100 sexual partners.[30]

To be perfectly clear: My point here is not to demonize gay men or to say that they are only focused on sex. That is certainly not the case. Rather, my point is this: To say that the issue before us is only one of *identity* and not *behavior* is to be disingenuous, not to mention completely buying into today's "It's all about equality and tolerance" mantra. There is much in gay culture that *is* about sex, more so than in the heterosexual world, and we simply need to be honest in our discussion.

PROMISCUITY HAS A PRICE

Gay activist and author Gabriel Rotello states candidly:

> HIV truly strikes us where we live. Its means of transmission – sex – is the very thing that to many of us defines us as gay men, drives our politics and our erotics, gives us our modern identity, provides the mortar of much of our philosophy and community, and animates much of our lives.[31]

Rotello recounts:

> Laurie Garrett reports that Dr. June Osborn, an NIH researcher who was one of the first to sound the alarm about STD transmission in gay core groups, had a hard time maintaining a handle on the level of multipartnerism. "Every time we do an NIH site visit, the definition of 'multiple sex partners' has changed," Osborn said in 1980. "First it was ten to twenty partners a year. That was nineteen seventy-five. Then in nineteen seventy-six it was fifty partners a year. By nineteen seventy-eight we were talking about a hundred sexual partners a year and now we're using the term to describe five hundred partners in a year. I am," pronounced Osborn, "duly in awe."[32]

A comprehensive 1987 study, the Multicenter AIDS Cohort Study, indicated that more than three-quarters of the nearly 5,000 gay men interviewed "reported having 50 or more lifetime sexual partners, and over 80 percent had engaged in receptive anal intercourse with at least some of their partners in the previous two years."[33] A 1997 survey of 2,583 sexually active homosexual men in Australia – and thus almost twenty years after AIDS was recognized – revealed that, "Only 15% of the men reported having fewer than eleven sex partners to date, while on the other end of the spectrum 15% had over 1000 sex partners. A whopping 82% had over 50 partners and nearly 50% had over 100."[34]

A major study entitled *Sex in America* indicated that gays and lesbians, combined as one group, had *twelve times* as many lifetime sexual partners as heterosexuals and that they had *seven times* as many sexual partners in the twelve months prior to the study. Even more striking was the fact that heterosexual couples were *forty-one times* more likely to be monogamous than homosexual couples. In fact, in the 1984 volume *The Male Couple* by D. McWhirter and A. Mattison – a volume often cited by conservatives – the authors, themselves a gay couple, found that,

> . . . of the 156 couples studied, only seven had maintained sexual fidelity; of the hundred couples that had been together for more than five years, none had been able to maintain sexual fidelity. The authors noted that "The expectation for outside sexual activity was the rule for male couples and the exception for heterosexuals."[35]

More recent studies and articles have confirmed this trend,[36] some of them including candid admissions that homosexual couples – especially male – play by a different set of rules. Typical is this 2003 study:

> Three-quarters of Canadian gay men in relationships lasting longer than one year are not monogamous, according to a limited study presented during the American Sociological Association conference held in Atlanta this week.
> Barry Adam, a gay professor at the University of Windsor in Canada, last year interviewed 70 gay men who were part of 60 couples for his study, "Relationship Innovation in Male Couples."
> . . . "Those who were monogamous were more likely to be younger, more likely to be in newer, shorter relationships — that is, under three years — and more likely to come from Latino or Asian immigrant groups who said a more romantic approach is what they were used to," Adam said.
> . . . "One of the reasons I think younger men tend to start with the vision of monogamy is because they are coming with a heterosexual script in their head and are applying it to relationships with men," Adam said. "What they don't see is that the gay community has their own order and own ways that seem to work better."[37]

Yes, the gay community has its own order and its own ways, including a new definition of monogamy, which includes things like, "We are monogamous. We only have three-ways together and are never sexual with others apart from each other."[38]

And how many gays would still agree with the sentiments expressed by pioneer gay activist Jack Nichols?

> Nonprocreative same-sex relationships have a particularly redeeming quality, namely, that they take place between people who are the same and can therefore, theoretically at least, welcome others into affectional relationships that bypass exclusivity. This, conceivably, could promote a maximization of affection through communal contact, replacing today's failing models of exclusive, neurotic, narrow, monogamous duos.[39]

Rutgers University English professor Michael Warner would surely concur, arguing that "marriage is unethical. At a time when the largest gay organizations are pushing for same-sex marriage, I argue that this strategy is a mistake and that it represents a widespread loss of vision in the movement." He goes "so far as to offer a principled defense of pornography, sex businesses, and sex outside the home."[40]

In a candid interview recorded in June, 2009, lesbian (or, bisexual) author Camile Paglia expressed admiration and even envy for gay male couples who find it much easier to have affairs – while still considered couples – than do lesbians. Commenting on the breakup of her fifteen-year lesbian relationship, she explained:

> . . . Alas, I know people are going to get mad at me for this, alright, uhh, but . . . I question . . . if there's long term lesbian relationships in terms of whether the spark can really be kept going. I mean, I think that, when I see men couples together – like I have friends who are male couples – they have a much more kind of open and sophisticated lifestyle which is closer to the French model where, umm, you have these like deep personal relationships and, umm, bondings that go on with our famous literary examples, there's so many you could name, from Ginsberg . . . to Gore

Vidal. And I think that, you know, gay men just have this attitude well, of course, you know romantic adventures and you know, the odd fling, is sort of factored into it. And it's easier for men to do that.

But I think with women it's not so easy, 'cause women are much more emotionally bonded. So, with women it's like deep and it's for life, and therefore in my opinion, it's harder for women to get the balance between sexual passion and the deep spiritual commitment. . . . I envy gay men this ability, because I think that if that were possible with lesbians we would just be going on [speaking of the breakup with her partner]. But I don't think this is possible. . . . A fling for a lesbian couple is a betrayal. It's a betrayal . . . it's a betrayal of intimacy. Whereas the gay men, possibly because of the compartmentalization of male sexuality that I talked about in *Sexual Personae*, where it's just a matter of, like, you know, it's like . . . the random, mischievous sex organ just doing its thing, and it's like, it doesn't go very deep. . . . It's one of the many things I've envied about gay men.[41]

Paglia's anecdotal observations confirm what other studies have found: Gay male couples commonly have a different definition of "monogamy" than do straight couples. To quote Kirk and Madsen again (in terms strikingly similar to Paglia's reference to "the random, mischievous sex organ just doing it's thing"), "Sooner or later, the roving penis rears its ugly head." They further noted that, "Yes, that wayward impulse is as inevitable in man-to-man, affairs as in man-to-woman, only, for gays, it starts itching faster." Thus, "Many gay lovers, bowing to the inevitable, agree to an 'open relationship,' for which there are as many sets of ground rules as there are couples."[42]

But that's certainly not a message you'll get from gay activists or the media, who are constantly showing us touching pictures of Jim and John who have been together for the last thirty years and now at last can seal their love with marriage. Well, faithful, truly monogamous, long-term Jim and John may exist, but they are quite a rare species in the gay male world. As a Hollywood actor related to me with sadness, "A gay colleague once told me, 'For every ten men I'm with (sexually), I'll only see one of them again. And for every ten of those men, only one of them will end up being my friend.'"[43]

To the extent that this is representative of even a minority of gay men, it reminds us that we can't focus only on identity; behavior is an issue as well.[44] And it would be ludicrous to think that, with the advent of same-sex marriage or civil unions in some countries and states, gay male promiscuity will suddenly and dramatically decline.[45] That hasn't happened yet.

A 2009 article in the *International Journal of STD and AIDS*, based on surveys of 5168 men in the UK from 1999-2001, reported that

> For the preceding 5 years the median numbers of partners for heterosexual, bisexual and exclusively homosexual men were 2, 7 and 10, respectively. Thus the bisexuals and exclusively homosexual had 3.5x and 5x as many partners as the heterosexuals.[46]

Five times as many sexual partners for gay men as compared to straight men is hardly an insignificant statistic, and yet in repeating these figures, I have no desire to demonize the LGBT community or to give the impression that the majority of gay men have had multiplied thousands of sexual partners. And I am not trying to make an overall moral comparison between heterosexuals and homosexuals based on this criterion alone, as if sexual promiscuity was the biggest and only sin.[47] There are other plenty of other behaviors and attitudes and actions that matter, and there are *plenty* of promiscuous, lust-filled, and deviant heterosexuals.

THE CONNECTION BETWEEN HOMOSEXUAL IDENTITY AND HOMOSEXUAL PRACTICE

Then why bring this up at all? For three primary reasons: 1) Homosexual identity is largely connected to homosexual practice, despite the popular emphasis on identity rather than behavior. The two cannot be so easily separated. 2) The idea that there are no real differences between heterosexual couples and same-sex couples (especially male) is simply not true. 3) Eric Marcus and other gay authors and activists paint a false picture about male homosexual behavior, be it intentionally or not. Indeed, the casual, even nonchalant nature of some of Marcus's answers underscores the point that highly promiscuous behavior is made to seem commonplace, while other aspects of his answers actually obscure the truth.

For example, Marcus implied that in order for the average gay man to have sex, he needs to get a date. This is certainly not true for many homosexuals (and I'm not referring to hiring prostitutes, which is practiced by both heterosexuals and homosexuals). As a researcher who was once actively involved in the gay community asked me, "Have you ever compared the Craigslist category postings for 'men seeking men' or 'casual encounters' versus the analogous postings for 'men seeking women'?! The qualitative difference between the two will shock you." (To be perfectly honest, I've never looked at either listing, but I take this man at his word. Feel free to prove him wrong!)

Marcus himself points to this reality in his response to the very next series of questions: "What are gay bathhouses and sex clubs? Why do gay men go there? Do women go to these kinds of places?" He answers:

> Gay male bathhouses and sex clubs are actually two different things. A gay bathhouse is typically set up like a health club and may have a weight room, a TV room, a sauna, a steam room, a swimming pool, and other amenities. It may also have cubicles with beds that you can rent. When you enter a bathhouse you're assigned a locker, where you put your clothes.
>
> The reason gay men to go bathhouses is generally to have sex, not lift weights. So once your clothes are in your locker, the search for a sexual partner or partners begins.

Marcus then observes, "There is no lesbian equivalent of gay male bathhouses."[48] Neither is there a heterosexual equivalent of gay male bathhouses![49] Yet Marcus describes this impersonal, extremely promiscuous behavior in the most offhanded way, as if it were perfectly normal, whereas in reality it greatly undercuts his claim that heterosexuals and homosexuals are basically the same in terms of their sexual activity.

REDEFINING MONOGAMY

And, as noted above, even among committed gay, male couples, the rate of infidelity is markedly higher than among heterosexual couples, in many cases calling for a redefining of monogamy, the primary dictionary definition of which is: "The practice or condition of having a single sexual partner during a period of time."[50] In gay terms it often means, "The practice or condition of living together with and being emotionally attached to one *primary* sexual partner during a period of time."[51] Indeed, some "committed" gay couples speak of having "open" relationships, of which gay author and activist Michelangelo Signorile states:

> For these men the term "monogamy" simply doesn't
> necessarily mean sexual exclusivity....The term "open
> relationship" has for a great many gay men come to have
> one specific definition: A relationship in which the partners
> have sex on the outside often, put away their resentment
> and jealousy, and discuss their outside sex with each other,
> or share sex partners.[52]

As noted in a January 28, 2010 article in the *New York Times*, "When
Rio and Ray married in 2008, the Bay Area women omitted two words from
their wedding vows: fidelity and monogamy."[53] The article, by Scott James,
was entitled, "Many Successful Gay Marriages Share an Open Secret" – note
that word "open" – and makes some startling admissions:

> A study to be released next month is offering a rare glimpse
> inside gay relationships and reveals that monogamy is not a
> central feature for many. Some gay men and lesbians argue
> that, as a result, they have stronger, longer-lasting and more
> honest relationships. . . .
> New research at San Francisco State University
> reveals just how common open relationships are among
> gay men and lesbians in the Bay Area. The Gay Couples
> Study has followed 556 male couples for three years —
> about 50 percent of those surveyed have sex outside their
> relationships, with the knowledge and approval of their
> partners.
> That consent is key. "With straight people, it's called
> affairs or cheating," said Colleen Hoff, the study's principal
> investigator, "but with gay people it does not have such
> negative connotations."

But is this really a new revelation? According to the article,

> None of this is news in the gay community, but few will
> speak publicly about it. Of the dozen people in open
> relationships contacted for this column, no one would agree

to use his or her full name, citing privacy concerns. They also worried that discussing the subject could undermine the legal fight for same-sex marriage.

So then, gay "marriage" really isn't entirely the same as male-female marriage after all, and what "straight people" call "affairs or cheating" is often accepted, with certain guidelines, in "committed" gay relationships.[54] (In an important essay that discusses other, relevant issues, gay scientist Dr. Simon LeVay, points out some of the very real differences that exist between heterosexual couples and same-sex couples.)[55]

Marcus claims that, "The popular myth is that gay men have enormous sexual appetites and have sex all the time. The truth is dull to report. Gay men and heterosexual men are different only in whom they desire, not how much they desire."[56] To be sure, not all "gay men have enormous sexual appetites and have sex all the time," but without question, a disconcertingly large percentage of gay men are inordinately promiscuous. And, as stated above, one reason for this is that heterosexual men have sex with women, who tend to bring a tempering aspect to the relationship, whereas this tempering aspect is lacking in homosexual relationships. (This, by the way, is one reason that marriage is designed to be the union of a man and a woman, along with the even more compelling fact that only male-female relationships can naturally procreate.)[57]

LET THE TRUTH BE TOLD

And so, Kirk and Madsen, who provided brilliant strategies to help the homosexual community depict itself as being essentially the same as the heterosexual community (with the sole exception of sexual orientation) still admitted,

> Alas, it turns out that, on this point, public myth is supported by fact. There *is* more promiscuity among gays (or at least among gay men) than among straights . . . . Correspondingly, the snail trail of promiscuity – sexually transmitted disease – also occurs among gay men at a rate five to ten times higher than average.[58]

Did you catch that? STD's occur "among gay men at a rate five to ten times higher than average," which would certainly be cause for alarm. Far more shocking – and tragic – is the fact that AIDS and HIV occur among gay men at a rate *more than 400 times higher than average.* More than four hundred times![59]

Kirk and Madsen cite a study indicating that, "roughly four in ten gay males, and over half of all lesbians, were found to be leading decidedly *un*promiscuous sex lives. The rest ranged from the most typical pattern – singles who occasionally dated and had sex, just as straight singles do – to the most exotic: hungry male adventurers who sought out multiple, anonymous sexual encounters on a daily basis."[60] Read those words again: *multiple, anonymous sexual encounters on a daily basis.*

Is such behavior heard of among even the most highly sex-focused, heterosexual males?[61] And why have some gay seminars offered to school children as young as twelve years old included the subject of "fisting" – the well-known homosexual practice of forcing one's entire fist into another person's rectum?[62] And what should we think of "circuit parties," in which up to 25,000 gay and bisexual men gather for a weekend of almost non-stop dancing and – in most cases – numerous sexual encounters, usually fueled by high levels of drug use?[63]

To be fair, I should note again that, in the words of gay blogger Timothy Kincaid, there are plenty of gay couples who "are home barbecuing and walking the dog. And there are bowling leagues and ski clubs and church groups and social networks" (meaning, for gays, or populated by gays). And, he points out correctly, there is plenty of heterosexual promiscuity: "We have no monopoly on 'having to sleep with as many people as possible' in order to feel good about one's self." Still, he added, "we as a community play our part in the confusion. Far too often we act as though getting the next hot guy is what it means to be gay (women do this less) and confirm these ideas [of extreme gay promiscuity]."[64]

Indeed, despite exaggerated, stereotyped images of homosexual behavior in the eyes of straights, Kirk and Madsen acknowledge: "The fact remains: what straights have now heard about gay sex is not so far removed from the barnyard."[65] They note that much of this was hidden from the public eye, but then "AIDS yanked aside the curtain." (What follows is extremely graphic.)

> Brochures alerting the public to 'safe sex' practices for the epidemic began to make only too clear what had been going on in darkened corners: gays should stop licking one another's anuses; gays should stop shoving their fists up

one another's rectums; gays should stop urinating into one another's mouths; gay sadists should stop drawing blood during their tortures of gay masochists, etc., etc.[66]

Of course, they note,

Just as most straights do, the vast majority of gays wince to hear such a list, and have had little or no personal experience with the activities it proscribes. But because ignorant heterosexuals have no way of knowing which gay behaviors are common and which rare, they seem inclined to assume that the grossest, kinkiest practices they've heard about are enjoyed nightly by *all* gay people.[67]

Still, even with these clear caveats, which mirror the comments of Joe Dallas, cited above, Kirk and Madsen confess:

Of all the misbehaviors we decry, *self-indulgence is perhaps most characteristic of gays, and of the gay community as a whole* [my emphasis]. Indeed, it was institutionalized, long ago, by the gay media and arbiters of Political Correctness, as a central tenet of gay liberation. . . . In a community in which every gay wants to be "p.c.-er than thou," any self-restraint is, itself, suspect of being a sign of self-hatred and bluenosery – so one virtually *must* act out one's most fleeting impulses in order to prove that one isn't a hung-up, judgmental old poop.[68]

How sad it is to read Kirk and Madsen's report that AIDS killed off many of the most sexually active homosexuals, reducing – albeit temporarily – some of the highest levels of promiscuity.[69] Of interest in this respect is the thesis of Patrick Moore, *Beyond Shame: Reclaiming the Abandoned History of Radical Gay Sexuality*.[70] As explained by reviewer Edmund White, "Patrick Moore boldly argues that the promiscuous gay men of the 1970s were actually artists and that AIDS derailed an esthetic community and sexual adventure."[71] Artists? Really? The "adventure" was certainly costly.

WE'RE IN THE 21ST CENTURY AND THE NEWS IS STILL NOT GOOD

Sadly, the new millennium did not bring about much of a change in the male homosexual community in terms of reducing promiscuity and the spread of AIDS, and recent reports from San Francisco have drawn attention to an alarming increase in STD's among the gay men there.[72] On a national level, a December 15, 2000 article in the gay *New York Blade News* stated that,

> Reports at a national conference about sexually transmitted diseases indicate that gay men are in the highest risk group for several of the most serious diseases. . . . Scientists believe that the increased number of STD cases is the result of an increase in risky sexual practices by a growing number of gay men who believe that HIV is no longer a life-threatening illness.[73]

Outside of the USA, an August 14, 2005 article announced:

> A SERIOUS sexual disease which can lead to insanity and death if left untreated has increased 14-fold among gay men in the past four years in Scotland.
>
> New figures have revealed that while little more than a dozen cases of syphilis were recorded in 2001, by last year that total had soared to 186.
>
> The majority of cases are centred in Scotland's two largest centres, with a 900% increase in four years in Glasgow and a 500% increase in Lothian in three years.
>
> Experts say that the disease is being diagnosed primarily in gay men, and warn it indicates that they are taking risks with their health by having unprotected sex.[74]

Worse still, according to a 2002 report from the Center of Disease Control and Prevention, "even though AIDS incidence (the number of new cases diagnosed during a given period, usually a year) is declining, *there has not been a comparable decline in the number of newly diagnosed HIV cases among youth.*"[75] The CDC estimates that "at least half of all new HIV infections in the United States are among people under twenty-five, and the majority of young people are infected sexually."[76] And so, despite increasing levels of social acceptance of homosexuality and despite major advances in the gay activist agenda, gay men in particular continue to be notoriously promiscuous – and tragically unsafe in their sexual practices.[77] Indeed, the headline to a September 27, 2010 article stated, "HIV Infection in Gays Increasing at an Alarming Rate."[78]

A recent scholarly article suggests that the three primary reasons given for unsafe gay sex are: AIDS optimism (meaning that there is less concern about the potentially fatal consequences of AIDS), condom fatigue (meaning that over a period of time, the men grow weary of using condoms), and low self-esteem (meaning that a gay man with low self-esteem will not want to put off his partner by refusing to have unprotected sex).[79]

This is important when we remember that some researchers and activists have blamed gay promiscuity on *society as a whole*. In other words, because gays have been rejected, marginalized, misunderstood, and oppressed by the society, and not allowed to marry, their promiscuity should be understood as a reaction to that society and a result of their mistreatment. While there may be some truth to this claim in individual cases, studies indicate that "out of the closet" gay men apparently engage in far more frequent and risky sex than do "closeted" gays.[80] Indeed, it is often in the most "liberated" homosexual circles – such as the San Francisco gay community – that things are so often out of control sexually. And reports issued in 2008 and 2009 confirm theses alarming trends (see Chapter Twelve, below, for more).

The undeniable conclusions would appear to be that: 1) Sexual license among promiscuous gay males remains rampant; and 2) gay sexual practices are fraught with health risks. Yet to say such things today is to be branded a bigoted homophobe. In reality, however, pointing out the dangers of certain homosexual practices is an act of love, not hate or irrational fear. Indeed, if we truly care about gay men – and are prepared to love them in a self-sacrificing way – then we should compassionately and candidly speak with them about the dangers they routinely expose themselves (and others) to through their sexual practices.

Gay journalist Matt Comer makes some interesting, candid comments about promiscuity among gay and bi men (while also expressing his views about "the Religious Right"):

> Whether gay and bi men want to admit it or not, the simple truth of the matter is that we all engage in a lot of sex. Is our promiscuity as bad as the Religious Right

claims? No, and who cares what they think anyway? We all know they lie and exaggerate for political power and earthly gain. Their opinions don't matter here. Forget them; we're talking about us.

But while we are talking we need to do it honestly. In our attempt to battle the Religious Right, conformists among our midst have turned our liberalized culture into a monastery.

"We can't talk about that," activists say. "We'll get attacked by the Right and give them ammunition."

This is an issue that is too important to be thrown into the closet. We shouldn't skirt around it or hide from it. Why? Because it limits our discussion, prevents true and honest reflection and hampers prevention and education.[81]

Outspoken gay activist Larry Kramer bemoaned the self-destructive state of affairs among many homosexuals, but not without emphasizing (and reiterating):

I love being gay. I love gay people. I think we're better than other people. I really do. I think we're smarter and more talented and more aware and I do, I do, I totally do. And I think we're more tuned in to what's happening, tuned into the moment, tuned into our emotions, and other people's emotions, and we're better friends. I really do think all these things.[82]

In other words, Kramer is an in-house critic – similar to Kirk and Madsen – and his greatest motivation is simple: ". . . I passionately and desperately want all my brothers and sisters to stay alive and well and on this earth as long as they want theirs to."[83] But he cannot deny the destructive, sex-driven pattern he sees among far too many gays:

In 1990, that is some nine years into what was happening [meaning, in terms of AIDS awareness], 46% of gay men in San Francisco were still f----g without condoms.

60% of the syphilis in America today is in gay men. Excuse me, men who have sex with men.

Palm Springs has the highest number of syphilis cases in California. Palm Springs?

I do not want to hear each week how many more of you are becoming hooked on meth. [For those who may be unaware, crystal methamphetamine is widely used by gay men as a sexual aphrodisiac.]

HIV infections are up as much as 40%.

You cannot continue to allow yourselves and each other to act and live like this! . . .

I do not understand why some of you believe that because we have drugs that deal with the virus more or less effectively that it is worth the gamble to have unprotected sex.[84]

And in another reminder that gay activism cannot be divorced from sex, what group of American citizens rejoiced when the Supreme Court in 2003 found an alleged constitutional right to sodomy in the "Lawrence vs. Texas" case? It was gay men in particular, since the "right" to have anal sex under the protection of the United States government was hailed as a significant, landmark breakthrough.[85] For years this had been a key element in the gay agenda.[86]

At this point you might be saying, "Enough already. I get the point. Lots of gay men are extremely promiscuous and all too many of them engage in high-risk sex. What's that got to do with the issue of civil rights for gays and lesbians? What's the big deal?"

PUTTING THE ISSUES IN FOCUS

Simply this. If the issue before us was only one of treating gays and lesbians with civility and decency, I would be championing their cause. (In fact, that's a cause that I *do* champion.) If the issue before us was simply one of repudiating and eliminating all violence against gays and lesbians, I would be raising my voice – as I have in the past and will continue to do so in the future – against all such heinous acts. But that is not the whole picture. Instead, much of today's debate is actually *sex driven*. In other words, a lot of this really *is* about sex, and to ignore that is to ignore reality.

Put another way, this is also a question of fundamental "rights," specifically, Why should people be put into a special class of citizens – equivalent, say, to race or ethnicity – based upon the way they have romantic and sexual relationships? Recent studies of lesbianism have pointed to a remarkable amount of sexual orientation fluidity for many women, with some women being exclusively heterosexual for years before becoming same-sex attracted, while others went from exclusively lesbian to bisexual or primarily heterosexual in their attractions.[87] As one bisexual woman commented, "I fall in love with a person, not a gender."[88] (Before her current relationship to a woman, she had been a satisfied heterosexual.)

WNBA basketball superstar Sheryl Swoopes had been married for three years to her high-school sweetheart and thought of herself as a heterosexual, but then fell in love with a woman and came out as a lesbian in 2005. She stated, "I can't help who I fall in love with. No one can," also explaining, "Discovering I'm gay just sort of happened much later in life."[89] Should we then redefine marriage to accommodate these changes? On what basis?

It is well known that a substantial number of lesbians have serious issues with men, many of them having been raped or abused or taken advantage of by a male figure earlier in life, contributing to their same-sex attraction (and opposite-sex revulsion; see further, below, Chapter Thirteen, for some examples). Given that some lesbians are repulsed by men because of earlier, negative experiences in life, while other women go from heterosexual to lesbian, why should all lesbians – who are treated universally as if they were born this way and cannot change – be entitled to special civil rights? Do you see the point I am making?

Am I willing to stand up for gays and lesbians when they are attacked and hated, when they are treated like the worst of all sinners, when they are persecuted and reviled? Absolutely! Am I willing to stand up and fight so that men can have sex with men and women can have sex with women – even intimate, loving sex? Absolutely not. And am I willing to lend my support to an agenda that, quite frequently, opens the door to all kinds of sexual perversions? God forbid.

Yes, I'm fully aware that the mainstream American media bombards us with pictures of gay weddings and gay couples, all of whom appear to be blissful in their union, the model of happy, fulfilled, and deeply devoted people, and I don't doubt that many of them really are devoted to each other. And we are told that this is only a question of love, equality, and tolerance, having virtually nothing to do with sex.

We see images of, say, Milly and Molly with their eighteen year-old daughter (presumably from a previous marriage by one of the partners), sitting on their front porch together with their Labrador Retriever, as solid as any family you know. The front cover of *People Magazine* (August, 2008) showed off the wedding pictures of Ellen DeGeneres and Portia DeRossi – in fact, "Oprah Winfrey spent an entire hour showcasing their relationship in an episode pointedly titled 'Ellen DeGeneres and Her Wife, Portia de Rossi'"[90] – while *Newsweek*'s December 15, 2008 issue, which actually claimed that the Bible *supported* same-sex marriage, featured a full-page replete with touching, gay-wedding photos.[91]

But do these blissful pictures (which may, indeed, represent couples deeply in love), fairly represent all, or even most of the LGBT community? Or is there another side to the story that also needs to be told, a story almost always overlooked by the mainstream media and virtually unknown to the average American?

NOT YOUR AVERAGE SOCIAL ACTIVIST CONFERENCE

Consider the annual "Creating Change Conference" held by the National Gay and Lesbian Task Force, one of the major gay activist events of the year. The theme of the 2010 conference, held in Dallas, Texas from Feb. 3-7, was, "Live Large. THINK BIG." Yet the front cover of the conference program book featured two prominent captions: "ACTION is HOT," and "Power is sexy."[92] How common is this for a civil rights, equality conference?

A welcome letter from Dallas mayor Tom Leppert (Feb. 3, 2010) stated that, "The Creating Change Conference has a long history of nurturing political skills and leadership within the LGBT community, and we are pleased that you chose Dallas for this year's event."[93] Yet this conference devoted to "nurturing political skills and leadership within the LGBT community" has some very peculiar elements to it.

Really now, how many political activist conferences print out warnings against sexual harassment for conference attendees? But the NGLTF found it necessary to do so, listing these specific examples of "unwelcome behavior of a sexual nature" in their program book:

- Touching someone without their permission (grabbing, hugging, petting)
- Sexual propositions
- Sexually offensive pictures, magazines, notes, calendars, cartoons, or jokes
- Unwanted flirtations or advances
- Graphic comments about an individual's body or dress

- Verbal abuse (including sexual insults and namecalling)
- Repeated pressure or requests for sexual activities
- Rewards for granting sexual favors or the withholding of rewards for refusing to grant sexual favors[94]

And remember: This is a major, political, gay activist conference, yet it is understood that unwelcome sexual behavior could very well be an issue too. After all, this *is* about sex and sexuality, at least on some unavoidable level. (On a more minor level, note that in order to acknowledge the needs of transgender people, all restrooms are designated as "gender neutral," the program book explaining, "Regardless of what bathroom you are in, please let everyone pee in peace.")[95]

How many other political activist conferences feature a Saturday night, "Mas-Queer-Ade Ball?"[96] How many offer fourteen different workshops under the heading of Sexual Freedom? Some of the workshops offered include:

- Creating Communities of Resistance/Change through Innovative Sex Organizations and Businesses
- Sexual Liberation as a Framework for Change
- Young and Poly
- Mapping Your Desire
- Kink, Race and Class
- Our Common Cause – A place for polyamorous/ non-monogamy communities in the LGBTIQA movement
- Polyamory/Nonmonogamy Caucus
- Sex Workers' Caucus
- Leather Caucus[97]

And yet we are told that GLBT issues are simply matters of social justice and *not* sexually focused (or, often sexually aberrant) matters as well. This is simply not true, as evidenced by the subject matter of just this one workshop (a workshop, I remind you, that is *not* being offered at a gay sex fair somewhere but rather at perhaps the most prestigious, political activist conference in the entire GLBT movement). Note the subject matter well, and then note who is presenting it:

Leather Caucus

Sexual Freedom

Whatever your kink – come meet your peers – fetishists of every stripe, the tippity tops, the brash bottoms, the doms and dommes, the bois, the high femmes, the givers and takers, the lovers of pain and pleasure. We'll all be here, queer and fabulous.

Presenters: Jaime M. Grant, Director of the Policy Institute, National Gay and Lesbian Task Force, Washington, DC.[98]

Grant is obviously a mainstream player in a mainstream (indeed, flagship) GLBT political organization who is giving a presentation on bizarre sexual practices, including sado-masochism – but, we're told, it's not about sex!

The Creating Change Conference even has an annual Leather Leadership Award, this year awarded to Hardy Haberman, "a member of many BDSM/Fetish organizations including Leather Rose Society, National Leather Association-Dallas, Discipline Corps and a founding member of Inquisition-Dallas."[99] (Remember that BDSM stands for "Bondage, Discipline, Sadism, Masochism." As for Inquisition-Dallas, it is described on its website as a "Social club dedicated to safe sane and consensual BDSM activities.") This is what the NGLT awards and celebrates?

A presentation of the Sexual Liberation Institute makes these fascinating points:

The modern movement for LGBT liberation was touched off by a rebellion against police-abuse aimed at gender expressions and sexual practices that were deemed 'deviant' by the dominant culture. Our movement was founded by outsiders who refused to be marginalized, targeted and victimized for their sexual practices and their gender non-conformity. Fast forward to 2009. We have many gains to be proud of as we look back and assess the modern movement – legal, social and cultural leaps that were unfathomable in the cramped quarters of queerness in 1968. But as we look around at our fierce battles to win marriage rights, establish and protect our families, and secure the economic well-being of our diverse households, one is struck by the near-erasure of LGBT sexuality in these struggles, and by the silencing of frank dialogue about sexual diversity and sexual practices in our communities.

Do we still believe that LGBT people have a unique contribution to make in American life in the areas of sexual liberation and sexual expression? Or is our desire irrelevant to the quest for "equality"? . . . The personal is still political. Come to this workshop and find out how to connect the dots between claiming your power in the bedroom and seizing power in the streets or the halls of justice.[100]

Are you starting to connect the dots more clearly? GLBT activism and sexual issues *are* joined at the hip.

We pointed out in Chapter Eight that major gay pride events and parades have often been marked by the flaunting of all kinds of sexuality and sexual perversions, in stark contrast with other public events and parades in the secular and religious world. In the same way, watershed gay literature is all too frequently marked by a pronounced emphasis on sex – often in its most perverse, degraded forms, while even "queer theology" is often shockingly sex-centered.[101] Do you think I'm exaggerating?

THE SEXUAL FOCUS OF A FAMOUS MANIFESTO

One of the landmark documents in the gay revolution is Carl Wittman's "Refugees from Amerika: A Gay Manifesto," written from San Francisco on January 1, 1970.[102] As far as manifestos go, it is one of many, with typically radical language and a piercing criticism of the "status quo."[103] What is unique about the *Gay Manifesto* is its emphasis on sexual issues, with one of Wittman's seven headings devoted entirely to sex (#5, On Sex) while several others directly touch on sexual issues (see #1, On Orientation, which deals with homosexuality, heterosexuality, and bisexuality; #2, On Women, which includes discussion of lesbianism; #3 On Roles, which mocks the institution of marriage and also deals with "closet queens").

Why so much sex talk in a programmatic document? The answer is simple: It is because sexual issues often occupy a prominent position in gay and lesbian literature, ideology, and even theology (yes, theology; see Chapter Ten, and see also below).

The Gay Today website provides a typical example. GayToday.com claims to be "an indispensable resource for anyone interested in gay life in

America" with "nothing else like it on the Internet."[104] Not surprisingly, the website prominently features a "Sex Talk" column, and it is sex talk with no holds barred.[105] This is part and parcel of being "gay today."[106]

Look at this selection from Wittman's manifesto and then ask yourself, Why hasn't the *Gay Manifesto* been repudiated by the larger gay community? Why is it still viewed as an important historical document, one that even has lasting relevance? And why are such topics germane to *this particular* manifesto? Read this extended selection carefully:

> A note on exploitation of children: kids can take care of themselves, and are sexual beings way earlier than we'd like to admit. Those of us who began cruising in early adolescence know this, and we were doing the cruising, not being debauched by dirty old men. Scandals such as the one in Boise, Idaho - blaming a "ring" of homosexuals for perverting their youth - are the fabrications of press and police and politicians. And as for child molesting, the overwhelming amount is done by straight guys to little girls: it is not particularly a gay problem, and is caused by the frustrations resulting from anti-sex puritanism.
>
> 5. *Perversion*: We've been called perverts enough to be suspect of any usage of the word. Still many of us shrink from the idea of certain kinds of sex: with animals, sado/masochism, dirty sex (involving [urine] or [fecal matter]). Right off, even before we take the time to learn any more, there are some things to get straight:
>
> 1. we shouldn't be apologetic to straights about gays whose sex lives we don't understand or share;
> 2. it's not particularly a gay issue, except that gay people are probably less hung up about sexual experimentation;
> 3. let's get perspective: even if we were to get into the game of deciding what's good for someone else, the harm done in these 'perversions' is undoubtedly less dangerous or unhealthy than is tobacco or alcohol.

4. While they can be reflections of neurotic or self-hating patterns, they may also be enactments of spiritual or important phenomena: e.g. sex with animals may be the beginning of interspecies communication: some dolphin-human breakthroughs have been made on the sexual level; e.g. one guy who says he digs s--t during sex occasionally says it's not the taste or texture, but a symbol that he's so far into sex that those things no longer bug him; e.g. sado/masochism, when consensual, can be described as a highly artistic endeavor, a ballet the constraints of which are thresholds of pain and pleasure.

Sex with animals may be the beginning of interspecies communication? Some dolphin-human breakthroughs have been made on the sexual level? Sado-masochism, when consensual, can be described as a highly artistic endeavor? Kids are sexual beings way earlier than we'd like to admit?

Why in the world is this material part of the *Gay Manifesto*? And what other manifesto would make reference to a man ingesting the feces or urine of his sexual partner? Once more I ask: Where is the gay repudiation of the *Gay Manifesto*?[107]

How far would the Civil Rights movement have gotten with a manifesto including material like this? Who could even imagine such a thing? It would have completely discredited every noble cause represented by that nation-changing movement. Yet somehow this trash remains part of the heritage – the proud heritage – of the gay rights movement.

Do you think I'm being unfair? I remind you that I am not trying to argue that most gays are into sex with animals – of course not! – or that gay sex normally includes sado-masochism. Absolutely not. And I am not making the claim that gay and lesbian couples never experience intimacy, affection, and love through sexual acts. To the contrary, I'm sure that many gay couples experience these emotions on a very deep level. Rather, to reiterate, my point is that *sexual issues* cannot be disassociated from the larger gay agenda and that homosexuality, in many ways, really *is* about sex. (At the very least, it must include the issue of sex.)

SOME SYNAGOGUES AND CHURCHES WITH A DIFFERENCE

Because sexual issues are often front and center in gay and lesbian culture, a prominent gay man like Allen Ginsberg, the celebrated Beat poet and convert to Buddhism, will be lauded and applauded even in *religious* gay circles, despite the fact that he was a member of the infamous NAMBLA, the North American Man-Boy Love Association.

The NAMBLA website quotes Ginsberg as stating that

> Attacks on NAMBLA stink of politics, witchhunting for profit, humorlessness, vanity, anger and ignorance ... I'm a member of NAMBLA because I love boys too -- everybody does, who has a little humanity.[108]

He also objected to

> . . . the whole labeling of pedophiles as 'child molesters.' Everybody likes little kids. All you've got to do is walk through the Vatican and see all the little statues of little prepubescents, pubescents, and postpubescents. Naked kids have been a staple of delight for centuries, for both parents and onlookers. So to label pedophilia as criminal is ridiculous."[109]

Yes, Ginsberg was not only a highly influential figure in the counterculture revolution of the 1960s and beyond, but he was a known pedophile – not to mention the author of some extraordinarily vulgar poems, the most famous being the controversial, seminal work "Howl." Yet Congregation Beth Simchat Torah, the world's largest gay and lesbian synagogue – boasting 3,500 members – announced this special event for their 20's and 30's group on August 1, 2005: **Allen Ginsberg on Film**: "Join us for an evening viewing of legendary Beat poet Allen Ginsberg's appearances on film, with a lively discussion to follow. This event is hosted by Bob Rosenthal, a poet and the director of the Allen Ginsberg Trust."[110] A synagogue-organized social event centered on Allen Ginsberg? This would certainly cause Moses to blush – or, more likely, pass out – not to mention the concept of a gay and lesbian synagogue itself.

I ask again: Do you think I'm being unfair? Then consider some of the seminars offered at the 2005 Annual Conference of the Metropolitan Community Churches, the world's largest "gay Christian" denomination, with more than 250 affiliated churches as of 2010.

Some of the conference seminars sound exactly like what would be expected at a Christian conference, discussing issues like which hymnals to use in the services and the need to establish new churches. Other teaching sessions, however, indicate that, *even in church seminars*, much of the discussion really is about sex.

The 2005 conference included such topics such as:

- Queer Power Dynamics
- Manifest Love: Toward the Creation of a More Loving Gay Male World
- Bisexuals: The Invisible Queers --or-- [It's not about] ANYTHING THAT MOVES
- Having Healthy Sexuality for Women who Partner with Women.[111]

These, however, are relatively tame. Consider the following which, I remind you, were presented at the preeminent conference of the largest "gay Christian" denomination:

Leather Tribe 101
Tony Shull, Rev. Lee Carlton, Rev. Kurt Kreiger and Pat Baillie
Our goal is to explore the spiritually diverse lives that the leather-folk and bear groups bring to our fellowship. We will look at what bands us together as a community within a community, and how we create what is one of the strongest and most socially active groups both in and out of MCC. Four panel members from a broad spectrum of spiritual backgrounds in MCC will share their experiences. The panel discussion will be followed by a Q&A.[112]

For those who are unaware,

"Leather" is a blanket term for a large array of sexual preferences, identities, relationship structures, and social organizations loosely tied together by the thread of what is conventionally understood as sadomasochistic sex.[113]

As for "bear groups,"

Bear culture has its origins in informal "chubby and chubby-chaser" networks among gay men in the late 1960s and early 1970s. Big men and their admirers played a role in the increasing diversification and specialization of identity-based gay organizations in the mid-1970s.[114]

Yet a "Christian" seminar was offered "to explore the spiritually diverse lives that the leather-folk and bear groups bring to our fellowship." In fact, Rev. Troy Perry, the founder of the MCC Churches, actually contributed a chapter to the book *Leatherfolk*, in which he speaks of his own "journey into leather," which, by definition, includes sado-masochism.[115] Yes, the gay magazine *Frontiers* (October 1, 1999, 51) referred to Perry – one of the most influential "gay Christian" leaders in the world – as a "big ol' leather queen"![116]

It is therefore no surprise that a pro-polyamory seminar was also offered at the MCC conference:

Building Closets or Opening Doors (Polyamory)
Fran Mayes
Have we who know the freedom of coming out to live without fear or shame created our own MCC closets? The stories of some of us who love and/or partner with more than one other person will be presented as told to me for my dissertation "Polyamory and Holy Union in UFMCC". Chosen families in light of the Bible, a theology of sexuality, history, and worldwide practice.[117]

Yes, "polyamory" – in other words, having multiple sexual partners (loving, of course!) – was also a topic of discussion at the MCC conference, and church members were encouraged to come out of the closets with their ongoing, multiple sexual relationships.[118]

And still, there is more. Other seminars included:

Finding God in Your Erotic Experience

Rev. Dr. Bob Goss
This workshop explores the connection between spirituality and sexuality, the escape from erotophobia and shame, the reclamation of sexual pleasure as an original blessing, coming out to God, how to become an erotic contemplative, and the connection of sexuality to justice issues. Deep sexuality and deep spirituality emerge from the same divine source and converge in our progress on the spiritual path. Can we speak of multiple configurations of erotic relationships and the Christian life?

Our Gay Gaze: Using Your Eyes in Whole New Ways to Get What You Want
Dave Nimmons
From glances to gaydar, lingering stares to winks, gay men have made eye contact an art form, with its own power, language, rituals, and conventions. Yet as we use our eyes to connect, we sometimes foreclose connection, impede contact and friendliness, preclude openness and warmth. Whether you're cruising for sex, intimacy, or spirit, this experiential, intimate session will open your eyes about how to use your gaze to get what you most need. You won't ever see gay men the same way again.[119]

What in Jesus' name (literally!) is going on? "Whether you're cruising for sex, intimacy, or spirit, this experiential, intimate session will open your eyes about how to use your gaze to get what you most need." Cruising for sex? Committed Christians cruising for gay sex and using their gaze to get what they most need? How can this be?

For those of you who consider yourselves Christian, can you imagine seminar topics such as these being offered at your denomination's annual conference, even if your denomination is extremely liberal? Why so much emphasis on sex?

PERVERSION FROM THE PULPIT
Another respected leader in the MCC is Dr. Neil G. Thomas, pastor of Metropolitan Community Church Los Angeles. His Doctor of Ministry dissertation, *Queer Theology: An Introduction*,[120] contains three sermons he

preached to his Los Angeles congregation entitled "Queering the Trinity." One of those sermons contained these remarkable lines:

> Our religious participation in community must cause us to think about who is Jesus, what did Jesus do, and how did Jesus queer the experience of God then and how I get to queer it today.

This question bears repeating: "How did Jesus queer the experience of God then and how I get to queer it today?" What exactly does Dr. Thomas mean? He asks:

> How do I change dominant culture? How do I change family dynamics from the established models, specifically, one mother, one father and 2.2 children? How do I get to do that in my world where two moms or two dads bring their children into church, as well as a mum and a dad?

Perhaps that sounds like a reasonable question to some, but this is only the beginning of an increasingly perverse statement. Please read these words slowly and carefully, and remember: The man who wrote these words is the pastor of a "gay Christian" church, and he raises these issues as valid pastoral concerns.

> How do I get to queer the whole experience of life by showing up and being authentically who I am as a leather man, as a drag queen, as an openly gay man, as a lesbian, as someone who is bisexual or transgender or intersex or questioning or who has no self identity yet whatsoever? How do I bring my whole self, authentic and spiritual, when I am not in a coupled relationship but I'm in a poly-amorous relationship [meaning, having multiple sexual and romantic partners outside of wedlock]? How can I be authentically myself when I bring my non-stereotypical family into church and that same family decides to come and receive communion together. How do I get to challenge my own theology when someone who is in a sadomasochistic relationship comes to communion

and the person who plays the role of 'S' [meaning, slave] kneels before the celebrant to receive communion, awaiting permission from his/her 'M' [meaning, master]?[121]

No, your eyes did not deceive you. You read what you think you just read. A man claiming to be a Christian pastor calls on his parishioners to be "authentic" and to attend church services in an "authentic" way, whether that means "as a leather man" or "as a drag queen," among other things. Yes, "being authentically who I am" is what matters, and that includes coming to church to receive holy communion as a "non-stereotypical family," even a poly-amorous "family" – perhaps consisting of Joe, who is heterosexual, and his wife Sally, who is bisexual, and her lover Molly, who is lesbian, and her friend Jane, who is heterosexual, and who also sleeps with Joe – and they all want to take communion as a family, together with all their children. (Do you think this church has the Ten Commandments hanging on the wall? Do you think, "Thou shalt not commit adultery" is one of their favorite verses?)

Dr. Thomas, however, has to take things one step further in what must be one of the most perverted images ever associated with the Eucharist. (For those not familiar with Christian teaching, Holy Communion, also called the Lord's Table or the Eucharist, is a remembrance of the death of Jesus, with the bread representing – or for Catholics, actually becoming – his body and the wine or grape juice representing – or becoming – his blood. It is considered a sacred act to eat the bread and drink the wine.)[122] Thomas speaks of a couple who are in a sadomasochistic relationship and who are about to receive communion. The "slave" (who is the one who receives sexual pleasure by being whipped or beaten or tortured), kneels before the person handing out the bread and wine – which represents, I remind you, the body and blood of Jesus – awaiting approval to partake of communion from his or her "master" (who is the one who receives sexual pleasure by doing the whipping or beating or torturing). And so a couple involved in a demeaning, perverted, truly sick sexual relationship receives communion in a church service, living out their perverted identity for all to see. *Such twisted images could only be conceived in a homosexual "church."*

PERVERSE EDUCATION

And if sexual issues are not so central in homosexual circles, how can we explain a college conference like this?

From February 6-8 [1998], the University of California-Santa Cruz hosted, Exposed! The University of California Lesbian, Gay, Bisexual, and Transgendered Annual Conference and General Assembly. The conference, which was attended by high school and college students, featured screenings of Blood Sisters: Leather Dykes & Sadomasochism and Daddy and the Muscle Academy. Workshops at the gathering included "Latex Lovers: A Workshop on Queer Womyn Safe-Sex," "Transgender Workplace Issues," and "Town, Gown, and T-Rooms: the University and Public Homosexual Sex." . . . [123]

And if sexual reeducation is not a major goal of gay activism, how can we explain the fact that the Gay, Lesbian, and Straight Educational Network (GLSEN) recommended some of the following books for school children? (What follows is graphic and very disturbing.)

- *Reflections of a Rock Lobster*, containing passages like this, which describes the sexual adventures of a *first grade boy*: "My sexual exploits with my neighborhood playmates continued. I lived a busy homosexual childhood, somehow managing to avoid venereal disease through all my toddler years. *By first grade I was sexually active with many friends.* In fact, a small group of us regularly met in the grammar school lavatory to perform fellatio on one another. A typical week's schedule would be Aaron and Michael on Monday during lunch; Michael and Johnny on Tuesday after school; Fred and Timmy at noon Wednesday; Aaron and Timmy after school on Thursday."[124]
- *In Your Face*, with passages like this, in which the male narrator describes how he lost his virginity at the age of 16 to a 25 year-old man he met at a gay youth group: "I don't remember exactly when I started coming out, but I joined this youth group called Positive Images; it's the Sonoma County gay/lesbian/bisexual youth group. I got a boyfriend instantly; he picked me up right away, right when I joined the group. He was

older; he was twenty-five, I was sixteen. He was just really supportive of me. I went with him to this gay prom in Sonoma County called the Rainbow Prom in the middle of May. So there was one night when I stayed at my boyfriend's house. I lost my virginity to him a couple weeks before that, and so I stayed at his house, and I was feeling good when I went home the next day. It was the first time that I actually spent the night there and stayed the whole night. So I went home and I was in a great mood."[125]

- *Passages of Pride*, with passages like this, describing a homosexual encounter between a minor and a stranger: "Near the end of summer, just before starting his sophomore year in high school, Dan picked up a weekly Twin Cities newspaper. Scanning the classifieds, he came upon an ad for a 'Man-2-Man' massage. Home alone one day, he called the telephone number listed in the ad and set up an appointment to meet a man named Tom. Tom offered to drive to Zimmerman. So, over the phone, Dan directed him to a secluded road in his subdivision. "Stop where the pavement ends," Dan told him. A couple of nights later, Dan pulled the broken screen from his bedroom window and slipped out of the house while his parents slept. He hurried to the prearranged rendezvous spot, and there, in the dark of night, he met Tom for the first time, man-to-man. In the back of Tom's van, the two had sex.[126]

What kind of educational organization would recommend such filth to be read by school children? It is spelled GLSEN, which appears to stand for the Gay and Lesbian *Sex* Education Network more than the Gay, Lesbian, and Straight Educational Network. And remember: These samplings represent only a tiny selection of just a few books on a long reading list, and it was a list that came to national attention in 2009 because President Obama's "Safe School Czar," Kevin Jennings, was the head of GLSEN at the time these books were recommended, prompting calls for his ouster.[127] Rather astonishingly, Martin Garnar, the chairman of the American Library

Association's Intellectual Freedom Committee launched a defense of Kevin Jennings, GLSEN, and these sexually explicit books:

> Though Jennings' and GLSEN's critics claim to be upholding American morals and values by condemning the GLSEN book list, they are actually undermining the values of tolerance, free inquiry, and self-determination that inform and sustain our democratic way of life in the United States.[128]

So it is those of us who are offended by this vulgar and pornographic trash – *part of a children's reading list* – who are undermining important American values. How utterly unpatriotic!

WHEN GAY THEOLOGIANS GATHER

And what happens at the world's largest gathering of biblical and religious scholars, the annual joint conference of the Society of Biblical Literature (SBL) and the American Academy of Religion (AAR)? (Take a deep breath and read on. This is *not* pleasant stuff, especially for the spiritually sensitive.)

This is a sampling of the papers and topics to be read and discussed in the "Gay Men's Issues in Religion Group" at the 2004 AAR conference, with brief excerpts of the descriptions following. (It would not be redundant for me to say yet again, "I'm not making this up!" This is intended to be a serious gathering of serious scholars. Seriously!):

> Donald L. Boisvert, Concordia University, Presiding
> **Theme: *Power and Submission, Pain and Pleasure: The Religious Dynamics of Sadomasochism***
>
> *"Sadomasochistic or bondage/dominance practice (sometimes also referred to as 'leather sexuality') . . . offers particularly potent location for reflecting on gay men's issues in religion."*
>
> Justin Tanis, Metropolitan Community Church
> ***Ecstatic Communion: The Spiritual Dimensions of Leathersexuality***
>
> *"This paper will . . . . look briefly at the ways in which leather*

is a foundation for personal and spiritual identify formation, creating a lens through which the rest of life is viewed. . . . All of this based within the framework of a belief in the rights of individuals to erotic self determination with other consenting adults, rather than apologetics for those practices and lives."

Thomas V. Peterson, Alfred University *S/M Rituals in Gay Men's Leather Communities: Initiation, Power Exchange, and Subversion*

"This paper uses S/M rituals within the gay men's leather community to explore how ritual may subvert cultural icons of violence by eroticizing power. . . . Those who exercise power and acquiesce to it in leather rituals meet as respected equals and negotiate the limitations of power according to mutual desires."

Ken Stone, Chicago Theological Seminary
"You Seduced Me, You Overpowered Me, and You Prevailed": Religious Experience and Homoerotic Sadomasochism in Jeremiah

"[Jeremiah 20:7-18] can be construed more usefully as a kind of ritual S/M encounter between the male deity Yahweh and his male devotee. This possibility provides a lens with which to interpret both other passages in the book of Jeremiah and the dynamics of power and submission in religious experience."

Timothy R. Koch, New Life
Metropolitan Community Church
Choice, Shame, and Power in the Construction of Sadomasochistic Theologies

"One of the constitutive elements of sado-masochistic interactions is the removal of the masochist's choices, making it possible for both masochist and sadist to proceed in a spiritually powerful state of relative shamelessness. These axes of choice, shame, and spiritual power are especially relevant to the experiences of gay men."

Julianne Buenting, Chicago Theological Seminary
Oh, Daddy! God, Dominance/Submission, and Christian Sacramentality and Spirituality

"This paper explores BDSM (bondage/dominance, sadomasochism) as potentially transformative encounter in relation to themes of trust and surrender, suffering and pleasure, self-shattering and self-donation found in Christian sacramentality and mystical spirituality. . . . Queer understandings of BDSM offer relational conceptualizations that may be helpful for Christian understandings of our relationship with the divine (and vice versa). Special attention will be given to the characteristics and role of the dominant (top/ master/daddy) as these relate to Christianity's use of dominant imagery for God."

Kent Brintnall, Emory University
Rend(er)ing God's Flesh: The Body of Christ, Spectacles of Pain, and Trajectories of Desire

"This paper substantiates the claim . . . that sado-masochistic homoerotic desire is part of what makes the spectacle of the crucifixion attractive and desirable."

Jay Emerson Johnson, Pacific School of Religion, Presiding
Theme: *Differing Accents: Queering White, Gay, Male Religious Discourse*

Katharine Baker, Vanderbilt University
The Transvestite Christ: **Hedwig and the Angry Inch** *Perform Queer Theology*

"In the rock musical Hedwig & The Angry Inch, Hedwig, the protagonist, re-signifies his identity through gender-bending transvestism and doctrine-deconstructing re-appropriation of Christian theology. This essay documents his evolution in the terms of Bourdieu, Butler and Queer Theology."

Burkhard Scherer, Canterbury
Christ Church University College
Transgenderism, Homosexuality, and the Pandakas: Gender Identity and "Queer" Sexual Conduct in Early Buddhism and Beyond

Donald L. Boisvert, Concordia University, Montreal, Presiding
Theme: *Love Is a Many Splendored Thing: Varied Views on Polyamory*

Julianne Buenting, Chicago Theological Seminary
(Marriage) Queered: Proposing Polyfidelity As Christian Theo-Praxis

"Lesbian-gay-bisexual-transgender (LGBT) political advocacy . . . have reflected the unexamined assumption that monogamy is the sole and ideal pattern for Christian sexual relationships. This paper troubles that assumption. . . . I conclude by proposing polyfidelity as a queer Christian sexual theo-praxis of marriage."

Robert E. Goss, Webster University
Proleptic Sexual Love: God's Promiscuity Reflected in Christian Polyamory

"I will argue that Christian religious communities, with their erotic and polyamorous relationships, symbolize the breadth of God's inclusive and promiscuous love."

Jay E. Johnson, Richmond, CA
Trinitarian Tango: Divine Perichoretic Fecundity in Polyamorous Relations

"Christian traditions abruptly stop short of applying this Trinitarian logic to human sexuality. It is well worth asking whether polyamorous sexual relations reflect the "imago Dei" -- indeed, the "imago Trinitate" -- better than the dyadic model of romantic love, commonly constructed as the Christian ideal."

Mark D. Jordan, Emory University
"One Wife": The Problem with the Patriarchs and the Promiscuity of Agape

"Traditional Christian arguments for restricting marriage to two, and only two, . . . leave a gap through which we can construct a theology of polyamory. So does the Christian ideal of the agapic community, which may be the main source and encouragement for this new theology."

Ronald E. Long, Hunter College
Heavenly Sex: The Moral Authority of a Seemingly Impossible Dream

I would suggest that all sex be thought of as a form of meeting, so that sexual "introductions" might be seen as ends in themselves, and sex within a relationship as meeting in depth. We might also think of a man's erection as his wearing his heart on his sleeve, distortions taking place when he forgets.[129]

Perhaps this is all a dream? Perhaps this is taking place on another planet somewhere? Perhaps there is no such thing as gay religious scholars arguing that the Trinity provides a striking image of a threefold sexual tryst, or that the crucifixion of Christ has special appeal because of homoerotic, sado-masochistic desires, or that God Himself is promiscuous and provides a model for having multiple sexual partners, or that perverse acts of bondage, discipline, and sado-masochism are a path to mystic spirituality, or that the dominant, "top" figure in bondage sex presents a good image of our Heavenly Father, or that there is a transvestite theology and a transvestite Christ.

I would love to tell you that this is not so, but sadly, tragically, it is, and many of the theologians and professors and scholars presenting these papers teach at some of the leading seminaries and universities in our land. And all of them were part of the "Gay Men's Issues in Religion Group" at the 2004 annual conference of the American Academy of Religion.

Go ahead and tell me it's not about sex, or that sex is not a major driving factor. And let the larger gay community *prove* that it's not about sex by demonstrating that gay men are no more promiscuous than heterosexual men, that committed gay couples (especially male) are just as faithful as committed heterosexual couples, that gay literature and scientific studies clearly, decisively, and unequivocally shut the door on "man-boy love,"[130] that there is not a strongly sexual side even to many segments of "gay Christianity," that perverse and blasphemous papers will no longer be presented by gay theologians. . . .

I'm not holding my breath.[131]

*FACT: Sexual orientation is neither a choice, nor is it something
that can be changed through prayer or therapy. All attempts to do so are rooted
in shame, religious bigotry, political propaganda and ignorance.*

Wayne Besen, on WayneBesen.com

*All ecclesial attempts to change gay/lesbian sexual identities to heterosexual
or demand that queers practice celibacy disembody them as human beings.*

Robert Goss, *Jesus Acted Up*

*They have the right to be homosexual and we have the right to walk away from
homosexuality. We respect that people have to make that decision for themselves.*

Ex-gay Mike Haley, with Focus on the Family

*Reparative therapists are detestable, money–hungry con artists who lure and
bamboozle susceptible people with misleading promises and false hope. One reason
these quacks practice their chicanery is to cash in on this lucrative industry, but one
cannot dismiss raw hatred as the primary motive that drives these charlatans to
extreme lengths to denigrate lesbians and gay men.*

Wayne Besen, *Anything But Straight*

*Tolerance and diversity includes those men and women
who seek sexual orientation change.*

Joseph Nicolosi, Ph.D, former president of NARTH,
in his Open Letter to Gerald Koocher
President of the American Psychological Association
APA Convention, August 11, 2006

*To quote the gay rights protesters,
I'm here,
I'm no longer queer,
GET USED TO IT!*

"An open letter to all those who oppose sexual reorientation,"
From "the blog of a former gay guy" (Jake, living in the UK)

12

The "Ex-Gay" Movement: Fact or Fiction?

If there is one topic that stands out as especially controversial in the whole debate about homosexuality, it is the question of whether a homosexual can truly change and become heterosexual. To many gays and lesbians, even to suggest such a thing is to betray one's ignorance and insensitivity.

"Of course we cannot change," they would state emphatically, "and it is downright cruel even to suggest the possibility that we subject ourselves to the damaging effects of 'reparative therapy' or so-called spiritual transformation.[1] Many of us have gone that route under pressure from family or friends or because of our own internalized homophobia, and not a single one of us has ever truly changed. Not one! There is not one single bona fide example of an exclusively homosexual individual becoming exclusively heterosexual. To the contrary, many of us have been scarred for life, and a good number – too many to count – have committed suicide as a result of these wrongheaded techniques. I can't believe you're even dignifying the debate by asking the question again. This was settled a long time ago!"[2]

Kevin Naff expressed this clearly in his *Washington Blade* editorial entitled, "Lock up the 'ex-gays'," with the subtitle, "Reparative rhetoric is dangerous and flawed and repudiated by mental health organizations, but that's not stopping the 'ex-gay' crusade." Naff wrote:

I can endure hours of evangelical Christian diatribes about the evils of the "gay agenda." Or quietly suffer the barbs of pandering politicians looking to win elections on our backs. Or turn the other cheek when a gaggle of ministers calls a news conference to announce their support for a ban on gay marriage.

Even the Washington Times' practice of putting the words gay marriage in quotation marks has ceased to send my blood pressure soaring.

There remains just one assault on the dignity of gay men and lesbians that still drives me into fits of rage: the "ex-gay" movement. The quotation marks are deliberate — and appropriate, because there is no such thing as "ex-gay." There is "repress-my-innate-immutable-characteristics-and-deny-their-existence," but no such condition as "ex-gay."[3]

So firm is this conviction that Eric Marcus, in his book *Is It a Choice?*, indicates that neither man nor God can change someone's sexual orientation. Answering the question, "Aren't there psychiatrists and psychologists who say they can 'cure' homosexuality," he states emphatically,

> . . . no matter what anyone claims, you cannot change a person's sexual orientation. In other words, you cannot eliminate a person's feelings of attraction for the same gender any more than you can eliminate a person's feelings of attraction for the opposite gender."[4]

As to the question, "Can you become heterosexual through prayer," Marcus replies, "Prayer may do a lot of things, but one thing it won't do is make a homosexual into a heterosexual."[5]

So then, it is impossible even for God Himself to change a homosexual, although, by very definition, He is the Creator of the universe, through whom all things are possible, and the one who will one day raise the dead. But He cannot change someone's sexual orientation. In fact, sociology professor and liberal "evangelical prophet" Tony Campolo suggests that, while all things are possible with God, most of those professing to be former homosexuals were probably bisexuals in the past, since it is extremely rare for a homosexual person to become heterosexual.[6]

"SCIENCE TELLS US THAT GAYS CAN'T CHANGE!"

The predominant – one could almost say "official" – view of the gay community is this: "Right-handed people can't choose to be lefties, those with brown skin can't choose white and gays can't choose to be straight. Yes, it really is that simple."[7] Supporting this position are a host of voices, from Dear Abby to gay theologians to national psychiatric and medical organizations.

Naff summarizes the general sentiment:

> AT A TIME when conservative Christians are resurrecting the debate over evolution, pesky details like science matter little to the "ex-gays."
>
> Every reputable medical institution, including the American Psychiatric Association, the American Psychological Association and the American Medical Association, has repudiated reparative therapies as dangerous.[8]

Another article repeats this information in expanded form:

> There is no reliable scientific research to indicate that any change in sexual orientation has occurred as a result of these programs. . . .
> "Ex-gay" programs have been denounced by every respected medical and mental health care organization and child welfare agency in America . . . .
> "The reality is that homosexuality is not an illness. It does not require treatment and is not changeable." *American Psychological Association 1998*
> "Clinical experience suggests that any person who seeks conversion therapy may be doing so because of social bias that has resulted in internalized homophobia, and that gay men and lesbians who have accepted their sexual orientation positively are better adjusted than those who have not done so." *American Psychiatric Association, 1994* . . .
> "The psychosocial problems of gay and lesbian adolescents are primarily the result of societal stigma, hostility, hatred and isolation." *American Academy of Pediatrics, 1993. . . .*[9]

Marcus quotes Dear Abby with approval: "I've always known," she wrote, "that there was nothing wrong with gay and lesbian people, that this is a natural way of life for them. Nobody molested them, nobody talked them into anything. They were simply born that way." Indeed, "Any therapist who would take a gay person and try to change him or her should be in jail. What the psychiatrist should do is to make the patient more comfortable with what he or she is – to be himself or herself." To this Marcus exclaims, "Amen!" – presumably with reference to Dear Abby's remark about jailing reparative therapists as well.[10]

According to *Just the Facts*, a publication of the gay educational organization GLSEN:

> The most important fact about "reparative therapy," also sometimes known as "conversion" therapy, is that it is based on an understanding of homosexuality that has been rejected by all the major health and mental health professions. The

American Academy of Pediatrics, the American Counseling Association, the American Psychiatric Association, the American Psychological Association, the National Association of School Psychologists, and the National Association of Social Workers, together representing more than 477,000 health and mental health professionals, have all taken the position that homosexuality is not a mental disorder and thus there is no need for a "cure."[11]

And in an interview with the *New York Times*, Kevin Jennings, then Executive Director of GLSEN (the Gay, Lesbian, and Straight Education Network) declared:

> All reputable health and education professional organizations have clearly and unequivocally denounced this 'treatment' as quackery. Attempts to change young people's sexual orientation through 'reparative therapy' have raised serious questions about its potential to do harm.[12]

So, reorientation therapy is nothing less than quackery, as confirmed by "all reputable health and education professional organizations." Worse still, it is dangerous: "There is freedom from the cycle of pain, shame and fear caused by restorative therapy," says Marc Adams, self-described as a "p.k." (meaning, "pastor's kid"), and a "former heterosexual lifestyle simulator, christian [sic] school survivor, author, free." He continues, "If you're gay or think you might be gay, you don't have to allow yourself to be recruited into a simulated heterosexual lifestyle."[13]

As stated by PFLAG (Parents, Families & Friends of Lesbians & Gays):

> Ex-gay ministries use out of date, and scientifically disproved medical theories and radical religious beliefs to justify trying to alter gay, lesbian, bisexual, and transgender peoples' natural sexual orientation or gender identity....
>
> "Reparative therapy" is unethical; it does not work and it is dangerous and destructive. The damage that can be done by so called reparative therapy is real. It can destroy someone's self esteem and faith and may lead to self-destructive and suicidal behavior.

It is critical that we answer the lies about "reparative therapy" and "ex-gays" in our local communities, whether in the media or in conversation....[14]

Ironically – but not surprisingly – some of the very people who denounce "reparative therapy" as quackery, even calling for the imprisonment of those who offer this service, are the same people who applaud what is called "gay affirmative therapy." Under the heading of "Gay Mental Health," the Gaylife website states:

There are some people who think that by seeking or needing a mental health professional they are somehow "crazy" or unable to control their own lives. This is a huge misconception. Many gay people seek gay affirmative therapy to help them through the unique challenges posed by our sexual orientation; normal issues faced by many. Sometimes coming out or previous abuse or even feelings surrounding being gay at work can be a minor setback or huge roadblock to leading a healthy gay lifestyle. Gay affirmative therapy can help.[15]

Following this comment, the services of psychotherapists Fran Brown and Joe Kort are advertised, and the blurb for Fran offers, "Quick therapy tips for gay men struggling with heterosexual to gay transitions, same-gender parenting and coming out."[16]

So then, therapy for "gay men struggling with heterosexual to gay transitions" is good and praiseworthy (although, some of *this* therapy has ended in suicide too),[17] but therapy for gay men struggling with homosexual to heterosexual transitions is nothing more than murderous, deplorable quackery.[18] Dr. Kort has even written a book called, *Gay Affirmative Therapy for the Straight Clinician: The Essential Guide.*[19] How interesting!

THE SINISTER FORCES BEHIND THE EX-GAY MOVEMENT

What do many gay leaders believe to be the driving force behind the "ex-gay" movement? According to an official report from the National Gay and Lesbian Task Force, Political Research Associates and Equal Partners in Faith entitled *Calculated Compassion: How the Ex-gay Movement Serves the*

Right's Attack on Democracy, the motivation is quite ugly:

> The ex-gay movement portrays itself as a haven for "hope
> and healing for homosexuals." The report documents that
> the ex-gay movement actually serves as a camouflage for a
> retooled and reinvigorated assault by the religious right on
> the legal protections against discrimination for gay, lesbian,
> bisexual, and transgender persons. . . .
> **The ex-gay movement is part of a broader social
> and political movement that is authoritarian and anti-
> democratic.** The ex-gay movement is an integral part of the
> Christian Right which promotes Christian nationalism, an
> ideology that seeks to use government laws and regulations
> to impose fundamentalist Christian values on the entire
> nation. If the Christian Right has its way, the constitutional
> walls separating church and state would be eliminated.
> The ex-gay movement is also located within the political
> Right's larger social change movement, which is pursuing
> an anti-democratic and authoritarian agenda of sweeping
> social, political, cultural, and economic changes.[20]

Gay theologian Dr. Rembert Truluck espouses a similar position, writing
about "the homophobic religious drive of the 'Ex-Gay' movement to destroy
homosexuals."[21] At the base of this, it is alleged, is greed. As gay activist Ray
Hill explained, the motivation for a Focus on the Family "Love Won Out"
conference in his own city of Houston was simple:

> Focus on the Family charges big bucks for this seminar.
> And Grace Community Church, which is hosting the
> thing, is worried it will take a bath. So the billboards have
> been put up so the church won't suffer. . . . I don't know if
> they're going to get enough suckers in to make it profitable,
> but they're trying. This is all about money.[22]

In the words of Wayne Besen, author of *Anything But Straight: Unmasking
the Scandals and Lies Behind the Ex-Gay Myth*, and founder of Truth Won
Out:

Today they [speaking of Dr. James Dobson's Focus on the Family] continue to ignore mountains of evidence pointing to the failure of the ex-gay ministries because the truth interferes with their presumably biblically inspired mandates to raise heaps of money and deny gay people civil rights. If lives are destroyed in the process, so be it. . . .

One way Focus became so powerful was by using divisive social issues, such as homosexuality, to scare money out of their followers.[23]

According to the gay-affirming camp, then, there is nothing altruistic in the ex-gay movement, nothing motivated by compassion and concern, nothing that comes from a heart of genuine love, nothing arising from a desire to share positive change with others. Rather, it is a movement bent on destruction, and as such, it is sometimes murderous in its effects, especially in its fundamentalist Christian strain. In support of this, Eric Marcus, after stating that even prayer can't change a homosexual, recounts the tragic story of the suicide of a young gay man raised in a fundamentalist Christian home. His mother subsequently blamed her beliefs for her son's death.[24] Reorientation therapy, or, in its spiritual manifestation, transformation through faith, kills!

WAYNE BESEN LEADS THE CHARGE

Championing this position is Besen, who received national attention after photographing John Paulk leaving a gay bar in Washington, DC in September, 2000. (Besen had been notified by a friend, who spotted Paulk there, after which Besen hurried over to the bar.) This was highly significant, since at that time, Paulk had been hailed as the poster boy of the ex-gay movement. (For further discussion on Paulk, see below.)

Besen describes part of what he shouted to Paulk that night, as he urged him to quit denying his homosexuality and return to the fold:

This was a man whom I believed may have ruined many lives and profited from his lies through his job with Focus on the Family. I confronted him, yelling at the top of my lungs.

"How many young men and women have committed suicide because of you? How many parents refuse to speak to their gay children because you have convinced them their kids can change when they cannot? Your work is killing people, yet you have the chutzpa and audacity to go to a gay bar? Your gig is over! Let us help you come out, so you can undo all of the damage you have done![25]

In the official statement released on September 21, 2000 by Focus on the Family, Paulk remembers Besen "screaming, 'John Paulk, you are guilty of murdering thousands of people with your message' . . . ." It would appear that Besen would not differ with that assessment, especially in light of a column he wrote for his website on July 15, 2005.

Besen reported:

A 21 year old Tampa man is charged with murder after his 3-year old son was pummeled into unconsciousness and then died. The toddler's mother, Nysheerah Paris, testified that her husband thought the boy might be gay and would force him to box.

Nysheerah Paris told the court that Paris would make the boy fight with him, slapping the child in the head until he cried or wet himself. She said that on one occasion Paris slammed the child against a wall because he was vomiting.[26]

What a tragic, sickening story, a story all the more exacerbated by the fact that: 1) there was a pattern of violence in the home; 2) the child had been removed from the custody of the parents before; and 3) the mother chose not to report the father's violence against his son because she feared that the boy would be taken away again. (She was actually charged with felony child neglect.)

But the father is not the only guilty party in this story. According to Besen:

This is clearly the result of James Dobson and Joseph Nicolosi's "ex-gay" therapy taken to the extreme. While these men and the groups they represent are in no way directly responsible, they have created a world where there is almost nothing worse than being gay - in some circles. Any remedy - no matter how bizarre - is fair game if it will supposedly help one become heterosexual. By the way, what they do doesn't work.[27]

You might want to read that first line again: "This is clearly the result of James Dobson and Joseph Nicolosi's 'ex-gay' therapy taken to the extreme." Yes, even though Dobson and Nicolosi "are in no way directly responsible," they are in every way *indirectly* responsible, since "they have created a world where there is almost nothing worse than being gay - in some circles."

So, a father prone to violence, who allegedly slammed his toddler against the wall for vomiting and slapped him around because, according to other reports, he didn't want him to be "a sissy," actually did so because Drs. Dobson and Nicolosi "have created a world where there is almost nothing worse than being gay." It's these right-wing Christian monsters who are ultimately responsible for this little boy's terrible death! The boy's father was only taking their teachings "to the extreme." (I remind you that this is not just rhetoric to Besen and those who share his views. They really believe what they are saying, as highlighted by a blurb on the back of Besen's *Anything But Straight* book by gay activist Donna Red Wing. She stated that the book, "Sheds light on one of the most insidious movements of the radical right.")

Besen continues:

> Ironically, Nicolosi, leader of The National Association of Research and Therapy of Homosexuality (NARTH), takes patients as young as three, calling them "prehomosexual boys". Once in his clutches he works to butch them up.
>
> Ex-gay therapy is unethical and in some cases a threat to the people it purports to help. It is a legal case waiting to happen. These quacks should be put out of business sooner than later. Not because they have a different, skewed point of view. But because they abuse patients and destroy lives, while lining their pockets by exploiting desperate and vulnerable people.[28]

He has certainly made himself clear.

At this point, even the most casual reader will have noticed several recurring themes in the gay critique of all methods attempting to change sexual orientation: 1) Reorientation therapy is medical quackery; 2) its practitioners should be locked up or put out of business; 3) what these therapists do is abusive and destructive; 4) their primary motivation is greed. This is certainly the gay mantra on the subject of reorientation therapy.[29]

Of course, some immediate questions come to mind after reading Besen's report on the murder of the three year-old boy: Did this violent father actually know about the teachings of reorientation therapy, especially in its Christian forms? If so, did he actually think that brutally slapping his son around was part of such treatment? If not, is it at all possible that this same man living one generation ago or five generations ago might have had the same extreme, violent reaction to the possibility that his boy was a "sissy"? In other words, is it possible – or strongly probable – that this violence was totally unrelated to the teachings of Dobson and Nicolosi? And does Dr. Nicolosi actually broadcast the (alleged) fact that he takes in patients as young as three years old, and does he actually "work to butch them up," perhaps slapping them around as well?

ARE JAMES DOBSON AND JOSEPH NICOLOSI GUILTY?

Some of you reading this book will say, "It is ludicrous to connect these actions to Dobson and Nicolosi!", but some others will differ strongly with that assessment, as illustrated by some of the responses to Besen's article posted on his website.[30] One reader named Peter, was exasperated with the article:

> Wayne, this is pathetic. Can you directly link NARTH to this brutal murder? If not your assertions are just ludicrous, on the level of me associating you and your website with the beating up of any ex-gay anywhere. Frankly, this kind of innuendo is just beneath most of the rest of us.[31]

He was quickly rebuffed by another reader, who blasted Peter personally:

> Peter is just plain moronic, and probably a NARTH supporter. Having read the post, Wayne never linked the two. But, he did point out that the similarities in the cases.

Peter responded by quoting the article again, followed by his own comments:

> "This is clearly the result of James Dobson and Joseph

Nicolosi's 'ex-gay' therapy taken to the extreme. While these men and the groups they represent are in no way directly responsible, they have created a world where there is almost nothing worse than being gay - in some circles. Any remedy - no matter how bizarre - is fair game if it will supposedly help one become heterosexual." And that isn't trying to associate NARTH with this? Ridiculous.

Unfortunately, Peter's fair and logical deduction stood alone, and he was further lambasted by another posting:

I totally disagree with Peter. NARTH (ie Focus on the Family, Research Council, Concerned Women and the like) has created an environment for this heinous abuse to occur and I DO hold them responsible for creating this. No two ways about it, a powerful organization convinces people that gays are a threat and are to be hated, the masses will hate them. I am personally sickened by what organized fundamentalist religion is doing to us. It is inexcusable, inhumane and certaining [sic] anything but christian [sic] in nature. It is time they were held accountable for the environment of harassment and belittlement they have created for gay people. The print material let alone the hate speeches spewing from these low lifes [sic] is akin to racism and should be illegal. It has nothing to do with religious freedom, it is simply power and greed and it is very shameful.

How consistent the gay argument is. These religious organizations are responsible for murder, they teach that gays should be hated and they themselves spew hate speech, their activities should be illegal (just like the therapists, who should either be put out of business or locked up), and they are motivated by power and greed. In the words of Arnold, adding his comments immediately after Peter's first post, "Put the abusive &*!%ers out of business!!! Murderers!!"

WHAT DOES KATIE COURIC HAVE TO SAY?
Now, lest you think that it's only Besen and those posting on his site

who think like this, it was none other than Katie Couric who suggested that conservative Christian groups were somehow responsible for creating the climate that led to the brutal murder of Matthew Shephard (in whose name and memory the Hate Crimes Bill was passed in 2010). To quote her comments from the *Today Show*, October 13, 1998, "The tragic beating of the college student in Wyoming has some activists in this country saying there is a climate of anti-gay hate that's been fostered by a provocative advertising campaign by the political Right in this country."

This followed Couric's October 12, 1998 interview with the governor of Wyoming, during which she asked whether "'conservative political organizations like the Christian Coalition, the Family Research Council and Focus on Family [sic.] are contributing to this anti-homosexual atmosphere' by suggesting that homosexuals can change their sexual orientation."[32] This was on the *Today Show*!

Returning to Besen's site, another reader had this to say about Peter, taking direct – and vulgar – aim on him as a person and repeating the charge that some Christian organizations have created the climate for murder:

It is clear that Peter is a self-loathing apologist. It is clear that people like him are the reason the right remains ahead of us. He just doesn't have enough fight or guts to make a real difference. YES, Focus on the Family does create the climate for murder. Petey, can we say denial??? What is "beneath us" is to keep taking it up the a-- by James Dobson. Or maybe that is what you r in 2?

The most articulate – and possibly telling – reply came from Julie Johnson, aka "The Great Spoon":

Oh Peter, Peter, Peter! Let me begin by asking you something no one has asked you yet...just what sort of proof would you require to believe that there could reasonably be a link between the reparitive [sic] therapy movement and this murder?

To be fair Peter, Wayne did stipulate that Nicolosi et al were "in no way" responsible for this crime. [Actually, that is not what Besen said. He said that they were "in no way directly responsible."] Something I am beginning to believe that you have purposefully decided to forget. Wayne was VERY clear about that. HOWEVER he did lay a certain level of blame at their feet for creating a culture in which such a crime could be considered to be a reasonable course of action by a small, poorly educated, unintelligent, unusually fanatically devoted faction of the Religious Right. By the very actions of Dr. Dobson, Mr. Nicolosi, et al, in publishing testimonials of accepting 3 year olds into their "therapy" did they NOT fertilize the fevered imaginations of such *already* disturbed individuals? Should they NOT beheld [sic] up to *social* condemnation for making such inappropriate public statements that could and would be taken completely wrong? Seriously, is it not entirely appropriate? Or are they somehow immune from this social oversight because they are wrapped in the mantle of "freedom of religion"?

One other question... is it your assertion that the parents of the murdered child would have had NO knowledge of reparitive [sic] therapy and/or it's [sic] common techniques and practices at all? If that is your position then would you mind explaining just how people who regularly attend a deeply fundamentalist church would or *could* miss out on getting this information?

It is really enlightening to read this post, and it provides insight into the minds of some gay and lesbian Americans. Notice Johnson's assumption that the father was part of a "small, poorly educated, unintelligent, unusually fanatically devoted faction of the Religious Right." How did she know that? And notice also the assumption that Nicolosi – with Dobson now thrown in for good measure – actually *publishes* "testimonials of accepting 3 year olds into their 'therapy.'" What is her source of information? Even Besen's statement didn't go that far.

But there is something even more remarkable. According to Johnson, anyone going to a "deeply fundamentalist church" could not possibly miss out on "getting this information," namely, the information about "reparative therapy and/or its common techniques and practices." Amazing! Survey ten thousand such churches and you will find that hardly anyone in these congregation has ever *heard* of reparative (or, reorientation) therapy, let alone is familiar with "its common techniques and practices" (and notice the assumption that these so-called "common techniques and practices" would somehow include physical violence). Not only so, but if you were to ask someone in a "deeply fundamentalist church" the question, "Can a homosexual be changed?" the almost universal answer would be, "Yes, through faith in Jesus Christ." The issue of reorientation therapy would not likely come up once in a hundred conversations.[33]

If "deeply fundamental" churches should be faulted, it is for *ignorance* about homosexuality – and in some cases, hostility towards homosexuality.[34] But it is as likely that the average person attending a "deeply fundamental church" knows any more about "reparative therapy" than they know about the molecular structure of a fly. Yet similar charges will surely be repeated over and over again, as if the mere repetition of them made them true. And this leads to a question, or really, a series of questions.

WHY SUCH A PASSIONATE DENIAL OF "EX-GAY"?

Why is the gay denial of the ex-gay movement so fervent and passionate? Why is it so enflamed with serious charges like quackery, murder, abuse, greed, and lies? Why is the rhetoric so extreme, and why do so many gays and lesbians seem to be in such lockstep in their statements about so-called reorientation therapy or spiritual transformation?

It is one thing to say, "I don't believe people can change their sexual orientation, and any attempts to do so are potentially harmful." It's quite another thing to claim that professional therapists and ministers who try to help people with unwanted same-sex attractions are greedy liars, frauds, and even murderers. Is there more to the story than meets the eye? Is there, perhaps, another important side to the story that is not being told?

According to Besen, the answer to the last two questions is No, articulated at length in *Anything But Straight*. There is, he would emphasize, no such thing as ex-gay. Period. As expressed with his typical forthrightness, Besen wrote that ex-gay ministries "have a zero percent success rate and victimize innocent people who are told they need to change or they are going to Hell. . . . At some point, they will be rightfully sued out of existence for fraud and malpractice."[35]

So, the whole concept of "ex-gay" is a lie-filled, scandal-riddled myth, and any debate about the subject should stop once and for all. Yes, anyone who claims to be a former homosexual is either lying to himself, lying to others, or both. It's that simple.[36] In the words of Rembert Truluck, this movement is really "The Ex-Gay Fraud."[37]

Consider some of the evidence cited by Besen as well as other gay activists, beginning with the case of John Paulk. He was a former transvestite prostitute who went under the name Candi but who claimed to experience a religious and sexual transformation, after which he married a former lesbian (now Mrs. Anne Paulk), had children, and appeared with his wife in 1998 on the front cover of *Newsweek* magazine with the caption "Can Gays Change?"[38]

A few years later, Besen was informed by a colleague that Paulk had walked into a gay bar in Washington, DC and, according to Besen, flirted with some of the men there. Besen writes,

> In his years as a member of the religious right, Paulk surely did go through many life changes, both positive and negative. He undoubtedly changed his religion, marital status, and philosophy. He admirably changed his decadent lifestyle riddled with drug abuse and prostitution. And by leaving Candi behind, his drag queen alter ego, he even changed his wardrobe. Despite his loud and very public protestations, however, Paulk never changed his sexual orientation. Paulk is now "living proof" that changing sexual orientation is highly unlikely – and certainly not through the ex-gay ministries or reparative therapy.[39]

As for ex-gay ministries such as Exodus International, Besen and others would tell us that their claims are also totally bogus, highlighted by the well-known (and, in the gay community, much-publicized) fact that one of the original board members of Exodus, Michael Bussee, along with one of his ministry helpers, Gary Cooper, eventually renounced the ministry, claiming that it had not helped them or anyone else. Both of them left their wives and became partners in 1982, with Cooper dying of AIDS seven years later.[40]

Throughout Besen's book, he offers similar anecdotal evidence, the results of "four years examining the phenomenon of 'ex-gay' ministries and reorientation therapies – interviewing leaders, attending conferences, and visiting ministries undercover as he accumulated hundreds of hours of research."[41] So persuasive is his evidence that Andrew Tobias, author of *The Best Little Boy in the World Grows Up*, exclaimed in his endorsement, "If there is anyone left in America who believes sexual orientation is a matter of choice, he or she should read this book."[42]

To repeat the message once more: Don't listen to anyone who claims that his or her sexual orientation has changed. The claim simply isn't true. End of subject, case closed, discussion finished.[43]

ASKING SOME HONEST QUESTIONS

Personally, I don't doubt Besen's sincerity. He genuinely believes he is right in his assessment. What do you do, though, when a person claiming to be a former homosexual seems quite credible, not to mention gracious and loving, especially towards the gay community? And what happens when it is not just one person, but five, or ten, or fifty, or one hundred, or one thousand, or more, all claiming to be "ex-gay" (or, whatever terminology they choose to use)?

Is it fair or right or honest or ethical to ignore these other voices which today number in the multiplied thousands? On what basis should we silence and even ridicule these men (and women) who say that they were once practicing homosexuals but have been dramatically changed? If this were a legal debate, wouldn't a court of law insist on hearing their testimony? If this were being decided in the court of public opinion, wouldn't people demand to hear both sides? And given that two of the most unceasing mantras of gay activists and their allies on the political Left are "tolerance" and "diversity," why are the stories and voices of those who sincerely claim to have walked away from homosexuality not celebrated – much less tolerated – for the "diversity" they bring to the table? And doesn't the over-the-top nature of the anti-ex-gay rhetoric raise questions about its accuracy?

Why is it, then, that the very mention of "ex-gays" creates such a firestorm of emotion and controversy? And why is a therapy that is, in fact, supported by scientific research in scholarly journals, practiced by trained professionals, and backed by a sizable amount of clinical data simply branded "quackery"?[44] (For the scientific and clinical data, see below, Chapter Thirteen.) And why are testimonies from those claiming to have experienced a spiritual and sexual transformation often swept under the carpet, even when independent investigations confirm the reliability of their accounts?[45]

On the one hand, I can only imagine the trauma suffered by those gay men and women who would say that they tried to change and even wanted to change but discovered after much persistent effort that they could not change.[46] A very few even underwent electroshock treatment (which, by the way, is still used today as a remedy for other mental health problems) with the hope of altering their neurochemical brain connectivity in the hope of changing their sexual orientation, all to no avail.[47] For such people, to speak of "ex-gays" is to open up an old wound and douse it with salt, adding insult to their injury.

For others, even to discuss the possibility of homosexuals changing is to go back to the dark ages of social and scientific oppression, to revive an old canard that should have been buried years ago. Why dignify such intellectual rubbish? And why resurrect the torment these people were forced to live with through their childhood and adolescence and young adulthood – and possibly even through an unsuccessful heterosexual marriage? Why dangle the carrot of change before them once again? Or why hit them over the head with the expectation of change once more? Haven't we learned anything in the last forty years?

Bruce Bawer has expressed this position with tremendous force:

> Of course, almost all psychologists and psychiatrists nowadays recognize that "therapy" designed to make gay people straight doesn't do any such thing. To be homosexual is not just to experience sexual attraction to another person of the same sex; it is to feel the same comfort, rightness, and wholeness in a same-sex relationship that a straight person feels in an opposite-sex relationship. What "ex-gay therapy" does is to build up precisely those unhealthy elements of a gay person's psyche – his or her self-hatred and willingness to live a lie – that psychotherapy should seek to dissolve. To encourage such "transformation," and to celebrate such a person's marriage to a person of the opposite sex, is to embrace a lie about that person and to do something that is cruel to both parties in the marriage. . . .
>
> [Dobson's] organization's propaganda about homosexuality shows that Dobson is more willing to sacrifice the lives of gay youth – who, devastated by hatred, commit suicide at an alarming rate – than to change societal attitudes that cause them to take their lives. He needs gay people – including gay youth – as scapegoats, in the literal ancient sense of the word: people who are sacrificed to keep society together. We look back at other cultures, such as the Egyptians and Romans, and are appalled at the brutality that made possible, say, the sacrifices of virgins to the gods,

the working of slaves to death to build the pyramids, and gladiators' deaths as a form of public entertainment. Yet the way legalistic Christians have been encouraged to victimize gay people is no less horrific. The only difference is that the worst abuse takes place behind closed doors, where parents, affirmed by the likes of Dobson in their antigay hatred, put their own children through unimaginable psychological torment that often leads to self-slaughter.[48]

IS COMPASSION A ONE-WAY STREET?

Certainly, compassion requires that we understand the sensitivities of homosexual men and women who are hurt or offended by the claims of ex-gays and that we do not glibly say, "Well, you can change if you want to," as if it was as easy as snapping one's fingers. But doesn't compassion (and fairness) also require that we hear from those who say they *have* changed, that after years of torment and pain or inner conflict and confusion they have found freedom and wholeness?

It was bad enough that many of them suffered misunderstanding, hatred, or even physical violence growing up. It was bad enough that they had to deal with the trauma of coming to terms with their same-sex desires and attractions. And it was bad enough that, after all that, they had to go through yet another traumatic journey, questioning the rightness of their "coming out" and then enduring a major internal struggle in their pursuit to experience sexual orientation change (or, simply, to steward their sexuality in alignment with their faith and values). But it is absolutely inexcusable that *now*, after all their struggles, when they finally claim to have found true peace and happiness, they are vilified by the very group of people that should be most sympathetic to their stories, the very group of people who is constantly calling for tolerance and understanding, the very group of people who should be able to identify with the struggles through which they have passed.

Bob Davies, Executive Director Emeritus of Exodus International, expressed his desire that the GLBT community

would acknowledge that all people have as much right to pursue a heterosexual lifestyle as they do to pursue homosexuality. Former homosexuals and lesbians should not be harassed and castigated by the gay community. But I have never heard any gay or lesbian leaders speak out against the violence (such as bomb threats and physical/verbal abuse) which some people perpetuate against Exodus ministries.[49]

Is there only compassion for gays as long as they remain gay? Does consideration and respect cease when a formerly-gay-identified person says they have become heterosexual and are happy and content with their sexual orientation? Must the standard gay response be to call all ex-gays liars?[50]

Ex-gay Rich Wyler (at the time using the pseudonym Ben Newman) writes:

> Given the vehemence with which Besen blasts any perceived slight against homosexuals or gay culture [in his book *Anything But Straight*], the blatant and hostile stereotypes and generalizations that he directs at ex-gays and reparative therapists represent the worst kind of double standard:
>
> - "Most (ex-gays) are suffering unbelievably dark, lonely, miserable lives" (p. 37).
> - "Most (ex-gays) are chronically depressed" (p. 40)
> - "The vast majority of the (ex-gay ministry) leadership and nearly all of the spokespeople ...(are) self-destructive, unstable individuals who lack self-control and have decimated their personal lives" (p. 42)
> - "A significant number appear to have problems with mental illness" (p. 42).
> - "Little evidence supports the existence of 'normal' ex-gays" (p. 56).
> - "Most ex-gays are not looking for a religion, but a regimen. They are learning scripture because they seek structure. When they claim they are searching for God, they really mean they are searching for guidance" (p. 48). (Apparently, Besen is a mind reader who can divine what seekers are "really" seeking.)
> - "They have left behind colorful, three-dimensional lives of uncertainty and despair for monochrome, one dimensional lives of relative stability and security"

(p. 52). (This may be the most bizarre sentence in the entire book. Colorful, three-dimensional lives of *uncertainty and despair*? What kind of a color is *that*?)

- (Ex-gays) "are stuck in a *lifestyle* that demeans, diminishes and dehumanizes them for who they are" (p. xviii, emphasis added).
- Reparative therapy clients are "hapless victims" with "fragile minds" (p. 156).

Imagine the howls of protest if these same aspersions were directed at gays instead of ex-gays![51]

To be sure, there are gays and lesbians who feel personally attacked the moment the possibility of change is raised, since, if change were possible, then the very basis of their worldview and the things they are campaigning for – "civil rights" because of unalterable sexual orientation – would theoretically be undermined and go out the window. But there are many other gays and lesbians who still struggle with their identity and who would really embrace change if they thought it were possible. Shouldn't they be willing to give the ex-gays an honest hearing?

Think back for a moment to the story of John Paulk. Here is a man who desperately wanted to change, who was *not* at peace with being a transvestite prostitute named Candi, and who claims to have been transformed through a personal relationship with Jesus to the point of being a happily married husband and father. Apparently during one weak moment – temptation is nothing new, regardless of one's sexual orientation – he went into a gay bar and allegedly flirted with a few men, subsequently admitting to the error of his way, both publicly and privately. That was his one "moral failure," and with all the hostility directed towards him, to my knowledge, there is still not a single man who claims to have had any sexual contact with him since his conversion. Not one! The worst charge brought against him was that he went into a gay bar a single time and, perhaps, flirted with some of the men.

In his own book, written before his confrontation with Besen, he had already described a time when he was strongly tempted to go into a gay bar but cried out to God for strength to resist and was able to do so. This time, he succumbed to the temptation bringing reproach on himself and the ministry that he served. (Remember: It is possible to be primarily heterosexual in orientation and yet be tempted with homosexual desires or thoughts, just as it is possible for anyone who once lived in a certain lifestyle to be tempted to return to it, even after making a clean break.) Thankfully, rather than slipping back into his old lifestyle, he submitted to a process of discipline and ministry probation, being fully restored today.[52]

Isn't it cruel, then, for the gay and lesbian community to throw stones at him and seek to exploit his one lapse of moral judgment, a lapse that close to ten years later has, apparently, never been repeated? Why demonize a man who is at peace with himself, in love with his wife, and devoted to his kids – and who can hardly be accused of making money off of his story, since he no longer holds a prestigious ministry position? Isn't there something revealing about the ugliness of the charge that, after fifteen years of happy marriage, "Today [John Paulk and his wife] both don the drag of being heterosexually married"?[53] Doesn't the nasty tone sometimes directed against him reveal the underlying problem, namely, the *denial* of any ex-gays by the gay community?[54]

THE KIND OF CHANGE YOU CAN BELIEVE IN

Bob Davies makes an insightful point:

This, of course, is where ex-gay ministries are ridiculed by pro-gay organizations. They say that, if we continue to experience ANY kind of gay thoughts or temptations, then we have not really changed. I find this to be totally unrealistic! I cannot think of any other kind of therapy where, if there are occasional thoughts of the past--or even behavioral lapses--the therapy is immediately said to be totally 'unsuccessful.'

Think about it for a minute. What about AA--do people give up because they have had one drink? Is the whole organization "trashed" in the media because they do not have a 100% success rate?

What about programs for those overcoming sexual addiction? Or drug abuse? Or weight control? Although these issues are not exactly parallel to homosexuality, I believe the general principle is the same: Finding "recovery" is an ongoing process which may indeed be lifelong.

Change is not immediate. Change is not total. But change is real and significant. Ask any of our leaders, for example, who were once firmly entrenched in the gay community and today are happily married and raising their families! They may occasionally be tempted by their past. But they have still experienced genuine change![55]

Ex-gay Jeff Johnston outlined the kind of change often experienced by Christians who overcame same-sex attraction:

- Change in behavior (meaning, no longer committing homosexual acts or being enslaved to sexual desires)
- Change in motivation ("from initial fear and shame to a love for God and desire to follow Him")
- Change in identity ("Many men who come out of homosexuality do not think of themselves as 'gay' or even 'ex-gay' any more. They are sons, fathers, friends, husbands – men.")
- Change in attitude (from feeling "victimized and rejected" to being emotionally healed and filled with gratitude and joy)
- Change in relationships with men and women (developing healthy, non-sexual relationships with those of the same sex)
- Change in relationship with God (from viewing Him as "angry, uninvolved, or uncaring," to knowing Him as a loving Father)
- Change in homosexual attractions ("For many, same-sex attractions do change dramatically, and attractions for [the opposite sex] develop.")[56]

Despite this evidence – which is quite well attested – most gays and lesbians do not believe that homosexual attractions can change, and gay opposition to the ex-gay movement is so intense – not to mention the pervasive acceptance by the media of the gay dogma that homosexuality is immutable– that the very idea existence of an "ex-gay" or "former homosexual" is greeted with scorn: "There is no such thing as a former homosexual! Anyone who claims to be ex-gay was either never gay in the first place, or they were bisexual, or they are lying to themselves or to others. Ex-gays do not exist!"

Many ex-gays have written to Dear Abby, telling her that her pronouncements on the biological nature of homosexuality are amiss and that change is possible, but to date, she remains unmoved, despite the many firsthand testimonies she has received.

AN UNETHICAL, DOUBLE STANDARD?

Why this outright dismissal (and even mockery) of evidence? Why such fierce resistance from many in the gay community? Why the impassioned attempts to silence and wipe out the ex-gay movement? Could it simply be that the very existence of an ex-gay movement completely undermines the whole argument of inalienable, immutable orientation? Could it be that even one true ex-gay testimony causes the entire ideological house of cards to collapse? Could this be part of the driving force to discredit and denounce former homosexuals in the most extreme and angry terms, even on the subconscious level?

And to think: There are quite a few gay activists – including some in the psychiatric field itself – who have sought to make it illegal for a trained professional to counsel a gay man or woman who desires to change. Illegal![57] In fact, in 2006, the American Counseling Association (ACA) passed a resolution in which any counselor willing to help a client deal with unwanted same-sex attractions could be guilty of a violation of ethics.[58]

The truth be told, it is the ACA's decision that is a violation of ethics, but that's how dramatically things have been turned on their heads, to the point that it is considered praiseworthy to help people "come out" and fully embrace being gay (or lesbian or bisexual or transgender) – despite their moral or religious or social values – but it is blameworthy to help people overcome their unwanted same-sex attractions, helping them to live in harmony with their moral or religious or social values. How can this be?

According to Professor Gregory Herek of the University of California,

> The mainstream view in psychology and psychiatry is that people who are troubled about their homosexual orientation have internalized society's prejudice against homosexuality, and that the appropriate task of a therapist is to help them to overcome those prejudices and to lead a happy and satisfying life as a gay man or lesbian.[59]

Psychologist Douglas C. Haldeman noted that Christian psychologist Mark Yarhouse

contends that some people simply find homosexuality at

odds with their "values framework" and so freely seek to become heterosexual. But from where do gay, lesbian, and bisexual people derive their "values framework," if not the homophobic world around them?[60]

These are absolutely remarkable statements, as both Herek and Haldeman claim that the only possible reason a person would not be at home with his or her homosexuality is the influence of a homophobic society. (Just think about that for a moment. It really is incredible that people can believe this.) In other words, "It is impossible that you could have a real objection to homosexuality based on a deeply-held moral or religious conviction. No! Such convictions are simply the result of internalized homophobia, since no one in his or her right mind, free from society's prejudices, could have any possible compunction with being gay." And Herek and Haldeman are respected (and quite representative) leaders in their fields.[61]

THE EX-GAYS AND THEIR CRITICS: A CONTRAST IN TONE AND SPIRIT

Wayne Besen's website is filled with reports of his tireless anti-ex-gay activities, such as this news release from October, 14, 2004:

FORT LAUDERDALE, Fla. - Author Wayne Besen today criticized an out of court settlement in the Tampa-area allowing divisive hate group Focus on the Family to advertise their ex-gay hoax. The settlement will let FOF promote a dangerous product, mislead area-residents on gay life and perpetuate outdated myths.[62]

Notice the amount of invective in just two sentences: "divisive hate group"; "ex-gay hoax"; "a dangerous product"; "mislead"; "perpetuate outdated myths." The news release further quotes Besen as saying:

This is analogous to Pinellas County allowing cigarette companies or asbestos manufactures to market their potentially deadly wares to children. Focus on the Family traffics in hate, peddling a harmful product that has likely ruined many lives. What they do is scientifically empty and their claims of sexual conversion have been shown to fail.[63]

This is *not* being said tongue in cheek.[64]

When MTV-Viacom announced the launching of an all-gay cable network called Logo, Besen jokingly offered some suggestions for new shows, including:

> **Survivor:** In this highly anticipated show, 10 "ex-gays" will be airlifted and placed on an island stocked with sex addicted A&F [Abercrombie & Fitch] Models. Each time an ex-gay breaks down and sodomizes, he is booted off the island. This show should have extraordinary ratings, but there is a reasonable fear that none of the ex-gays will make it to the second episode.[65]

Why such scorn and derision? As I asked in another context in this book, what if the shoe were on the other foot?

How do gays react to heterosexual scorn and derision – in other words, to so-called "homophobic" words and deeds? How do they react to attempts to silence their voices and exclude their views? They cry foul every way they know how, complaining of intolerance, bigotry, and hatred, and in some cases, they are right. Yet when the "persecuted" become the "persecutors," they become guilty of the very things they condemn in others. How hypocritical! Perhaps a nerve is being hit?

A statement on an ex-gay website reads:

> Individuals who have transitioned out of a former homosexual identity and lifestyle, or who choose to pursue alternatives to homosexuality, deserve compassion and respect. Their choices should not subject them to discrimination, ridicule, marginalization, or make them the target of hate speech or accusations of homophobia. Demands for tolerance by one group can never justify intolerance or ridicule of another."[66]

Who can argue with this?

Jeff Konrad, an ex-gay author, begins his book, *You Don't Have to Be Gay* with this proviso:

FOR THE RECORD
This book is not an attack against those who have embraced homosexuality. If you are happy with your homosexual identity, *You Don't Have To Be Gay* is not for you.

The sole purpose of this book is to educate people about the root causes of homosexuality, to offer sound counsel on how a person struggling with homosexual feelings and desires can overcome them, and to help those who are not happy as homosexual to change their identity.

Extreme care was taken in considering the title for this book. It is not meant to be accusatory in any way. *You Don't Have To Be Gay* is a straightforward statement concerning homosexuality. It isn't, "You **shouldn't be gay**," but rather, if you really don't want to, "You **don't have to be** gay."[67]

Do these sound like the words of a fraud, a liar, a bigoted member of the sinister, radical right?

Listen also to the voice of Mike Haley, a former homosexual who was transformed after years of interaction with Konrad, and who once served as the manager of the Homosexuality and Gender Issues Department at Focus on the Family. Haley writes:

For 12 years, I lived as an active homosexual. I know the subculture. I've felt what homosexuals feel – the hurt, rejection, anger, broken relationships, and the intense desire to be loved for who they are. I also know how their friends and loved ones feel when someone close to them "comes out" about their homosexuality. I know how the church often seems like the last place to go for help.[68]

Answering the question, "Do homosexuals choose to be gay?", Haley responds:

Let me answer this one directly: *No!* And in case you didn't hear me, let me speak up: NO!

This continues to be one of the myths of homosexuality

that uninformed people perpetuate. Christians or conservatives may say to a homosexual, "I have a heart for those in your community, and I love *you*." And then as if to drive a splinter under the fingernail of the hand they've just reached out to hold, they add: "But you and your friends have to realize that homosexuality was your choice."

Ouch.[69]

As for the question, "How can we help someone who has tried to overcome homosexuality and failed – especially since she has been hurt by the response of churches and other Christians?", Haley notes:

> At the 1995 Exodus International conference in San Diego, a pastor walked to the podium, leaned against it as if he were talking to friends, and uttered some of the most powerful words I've ever heard: "On behalf of Christian leaders and pastors, as well as any calling themselves Christians across this country, who have been guilty of showing a lack of attention to your dilemma and dismissed you as unimportant, for any of the unbalanced messages we've spoken that have hurt your and for ways we've offended you without even knowing it, I ask for your forgiveness – I truly am sorry."
>
> …That's what you and anybody else who wants to reach into the life of someone struggling with homosexuality need to do too. Validate your friend's pain and be a true ambassador for Christ.[70]

According to Besen and others, people like Haley should be locked up and ministries like Exodus International should be shut down. For what? For reaching out to gays and lesbians with tenderness and compassion? For saying, "I understand your pain, I once lived where you live, and I would love to tell you how my own life has been wonderfully changed"? When did this become criminal?

Without question, Haley's message and tone do not line up with the portrayal of ex-gay ministries by Besen and other gay leaders. Yet Haley's words and sentiments are representative of virtually all ex-gay ministries, ministries that are vilified as part of an insidious, hate-filled, terribly destructive, fraudulent empire. Could it be that those crying "Fraud!" have themselves been misled?[71]

If you had no way to evaluate the evidence other than the credibility of the witnesses, would you believe Wayne Besen or would you believe Mike Haley? What about Ben Newman (Rich Wyler)? Do you find him to be credible – as he speaks for himself and others – or is he a fraudulent bigot as well?

> In sharing our experience, we are not necessarily suggesting that *everyone* can change. Nor are we saying that everyone *should* try to change. We are only sharing our own experience, about what was right for us and what worked for us. We have no desire to try to convince people who are happy living a gay life that they should be dissatisfied. If "gay" works for them, great. We are not suggesting that those who embrace and accept a gay identity and choose to live as homosexuals are sick, or wrong, or somehow "less than" others. They are as deserving of respect as we are.
>
> Homosexuality just wasn't right for us. It conflicted with our deeply held beliefs, our life goals, and our intrinsic sense of our true, authentic selves.
>
> And so we pursued change -- and ultimately found that by facing and addressing deep emotional wounds, fears and other root problems, our homosexual desires started to diminish and then to disappear, while heterosexual feelings began to emerge and increase. True, we found the journey was often difficult and frightening, but the destination has brought us immeasurable peace and joy. In fact, if there is one consistency in the scores of published testimonials by those who have succeeded at change, it is their universal claim that their lives are better now.[72]

Are these the words of a dangerous liar?

And what about the words of the allegedly greed-driven, hateful, homophobic, *therapists*. What do they have to say about their gay clients? Quotes like this, from an Orthodox Jewish therapist, are typical: "These individuals are among the finest people I know. *I believe that they are very lofty souls*, and I suspect that is why God has given them this challenge."[73]

One man with unwanted same-sex attractions, who has interacted with many therapists, assured me that such gracious attitudes are quite typical: "Every SRT [sexual reorientation] therapist I've met, worked with or corresponded with has been incredibly compassionate."[74] Somehow, I'm not feeling the homophobic hatred!

A HEARTFELT LETTER OF APPEAL

After *Nightline* aired a show focusing on the Journey into Manhood (JiM) weekends, which are designed to help men deal with unwanted same-sex attractions, a former JiM participant wrote an email to Dr. Jack Drescher, a gay activist and professional therapist (see, below, Chapter Thirteen, for more on him), who spoke against the JiM program on *Nightline* characterizing it as "dangerous."[75] His sincere and passionate letter of November 14, 2010 should be taken to heart:

> Dear Dr. Drescher,
>
> With all due respect, your comments on the ABC Nightline program highlighting the Journey into Manhood weekend (as well as several similar ones you have made to the same effect about reparative therapy) as being "dangerous" are ill-informed and simply naïve.
>
> ....I attended JiM 16 in 2005 and it made a significant difference in my life. I always thought that professionals such as you would be interested in a client being able to obtain his/her goals in life, and would be equally interested in knowing what worked for them in order to accomplish their objectives.
>
> I don't know why you insist on being so adamantly opposed to this work. Do you really not care about people like us at all? . . . If men like us want to deal with unwanted SSA, why should you object? Frankly, it should mean everything to you, but apparently it means nothing. The APA should be interested in helping men like us to accomplish what we want for our own lives; instead you oppose us and call a process that has worked for us to be "dangerous". I'll tell you what Jack: my life was a whole lot more dangerous when I was living a lifestyle not meant for me than it is now when I live as a husband and father. Why

DON'T you seem to care about that?

My own personal life is a testimony to the accuracy of the presentation on the Nightline program and the efficacy of the concept that people can change. I never wanted to be "gay." I lived a double life for a long time. By exercising my free will, I choose to neither identify nor believe I was gay; rather I chose to live a heterosexual life and to conform my inner most feelings and emotions to that view. The path I chose was consistent with the APA 1973 decision removing homosexuality from the DSM. It there stated, "Psychiatrists ... will continue to try to help homosexuals who suffer from what we can now refer to as Sexual orientation disturbance, helping the patient accept or live with his current sexual orientation, OR IF HE DESIRES, HELPING HIM TO CHANGE IT" (emphasis mine). The APA did not opine, as you do, that such therapy is dangerous. Rather the concept of "dangerous" is a spin that you and your colleagues have created to deter people like myself from exercising our free rights of patient determination.

Through counseling, experiential weekends such as JiM, and other strategies prevalent within the "ex-gay" movement, I have succeeded in not only changing my behavior patterns but have also changed my sexual fantasies, arousals, and identity. I have done it, and I'm happier for it – does that not matter to you?

If it really doesn't matter to you, then I can only conclude that you have a personal agenda and will press forward with your own unsubstantiated beliefs regardless of evidence to the contrary. If you were a true science oriented professional guided by clinical results and honest inquiry, you would be interviewing men like us and asking lots of questions. What you say can't happen IS in fact happening right before your eyes!

You simply choose to turn your head the other way. Is there no honesty in your profession anymore? If people in my own profession ignored the facts in a similar way, we would be driven out of leadership.

I am simply aghast at your response on Nightline and

the audacious position other gay advocates within the APA
have taken. You have apparently ceased searching for truth
and have unfortunately replaced integrity with pushing a
politically correct social agenda instead.

You're more than welcome to call and discuss this with
me, but I will not be surprised if you don't.

Sincerely,
Steve[76]

A CLOUD OF WITNESSES YOU CAN'T IGNORE

Take a few minutes and go to the Exodus International website and
read the stories of Alan Chambers and Dottie Ludwig and Linda D. Carter
and Dennis Jernigan and Mario Bergner and Michelle Ferguson and Ethan
Martin and Rebekah Johnson and Chris Stump and Elaine Sinnard and
David Kyle Foster and Randy Thomas and Phil Hobizal and Michael Babb
and Jason Thompson and Mike Jones and Sunny Jenkins and John Smid and
Alan Medinger and Michael Newman and Patricia Allan Lawrence and Rob
G. and Darryl L. Foster and Amy Tracy and D. Freeman and Penny Dalton
and Christine Sneeringer and Anne Paulk and Roberta Laurilla and Patty
Wells and Marcus Mitchell and Nate Oyloe and Melissa Fryrear and Bob
Davies and Starla Allen and Michael Lumberger and Bob Ragan and Kristin
Johnson and David Fountain and Mike Goeke and Randy Thomas and Mike
Ensley and Yvette Schneider and Christopher Yuan and Jeff Buchanan and
Jeff Johnston and Joe Dallas and Veronica Hagberg and James Wimbush and
Janet Boynes and Jayson Graves and Stephen Black and Drew Berryessa.[77]
Are all of them frauds, liars, and deceivers? Are all of them greedy for gain?[78]

Really now, we're not dealing here with alleged sightings of Bigfoot or
the Loch Ness monster. The evidence is there for all to see – first-person
accounts, not second-hand stories – and these testimonies are just the tiniest
tip of the iceberg. There *is* such a thing as ex-gay.[79]

The very nature of the ex-gay movement would tell you that something is
fishy with the virulent gay denial of ex-gay. Just think: Exodus International,
which celebrates its thirty-fifth anniversary in 2011, receives tens of thousands
of requests each year from people wanting help with issues relating to
homosexuality, not just from family members of friends of gays and lesbians,
but, primarily, from gays and lesbians themselves (or people who experience
and/or struggle with same-sex attraction). As of 2010, Exodus worked with

more than 125 non-profit ministry centers worldwide, most of them in North America, with thousands of people claiming to have experienced change. Are all of them simply going along with a big lie? Have all of them made a tacit commitment to deceive the masses? Even the most wild-eyed conspiracy theorist would have a hard time swallowing that.

Are organizations such as PFOX, claiming to be both parents and friends of both ex-gays and gays, also sharing in this mass deception?[80] And is JONAH, the acronym for Jews Offering New Alternatives to Healing, also in cahoots with this ruse?[81] What about the Presbyterian organization OneByOne, or the Mormon organization Evergreen International, or the African-American Christian organization Powerful Ministry Change Group, or non-religious organizations such as Gender Menders or People Can Change, or the German Institute for Youth and Society – just to name a few.[82] Are all of them giving their time and money and effort – and often reputation – to a cause they all know to be untrue? It is preposterous even to ask the question.

And when the scientific data is also factored in,[83] the conclusion is irresistible: It is possible – albeit sometimes very difficult – for someone who has embraced a gay identity to live a satisfied, non-homosexual lifestyle. And for those wanting to change (and/or steward their sexuality in alignment with their faith values and ethics), there is hope.[84] As for those building their whole agenda on the argument that homosexuality is innate and unchangeable, the ex-gay movement is living proof that the very ideological foundations of that agenda are faulty, unable to sustain the massive weight that is being placed upon them.

In reality, the gay agenda and the ex-gay movement cannot coexist together in truth – their positions are mutually contradictory – which is one reason why there is such a concerted effort from many gay leaders to silence or discredit the voices of thousands of ex-gays: The success of the ex-gay movement is a direct threat to the gay activist cause. Otherwise, why call for ex-gays to be locked up? Why call them murderous and dangerous? Why mock their stories, judge their motives, and attack their personal lives? Is it just that the anti-ex-gay crowd really doesn't believe in "ex-gay therapy"? Is there nothing more to the intensity of the rejection of "ex-gay"?

According to the prevailing, politically correct sentiments of today:

- Gay is good; ex-gay is bad.
- To be gay is a source of pride; to be ex-gay is a source

of shame.
- Gays should be embraced; ex-gays should be excluded.
- The claims of gays are true; the claims of ex-gays are false.
- Gays deserve tolerance; ex-gays deserve intolerance.
- Gay activists are motivated by love; ex-gay activists are motivated by greed.
- Gays have a healthy self-image; ex-gays suffer from internalized homophobia.
- Any doctor who states that gays cannot change is telling the truth; any doctor who states otherwise is a liar and fraud.
- Those practicing gay-affirmative therapy are performing a noble service and should be commended; those practicing reparative therapy or other forms of sexual orientation change are quacks who should be locked up.
- Diversity requires that gay educational programs be introduced in the schools, beginning with kindergarten; diversity also requires that *no* ex-gay programs or materials be allowed in the schools under any circumstances.

There *is* something insidious going on, but it is *not* the ex-gay movement in either its religious or mental health/counseling–based forms. Do you care to hear more? Then keep reading.

*... [The American Psychological Association] did not take
a stand on rebirthing therapy that resulted in a Denver child's suffocation when
the birth process was simulated with tight blankets. . . . it left it up to the courts
with no help from psychology. However, the leadership in the APA has not
hesitated to attack therapists practicing reparative therapy, treatment to help
willing patients to overcome same sex attraction. On the other hand, therapy
to help patients "come out" is highly encouraged, making sexual preference
a one-way street. The APA Council came within a couple of votes of
declaring reparative therapy to be unethical, and the leadership vows
to try again. In the meantime the attacks on reparative therapy have
made patient choice more difficult, rendering the APA rather than
the consumer the de facto determiner of therapeutic goals.*

Dr. Nicholas Cummings,
Gay marriage advocate and former president of the APA
Addressing the APA Convention, New Orleans, August 12, 2006

*In all, I received about 120 letters...Several writers suggested
I was a "Nazi" and "bigot," and one compared me with the Taliban.
A surprising number of letters asserted that gays have a right to be rude
or abusive because they themselves have been abused.*

Dr. Robert Epstein, the pro-gay editor-in-chief of *Pyschology Today*,
after an ad for *A Parent's Guide to Preventing Homosexuality* ran in the magazine

*Gay marriage is one of the most militant stances within the APA, strongly
implying that anyone who might be in opposition is homophobic.*

Drs. Nicholas A. and Janet L. Cummings,
Psychology's War on Religion

*Gay activism was clearly the force that propelled
the APA to declassify homosexuality.*

Dr. Simon Levay, *Queer Science*

13

The Stifling of
Scientific Debate

n 1973, the American Psychiatric Association (APA) decided that homosexuality was not a mental illness, removing it from the *Diagnostic and Statistical Manual of Mental Disorders* (*DSM*) in 1974.[1] This marked a turning point in the gay liberation movement, since the *DSM* is considered the Bible of psychiatry and psychology, and once the APA made its landmark ruling, other organizations soon fell in line, including the American Psychological Association (also called the APA) in 1975, the National Association of Social Workers in 1977, and the National Psychoanalytic Association in 1991.

Over the years, the American Psychiatric Association has become quite aggressive in its stance:

> Whereas homosexuality per se implies no impairment in judgment, stability, reliability, or general social or vocational capabilities, the American Psychiatric Association calls on all international health organizations, and individual psychiatrists in other countries, to urge the repeal in their own country of legislation that penalizes homosexual acts by consenting adults in private. And further, the APA calls on these organizations and individuals to do all that is possible to decrease the stigma related to homosexuality wherever and whenever it may occur.[2]

Before 1973, homosexuality was viewed as a mental disorder or disease by the mental health profession, akin to schizophrenia or manic depression. As explained on the Rainbow History website:

> The American Psychiatric Association's definition of homosexuality as an illness in its second Diagnostic and Statistical Manual of Mental Disorders (1968) provided crucial underpinnings for federal discrimination against homosexuals. From the late 1940s, civil laws had in many states criminalized homosexuality defining it as a sexual pathology and providing imprisonment and institutionalization as punishment. A core of American psychiatrists and psychologists provided written arguments supporting the definition of homosexuality as an illness.[3]

Writing in 2006, pioneer lesbian activist Barbara Gittings provided more details:

> When our American movement for full civil rights and equality for homosexuals got launched fifty-six years ago, we had a huge range of basic problems to tackle. We were denounced as immoral and sinful. We were punished as criminals and lawbreakers. We were labeled "sick" and needing a "cure." We were mostly invisible as gay, which made it hard for gay men and lesbians to develop good social lives and to create a movement to battle injustice and prejudice.
>
> It's difficult to explain to anyone who didn't live through that time how much homosexuality was under the thumb of psychiatry. The sickness label was an albatross around the neck of our early gay rights groups – it infected all our work on other issues. Anything we said on our behalf could be dismissed as "That's just your sickness talking." The sickness label was used to justify discrimination, especially in employment by our own government.[4]

But with the APA ruling, things changed dramatically, to the point that in a major position paper in 2009, the American Psychological Association stated as "scientific fact" that:

> Same-sex sexual attractions, behavior, and orientations per se are *normal* and *positive* variants of human sexuality; in other words, they are not indicators of mental or developmental disorders.[5]

Yes,

> The longstanding consensus of the behavioral and social sciences and the health and mental health professions is that homosexuality per se is a *normal* and *positive* variation of human sexual orientation . . . . Homosexuality per se is not a mental disorder (APA, 1975). Since 1974, the American Psychological Association (APA) has opposed

stigma, prejudice, discrimination, and violence on the basis of sexual orientation and has taken a leadership role in supporting the equal rights of lesbian, gay, and bisexual individuals (APA, 2005).[6]

. . . THEREFORE, BE IT RESOLVED, That the American Psychological Association affirms that same-sex sexual and romantic attractions, feelings, and behaviors are *normal* and *positive* variations of human sexuality regardless of sexual orientation identity. . . .[7]

Not surprisingly, websites posting information like this are now quite common:

Is Homosexuality a Mental Disorder? No. All major professional mental health organizations have gone on record to affirm that homosexuality is not a mental disorder. **Is It an Emotional Problem?** No. Psychologists, psychiatrists, and other mental health professionals agree that homosexuality is not an illness, mental disorder, or an emotional problem. Over 35 years of objective, well-designed scientific research has shown that homosexuality, in and of itself, is not associated with mental disorders or emotional or social problems.[8]

Not everyone, however, agrees with this assessment and, to put it mildly, there *is* another side to the story. In fact, there are several other sides to the story, and some of them are hardly flattering to the gay activist cause.

THE BACKGROUND TO THE APA'S LANDMARK DECISION

Let's go back to the 1973 landmark decision of the American Psychiatric Association. It is an open secret that this much-heralded decision was as least as much political as it was scientific, with disruptive, gay activist pressure playing a major role. The Rainbow History Project celebrates these pressure tactics, reprinting some of the classic, activist reports from the past. One of those reports, called "Zapping the Shrinks" (originally published May 3, 1971), boasts about the "disruption by gay activists at the [APA's] 1970 convention in San Francisco."[9] Their actions caused quite a commotion!

At the 1970 APA gathering, the activists carried out a special "zap" during a high point of the conference. (Zaps, as noted in Chapter Five, were "militant, but non-violent, face-to-face confrontations with homophobic persons in positions of authority.")[10] The gay intruders burst into the conference hall and pushed their way past a number of elderly psychiatrists who tried to stop them. And there was no mistaking who the intruders were: "Half of the men were in really fabulous drag with wildly painted faces, that accentuated the spontaneous, liberating attitude of brothers in drag ..."[11] This is some of the background leading up to the APA's momentous decision to remove homosexuality as a mental disorder from the *DSM*.

But the gay strategy accomplished its goals, with a number of psychiatrists agreeing to hear out the activists, amid threats of further disruption if they chose not to do so. And in a famous moment in psychiatric history, Dr. John E. Fryer gave a presentation to the APA in 1972 as "Dr. H. Anonymous," wearing a bizarre mask and using a microphone that altered the sound of his voice. He began his speech by saying, "I am a homosexual. I am a psychiatrist."[12]

By 1973, leadership within the APA was ready to revise its views on homosexuality, but not without a firestorm of controversy, a firestorm that is still smoldering today. Prof. Ronald Bayer, author of the definitive work on the events surrounding the APA's 1973 ruling, explained:

In 1973, after several years of bitter dispute, the Board of Trustees of the American Psychiatric Association decided to remove homosexuality from the *Diagnostic and Statistical Manual of Psychiatric [sic] Disorders*, its official list of mental diseases. Infuriated by that action, dissident psychiatrists charged the leadership of their association with an unseemly capitulation to the threats and pressures of Gay Liberation groups, and forced the board to submit its decision to a referendum of the full APA membership. And so America's psychiatrists were called to vote upon the question of whether homosexuality ought to be considered a mental disease. The entire process, from the first confrontation organized by gay demonstrators at psychiatric conventions to the referendum demanded by orthodox psychiatrists, seemed to violate the most basic expectations about how questions of science should be resolved. Instead of being engaged in a sober consideration of data, psychiatrists were swept up in a political controversy. The American Psychiatric Association had fallen victim to the disorder of a tumultuous era, when disruptive conflicts threatened to politicize every aspect of American social life. [Bayer is referring here to the massive anti-war protests that were also prevalent at that time, among other things.] A furious egalitarianism that challenged every instance of authority had compelled psychiatric experts to negotiate the pathological status of homosexuality with homosexuals themselves. The result was not a conclusion based on an approximation of the scientific truth as dictated by reason, but was instead an action demanded by the ideological temper of the times.[13]

It is against this politically-charged, highly-pressurized, hardly-scientific backdrop that this landmark decision was made, initially by the APA's Board of Trustees, resulting in howls of protest from many other APA members. One psychiatrist complained:

> I think the Board of Trustees did not have the strength and guts to resist superficial social pressure from homosexuals who, having a collective Oedipal complex, wish to destroy the American Psychiatric Association. It is a bad day for psychiatry.[14]

"The dissenters," Bayer explains, "were haunted by the specter of a politicized psychiatry that would be defenseless against an endless wave of protests. 'It now seems that if groups of people march and raise enough hell they can change anything in time.... Will schizophrenia be next?'"[15]

A more somber warning was sounded by Dr. Abram Kardiner, described by Bayer as "a senior figure who had pioneered in the effort to merge the insights of psychoanalysis and anthropology," who viewed "homosexuality as a symptom of social disintegration."[16] Writing to the editors of *Psychiatric News*, the official publication of the APA, he argued:

> Those who reinforce the disintegrative elements in our society will get no thanks from future generations. The family becomes the ultimate victim of homosexuality, a

result which any society can tolerate only within certain limits.

If the American Psychiatric Association endorses one of the symptoms of social distress as a normal phenomenon it demonstrates to the public its ignorance of social dynamics, of the relation of personal maladaptation to social disharmony, and thereby acquires a responsibility for aggravating the already existing chaos.[17]

Those protesting the Board's decision were able to push for a referendum on the question of homosexuality, and so, for "the first time in the history of healthcare . . . a diagnosis or lack of diagnosis was decided by popular vote rather than scientific evidence."[18] Now both sides were upset. Board members who ruled that homosexuality was not pathological were mortified that a scientific matter would be put to vote; those opposing the ruling were mortified that the APA Board could have caved in to gay activist pressure in the first place.

Understandably, gay activists were alarmed by the call for a vote, and behind the scenes, the National Gay Task Force (NGTF) helped compose and fund a letter to be sent out to all APA members, urging them to back the Board's decision. But the NGTF was careful not to let the APA members know that it had anything to do with the letter since to do so would have been suicidal.

The letter stated that

it would be a serious and potentially embarrassing step for our profession to vote down a decision which was taken after serious and extended consideration by the bodies within our organization designated to consider such matters.[19]

And so, a critically important letter ostensibly conceived and mailed by its signers (all of whom were key members of the APA's Board of Trustees) was in fact the brainchild of gay activists.

Obviously, the role of the NGTF needed to remain hidden, even though both the APA officers "as well as the National Gay Task Force, understood the letter as performing a vital role in the effort to turn back the challenge"[20] of the referendum to reverse the APA's decision normalizing homosexuality.

But, as Bayer points out, "at least one signer had warned privately that to acknowledge the organizational role of the gay community [in the composition and distribution of this letter] would have been the 'kiss of death.'"[21] What a subterfuge!

Now, step back for a moment and think about how much is made of the APA's landmark, 1973 decision – it was *the* decision that marked a sea change in research about homosexuality – then ask yourself: How seriously should this decision be taken in light of the extreme gay activist pressure that surrounded it?

Ultimately, when the referendum vote was taken, the ruling was upheld 5,854 to 3,810, with 367 abstaining,[22] meaning that despite the external pressure that was applied, despite the turbulent political and cultural climate, despite the gay-sponsored letter that went out, almost 40% of the psychiatrists still differed with the decision. And four years later, according to a survey conducted by the journal *Medical Aspects of Human Sexuality*, "69 percent of psychiatrists disagreed with the vote and still considered homosexuality a disorder."[23]

This is a major scientific breakthrough? This represents some kind of academic consensus? This is the decision that moved homosexuality from the category of abnormal to normal? This is the historic ruling that carried the other mental health organizations in its wake? Talk about a tainted moment in scientific history!

SOME SHARP REACTIONS TO THE APA DECISION

According to Dr. Charles Socarides, at that time considered by many to be a leading authority on homosexuality,[24] the APA's decision "involved the out-of-hand and peremptory disregard and dismissal not only of hundreds of psychiatric and psychoanalytic research papers and reports, but other serious studies by groups of psychiatrists, psychologists and educators over the past seventy years..."[25]

To be sure, "To those who viewed the 1973 decision sympathetically, psychiatry had displayed a remarkable capacity to acknowledge the significance of new research findings and to rethink its approach to sexuality."[26] As stated by Dr. Judd Marmor, an advocate for depathologizing homosexuality in the early 1970's who takes issue here with Bayer's account,

> The fact is that the decision to remove homosexuality from the DSM was *not* based on gay political pressure but on

835

scientific correctness, and only after a full year of exploratory hearings and study of the issue by the APA's Committee on Nomenclature, a year during which it heard presentations both by proponents and opponents of depathologization.[27]

Others within the APA, however, were outraged by what they considered to be a wholly non-scientific decision that was not supported by clinical evidence, and eventually, the rift proved so severe that a number of leading psychiatrists formed the National Association for the Research and Therapy of Homosexuality (NARTH) in 1992.[28] Most notable among the founders were Dr. Benjamin Kaufman, then Clinical Professor, Dept. of Psychiatry, University of California at Davis School of Medicine, and Dr. Charles W. Socarides, then Clinical Professor of Psychiatry, Albert Einstein College of Medicine / Montefiore Medical Center.

NARTH's fundamental tenets include the following: 1) Homosexuality is a disordered condition; 2) homosexuals can potentially change; and 3) if a homosexual client desires to change, then the doctor working with that client should assist him or her in their endeavors. According to their mission statement,

> We respect the right of all individuals to choose their own destiny. NARTH is a professional, scientific organization that offers hope to those who struggle with unwanted homosexuality. As an organization, we disseminate educational information, conduct and collect scientific research, promote effective therapeutic treatment, and provide referrals to those who seek our assistance.
>
> NARTH upholds the rights of individuals with unwanted homosexual attraction to receive effective psychological care and the right of professionals to offer that care. We welcome the participation of all individuals who will join us in the pursuit of these goals.[29]

For holding to these views, which NARTH believes are fully supported by the best scientific studies, the organization is under constant criticism and ridicule, with their smallest misstatements greatly magnified by the LGBT community, a community largely silent when the APA issued a report stating that adult-child sexual encounters were not harmful to the children.[30] But who said anything about being fair and balanced?

FROM RADICAL ACTIVISM TO RULING ORTHODOXY

The reality is that the radical activism of the 1970's has become the reigning orthodoxy of today, to the point that dissenting voices are summarily marginalized and even silenced. As noted in 2004 by Dr. Robert Spitzer, one of the men who was instrumental in declassifying homosexuality as a mental disease in 1973,

> There is a gay activist group that's very strong and very vocal and recognized by the American Psychiatric Association... there's nobody to give the other viewpoint...There may be a few people...but they don't talk.[31]

As Benjamin Kaufman explained:

> I saw that I could not turn to the American Psychiatric Association, or any other such professional organizations. All had totally stifled the scientific inquiry that would be necessary to stimulate such a discussion. It remains very politically incorrect–very marginalizing–to even make the suggestion of a dialogue that opens up the question of the normality of homosexuality.[32]

This was echoed by Drs. Rogers H. Wright and Nicholas Cummings, both self-described life-long liberals and both former presidents within the American Psychological Association. In fact, Cummings was the first president of the APA's Task Force on Gay and Lesbian Issues. They wrote:

> Within psychology today, there are topics that are deemed politically incorrect, and they are neither published nor funded. Journal editors control what is accepted for publication through those chosen to conduct peer reviews. ... censorship exists . . . .[33]

In fact, when Wright and Cummings were trying to solicit other professionals to contribute to their important volume, *Destructive Trends in Mental Health: The Well-Intentioned Path to Harm*, "many of [them] declined to be included, fearing loss of tenure or stature, and citing previous ridicule and even vicious attacks. . . ."[34]

Wright and Cummings noted that

> Political diversity is so absent in mental health circles that most psychologists and social workers live in a bubble. So seldom does anyone express ideological disagreement with colleagues that they believe all intelligent people think as they do. They are aware that conservatives exist, but regard the term "intelligent conservative" as an oxymoron.[35]

Thus, "Diagnosis today in psychology and psychiatry is cluttered with politically correct verbiage, which seemingly has taken precedence over sound professional experience and scientific validation."[36] In fact, in a 2008 interview, Cummings stated that when he served as first president of the APA's Gay and Lesbian Task Force,

> In that era the issue was a person's right to choose a gay life style, whereas now an individual's choice not to be gay is called into question because the leadership of the APA seems to have concluded that all homosexuality is hard-wired and same-sex attraction is unchangeable.
>
> My experience has demonstrated that there are as many different kinds of homosexuals as there are heterosexuals. Relegating all same sex-attraction as an unchangeable--an oppressed group akin to African-Americans and other minorities--distorts reality. And past attempts to make sexual reorientation therapy "unethical" violates patient choice and makes the APA the de facto determiner of therapeutic goals.[37]

It has even been claimed that there is explicit discrimination against conservative Christian students on the graduate level, a claim backed by the well-known study of J. D. Gartner, "which empirically demonstrated the discrimination against those with conservative views in graduate school admissions."[38]

Summarizing the evidence of Gartner's study, Prof. A. Dean Byrd (a past president of NARTH) noted that

465

Professors in APA-approved clinical psychology departments were provided with graduate school applications including grade-point-averages, GRE scores and personal statements that differed only in whether the applicant volunteered that he was a conservative Christian.[39]

According to Richard E. Redding, writing in the *Destructive Trends* volume,

Professors rated the nonconservative applicants significantly higher in all areas, had fewer doubts about their abilities, felt more positively about their abilities to be good psychologists and rated them more likely to be admitted to their graduate program. The findings suggest an admission bias against religious conservatives, which violates the APA's ethical principles and antidiscrimination laws.[40]

He added this cautionary warning:

We should encourage conservatives to join our ranks and foster a true sociopolitical dialogue in our research, practice, and teaching. It is in our self-interest to do so. Otherwise, we pay a terrible price that is a consequence of partisan narrow-mindedness. Political narrowness and insularity limit and deaden a discipline.[41]

STRONG WORDS OF WARNING FROM LEADING PSYCHOLOGISTS

Cummings felt so strongly about these issues that he co-authored another volume (with Dr. William T. O'Donahue) entitled *Eleven Blunders that Cripple Psychotherapy in America: A Remedial Unblundering.*[42] The chapter on "Political Correctness: We No Longer Speak as a Science and Profession" is especially damning, as Cummings and O'Donahue deal with topics such as:

- Political Correctness Uses Intimidation, Speculation, and Junk Science (189)

- Political Correctness Is Red-Green Colorblindness (189-93)
- Political Correctness Invades Psychology: A Historical Perspective (193-97)
- Boomer Ideology Trumps Psychology (197-98)
- Psychology Has Replaced Science with Political Correctness (199-215)

This last section includes these sub-headings:

- Political Correctness Inhibits Much-Needed Research (201)
- Political Correctness Can Harm Patients (206)
- Political Correctness Deliberately Slants Knowledge (208)
- Political Correctness Could Destroy the Profession (209)
- Political Correctness Intimidates and Limits Students' Critical Thinking (212)

As an illustration of the extent that politically correct (= gay activism affirming) intimidation exists today in his field, Cummings wrote that,

As one who lived through the era of McCarthyism, as egregious as that was, it was not as bad as the unspoken intimidation that exists today. In the 1950s I knew the enemies that would restrict my freedom: the John Birch Society, the KKK, the American Nazi Party, Stalinists, the evangelists in the revival tent down the street. Now the intimidator is more likely to be my colleague in practice, my fellow faculty member, and my own APA.[43]

And I remind you: Dr. Cummings remains a committed liberal, and he agrees with the decisions of both APA's to no longer regard homosexuality as a psychiatric disorder. His issues with that decision have to do with: 1) the way the decisions were made; 2) the failure to back up those decisions with solid research, even though such research was required by the American Psychological Association as a follow-up to its decision; and 3) the political correctness that stifles true diversity among the mental health professionals.[44] This, then, is quite a critique from a respected insider. But Cummings minced no words:

> How far we have fallen is illustrated by the 2003 publication in a prestigious APA journal by four prominent psychologists who found that on their test the personality of Ronald Reagan was almost identical with those of Hitler, Stalin, and Mao.[45]

When Cummings inquired as to why the media didn't take much notice of the report, one editor told him that "psychology is not that important to the public anymore."[46] For Cummings, the profession has greatly disqualified itself, with political correctness being a major factor in the equation: "The public can no longer trust organized psychology to speak from evidence rather than from what it regards to be politically correct."[47]

Dr. Robert Perloff, the 1985 president of the American Psychological Association, and a founding (and longtime continuing) member of the APA's Gay and Lesbian Caucus was even more blunt in a speech delivered to the APA in 2001: "The APA is too god----n politically correct...and too god----n obeisant to special interests!"[48] (Note that Perloff "is also a recipient of the American Psychological Foundation's Gold Medal Award for Lifetime Achievement in Psychology in the Public Interest. In bestowing the award, the Psychological Foundation recognized Perloff for his noted 'love of social justice' and his career-long struggle to champion 'the rights and dignity of women, minorities, and homosexuals.'")[49]

Regarding the attempt of psychologists and psychiatrists to bar any type of reparative therapy or sexual reorientation counseling for homosexuals wanting to become heterosexual, Perloff stated: "It is considered unethical... *That's all wrong.* First, the data are not fully in yet. Second, if the client wants a change, listen to the client. Third, you're barring research."[50] He also asked, "How can you do research on change if therapists involved in this work are threatened with being branded as unethical?"[51]

With regard to the APA's shunning of NARTH, Perloff said:

> I believe that APA is flat out wrong, undemocratic, and shamefully unprofessional in denying NARTH the opportunity to express its views and programs in the APA

Monitor and otherwise under APA's purview.[52]

To this day, gay activism continues to fuel the fires of this extreme political correctness.

It is common to hear claims that the American Academy of Pediatrics, the American Association of School Administrators, the American Counseling Association, the American Federation of Teachers, the American Psychological Association, the American School Counselor Association, the American School Health Association, the Interfaith Alliance Foundation, the National Association of School Psychologists, the National Association of Secondary School Principals, the National Association of Social Workers, the National Education Association, and the School Social Work Association of America all agree that homosexuality cannot be changed and that all attempts to do so are harmful.[53]

Viewed from another vantage point, however, what this really means is this: Once a big domino falls – in this case, the American Psychological Association, or, before that, the American Psychiatric Association – the rest of the dominos will soon fall too. Boom! It's as easy as that, unless, of course, you actually believe that each of the organizations just listed engaged in their own, careful, sexual orientation research over a period of many years and independently came to the same conclusions – which is about as realistic as believing that all salesmen at all car dealerships have independently researched all competing car manufacturers and, after exhaustive study, come to the conclusion that the cars they are selling are the best. Right![54]

WHEN HELPING HOMOSEXUALS BECOMES A CRIME
Shortly after the APA declassified homosexuality as pathological in 1973, a psychiatrist wrote a somewhat prophetic letter of protest to *Psychiatric News*:

> The Board of Trustees has made a terrible, almost unforgivable decision which will adversely affect the lives of young homosexuals who are desperately seeking direction and cure. That ... decision will give young homosexuals an easy way out and make the job of practicioners like myself much more difficult.[55]

In hindsight, "much more difficult" has proven to be quite an understatement. As noted by Dr. Gerald Schoenewolf in a 2009 article,

> Over the years a number of gays (usually with strong bisexual features) have come to my office for treatment specifically because they wanted to be straight. They wanted to make love to a woman, have a family and live a straight lifestyle. What was I supposed to say? "Sorry, you're only allowed to be gay!"[56]

The politically correct answer is, "Yes! You're only allowed to be gay, and I'm only allowed to help you embrace your homosexuality. Any attempts to change your sexual orientation are harmful and dangerous."

Ex-gay Rich Wyler relates what happened to him the first time when, as a gay man, he met with a therapist named Matt:

> **The APA's Disclaimer: This Won't Work and Might Hurt**
> The first order of business on my first visit with Matt was for me to sign a release form required by the American Psychological Association. Reparative therapy was unproven, the form said; the APA's official stance was that it didn't believe it was possible to change sexual orientation; attempting to do so might even cause psychological harm.
>
> Yeah, right, I thought, as if the double life I was living was not causing psychological harm enough.[57]

The absurdity of all this was not lost on conservative journalist Matthew Cullinan Hoffman. The beginning of his article, "The Psychological Profession and Homosexuality: Lunatics Running the Asylum?" reads like a very poor joke, but it's neither a joke nor funny:

> A man goes to a psychologist with a problem. "Doctor," he says, "I'm suffering terribly. I feel like a woman trapped inside the body of a man. I want to become a woman."
>
> The psychologist responds: "No problem. We can discuss this idea for a couple of years, and if you're still sure you want to be a woman, we can have a surgeon remove your penis, give you hormones for breast enlargement and make other changes to your body. Problem solved."

Gratified, the first patient leaves, followed by a second. "Doctor," he says, "I feel terrible. I'm a man but I feel attracted to other men. I want to change my sexual preference. I want to become heterosexual." The psychologist responds: "Oh no, absolutely not! That would be unethical. Sexual orientation is an immutable characteristic!"[58]

So, gender is now changeable, but not sexual orientation. How extraordinary![59]

A PRO-GAY PSYCHIATRIST BECOMES THE TARGET OF GAY ACTIVISTS

Ironically, almost thirty years after he helped pave the way for the American Psychiatric Association's acceptance of homosexuality as normal, Robert Spitzer became the object of scorn and ridicule when he published a study indicating that some gay and lesbians were, in fact, successful in making changes in their orientation. This was psychiatric heresy. How dare he publish such findings!

So, Spitzer, a longtime hero of gay activism was now vilified as "an over-the-hill stage horse galloping toward the limelight, or a court jester hoodwinked by a scheming religious right."[60] Not only so, but the journal which published his article (*Archives of Sexual Behavior*) also printed twenty-eight peer-commentaries on his article in the very same issue (a highly unusual procedure, to say the least), and a whole issue of the *Journal of Gay and Lesbian Psychotherapy* was devoted to critiquing his study. And all this was done despite the fact that: 1) Spitzer remains a strong advocate of "gay civil rights"; 2) he has raised concerns about the use of his study by religious conservatives; and 3) he remains a committed liberal. But the simple fact that he claimed some gays could change was an unforgivable sin.

All the contributors to the issue of the *Journal of Gay and Lesbian Psychotherapy* devoted to critiquing Spitzer were gay activists and/or strongly gay affirming, including men like Dr. Theo Sandfort, an advocate of "man-boy love" and a former editor of the *Journal of Paedophilia*, and Dr. Charles Silverstein, author of *The Joy of Gay Sex*, to name just two.[61] The deck was clearly stacked against Spitzer.

And what, exactly, was Spitzer's crime? It was making statements such as this:

Like most psychiatrists, I thought that homosexual behavior could be resisted, but sexual orientation could not be changed. I now believe that's untrue--some people can and do change."[62]

Such conclusions are forbidden! Indeed, the moment news of his study was released, despite Spitzer's measured conclusions (which stated that some "highly motivated" gay people can "apparently make sustained changes in sexual orientation"), both he and his study were vilified by gay leaders: As noted by Deroy Murdock, "The fire and brimstone quickly erupted."

"I'm appalled, absolutely appalled — it's not scientific, it's not valid, it's what's known as anecdotal data," Dr. Barbara Warren of the Lesbian and Gay Community Services Center in Manhattan told the New York Post's Kate Sheehy. "I cannot believe Columbia would allow any of its professors to do anything like this."

How dare Columbia allow one of its very own to release such a horrific study!

"This study makes it clear that until society is free from anti-gay prejudice, people will feel compelled or can be coerced into attempting to change and claim success even if it has not occurred," said Wayne Besen, Associate Director of Communications for the Human Rights Campaign. An HRC news release adds: "The validity of the study is questionable because of the author's anti-gay views, close ties to right-wing political groups and lack of objective data."[63]

Seriously? Since when did Robert Spitzer, a pioneer of gay rights in psychology and, to this day, someone who is quite wary of conservative political and religious organizations, have "anti-gay views" and "close ties to right-wing political groups"? And since when was he guilty of issuing studies with a "lack of objective data"? Not only was the HRC's attack totally gratuitous, but based on their logic, the many pro-gay studies, conducted by gay and lesbian scientists and issued or funded by gay and lesbian organizations, should be rejected out of hand.

Of course, those opposed to the Spitzer study claimed that his methodology was seriously flawed, notwithstanding the fact that: 1) he had been one of the most esteemed leaders in the APA; 2) he had more than 250 academic publications to his credit; and 3) he had no ulterior motive in carrying out his research and simply followed the evidence whichever way it went. (You can be quite sure that if his study concluded that gays could *not* change, his methodology would not have been critiqued by gay-affirming psychologists, nor would whole journal issues have been devoted to challenging his research.)

It's also instructive to note that an article by two openly gay psychologists, Ariel Shidlo and Michael Schroeder,[64] came out about the same time as Spitzer's study and argued that it is dangerous for therapists to try to change someone's sexual orientation. And their article was highly praised by some of the same people who vilified Spitzer's study. Yet the Shidlo-Schroeder study was no more scientifically rigorous than was Spitzer's and, whereas Spitzer began his study without a personal bias in the issue, Shidlo and Schroeder unabashedly had a point to prove.[65]

What then was the difference? It was simply that Spitzer wanted to see if some homosexuals could actually change (and concluded that some, indeed, did), whereas the Shidlo-Schroeder study had *as its goal* proving that "reparative therapy" was harmful. In fact, the original name of Shidlo and Schroeder's article was "Homophobic Therapies: Documenting the Damage." And their research was hosted by the National Gay and Lesbian Health Association and the National Gay and Lesbian Task Force.[66] Need I say more?

To be clear, Spitzer's study relied on interviews he had conducted with 247 gays and lesbians over a period of 16 months, which is one of the reasons that other researchers criticized his work. How could he tell if the people were being truthful in their responses? But Shidlo and Schroeder also relied on interviews they had conducted – and which took them a similar amount of time to find willing participants, a common critique of Spitzer's study – yet their report is commonly quoted as fact. Why? It would appear that when a person tells you that he or she used to be gay (or, had some level of change in their sexual orientation), they are not to be trusted, but when a gay person tells you that he or she was harmed by reparative therapy, they are definitely telling the truth.[67] And, in terms of the prominent use made of the study to demonstrate the alleged, universal damage of reparative therapy, Prof.

Warren Throckmorton rightly observed, "You could make a case that riding in cars is invariably harmful if you only studied those who were in automobile accidents. But would that be scientific?"[68]

Psychologist Louis A. Berman, author of a major book on homosexuality called *The Puzzle*, made these interesting comments when asked, "Why has there been so little research on homosexuality?"

> Research in this area is taboo... off limits in most psychology departments. One of the arguments of my book is that we need more research in the development of sexual orientation and in orientation therapy.
>
> Gays, gay advocates, and gay-friendly people sit on the research boards that decide which grant applications are approved and which are not. A young psychologist whose doctoral research was on the origin or change of sexual orientation might have a hard time finding a job. It is politically correct nowadays to believe that *[homo] sexual orientation is not a problem*, that gay is just as good as straight. If, on the other hand, homosexuality is really an attempt to overcome *a feeling of deficit*, then straight is better than gay, in the sense that homosexuality burdens the individual with problems and risks that he would not otherwise face.[69]

There really is a Catch-22 situation here, since we are told that homosexuality is good and that it can't be (and shouldn't be) changed, but anyone wanting to do research to question those premises is often marginalized in academic and professional circles. How then can serious research be done?

THE THEATER OF THE ABSURD

Of course, this pressure is often felt beyond the pale of academia, and at such times the story of extreme, anti-ex-gay, political correctness actually becomes comedic. Roberto Marchesini penned this 2009 report from Italy:

> Italy's "Festival di San Remo," the most important musical happening in my country which is seen on T.V. by millions of Italians, became the unlikely platform this year for a powerful ex-gay testimony. The singer, Giuseppe

Povia, winner of the festival in 2006, presented a song entitled, "Luca Era Gay" (Luca was once gay) . . . . The title of his song, implying that some gays can change to heterosexuality, was sufficient to destabilize the Italian gay movement. Gay activists threatened to block the festival, and Europarlimentary member Vittorio Agnoletto asked for a European resolution to stop Povia from performing the song. Povia, himself, received death threats. The gay association "Everyone" denounced Povia to the Procura of the Republic for alleged "homophobia." These efforts failing, gay activists then asked the Festival organizers to "counterbalance" Povia with a song by a gay singer, about "the perfection of homosexual love." That effort too, failed.[70]

All this because a popular singer was going to perform a song entitled Luca Was Once Gay!

Finally, on February 17th., Povia sang his song on the first evening of the Festival. "Luca Era Gay" recounts the transformation of a man named Luca from the gay lifestyle. Without the help of psychologists and psychiatrists, he digs deep within himself to understand the sources of his homosexual attractions. An emotionally disconnected, detached father and a smothering mother, he says, created confusion about his sexual identity . . . . The music, a soft rap with dramatic tunes, carries a direct and honest text while never judging homosexually oriented people for their own personal lifestyle choices.[71]

And not only does Povia *not* judge homosexually oriented people, but he states emphatically towards the end of the song, "This is my story. Only my story. No disease. No healing."

All this, however, was just too much:

Before Povia's song was aired, the Italian comedian Roberto Benigni presented a twenty-minute show in which he condemned Povia, saying that homosexuality isn't a sin and that gays have been persecuted historically "because they love someone." He then read an excerpt from Oscar Wilde's "De Profundis."

After Povia's song, contrary to all custom, the conductor gave the microphone to Franco Grillini, former parliamentary member and former president of ARCIgay, the foremost gay association in Italy. Grillini said he had received a cellphone message from a friend (although all celphones were supposed to be turned off during the festival...), who had cried when he had just heard Benigni reading "De Profundis," because it brought to mind his partner who had died of AIDS. Grillini concluded by saying that Povia must learn what gay love is.

Then, the unforeseeable happened: people in the theater started to hiss at Grillini (in Italy, hissing is like booing)! The crowd's sympathy was with Povia, not with the gay activist.[72]

Think of it: There were death threats against the popular performer; a comedian presented a twenty minute anti-ex-gay diatribe before the song; then a presentation was made after the song by a leading gay activist stating that Povia must learn what gay love is. (This is *not* some fictional account taken from the Homophobe's Handbook of Paranoia. This really happened.) And what was Povia's terrible crime? Like Dr. Robert Spitzer, he said that some gay men can and do change. The reaction to his song was nothing less than hysterical.

The end results, however, were heartening:

Povia's song went on to the finals and Saturday night, won second place in the San Remo Festival, while outside the theatre, gay activists continued to protest against him. Povia himself said: "I too had a gay phase--it lasted seven months and then I got over it."

The popularity of "Luca Era Gay" has given courage and dignity to the ex-homosexual community in Italy, who, until now, have been thoroughly intimidated by gay activists. The text's real-life insights regarding the ex-gay experience are undeniable.[73]

And in an act of real artistic boldness, when Povia finished his song, he placed a large sign on his chair that read: NO MAN CAN TELL ANOTHER MAN WHO HE IS AT HIS CORE. Could you imagine seeing something like this on American Idol?

"But wait one second," someone protests. "I know this story sounds extreme, and I recognize that there's a lot of political correctness out there today, but you can't deny that a major study released in 2009 has demonstrated conclusively that gays can't change and that efforts to promote such change should be strongly discouraged."

WHAT ABOUT THE APA'S 2009 STUDY?

Actually, once again, there's more to the story than meets the eye. First, may I ask who published this study? It was none other than the strongly pro-gay American Psychological Association. That's right. This study was funded and conducted by an organization that has been blasted by some of its former leaders as being politically correct to the point of stifling other viewpoints, especially when it comes to gay-related issues.

"But," you protest again, "there was a specially appointed task force that took almost two years to investigate the evidence."

True enough, but who was on the task force that was appointed to investigate whether sexual orientation could be changed? All gay, lesbian, and gay-affirming psychologists, with no dissenting viewpoints allowed onto the panel. And almost every one of them had a long, proud, and well-known history of gay psychological activism. Yes, *this* was the APA's handpicked task force to investigate whether gays could change their sexual orientation.

Assembling a task force like this would be similar to asking decorated, American World War II veterans to investigate whether our country's role in that war was justified, or asking radical feminist leaders to investigate whether women were being treated fairly in the workplace, or asking Al Gore and Greenpeace to investigate whether man-made global warming existed. You could predict the results of the studies before they ever started, and that's exactly what happened with the APA. It didn't take a rocket scientist to calculate what their conclusions would be.[74]

In fact, the APA's bias was so blatant that when the task force was formed in 2007, some members urged the APA to include at least one highly-qualified advocate of sexual orientation change, but the request was denied.[75] One of the task force members, gay activist Dr. Jack Drescher, even participated in an "Anti-Heterosexism" conference held in protest of NARTH's annual conference barely three months after the APA issued its report in August of 2009.[76] The conference, which was held on Nov. 20-22, 2009, was called "From Straight Rackets to Straight Jackets," and Drescher's presentation was titled, "Straight Jackets: A Psychiatrist Deconstructs Sexual Conversion Therapies." So much for unbiased research.

The task force chairperson was the lesbian psychologist Dr. Judith M. Glassgold. Together with Jack Drescher, she edited the book *Activism and LGBT Psychology*.[77] So *two* of the *six* members of the task force (meaning one-third, for those not good at math) co-authored a book on gay psychological activism, and they both had written a number of other articles or books that reflect their activist mentality. In fact, Drescher had already written articles and edited books warning that attempts to change one's sexual orientation were harmful,[78] also referring to ex-gays as "so-called ex-gays."[79]

Another task force member was Dr. Beverly Greene, an African American woman (presumably lesbian). She is the author of articles such as "Beyond Heterosexism and Across the Cultural Divide: Developing an Inclusive Lesbian, Gay, and Bisexual Psychology. A Look to the Future," and "Lesbian Women of Color: Triple Jeopardy," in the book *Classics in Lesbian Study*.[80]

Also on the task force was Dr. Roger L. Worthington, the Assistant Deputy Chancellor and Chief Diversity Officer at the University of Missouri (for the gay-charged meaning of "diversity," see above, Chapter Eight) and co-author of the article "Becoming an LGBT-affirmative career advisor: Guidelines for faculty, staff, and administrators." Worthington had previously criticized Robert Spitzer's research which had indicated that some gays could, in fact, change (discussed above). He wrote, "I have argued that a host of scientific and conceptual flaws are inherent to the work reported by Spitzer."[81] He even expressed his concern that Spitzer's study could receive ongoing "widespread publicity" that would draw positive attention to sexual reorientation therapy.[82]

Then there was Dr. Lee Beckstead, described as "gay-affirming" on the gay watchdog website Box Turtle Bulletin, which reported that, "Dr. Beckstead is a counseling psychologist who has focused his research and clinical work on helping gay, lesbian, bisexual, and transgender people with strong religious affiliations."[83]

And then there was the staff liaison, Dr. Clinton W. Anderson, a well-known gay activist. According to the APA website,

He has vigorously advocated for LGBT issues on several fronts and has been a model and mentor for many LGBT psychologists within APA governance. . . .

Dr. Anderson's lobbying efforts led to passage of the Hate Crimes Statistics Act which is the first federal statute to recognize the categories of gay, lesbian, and bisexual people.

By bringing together national stakeholders the CDC funded Healthy Lesbian, Gay, and Bisexual Students Project was inaugurated which is designed to strengthen the capacity of our nation's schools to prevent behavioral health risks for lesbian, gay, and bisexual students.

His office has been responsible for more than a decade of public education and advocacy on behalf of lesbian and gay parenting.[84]

These, then, were the members and the liaison of the APA's task force appointed to study the possibility of change in sexual orientation. Could they fairly be called unbiased?

UNBIASED SCIENTIFIC RESEARCH?

Earlier in this chapter, I made reference to Matthew Hoffman's article entitled "The Psychological Profession and Homosexuality: Lunatics Running the Asylum?" In a similar vein, registered nurse and medical reporter Kathleen Melonakos had previously written,

I do not think it is far-fetched to use the analogy that the "drunks are running the rehab center," in reference to the [two] APA's--at least as far as homosexuality is concerned. Active homosexuals can hardly be objective about an addictive behavior they engage in themselves.[85]

According to Dr. Joseph Nicolosi, one of the founding members of NARTH:

The fact that the Task Force was composed entirely of activists in gay causes, most of whom are also personally gay, goes a long way toward explaining their failure to be scientifically objective.

To be "gay-identified" means to have undergone a counter-cultural rite of passage. According to the coming-out literature, when a person accepts and integrates a gay identity, he must give up the hope of ever changing his feelings and fantasies. The process is as follows: the adolescent discovers his same-sex attraction; this causes him confusion, shame and guilt. He desperately hopes that he will somehow become straight so that he will fit in with his friends and family. However, he eventually comes to believe that he is gay, and in fact can never be otherwise. Therefore, he must accept his homosexuality in the face of social rejection, and find pride in his homoerotic desires as something good, desirable, natural, and (if he is a person of faith) a gift from his creator.

The majority of the Task Force members clearly underwent this same process of abandoning the hope that they could diminish their homosexuality and develop their heterosexual potential. Coming to the Task Force from this perspective, they would be strongly invested in discouraging others from having the opportunity to change -- i.e., *"If it did not work for me, then it cannot work for you."*[86]

Even some of those who felt the APA's study was objective agreed that it would have certainly helped their credibility to have had at least one dissenting voice on their six person task force.[87] But now that the APA report is out, we are supposed to embrace its conclusions without question. After all, this is the APA!

It should also be noted that the results of the APA report were reported in exaggerated form by the media, with blaring headlines such as: "Psychologists repudiate gay-to-straight therapy" (AP News), and "Psychologist group rejects so-called 'gay therapy'," and "APA exposes 'ex-gay' myth."[88] In reality, while discouraging "gay-to straight" therapy, the report said there was *insufficient evidence* that the therapy actually worked. As explained by Dr. Warren Throckmorton,

> Regarding these change efforts, the APA task force reported that "there is insufficient evidence to support

the use of psychological interventions to change sexual orientation." On that basis, the APA recommended that therapists should "avoid telling clients they can change from gay to straight."[89]

This is hardly a complete repudiation of such therapy. Why wasn't this reported accurately?

Not surprisingly, the misleading headlines had their effect. Just a few weeks after the APA's report was released, one reader commenting on an article posted on Advocate.com asked, "Didn't the APA already rule that 'ex gay therapy' didn't work? Therefore, logically, there is no such thing as an ex gay."[90] Such are the popular perceptions: The APA already "ruled" on this.

The report also concluded that there was insufficient evidence that sexual reorientation therapy caused harm, yet this too was not reported accurately (if at all), despite the fact that many voices had been proclaiming for years that the harmful effects of "reparative therapy" were thoroughly documented and apparently indisputable. (The online comments of another reader, named Justin, on Advocate.com, reflect the typical mentality among gays: "There is no 'ex-gay.' Just individuals subjected to the near equivalent of psychological torture and brainwashing of a most virulent and unforgivable nature.")[91]

So, the accusation that all professional attempts to change a person's sexual orientation were harmful continue to be trumpeted, while the APA's verdict that the evidence of harm was inconclusive has barely been whispered.

One endorsement of *Sexual Conversion Therapy*, the 2002 book edited by gay psychologists Ariel Shidlo, Michael Schroeder, and Jack Drescher, exclaimed:

VIVID . . . documents the harm that conversion therapy may produce in the lives of gay, lesbian, and bisexual individuals.

Another endorsement stated,

This book gives voice to those men and women who have experienced painful, degrading, and unsuccessful conversion therapy and survived. The ethics and misuses of conversion therapy are well documented, as are the harmful effects.[92]

Yet even the heavily-slanted APA Task Force, with this same Jack Drescher as a vital part of it, stated that the evidence for harm was inconclusive. Why wasn't this shouted from the roof tops?[93] And why didn't the APA conclude that more research was needed, rather than making sweeping recommendations based on "inconclusive" findings?[94]

To be sure, it is reasonable to believe that the Task Force members sought to act with professional integrity in performing their research and issuing their report. But does anyone doubt for a moment that, if the Task Force panel was composed entirely of conservative religious psychiatrists or reorientation therapy advocates that the results would not have been markedly different, despite equally high levels of professionalism?

HOMOSEXUAL ATTRACTIONS ARE "NORMAL" AND "POSITIVE"?

And what are we to make of the oft-repeated statement in the APA report that, "Same-sex sexual attractions, behavior, and orientations per se are normal and positive variants of human sexuality."[95] Normal and positive? The report explains, "in other words, they are not indicators of mental or developmental disorders." But is this all that is meant by "normal and positive"?

Let's consider these statements for a moment. Both APA's now agree that:

> There is no consensus among scientists about the exact reasons that an individual develops a heterosexual, bisexual, gay or lesbian orientation. Although much research has examined the possible genetic, hormonal, developmental, social, and cultural influences on sexual orientation, no findings have emerged that permit scientists to conclude that sexual orientation is determined by any particular factor or factors. Many think that nature and nurture both play complex roles....[96]

So, these psychiatrists and psychologists acknowledge that upbringing or life experiences may cause or contribute to someone's homosexual orientation, at least in some individuals. Many professional therapists would also attest to this, with some arguing that "nurture" plays a more dominant role in determining homosexual orientation than does nature.[97] Sadly, many gays and lesbians report traumatic experiences in their past, such as rape and other forms of sexual abuse, meaning that these negative experiences may have played a formative role in the development of their same-sex attractions. Stories like this are hardly exceptional:

> Jennifer was physically abused by her father in high school; Thom was molested by his neighbor for five years; Cynthia was fondled by her cousin from age seven to age thirteen; Rich was raped by his uncle from elementary school to high school. Each one of them today says that they choose to be part of the GLBT community not because they feel they were born gay but because of their abuse.[98]

On what basis, then, are the sexual orientations of these people deemed "normal and positive?" It could well be argued that without these hurtful experiences, these particular individuals would not have developed same-sex attractions. Why then describe their attractions as "normal and positive variants of human sexuality"? Isn't there something aberrant (and therefore *abnormal*) about a woman not being able to have intimate relations with a man, or a man not being able to have intimate relations with a woman, rooted in traumatic childhood sexual abuse? Isn't there something aberrant (and therefore *abnormal*) about two people of the opposite sex being unable to function according to their biological design? How is this "normal and positive"?

It appears that there have been same-sex attracted people throughout history, but until recently, they could not have children of their own, meaning that they could not reproduce offspring for the next generation. And even today, the child of a same-sex couple is not fully "their own" child but rather, at best, it is the biological child of only one of them (and, in many cases, also the child of an unknown stranger). Is this "normal and positive"?

"BENEFICIAL, HELPFUL, AND PRODUCTIVE"?

Let's take this a little further and focus on the word "positive," which is defined as "beneficial" or "helpful," with synonyms such as "constructive, good, practical, productive, progressive, sound, useful." Antonyms to positive include "disadvantageous, negative, unhelpful."[99] So, the APA is telling us that same-sex attractions *and behaviors* are beneficial and helpful and that they are not disadvantageous, negative, or unhelpful. Really?

According to an August 14, 2009 report,
Gays and lesbians get mental health treatment at twice the rate of heterosexuals, a new study concludes. The group least likely to seek treatment? Heterosexual men.
Researchers at the UCLA School of Public Health studied data from over 2,000 people and found that 48% of lesbian, gay, and bisexual men and women have received treatment in the past year, compared to 22% of straight people.[100]

This is positive? This is *not* disadvantageous or negative?
Not surprisingly, one of the authors of the report, Susan Cochran, professor of epidemiology at the UCLA School of Public Health, stated that,

> The pervasive and historically rooted societal pathologizing of homosexuality may contribute to this propensity for treatment by construing homosexuality and issues associated with it as mental health problems.[101]

So, the fact that such a high percentage of gays and lesbians are undergoing treatment is probably the fault of our homophobic society and is not reflective of the emotional or mental problems related to being gay or lesbian.

Other researchers have come to different conclusions, arguing:

> The usual hypothesis is that societal discrimination against homosexuals is solely or primarily responsible for the development of this pathology. However, specific attempts to confirm this societal discrimination hypothesis have been unsuccessful, and the alternative possibility— that these conditions may somehow be related to the psychological structure of a homosexual orientation or consequences of a homosexual lifestyle—has not been disconfirmed. Indeed, several cross-cultural studies suggest that this higher rate of psychological disturbance is in fact independent of a culture's tolerance of—or hostility toward—homosexual behavior. We believe that further research that is uncompromised by politically-motivated

bias should be carried out to evaluate this issue.[102]

What about the well-known health risks of gay sex, in particular men having sex with men? Is this "positive"? Is this all the fault of "homophobia"?[103] A May 11, 2006 report on Advocate.com carried the headline, "Rise in U.S. syphilis rates linked almost entirely to gay and bisexual men." The statistics were staggering:

> The overall rate of syphilis diagnoses increased in the United States from 1999 to 2004, but the rise is attributed almost exclusively to gay and bisexual men, among whom syphilis infections have dramatically risen, researchers said this week at the National STD Prevention Conference in Jacksonville, Fla. Infection rates actually fell in most other populations during that time frame, including among women, African-Americans, and babies born to women infected with the STD. The overall U.S. syphilis rate rose from 2.4 cases per 100,000 people in 1999 to 2.7 cases per 100,000 people in 2005. But the rate fell by about one third among African-Americans and by more than half among women during that time frame.
>
> In 1999 men who have sex with men represented about 5% of all new syphilis diagnoses, but that percentage increased to 64% of all new cases by 2004. More than half of the new syphilis cases were reported in just 20 counties across the country, with Los Angeles County at the top of the list for new cases.[104]

This really is tragic. Gay men make up roughly 3% of the population, and yet 64% of all new syphilis cases in 2004 were reported among them. And these statistics have continued to rise. As noted in an August 8, 2008 report in Q-Notes:

> Gay and bisexual men, as well as men who have sex with men (MSM), are at a higher risk of contracting syphilis, as officials have seen infection rates in these communities rise for seven straight years. Numbers released by the Centers for Disease Control and Prevention show that syphilis

infections are up 81 percent. Gay and bisexual men and MSM represent 65 percent of the total number of cases.[105]

There is nothing positive about this.

But the news gets worse. On August 28, 2009, the results of a study from the Centers for Disease Control were released. As reported in the gay Southern Voice (a website replete with ads featuring same-sex couples in loving embrace):

> Gay and bisexual men account for half of the new HIV infections in the U.S. and have AIDS at a rate more than 50 times greater than other groups, according to Centers for Disease Control & Prevention data presented at the National HIV Prevention Conference this week in Atlanta.
> . . .
> While the CDC data has continually reported gay and bisexual men and other MSM of all races as the groups with the highest numbers of new HIV cases each year, AIDS activists said this was the first time the CDC clearly stated with a concrete rate how the disease is impacting gay and bisexual men. Gay and bisexual men are also the only risk group in which new infections are increasing.[106]

What is positive about this? And note that new infections are increasing at the same time that American societal acceptance of homosexuality is increasing. Surely these alarming health risks and heartbreaking statistics cannot be blamed on homophobia. They *can*, however, be blamed squarely on gay sex practices, which are directly related to same-sex attractions.

According to a report issued by the FDA (US Food and Drug Administration),

> Men who have had sex with men since 1977 have an HIV prevalence (the total number of cases of a disease that are present in a population at a specific point in time) 60 times higher than the general population, 800 times higher than first time blood donors and 8000 times higher than repeat blood donors (American Red Cross). Even taking into account that 75% of HIV infected men who have sex with

men already know they are HIV positive and would be unlikely to donate blood, the HIV prevalence in potential donors with history of male sex with males is 200 times higher than first time blood donors and 2000 times higher than repeat blood donors.[107]

I ask again: Is this positive? The simple facts are that gay men are decidedly more promiscuous than straight men[108] and that gay sex has decidedly more health risks than heterosexual sex, even in "monogamous," committed relationships.[109] In fact, a report published in 2007 by the *International Journal of STD & AIDS* found that,

> HIV-positive men who have sex with men are up to 90 times more likely than the general population to develop anal cancer. Detection of precancerous changes (anal dysplasia) by anal cytology [essentially an anal canal Pap smear] is a relatively new procedure and one that has yet to enter standard practice.[110]

And on March 10, 2010, the American government released a report stating that,

> A data analysis released today by the Centers for Disease Control and Prevention underscores the disproportionate impact of HIV and syphilis among gay and bisexual men in the United States.
>
> The data, presented at CDC's 2010 National STD Prevention Conference, finds that the rate of new HIV diagnoses among men who have sex with men (MSM) is more than 44 times that of other men and more than 40 times that of women. . . . The rate of primary and secondary syphilis among MSM is more than 46 times that of other men and more than 71 times that of women, the analysis says.
>
> . . . "While the heavy toll of HIV and syphilis among gay and bisexual men has been long recognized, this analysis shows just how stark the health disparities are between this and other populations," said Kevin Fenton,

M.D., director of CDC's National Center for HIV/AIDS, Viral Hepatitis, STD, and TB Prevention.[111]

There is one word that sums this up, and that word is *negative*, not *positive*.[112]

The comprehensive review of 100 years of literature by NARTH researchers yielded the following conclusions:

- Despite knowing the AIDS risk, homosexuals repeatedly and pathologically continue to indulge in unsafe sex practices.
- Homosexuals represent the highest number of STD cases.
- Many homosexual sex practices are medically dangerous, with or without protection.
- More than one-third of homosexual men and women are substance abusers.
- Forty percent of homosexual adolescents report suicidal histories.
- Homosexuals are more likely than heterosexuals to have mental health concerns, such as eating disorders, personality disorders, paranoia, depression, and anxiety.
- Homosexual relationships are more violent than heterosexual relationships.[113]

The report also emphasized that, "Societal bias and discrimination do not, in and of themselves, contribute to the majority of increased health risks for homosexuals."

How, then, can same-sex attractions and behaviors be deemed "positive"? Dr. Louis Berman observed that,

It's no wonder that [male] homosexuals are more likely to become alcoholics, drug abusers, and are even more likely to become suicidal. The evidence very strongly suggests that straight is better than gay--and that is why my book [*The Puzzle*] pleads for more research on the psychological determinants of sexual orientation, and on the improvement of reorientation therapy.[114]

But to say that "straight is better than gay" – in any sense of the word – is be to rejected as a homophobe, even if the intent is to provide real help to gay men, as is clearly the case with Dr. Berman.

According to a report presented at a bisexual health summit held in August, 2009,

> Research presented by Cheryl Dobinson, MA, and Stewart Landers, JD, MCP, from their two separate studies was remarkably similar. Bisexuals reported suffering from depression and anxiety in higher rates than heterosexuals or lesbians and gay men. In terms of attempting or thinking of attempting suicide, bisexual men were 7 times higher, while gay men were 4 times higher, than straight men; bisexual women were 6 times higher, while lesbian women were 4 times higher, than straight women. An Australian study revealed that middle-aged bi women were 24 times more likely to engage in self harm, like cutting, than straight women, as a coping mechanism.[115]

The research also "revealed that only 26% of bisexuals did *not* experience child sexual abuse" – meaning that 74% of bisexuals *did* experience child sexual abuse.[116] What does this tell us about the impact of "nurture" on sexual orientation, at least in a large number of cases? And how can any of this be deemed either "normal" or "positive"?[117]

It might even be theorized that bisexuals should suffer less social stigma, since they experience opposite-sex attractions (at least, at different times in their lives) and could therefore appear to be heterosexual, even enjoying the social benefits of heterosexual marriage. Yet in some studies, they have topped the charts in terms of mental and physical health problems. This is neither normal nor positive.[118]

To say all this, however, is off-limits and to be quickly labeled homophobic and "anti-gay." And to go one step further and say that more research is needed to determine the causes of homosexuality so as to help people with unwanted same-sex attractions change is to speak psychological and psychiatric – and professional – blasphemy.

"How dare you utter such things," says the LGBT community. "The APA has ruled that our sexual orientations and behaviors are normal and positive, and no amount of mental or physical or societal data you can present, no matter how negative it might be, can change that. The only problems we have are *your* fault, and if you would just celebrate our multifaceted sexual orientations and attractions and behaviors, everything would be just fine."

YOU ARE FORBIDDEN TO SEEK HELP TO CHANGE!

What about people with unwanted same-sex attractions? Should they be encouraged to seek help to change? "Absolutely not!", we are told. "They need to be counseled to embrace their homosexuality as a gift. (If they are spiritual people, they should embrace it as a gift from God.) Remember: Same-sex attractions are normal and positive!"

So, those suffering emotional problems because of their homosexuality – evidenced by the disproportionately high number of LGBT's undergoing treatment – must remember that their same-sex attractions are normal and positive.

And those suffering physical problems because of their homosexuality – evidenced by the disproportionately high number of gays with HIV and AIDS – must remember that their same-sex attractions are normal and positive.

And those suffering spiritual problems because of their homosexuality – the results of intense, internal conflicts based on their religious and moral beliefs – must remember that their religions have it all wrong and that same-sex attractions are normal and positive.

Such is the politically correct verdict of modern psychology and psychiatry. And this kind of thinking is supposed to be *helping* people?

Kathleen Melonakos noted that:

A careful reading of the articles opposing reorientation therapy reveals their authors' rationale that they find such therapy to be "oppressive" to those who do not want therapy.[119]

What if this logic was applied to any other lethal illness? What if doctors said, "We refuse to treat cancer (or, say, alcoholism) because we only achieve a 50% cure rate – and many people who don't want to be cured find it oppressive that we do cure the others?" Why wouldn't the lawsuits for malpractice be filed?[120]

Helping people, however, is obviously not the issue, since homosexuals don't need to be helped, seeing that their orientation and behavior are "normal, natural and positive." No, it is the homophobes who need to be helped, since they are the ones who are disordered, not those in the GLBT community – and to say otherwise is to be guilty of psychiatric heresy.

Yes, it is "homophobia" which today is labeled a disorder,[121] and in the words of Dr. Richard Isay, a leading gay psychiatrist, "homophobia . . . is a psychological abnormality. Those afflicted should be quarantined and denied employment."[122] With attitudes like this, is it any surprise that true scientific inquiry has been stifled? Even rational scientific *discussion* has been stifled, as reported by the *Washington Times* on May 8, 2008 with the headline, "Gay Activists Shut Down APA Panel":

> The American Psychiatric Association suddenly canceled an upcoming workshop on religion and homosexuality during its annual conference here after gay activists campaigned against the two evangelicals slated to appear on the panel.
>
> Planners of the symposium, "Homosexuality and Therapy: The Religious Dimension," originally slated for 2 to 5 p.m. Monday at the Washington Convention Center, at first ignored calls from some gays to cancel the event.
>
> But when its star panelist, the openly gay New Hampshire Episcopal Bishop V. Gene Robinson, dropped out last week, plans for the symposium collapsed amid an avalanche of criticism from gays.
>
> "It was a way to have a balanced discussion about religion and how it influences therapy," said David Scasta, a former APA president and a gay psychiatrist in charge of assembling the panel. "We wanted to talk rationally, calmly and respectfully to each other, but the external forces made it into a divisive debate it never intended to be."

It appears, however, that to "talk rationally, calmly and respectfully to each other" was not the goal of the gay activists:

> An April 24 article on www.gaycitynews.com called the event "junk science on stage" and "psychiatrists allow ex-gay end run." A Wednesday piece in the Washington Blade, a gay newspaper, said the panel could legitimize

"homophobic views."

So, even public *dialogue* is now off limits.

According to Scasta, the openly gay organizer of the cancelled event,

> This was supposed to reduce polarization, which has hurt the gay community. They are blocked into this bitchy battle and they are not progressing. They are not willing to do missionary work and talk to the enemy. They have to be willing to listen and change themselves.[123]

Rev. Dr. Albert Mohler, one of the scheduled participants, echoed these sentiments:

> It is clear which side of the argument [was] unwilling to show up for this conversation. It is a tragedy the APA cannot hold a conversation on a matter of this importance without facing such internal political pressure that it becomes impossible for this symposium to be held.[124]

So, this is where we have come to, and this is the current state of what is supposed to be rational, unbiased, scientific, inquiry. The pressure worked back in 1973, and it's still working today.[125]

But the political strong-arming gets worse. Don't stop reading now.

*Edinburgh University has banned copies of the Bible
from student dormitories after condemning the Christian Union for violating
its "equality and diversity policy" by claiming that "any sexual activity outside
heterosexual marriage is not God-ordained."*

Jonathan Luxmoore,
"The Dawkins Delusion: Britain's Crusading Atheist,"
Commonweal 134, April 20, 2007

*A Canadian professor has been fined two weeks pay
by a Nova Scotia university for telling a student that homosexuality is an
unnatural lifestyle. . . . Cape Breton University (CBU) fined veteran history
professor David Mullan $2,100 in response to two human rights complaints
filed by a homosexual student who coordinates the campus' Sexual Diversity
Office. The student took umbrage at two letters the professor had written
to his former Anglican bishop two years ago.*

Reported by Agape Press, July 26, 20062

*Ex-gay messages have no place in our nation's public schools.
A line has been drawn. There is no "other side" when you're talking
about lesbian, gay and bisexual students.*

Kevin Jennings, founder of GLSEN, *Washington Times*, July 27, 2004

*One reason I so dislike recent gay activism is that my
self-identification as a lesbian preceded Stonewall: I was the only openly gay
person at the Yale Graduate School (1968-72), a candor that was professionally
costly. That anyone with my aggressive and scandalous history
could be called "homophobic," as has repeatedly been done,
shows just how insanely Stalinist gay activism has become.*

Camille Paglia, *Vamps and Tramps*

14

Big Brother is Watching, and He Really Is Gay

T he two teenage girls were terrified, having spent eighteen days in jail before appearing in court with shackles on their ankles, charged with a felony hate crime. When the judge announced that they could return home until their sentence was passed – meaning, confined to home detention with electronic monitoring – the girls sobbed uncontrollably. "Prosecutors eventually dropped the felony hate-crime charge in exchange for a plea bargain, in which the girls pleaded guilty to lesser misdemeanor charges of disorderly conduct and resisting arrest (the girls fled the scene when a police officer arrived; they did not strike an officer)."³

They were eventually sentenced to one-year of probation, forty hours of community service, and ordered to write letters of apology to the arresting officer and to a boy who was offended by their actions. And what exactly was their crime? Prof. Robert Gagnon tells the story:

> In 2007 two 16-year old girls from Crystal Lake South High School (Ill.) were arrested on felony hate crime charges for distributing about 40 fliers on cars in the student parking lot of their high school. The fliers contained an anti-homosex slur (the media have not reported what precisely the slur was) and a photo of two boys kissing, one of whom was identified as a classmate. The fliers contained no threats of violence. One of the girls was apparently getting back at a boy with whom she had once been best friend.
> . . . The girls told the court that the whole matter was a joke that they took too far. State Attorney Louis Bianchi told the press that he still felt the hate crime charge was justified, while acknowledging that the plea bargain was fair for juveniles.⁴

And for this they were incarcerated for eighteen days in a juvenile detention center, shackled like dangerous criminals, and put on probation for one year.

To be sure, gay kids in school (along with kids perceived to be gay) have suffered more than enough harassment at the hands of their schoolmates, and to reiterate what we have said elsewhere in this book, there is no place for bullying and harassment in our schools. But in terms of the case at hand, the punishment hardly fits the crime – if it was really a crime at all.

According to some state officials, however, the girls most definitely committed a crime, and a hate crime at that:

> Assistant state's attorney for McHenry County, Thomas Carroll, commented: "You can be charged with a hate crime if you make a statement or take an action that inflicts injury or incites a breach of the peace based on a person's race, creed, gender, or perceived sexual orientation." Another assistant state's attorney, Robert Windon, said: "We do not feel this type of behavior is what the First Amendment protects." State's attorney Lou Bianchi insisted: "This is a classic case of the kind of conduct that the state legislature was directing the law against. This is what the legislators wanted to stop, this kind of activity."[5]

Does anyone think that Carroll, Windon, and Bianchi would have reacted like this if the case involved anti-Christian flyers that were put on cars as opposed to anti-gay flyers, making fun of the faith of a Christian young man (be it done in jest or otherwise)? But such is the climate today that one of the worst accusations that can be brought against you is that you are anti-gay.

THE CONSEQUENCES OF USING THE NEW "F-" WORD

Just think of the almost hysterical reaction that followed the revelation that actor Isaiah Washington, star of ABC's *Grey's Anatomy*, referred to (then-closeted) gay co-star T. R. Knight with what is now called "the f- word" (meaning, faggot) during a heated, on-set incident. He then compounded his transgression by actually pronouncing the forbidden word in a backstage interview with reporters at the Golden Globes' event, held on Monday night, January 15th, 2007: "No, I did not call T.R a faggot. Never happened, never happened."[6] Not only was he lying (apparently), but he actually mentioned the unmentionable word.

ABC was quick to express its outrage:

> "We are greatly dismayed that Mr. Washington chose to use such inappropriate language at the Golden Globes, language that he himself deemed 'unfortunate' in his previous public apology," the network said in a statement.
> "His actions are unacceptable and are being addressed,"

the statement concludes.[7]

Neil Giuliano, president of GLAAD (the Gay & Lesbian Alliance Against Defamation) referred to the situation as "deeply troubling" and stated that Washington's repeated use of the word was "inexcusable," asking for a meeting to discuss "the destructive impact of these kinds of anti-gay slurs."[8]

Then, on Thursday, January 18th, Washington came clean, expressing how deep his problems really were:

> In his apology Thursday, Washington acknowledged "repeating the word Monday night."
> "I apologize to T.R., my colleagues, the fans of the show and especially the lesbian and gay community for using a word that is unacceptable in any context or circumstance. I marred what should have been a perfect night for everyone who works on 'Grey's Anatomy.' I can neither defend nor explain my behavior. I can also no longer deny to myself that there are issues I obviously need to examine within my own soul, and I've asked for help."[9]

He actually went for professional counseling and rehabilitation. Despite his apology, however, and despite his efforts to make amends with the GLBT community – not to mention his prominent role in *Grey's Anatomy* – ABC fired him.[10]

To be sure, it is inexcusable to slur someone with a word that people find so offensive, just as it would be inexcusable for a white person to use "the n-word" in referring to a black person. It's the reaction here that is so extreme and is symptomatic of the larger, "Big Brother Is Gay Syndrome."

Simply stated, since when does using an insulting word in the midst of an angry argument call for an over-the-top apology like this: "I can . . . no longer deny to myself that there are issues I obviously need to examine within my own soul . . . ." Since when does it call for professional counseling (to understand why he used "the f- word," as opposed to getting help with anger management)? People say and do stupid things all the time, but when it comes to offending gays, a line of hyper-sensitivity has been crossed. (To repeat yet again: I understand why there is such sensitivity and I actively work to educate others about the struggles endured by the GLBT community. I am simply highlighting the extreme over-reaction to anything perceived as demeaning or offensive to gays.)

A DOUBLE STANDARD HERE?

But there's more. Within gay culture, "the f- word" has often been used in self-description, most famously in Larry Kramer's 1978 novel *Faggots*. Is one no longer allowed to refer to his book by name? (Apparently, Naomi Wolf didn't think so, beginning her Foreword to Kramer's 2005 book, *The Tragedy of Today's Gays*, with these words: "Of course, I had heard of *Faggots*, growing up as I did in San Francisco in the 1970's . . . .").[11]

In 1999, Michael Thomas Ford, author of *Alec Baldwin Doesn't Love Me: And Other Trials from My Queer Life*, wrote his follow-up book entitled *That's Mr. Faggot to You: Further Trials from My Queer Life*. The positive review in *Publisher's Weekly* began by saying: "Cranky, bemused and extremely funny, Ford . . . is brilliant even on potentially mundane topics like high school reunions ('Michael Thomas Ford is very proud to announce that he is still queer... [and] happier, more successful, and a great deal more attractive' than his former schoolmates') . . . ."[12]

Why wasn't *Publisher's Weekly* outraged by Ford's use of the forbidden word? Why could Ford use it so freely in 1999, but today, it can't even be uttered? And speaking of today, why was it OK for gay columnist Dan Savage to describe himself (and others of his ilk) as "radical sex-advice columnist faggots" on Keith Olbermann's TV show on January 4th, 2010?[13] How dare he utter that word, even if, as he later explained, he was talking about the way he was viewed by conservative Christians?[14] How could he be so glib? And was it right for him to turn the tables and, in a backhanded way, basically blame and malign Christians for his usage of the term?

Most importantly, let's say we all agree that the word "faggot" should not be used, especially in an insulting way. Certainly, I would think that any civil person would agree with dropping the word entirely as an insult or slur. Why, then, is it OK to bash and mock and ridicule others in the crudest, crassest, and cruelest ways – especially if they are religious conservatives – while it is now politically incorrect to say (even playfully) something like, "That's so gay"? It is common to see conservative women vilified with "the c- word" on gay websites – a word even more crass than "the f- word" – and yet rarely is a word of gay protest raised against this kind of invective.[15] Yet we who take respectful issue with gay activism are branded hypocrites.

On January 18, 2010, MSNBC's Keith Olbermann let loose against Massachusetts Republican candidate Scott Brown, stating, "In short, in Scott

Brown we have an irresponsible, homophobic, racist, reactionary, ex nude model, teabagging supporter of violence against women...".[16] This, to be sure, is more extreme than privately using "the f- word" in the heat of anger, and Olbermann did this on national TV. To add insult to injury, the next day he offered an apology – for leaving out the word "sexist" (along with failing to mention another derogatory story about Brown).[17] Did Olbermann lose his job over this? Was the outrage against him anywhere near as shrill as the outrage against Isaiah Washington? Why the glaring double standard?

And why is it acceptable for the GLBT community and its straight allies to bully their opponents if bullying is always wrong? As noted in a March 7, 2007, *Chicago Tribune* article, "Ellen Waltz, a Deerfield [IL] mother of eight, said the climate has changed so much that students who believe that homosexuality is immoral and violates their religious beliefs are now the ones being bullied."[18]

Isaiah Washington's *faux pa* cost him his job and blemished his career. The error of the two high-school girls almost cost them their freedom – and we have barely begun to scratch the surface of the seismic shift that is taking place today. But this is a story that has played itself out time and again: Those who have been oppressed, suffering humiliation and discrimination and violence, once they are liberated, become the oppressors. Those who had no rights and were powerless, once they are in power, quickly take away the rights of others. Who can forget Orwell's classic telling of this story in *Animal Farm*?[19]

To be sure, it is impossible to listen to the GLBT community without feeling the weight of the rejection, abuse, mockery, and even violence that many of them have suffered (and, all too often, continue to suffer) through their lives. They carry the wounds inflicted on them by cruel classmates, mean-spirited clergy, bigoted employers, and even well-intended but hardnosed parents. Rejection stings, sometimes to the point of hopelessness, despair, and suicide. If you are a caring, fair-minded person, the pain of the GLBT community must hurt you as well.

WHEN THE OPPRESSED BECOME THE OPPRESSORS

Unfortunately, as frequently happens, those who have been the most oppressed quickly turn the tables when they come into places of influence. As Paulo Freire bemoaned,

> . . . almost always, during the initial stage of the struggle,

the oppressed, instead of striving for liberation, tend themselves to become oppressors, or "sub-oppressors." The very structure of their thought has been conditioned by the contradictions of the concrete, existential situation by which they were shaped.[20]

As expressed concisely by jurist and author Marvin Frankel, "The powerless call out for tolerance. Achieving power, they may soon forget."[21]

Today, those who have come out of the closet are trying to put their ideological opponents into the closet; those preaching tolerance have become the most intolerant; those calling for inclusion are now the most exclusionary; those celebrating diversity demand absolute uniformity.[22]

In the words of conservative gay journalist Charles Winecoff,

Because gay is no longer taboo in America, the community has shifted its focus from supporting 'difference' to espousing a blanket Leftist agenda – *in essence, suppressing diversity* - and driving many of its own into a new (conservative) closet.[23]

College professors have felt the heat of this repressive new order; researchers and scientists have encountered its ire; ministers have found themselves muzzled; teachers have been intimidated; employees have lost their jobs; even parents have been told they cannot exercise their rights. Queer has become something to fear, and gay is beginning to rule the day. The tables have been turned – dramatically. Who would have imagined?

Do you think I'm blowing things out of proportion? Do you think it's impossible that a tiny minority can have such a dominating influence over the great majority? The facts speak for themselves.

FAITH ORGANIZATIONS ARE LOSING THEIR RIGHTS

An April 9, 2009 article in the (certainly not conservative) *Washington Post* documented how "Faith organizations and individuals who view homosexuality as sinful and refuse to provide services to gay people are losing a growing number of legal battles that they say are costing them their religious freedom."[24]

Correspondent Jacqueline L. Salmon cited these representative examples:

- A Christian photographer was forced by the New Mexico Civil Rights Commission to pay $6,637 in attorney's costs after she refused to photograph a gay couple's commitment ceremony.
- A psychologist in Georgia was fired after she declined for religious reasons to counsel a lesbian about her relationship.
- Christian fertility doctors in California who refused to artificially inseminate a lesbian patient were barred by the state Supreme Court from invoking their religious beliefs in refusing treatment.
- A Christian student group was not recognized at a University of California law school because it denies membership to anyone practicing sex outside of traditional marriage.[25]

So much for freedom of conscience!

The article ended with this telling quote from Marc Stern, general counsel for the American Jewish Congress: "When you have a change that is as dramatic as has happened in the last 10 to 15 years with regards to attitudes toward homosexuality, it's inevitable it's going to reverberate in dozens of places in the law that you're never going to be able to foresee."[26] In confirmation of this, Georgetown Law Professor Chai Feldblum, appointed by President Obama to serve on the U.S. Equal Employment Opportunity Commission, famously remarked that when push comes to shove, when religious liberty and sexual liberty conflict, "I'm having a hard time coming up with any case in which religious liberty should win."[27] In more technical terms, she wrote, "Protecting one group's identity liberty may, at times, require that we burden others' belief liberties."[28]

Writing in the *Washington Post* eighteen months later, political science professor Matthew J. Franck drew attention to other egregious cases, including:

At [a] midwestern state university, a department chairman demurs from a student organizer's request that his department promote an upcoming "LGBTQ" film festival on campus; he is denounced to his university's chancellor, who indicates that his e-mail to the student warrants inquiry by a "Hate and Bias Incident Response Team." . . .

On a left-wing Web site, a petition drive succeeds in pressuring Apple to drop an "app" from its iTunes store for the Manhattan Declaration, an ecumenical Christian statement whose nearly half-million signers are united in defense of the right to life, the tradition of conjugal marriage between man and woman, and the principles of religious liberty. The offense? The app is a "hate fest." Fewer than 8,000 people petition for the app to go; more than five times as many petition Apple for its reinstatement, so far to no avail.[29]

Not only did the incident with the Manhattan Declaration expose a glaring double standard within Apple (since numerous, sexually explicit gay apps have *not* been removed, including apps with information on gay bathhouses for anonymous sexual encounters, despite complaints regarding their offensive content), but it also exposed the mindset of gay activist groups (and their allies) that encouraged Apple to remove the Manhattan Declaration app: All opposing views must be silenced!

As expressed by the website that started the campaign to remove the app:

Let's send a strong message to Apple that supporting homophobia and efforts to restrict choice [meaning, the 'right' to abortion] is bad business.[30]

This was seconded by GLAAD (the Gay Lesbian Alliance Against Defamation):

Apple's action sent a powerful message that the company stands against intolerance. . . . Join GLAAD in thanking Apple for their action to remove the app and urging them to stay strong in the face of anti-gay activism.[31]

So, if you support the institution of marriage as we have known it from the beginning of human history and if you dare take issue with the goals of gay activism, prepare to be censored – or worse.

WHATEVER HAPPENED TO FREEDOM OF SPEECH?

Consider the case of Crystal Dixon, an African American woman who was formerly Associate Vice President of Human Resources at the University of Toledo. When Michael S. Miller, editor in chief of the *Toledo Free Press*, wrote an editorial in which he likened the "gays rights struggle" to "my black friends' struggles and my wheelchair-bound friends' struggles," Dixon took exception to this and penned an op-ed piece for the newspaper. She wrote:

> I respectfully submit a different perspective for Miller and Toledo Free Press readers to consider. … First, human beings, regardless of their choices in life, are of ultimate value to God and should be viewed the same by others. At the same time, one's personal choices lead to outcomes either positive or negative.
>
> As a black woman who happens to be an alumnus of the University of Toledo's Graduate School, an employee and business owner, I take great umbrage at the notion that those choosing the homosexual lifestyle are "civil rights victims." Here's why. I cannot wake up tomorrow and not be a black woman. I am genetically and biologically a black woman and very pleased to be so as my Creator intended. Daily, thousands of homosexuals make a life decision to leave the gay lifestyle evidenced by the growing population of PFOX (Parents and Friends of Ex Gays) and Exodus International just to name a few.[32]

She then cited statistics indicating the relatively high wages earned by gays and lesbians, especially when compared with the relatively low wages earned by black Americans, and also addressed what she believed to be God's intended natural and biological design for human sexuality, writing,

> [T]here are consequences for each of our choices, including those [which] violate God's divine order. It is base human nature to revolt and become indignant when the world, or even God Himself, disagrees with our choice that violates His divine order."[33]

And for writing these words, which expressed her strong religious convictions, not those of her employer (whom she did not mention), she was fired by the university. Really!

Just consider the absurdity of this situation. She had obviously worked hard over a number of years to rise to the important position she held. She apparently had a good, proven track record. So, even if she wrote something in her local newspaper that was, say, racially or religiously insensitive, one would think that she might be corrected or even disciplined, but not fired. The fact is, there was nothing intolerant or hateful with what she wrote, yet she was fired nonetheless. Her transgression was simple and, these days, unforgivable: She said that homosexuality was neither innate nor immutable, she differed with the comparison between homosexuality and skin color, and she did not equate today's "gay rights" movement with the black Civil Rights movement.

Even if some of her statements or statistics could be challenged (e.g., on the degree to which homosexuality is a choice, or on the numbers of those leaving homosexuality, or on the earning power of gays and lesbians), there was nothing in her words that could rightly be labeled hateful or intolerant – at least, that's what reason and common sense would say.

What, then, was the response of members of the GLBT community to her firing?[34] Alvin McEwen, a black, gay blogger who it quite antagonistic towards pro-family organizations and individuals,[35] had some misgivings about her dismissal, wishing there could have been some sort of compromise, but his conclusions were clear:

> I ... feel that the University had an obligation to investigate whether or not Dixon could do her job fairly in light of her comments.
>
> And as of right now, I agree with the decision to let her go. . . .
>
> But to those who will spin this case as one of "an attack on free speech," how would you feel if her comments had been against Christians, or Muslims, or any other groups; people whose interests she was hired to look after while they are students at the university.
>
> Ms. Dixon has a right to free speech, but that doesn't trump her responsibility to the students, whether or not they are gay. Their well-being takes precedent over everything.
>
> She is **not** the victim here.[36]

But how *could* she be the victim? She was "anti-gay"! And so, whatever happened to her was well-deserved. Perhaps Camille Paglia's comment (cited in the opening quotes of this chapter) speaking of "how insanely Stalinist gay activism has become," is making more sense to you now.

Not surprisingly, almost all of the 68 comments that followed McEwen's article agreed with Dixon's firing, typified by this one:

> The University of Toledo should be commended for terminating the employment of Crystal Dixon. Dixon is clearly a religious zealot and a bigot. She is unfit to hold any human resources position let alone serving as associate vice president for human resources of a large public university. [Links are then listed that allegedly support this claim.][37]

Presumably, one could be a gay zealot and be fit to hold an important human resources position, but if you are a religious zealot you are thereby a bigot, and obviously unfit to hold such a position.

According to someone named Thomas, posting on the award-winning, gay activist, JoeMyGod website,

> No one is entitled to a job. And if you run around spewing "values" that are diametrically opposed to those of your employer, it's pretty reasonable to expect to be fired. This is especially true if you spew bigoted debunked science and your employer is a university.[38]

Other comments responding to McEwen's article made clear that Christian conservatives would be quick to seize on this case:

> "She is not the victim here."

> But, within a week she will be the christianist right's new martyr-cum-tool.[39]

> Yep, the wingnuts certainly will frame this as a free speech case. They love to yell "free speech" in cases like this ... as though the freedom of [speech] meant speech without consequences for the things one says.

> In Ms. Dixon's case, her job was responsibility for ensuring the protection of the civil rights of glbt folks on campus. She was clear; she did not believe the glbt folks had any

civil rights worthy of protection. How could she accept pay for protecting those rights she did not believe they had? As a Christian, I would have thought she would have quit her job long ago rather than work under a lie. Oh well.

If it is true she was terminated, it was a fair decision.[40]

WAS CRYSTAL DIXON'S FIRING FAIR?

A fair decision? Really? In point of fact, Dixon's university job was not focused on "ensuring the protection of the civil rights of glbt folks on campus." Rather, her responsibilities included recruitment, hiring, benefits, compensation, labor relations, and training. Was she impaired from doing any of this with excellence because of the personal and religious views expressed in her editorial? Certainly not. She had worked in human resources for twenty-three years, and at no time was there ever a complaint against her in terms of unfair treatment of GLBT's. She advocated for equal employment for all, regardless of race, religion, political affiliation, disability, sexual orientation, or any number of other beliefs, practices, viewpoints, or genetic conditions, and she submitted to and supported the school's work policies. Even in her editorial, she stated clearly that "human beings, regardless of their choices in life, are of ultimate value to God and should be viewed the same by others."

Now, as a Christian, she would presumably believe that it would be better to follow Jesus than Muhammad, but that wouldn't imply that she would advocate for unfair treatment for a Muslim employee. Where is the connection? Conversely, a fair-minded Muslim who felt that adherence to the Koran was God's way could serve in a human resources position as well. And as far as saying that "gay rights" were not the same as the Civil Rights movement, she was saying what many African Americans firmly believe. (To quote a letter to the editor of the *Orange County Register*: "I am not homophobic; I do not fear homosexuals, I just wish they would stop attempting to hijack the pain, deaths, suffering and struggles of the African American people in this country.")[41] She was also stating something that was factually true.

As Prof. Gagnon explained in his open letter to university president Lloyd Jacobs:

> Ms. Dixon is absolutely right that sexual orientation is not akin to race or sex. Unlike a homosexual orientation, race and sex are 100% congenitally predetermined, cannot

be fundamentally changed in their essence by cultural influences, and are not a primary or direct desire for behavior that is incompatible with embodied structures.[42]

So how does her belief that skin color is not the same as homosexuality impinge on her ability to do her job? It clearly does not, unless, at the University of Toledo, one is not allowed even to question the sacred cows of gay correctness – and that was clearly the case. The statement of President Jacobs, says it all:

"Her comments do not accord with the values of the University of Toledo. It is necessary, therefore, for me to repudiate much of her writing," he said.

"Our Spectrum student group created the Safe Places Program to 'invite faculty, staff and graduate assistants and resident advisers to open their space as a Safe Place for Lesbian, Gay, Bisexual, Transgender, Queer, and Questioning [LGBATQ] individuals.' I took this action because I believe it to be entirely consistent with the values system of the university. Indeed, there is a Safe Places sticker on the door of the president's office at the University of Toledo," Jacobs said.

"We will be taking certain internal actions in this instance to more fully align our utterances and actions with this value system," he said.[43]

Big Brother is definitely watching, and he most definitely is gay. If you work for the university, your utterances and actions must mimic the standard gay mantras or you'll soon find yourself out of a job.

THE INTOLERANCE OF "DIVERSITY"

Did I already say that "a queer new order rules the day?" Well, this seems to be a good place to repeat it. Certain things simply cannot be questioned, and yet this groupthink is being carried out in the name of diversity and inclusion and tolerance. (Should we be the least bit surprised that the "President's Council on Diversity" is one of the resources listed on the university's LGBT Initiatives page?)[44]

And who is this "Spectrum student group" to which President

Jacobs made reference? According to their own description, "This student organization represents, advocates for and promotes a positive environment for the gay, lesbian, bisexual, transgender, intersex, queer, questioning, same-gender-loving, two-spirit and straight ally community at UT."[45]

So, the president of the University of Toledo took great exception to the statements expressed by Crystal Dixon, statements which doubtless represent the views of tens of millions of civil-minded Americans, choosing instead to show his solidarity with a group that advocates for cross-dressing, "same-gender-loving," and (Native American) "two-spirit" ideologies, among other queer things listed. This is now the mindset of many an American university today. Tolerance is a one way, very gay street.

But there's more. According to the Spectrum Constitution:

> The purpose of Spectrum is to create a positive, supportive environment for all gay, lesbian, bisexual, transgender, questioning and ally students at the University of Toledo. Spectrum will strive to promote awareness through social and political activism of the contributions of all queer people locally, nationally, and internationally, and to encourage campus and community acceptance through educational outreach.[46]

So, Spectrum – and by extension, President Jacobs and the University of Toledo – supports "social and political activism" that will promote awareness "of the contributions of all queer people locally, nationally, and internationally," and strives to have a campus atmosphere where everyone can freely explore and discover and express their queer-related sexualities. But the moment a faithful employee, writing as a private citizen, dares to say that homosexuality is not immutable or that homosexual feelings are not the same as skin color or that gays, in general, earn far more than blacks, or that homosexuality is not simply an acceptable equivalent to heterosexuality, there is but one recourse: termination![47]

The story really does read like science fiction, like a very queer *1984*, but it's not, and happenings like this are not uncommon, be it on university campuses (and other educational institutions, right down to nursery schools), in places of business, in the political world, in the media, or in the society as a whole. Free speech *is* being muzzled, freedom of conscience *is* being removed, and freedom of religion *is* being threatened – and I write this as an observer of what has already happened rather than as some kind of conspiratorial, sky-is-falling, alarmist.

It is with good reason that Gagnon began his open letter to President Jacobs by saying,

> I have read of your action in connection with Ms. Crystal Dixon, Associate Vice President of Human Resources at the University of Toledo. Your suspension of Ms. Dixon for rejecting an equation of homosexuality with ethnicity constitutes, in my view, a gross injustice and an expression of the very intolerance that you claim to abhor. It is also predicated on a lack of knowledge and, as such, an abundance of prejudice.[48]

I have found it interesting to observe a subtle but clear progression of attitude over the last few years. Initially, those I interacted with in the GLBT community, along with their straight allies, assured me that things like Dixon's firing would never happen, that nobody was trying to put conservative religious people in the closet. Then, as the evidence became clear that these things really were happening, more and more of these same people began to say, "You bigots deserve to be put into the closet!"

Consider one of the comments from a gay website, cited above, with reference to the Crystal Dixon firing, where it was noted that some people thought that "freedom of [speech] meant speech without consequences for the things one says." The real question is, Why should there be job-related consequences for taking respectful issue with the positions of gay activism? Have all gay axioms and positions been proven to be indisputably and irrefutably true? If not, why is it forbidden to question or disagree?

THE SOUTHERN POVERTY LAW CENTER DEBUNKS ITSELF

Well, according to the (once-highly-respected) Southern Poverty Law Center (SPLC), it *is* forbidden to question or disagree with standard gay axioms. Not only so, but to do so is to be guilty (officially!) of hate speech and, if it is a group or organization that dares to differ with the standard gay line, then the SPLC will classify that group as a hate (or, anti-gay) group.

A recent SPLC Intelligence Report (Winter 2010, Issue Number: 140), included an article authored by Evelyn Schlatter and Robert Steinback entitled "10 Anti-Gay Myths Debunked," purporting to give "the truth behind the propaganda."[49] In reality, the article is so poorly documented and weekly reasoned that it is actually a work of gay-slanted propaganda itself. Yet according to a November, 2010 press release, the SPLC is listing organizations as hate groups

> *based on their propagation of known falsehoods* — claims about LGBT people that have been thoroughly discredited by scientific authorities — and repeated, groundless name-calling," claiming that these groups continue "to pump out demonizing propaganda aimed at homosexuals and other sexual minorities.[50]

Let me emphasize those words again: "based on their propagation of known falsehoods," one of which is that "No one is born a homosexual." Yes, if you make the claim that "No one is born homosexual" – a claim seconded by the clear majority of scientific researchers (see above, Chapter Six) – you are propagating known falsehoods and pumping out demonizing propaganda. And the SPLC really means this! Worse still, some people will even take them seriously.

And what is the "truth behind the propaganda" offered by the SPLC to refute the demonizing myth that "No one is born homosexual"? It is this:

> The American Psychological Association (APA) acknowledges that despite much research into the possible genetic, hormonal, social and cultural influences on sexual orientation, no evidence has emerged that would allow scientists to pinpoint the precise causes of sexual orientation. Still, the APA concludes that "most people experience little or no sense of choice about their sexual orientation."[51]

In other words, we still don't know what causes homosexuality, but if you say that no one is born homosexual, despite the fact that we can't offer proof that anyone *is* born homosexual, you are spreading destructive myths and demonizing propaganda and you are thereby deemed to be a hate (or, anti-gay) group. How utterly ludicrous – but I remind you again: Some people actually take the SPLC's listings seriously. Rather than debunking anti-gay myths, the SPLC has really debunked itself.[52]

EXPOSING THE DOUBLE STANDARD

Returning to Crystal Dixon's dismissal, what would have happened if she had written an editorial defending same-sex marriage and speaking against alleged Christian bigotry toward gays? And what if she had written this as an openly lesbian woman? Can anyone imagine that she would have been fired for doing *that*? Can anyone imagine that the university would have decided that she was not qualified to care for her Christian employees? The thought of it is totally laughable. So much for free speech having consequences!

"But," I can hear a reader protest, "you're missing the point again. We're talking about fairness and equality and justice. When you stand against those foundational, American values, of course you will be opposed, and of course there will be consequences."

Actually, the objection proves the point. In other words, from the GLBT perspective, there *is* no other side, no valid, moral reason to object to same-sex marriage, no valid, moral reason to deny the equation of skin color with sexual orientation, no valid, moral reason to say that it's best for a child to be raised by a mom and a dad – just to mention a few of the most volatile issues. To quote President Obama's Safe School Czar, Kevin Jennings, again, "Ex-gay messages have no place in our nation's public schools. A line has been drawn. There is no 'other side' when you're talking about lesbian, gay and bisexual students."[53] A line most certainly has been drawn, and the sooner we realize it, the better.

Remember: We're not talking about whether a qualified lesbian student should be allowed entry into a graduate school program or whether a gay man should be allowed to buy a house in your neighborhood. We're talking about things like whether an employee, when asked pointedly about his views on homosexuality, is allowed to say to his lesbian supervisor, "According to my faith, I don't agree with it," without being fired. We're talking about whether a pastor is allowed to write an editorial in a local newspaper expressing his differences with gay activism without being fined and banned for life from speaking against homosexuality. We're talking about whether a graduate school student in counseling is allowed to follow her professor's suggestion – and her professional ethical dictates – and request that a homosexual counselee be referred to another counselor who would affirm his homosexuality, without being kicked out of the program.

You might say, "But those things surely aren't happening. They're obviously figments of the very fertile imagination of the religious right."

Check again, my friend. Each of these situations – which could easily be multiplied – took place in the United States and Canada within the last few years. Let's take a look at them one at a time.

ANTI-RELIGIOUS DISCRIMINATION IN THE WORKPLACE

According to Carl Michael, reporting on November 2, 2009:

> A Massachusetts man has been fired from his sales position at the Logan Airport branch in Boston of Brookstone allegedly for telling a female manager that his Christian faith says homosexuality is wrong.
>
> Peter Vadala was fired, and the company says he violated a tolerance policy. But Vadala reports his dismissal came because he expressed his Christian view of homosexuality after a female manager made repeated references, as she approached him four times during work hours, to her plans to marry her lesbian partner.
>
> "At the start of the day, she told me she was getting married. I told her 'Congratulations,' and asked, 'Where's he taking you on your honeymoon?'" Vadala said.
>
> "She replied that her partner was a 'she,'" he continued, "So I immediately tried to change the subject.
>
> "I think she knew I was uncomfortable talking about it," he continued. "But, she brought it up to me three more times during the day.
>
> "After the fourth time she told me about her plan to marry her partner, I told her, 'I think homosexuality is bad stuff,'" Vadala said.
>
> "That's what I said. I wasn't rude about it and I didn't act disrespectfully to her," he said. "All the woman said to me as she left the store was, 'Human Resources buddy. You keep your opinions to yourself!'"[54]

According to a video interview provided by Vadala, he was trying to avoid the subject since he didn't feel that such controversial subjects should be brought up in the workplace, but ultimately, after being approached about his supervisor's same-sex marriage plans, he politely expressed his views.[55] For this he was fired – and in the opinion of gay blogger Timothy Kincaid, Vadala deserved to be fired.

According to Kincaid, this was Vidala's perpsective, as expressed during his interview:

> He sees "that type of behavior" (her engagement) as immoral. He believes that controversial issues (her engagement) have no place in the workplace, particularly in Boston. And he is entitled to never have to be exposed in the workplace to ideas that contadict [sic] his opinions. To exist as a lesbian – and not keep it a secret – is to harass Vidala. And he was only expressing his offense when they retaliated against him. Unfairly.[56]

Or is Kincaid missing something? Perhaps this is the more accurate perspective: First, there was no reason for this supervisor to repeatedly bring up her "marriage" plans to this worker, especially when his body language indicated that he was uncomfortable with the subject. Isn't this a form or harassment? Second, if it was fine for her to share her views with him, based on her outlook on life, why wasn't it fine for him to share his views with her, based on his outlook on life? Why was her speech protected but not his? Third, in the video, Vidala expressed his overall thoughts on Christianity and homosexuality, thoughts which he did not articulate in the workplace. Why should he be fired for beliefs he held outside of the workplace, unless, of course, one's *thoughts* can be on trial these days as well?[57]

For Kincaid, however, this case once again exposes the bigotry of the conservative right:

> The anti-gay activist[s] will champion Vidala, just as they do anyone who is "martyred to the homosexual agenda." He will be Example A of what will happen if your state allows gay citizens to have the same rights as heterosexual citizens: religious freedom will suffer!!
>
> But they will not be telling the truth; Vidala did not suffer for his beliefs.
>
> Peter Vidala was not fired because he disapproved of homosexuality; rather, he was fired because [he] couldn't

care less about the best interests of his employer. He selfishly decided that he didn't have to be civil at work, he simply had to tell his superior that her life was deviant and immoral. It's his Christian duty.

And, besides, why should he be punished? She needed it, you know.[58]

Would a corporate "sigh" be appropriate here? "Vidala did not suffer for his beliefs"? Really now, is there no ability for gay activists to see the other side of things, no ability to realize just how twisted the standards have become, no ability to recognize that there was incivility towards Vidala, no ability to understand that an employee is not bound by law to affirm or celebrate the sexual orientation of a co-worker or employer?

Let's say the supervisor was heterosexual and had mentioned several times to Vidala that she was looking forward to sleeping with her boyfriend that weekend and, after the fourth time of being told the same story, he replied, "You know, I think that sex outside of wedlock is bad stuff." Would he have been fired? Would this have been promptly (and gleefully) reported to Human Resources? What if the supervisor was a man involved in a polyamorous relationship and mentioned repeatedly through the day that he was really enjoying his open, loving relationship with three other women? If Vidala finally expressed that, in his view, this was "bad stuff," would he have been terminated?

These questions, of course, are speculative (although the answers, I believe, are self-evident). What is certain is that gay activists feel that the firings of Peter Vidala and Crystal Dixon were fair and just. That is to say, "You are not martyrs. You are bigots, and bigots belong in the closet!"

ANTI-RELIGIOUS DISCRIMINATION IN CANADA

Turning our attention now to Canada, Dr. Chris Kempling, himself a victim of unfair treatment there, observed,

It has become increasingly difficult to speak publicly about [sexual] orientation change or make any valid criticism of homosexual behavior in Canada. Homosexual activists have been quite successful in pressing their agenda to normalize their lifestyle and have worked vigorously to silence opponents.[59]

Specifically, Robert Gagnon notes that: "...among those fined thousands of dollars and threatened with imprisonment for repeat offenses of speech are:

Father Alphonse de Valk and *Catholic Insight Magazine* for speaking against homosexual behavior.

Bill Whatcott, a Catholic activist, for producing pamphlets that called homosexual practice immoral (Whatcott was also "banned for life" from criticizing homosexuality).
Stephen Boisson, a pastor, for a letter to a newspaper denouncing homosexual practice as immoral (also ordered to desist from expressing his views on homosexual practice in any public forum. ...).[60]

Let's focus on the case of Rev. Stephen Boisson, formerly Central Alberta Chairman of the Concerned Christian Coalition. In 2002, he wrote a strongly-worded letter to a local newspaper in which he spoke against homosexuality and homosexual activism. Boisson supplies the background to his letter:

At the time this letter was published, homosexual marriage, homosexual adoption, gay books being added to the public school curriculum etc. were topics of debate across Canada. In addition, the [eventual] complainant against me, Darren Lund, had invited a pro-homosexual minister into the public school where he taught (in my city) to teach the pro-homosexual interpretation of the Bible. He offered no alternate theological opinion to these impressionable young minds.[61]

This is how the letter was published in the *Red Deer Advocate*, June 17, 2002:

Homosexual Agenda Wicked –
Disclaimer: I do not encourage, condone, support or approve of ANY violent act towards ANY individual(s) unless in self-defence or the defence of the innocent.
The following is not intended for those who are

suffering from an unwanted sexual identity crisis. For you, I have understanding, care, compassion and tolerance. I sympathize with you and offer you my love and fellowship. I prayerfully beseech you to seek help, and I assure you that your present enslavement to homosexuality can be remedied. Many outspoken, former homosexuals are free today.

Instead, this is aimed precisely at every individual that in any way supports the homosexual machine that has been mercilessly gaining ground in our society since the 1960s. I cannot pity you any longer and remain inactive. You have caused far too much damage.[62]

He stated that, "My banner has now been raised and war has been declared so as to defend the precious sanctity of our innocent children and youth, that you so eagerly toil, day and night, to consume." And, he added, "Know this, we will defeat you, then heal the damage that you have caused."

He claimed that, "From kindergarten class on, our children, your grandchildren are being strategically targeted, psychologically abused and brainwashed by homosexual and pro-homosexual educators." Specifically, he charged that "children as young as five and six years of age are being subjected to psychologically and physiologically damaging pro-homosexual literature and guidance in the public school system; all under the fraudulent guise of equal rights. Your children are being warped into believing that same-sex families are acceptable; that men kissing men is appropriate." And, "Your teenagers are being instructed on how to perform so-called safe same gender oral and anal sex and at the same time being told that it is normal, natural and even productive. Will your child be the next victim that tests homosexuality positive?"

And he raised an urgent warning,

Come on people, wake up! It's time to stand together and take whatever steps are necessary to reverse the wickedness that our lethargy has authorized to spawn. Where homosexuality flourishes, all manner of wickedness abounds.... Don't allow yourself to be deceived any longer. These activists are not morally upright citizens, concerned about the best interests of our society. They are perverse, self-centered and morally deprived individuals who are spreading their psychological disease into every area of our lives. Homosexual rights activists and those that defend them, are just as immoral as the pedophiles, drug dealers and pimps that plague our communities.[63]

His closing words were passionate: "It's time to start taking back what the enemy has taken from you. The safety and future of our children is at stake."

What did you think of Boisson's letter? Some of you might nod your heads in total agreement, affirming every sentence of his letter and even pointing to this very book as evidence of his charges. Others might shake your heads in absolute disbelief, appalled (but not surprised) that someone claiming to be a reverend could utter such hate-filled, bigoted, homophobic words. But either way, was Boisson guilty of a crime? Haven't equally spirited, strongly opinionated letters been published for years in North American newspapers?

One gay blogger felt that Boisson clearly crossed a line, explaining,

I'm not sure how easily understood this is unless you are one of the people threatened by the letter, but being called "as immoral as pedophiles, drug dealers and pimps" and then having a call to action issued against you as open-ended as "take whatever steps are necessary to reverse the wickedness [of the] homosexual machine" is scary.[64]

Certainly, I can see how Boisson's letter would raise serious concerns for Canadian gays and lesbians, despite his loud and clear disclaimer that he strongly opposed all acts of violence (aside from self-defense or defending the innocent). And I for one would have chosen different words in raising my concerns. But once again, the question is: Did Boisson commit a crime?

Darren Lund, the aforementioned local teacher who had a pro-gay minister address his schoolchildren (and who is now a professor at the University of Calgary), felt that a crime had been committed, filing a complaint. Boisson was eventually found guilty by the Alberta Human Rights Tribunal on November 30, 2007. According to the Tribunal, Boisson's letter violated the *Alberta Human Rights, Citizenship, and Multiculturalism Act*, which read in part:

> No person shall publish ... or cause to be published ... before
> the public any statement ... that ... is likely to expose a person
> or a class of persons to hatred or contempt because of the
> sexual orientation ... of that person or class of persons.[65]

The details of the verdict, announced May 30, 2008, were chilling:

> Mr. Boissoin and The Concerned Christian Coalition
> Inc. shall cease publishing in newspapers, by e-mail, on
> the radio, in public speeches, or on the Internet, in future,
> disparaging remarks about gays and homosexuals. Further,
> they shall not and are prohibited from making disparaging
> remarks in the future about ... Lund or ... Lund's witnesses
> relating to their involvement in this complaint. Further, all
> disparaging remarks versus homosexuals are directed to be
> removed from current Web sites and publications of Mr.
> Boissoin and The Concerned Christian Coalition Inc. ...
> [Fines were doled out as well.][66]

In other words, Rev. Boisson, you shall herewith be silenced and
absolutely forbidden from saying a single word that reflects negatively on the
GLBT community, regardless of what the Bible says and regardless of your
Christian convictions. As noted by Eugene Volokh, a gay-friendly, free speech
expert and Professor of Law at UCLA,

> This is a breathtakingly broad prohibition, which extends
> far beyond the terms of the (already troubling) statute.
> Boissoin and his group aren't allowed to saying anything
> "disparaging" about homosexuals, which presumably would
> even extend to statements such as "homosexuals are acting
> sinfully" or "The Bible, which I believe should be our moral
> guide, condemns homosexuality."[67]

So extreme was the ruling that even the JoeMyGod website took
exception:

> What Boissoin and his ilk say is obviously repugnant and
> should be loudly denounced. But the conservative Christian

group Real Women Of Canada is right when they say, "People in a democracy should be able to have an opinion on homosexuality or on gardening or on anything without being charged or paying money out to protect oneself."[68]

What do you know! JoeMyGod and I find something on which we agree. Thankfully, after further legal efforts on behalf of Boisson (costing thousands of dollars), on December 3, 2009, the Court of Queen's Bench of Alberta overturned the ruling of the Alberta Human Rights Commission, stating:

> That the language of [Stephen Boisson's letter] may be jarring, offensive, bewildering, puerile, nonsensical and insulting may be of little doubt, but the language does not go so far as to fall within the prohibited status of "hate" or "contempt."[69]

Yes, this is one small victory for freedom of speech and religion (albeit in the most insulting and belittling terms), but it goes squarely *against* the strong Big Brother mentality that has been dominating Canada in recent years. Little did Boisson imagine that his letter would spark a backlash that hung over him for *seven years* of his life.

As reported in the Canadian Press:

> The Canadian Constitution Foundation, a free-speech advocacy group, issued a news release saying it was pleased with Thursday's ruling. "Unfortunately, the law that was used against Rev. Boissoin to subject him to expensive and stressful legal proceedings for more than seven years is still on the books," said executive director John Carpay.
>
> That law — the Alberta Human Rights, Citizenship and Multiculturalism Act — says no one can publish a statement that is likely "to expose a person or a class of persons to hatred or contempt" for reasons including sexual orientation.
>
> "In spite of today's court ruling, Albertans need to continue to exercise extreme caution when speaking about public policy issues, lest they offend someone who then files

a human rights complaint," said Carpay. "No citizen is safe from being subjected to a taxpayer-funded prosecution for having spoken or written something that a fellow citizen finds offensive."

Many other cases from Canada could be cited, dating back well over a decade, but one more will suffice. In 1997, Hugh Owens, after being grieved over public displays that he witnessed during Homosexual Pride Week in Regina, Saskatchewan, placed an advertisement in the local newspaper, simply listing Scripture references dealing with homosexual behavior – the verses themselves were not even printed – next to an equal sign and a picture of two men holding hands, encircled by the universal sign for "no" (i.e., a circle with a slash through it). Three gay men filed a complaint and Owens was found guilty by the court in June, 1997 and ordered to pay a fine of $1500 to each of the men. According to the ruling, and following the Human Rights Code, the combination of the "no" sign and the Scripture references were deemed hate speech.[70] It was not until 2006 – *nine years* after the ad was published and *nine years* after the initial decision against Owens was rendered – that the Court of Appeals ruled in his favor.[71]

BIG BROTHER RAISES HIS HEAD IN QUÉBEC

Perhaps this can be called "free speech with a price" – and quite a hefty price at that. And things might only be getting worse in Canada. As reported on a Québec government website, "On December 11, 2009, the Minister of Justice, Attorney General of Québec and minister responsible *for the fight against homophobia*, Kathleen Weil, released the first-ever Québec policy against homophobia."[72]

According to Attorney General Weil:

> Over the last thirty years, Quebec has introduced a range of legislative measures leading to recognition for the legal equality of the sexual minorities. Despite this fact, full social acceptance for sexual diversity has yet to be achieved.... As the minister responsible for the fight against homophobia, I am proud to present the **Quebec Policy against Homophobia.** It relies on the participation of all institutions, and all Quebecers, to create a society free of prejudice with regard to sexual diversity. This is a key

issue, since it involves the right of all individuals to achieve their potential and participate fully in all aspects of life in society, whatever their sexual orientation or identity.[73]

This does not bode well for those who do not endorse all sexual orientations and behaviors and who are now, de facto, branded "homophobes," people whom the government is determined to fight against. In fact, if the government has its way, alleged homophobes will be fought against by the nation as a whole, as the new policy states that it is "the responsibility and commitment of all institutional and social players, and of the general public, to combat homophobia."[74] If you are perceived to be a homophobe, Big Brother is coming your way. (Note that the term "homophobe" and its variants occur *234 times* in the thirty-five page document.)[75]

Of specific concern is the policy's targeting of "heterosexism," defined there as,

> Affirmation of heterosexuality as a social norm or the highest form of sexual orientation; social practice that conceals the diversity of sexual orientations and identities in everyday representations, social relations and social institutions, in particular by taking for granted that all people are heterosexual.[76]

So, the government of Québec is calling on all its citizens, "whether in terms of largescale measures or simple day-to-day actions,"[77] to combat the idea that heterosexuality is "a social norm or the highest form of sexual orientation." That is saying something. Yes, it is now "homophobic" to say that male-female relationships and sexual unions, which are practiced by roughly 97% of the population and are the natural means of human procreation, are the social norm.

As acutely observed by Professor Douglas Farrow:

> Only when we pause to take this in – the Government of Québec has rejected heterosexuality as a social norm! – does the full scope of this absurd war begin to appear. Québec society, like every other society in the world, has been built on heterosexuality as the social norm. Québec citizens, like citizens of every other society in the world,

are the product of parents and grandparents and great-grandparents who all took heterosexuality as the social norm. Every native-born Québecer, and every immigrant too, knows that his or her own origins are heterosexual. But the Government of Québec, giving a mind-boggling twist to the doctrine of original sin, has declared all the implicit and explicit "heterosexism" that is built into these undeniable facts an enemy of the state. In its breathtaking stupidity it has declared war, not only on its own citizenry, but on nature itself.[78]

As for the implications of the bill war on "homophobia," Farrow states:

. . . there can be no obscuring the fact that the Québec policy against homophobia is an official endorsement of – indeed, the assumption of full responsibility for – the activist agenda of so-called LGBT groups. As such, it is also a declaration of war by the Charest government on all groups and citizens who oppose that agenda. That this war must be fought on a broad front is not denied:

Some widely held beliefs about sexual minority members are still common in Québec. For example, it is still possible to hear people say that homosexuality is an illness, morally wrong or a form of deviant behaviour, and that people choose their sexual orientation. These beliefs, often instilled in the past, tend to marginalize sexual minority groups and prevent full recognition of their social equality.[79]

So, the government of Québec is now at war with anyone who feels that homosexuality is an illness or morally wrong or deviant or in any way chosen, and it will use all of its power to eradicate such thinking. Big Brother would be proud! In fact, some of the bill's language could have been written by the Thought Police themselves:

The fourth guideline—Ensure a concerted approach—reflects the government's intention to take the lead in the fight against homophobia, and to rally all players in society. Systemic investigations must be one of the actions given priority. They allow an analysis of the individual and institutional practices, decisions and behaviour patterns that have a discriminatory effect on a given group. Investigations of this kind, discrimination testing and an ongoing scan of concepts and tools relating to homophobia against women and men will improve the documentation of the current situation of sexual minority members.[80]

This is positively chilling. The entire society is being rallied together in a systematic inquisition to rid society of "homophobia" and "heterosexism."

So disturbing was the bill that it caught the attention of CultureWatch blogger Bill Muehlenberg in Australia, inspiring him to write an article entitled, "Heterosexuality: The New Hate Crime." He commented:

Even if only a fraction of [what is written in the bill] is true, this is scary as all get out. This matches anything envisaged by Aldous Huxley, George Orwell, and other fiction writers warning of future totalistic regimes. This is mind moulding at its worst.

Imagine that! Anyone who even affirms that homosexuality is in anyway other than absolutory hunky dory must be punished and re-educated. This is Big Brother at its worst. And get this: even to suggest that homosexuality is a choice will bring on the wrath of the state thought police. But what about the many homosexuals themselves who have suggested that choice plays an important role in their lifestyle? Will they be punished as well?[81]

According to Québec's premier, Jean Charest, after more than thirty years of work, "we can proudly state that we have achieved full legal equality for the sexual minorities, whether lesbian, gay, bisexual, transsexual or transgender."[82] That, however, was apparently not enough: Every manifestation of alleged homophobia – including that foul concept called heterosexism – must be eradicated. Heterosexists of Québec, beware. It is with good reason that Farrow stated in a footnote to his article,

It goes without saying that the views expressed here are strictly my own; whether it goes without saying that I am still a free citizen with a right and – on a subject of such importance – a duty to speak my mind, we shall see.[83]

ANTI-RELIGIOUS DISCRIMINATION IN A UNIVERSITY'S COUNSELING PROGRAM

And what about the last example I cited above, namely, that of a graduate school student in counseling who was kicked out of school because, although willing to counsel a gay man, she was not willing to affirm his homosexuality? The case involves another African American woman, Julea Ward, who was expelled from Eastern Michigan University on March 12, 2009 after refusing to renounce her beliefs at a meeting that can best be described as a school tribunal (or perhaps "inquisition" would be a better word?).

As reported by the Alliance Defense Fund Center for Academic Freedom, their attorneys

filed a lawsuit against Eastern Michigan University Thursday [April 2, 2009] after school officials dismissed a student from the school's counseling program for not affirming homosexual behavior as morally acceptable. The school dismissed Julea Ward from the program because she would not agree prior to a counseling session to affirm a client's homosexual behavior and would not retract her stance in subsequent disciplinary proceedings.[84]

David French, senior attorney with the ADF, stated,

Christian students shouldn't be penalized for holding to their beliefs. When a public university has a prerequisite of affirming homosexual behavior as morally good in order to obtain a degree, the school is stepping over the legal line. Julea did the responsible thing and followed her supervising professor's advice to have the client referred to a counselor who did not have a conscience issue with the very matter to be discussed in counseling. She would have gladly counseled the client if the subject had been nearly any other matter.[85]

What makes this case all the more galling is that Ward had asked her supervising professor for advice in terms of how to handle the situation – she was happy to counsel the gay man but not to affirm his homosexual relationships – and was advised, based on professional ethical standards, to refer the client to another counselor. But she crossed that forbidden line, since "EMU requires students in its program to affirm or validate homosexual behavior within the context of a counseling relationship and prohibits students from advising clients that they can change their homosexual behavior."[86]

But it gets worse still. Listen to this disturbing report from the ADF:

> EMU initiated its disciplinary process against Ward and informed her that the only way she could stay in the graduate school counseling program would be if she agreed to undergo a "remediation" program. Its purpose would be to help Ward "see the error of her ways" and change her "belief system" as it relates to counseling about homosexual relationships, conforming her beliefs to be consistent with the university's views. When Ward did not agree with the conditions, she was given the options of either voluntarily leaving the program or asking for a formal review hearing.[87]

At the risk of overkill, I assure you that your eyes are not playing games with you. In order to remain in the counseling program she needed to undergo a "remediation program," needed to "see the error of her ways," and needed to change her "belief system." In other words, in order to graduate with a counseling degree from Eastern Michigan University, she needed to repudiate her Christian beliefs, and we're not talking about believing that witches should be burned at the stake or that homosexuals should be drawn and quartered. We're talking about being unable to affirm someone's same-sex relationship. According to EMU, that wasn't just academic heresy, that was academic suicide.

Rather than leave the program voluntarily (which, in my humble opinion, would have been complete capitulation to injustice and intolerance),

> Ward chose the hearing, during which EMU faculty denigrated her Christian views and asked several inappropriate and intrusive questions about her religious beliefs. The hearing committee dismissed her from the

counseling program on March 12. Ward appealed the decision to the dean of the College of Education, who upheld the dismissal on March 26.[88]

So, university faculty members were free to denigrate this woman's religious beliefs and ultimately kick her out of the program simply because her religious convictions – which were never once expressed in mean-spirited or bigoted terms – did not allow her to affirm a client's homosexual relationship. (Again, she was perfectly willing to counsel the client without affirming that relationship, and she simply followed her professor's advice that the client be referred to another counselor.)

This is outrageous, plain and simple, and it is for good reason that, "Lawmakers in Michigan are preparing to call on the carpet leaders of taxpayer-supported universities across the state" because of the Julea Ward case.[89] As of July 28, 2010, however, things are not looking good, as a federal judge ruled *against* Ward and in favor of the university. This prompted ADF attorney Jeremy Tedesco to warn,

> Public universities are imposing the ideological stances of private groups on their students," he said. "If you don't comply, you will be kicked out. It's scary stuff and it's not a difficult thing to see what's coming down the pike.[90]

The ADF is appealing the ruling, but be assured: Big Brother is getting more entrenched by the day.[91]

ANTI-RELIGIOUS DISCRIMINATION ON THE COLLEGE CAMPUS

Perhaps even more unsettling was the case of Emily Brooker, although this one had a more positive outcome. While a freshman at Missouri State University,

> one of Emily's professors had directed her students to go out into the community, find a public place, and act out some homosexual behavior. Hold hands with a classmate of the same gender, or kiss them, or whatever, and see how other people react to what you're doing. Write up your experiences, and turn them in for your grade.[92]

As a conservative Christian, Emily was stunned by the assignment, but she took the easy way out, writing a fictional paper that she knew would please her professor and earning an "A" for her work. But she knew she had missed an opportunity to speak up for what was right.

Three years later, in the last semester of her senior year and just a few weeks before graduation, another of Emily's professors "commissioned his students to write letters to the Missouri legislature advocating foster care and adoption rights for same-sex couples." Yes, they were *required* to write these letters, regardless of their personal views.

> During a lull in the class, Emily respectfully approached the professor and told him she couldn't do what he asked, offering to do another assignment, or even everything involved in this one – short of actually signing and sending the letter.
>
> "It's good to learn about different walks of life," she said, "but for me to go out into the community and endorse something … I cannot do that, if I don't believe in it."
>
> "I am a Christian," Emily said, "and, yes, my Christian beliefs do guide where my life goes. But this is a right-and-wrong thing. I just cannot support this, and you cannot tell me how to stand on a political issue."
>
> When a little further back-and-forth established that Emily wasn't going to change her mind, the professor abruptly ended class and stormed out in a fury.[93]

What happened next was nothing less than remarkable. The professor filed a Level 3 grievance against Emily (this was the most serious complaint possible), and she was called before a school tribunal (shades of Julea Ward!) and interrogated for her religious beliefs.

As reported by the Alliance Defense Fund:

> Interestingly, the "ethics committee" was not overly concerned with how it conducted its own affairs. The group didn't put its request in writing, wouldn't tell Emily what the complaint was, and gave her considerably less than 30-days' notice – all university requirements. They refused to let Emily bring an attorney, or even her parents,

to the meeting, and they refused to let anyone record the proceedings.

Instead, the Social Work Sanhedrin devoted two-and-a-half hours to browbeating Emily about her Christian faith.
"Do you think homosexuals are sinners?"
"Are you a sinner?"
"What's the difference between you and them?"
"Are we sinners?"
As the questions intensified, tears rolled down Emily's face ... but she held her ground.
"You haven't changed your mind?" one of the professors said, at last.
"No," Emily said. "And I'm not going to."
The committee came up with a few academic hoops for Emily to jump through before graduation, then dismissed her, threatening to withhold her diploma.[94]

Yes, this really happened at a university here in America – and it was all carefully documented by the attorneys from the Alliance Defense Fund when they took up Emily's case. In fact, attorney David French noted that when the university president received the lawsuit, "he launched an immediate internal investigation, found that Emily's claims were accurate, said so publicly, suspended the professor involved, (and) placed the entire department under investigation." Not only so, but "He also took one more extraordinary step – offering to pay for Emily's graduate school education and expenses at any other public school in the state."[95]

Thankfully, justice was done, but not before Emily was subjected to mental and emotional cruelty and the ridiculing – more than that, the call to renounce – her Christian convictions. What a horror! But things have degenerated so much on many of our campuses that the reverse scenario would be utterly unthinkable.

What would have happened if the professor had required all his students to write letters to their legislators *opposing* adoption and foster care rights for same-sex couples? And what if a lesbian student said that she could not write such a letter in good conscience? And what if that lesbian student was then called on the carpet for her actions and brought before an ethics committee, taunted for her sexual orientation and reduced to tears because she refused to renounce her homosexuality? There would have been a national outcry, to say the least, and gay activist groups across the land would have called for severe sanctions against the school.

UNIVERSITY PROFESSORS FIRED!

Yes, Big Brother has established his presence on the college campuses, both in America and around the world. In fact, the first nine days of July, 2010 saw not one but *two* dismissals of college professors because of comments they made concerning homosexuality and, to be frank, their firings were nothing less than outrageous.

On July 5th, Hillel Fendel reported from Israel that, "Ben Gurion University has fired a professor for stating his opinion that the development of children raised by homosexual parents could be harmed, and that sexual inclinations can be restrained and chosen."

The professor in question, Dr. Yeruham Leavitt, had taught a class on medical ethics for pharmacological students at the university for many years. In fact, this was his sole class. What then was his crime?

> Several weeks ago, the topic was fertilization methods for homosexual couples, and a female student noted her concern . . . for the development of children raised by homosexual parents. Another student, a declared homosexual himself, objected, at which point, Prof. Levitt [sic] intervened and vindicated the first student's concerns. He affirmed the chance of harm to the development of such children and that their ability to lead a normal family life could be affected. He added that sexual inclinations can be restrained and chosen.[96]

When several students complained about these comments, he was fired by the head of the School of Pharmacology, Prof. Riad Agbariya, despite Prof. Leavitt's explanation that "it is acceptable for a lecturer to express his opinion in classes on ethics,"[97] and despite strong protests from other professors as well as from the Legal Forum for the Land of Israel. Prof. Leavitt even offered an apology – what else is new? – and noted that his statement in class was meant "to show that all sexual urges could be overcome, including homosexual ones."[98]

But there's more to the story. Only a few weeks earlier,

another Ben Gurion lecturer, Dr. Neve Gordon, head of the Department of Politics and Government, escaped being fired even though he called for a political boycott against Israel. University Rector Prof. Weinblatt said at the time, "We live in a democratic country in which there is freedom of expression for all, even for those whose opinions are not appreciated by all."[99]

So, it is acceptable for an Israeli professor to call for *a political boycott of his own country*, but it is unacceptable for another Israeli professor at the same university to opine that children raised in same-sex households could be harmed developmentally and that sexual inclinations can be restrained and chosen. To modify Rector Weinblatt's words, "We live in a democratic country in which there is freedom of expression for all, even for those whose opinions are not appreciated by all – unless those opinions happen to reflect negatively on homosexuality or homosexual practice." The Legal Forum vowed to take this case to the Israeli Supreme Court if the university does not reverse its decision.

Back in the States, on July 9th, an adjunct professor of Catholicism at the University of Illinois was fired for stating that, according to Catholic teaching, homosexual acts are morally wrong. (No, this is not a typo. A professor of Catholic thought was fired for teaching what Catholicism teaches.)

Kenneth Howell, had been an adjunct lecturer in the Department of Religion for nine years, "during which he taught two courses, Introduction to Catholicism and Modern Catholic Thought. He was also director of the Institute of Catholic Thought, part of St. John's Catholic Newman Center on campus and the Catholic Diocese of Peoria. Funding for his salary came from the Institute of Catholic Thought."[100]

So, he was responsible for teaching what Catholics believe, and in a lengthy email to his students in preparation for a test, he explained that, "Natural Moral Law says that Morality must be a response to REALITY. In other words, sexual acts are only appropriate for people who are complementary, not the same."

When one student complained (on behalf of a gay student who wished to remain anonymous), Howell was told that he would no longer be teaching at the university, despite his explanation that

My responsibility on teaching a class on Catholicism is

to teach what the Catholic Church teaches. I have always made it very, very clear to my students they are never required to believe what I'm teaching and they'll never be judged on that....

I tell my students I am a practicing Catholic, so I believe the things I'm teaching. It's not a violation of academic freedom to advocate a position, if one does it as an appeal on rational grounds and it's pertinent to the subject.[101]

So, a Catholic professor teaching Catholicism within a university's Department of Religion is dismissed for accurately teaching what Catholics believe about same-sex acts. And to think: On a daily basis all over America, college professors mock belief in God and attack organized religion; vilify political leaders (especially conservative ones) and denigrate American government policy; encourage (hetero)sexual experimentation and celebrate homosexuality – without the slightest penalty for their actions.[102] But the moment a professor crosses the gay line, he loses his job. If this not an example of gross academic injustice and inequality, then nothing is, and it was only after a public outcry – largely sparked by aggrieved students – coupled with a complaint from the Alliance Defense Fund, that the university reinstated Prof. Howell.[103]

FRIGHTENING NEWS FROM THE UK

What can we expect next? Well, let's look across the pond to England, another nation where the thought police (literally) are alive and well, we can get a good idea of what's coming our way.

After expressing his shock at the Québec bill, Bill Muehlenberg noted:

In the UK an MP has actually said that his party would ensure that faith-based schools would be forced to comply with PC views on homosexuality. This is how one article describes this:

"UK Liberal Democrat leader Nick Clegg says his party (the third largest in the UK) would legislate to legally oblige faith schools to teach that homosexuality is normal and without risk to health. In a magazine interview, Clegg outlined proposals to advance 'gay rights', including forcing all schools to implement anti-homophobia bullying policies and to teach that homosexuality is 'normal and harmless.'"[104]

So, if this MP has his way, faith-based schools will not be allowed to teach their faith. But this is hardly an isolated sentiment. Consider these examples from the UK as summarized in a December, 2009 report called *Marginalising Christians: Instances of Christians being sidelined in modern Britain*.[105] The report was produced by The Christian Institute, a non denominational, conservative Christian charity.

IN THE SCHOOLS

At George Tomlinson Primary School in Waltham Forest, East London, March 2009 was designated as LGBT History Month, because of which some Christian and Muslim parents pulled their kids out of class during one especially offensive week. The school decided to take action against them:

> A Waltham Forest Council spokesman confirmed that the withdrawals were being treated as "unauthorised absences" and that "action has been taken". Although the Council refused to say how they planned to punish parents, the Council website said that parents of truant children can be asked to sign a contract, fined on the spot or taken to court.[106]

How dare you act responsibly as parents and take your kids out of classes you find to be morally and religiously objectionable. You are henceforth forbidden to so.

Yet parents can withdraw their children from *Christian* assemblies, and teachers can opt out as well:

> In 2005 a group of Christian Year Nine girls at a school in Stoke Newington were forced to remain in an LGBT History Month assembly despite their parents' wishes that they should not attend. Parents with objections to Christian assemblies are permitted to withdraw their children. Teachers are also permitted to opt out.[107]

HARASSMENT BY THE POLICE

According to the Association of Chief Police Officers (ACPO) a homophobic incident is described as: "Any incident which is perceived to be homophobic by the victim or any other person." The sky, therefore, is the limit, and the perception of the offended person can be more important than the actual facts of the case. The Christian Institute rightly notes:

> This definition, coupled with the pressure placed upon the authorities to respond to complaints, has caused significant problems. By emphasising the perception of the victim, or any other person, regardless of the context or content, any semblance of objective legal reasonableness is stripped away. The ACPO guidance effectively encourages the police, on hearing a complaint, to confront individuals over their views on homosexuality, even when no crime has been committed.[108]

So, the thought police are going one step further, moving beyond the question of what the *alleged offender* was thinking. They are now investigating what the *alleged victim* thinks the alleged offender was thinking. The infringements of religious liberty have become so serious that on August 23, 2009, BBC Radio 4 devoted a special program to the problem, "highlighting religious liberty issues, including police interference, faced by Christian street preachers."

> The report acknowledged Britain's "long and honourable" tradition of street preaching and asked if street preachers were victims of "21st Century intolerance". Reporter Trevor Barnes investigated recent examples of street preachers facing interference from police and public authorities, and said that hate crime legislation was "complicating the picture".
>
> The report included a recording of an incident where a street preacher was told by police officers that it is a criminal offence to identify homosexuality as a "sin". The warning was directed at Open-Air Mission (OAM) evangelist Andy Robertson, even though he had not mentioned homosexuality in his preaching.[109]

When the famously liberal BBC talks about street preachers being victims of "21st Century intolerance," you know things have gone awry. And can you imagine policemen informing a preacher that it's a *criminal offense* "to identify homosexuality as a 'sin'"? (And let's not forget that the preacher never even mentioned the subject in his preaching.) But since the Bible does speak of homosexual practice as sinful, is it now a criminal offense in England even to quote certain verses from the Bible in public?

But there's more. Pauline Howe, then a 67 year-old grandmother, handed out religious literature in protest of a gay pride event in the city of Norwich on July 25, 2009, for which she was verbally abused. But when she complained to her local council, expressing her strong views in a letter, she was investigated for "homophobic hatred." Honestly!

And what did she write in her letter? Did she call for violence against gays and lesbians? Did she call for the criminalization of homosexual practice? Not at all. In fact, she explicitly stated that she wasn't trying to prevent what people did in the privacy of their own homes. She simply described homosexual practice negatively (using biblical terminology) and made the claim that it "contributed to the downfall of every empire and said that gay sex was a major cause of sexually transmitted infections."

Now, you may or may not agree with what she wrote, but either way, you can't accuse this grandmother of committing a crime. But that's exactly what the local council did!

> In September [2009] she received a reply from the Deputy Chief Executive at the Council warning that she could face being charged with a criminal offence *for expressing such views*. Weeks later two police officers knocked on her door and interviewed her in her home. They said her letter was homophobic and may be treated as a 'hate incident'.[110]

So, even expressing such views put her in danger of committing a "hate incident," to the point that two policemen *came to her house* to interview her. To repeat one of the most common statements in this book: I am not making this up. Even gay activist Ben Summerskill felt that the reaction against Mrs. Howe was "disproportionate."[111]

Sadly, such incidents are not isolated. "In 2005 elderly Christians Joe and Helen Roberts, of Fleetwood in Lancashire, were subjected to 80 minutes of questioning by police officers." And what was *their* crime?

The police were sent to the couple's home after the couple had telephoned the local council to express their disagreement with its 'gay rights' policy. There was never any accusation that the couple had been impolite in their tone. The two officers, from Lancashire Constabulary, told the Roberts they were responding to a reported "homophobic telephone call". They said the couple were close to committing a 'hate crime' which carried a seven-year prison sentence and were "walking on eggshells".[112]

Doesn't this sound like it is straight out of the pages of a very gay *1984*? It was only as a result of legal action taken by the Roberts that, "In December 2006, in an out-of court settlement, the police and council both admitted they were wrong in how they treated the Roberts." Without the legal pressure, the police refused to acknowledge any wrongdoing in the matter.[113] Incredible!

Not even Church Bishops are beyond the reach of Britain's thought police. In November, 2003, the Right Reverend Dr. Peter Forster, Bishop of Chester, was quoted as saying, "Some people who are primarily homosexual can reorientate themselves. I would encourage them to consider that as an option but I would not set myself up as a medical specialist on the subject – that's in the area of psychiatric health." Again, you might agree or disagree with this position, but there is no possible way that such a comment could spark *legal* controversy, right? Guess again!

Even this innocent comment – one that many psychiatrists and ministers would support – prompted a police investigation after a complaint was lodged against the bishop. (Yes, in England, you can actually file a complaint to the police for a statement like this.)

> Just days later the Chief Constable, Peter Fahy, attacked the Bishop publicly, saying: "All public leaders in Cheshire need to give clear leadership on the issue of diversity". He also attempted to link the Bishop's remarks with crimes against homosexuals "generated by hate and prejudice". The police passed a file to the Crown Prosecution Service which decided not to prosecute. The police eventually admitted no crime had been committed.[114]

So, the local police decided to lecture the bishop publicly, calling on him to "give clear leadership on the issue of diversity" – which, apparently, doesn't include the possibility that some people who are "primarily homosexual" in their sexual attractions can experience a change. So much for "diversity"! Not surprisingly, the bishop's utterly innocuous comments were linked by the constable with "crimes against homosexuals 'generated by hate and prejudice.'" But of course!

British police also took it on themselves to lecture Lynette Burrows, an author and champion of family values, after she participated in a talk show on BBC Radio 5 Live, December, 2005, discussing the issue of civil partnerships. What exactly prompted this police action? She explained during the program that "she did not believe that adoption by a homosexual couple was in the best interests of a child."

> The following day, Mrs Burrows was shocked to receive a telephone call from the police who said a member of the public had made a complaint about her 'homophobic' comments. Mrs Burrows says the police officer proceeded to read her a "lecture about homophobia" and told her that the incident would be noted on police records. Mrs Burrows felt intimidated by the phone call.[115]

And you thought I was exaggerating.

Of course, someone will say, "Look, this is happening in England, not America, so you really can't compare the two." But the fact is that similar things *are* taking place in America, even if they are not yet as extreme. (Recall the arrest of the "Philly Five," which included a grandmother, in October, 2004, for preaching and holding signs at a large gay pride event in Philadelphia. Before a judge threw out the charges against them, they faced the potential of *forty-seven years* behind bars.)[116] More importantly, if I told the people of England twenty years ago that such things would be happening in their country today, they would have laughed me to scorn. Fellow Americans, this is coming our way, and to a large extent, it is already here.

Getting back to jolly old England, even members of Parliament are not exempt from Big Brother's gaze:

> In 2008 the police investigated Northern Ireland MP Iris Robinson for expressing her religious beliefs about

homosexuality on a BBC radio show. Officers from the 'serious crime branch' of the Police Service of Northern Ireland held interviews about the incident. As part of a BBC Radio Ulster debate, Mrs Robinson used the biblical word 'abomination' to describe homosexual practice. She also recommended that homosexuals seek counselling if they are struggling with unwanted same-sex attraction.[117]

So, referring to homosexual practice as an "abomination" (as in Leviticus 18:22 and 20:13) can merit interrogation from the "serious crime branch," even if you are a political leader.

Here are just a few more examples from the UK, taken from the report we have been citing.

ROMAN CATHOLIC FIREMEN PUNISHED

At the annual gay pride event in Glasgow, it was common for the Roman Catholic Church to be mocked.[118] Not surprisingly, when the city ordered their firemen to march in the 2006 gay pride parade, a number of them refused, including several Roman Catholics. Instead, they handed out safety leaflets – not anti-gay leaflets – on a nearby street. And for this they were punished!

> The men were consequently given written warnings and were ordered by their employer, Strathclyde Fire Board, to undergo 'diversity' training. Strathclyde Firemaster Brian Sweeney said at the time that the incident would be "placed on their personal record file" and could damage their careers.

Forced "diversity" training? A lifetime blemish on their personal record? It looks like Big Brother has infiltrated the fire department as well as the police department. Once again, it was only under legal pressure that an apology was issued to one of the men involved.

> One of the firemen, John Mitchell, sought to overturn the disciplinary decision. After several unsuccessful internal appeals, he took the matter to an Employment Tribunal. Days before the hearing was due, Strathclyde Fire Board

admitted they had failed to take account of his religious beliefs. Mr Mitchell was awarded damages and received an apology from his employers.[119]

CHRISTIAN EMPLOYEE FACES FIRING

For all those who think that "diversity" laws (again, meaning pro-gay-activist laws) could not affect religious or charitable organizations, think again.

> In March 2009 a Christian charity worker in Southampton was suspended under 'diversity' rules after answering a colleague's questions about his beliefs on sexual ethics. David Booker has worked as a hostel support worker for four years. He was told that expressing his religious beliefs on same-sex unions broke the charity's Culture and Diversity Code of Conduct.[120]

So, a Christian charity worker serving at a hostel loses his job because he expressed his religious beliefs to a colleague in a private conservation. He was found to be in violation of (Big Gay Brother's) Culture and Diversity Code of Conduct.

You might say, "But surely there's more to the story than this. He must have acted with prejudice against someone in the hostel or made a gay client feel uncomfortable by sharing his beliefs with him." To the contrary, he was suspended for sharing his views in a private conversation with a colleague – and his views were hardly "homophobic."

> The allegations followed a discussion with colleague Fiona Vardy during which Mr Booker answered questions about Christian teaching on same-sex relationships. The free-flowing conversation lasted 35 minutes, and Mr Booker answered his co-worker's questions while making clear that he had homosexual friends and was not homophobic. However, the following day he was told he was being suspended. His employers say they took the decision to "safeguard both residents and staff" at the Southampton Street hostel.[121]

Are you kidding me? The employers did this to "*safeguard* both residents and staff?" Safeguard them from what? This utterly unmerited stifling of this employee's speech leaves me speechless. Yet there's more. (And I remind you: This is just a sampling from the UK, not even citing every relevant instance found in just one report.)

DEMANDS PUT ON CATHOLIC ADOPTION AGENCIES

For decades, faith-based adoption agencies in the UK have been placing children in the homes of married couples only in keeping with their belief that this is the best environment for the adopted child. "In 2007 the Government introduced the Sexual Orientation Regulations which outlaw discrimination against homosexuals in the provision of goods, facilities and services." Because of this, faith-based adoption agencies requested an exemption so that they would not be required to place children into same-sex households, an entirely reasonable request. After all, there were other agencies from whom same-sex couples could adopt children, and there was certainly no need to require faith-based agencies to violate their faith.

Well, what is logical and reasonable in one world has become discriminatory and homophobic in another, and thus,

> in January 2007 the Government announced there would be no such exemptions. Instead the Government said faith based adoption agencies would have until the end of 2008 to change their practice or face the prospect of legal action. These agencies have played a key role for many years in finding homes for hard-to-place children. Yet because the Regulations made no accommodation for religious beliefs on sexual ethics most have either ceased operating or cut ties with the Roman Catholic Church.[122]

So, in the name of outlawing discrimination against homosexuals, discrimination was now practiced against religious organizations, and in the end, it is the children who are hurt most. (This parallels what happened to Catholic Charities of Boston, previously one of the nation's largest adoption agencies, with adoption work being part of its founding mission. When the state refused to grant them a religious exemption so they would not be forced to place children in same-sex households, they ended their adoption efforts.)[123]

CHRISTIAN ELDERLY CARE HOME LOSES FUNDING

William Wilberforce is one of the most heralded names in British history, the man responsible for outlawing slave trade and slavery in the British Empire in the 19th century. The 2006 movie *Amazing Grace* introduced him to our contemporary generation.

As a Christian leader in Parliament, Wilberforce was involved in many other charitable causes, including the founding of Pilgrim Homes, which "provides residential care for elderly Christians, meeting their spiritual as well as physical needs." And because these homes provide a specific, spiritual purpose, "all residents must be personally committed to the Protestant Christian faith," just as in, say, a home for elderly, religious Jews, only religious Jews would be admitted.

Of the ten UK homes operated by Pilgrim Homes, one is located in Brighton, housing more than eighty people, including retired missionaries and a retired church minister, and the home receives roughly $20,000 from the local council to support the costs of a caretaker.

At this point, you're probably wondering how in the world the thought police intruded themselves into a 200-year-old Christian home for the elderly. Well, wonder no more. What follows is even hard for me to believe, which is saying a lot.

> In 2007 Brighton Council demanded that Pilgrim Homes should question elderly residents every three months about their sexual orientation; use images of LGBT couples in its promotional literature; publicise LGBT events to elderly residents; and force staff to attend a Stonewall presentation on LGBT issues.[124]

Honestly, if I were making something up, I would not make up something this outlandish, over the top, and outrageous. And, to be perfectly candid, when I read the report carefully, I said to myself, "There must be more to the story." And then the light went on: There *is* more to the story. Brighton is one of the gayest cities in England! This blurb from the gay.brighton.co.uk website says it all:

> The City of Brighton & Hove acts as a magnet for lesbians and gay men from all over the world attracted to its bohemian atmosphere, open minded attitudes and raffish

air. *Brighton has now long been known as Britain's number one gay resort.*[125]

In fact, BBC News referred to Brighton (and Hove) as "the gay capital" of the UK, and it was there that Britain's first "gay weddings" were celebrated after the nation's Civil Partnership Act was passed.[126] How dare a specifically Christian home for the elderly exist in this bastion of gay activism. How dare these Christians practice such "institutionalized homophobia" (the specific charge that was raised against them).

In keeping with their religious convictions, Pilgrim Homes refused to comply:

> Pilgrim Homes notified the Council that the home would not comply with its demands because to do so would unduly distress the elderly residents and undermine the home's religious ethos. The Council pulled the £13,000 grant and accused the home of "institutionalized homophobia" using the Macpherson definition of institutional discrimination. Despite attempts to resolve the matter over an 18-month period, Pilgrim Homes eventually felt they were left with no other option than to take legal action against the Council.
>
> Before the matter reached court, Brighton Council agreed to restore the funding and withdraw its demands and its accusation of institutionalised homophobia.[127]

Once again, it was only as a result of court action that the matter was dropped, but in the process, the bullying, intimidating, our-way-or-the-highway nature of British gay activism was clearly revealed, providing a classic example of outright anti-religious discrimination. This, apparently, is what is meant in Brighton's claim, cited above, to be famous for its "open minded attitudes" – apparently in an Orwellian sort of way.

And the end is not in sight. According to a headline carried by *The Telegraph*, May 2, 2010:

Christian preacher arrested for saying homosexuality is a sin

A Christian street preacher was arrested and locked in a

cell for telling a passer-by that homosexuality is a sin in the eyes of God.

According to the story,

Dale McAlpine was charged with causing "harassment, alarm or distress" after a homosexual police community support officer (PCSO) overheard him reciting a number of "sins" referred to in the Bible, including blasphemy, drunkenness and same sex relationships.

The 42-year-old Baptist, who has preached Christianity in Wokington, Cumbria for years, said he did not mention homosexuality while delivering a sermon from the top of a stepladder, but admitted telling a passing shopper that he believed it went against the word of God.[128]

After a woman who heard him preaching issued a complaint, he was approached by a police community support officer (PCSO) who stated that he was homosexual and "identified himself as the Lesbian, Gay, Bisexual and Transgender liaison officer for Cumbria." When McAlpine continued to preach (but, according to him, without mentioning homosexuality), he was approached by three uniformed officers who "arrested Mr McAlpine and put him in the back of a police van."

At the station, he was told to empty his pockets and his mobile telephone, belt and shoes were confiscated. Police took fingerprints, a palm print, a retina scan and a DNA swab.

He was later interviewed, charged under Sections 5 (1) and (6) of the Public Order Act and released on bail on the condition that he did not preach in public.[129]

Big Brother is serious!

And what were some of the responses to this article on a gay and lesbian news website?

Good for England. I wish they would enforce a law like that here in the US. Stop the hate!

The Romans had a solution to their "christian problem." Bring back the lions.[130]

And still there's more. On October 31, 2010, another shocking news story came in from the UK, perhaps going one step further than anything so far. The headline read, "Christian couple in fostering fight," and the story reported that, "Eunice and Owen Johns said their local council's fostering panel rejected them as carers because they could not tell a child a homosexual lifestyle was acceptable." (This is another sentence you might want to read again to make sure your eyes were not deceiving you.)

What exactly does this mean?

> The Pentecostal Christian couple from Derby, who have fostered almost 20 children in the past, are not homophobic [note that this caveat needs to be included!], according to a legal representative.
>
> But they are against sex before marriage - and by marriage, they do not recognise civil partnerships between gay couples.
>
> Their beliefs are at odds with Derby City Council's equality policy, which was drawn up under the terms of the Sexual Orientation Act.[131]

So, in order for this highly experienced foster care couple to be able to take in another needy child, they must affirm the rightness of homosexual practice. And how does gay activist leader Ben Summerskill feel about this case? He agrees with the decision, explaining, "Too often in fostering cases nowadays it's forgotten that it is the interests of a child, and not the prejudices of a parent, that matter."[132] What an extraordinary – and almost unbelievable – reversal of thinking.

These days, it is considered bigoted and intolerant to question the propriety of a same-sex couple adopting a child, even though that child will be deprived of either a mother or a father and will never witness the proper social interaction of a husband and wife in the home. Yet it is socially acceptable, even admirable – and perhaps even enforced by the law – to say, "It is harmful for a child to be adopted by a Christian couple that does not affirm sex outside of marriage by anyone, gay or straight, and that does not affirm homosexuality and homosexual practice." What kind of world are we living in?

"WHEN THE THOUGHT POLICE COME KNOCKING ON YOUR DOOR"

The really frightening thing is that it would be easy to write an entire book focusing on the subject matter of this chapter alone, and the book could be much longer than this present book – and this is one long book![133]

I could have cited scores of examples of universities in America and abroad where free speech is being shut down or muzzled, of employees losing their jobs because they took exception to gay activism in the work place, of educators being silenced for privately expressing their differences with homosexual practice, of Christian organizations being censured for holding to their convictions, and of religious leaders being silenced and harassed -- but by this point, I think you've heard enough.[134]

So I'll end here with the words of a children's play, produced by gay activists, followed by a warning from Australia. The play in question received widespread attention when Fox News picked up the story back in 2002. Here's the relevant background.

In October, 2001, Gray Davis, then governor of California, signed into law several bills that added "hate crimes" to the list of crimes included in "safe school" programs.[135] Not long after this, a presentation called Cootie Shots was performed in many of the schools, involving children as young as seven (meaning, second graders).

> FOX News' William La Jeunesse reported: "Performed in hundreds of classes, 'Cootie Shots' include skits in which a transsexual boy says proudly, 'Let them say I'm a girl. What's wrong with being like a girl? Let them laugh, let them scream, they'll all be beheaded when I'm queen.' In another, a girl says, 'The one I love she wears a dress.' And in 'What's With the Dress, Jack?' Jack says, 'It shows off my legs.'"[136]

"Let them laugh, let them scream, they'll all be beheaded when I'm queen." What a line! And seven-year-old kids were exposed to this?

To be sure, I don't expect to have my head chopped off for differing publicly with the goals of gay activism (after all, I have never accused gay activists of being jihadists or Taliban, among whom beheading is a common practice, although I have often been called those names by gay activists). But the day is not far off – in many respects, it is already here – when you and I can expect to be harassed or fired or interrogated or fined or jailed or attacked for actively holding to views like, "Marriage is the union of a man and woman only," or, "It's best for a child to be raised by his or her mother and father," or, "I believe that homosexual practice is wrong."

Recently, in Australia, Bill Muehlenberg addressed the consequences of a just-passed government policy, writing,

> Let me tell you in advance something you will need to know. If in the near future you notice that no new articles are being added to this website, and no new comments are being posted, there will be one very good reason for this: I will be in jail, or fighting a lengthy court battle, because of Victoria's new [Equal Opportunity Commission] law which was just passed.[137]

According to this law, the government now has:

- The power to enter a church or meeting for the sole purpose of assessing what is said.
- The right to demand that a religious organisation hand over files.
- The right to compel church folk to attend a hearing at the Commission without any complaint being made.
- The power to initiate a complaint of discrimination.[138]

Muehlenberg's column was appropriately entitled, "When the Thought Police Come Knocking on Your Door." You have been forewarned.

*In recent years gender identity has galvanized
the queer community perhaps more than any other issue. The questions go
beyond the nature of male or female to a yet-to-be transverse region that lies
somewhere between and beyond biologically determined gender.*

From the back cover of *Genderqueer: Voices Beyond the Sexual Binary,*
edited by Joan Nestle, Clare Howell, and Riki Wilchins

*We are transgendered men (female-to-male, or FTM).
My boyfriend is the mother of my child.*

Patrick Califia-Rice, "Two Dads with a Difference—
Neither of Us Was Born Male,"
Village Voice, June 21-27, 2000

*For clarity, though, I still refer to her as my dad
or my father when talking to other people; after all, that's who she is.*

Noelle Howey, in *50 Ways to Support Gay and Lesbian Equality*
(her father underwent sex-change surgery)

*Sally considers himself a gender outlaw,
playing outside the traditional definitions of man and woman.
Sally runs his business as a man and has not had sex change surgery
but considers himself a woman.*

"Canadian Transgender Activists Urge Legal Protection for Gender Fluidity,"
reported by NARTH, September 19, 2005

15

GLBT and Beyond: Reflections on Our Current Trajectory

W hen Korean Airlines flight 007 began to veer ever so slightly off its flight path from Anchorage, Alaska to Seoul, Korea early in the morning of September 1, 1983, there seemed to be little reason for concern. And so, 28 minutes into its journey, when it was 5.6 miles north of its expected route, there was neither urgency nor panic. But that slight deviation continued to get more and more pronounced: 5.6 nautical miles soon became 60 nautical miles; 60 became 100; 100 became 160, until the plane crossed into Soviet airspace over Kamchatka. The end was tragic.

The Soviet military, claiming that this was an intentional American provocation, shot down KAL 007, taking the lives of all 269 passengers and crew, including 22 children (the youngest being 8 months old) as well as an American Congressman. When the plane finally went down, it was more than 300 miles off track, and so, that slight variation from the proper trajectory became a major deviation, until a terrible tragedy occurred.

The lessons we can learn from this are obvious. A small error multiplied becomes a large, consequential error. A slight deviation from the path becomes enormous and even deadly over the course of time. Any marksman will tell you that the tiniest miscalculation in aim will result in a badly missed target. It's all about the trajectory: If followed to its natural and logical conclusion, where will the current direction take us?

And herein lies the problem. When it comes to "accepting homosexuality," most Americans want to be civil, fair-minded, and tolerant. Who among us enjoys being called a bigot? Who among us wants to be accused of prejudice and hate? After all, the argument goes, gays and lesbians are just like everybody else, and they deserve the same rights heterosexuals have, including the right to marry the person they love and make a lifetime commitment together.

And just think of the children who are harassed at school every day and called "sissies" and "faggots" just because they are "different." We need to put an end to this mental – and sometimes physical – abuse. And we need to help those who say they are trapped in the wrong body. Can you imagine the torment they live with? Surely hormone therapy and sex reassignment surgery are a godsend for people like that.

We are an enlightened people, after all. We have outgrown slavery and segregation and the oppression of women. It is high time we outgrow the small-minded thinking that discriminates against people based on sexual orientation and gender identity/expression. The business world has caught on. The educational system has caught on. The media has caught on. Young people have caught on. Other nations have caught on. How long will we hold on to our outmoded fundamentalist narrow-mindedness?

In October, 2008, I was handed a book entitled *Crisis: 40 Stories Revealing the Personal, Social, and Religious Pain and Trauma of Growing Up Gay in America*. In fact, the book was presented to me as a gift by one of the contributors.[1] The book's dedication is touching:

> There are teenagers all over the world today in crisis mode because they fear what will happen if others discover their sexual orientation. They suffer debilitating depression, isolation, and possibly even suicidal thoughts. I dedicate this book to them in the hopes that not one more teenager will have to live the way I did in my teenage years....

The book's back cover makes this heartfelt appeal:

> A MENTAL HEALTH CRISIS FACES AMERICAN TEENS RIGHT NOW – and it is one we can solve. Hundreds of thousands of gay teens face traumatic depression, fear, rejection, persecution, isolation – usually alone. Studies show they are 190 percent more likely to use drugs or alcohol and four times more likely to attempt suicide. Homophobia and discrimination are at the heart of their pain. Love, support, and acceptance – all within our power to give – can save them.

Surely, then, there is only one possible course of action we can take: We must accept homosexuality and transgenderism without reservation. There is obviously no other choice.

DO WE REALLY WANT THIS QUEER NEW WORLD?

Not so fast, my friend. There are massive and costly consequences to this deviation from the basic, male-female ordering of human life and society, and so, before we proceed any further – and with due respect to the many legitimate questions that must be addressed, including how to help the troubled gay and lesbian teens just described – we should first look ahead and see where we're headed. In fact, the future is already here: Welcome to a

queer new world!
Already in 2001, Richard John Neuhaus could write:

> "The Transgender Revolution" is the latest political cause
> being promoted by those of heightened consciousness.
> Columnist John Leo notes that San Francisco now pays
> for city employees who want sex-change operations, and
> a number of television shows are in the works portraying
> the joys of transgendered liberation. The *Los Angeles Times*
> had a sympathetic story on a husband and wife who are
> both having the operation. They will stay married, but the
> husband will become the wife and vice versa.[2]

Yes, from "transgendered liberation" to husband and wife swapping in the
same marriage (!), we have entered some unchartered territory. We had better
think twice before we proceed.

What does this queer new world look like on an up close and personal
level? Consider the story of Patrick (originally Patricia) Califia, an extreme
story, to be sure, but fully accepted in many gay circles and, without a doubt,
a glimpse into where our current trajectory is taking us. As described on
Patrick's website (and only excerpted here; the more you read, the more
bizarre the story gets):

> Patrick Califia is a bisexual transman and prolific author
> of essays, fiction, and poetry. He is also a licensed marriage
> and family therapist in the state of California, the divorced
> father of a three-year old autistic little boy, and a pagan
> minister through the Fellowship of the Spiral Path. . . .

A bisexual transman? What exactly is that? But this is only the beginning:

> He came out as a lesbian in 1971. . . . But a few years later
> he was persona au gratin [sic] among lesbian separatists
> everywhere because he had come out as a sadomasochist
> and started writing political screeds that were an opening
> salvo in the Lesbian Sex Wars. . . .
> During his late twenties, Patrick was affiliated with
> the gay men's leather community (that means he was tying

up, whipping, and fisting gay men) and had a hard time reconciling those interests with a lesbian identity. . . .

Are you following this? *He* came out as a lesbian? How is that possible? Well, *he* was a *she* at that time, and *she* came out as a lesbian. Does that help? But then *she* "was affiliated with the *gay men's* leather community." Talk about gender confusion and sexual obsession! In keeping with being part of the gay leather community, *he*, who was still biologically a *she*, "was tying up, whipping, and fisting gay men."

Out of Patrick's identity "as a leatherdyke," three volumes of short fiction were written, *Macho Sluts, Melting Point,* and *No Mercy,* along with a novel, *Doc and Fluff: The Dystopian Tale of a Girl and Her Biker,* followed by *Sex Changes: The Politics of Transgenderism.* This book appeared "during a time in his life when Patrick assumed he would never transition." Then the crisis came:

> So sometime after Patrick had been clean-and-sober for a decade and had gotten his master's degree and therapy license and was dating yet another tranny boy, he started having hot flashes and went to see the doctor. The doctor said, "You are perimenopausal. Shall we start you on estrogen?" Patrick left the office in an agitated state, went home, and cried for three hours. Several things became clear. (1) Having once suffered through the alienating and revolting side effects of having active ovaries, Patrick could never again put estrogen in his body on purpose. (2) When he told his parents, as a four-year-old child, that he was not a girl and would grow up to be a boy, he really meant it. (3) Living as a strong feminist and a very different kind of woman had not made his gender issues go away. (4) The only thing left to try was testosterone. . . .
>
> Patrick began taking testosterone about five years ago. (He is 49 as of 2003.) He had chest surgery two years ago but remains fascinated by other people's [breasts]. Today, he looks like a bearded, nearsighted daddy bear who has a lot of dirty thoughts and knows what to do about them. He's a sadistic but forgiving fag who also likes to have sex with girls of all genders. He is still a feminist and is quite

comfortable with his lesbian past . . . .

While he is pretty happy with all of the physical changes that making a gender transition have given him, he is also aware that 9,999 out of 10,000 men agree that they have penises, and he wants one too. [He then offers to pay for one if enough people send him the money].[3]

Does Patrick's story sound over the top? Without a doubt. Is it representative of most gays and lesbians and even transgendered individuals? Certainly not. But once the door is opened to legitimizing homosexual practice, "bisexual transmen" and "leatherdykes" are just an inevitable part of the larger gender variant family.

The trajectory has been set, and the only thing uncertain is the final end of the journey. But make no mistake about it: A queer new world is here already.

Not surprisingly, Patrick, clearly a troubled soul, appeared as a transgender poster boy in a June, 2000 *Village Voice* article entitled, "Two Dads with a Difference— Neither of Us Was Born Male." He stated there, "We are transgendered men (female-to-male, or FTM). My boyfriend is the mother of my child."[4] And what happens to the children raised by "dads" (or "moms") like these?

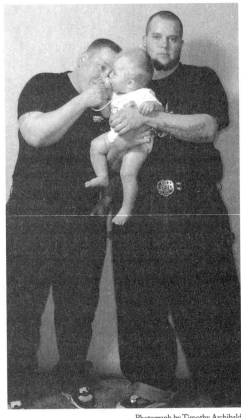

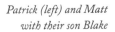
Patrick (left) and Matt with their son Blake

Photograph by Timothy Archibald

Yes, once we open the door, there is no stopping the flood. Is this really the way we want America to go? Is this really the world we want to bequeath to our children and grandchildren? Gay columnist Dan Savage wrote a satirical book entitled *The Kid: What Happened After My Boyfriend and I Decided to Go Get Pregnant*, but this is hardly a laughing matter.[5] And if we are still in the early stages of the deviation from the norm, where will things end up?

EMBRACING "GAY AND LESBIAN" IS NOT ENOUGH

Author and gay activist Dr. Mel White is quite clear that embracing homosexuality means more than just recognizing the categories of gay and lesbian:

> While throughout [my book] *Religion Gone Bad* I use "gay" and "gay and lesbian" or "lesbian and gay," I want to make it clear up from that I'm not just talking about gay men and lesbians but about all my lesbian, gay, bisexual, transgender, transsexual, intersex, queer, and questioning sisters and brothers. The "LGBT" alphabet soup option is an ugly abbreviation for a beautiful community. It leaves out other important sexual and gender minorities.[6]

So, get ready to meet and embrace and accept as perfectly normal a whole "beautiful community," including "lesbian, gay, bisexual, transgender, transsexual, intersex, queer, and questioning" – just to name a very, very few. No doubt, there are many beautiful people among them, but that hardly means that each of their sexual orientations and identities and proclivities must be recognized, endorsed and celebrated by society or that their sexual orientations or identities or proclivities are what make them beautiful. Really now, is it beautiful for a grown man to surgically mutilate his penis and wear a dress?

In the not too distant past, some gay activists told us that the real problem was that we viewed heterosexuality as normal and homosexuality as aberrant. The solution, we were given to understand, was simply to normalize homosexuality. But it now appears that was just a first step. As noted by Dr. Christl Ruth Vonholdt,

> In recent years there was an increasing shift away from

man and woman as basic anthropological realities, towards heterosexual and homosexual identities which supposedly exist on an equal level. However, this, too, has now become outmoded. For quite a while now German universities no longer offer just Gay-Lesbian Studies, but Queer Studies. Queer theories deny that humankind should fall into two gender categories. Instead of acknowledging mutually complementary manhood and womanhood, such theories hold that there are a variety of different genders which are all on a par with each other: heterosexuals, homosexuals, bisexuals, transsexuals, transgender sexuals, intersexuals and cross-dressers, to name but a few.[7]

Are we truly ready for what's coming?

WHEN "HONOR YOUR FATHER" BECOMES COMPLICATED

Virtually all of us know that one of the Ten Commandments is to "Honor your father and mother." In this queer new world, this is easier said than done. Author Noelle Howey shares her own experience:

Fourteen years ago, my father became a woman. In the process, she acquired a stylish new wardrobe. Pumps and flats. Various and sundry plastic surgeries. A new taste for flower arranging. Though itmay be difficult to believe, I found none of these changes jarring. For me, the biggest challenges were semantic. Using "she," not "he," "woman," not "man" – and figuring out what in the heck to call her.

What was this daughter to do?

Names, like pronouns, were initially a challenge for us. The conundrum might have been solved by defaulting her title to "Mother," as most kids of transsexuals are inclined to do. Call us old-fashioned, but my father and I had little intention of altering the name of our relationship, regardless of peer pressure. I already had a mother, who was more than a bit proprietary about the title. Also, I *had* a father. She might have changed her gender, but that didn't change who originally brought the sperm to the party.

So, calling her father "Mother" wasn't going to work – after all "she" was still her father, the one "who originally brought the sperm to the party." But how could she call this slickly-dressed lady "Dad"? That's not what dads are like!

> Of course, calling her "Dad" was initially a bit of a mind bender: every image I had of fathers – from a smirking Bill Cosby in geometric sweaters to suburban dads slinging burgers over a grill – was incongruent with this attractive lady in her ultrasuede pantsuit. Father's Day sales featured key-hole saws and paisley ties, not bath beads and personalized bouquets. I didn't want to call my dad "Christine" either, as if she were just any woman I knew. Finally, I settled on the shortened and softened "Da," which wasn't as frontier woodsman-esque as "Pa" or as baggage laden as "Dad," but still felt fatherly all the same. For clarity, though, I still refer to her as my dad or my father when talking to other people; after all, that's who she is.[8]

Yet there's more: Her father, now a woman, still likes women, leading to the inevitable question, "Why not stay a man?"

> . . . Yes, my dad is female. . . . Were I to make a list of the things that fascinate me about my father, her gender and sexual orientation (she likes women, by the way) wouldn't even crack the Top Ten.[9]

But this is only the beginning. Even simple prayers and old hymns become complicated. Consider the classic prayer taught by Jesus, often called "the Our Father" because it opens with the words, "*Our Father,* who art in heaven." In gay liturgy this becomes "*Our Creator,* who art in heaven." God as "Father" has to go! In the same way, a beloved old hymn, still found in gay hymnals, must be changed from "Great is Thy faithfulness, *O God my Father,*" to "Great is Thy faithfulness, *God my creator*" (my emphasis).[10]

As subtle as this change is, the semantic shift is dramatic. Thinking of God as Father evokes images of tenderness and intimacy and care and nurture; thinking of Him only as Creator is a very different thing. Does this change reflect the lack of a healthy father figure among many of those who profess to be "gay Christians"? Or is there simply a problem with affixing any "gender identity" to God?[11] Everything must change in this queer new world.

PRAYERS FOR SEX-CHANGE SURGERY AND ANONYMOUS GAY SEX

And so, Reform Judaism now has a series of blessings to be recited over sex-change surgery, part of the revised, 500-page manual, *Kulanu* [meaning, "All of us"]: *A Program for Implementing Gay and Lesbian Inclusion*.[12] Can you imagine praying a prayer whose sentiments are roughly equivalent to, "God, we ask You to bless our efforts as we radically alter Your creation and design through mutilating surgeries of perfectly healthy body parts and organs in keeping with our preferences and needs"?

Yet even this pales in comparison with the new prayerbooks released by gay synagogues in San Francisco and New York. They contain a blessing for "unexpected intimacy," meant to be recited *"after engaging in anonymous sex*, though those involved in the project say it could also be said for other meaningful encounters with strangers."[13] So gay synagogues have now invented a prayer to be recited *after having sex with a stranger.* Talk about trying to sanctify the obscene!

The prayer, titled "Kavannah [Devotion] for Unexpected Intimacy," goes on to ask God -- "who created passion and wove it throughout creation" -- to permit the encounter to be a blessing "that allows us to both touch and see the Divine."

Proponents of the siddur [prayerbook] see the prayer -- included in a section of innovative blessings meant to enhance life-cycle moments -- as an effort to elevate a practice that, in some quarters, is viewed as integral to gay culture....

The point of the prayer for unexpected intimacy is "that all aspects of our lives are holy if we approach them with a sense of the sacred," said Rabbi Camille Angel of [the gay synagogue] Sha'ar Zahav.

"The fact of the matter is we have emotional, sexual,

intellectual encounters that are Martin Buber's I-Thou, which ennoble us and draw us to our highest potential," she said. "Whether they ever happen again, the experience itself can change us and be a blessing in our lives."[14]

I am not making this up. Two people have anonymous sex and then pray that their promiscuous act of fornication or adultery will allow them both to "touch and see the Divine"?[15]

And yet there is more. In a classic example of the (very black!) pot calling the (even more black!) kettle black, Rabbi Steven Greenberg, best known for being the world's first openly gay, Orthodox rabbi took issue with the prayer, even though he understood the motivation behind it. In his view, the blessing "contorts" the idea of holiness:

> The more common reality of anonymous sex is that it is a form of mutual objectification and so must be the opposite of holiness. . . . What is missing from this prayer is that holiness grows incrementally as we move beyond the momentary, the sensual and the strange.[16]

So then, in order for a gay relationship to be marked by "holiness," it must be long term, meaning that, over the course of time, the act of two committed men engaging in anal intercourse becomes sacred in God's sight, worthy of a prayer of thanksgiving. *The very thought of this is repulsive.*

Are we sure this is the direction we want to go? Is this really the heritage we want to leave with the next generation?

CHICKS ARE DUDES AND DUDES ARE CHICKS

In the words of sixteen year-old Leanne Reyes, who voted for Cinthia Covarrubias (a female!) to be high school *prom king*, "It's not like the stereotype where the [prom] king has to be a jock and he's there with the cheerleaders anymore. We live in a generation now where dudes are chicks and chicks are dudes."[17] In fact, we live in a generation where some chicks think that they are gay dudes trapped in a chick's body!

Consider these descriptions of contributors to the *Genderqueer* book:[18]

> I identify as a queer girl who is openly attracted to male, female, and trans-identified people. Given this vision of

myself, on any given day I am called upon to present and self-identify as a sex-worker [= prostitute] (I use the name Faith) or an activist and social worker. (275)

Debbi Fraker lives in East Point, Ga., in a polyamorous and gender-variant family of four women. (104)

When she wrote this, Mollie Biewald was a 15-year-old dyke artist with a passion for genderf---, filmmaking, and 'zines. (120)[19]

Raven Kaldera is a trans/intersexual FTM [Female-to-Male], organic farmer and homesteader, a member of the board of directors of the American Boyz, and author of *Hermaphrodeities: The Transgender Spirituality Workbook.* (156)

The subheading to the chapter "Queerer Bodies" by Riki Wilkins says it all: "When I Was in Gender and You Were the Main Drag."[20] *When I was in gender?* What does this mean? What is coming next? Do you really want to know?

Within months of California's Supreme Court determining that there was a constitutional right to same-sex marriage – a ruling rightly described as "legal jujitsu" by a dissenting judge[21] – a first grade class in San Francisco (meaning six year-old children) was brought to attend the "marriage" of the teacher to her lesbian partner. After all, it's legal now![22] Not to be outdone, a *kindergarten* teacher had his five-year old kids fill out gay advocacy cards in preparation for a special Gay Day at school – called for without any parental notification.[23] And why not?

The tragic flight path of KAL 007 initially veered just 5.9 miles off course, but that 5.9 miles soon became 50 miles, then 100, then 200, then more. How far have we already deviated from the path? Where will this current trajectory take us? If our college kids can describe themselves as "genderqueer dykes" and "transgender gay males," what is coming next? How about the "trans child"? How about "queer in the crib?"

THE QUEERING OF OUR CHILDREN

Actually, "Queer in the Crib" was the title of Julia Reischel's June 19th, 2007 *Village Voice* article in which she explained:

Long enshrined alongside sexual orientation as the T in

LGBT, today transgender is almost trendy. Oprah's done several shows on the topic; trans people are coming out at work at the *Los Angeles Times* and Fortune 500 companies across the country; and the rising number of transmen at women's colleges in the Northeast is forcing schools like Smith and Mt. Holyoke to rethink the use of pronouns entirely. [Did you catch that? "Transmen" at women's colleges forcing the rethinking of pronouns entirely?] Newspapers and magazines have seized on trans as the new gay—the latest, freshest deviant identity to be dissected and exhaustively profiled. At the top of the hot-story list is the tale of the trans child.[24]

So, not only is queer hipster these days (see above, Chapter Nine), but "transgender is trendy . . . the latest, freshest deviant identity to be dissected and exhaustively profiled," while "the rising number of transmen at women's colleges in the Northeast is forcing [some of them] to rethink the use of pronouns entirely." So much for referring to your roommate at an all girls college as "she" or "her"; she might be a transman after all. Come to think of it, so much for the concept of an all girls college! After all, what *is* a girl?

But we must not forget the "trans child," and as an exclamation point to the "Queer in the Crib" article, the *Village Voice* cover was adorned with a picture of a young boy dressed in leather, with a whip in his hand and handcuffs around his waist, a tip of the hat to the sado-masochist, gay leather community – in Patrick Califia's words, the community known for "tying up, whipping, and fisting" each other. Yet here, it is a little boy dressed up as a gay leather man![25] (See picture on next page.)

I ask again: Is this the way we want to go?

According to a story run on KUSA-TV in Denver, Colorado, February 7, 2008, parents were shocked to hear that an *eight-year-old boy* was returning to his school *as a girl*. In the words of the father of a girl who was going to be this boy's classmate, "I do think that there's going to be an acknowledgment that, 'Why are you in a dress this year when you were in pants last year?'"

The school leadership, however, felt they had everything covered: They were preparing two unisex bathrooms for him to use, teachers would only refer to him by his new female name rather than use "he" or "she" pronouns, and, "mental health professionals" would be available for the other students, staff, and parents if there were "any concerns at all."[26]

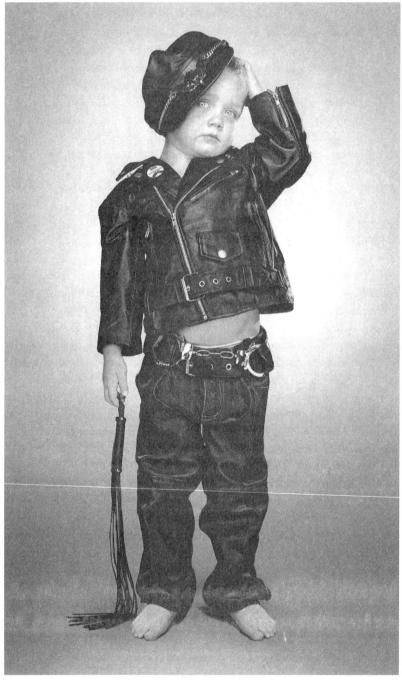

Photograph by David Yellen

How utterly twisted! Rather than this troubled eight-year-old boy receiving the help of mental health professionals to come to terms with the unchangeable and objective reality of his biological sex, it was *all the other students*, along with concerned parents and staff, for whom help would be available to help *them* conform to this confused child's subjective feelings.

A MAYOR WITH A DIFFERENCE

In November, 2008, Stu Rasmussen was elected as mayor of the small town of Silverton, Oregon, a position he had previously held in the 1990's. But now, as news commentators observed, he was a different man. No, he had not changed political parties, but he now dressed as a woman (with long hair and tight skirts) and he had "acquired cleavage," although he still considered himself heterosexual and even had a girlfriend. Cross-dressing, cleavage-showing Stu was the first openly transgender mayor in America, and considered to be the most popular guy in town.[27]

But the story gets more bizarre. On August 3, 2009, he was censured by the city council after making an appearance at a children's meeting in an inappropriate outfit, specifically, an open-backed bathing suit, a mini-skirt, and high-heels. Those criticizing Mayor Stu, however, were careful to point out that they had no problem with him dressing as a woman at this children's meeting. They only had a problem with him dressing *immodestly* as a woman.[28] I kid you not!

We have already veered dangerously off course, and either we make a serious course adjustment now or we suffer the consequences. The very foundations of human society are undermined once we deviate from the foundational path of male and female.

MALE AND FEMALE CATEGORIES MUST GO

In Ontario, Canada, as a result of the legalization of same-sex marriage, all references to terms like *husband*, *wife*, and *widow* were removed from the law books in 2005.[29] In Spain, birth certificates were changed from "Father" and "Mother" to "Progenitor A" and "Progenitor B," while in America, the State Department made this startling announcement on January 7, 2011:

> The words "mother" and "father" will be removed from U.S. passport applications and replaced with gender neutral terminology, the State Department says.
> "The words in the old form were 'mother' and 'father,'"

said Brenda Sprague, deputy assistant Secretary of State for Passport Services. "They are now 'parent one' and 'parent two.'"

A statement on the State Department website noted: "These improvements are being made to provide a gender neutral description of a child's parents and in recognition of different types of families."[30]

Subsequent reports claimed that Secretary of State Clinton, "In a bid to forestall a backlash from congressional conservatives" ordered that "the form will now ask for the names of the child's 'mother or parent 1' and 'father or parent 2.'"[31]

Did you think something like this could ever happen in America? Well, it has! And let's not forget that in California, for a short time in 2008, marriage certificates were changed from "Bride" and "Groom" to "Partner A" and "Partner B." (In another interesting twist, when heterosexuals protested this change, the marriage certificates were modified to have "Bride" and "Groom" on each side of the form, thus there could be two brides or two grooms.)

Once we recognize homosexuality as no better or worse than heterosexuality, we have let the cat out of the bag (or, more accurately, opened a veritable Pandora's box), leading to an almost endless list of gender possibilities. In fact, a law was almost passed in New York City that would have allowed people to change the gender *on their birth certificate* without even undergoing sex-change surgery!

According to a November 6, 2007 article in the *New York Times* by Damien Cave, "Separating anatomy from what it means to be a man or a woman, New York City is moving forward with a plan to let people alter the sex on their birth certificate even if they have not had sex-change surgery."[32] Did you get that? "Separating anatomy from what it means to be a man or a woman. . . ." Where in the world will this lead us? If anatomy no longer delineates gender/sex, then how *do* we delineate it? How do we decide who is male and who is female? Let's come back to reality, friends.

In the days before ultrasounds, parents only learned the sex of their baby when it was born, with the extended family waiting on pins and needles to hear the words, "It's a boy!" or, "It's a girl!" And how did the doctor and the parents figure this out? They took a look! Boys have male organs and girls have female organs. How simple! And that's how a doctor reading an ultrasound tells the parents the exciting news today: You're going to have a girl (or a boy).

Now, however, we're supposed to separate anatomy from gender/sex. We're supposed to say (using language cited in Chapters Three and Nine), "Well, the plumbing is definitely male (or, female), but we have no idea if it's really a boy (or, girl). We'll just have to let this child decide for him/herself when he/she gets older." In the words of a famous sportscaster, "Are you kidding me?"

In October, 2006, New York City's Metropolitan Transit Authority legalized the use of the bathroom of your choice for transgender individuals, with one article running the headline, "Be careful, ladies –it's his bathroom, too." Yes,

> If you happen to be passing through Grand Central Station and nature calls, you just might want to hold it until you get home, because, this week, officials with the Metropolitan Transportation Authority decided that transgendered people have the right to use the bathroom – men's or women's – of their choice on New York's subway system.[33]

But the new proposal went even further, allowing a man to change his birth certificate gender to female (and vice versa) without even having sex-change surgery.

Thankfully, the plan drew such an outcry that it was ultimately dropped (for the moment), but according to the plan, a person simply needed to provide "affidavits from a doctor and a mental health professional laying out why their patients should be considered members of the opposite sex, and asserting that their proposed change would be permanent" (after living as a member of the opposite sex for at least two years).

The article quotes Joann Prinzivalli, 52, a lawyer for the New York Transgender Rights Organization, identified as "a man who has lived as a woman since 2000, without surgery" (in other words, a cross-dresser, or, using the older lingo, a transvestite). He claimed that

> the proposed changes amount to progress, a move away from American culture's misguided fixation on genitals as the basis for one's gender identity.
>
> "It's based on an arbitrary distinction that says there are two and only two sexes," she said. "In reality the diversity of

nature is such that there are more than just two, and people who seem to belong to one of the designated sexes may really belong to the other."[34]

Yes, it's those pesky genitals again! What in the world do genitals have to do with gender/sex anyway? Indeed, Dr. Thomas R. Frieden, New York's health commissioner, explained that, "Surgery versus nonsurgery can be arbitrary. Somebody with a beard may have had breast-implant surgery. It's the permanence of the transition that matters most."[35]

Somebody with a beard and with breasts? This is something we should accept as normal?[36]

(left) Women marching at the Transgender Pride Parade, Northhampton, MA, June 7, 2008, one with a beard and the other with her breasts removed. Photographs courtesy of MassResistance. (right) A female "drag king" with breasts removed, performing at Pride Charlotte, August 26, 2006. Photo courtesy of N. Gurian Brown.

SEX-CHANGE SURGERY AND THE PREGNANT "MAN"

How about the real life story of a former beauty queen who had her breasts cut off but left her reproductive organs intact, then underwent hormonal treatment to grow facial hair, then, after changing her identity to that of a man, married a woman who was unable to have children, then got artificially inseminated and had a baby. Yes, it is none other than the so-called "Pregnant Man," in reality, a woman with her breasts chopped off, sporting a beard and female private parts, and married to another woman – but not according to many media reports, which glorified "Thomas":

> Tune in to *Pregnant Man* on Discovery Health Channel to
> see the story of a man, Thomas Beatie, and his labor of love
> - an extraordinary pregnancy. . . . Exclusive documentary
> featuring Thomas Beatie – history's first pregnant man
> – and his wife, Nancy, through the final weeks of his
> pregnancy, the landmark birth of their child and their
> eventual return home.[37]

So the "Pregnant Man" has become a celebrated media star (and is now
the mother of two), yet few if any seem to asking the obvious question: What
about the child born to a mother who claims to be a man while the child's
other parent is a woman who functions as the wife of the male mother?[38]

We have really deviated from the path and have strayed off into tragically
dangerous territory. Can I dare ask what is next? Even the current craze with
sex-change surgery is more than enough.

Of course, "sex-change surgery," can sound a little harsh, so a preferred
term to use is, "sex reassignment surgery" (abbreviated as SRS). Nothing major
here; you've just been reassigned sexually, like being reassigned in the military
or in the sports or business world. But even the term "sex reassignment
surgery" could put some people off, so the Human Rights Campaign (HRC),
among others, is championing the use of the term "transitioning." How
non-descript, harmless, and nonthreatening! The HRC even produced an
eleven-page booklet laying out guidelines for employees "transitioning" in the
workplace.[39]

As defined in the Workplace Gender Transition Guidelines:

> The term "transitioning" refers to the process through
> which a person modifies his or her physical characteristics
> and/or manner of gender expression to be consistent with
> his or her gender identity. This transition may include
> hormone therapy, sex-reassignment surgery and/or other
> components and is generally conducted under medical
> supervision based on a set of standards developed by
> medical professionals. The transition process typically
> includes a one-year "real-life experience" in which the
> individual lives and presents consistently with their gender
> identity under medical supervision (3).

It's really no big deal. Just another medical procedure. There's nothing to it at all. Just dress up and act like the opposite sex *in the workplace* for one year, then go ahead and mutilate, er, modify perfectly healthy body parts to make your transition complete. And the employer, of course, is fully expected to not only pay for this through company-sponsored insurance, but comply fully with the employee's "transition" in every way demanded:

> **Leave Benefits for Transsexual Employees** Managers should provide sufficient flexibility to meet the employee's needs for appointments. Time off for medical procedures is to be treated the same as other scheduled medically necessary procedures (7).
>
> **The First Day of Full-Time Workplace Gender Transition** On the first day of transition, the employee's manager should take these steps, much as he or she would for a new or transferred employee: 1. Issue a new company identification badge with a new name and photo. 2. Place a new nameplate on door/desk/cubicle/workstation. 3. Update any organization charts, mailing lists and other references to the new name (10).

As an employer, you had better have your ducks in order, and that means company policies in place for name change (say, from Joe to Jane), new identification badges (highlighting the new appearance), and special bathroom accommodations (after all, how can someone in the midst of sex-change be expected to use either a men's or women's bathroom?), just to name a few. As the HRC Corporate Equality Index for 2010 asks:

> Does your business have written gender transition guidelines documenting supportive policy or practice on issues pertinent to a workplace gender transition (including guidance on restroom and facilities access, dress code and internal record keeping that fully recognize an employee's full-time gender presentation and maximize privacy for the employee)?[40]

And if, as a fellow-employee, you're uncomfortable with your co-worker's "transition," you could be in serious trouble. You could even lose your job:

Employees who raise concerns about a transgender co-worker should be provided [COMPANY]'s equal employment opportunity policy, harassment policy and other related policies. They should be informed that they must work cooperatively with their co-workers regardless of their gender identity and that failure to do so could result in corrective action, including termination of their employment (*Workplace Gender Transition Guidelines*, 7).

Yes, you had better watch what you say and how you say it:

Note on pronouns: If a co-worker is transitioning and you are not certain which pronouns to use, it is appropriate to respectfully ask his or her name and which pronouns you should use. In general, it is considered insensitive to refer to someone by the wrong pronouns once you have established which set of pronouns he or she prefers. Again, transitioning employees should be prepared to help educate their co-workers (7).

And what happens to employees who have moral or religious compunctions about violating their consciences and being forced to call a male co-worker "she" or "her", or a female co-worker "he" or "him"? Must they go along with the program? In Colorado, the answer is yes, after this pronoun requirement became law in 2008 as part of the state's "nondiscrimination" law (SB-200).[41]

As for the HRC, let's remember that this gay activist organization is a darling of corporate America, underwritten by some of the nation's largest companies (see above, Chapter Eight). Even Pepsi Cola has contributed as much as $500,000 at a time to the HRC,[42] an organization that avidly promotes the mutilation of one's sexual organs through surgery and encourages the LGBT community to avoid doing business with companies that do not comply with their guidelines.[43]

Yet sex-change surgery, so increasingly common in our day, is a radical assault on the fundamental and most basic categories of humanity. This surgery is also very much in harmony with the GLBT attempt to deconstruct the male-female foundations of human society, even if some people feel that "sexual reassignment" is their only path to sanity and wholeness.

WHERE THE GAY REVOLUTION IS GOING

Forty years ago, it was only radical gay activists who called for such an extreme deconstruction, as seen in the 1970, Marxist-influenced, Gay Revolution Party Manifesto:

> Gay revolution will not produce a world in which women will receive "equal pay" for work traditionally assigned to their gender, nor in which they will become "equal partners" in the nuclear family. Rather, it will mean that biological sex will have nothing to do with occupation, and that there will be no families.
>
> Gay revolution will not lead to freedom of association for gay people in a predominately straight world, nor will it lead to straight-defined homosexuality with marriages and exclusive monogamy. Gay revolution will produce a world in which all social and sensual relationships will be gay and in which homo- and heterosexuality will be incomprehensible terms.[44]

Today, it is university faculty like Dr. Barb Burdge, Assistant Professor of Social Work at Manchester College, who are writing articles like, "Bending gender, ending gender: theoretical foundations for social work practice with the transgender community."[45] (Prof. Burdge, it should be noted, is a lesbian.) A review of her article states:

> Burdge says that [the] current view of gender - the social construct of dividing humans in to male and female - is oppressive and should be rejected altogether. She believes social constructionism and queer theory provide methods for social workers to actively work to subvert "binary" concepts of male and female.
>
> She believes that transgendered individuals - which includes a whole range of individuals - should be affirmed and considered to be gender variant, not suffering from gender identity disorders. These individuals include "bigenders, gender radicals, butch lesbians, cross-dressing married men, transvestites, intersex individuals, transsexuals, drag kings and queens, gender-blenders,

queers, genderqueers, two spirits, or he-shes."[46]

If you were wondering where the deviation from the path *has already led us*, here it is: ending gender; bending gender; getting rid of the "oppressive" categories of male and female; opening the door to all kinds of gender variation, including: "bigenders, gender radicals, butch lesbians, cross-dressing married men, transvestites, intersex individuals, transsexuals, drag kings and queens, gender-blenders, queers, genderqueers, two spirits, or he-shes."

The new possibilities are endless, as are the new problems. As noted by Dr. Paul McHugh, a member of the President's Council of Bioethics, University Distinguished Service Professor of Psychiatry, and chairman of the Johns Hopkins psychiatric department:

> I've already heard of a "transgendered" man who claimed
> at work to be "a woman in a man's body but a lesbian" and
> who had to be expelled from the ladies' restroom because
> he was propositioning women there. He saw this as a great
> injustice in that his behavior was justified in his mind by
> the idea that the categories he claimed for himself were all
> "official" and had legal rights attached to them.[47]

Legal rights indeed! But perhaps we're being too impersonal. To put a name and face on "gender variation," consider the case of Renata Razza, who "was born female and came out as a lesbian at 15."

As reported in the leading gay publication, *The Advocate*, "Life in the T Zone," Razza's declaration to be a lesbian "took few by surprise":

> She'd always looked gender-ambiguous. But as time went
> on, Razza became more convinced that her internal self
> and her physical body didn't line up. So in 2003 she decided
> to start taking testosterone. But Razza, 33, doesn't identify
> as male, nor does he [sic] want to live life as a man. Instead,
> Razza wants to live in a space between male and female.
> His identity of choice? Gender-queer. If bisexuals defy the
> notion that a person can be attracted only to one gender,
> gender-queers explode the concept that a person has to
> be one gender. "People who identify as gender-queer,"
> says Lydia Sausa, a trainer at the California STD/HIV

Prevention Training Center, "are blending and blurring and living outside of gender dichotomies."[48]

Or, as explained by Randi S. on the ExGayWatch.com site,

> Being attracted to both genders it has not been a clear cut decision for me to seek a complete sex change. My therapist advised me that some people in my situation choose to live as 'she-males', taking hormone therapy but not actually having the surgery. I have seriously considered this 'third sex' option. . . I would love to be a genetic female but I can't force the public to accept me as such. I don't feel I should have to force fit myself into black and white roles [meaning male or female] just because other people need to categorize me in that way. . . . [49]

Yes, it's time for ending gender, bending gender, and blurring gender, living "in a space between male and female," and considering "she-male," "third sex" options.

TOWARD A GENDERLESS FUTURE?

And what exactly does it mean to "end" gender? Consider the case of Norrie May-Welby, who, early in 2010 became

> the first person to be officially designated as gender 'not specified' - being neither a man nor a woman.
> May-Welby, born a man 48 years ago in Scotland, became a woman at age 28 after a sex change operation in Australia. However, May-Welby did not feel comfortable as a woman and desired to become a 'neuter.'[50]

Not surprisingly, this story was headlined, "Norrie May-Welby: The World's First Legally Genderless Person."[51] (Bear in mind this person was born male, then "became female," before deciding that he/she was neither, and remember that no series of medical procedures or surgeries can ever alter a person's underlying chromosomal sex.)

An article on PinkNews.co.uk reported this landmark event using the bizarre pronouns usually reserved for transgenders, but in this case, applied to a "no-gender": "Three weeks ago, Scottish-born Norrie mAy-welby achived [sic] a world first when *zie* was granted a Recognised Details Certificate giving *hir* gender as 'not specified.'"[52] Really now, isn't all this just twisted and virtually incomprehensible? According to *Newsweek Magazine* (August 16, 2010), we better start getting used to it. In fact, the *Newsweek* article, "Are We Facing a Genderless Future?" began with the May-Welby story and ended with a quote from Dr. Jack Drescher: "There is no way that six billion people can be categorized into two groups," followed by these words, meant to be taken seriously: "Now if we could only figure out the pronoun problem."[53]

Leading lesbian author and activist Urvashi Vaid, praising the book *Genderqueer*, stated that, "Gender is a poorly understood yet rigidly defended system of power rooted in a binary that this book shatters."[54] In other words, let the male-female order be shattered once and for all!

And I repeat: This is where the deviation from the path has *already led us*. What is coming next? And what will the multiplication of all these "gender variant" people mean to the rest of society? What of the kids raised in any assortment of "gender variant" households? (What of the kids who are encouraged by their parents to identify as the opposite sex when only six or seven years old?) If the parents are uncertain of their sexual and gender identity (producing much internal conflict in their lives), what will happen to their children? And what will be the effect of the coming wave of "gender variant" professors and school teachers?

Actually, we need not speculate. This is old hat now. Consider, for example, Prof. C. Jacob Hale, who "teaches philosophy at California State University, Northridge, where he transitioned and received tenure (1995-1996). Active in trans community work, Hale also enjoys doing drag as Miss Angelika and hanging with genderqueer sex radical friends."[55] Yes, this is a tenured university professor, and quite an example at that: a woman who became a man but who enjoys doing drag as a woman. Parents, is this what you want your kids to emulate?[56]

Even the Orthodox Jewish Yeshiva University experienced shockwaves when a male professor returned from an extended break as a woman wearing a tight skirt. (Had the professor's skirt been lifted, it would have revealed that "she" was still a man where it counted. For a variety of reasons, the university has accepted this professor's decision to identify as a woman.)[57]

These people need compassionate, competent, professional and/or spiritual help, but instead, sex and gender have become the enemy, and if you're not happy being a man, then by all means become a woman. After all, "transitioning" is no big deal, right? Not so!

Tragically, ending, bending, blurring and even shattering gender is not enough. In many cases, healthy body parts must be chopped off and surgically changed, and hormonal medications must be taken for life – and all this because we opened the door just a crack.

THE CONSEQUENCES OF SEX-CHANGE SURGERY

The famous case of Dr. Renée Richards, formerly Dr. Richard Raskind, is enlightening. Richards became famous because "she" successfully fought to play as a forty year-old woman in the US Open after "her" original male identity was revealed. More recently, a 57 year-old, male-to-female golfer, now going by the name Lana Lawless, and who once was a male SWAT team member, was disallowed from playing in the LPGA, the Ladies Professional Golf Association. So Lawless claimed in court that "the organization's rules that a player must be 'female at birth' are outdated and discriminatory," and in late 2010, the LPGA capitulated as its players "voted to remove the 'female at birth' requirement from the tour's constitution at a year-end meeting at the LPGA Tour Championship."[58]

What's coming next to the LPGA tour? In all seriousness, what if a top male golfer ended up having sex change surgery after suppressing an alleged hidden, female identity for years and then wanted to join the ladies tour? Couldn't this happen too?

Returning to the story of Richards, Joyce Wadler, writing for the *New York Times* on February 1, 2007, observes that, three decades after the surgery, "one still has the uneasy sense, at times, of that impatient male surgeon trapped in her body trying to break out," noting that as her interview with Richards drags on, "her body language seems to become more traditionally male, suggesting an athlete who is wearying of the game."[59]

What prompted the interview was Dr. Richard's 2007 book, *No Way Renée: The Second Half of My Notorious Life,*[60] chronicling the long-term effects of her sex-change surgery, including the impact it had on her son, Nick Raskind, who is now an adult.

> Mr. Raskind was 3 years old at the time of the sex change, but was not told about it until he was 8. (When Dr. Richards saw her son during that period, she dressed as a man and wore a short gray wig.) Dr. Richards takes responsibility for her son's problems: getting tossed out of prep schools;

running away to Jamaica at 13. . . .

Mr. Raskind seems perfectly comfortable speaking about the woman who still considers herself his father — although he's annoyed that his problems were always blamed on the sex change. He also refers to Dr. Richards as "he."

Why?

"Because I have a mother that's a woman," he says. "My father could have an elephant change — he could be a dromedary — and he'd still be my father."[61]

So, perhaps not all sex-change operations end with the fairy-tale joy so commonly seen on the TV documentaries.

In the book,

Dr. Richards writes of life as a very young boy, when an older sister, "after pushing my penis into my body," would say "Now you're a little girl"; of their psychiatrist mother who occasionally dressed him in a slip. As an adult, there was off-and-on use of female hormones, which left Dr. Richard Raskind with breasts. He tried to compensate in the early years of his marriage by acting tough.[62]

Clearly, this was a person who needed real help – on the inside, not the outside – but instead, the reconstructing of a perfectly healthy body was chosen.

In her book, Dr. Richards never writes that she regrets having had her surgery, yet she lists so many regrets relating to her sex change that it is like someone who returns again and again to the edge of a great pit, but refuses to leap in. Those feelings were also evident in past interviews.

"In 1999, you told People—" the reporter begins.

Dr. Richards interrupts.

"—I told People what I was feeling, which I still feel: Better to be an intact man functioning with 100 percent capacity for everything than to be a transsexual woman who is an imperfect woman."

In the same interview, Dr. Richards talked about wishing for something that could have prevented the surgery.

"What I said was if there were a drug, some voodoo, any kind of mind-altering magic remedy to keep the man intact, that would have been preferable, but there wasn't," Dr. Richards says. "The pressure to change into a woman was so strong that if I had not been able to do it, I might have been a suicide."

Does she regret having the surgery?

"The answer is no."[63]

How sad! "Better to be an intact man functioning with 100 percent capacity for everything than to be a transsexual woman who is an imperfect woman." But with seemingly no other solution, Richards chose surgery over suicide.

We should have compassion for such people, whose struggles can hardly be imagined by most of us, but that compassion should motivate us to look for an answer to meet their real need rather than encourage them to chop off their breasts or cut off or mutilate their private parts, before reconstructive surgery makes them into something they were never born to be.[64]

Listen to the warnings of Danielle Berry, three years after undergoing male-to-female surgery. While acknowledging that there are "some perks" and that "I'm making it sound awful but it's not," Berry, in a remarkably sad moment of transparency, strongly urges caution to those wanting to undergo similar operations:

I'm now concerned that much of what I took as a gender dysfunction might have been nothing more than a neurotic sexual obsession. I was a cross-dresser for all of my sexual life and had always fantasized going fem as an ultimate turn-on. Ironically, when I began hormone treatment my libido went away. However, I mistook that relief from sexual obsession for validation of my gender change. Then in the final bit of irony, after surgery my new genitals were non-orgasmic (like 80% of my TG sisters).

So, needless to say, my life as a woman is not an ultimate turn-on. And what did it all cost? Over $30,000 and the loss of most of my relationships to family and friends. And the costs don't end. Every relationship I make now and in the future has to come to terms with the sex-change. And I'm not the only one who suffers. I hate the impact this will have on my kids and their future.[65]

Or consider these poignant remarks from the wife of a man who used to be Ted but underwent sex-change surgery and became Chloe (his wife's name is Renee):

I didn't want to accept it and begged, pleaded, cried. Please don't. Honor your mother and father. How can you do this, and the kids need a dad, and nothing I could say would change.[66]

This is painful to read. But Ted was determined to become Chloe, meaning that Renee was now married to a female, at least a female outwardly. She explained:

Chloe is completely a woman, and you would never think anything other than that but to me, I don't see that. I still hear my husband, same voice. I still see the eyes, I still see the same eyes.

I miss being able to go out on a date with my husband, and sit next to him and hug him and kiss him in public. I don't feel comfortable doing that.[67]

And there were implications for Ted/Chloe as well. It was "torturous" to see his wife recoil from him physically.

I still see her through the same eyes that Ted did. She's still the same gorgeous, you know, beautiful woman. So she's three feet away from me in bed and I want to go over there and I want to hug her, I want to kiss her, you know? And I can smell her. It's torturous. And when the lights are off, she says, I can still hear Ted's voice. And I can even smell, it's still the same. But she says, I'm not a lesbian.[68]

This is really tragic. And yet there's more. Ted and Renee have two sons, aged 7½ and 6 at the time an ABC TV special sought to put a positive spin on Ted's "transition" into Chloe. Despite Ted/Chloe's claim that he would teach his boys how to be men (really?), one of them commented, "It feels like having two moms and zero dads." As journalist and media critic Colleen Raezler noted in the title of her article on Ted and Renee, "When Dad Becomes a Woman, Things Aren't 'Perfectly Fine'," and no amount of media spinning can change that. Did Ted really have to become Chloe? Was he thinking about his family or was he thinking about himself?

HOMOSEXUALITY AS A GIFT FROM GOD?

On February 14th, 2008, I had a public dialogue with Mr. Harry Knox, Director of Religion and Faith for the Human Rights Campaign and now a member of President Obama's Faith Advisory Council.[69] In my opening presentation, I challenged Harry on a statement he had made on TV. He had said:

> What's clear from our experience and from science is that being gay or lesbian is an immutable, unchangeable gift from God, one for which I'm very grateful, and it would fly in the face of my respect for God to give that gift back. It would simply be unethical and hurtful to our relationship with the Creator to give back gifts that God has given us.[70]

Of course, I took issue with virtually every part of this statement, challenging the notion that science and experience have demonstrated that being gay or lesbian is immutable, asking him if he believed that all sexual orientations were gifts from God (such as pedophilia, to mention one among several), and questioning how he and the HRC could so aggressively support sex-change surgery when he claimed that, "It would simply be unethical and hurtful to our relationship with the Creator to give back gifts that God has given us." Really? As I asked Harry that night, "Isn't sex-change surgery the ultimate insult to the Creator? Why mutilate the beautiful and unique design made by God?"

Really now, isn't it hypocritical to thank God for the "gift" of being transgender or homosexual while going to radical extremes to reject the gift of a male or female body? And how wonderful a gift is homosexuality after all?

To illustrate my point to Harry, I shared the story of two gay men who desperately wanted to have a child. As reported in the *LA Times*, their attempt

> to bring a child into the world involved a woman they barely knew. After fertilizing her eggs in vitro using both men's sperm, another woman would carry the resulting embryos to term. They had no idea whose DNA would carry the day.
> [The birth of their son Jansen] marked the end of a four-year journey that involved three egg retrievals, 65 eggs, seven fertilization attempts, three surrogates and more than $200,000 in expenses.[71]

How costly, indeed, for two men to try to have a baby.

Prior to this attempt, one of the men's sisters had agreed to take on the role of surrogate mother, but the twins she conceived were born prematurely and died less than one week after being born. When they finally did succeed and produced a baby boy through a different surrogate mother, they decided not to know which one of them was the biological father. And this is somehow in the best interests of the child? The *Times* report continued, "As the new family settles in its Atlanta home, the surrogate continues to pump and freeze breast milk for Jansen. Each week she ships bottles from Massachusetts to Georgia packed in dry ice."[72]

To be perfectly clear, I don't doubt that these two men are doting fathers, but the whole story underscores clearly that God does not "bless" His human creation with homosexuality. And what about those who can't afford $200,000 to produce a child? And what of the fact that a child has been brought into the world by human choice that is guaranteed not to have a mother or even to know for sure who his father is? This is a blessing? Harry offered no response to this story.[73]

It is not society's fault that two men (or two women) cannot produce a baby (remember that this is the unbreakable rule for homosexual couples and the rare exception to the rule for heterosexual couples). And stories like this one, rather than generating support for the rightness of same-sex unions and families, actually underscore the beauty, wisdom, and simplicity of male-female complementarity.

Isn't there something precious about male-female distinctives? And aren't we headed in the wrong direction with our sex-change surgery emphasis, to the point that children as young as twelve have now opted for it? (This took place in Germany; the child waited until he was sixteen, as required by German law, to actually have the operation after making the decision and beginning hormone treatment at the age of twelve.)[74] And let's not forget the phenomenon discussed in Chapter Three, wherein the parents of some gender-confused children "are choosing to block puberty medically to buy time for them to figure out who they are, raising a host of ethical questions." Yes, ethical questions abound – entirely apart from religion – and we do well to look carefully at those questions.

LESSONS FROM JOHN HOPKINS UNIVERSITY

Listen again to Dr. Paul McHugh:

> When the practice of sex-change surgery first emerged back in the early 1970s, I would often remind its advocating psychiatrists that with other patients, alcoholics in particular, they would quote the Serenity Prayer, "God, give me the serenity to accept the things I cannot change, the courage to change the things I can, and the wisdom to know the difference." Where did they get the idea that our sexual identity ("gender" was the term they preferred) as men or women was in the category of things that could be changed?[75]

Yes, where did we get the idea that our sexual identity (or, gender) was something that we could simply change? Dr. McHugh relates that his colleagues in favor of sex-change operations would introduce him to some of their clients after surgery, but McHugh was not impressed.

Speaking of the days when virtually all sex-change surgery was male to female, McHugh explained that:

> The post-surgical subjects struck me as caricatures of women. They wore high heels, copious makeup, and flamboyant clothing; they spoke about how they found themselves able to give vent to their natural inclinations for peace, domesticity, and gentleness—but their large hands, prominent Adam's apples, and thick facial features were incongruous (and would become more so as they aged). Women psychiatrists whom I sent to talk with them would

intuitively see through the disguise and the exaggerated postures. "Gals know gals," one said to me, "and that's a guy."[76]

Well, perhaps that was in the old days. Perhaps with new and improved techniques and with countless thousands of operations performed around the world (both male to female and female to male), Dr. McHugh's views have changed. In fact, they have not, and he remains an outspoken critic of sex-change surgery. As he stated in an email to me dated November 18, 2009, "I hold that interfering medically or surgically with the natural development of young people claiming to be 'transgendered' is a form of child abuse."

In 1975, when McHugh became psychiatrist-in-chief at Johns Hopkins Hospital, he decided to "to test the claim that men who had undergone sex-change surgery found resolution for their many general psychological problems," demanding more information before and after surgery. With the help of a fellow psychiatrist, he "found that most of the patients [his colleague] tracked down some years after their surgery were contented with what they had done and that only a few regretted it."[77]

But that was only part of the story. McHugh notes that "in every other respect, they were little changed in their psychological condition."

They had much the same problems with relationships, work, and emotions as before. The hope that they would emerge now from their emotional difficulties to flourish psychologically had not been fulfilled. We saw the results as demonstrating that just as these men enjoyed cross-dressing as women before the operation so they enjoyed cross-living after it. But they were no better in their psychological integration or any easier to live with. With these facts in hand I concluded that Hopkins was fundamentally cooperating with a mental illness. We psychiatrists, I thought, would do better to concentrate on trying to fix their minds and not their genitalia.[78]

How profound! "We psychiatrists . . . would do better to concentrate on trying to fix their minds and not their genitalia." Who could argue with this?

As for the adults who came to us claiming to have discovered their "true" sexual identity and to have heard about sex-change operations, we psychiatrists have been distracted from studying the causes and natures of their mental misdirections by preparing them for surgery and for a life in the other sex. We have wasted scientific and technical resources and damaged our professional credibility by collaborating with madness rather than trying to study, cure, and ultimately prevent it.[79]

Collaborating with madness, indeed.

WHY NOT AMPUTATE OTHER HEALTHY PARTS OF THE BODY?

Yet there is more. Some people suffer with what is now called "Body Integrity Identity Disorder" (the technical name is apotemnophilia). They are otherwise normal people who are tormented by their limbs – I'm speaking of perfectly healthy and fully functioning arms and legs – and are obsessed with having them surgically removed. Their right leg must be severed below the knee, or their left arm must be removed. Only then will they be at peace. (In case you think I'm making *this* up, check out a serious academic article by Annemarie Bridy, "Confounding Extremities: Surgery at the Medico-Ethical Limits of Self-Modification."[80] For a scholarly article documenting the new trend in *castration* as a personal preference, see, "New Age Eunuchs: Motivation and Rationale for Voluntary Castration."[81])

And some of this obsession with amputation is motivated by erotic desire. To quote Dr. McHugh again: "The most astonishing example is the surgeon in England who is prepared to amputate the legs of patients who claim to find sexual excitement in gazing at and exhibiting stumps of amputated legs." For McHugh, it is high time to shut sex-change surgery down: "At any rate, we at Hopkins hold that official psychiatry has good evidence to argue against this kind of treatment and should begin to close down the practice everywhere. . . ."[82]

At this point, some of you will protest that I have just made an unfair and gratuitous leap from sex-change surgery to limb amputation and then back to sex-change surgery, but in reality, the two are closely connected. First, how different is it for someone to cut off a fully-functioning arm than to cut off a fully-functioning private part capable of reproducing? Why are we outraged that a doctor is willing to cut off the limb but fully accepting of the doctor willing to cut off the genitalia? As expressed by Selwin Duke,

Sure, it strikes us as the most horrid malpractice when a doctor amputates healthy body parts, such as a pair of legs. But, then, should we call it something else just because those healthy body parts are between the legs?[83]

Second, and more importantly, psychiatrists have identified similar mental and emotional traits in those who want to amputate limbs and those who want to change their sex. As expressed by one interview subject, "For me, having one leg improves my own sexual image. It feels 'right,' the way I should always have been, and for some reason, in line with what I think my body ought to have been like."[84] As explained by Dr. Christopher Ryan, a psychiatrist at the University of Sydney, "

"I am not saying we should unthinkingly cut off people's legs," Dr Ryan said.

"I realise that the idea strikes almost everyone as lunatic when they first hear it. However, there are a small number of people who see themselves, and have always seen themselves, as amputees," he said.

"They are often miserable their whole lives because of their 'extra limb', and we know that at least some of them feel much better if it is removed."[85]

The parallels with sex-change surgery are undeniable.[86]

In a December, 2000, article in *The Atlanta Journal Monthly* entitled, "A New Way to Be Mad," Prof. Carl Elliot, M.D., who teaches at the Center for Bioethics at the University of Minnesota, wrote:

In January of this year British newspapers began running articles about Robert Smith, a surgeon at Falkirk and District Royal Infirmary, in Scotland. Smith had amputated the legs of two patients at their request, and he was planning to carry out a third amputation when the trust that runs his hospital stopped him.

These patients were not physically sick. Their legs did not need to be amputated for any medical reason. Nor were they incompetent, according to the psychiatrists who examined them. They simply wanted to have their legs cut off. In fact, both the men whose limbs Smith amputated have declared in public interviews how much happier they are, now that they have finally had their legs removed.[87]

According to Frank York, commenting on Elliot's article, it was Dr. John Money, formerly a John Hopkins professor and the advocate of all forms of sexual expression (including pedophilia) and all kinds of sexual surgery, who "coined the term 'apotemnophilia,' to describe individuals who are fascinated by the idea of having their limbs cut off. Money described those who are sexually attracted to amputees as suffering from 'acrotomophilia.'"[88] (For more on Dr. Money, see above, Chapter Seven.) In short, "The wannabes Elliott talked to discuss their need to have their limbs removed because they believed they were incomplete persons with their arms or legs."[89]

And note this carefully. Elliot found that "comparison of limb amputation to sex reassignment surgery comes up repeatedly in discussions of ampotemnophilia, among patients and clinicians."[90] But of course! Both are connected to psychological disorders for which amputation – either of the limb or the private parts or the breasts – is *not* the solution.

"Transsexuals want healthy parts of their body removed in order to adjust to their idealized body image, and so I think that was the connection for me," the psychiatrist Russell Reid stated in the BBC documentary Complete Obsession. "I saw that people wanted to have their limbs off with equally as much degree of obsession and need and urgency." The comparison is not hard to grasp. When I spoke with [Columbia psychiatrist] Michael First, he told me that his group was considering calling it "amputee identity disorder," a name with obvious parallels to the gender-identity disorder that is the diagnosis given to prospective transsexuals. The parallel extends to amputee pretenders, who, like cross-dressers, act out their fantasies by impersonating what they imagine themselves to be.[91]

As Dr. McHugh observed in a related context:

> It is not obvious how this patient's feeling that he is a woman trapped in a man's body differs from the feeling of a patient with anorexia nervosa that she is obese despite her emaciated, cachectic state. We don't do liposuction on anorexics. Why amputate the genitals of these poor men? Surely, the fault is in the mind not the member.[92]

Yes, "the fault is in the mind not the member," and therefore, "We don't do liposuction on anorexics," and we are rightly outraged when a surgeon amputates the limb of a healthy patient. Yet we glorify sex-change surgery on TV documentaries and in the workplace, simply dubbing it "transitioning," with guidelines and procedures neatly in place – and punitive consequences for those in society who refuse to participate in the charade.

Something is terribly wrong with this picture, and the consequences of our deviation from the path are more costly than we could have predicted.[93]

A queer thing indeed has happened to America, and the end is nowhere in sight. To quote lesbian professor and social worker Barb Burdge again: "... challenging oppressive gender structures and making gender rights a priority are critical steps toward universal freedom from punishment for gender nonconformity." Thus she calls upon all social workers to join forces and

> challenge gender stereotyping unceasingly. Given the ubiquitous nature of gender stereotyping in our society, social workers need to be acutely perceptive and prepared to challenge gender stereotyping in any setting at any time. . . . Whatever the forum, we must be capable of sophisticated conversations on gender if we hope to cure the social diseases of sexism, homophobia, heterosexism, and transphobia. In all our communications, we can intentionally inject the language of diversity and inclusivity into a gendered world. In doing so, we can begin changing the broader gender discourse, lessening its oppressive power.[94]

War has been declared on the "gendered world," and what Burge advocates is nothing less than complete and radical social revolution. (Again, from a biblical perspective, by attacking and deconstructing male and female distinctives, an attack is made on the image of God, which is reflected in the uniqueness of males and females as well as the full expression of the divine image that comes from their union.)

Here we can learn a lesson from the courts, where opening the door in the name of "personal liberty" can have massive repercussions. As noted in the April 5, 2007 *Time Magazine* article by Michael Lindenberger, "Should Incest Be Legal?":

> When the Supreme Court struck down Texas's law against sodomy in the summer of 2003, in the landmark gay rights case of Lawrence v. Texas, critics warned that its sweeping support of a powerful doctrine of privacy could lead to challenges of state laws that forbade such things as gay marriage and bigamy. "State laws against bigamy, same-sex marriage, adult incest, prostitution, masturbation, adultery, fornication, bestiality, and obscenity are ... called into question by today's decision," wrote Justice Antonin Scalia, in a withering dissent he read aloud page by page from the bench.[95]

According to Lindenberger, Scalia and other "critics were right":

> Plaintiffs have made the decision the centerpiece of attempts to defeat state bans on the sale of sex toys in Alabama, polygamy in Utah and adoptions by gay couples in Florida. So far the challenges have been unsuccessful. But plaintiffs are still trying, *even using Lawrence to challenge laws against incest.*
>
> In Ohio, lawyers for a Cincinnati man convicted of incest for sleeping with his 22-year-old stepdaughter tell TIME that they will make the Lawrence decision the centerpiece of an appeal to the Supreme Court. "Our view of Lawrence is a fairly narrow one, that there is a Constitutional right under the 14th Amendment's due process clause that says private consensual activity between adults cannot be criminal," said J. Dean Carro, the lead lawyer for Paul D. Lowe, the former sheriff's deputy sentenced in 2004 to 120 days in jail after pleading no contest to incest.[96]

Similar arguments are now being used in some high-profile international cases, with the "right" to same-sex marriage being used to push open the door for the "right" to incestuous marriage. The trajectory is all too clear! A large group of mainstream gay activists, representing most of the leading GLBT-rights organizations, has been quite explicit too, saying that same-sex marriage is only a starting point:

BEYOND SAME-SEX MARRIAGE
A NEW STRATEGIC VISION FOR ALL OUR
FAMILIES & RELATIONSHIPS
July 26, 2006

> We, the undersigned – lesbian, gay, bisexual, and transgender (LGBT) and allied activists, scholars, educators, writers, artists, lawyers, journalists, and community organizers – seek to offer friends and colleagues everywhere a new vision for securing governmental and private institutional recognition of diverse kinds of partnerships, households, kinship relationships and families. In so doing, we hope to move beyond the narrow confines of marriage politics as they exist in the United States today.[97]

The battle lines have been drawn, and the ultimate victims will be the children.[98]

MOMS AND DADS MAKE A DIFFERENCE, FOR BETTER OR WORSE

Most kids, we can readily surmise, will not be happy to embrace Daddy as a woman or Mommy as a man. Indeed, a very friendly transsexual I recently met – a tall, deep-voiced man in his sixties wearing a long skirt and a wig, who identified himself as Roberta and who has been happily married to a woman for more than twenty-five years – stated that only some of his kids or grandkids know about "Roberta." In other words, some of the little ones would have a real problem finding out that "Grandpa" liked to go out in public wearing women's underwear, women's clothes, and a wig. But of course![99]

Most kids, despite the protestations of gay activists, really do grow up much more whole with their biological mother and father (as opposed to only one parent or two moms or dads).[100] There *is* something to the natural family and the natural order, and some of it transcends what can be expressed by all the scientific studies in the world.[101] As expressed by Dawn Stefanowicz, whose father was openly homosexual, "What makes it so hard for a girl to grow up with a gay father is that she never gets to see him loving, honoring, or protecting the women in his life."[102] And that makes a tremendous difference in a young woman's life.

Speaking from a more clinical perspective, Dr. Gerard J.M. van den Aardweg explained, "Homosexual parents who are emotionally central in a child's life cannot impart the gender confidence to it they miss themselves, and if it hadn't been for especially one supportive, respectful and encouraging young male friend, Dawn might have sled into a form of lesbianism."[103] As she herself expressed:

> I assumed and dreaded that I would have to experiment sexually to discover what my identity was. I felt uncomfortable and ambivalent in the company of female friends and ... didn't seem to live in the same world as these girls. The only time I could ever relax and be myself was in the company of a few boys who'd made it clear their interest in me was strictly platonic.[104]

Listen to the testimony of Denise Shick, whose father confided in her that he was a cross-dresser when she was only nine:

> My dad was a cross dresser when I was a child. This made me feel very uncomfortable around him growing up. This confused me with his role of a father in my childhood. I just wanted him to be my dad, a real dad. I desired to have a dad that made his daughter feel special and loved and cherished.

Of course she was confused. What should a little girl expect from her own father?

> I was determined that I must have been adopted because I really never felt loved by my dad. Every father loves their daughter I thought to myself. I felt that no father who loved their daughter would treat her the way he treated me.

> My love for him did not seem to be enough. I felt like no matter how much I tried to love him, be good or be as understanding as a child can be I could not fix him. . . .
>
> I would blame myself for his behavior, I thought maybe I had hurt him in some way that helped to cause this. Maybe I was a bad child in his eyes, maybe I was a disappointment to him as a daughter or I didn't love him enough. Why is he really like this?[105]

Years later, when Denise's father was dying of stomach cancer, she visited him often in the hospital, where he would lay in bed wearing a ladies nightgown and was called "Becky" and referred to as "she" by the staff. (Denise's dad also had grown breasts through hormonal treatment.) This one comment says it all: "The one memory I have that I felt so sad about was watching him take his bra off. You are never prepared to see your dad take his bra off."[106] This really is tragic.

The title of David L. Tubb's 2007 volume, *Freedom's Orphans: Contemporary Liberalism and the Fate of American Children*, eloquently describes the consequences of the breakdown of the traditional family unit. With regard to the theories put forward by Susan Moller Okin in her book, *Justice, Gender, and the Family*, Tubbs, who is the former editor of the *American Journal of Jurisprudence*, notes that "her desire to eradicate gender exceeds her desire to promote the welfare of children and prevents her from seeing how these new family forms are likely to affect them."[107]

To be sure, there are kids with severe problems who were raised in heterosexual homes, and there are well-adjusted kids who were raised in same-sex homes, but there are recurring patterns that cannot be denied: The children raised in same-sex homes are more prone to promiscuity, sexual experimentation, and crossing gender lines.[108] (Let's remember that we make our societal decisions based on the general rule, not the exception. For example, even though some people can drive at 120 mph without a problem, we establish speed limits for the safety of all drivers.)

Amazingly, some gay activists who were aware of these patterns among children raised in same-sex homes still reported a similar outcome in comparison with children raised by their biological parents, since they felt that the differences that did exist – the sexual experimentation, the greater tendency to gender fluidity, etc. – were actually positives, not negatives.

According to Prof. A. Dean Byrd, the meta-analytical study of gay researchers Judith Stacey and Timothy J. Biblarz

> found that lesbian mothers had a feminizing effect on
> their sons and a masculinizing effect on their daughters.
> They report: "...the adolescent and young adult girls raised
> by lesbian mothers appear to have been more sexually
> adventurous and less chaste...in other words, once again,
> children (especially girls) raised by lesbians appear to depart
> from traditional gender-based norms, while children raised
> by heterosexual mothers appear to conform to them."[109]

Yet for Stacey and Biblarz, this was not a negative, and they even suggested that same-sex parenting might be superior. As noted by Dale O'Leary:

> Paula Ettelbrick of the National Gay and Lesbian
> Task Force admitted that Stacey and Biblarz had "burst
> the bubble of one of the best-kept secrets" of the gay
> community – namely, that the studies it had been using
> didn't actually support the claims it was making. Not all
> gay activists saw this as a problem. Kate Kendall [sic], head
> of the San Francisco-based National Center for Lesbian
> Rights, who raises two children with her partner, took the
> Stacey-Biblarz article as good news:
>
> > There's only one response to a study that children
> > raised by lesbian and gay parents may be somewhat
> > more likely to reject notions of rigid sexual orientation
> > – that response has to be elation.[110]

Really now, life is not one big experiment, and we cannot tamper with the foundations of human society without grave consequences. As the old Chiffon Margarine commercial said, "It's not nice to fool Mother Nature!" Our flight path is already way off course, and now is the time to make a radical course correction.

MAKING A RADICAL COURSE CORRECTION

What will that look like? It will first take into account some of the important things we *have* learned from our GLBT friends: We must recognize that, while gays and lesbians do make lifestyle choices, most all of them did not consciously choose their sexual and romantic attractions (aka sexual orientation). That alone should give us pause for thought since, for better or worse, they were saddled with something they didn't ask for, and for some, the realization of their same-sex attractions was more of a nightmare than a dream. Doesn't that call for compassionate interaction rather than name-calling and attacks, especially with regard to children who appear to be "different"?

We must learn to treat everyone with dignity and respect, recognizing that all human beings are created in the image of God (to bring in a theological perspective). And for those of us who follow the Scriptures, we must recognize that homosexual desires are just another aspect of our broken world, as opposed to being the worst of all possible sins. How about befriending your gay or lesbian co-worker? How about having a meal together? How about taking an interest in their lives? And for people of faith, how about praying for them on a daily basis?

Just because many of us don't believe in redefining marriage or in legislating sexual orientation and gender identity into specially protected classes doesn't mean that we can't live in respect and civility with our GLBT neighbors, co-workers, and family members. And should anyone threaten to mistreat or harm them because of who they say they are or how they choose to live, we should be the first to advocate for their safety and defense. Every human being is entitled to fundamental protections under the law, and those of us in particular who claim to believe in God and His principles should be champions of justice for all.

But this is where we will be misunderstood, and this is where we will certainly be reviled, since if we are really motivated by love, we will not celebrate something that we believe is harmful any more than a doctor would celebrate obesity. Instead, we will draw a line in the sand with as much courage as compassion, and we will state clearly that the time has come to make a strategic adjustment to our trajectory before we pass the point of no return. Now is the time to regain our bearings.

EITHER "MALE AND FEMALE" OR . . .

Consider the simplicity and beauty of the divinely established order: "God created humankind in His own image, in the image of God He created them, male and female He created them" (Genesis 1:27, my translation). How simple, profound, and beautiful, even for those who do not follow the

Scriptures.[111]

Contrast that with the almost endless list of contemporary "gender identities" (and phases thereof) including (but not limited to): Androgeny, Androgenous, Bigendered, Bi-Dyke, Boi, Boidyke (or, Boydyke), Bro-sis, Butch, ButchDyke, Camp, Cross Dresser (CD), Cross-Living, Drag (In Drag), Drag King, Drag Queen, Dyke, FTM or F->M or F2M (Female to Male), Femme, Femme Dyke, Female Bodied, Female Impersonator (FI), Fetishistic Transvestite, Gender Illusionist, Gender Neutral, Gender-Bender, Gender-Blender, Genderqueer, Genetic Boy, Genetic Male/Man (GM), Genetic Female/Woman (GF/GW), Genetic Girl (GG), Grrl, Half-dyke, Heteroflexible, Hir, Intersex, MTF or M->F or M2F (Male to Female), Male Impersonator, Metamorph, Monogendered, Multigendered, Neuter, No-gendered, Non-op, Omnisexual, Pansexual, Pre-operative Transsexual (Pre-op TS), Polygendered, Post-operative Transsexual, Queer, Queerboi, Shape Shifter, Stem (a feminine-identified lesbian), Stud (a masculine-identified lesbian), Trannyboi, Trannydyke, Trannyfag, Transboi, Transgendered, Transgenderist, Transitioning, Transmale, Transsexual (TS), Transvestite, Transidentified, Trisexual, Two-Spirit, Ze.[112]

Which will it be? Either we reinforce "heteronormativity" – the recognition that heterosexuality is the intended norm for the human race – or we will have everything from A to Z (literally) and beyond. Really now, if we must accept, nurture, and even celebrate homosexuality – as so many gay activists, media moguls, educators, and politically correct gurus insist – then why mustn't we accept, nurture, and celebrate all "gender identities"? This is hardly a theoretical question: We can recognize heterosexuality as the norm and reach out to those who find themselves on the fringes, or we can open the door to gender madness.[113]

To repeat: There really is a divinely intended order for the human race, a male-female, heterosexual order, which "explains why a man leaves his father and mother and is joined to his wife, and the two are united into one" (Genesis 2:24, NLT; literally, "the two become one flesh") – uniquely fit for emotional and spiritual unity, uniquely fit to reflect the image of God together, uniquely fit to reproduce and bring forth new life, to "be fruitful and multiply" (Genesis 1:28) – which is more than just a biological process. It is a man and woman giving themselves to one another for life, becoming one in body and spirit, joining together in sexual love, producing a brand new life within the womb, then watching with wonder as the baby grows within its mother's belly, feeling it kick and move, counting the days until delivery, and then experiencing what truly feels like a miracle as a new human being bursts forth from the womb and is soon in the arms of its mom and dad, who are laughing and crying for joy and wonder.

This is the rhythm of life, expressed so beautifully in Paul Stookey's "Wedding Song (There Is Love)":

> Well a man shall leave his mother and a woman leave her
> home
> They shall travel on to where the two shall be as one.
> As it was in the beginning is now and til the end
> Woman draws her life from man and gives it back again.
> And there is Love,
> there is Love.[114]

This is why God made us male and female, and this is why the natural family is the ideal place for a child to be nurtured and raised, the daughters mentored by their mothers and the sons mentored by their fathers, with both mom and dad uniting to set an example for their children.[115] It truly is a beautiful picture. And to emphasize again, whereas it is the exception to the rule for a heterosexual couple to be unable to reproduce, it is the rule without exception for a homosexual couple, often leading to extreme measures, like this one, from Mexico:

> A fifty-year-old Mexican woman has given birth to a child whose biological father is her homosexual son, according to the Mexico City newspaper Reforma. . . . A childhood friend, who is married, contributed the ovum. Jorge's son was conceived through in-vitro fertilization . . . and implanted in his mother's womb. . . . The family says that they have documented the circumstances of the birth so that the child, whose name is Darío, will someday know the full truth about his origins.[116]

Poor Darío! But who can say this is "wrong" once we abandon the God-established order for relationships, marriage, and family? Darío's dad would surely call us bigoted and intolerant.

WE ARE ALREADY FAR DOWN THE SLIPPERY SLOPE

Or who can say that *this* report from England is wrong? "**Granny, 72, Having a Baby With Her Grandson.** A grandmother has shocked her friends and family after revealing she is having a baby with her own grandson."[117] What's so bad about this? Yet every gay person I know would be repulsed at this headline while at the same time telling me same-sex relationships were fine. Based on what criteria?

What if this story had been about a grandfather and his grandson, or about two brothers? On what basis would it be wrong for two men who *were* related to be in a consensual romantic and sexual relationship, while it would be right for two men who were *not* related to be in a consensual romantic and sexual relationship? Could it be that both are wrong, since both violate the divinely intended order of male-female, non-incestuous relationships?[118]

The shocking story from England continues:

> Pearl Carter, 72, says she has never been happier after beginning an incestuous relationship with her 26-year-old grandchild Phil Bailey.
>
> The pensioner [meaning, the retired person], from Indiana, US, is using her pension to pay a surrogate mother so they can have a child, reports New Zealand's New Idea magazine.
>
> She said: "I'm not interested in anyone else's opinion. I am in love with Phil and he's in love with me.
>
> "Soon I'll be holding my son or daughter in my arms and Phil will be the proud dad."
>
> Her lover is the son of Pearl's daughter Lynette Bailey - who she put up for adoption when she was 18-years-old.
>
> When his mother passed away, Phil tracked down his long lost grandmother and they quickly fell in love.
>
> Pearl told New Idea magazine: "From the first moment that I saw him, I knew we would never have a grandmother-grandson relationship.
>
> "For the first time in years I felt sexually alive."[119]

There was a time not too long ago when reports of two men wanting to have a child through the fertilization of a surrogate mother would have been greeted with shock, just as this grandmother-grandson story is met with shock today. Perhaps a few years from now consensual, adult, incestuous relationships will be greeted with a shrug of the shoulders or, worse still, with affirmation and approval. Why not? Isn't it all about two people (or more) being happy? Isn't it all about "the right to love"? Perhaps we don't even have to wait a few more years?

On December 14, 2010, newspapers reported that Columbia University professor David Epstein was charged with carrying on a three-year, consensual affair with his adult daughter. His attorney, Matthew Galluzzo, commented, "It's OK for homosexuals to do whatever they want in their own home. How is this so different? We have to figure out why some behavior is tolerated and some is not."[120]

Do we really have to figure it out? The reason that homosexual behavior is tolerated is because we have completely lost our moral bearings – and moral courage – in the face of the never-ending onslaught of gay activism, to the point that today, it is not enough that we tolerate homosexual acts. We must celebrate them!

The tragic reality, however, is simple: If we no longer recognize the inherent wrongness of homosexual acts, we will have little or nothing to say to those who clamor for the "right" to adult, consensual incestuous acts. As one radio host noted when reporting on this story, students commenting on "the Columbia University student newspaper website are mystified as to why it's illegal: 'Wait, why is consensual incest a crime? It might not be appealing to everyone, but if they're adults and they consent, who cares what they do?' This is a typical comment from a student on the site."[121]

The truth is that we are already well down the "slippery slope" (see above, Chapter Seven, with n. 90), and therefore it is no surprise that attorneys like Galluzzo are appealing to the Supreme Court decision of Lawrence v. Texas (for which see above) to argue that consensual, adult incest should not be prosecuted:

> In an interview with the Huffington Post, Galuzzo also questions whether "prosecuting incest was 'intellectually consistent' with the repeal of anti-sodomy laws that resulted from Lawrence v. Texas in 2003" and asserts that "what goes on between consenting adults in private should not be legislated" because the bedroom "is not the proper domain of our law."[122]

But of course! The same logic that justified homosexual practice between consenting adults also justifies incestuous practice between consenting adults. How much more proof do we need?

On February 20, 2007, Jerry Springer hosted a show entitled, "I'm Happy I Cut off My Legs," putting on display the truly tragic story of a man who identified as "Sandra." This masculine looking man sat in a wheelchair trying to look like a woman, wearing a dress which proudly exposed two stumps, having cut off his legs with a saw (really!) six years earlier. And he was quite happy with both of his radical life choices, first deciding that he was really a woman in a man's body (although he did not have sex-change surgery), and then deciding to cut off his legs.[123]

The show was as enlightening as it was pathetic. For Jerry Springer (and most of his audience), the fact that this man was wearing a dress and identifying as a transsexual was perfectly fine. He was sure that "he" was really a "she," and that's how "Sandra" wanted to live. More power to him! But the fact that he was tormented by the presence of his legs (from his knees down), moving him to saw them off, was a sign of mental illness or extreme stupidity, something to even be ridiculed and mocked. But why? After all, isn't it his own life and his own body? And isn't he much happier now?[124]

What happened, however, when his former wife and his daughter were brought onstage to confront him was truly eye-opening. They could care less that he cut off his legs. Yes, it was stupid, but that wasn't what concerned them. It was that this man – a husband and father – had driven his ex-wife and daughter to drugs, depression, and almost suicidal despair because he decided he was really a woman. That's what destroyed *their* lives. He, for his part, was sure he did the right thing.

What terribly twisted thinking for this man, and how very sad for all parties involved. But if cross-dressing and, more radically still, sex-change surgery are fine – after all, we have to be true to ourselves, and, in the end, "it's my life" – then the day will soon come when the mutilation of other body parts will be considered fine if it makes the person feel happy and whole. Why not?

Without the male-female order, there would be no human race (it still takes a sperm and an egg to produce a person), and the normalization and celebration of GLBT are a direct assault on the male-female order, leading to gender chaos, to the redefining of marriage, to the remaking of our educational system, to the rewriting of the Bible, to the enshrining of special gay rights even at the expense of religious rights and freedoms of conscience

– just to name a few.

IT'S NOT TOO LATE TO TURN THE TIDE

A queer thing, indeed, has happened to America, but there is a way forward (not backward), a better way, a "straighter" way. It is not too late to turn the tide, no matter how daunting the task might appear in light of the massive societal shifts that have taken place in the last generation. In times like these, when it is easy to be discouraged, we do well to recall the words of Mahatma Gandhi: "When I despair, I remember that all through history the ways of truth and love have always won."

Without a doubt, those of us who oppose the current trajectory of GLBT and beyond will be told that we are on the "wrong side of history," that we have branded ourselves as intolerant bigots, that we have marginalized ourselves to the point of no return. So be it. It is better to stand up for what is right than to have the approval of the masses. It is better to swim against the tide when it is going in the wrong direction then to be carried along with the (always fickle) whims of current public opinion.

Do we really have a choice? Can we simply sit back and let gender anarchy rule the day? What will we say to our children and grandchildren? How will we explain to them that it was on our watch that "Mother and Father" became "Parent A and Parent B"? That North American courts ruled that the public use of certain verses in the Bible was a hate crime punishable by law? That businesses were penalized because they would not support gay activism? That college professors were fired and university students dismissed because they took issue with homosexual practice? How will we justify our silence and inaction?

To be sure, our work is cut out for us. Some of us need to get involved in our schools, from pre-school to high school, while others need to make an impact on the colleges and universities. Still others need to help reshape the media and make our voices heard in the political realm and the business world. And all of us need to be a positive influence in society, giving attention to our own lives and marriages and families if they are out of order. (Fixing heterosexual marriage and sexuality is at the top of the list!) As for those of us who claim to be followers of Jesus, we should understand the import of his words, "You are the salt of the earth . . . . You are the light of the world" (see Matthew 5:13-16). Put another way by Dr. Martin Luther King, Jr., "The church must be reminded that it is not the master or the servant of the state, but rather the conscience of the state. It must be the guide and the critic of the state, and never its tool." Now is the time to put this into practice.

We need to recover scriptural truth in our houses of worship and win the battle of semantics – indeed, the battle for sanity – in the marketplace of ideas. And we need to do all this while walking in genuine love towards GLBT individuals, who will certainly view us as villains out to destroy their lives and steal their rights. Let us persevere through the inevitable vilification and misunderstanding that will be heaped upon us, and let us stand tall and unashamed.

History is awaiting our move.

FURTHER RESOURCES

I'm sure that many of you reading this book have been deeply troubled, often asking the question, "What can I do to help bring about positive change?"

To help answer that question, we put together a special resource section on our website, **aqueerthing.com**, that offers practical guidelines for positive involvement in all the major areas covered in this book, including: education, the media, religion, business, politics, and the courts. Just go to **aqueerthing.com** and click on **Get Involved**. There you will also find links to many other relevant websites and organizations, including those devoted to helping people with unwanted same-sex attractions.

We also invite you to submit your own suggestions for positive change, which we will be happy to post on the website if they prove helpful. And feel free to write to us if your own experience confirms what you have read here. When relevant, and with your permission, we will post some of your personal stories, but with full confidentiality and protecting your identity.

Should your local bookstore or library refuse to carry this book, send a note to our website and share the details, especially if the bookstore or library carries other titles that strongly endorse contrary positions. Surely in 21st century America there should be room for the respectful interchange of ideas!

The approach we have used in dealing with these difficult and often volatile issues – and which we commend to each of you – is "reach out and resist," meaning, *reach out* to GLBT individuals with sensitivity and kindness, and *resist* gay activism with courage. We trust that the resources offered at **aqueerthing.com** will help you to maintain that healthy balance.

ENDNOTES

Introduction

1   David Eisenbach, *Gay Power: An American Revolution* (New York: Carroll & Graf, 2006), 86.

2   Ibid., 90-91.

3   Ibid., 91.

4   Cited in ibid. A fascinating sidebar to this story is the claim that the death of Judy Garland – who was greatly loved by the gay community – just days before Stonewall helped provoke the riots (she died on June 22, 1969, at the age of forty-seven). See http://www.fordham.edu/halsall/pwh/index-icons.html, which notes that, "Her death days before the Stonewall Riots has been cited as part of the reason for intense emotions among the NY gay community in June 1969." Cf. also http://www.artsjournal.com/outthere/2009/06/did_judy_garland_cause_stonewa.html, "Did Judy (Garland) Cause Stonewall (Riots)?", both accessed May 18, 2010. There is a lively discussion on the Internet arguing for or against this theory.

5   *Gay Power*, 93.

6   Ibid., 94.

7   According to gay sources, the riots erupted again because of police provocation and even brutality; cf. Dick Leitsch, "Acting Up at the Stonewall Riots," in Mark Thompson, ed., *Long Road to Freedom: The Advocate History of the Gay and Lesbian Movement* (New York: St. Martin's Press, 1994), 28-29.

8   Eisenbach, *Gay Power*, 97.

9   http://latimesblogs.latimes.com/washington/2009/06/obama-gay-pride-remarks-lgbt.html, accessed April 30, 2010.

10   http://www.lyricsfreak.com/g/grateful+dead/truckin_20062376.html, accessed April 30, 2010.

11   http://www.baptistpress.com/bpnews.asp?id=28074, accessed April 30, 2010; for the American Family Association's prolonged battle with McDonald's, see, e.g, http://www.washingtonpost.com/wp-dyn/content/article/2008/07/03/AR2008070303769.html, July 4, 2008 (accessed April 30, 2010).

12   For one of his landmark speeches, see James Daley, ed., *Great Speeches on Gay Rights* (Mineola, NY: Dover Publications, 2010), 31-52 (Franklin Kameny, "Civil Liberties: A Progress Report," New York City, 1964).

13   Letter from Franklin E. Kameny, to Peter LaBarbera, May 31, 2008, http://americansfortruth.com/news/gay-icon-kameny-says-bestiality-ok-as-long-as-the-animal-doesnt-mind.html, accessed April 30, 2010. For Kameny, his sentiments expressed the best of "Americanism," and he took LaBarbera to task for his alleged misunderstanding of true Americanism.

14   See, e.g, http://www.wnd.com/index.php?fa=PAGE.view&pageId=121811, January 12, 2010 (accessed April 30, 2010). The full quote reads, "Your God of Leviticus (and of the whole Bible) is clearly a sinful homophobic bigot. He should repent of his sinful homophobia. He should atone for that sin, and he should seek forgiveness for the pain and suffering which his sinful homophobia has needlessly inflicted upon gay people for the past 4,000 years" (cited in ibid.). For a sympathetic portrayal of Kameny as a courageous gay rights hero, along with a sympathetic portrayal of the gay rights movement as a whole, see George Chauncey, *Why Marriage: The History Shaping Today's Debate Over Gay Equality* (New York: Basic Books, 2004), 5-58. For a classic Kameny speech, see "Civil Liberties: A Progress Report," in James Daly, ed., *Great Speeches on Gay Rights* (Mineola, NY: Dover Publications, 2010), 31-52.

15   http://latimesblogs.latimes.com/washington/2009/06/obama-gay-pride-remarks-lgbt.html (see above, n. 9).

Chapter 1

1   See, e.g., http://www.mcsweeneys.net/2005/4/28l.html, accessed April 30, 2010.

2   See, e.g., http://www.commonplacebook.com/jokes/gay_jokes/the_gay_agenda.shtm, accessed April 30, 2010. For an animated version, see http://www.truthwinsout.org/blog/2010/04/8128/, accessed May 1, 2010.

3   A search for the phrase "there is no gay agenda" yields multiplied thousands of hits on a wide variety of websites.

4   For an animated version with sound effects, see http://www.markfiore.com/animation/agenda.html, accessed April 30, 2010.

5   http://www.pamspaulding.com/weblog/2006/06/arm-yourself-with-copy-of-homosexual.html (June 25, 2006, accessed April 30, 2010); she decided to post several – mostly sarcastic – "gay agendas" until, she writes, "we get our hands on the real deal."

6   As stated by Jeffrey-John Nunziata, "Homo-hatred in America," http://www.impactpress.com/articles/octnov97/homohate.htm, "We as a nation and a people have a long way to go in regards to treating our gay, lesbian, bisexual and transgender brothers and sisters as equals. All they want to do is live out their lives just like you do. All they want is to love someone and be loved... so what if it is with a member of the same sex." According to openly gay Congressman Barney Frank, (speaking on the heels of the repeal of "Don't Ask, Don't Tell"), "the radical homosexual agenda" is "to be protected against violent crimes driven by bigotry, it's to be able to get married, it's to be able to get a job, and it's to be able to fight for our country. For those who are worried about the radical homosexual agenda, let me put them on notice. Two down, two to go." http://www.advocate.com/News/Daily_News/2010/12/22/Barney_Frank_Reveals_Gay_Agenda/, both accessed December 22, 2010.

7   http://www.waynebesen.com/2006/02/fundies-fuming-gay-actor-in-christian.html#11389087165433 1659#11389087165433331659, Feb. 2, 2006, accessed April 30, 2010.

8   Rev. Louis P. Sheldon, *The Agenda: The Homosexual Plan to Change America* (Lake Mary, FL: Frontline, 2005); Alan Sears and Craig Osten, *The Homosexual Agenda: Exposing The Principle Threat to Religious Freedom Today* (Nashville: Broadman & Holman, 2003); Dr. Ronnie W. Floyd, *The Gay Agenda: It's Dividing the Family, the Church, and a Nation* (Green Forest, AZ: New Leaf Press, 2004). Similar is the statement of Janet L. Folger, *The Criminalization of Christianity* (Sisters, Oregon: Multnomah Publishers, 2005), 16: "The *greatest threat* to our freedoms comes from the homosexual agenda" (emphasis in the original). More extreme would be the comment of Scott Lively, *Reprobate Theology: The Homosexual Seduction of the American Church* (Citrus Heights, CA: Veritas Aeterna Press, 2003), 1, "The 'gay' activists will be satisfied by nothing less than the total capitulation of the culture to their agenda." Cf. also Congressman William Dannemeyer, *Shadow in the Land: Homosexuality in America* (San Francisco: Ignatius, 1989); Peter Spriggs, *Outrage: How Gay Activists and Liberal Judges Are Trashing Democracy to Redefine Marriage* (Washington, DC: Regnery, 2004). Also quite representative would be Rod Parsley, *Silent No More* (Lake Mary, FL: Charisma House, 2005), chapter four, "Homosexuality: The Unhappy Gay Agenda," 69–88; David Kupelian, *The Marketing of Evil: How Radicals, Elitists, and Pseudo-Experts Sell Us Corruption Disguised as Freedom* (Nashville: WND Books, 2005), especially 17–38; Tristan Emmanuel, *Warned: Canada's Revolution Against Faith, Family, and Freedom Threatens America* (Canada: Freedom Press, 2006), especially 61–78; Roger Magnuson, *Informed Answers to Gay Rights Questions* (Sisters, OR: Multnomah, 1994), esp. 27–43, "The Agenda: What Homosexuals Really Want." See further O. R. Adams Jr., *As We Sodomize America: The Homosexual Movement and the Decline of Morality in America* (n.p.: n.p., 1998); note that this self-published study, available as an ebook, runs 649 pages.

9   http://dir.salon.com/story/news/feature/2004/09/13/coburn/index.html, cited in http://www.edgephiladelphia.com/index.php?ch=news&sc=&sc2=&sc3=&id=97955 (Oct. 21, 2009), "Anti-Gay Pol Reaches Out to GLBTs for Support Against ObamaCare," accessed April 30, 2010.

10   http://www.glaad.org/media/guide/offensive.php?, accessed August 19, 2006 but subsequently removed from the site. It was still listed on a Wikipedia article on "The Gay Agenda" (endnote 2) as of Oct. 26, 2009 and the text is still cited on numerous websites, including this gay activist blog: http://www.soulforce.org/forums/archive/index.php/t-1685.html, with reference to this same GLAAD web address. See also http://www.aglbical.org/2LANGUAGE.htm (accessed Oct. 26, 2009).

11   Jack Nichols, *The Gay Agenda: Talking Back to the Fundamentalists* (New York: Prometheus Books, 1996), 81 (the used copy of the book that I purchased turned out to be signed by Nichols to a friend). Cf. also Didi Herman, *The Antigay Agenda: Orthodox Vision and the Christian Right* (Chicago: University of Chicago Press, 1997).

12   http://rainbowallianceopenfaith.homestead.com/GayAgenda.html, accessed April 30, 2010.

13   This was part of a response to an email from Bill Bonilla to Dr. Mel White, the founder of Soulforce, dated Oct. 9, 2006, responding to a request to hold a campus debate with me on the subject of homosexuality and the Bible. Mr. Bonilla made the innocent mistake of making reference to "the homosexual agenda," drawing this response from Kara, assistant to Dr. White: "You clearly show your bias against the LGBT community with these words. It is only the extreme religious right who suggest that there is a homosexual agenda. Just as any self respecting black person would never deighn [sic] to discuss their humanity with the KKK, we do not chose to give fundamentalists a platform to promote their lies." In an email dated Oct. 12, 2006, Kara added, "Anyone who says there is a homosexual agenda, clearly does not know any gay people. There is no more a homosexual agenda than there is a heterosexual agenda.

There will be no debate, because we will no longer allow fundamentalists such as you, to call our faith and our lives into question." The response from Jeff Lutes of Soulforce, also on Oct. 12, 2006, was much more gracious, as was his personal e-interaction with me.

14   "The gay agenda revealed," http://www.advocate.com/exclusive_detail_ektid00818.asp, accessed April 30, 2010. He states, "There is no gay agenda--this is so clear, and it's the stance we must take. But there is an American agenda, a promise made by the founders that we are still striving to fulfill. Gays and lesbians have merely started to pursue the freedoms and exercise the rights granted in that document that the president wants to amend. How we get and pursue those rights and freedoms remains up for debate, and while there is not real unity in the gay community, there is one thing that ties us in the United States together: We are Americans first. It's time to remind the Right that our agenda is not based on sexual orientation but on a political and social promise, set forth by a group of insightful men a couple hundred years ago."

15   http://www.religioustolerance.org/hom_mar1.htm, accessed April 30, 2010.

16   http://www.aegis.com/news/ap/2004/AP041022.html, accessed May 1, 2010.

17   As quoted in the *Saginaw News*, February 3, 2005, http://afamichigan.org/index.php?p=3, accessed April 30, 2010.

18   http://www.gaytoday.com/garchive/viewpoint/071999vi.htm, accessed April 30, 2010. My appreciation to Katie George and Kim Stephen Allison, FIRE School of Ministry grads and former staff, for drawing my attention to this article.

19   Ibid. This material is also treated in my book *Revolution in the Church: Challenging the Religious System with a Call for Radical Change* (Grand Rapids: Chosen Books, 2002), 29-30. Also relevant is my lecture from February 20, 2007, "What the Church Can Learn from the Gay and Lesbian Community" (available only on DVD).

20   Available online at http://www.williamapercy.com/wiki/images/Refugees_from_Amerika.pdf, accessed April 30, 2010. Wittman died of AIDS in 1986; his manifesto has frequently been reprinted. See, e.g., Karla Jay and Allen Young, eds., *Out of the Closets: Voices of Gay Liberation* (New York: Douglas Book Corporation, 1972), 330-341.

21   See, conveniently, http://www.freerepublic.com/focus/f-news/908140/posts, accessed April 30, 2010.

22   See http://www.qrd.org/qrd/events/mow/mow-full.platform , accessed April 30, 2010.

23   At present, *The Advocate* does not have an online archive of all its past articles, but this article has been memorialized through its citation on conservative Christian websites, where it remains available. See, e.g., http://www.baptistpillar.com/bd0287.htm, accessed December 31, 2010.

24   Marshall Kirk and Hunter Madsen, *After the Ball: How America Will Conquer Its Fear and Hatred of Gays in the 90's* (New York: Penguin, 1989). For a full version of "Overhauling Straight America" online, see http://www.article8.org/docs/gay_strategies/overhauling.htm (with text highlighted by Mass Resistance, which stridently opposes gay activism), accessed April 30, 2010; the article, which is incorporated into chapter 3 of *After the Ball* ("Strategy: Persuasion, Not Invasion") was published in *Guide* magazine, November, 1987; Madsen wrote the article under the pseudonym Erastus Pill.

25   See n. 23, immediately above, for references.

26   *After the Ball*, xv, my emphasis.

27   Ibid., 163, my emphasis.

28   http://positiveliberty.com/2006/01/the-freemasonsthe-illuminatiand-hunter-and-madsen.html, accessed May 1, 2010. Steve Miller's comments were cited by Moore. To quote Miller more fully from Moore's site, Miller claims that when *After the Ball* was published it "didn't generate much buzz among the lefty lesbigay activists at the helm of 'the movement' and certainly was never adopted as any kind of a blueprint. Today it's all but forgotten. To suggest that this book is and has been driving a 'gay agenda' is bizarre to say the least. How gullible are these people?" A Google search of the phrase "'after the ball' kirk madsen" on May 1, 2010, yielded 4,070 hits, and the majority of those that I sampled were from conservative (Christian) websites, apparently confirming Moore's claim. What I have always wondered about was: 1) Since the book was a national bestseller, who actually read it? I would think that it was read far more by the gay community in 1989 than by the straight community (or at the least, widely read by gay leaders); in keeping with this assumption is the blurb from *The Advocate* praising the book: "Offer[s] some excellent suggestions as to how we may proceed in making America more tolerant of gay men and lesbians." Stronger still was the endorsement from the *Washington Post*: "Currently the object of lively debate in the gay community nationwide," while *Booklist* called it, "*The* gay non-fiction book of the year, and certainly the most sensible gay political book ever written" (emphasis in the original). 2) Kirk and Madsen speak of their participation in a "'war conference' of 175 leading gay activists, representing organizations from across the land" that took place in 1988, so it is only logical to think that some of their strategies were shared with the other activists there. In fact, the final statement drafted in this "war

conference" emphasized the importance of using the media to gain "full acceptance of us in American life" (*After the Ball*, 163). 3) Their strategies have been used with incredible effectiveness nationally. Is this just a coincidence? If it is "coincidence," it would mean that other gay activists and leaders and people of influence came up with similar ideas on their own, which is certainly possible, although not necessarily the most likely scenario. The bottom line is this: Strategies like those proposed by Kirk and Madsen *have* been implemented with great success as part of a gay vision to change society, otherwise known as a "gay agenda." (In a debate with Ryan Sorba recorded September 13, 2010, gay activist pioneer Frank Kameny also stated while "the entire conservative far right has read Kirk and Madsen and believes that gays believe it," neither he nor any of his associates ever read the book. Rather, he claimed, "They came up with no new ideas which we/I hadn't been pursuing . . . for thirty years, for twenty-five years before that, and a lot of others with me," and therefore bringing up the book – which Sorba did – "is really irrelevant to anything that's really going on in terms of the gay rights movement." See http://www.youtube.com/watch?v=R7hwt3IVres, beginning at the 2:37 mark, accessed October 19, 2010. This, once again, confirms the point I'm making: If Kirk and Madsen didn't invent the strategies, they helped articulate already extant strategies for advancing a gay agenda.)

29   http://www.waynebesen.com/columns/2005/06/visibility-is-victory.html, accessed May 1, 2010; for those few readers who might be ignorant of this, June has been widely designated "Gay Pride Month," hence Besen's "Happy Pride Month." Would it be fair to ask what the other eleven months stand for in terms of "pride" – be it ethnic, racial, or religious pride? Note that, beginning in June, 2009, President Obama officially recognized June as Gay Pride Month; see http://www.whitehouse.gov/the_press_office/Presidential-Proclamation-LGBT-Pride-Month/, accessed May 1, 2010. For Besen's statement in conjunction with the 2006 elections, see below, n. 92.

30   www.prideagenda.org, accessed May 1, 2010.

31   See http://www.gaypeopleschronicle.com/stories05/january/05jan14-st1.htm, accessed May 1, 2010; the article is by Eric Resnick. The twenty-two organizations are: American Civil Liberties Union Lesbian and Gay Rights Project; Equality Federation; Freedom to Marry; Gay and Lesbian Advocates and Defenders; Gay and Lesbian Alliance Against Defamation; Gay and Lesbian Victory Fund; Gay Lesbian and Straight Education Network; Human Rights Campaign; Lambda Legal; Log Cabin Republicans; Mautner Project; National Association of LGBT Community Centers; National Black Justice Coalition; National Center for Lesbian Rights; National Center for Transgender Equality; National Coalition of Anti-Violence Programs; National Gay and Lesbian Task Force; National Youth Advocacy Coalition; Parents, Family and Friends of Lesbians and Gays; Servicemembers Legal Defense Network; Sigamos Adelante--National Latino/Hispanic LGBT Leadership; Stonewall Democrats.

32   http://www.nationalreview.com/phi-beta-cons/242996/lgbtq-presidents-higher-education-thomas-shakely, my emphasis, accessed August 12, 2010. For this use of the word "diversity," see below, and more fully, Chapter Eight.

33   http://www.hrc.org/Template.cfm?Section=About_HRC, accessed August 29, 2006, but no longer accessible. Similar descriptions can be found throughout the HRC website.

34   See http://www.theagendaonxm.org/ for show archives.

35   http://www.thetaskforce.org/aboutus/whatwedo.cfm, accessed August 29, 2006, but carrying other information now, although, as with the HRC website, similar statements can be found throughout their website.

36   Ibid.

37   http://www.ilga.org/aboutilga.asp, accessed May 1, 2010.

38   http://old.ilga.org/aboutilga_results.asp?FileID=18, accessed May 1, 2010.

39   http://www.lambdalegal.org/, accessed May 1, 2010; note also that there is a strong, pro-homosexual slant among lawyers in the ACLU; see now Alan Sears and Craig Osten, *The ACLU Against America* (Nashville: Broadman & Holman, 2005).

40   See Paula Ettelbrick, "Since When Is Marriage a Path to Liberation?", in William Rubenstein, ed., *Lesbians, Gay Men and the Law* (New York: The New Press, 1993), 401-405. Dr. Ettelbrick has been a Professor of Law at the University of Michigan since 1994. Her comments here have often been quoted and turn up in many Internet articles on both sides of the issue.

41   http://www.pflag.org/index.php?id=13, accessed August 29, 2006, but no longer available here; the same information can now be found on other websites, such as http://www.madisonsos.org/index.php?page=natlorg, accessed May 1, 2010.

42   http://community.pflag.org/Page.aspx?pid=743, accessed May 1, 2010.

43   http://www.glsen.org/cgi-bin/iowa/all/about/history/index.html, accessed May 1, 2010.

44   See Chapter Three for more on this.

45   See Chapter Three for more on this.

46 This is an accurate assessment: "GLSEN's materials regularly undermine both parental authority and religious teaching. They seek to separate children from their families and from their faith upbringing." See http://mommylife.net/archives/2010/07/glsen_-_gay_act.html, accessed August 14, 2010.

47 See Chapter Three for more on this.

48 Their website is www.queertoday.com; for this description, originally found on their home page, see http://www.masstpc.org/mediawiki/index.php?title=Blogs, accessed May 1, 2010; for LGBTQIP, see Chapter Nine.

49 www.campuspride.net/**gaypril**.asp, accessed May 1, 2010, but without the "GayPril brings campus queers," quote, originally accessed August 29, 2006.

50 Ibid. According to an e-mail from Jordan B. Woods, Co-Chair of the BGLTSA for 2006 (see again Chapter Nine for explanations of acronyms such as these), Gaypril at Harvard has three objectives. First, it is to "increase visibility of queer issues and people at Harvard; second, to increase awareness through education and workshops about queer issues. . . . [the third objective is to] "simply celebrate and have fun." The goals in general fit with the constitution of the BGLTSA, which has in its mission statement, among other things, the commitment to "improving the visibility, strength, and support of the Harvard-Radcliffe undergraduate bisexual, gay, lesbian, transgender and queer communities." See http://www. harvardindependent.com/media/paper369/news/2005/04/21/News/Gaypril.In.Full.Tilt-935709. shtml, accessed August 29, 2006 but subsequently removed. For the last sentence, see http://wgs.fas. harvard.edu/icb/icb.do?keyword=k53419&tabgroupid=icb.tabgroup92526, accessed May 1, 2010.

51 http://www.glaad.org/Page.aspx?pid=1373, accessed May 1, 2010; the statement on their Mission s=page now reads, "The Gay & Lesbian Alliance Against Defamation (GLAAD) amplifies the voice of the LGBT community by empowering real people to share their stories, holding the media accountable for the words and images they present, and helping grassroots organizations communicate effectively. By ensuring that the stories of LGBT people are heard through the media, GLAAD promotes understanding, increases acceptance, and advances equality." See http://www.glaad.org/mission, accessed May 1, 2010.

52 http://www.glaad.org/about/pres_letter.php, accessed August 29, 2006, but subsequently removed.

53 Cited in my article "Charlotte Pride or Charlotte Shame," http://www.icnministries.org/revolution/ CharlotteShame.htm, accessed September 15, 2010; the *Observer* article is no longer available online.

54 See further, below, Chapter Six, where the "Gay is the new black" argument is analyzed.

55 http://faculty.smu.edu/dsimon/Change-Civ%20Rts.html, accessed May 1, 2010, my emphasis.

56 http://www.cccr.org/template/index.cfm, accessed May 1, 2010, my emphasis.

57 http://capmag.com/articlePrint.asp?ID=1211, accessed May 1, 2010.

58 http://www.usda.gov/news/pubs/97arp/arp8.htm, accessed May 1, 2010.

59 A Google search for "civil rights agenda" on May 1, 2010, yielded 359,000 hits.

60 See http://got.net/~elained/, accessed August 29, 2006, but access denied on May 1, 2010.

61 http://www.now.org/issues/peace/index.html, accessed May 1, 2010.

62 http://www.now.org/press/02-99/02-08-99.html, accessed May 1, 2010.

63 http://www.advocate.com/exclusive_detail_ektid00818.asp, accessed May 1, 2010. Note that Bouley's reference to gay Republicans as oxymoronic points to his assumption that the expected political allegiance of most gays is *not* with the Republicans, for obvious reasons.

64 In a mock – but quite realistic – confession of "a large group of same-sex-marriage activists . . . to a group of same-sex-marriage skeptics," Stanley Kurtz puts these words on the lips of the same-sex-marriage activists: "As gay marriage gains acceptance, we're going to have a polygamy-polyamory debate in this country. And among those sponsoring that debate will be many of the very same people and groups who've already pushed for same-sex marriage.

"So why haven't we told you all this before? Simple. We've been censoring ourselves for fear of scaring away public support for same-sex marriage. You see, it's all about timing. Our plan is to establish same-sex marriage first, and then, as our next step, to demand that the rights and benefits of marriage be accorded to all types of families. After all, when the call for yet another radical redefinition of marriage comes from married same-sex couples, it's going to be that much more persuasive. Up to now, truth to tell, if any same-sex marriage backers pushed this radical agenda in public, we pressured them to keep silent. But now we're telling you the truth." See "The Confession," October 31, 2006, http://article. nationalreview.com/296007/the-confession/stanley-kurtz, accessed May 1, 2010.

65 With reference to the radical language and goals of the Beyond Same Sex Marriage statement issued in July, 2006 (BeyondMarriage.org), Stanley Kurtz, "The Confession II," November 1, 2006, http:// article.nationalreview.com/296336/the-confession-ii/stanley-kurtz, accessed May 1, 2010, quotes the "conservative" gay advocate Evan Wolfson who acknowledged that, "Ninety percent of what's in that document could have been signed onto by virtually every person working in the gay movement today."

66 In the animated version of Mark Fiore's "Attack of the Gay Agenda," one of the men in the pictured gay couple says, "Leave us alone." See above, n. 4.

67 For psychological effect, students in Framingham, Massachusetts "were forced to answer a questionnaire that openly challenged the validity of their heterosexuality," or at least, was intended to demonstrate to them that homosexuality was just as innate and natural as heterosexuality and that all forms of "homophobia" were completely baseless. See Sears and Osten, *The Homosexual Agenda*, 65. For the full text of the questionnaire, see, e.g, http://safezone.slu.edu/downloads/program.heterosexual%20questionnaire.pdf (accessed May 10, 2010). A Google search performed on May 1, 2010 for the sentence (in quotation marks) "What do you think caused your heterosexuality," yielded 6,100 hits, which is quite telling.

68 See, e.g., Hans Clausen, "The 'Privilege of Speech' in a 'Pleasantly Authoritarian Country': How Canada's Judiciary Allowed Laws Proscribing Discourse Critical of Homosexuality to Trump Free Speech and Religious Liberty," *The Vanderbilt Journal of Transnational Law* 38 (2005), 443-504; it can be downloaded in PDF format at http://narth.com/docs/PrivilegeofSpeechClausen090.pdf, accessed May 1, 2010. See further Chapter Fourteen, below.

69 See Chapters Fourteen and Fifteen, for more on this.

70 For more on this, see Chapter Three, below.

71 See Debra J. Saunders, "Diversity Training," *The San Francisco Chronicle*, 23 June, 1996, cited by Josh McDowell and Bob Hostetler, *The New Tolerance* (Wheaton: Tyndale House, 1998), 75. See now http://articles.sfgate.com/1996-06-23/opinion/17777760_1_religion-and-politics-hate-public-school, accessed August 26, 2010.

72 See Folger, *Criminalization*, 17-18, with references. In 2003, these views were written into the Swedish constitution; see further below, Chapter Fourteen.

73 Ibid., 118-120.

74 Ultimately, under federal pressure, the Borough Council had to apologize to Michael Marcavage, the Christian leader in question, since the charges against him were found to be without merit. See http://www.alliancedefensefund.org/news/story.aspx?cid=3689, accessed May 1, 2010.

75 See Folger, *Criminalization*, 20-21.

76 http://www.telegraph.co.uk/news/uknews/1577982/Bishop-fined-in-gay-discrimination-case.html, accessed May 1, 2010.

77 See below, Chapter Fourteen, for details.

78 All these are cited verbatim from Folger, *Criminalization*, 26-27; see further Sears and Osten, *Homosexual Agenda*, for numerous examples, assembled carefully and without exaggeration by the authors, both of whom are attorneys. More broadly, see now Rev. Donald E. Wildmon, *Speechless: Silencing the Christians* (n.p.: Richard Vigilante Books, 2009). Even if some of the specific instances cited in these books could be challenged in terms of there being another side to the story, or if, in some cases, the Christians involved were not entirely "Christian" in tone, what cannot be denied is that: 1) There are many, undeniable cases of attempts to eradicate or greatly curtail the constitutional liberties guaranteed by our nation; and 2) free speech is not protected only when the speaker's tone is civil and gracious.

79 It has been suggested to me by a conservative attorney that "full circle" would be this: In the past, gays were put into jail for their open demonstrations and violations of the law; in the future, those who oppose them will be put into jail!

80 Quoted in George Archibald, "Changing minds: Former gays meet resistance at NEA convention," *The Washington Times*, July 27, 2004, p. A2.

81 For a thorough critique of Jennings' appointment, see Peter Sprigg, "Homosexual Activist Kevin Jennings not Fit for Dept. of Education," http://www.frc.org/get.cfm?i=IS09F01, accessed May 1, 2010.

82 Cited in Clausen, "Privilege of Speech," 447, n. 21. The lesson aide is entitled *Counseling Gay and Lesbian Youth*.

83 See below, Chapter Nine, for more on this.

84 See below, Chapter Eight, for more on this.

85 See below, Chapter Eight and Fourteen, for more on this. Cf. also Robert Weissberg, *Pernicious Intolerance: How Teaching to "Accept Differences" Undermines Civil Society* (New Brunswick, NJ: Transaction Publishers, 2008); Brad Stetson and Joseph G. Conti, *The Truth about Tolerance: Pluralism, Diversity and the Culture Wars* (Downers Grove, IL: InterVarsity, 2005); Jay Budziszewski, *True Tolerance: Liberalism and the Necessity of Judgment* (Brunswick, NJ: Transaction Publishers, 2000); Amy Orr-Ewing, *Is the Bible Intolerant? Sexist? Oppressive? Homophobic? Outdated? Irrelevant?* (Downers Grove, IL: InterVarsity, 2005).

86 See below, Chapter Two, for more on the accusation of "hate speech."

87 See below, Chapter Three, for more on this.

88   See below, Chapter Three, for more on this.
89   See below, Chapter Four, for more on this.
90   See below, Chapter Fourteen, for more on this.
91   See below, Chapters Two and Fourteen, for more on this.
92   Note that even in Foreman's statement, one has to read between the lines to understand what, exactly, the agenda would mean. For a "translation" of Foreman's agenda, see Peter LaBarbera, http:// americansfortruth.com/news/gay-agenda-what-gay-agenda.html, "'Gay Agenda' . . . What 'Gay Agenda'?," November 22, 2006 (accessed May 1, 2010). Foreman's statements make Kurtz's "gay" comments somewhat prophetic and all the more believable: "Up to now, truth to tell, if any same-sex marriage backers pushed this radical agenda in public, we pressured them to keep silent. But now we're telling you the truth." On October 20, 2006, in the gay *Washington Blade*, Wayne Besen was quoted as saying, "We're accused of having a gay agenda ... but this is the time when we really need one," cited in http://americansfortruth.com/news/homosexual-activists-already-planning-"gay-agenda"-for-democratic-controlled-house.html, accessed May 1, 2010.
93   Mel White, *Religion Gone Bad: The Hidden Dangers of the Christian Right* (New York: Jeremy P. Tarcher/ Penguin, 2006), 7.

Chapter 2
1   Marshall Kirk and Hunter Madsen, *After the Ball: How America Will Conquer Its Fear and Hatred of Gays in the 90's* (New York: Penguin, 1989), 153; for the text online, see http://www.article8.org/docs/ gay_strategies/after_the_ball.htm, accessed May 1, 2010; for more on gay influence on the media, see below, Chapter Five. For a gay denial that *After the Ball* was actually influential in gay activism, see above, Chapter One, n. 28.
2   See, respectively, http://www.jeffjacoby.com/784/phobic-in-the-wrong-places, accessed May 1, 2010, and Laura Schlessinger's Foreword to Richard Cohen, *Coming Out Straight: Understanding and Healing Homosexuality* (Winchester, VA: Oakhill Press, 2000), ix. For the "Stop Dr. Laura" campaign, see below, Chapter Five.
3   We'll discuss the semantic strategies put forth in *After the Ball* in greater detail in Chapter Nine, below.
4   See the revealing editorial of John McCandlish Phillips, "When Columnists Cry 'Jihad,'" published in the *Washington Post*, Wednesday, May 4, 2005, Page A19; http://www.washingtonpost.com/wp-dyn/ content/article/2005/05/03/AR2005050301277.html. Phillips was formerly a highly respected journalist for the *New York Times*. For background, see http://ashwoodjournal.blogspot.com/2009/06/john-mccandlish-phillips.html, both accessed May 1, 2010.
5   For the origin of the term homophobia, see *Gay Power*, 182-184; for more on the concept of "homophobia," see below, Chapter Nine.
6   For an articulation of some of his beliefs, see his debate with Rev. John Rankin, "Does God Hate Homosexuals," transcribed at http://www.mars-hill-forum.com/forumdoc/m070cont.html. To watch the debate online, begin at http://www.youtube.com/watch?v=hxmud2vMutc&feature=related, both accessed May 1, 2010. I am in fundamental agreement with the position of Rev. Rankin. It is quite surprising to know that in decades past, Phelps was a prominent civil rights attorney who was a champion of the black community; see http://us.cnn.com/2010/US/05/05/hate.preacher/index.html, accessed June 1, 2010.
7   Originally posted at http://www.godhatesamerica.com/ and posted frequently online on other sites. See, e.g, http://www.kare11.com/news/news_article.aspx?storyid=103703, accessed May 1, 2010.
8   Originally posted at http://www.godhatessweden.com/ but since posted on other sites, such as http:// erikwottrich.blogspot.com/2007/04/god-hates-sweden.html, accessed May 1, 2010.
9   As with the other comments just cited, these were originally posted on one of the various Phelps cites and then spread widely online. See, e.g., http://www.sodahead.com/entertainment/heath-ledger-is-now-in-hell-and-has-begun-serving-his-eternal-sentence-there-the-westboro-baptis/question-41292/ (KK's comment on January 30), accessed May 1, 2010.
10   See, e.g., http://watchingthewatchers.org/news/389/fred-phelps-swears-god-hates-america-fags, accessed May 1, 2010.
11   See http://www.pamspaulding.com/weblog/2005_06_01_pamspaulding_archive.html, accessed May 1, 2010.
12   Originally posted at http://www.godhatesfags.com, now posted at http://blogs.sparenot.com/index. php/workmen/?title=we-know-how-to-accomodate-the-sound-byte-generation&more=1&c=1&tb=1 &pb=1, accessed May 1, 2010.
13   http://www.mars-hill-forum.com/forumdoc/m070opgu.html, accessed May 1, 2010.
14   "Holy War: 'A Cause Worth Dying For,'" http://goqnotes.com/editorial/editorsnote_012608.html, ac-

cessed December 12, 2010.

15 http://askdrbrown.org/media/albums/COC/OfficialStatements/Statement%20to%20the%20Gay%20 and%20Lesbian%20Community.pdf, accessed December 12, 2010.

16 This is a verbatim transcript from the video of the night.

17 "Holy War," cited above, n. 14.

18 More recently, Matt Comer, while still claiming that I'm "preaching exclusion and hate and pushing people away from Christ rather than pulling them," and while making reference to my allegedly "hardened heart" could write: ". . . after years of interactions with Brown, I've finally come to see more and more of his own humanity, particularly a more private and sincere side of him I'd never seen before. I'm now convinced that Brown honestly does believe everything that comes out of his mouth." So, I'm *not* following "a carefully plotted and scripted message of 'compassion,' 'love' and 'gentleness'," as he previously thought. This being the case, Matt concluded that I must be deluded, since, from his vantage point, it would be impossible for someone to be as civil as me and yet as bigoted and intolerant without being deluded. Thus, he accuses me of coming from "some sort of deeply-rooted dislocation from reality," claims that my "words provide more than ample evidence of a journey into delusion," and speaks of my "unique brand of lunacy." But at least he now believes I'm sincere! See "A Prayer for Michael Brown," http://goqnotes.com/9424/a-prayer-for-michael-brown/, accessed December 12, 2010; for my response to this editorial, published by Q-Notes, in which Matt wrongly claimed that I compared "homosexuality to child rape," see http://goqnotes.com/9513/setting-the-record-straight/, accessed December 27, 2010.

19 See, respectively, "Michael Brown responds to the Southern Poverty Law Center article on ex-gays," http://wthrockmorton.com/2007/12/14/michael-brown-responds-to-the-southern-poverty-law-center-article-on-ex-gays/, December 14, 2007; and "The Fighting Words of Michael Brown," http://www.exgaywatch.com/wp/2008/01/the-fighting-words-of-michael-brown/ (January 24, 2008); for other articles attacking me on the Ex-Gay Watch site, see also "Pedophilia, Hedonism & Impending Confusion: Revisiting the Anti-Gay Rhetoric of Michael Brown," http://www.exgaywatch.com/wp/2008/02/pedophilia-hedonism-impending-confusion-revisiting-the-anti-gay-rhetoric-of-michael-brown/, February 29, 2008; and "Building 'London Bridges' with Dr. Michael Brown," http://www.exgaywatch.com/wp/2009/07/building-london-bridges-with-dr-michael-brown/, July 1, 2009. (All sites were accessed May 2, 2010.)

20 Using 300 words per page as a common figure for popular, printed books, this would mean that these two threads equaled a 500 page book! The Throckmorton thread was the result of interaction that took place over a period of about two weeks and totaled about 95,000 words; the Ex-Gay Watch interaction lasted only for several days (in terms of my active participation), totaling about 55,000 words.

21 http://www.exgaywatch.com/wp/2008/01/the-fighting-words-of-michael-brown/comment-page-5/#comment-27565, accessed May 2, 2010.

22 J. James, January 18, 2008, 4:05 PM, at http://wthrockmorton.com/2007/12/14/michael-brown-responds-to-the-southern-poverty-law-center-article-on-ex-gays/, accessed May 2, 2010.

23 http://www.topix.com/news/gay/2008/02/wheaton-college-invites-pro-gay-evangelical-speaker#comments, Comments #22 and 20, respectfully, accessed February 27, 2008, but since relocated or removed.

24 The HRC has responded to this kind of criticism by saying, "Homosexual rights are human rights," which, of course, does not actually address why the HRC does not invest one dollar a year in advocating for the rights of the poor, the rights of those persecuted for their religious beliefs, or the rights of women and minorities, or, for example, the rights of those being slaughtered in Darfur – with the exception of those people in these various groups who are gay! The HRC could also be asked, What about the rights of ex-gays? What about the rights of those who voted for Prop 8? Do those people not have human rights? In point of fact, everything the HRC does has one purpose only, and every dime they raise goes in one direction only: Advocating for homosexual rights in particular, not human rights in general. For gay blogger Andrew Sullivan's criticism of the HRC for still using the name "human rights" rather than being more forthright (obviously, he is criticizing them for reasons quite different from mine), see http://www.youtube.com/watch?v=8B_uLSHniik&feature=PlayList&p=1578CEEC64D9F97D&pla ynext_from=PL&playnext=1&index=16. Note that using "human rights" as a codeword for "gay rights" is not unique to the HRC. According to http://www.infoplease.com/ipa/A0761909.html, such use in America dates back to 1924, when the Society for Human Rights in Chicago became "the country's earliest known gay rights organization." For further details, see http://www.glapn.org/sodomylaws/usa/illinois/ilnews02.htm, all accessed May 2, 2010.

25 See http://demopedia.democraticunderground.com/discuss/duboard.php?az=viewall&address=3 9x206904, accessed May 2, 2010.

26 http://www.democraticunderground.com/discuss/duboard.php?az=register, accessed May 2, 2010.

27   http://www.youtube.com/watch?v=TuBzgQYy3YA, accessed May 2, 2010.

28   For more on Kim Pearson's work, see http://www.imatyfa.org/; for Dr. Marci Bowers's website, see http://www.marcibowers.com/.

29   http://www.youtube.com/watch?v=TuBzgQYy3YA (because of the amount of comments, it's necessary to scroll down multiple pages), accessed May 2, 2010.

30   Ibid.

31   Ibid.

32   http://www.youtube.com/user/1993Vanessa2009, accessed May 2, 2010, with updated personal information; the description cited here was accessed January 31, 2010 (presumably she was born in 1993). Just for the record, when I read posts like those of this teenager, I certainly don't feel like the victim. My sympathies are entirely with "Vanessa," and she has not wounded me in the least.

33   She states, "I strongly detest discrimination and that includes transphobia, homophobia, and racism. I get extremely infuriated when people are rude to an entire group of people, because they are either ignorant, childish, mislead by a childish source (such as Jerry Springer), insensitive, naïve, or automatically misinterpret something (like with the bible), or just plain sterotypical" (ibid.).

34   Dr. James Dobson, *Marriage Under Fire: Why We Must Win This Battle* (Sisters, OR: Multnomah, 2004), 72; for a listing of relevant studies on both sides of the same-sex marriage debate, see below, n. 56.

35   Ibid., 73. I am very much aware of the fact that many gays and lesbians do *not* appreciate this kind of compassion, as articulated by this review of Thomas E. Schmidt's study, *Straight and Narrow: Compassion and Clarity in the Homosexuality Debate* (Downers Grove, IL: InterVarsity Press, 1995), posted by Timothy Hulsey on Amazon.com: "Is Schmidt's book reliable, clear, and compassionate? A friend of mine took a swan dive off the fifth floor of a parking garage because his church and his family believed 'compassionate' theologians like Schmidt. Many Gays and Lesbians, also friends of mine, swear never to set foot in a Christian church again, precisely because they were traumatized by this kind of 'compassion.' And many Straight people – parents and friends of Gays and Lesbians who have learned that God loves homosexuals for who they are -- have left their churches because of this kind of 'compassion.'
"When I read a book like Schmidt's, and reflect that his is the line adopted by *liberal* Christian churches, I wonder if Gays and Lesbians aren't doing the best thing for their physical, mental and spiritual health when they reject Christianity outright. Fortunately, there are ministers like Rembert Truluck, church leaders like Bishop John Shelby Spong, and theologians like Daniel Helminiak, who exhibit true compassion on this issue. Christians who seek insight in the debate over homosexuality may do well to look to their examples."
Contrast these sentiments with those of an anonymous Amazon reviewer: "If you are looking for a book that 'justifies' homosexuality through misinterpretation of Scripture this is not the book for you. If you are looking for a book that 'justifies' your anger or resentment of homosexuals this is not the book for you. If you are a person who wants to better understand the issues surrounding the Christian faith and homosexuality this is an excellent book for you. Unfortunately, the critics of Schmidt's conclusion don't tackle his arguments, they merely resort to lumping him into a category (homophobe) they immediately dismiss. Those critics should read his book again because they missed his love and compassion for them as individuals regardless of whether they are homosexual or heterosexual." (I have corrected misspelled words in both reviews.)

36   All these quotes come from bulletin board postings re: the Sponge Bob controversy on talkleft.com/new_archives/009400.html, accessed May 2, 2010. A search for "Sponge Bob" and "Dobson" points to how wide spread the controversy became, with the common accusation being that Dobson called "Sponge Bob" gay.

37   David Henson, assistant views editor, *The Decaturian Online* (The Decaturian is a publication of Milliken University in Decatur, Illinois), www.deconline.com (but in perpetual maintenance mode for the last few months, and hence inaccessible), originally accessed February 1, 2006. Although there are many similar quotes about Dobson, this one caught my eye because it was from a campus newspaper.

38   See Chapter One, above, for more on this.

39   *The Tragedy of Today's Gays* (New York: Jerry P. Tarcher/Penguin, 2005), 38; for Kramer's retrospective thoughts on the speech that formed the text of the book, see ibid., 15-31. I would encourage all those who oppose "gay rights" to read Kramer's speech in order to get a better grasp on the state of America as seen by one influential (and, then, quite pessimistic) gay activist. Also enlightening from this perspective is Daley, *Great Speeches on Gay Rights*.

40   As a Jew, I am fully aware of the tragic fact that some homosexuals were also singled out for brutal torture, deprivation, and execution by the Nazis, being forced to wear the pink triangle just as Jews were forced to wear the yellow star (although there is some dispute as to the numbers of homosexuals killed by the Nazis). All the more then do I find it indefensible to compare defenders of traditional marriage

with Hitler and the Nazis, since the vast majority of those who differ with the gay agenda (including the sinister Christian right!) at the same time denounce all forms of violence that would be directed against homosexuals, welcoming them as fellow-citizens, co-workers, and often friends. Notwithstanding the unfairness of the comparison, it is regularly exploited in gay propaganda. See, e.g., Kirk and Madsen, *After the Ball*, 189, and note that Mel White, *Stranger at the Gate: To Be Gay and Christian in America* (New York: Plume, 1995), 321, lists as a strategy against the religious right, "Start your own version of a local 'to prevent gay/lesbian' holocaust museum. Demonstrate the similarity between Hitler's Third Reich and the current tactics of the religious right." See further, below, n. 62, with reference to the *American Taliban* volume of Markos Moulitsas. An anonymous Amazon.com reviewer of Dr. Jeffrey Satinover's important book *Homosexuality and the Politics of Truth* (see below, n. 45, for bibliographical details; the review was dated December 27, 2001) suggests reading the book as follows: "Every time you see the word 'homosexual,' substitute the word 'Jew.' Whenever you see 'homosexuality,' substitute the word 'Judaism.' Then close your eyes and pretend you are in Nazi Germany and you're listening to a lecture about 'the Jewish problem.' Then go home and read your bible, 'Mein Kampf.' After all, isn't it the revealed truth? Not too pretty a picture, is it? When authors write attack books that purport to tell the 'truth' about one group, no group is safe." Again, the moral equivalency argument here is extremely offensive, as if homosexuals make absolutely no choices in their course of action or lifestyle, whereas in Nazi eyes a Jew was a Jew regardless of where he or she had sought to convert to another religion, sever all connection to Judaism, or even completely renounce his or her Jewishness." See http://www.amazon. com/Homosexuality-Politics-Truth-Jeffrey-Satinover/dp/080105625X/ref=cm_cr_pr_product_top (scroll down the reviews by date), accessed May 2, 2010.

41   *Tragedy of Today's Gays*, 37. For the Larry Kramer Initiative in gay and lesbian studies at Yale, see below, Chapter Four.

42   http://voiceofrevolution.askdrbrown.org/2010/02/06/responding-to-the-critics-ihop-testimony-on-deliverance-from-same-sex-attraction/#comment-12604, accessed May 2, 2010.

43   http://lezgetreal.com/?p=26053, accessed May 2, 2010.

44   Ibid, with specific reference to http://voiceofrevolution.askdrbrown.org/2010/02/06/responding-to-the-critics-ihop-testimony-on-deliverance-from-same-sex-attraction/, accessed May 2, 2010 (this is the same article from which Evan Hurst's comments were cited, immediately above).

45   Jeffrey Satinover, M.D., *Homosexuality and the Politics of Truth* (Grand Rapids: Baker, 1996).

46   Ibid., 11.

47   Ibid., 15.

48   Ibid., 20-21.

49   http://www.amazon.com/Homosexuality-Politics-Truth-Jeffrey-Satinover/dp/080105625X/ref=cm_cr_pr_product_top, accessed May 2, 2010 (scroll down the reviews by date).

50   Ibid.

51   http://www.washingtonpost.com/wp-dyn/content/article/2008/07/03/AR2008070303769.html, accessed May 2, 2010.

52   Ibid.; McDonald's subsequently withdrew from the National Gay and Lesbian Chamber of Commerce.

53   On April 6, 2009, President Obama appointed Harry Knox to his Faith Advisory council.

54   The video of the dialogue can be viewed at http://coalitionofconscience.askdrbrown.org/resources/debate.html.

55   http://www.hrcbackstory.org/2008/02/hrcs-religion-and-faith-director-takes-on-leader-of-conservative-anti-gay-group-in-charlotte/, accessed May 2, 2010. In reality, what provoked Joe Solomonese's challenge to me was my aforementioned, five-night lecture series on "Homosexuality, the Church, and Society," in 2007, culminating with a lecture entitled, "Debunking the Myth of the Human Rights Campaign," on Friday, February 23, the night before the HRC's large, Carolinas fund raising dinner. (The timing of this on my part was, of course, intentional.) The next night, at the dinner, Solmonese challenged me directly (in my absence, but in the presence of the 1,200+ in attendance) saying, "And Pastor Brown, if you're here tonight [loud laughs] . . . do you remember Ted Haggard [hoots and applause]. If you're here tonight, know this: We are not afraid to take you on and take back the conversation about religion and faith in this country [cheers and applause]." In response to that challenge, we reached out to Mr. Solmonese suggesting that he send a representative or come himself and have a dialogue with me the following year, which led to the discussion with Harry Knox.

56   Even more inaccurate than the opening comments was the description of the debate and its alleged effects on some of our own college-age students (ibid.): "Speaking from his heart and out of his deep faith, Harry electrified the crowd and transformed many. . . . While those who came to support Harry were ebullient, Harry's words also seemed to leave Brown's students rattled as he clearly disturbed many of their set assumptions about religion and GLBT people. Indeed, Harry was nearly mobbed at the end

of the event by students who found themselves unexpectedly wrestling with the power of his words and clarity of his vision of justice." Scott Volk, the pastor of my home congregation in Concord, NC, read the HRC report the following Sunday morning, Feb. 17, and emailed me the reaction: "I read the HRC piece from their website to our church body, many of whom were there on Thursday night. I was actually surprised by the volume of gasps and incredulous laughter that came as they heard the HRC rendition of what transpired last Thursday. As I looked up after reading the first number of paragraphs, I was amazed at the number of heads that were shaking in disbelief.

"Here is what I liken it to: The New England Patriots write a game plan, predicting how the Super Bowl will turn out with them victorious. And then, after losing the game, they publish the plan and continue wearing their 'Super Bowl Champion' shirts" (this was immediately after the Patriots *lost* the Super Bowl to the NY Giants). See "Living in the Land of Make Believe: A Response to the HRC's Article on the Brown/Knox Dialogue," see http://www.icnministries.org/articles/SCOTTVOLKRESPOND-STOTHEHRC.pdf, accessed May 2, 2010 When I read the HRC report to the very students Harry had spoken to, they were even more incredulous, expressing nothing but love and pity for him.

57   Judge Marvin Baxter, one of the dissenting justices in this decision, labeled it an "exercise in legal jujitsu," claiming that it would "create a constitutional right from whole cloth, defeat the people's will and invalidate a statute otherwise immune from legislative interference." See, e.g., http://www.connor-boyack.com/blog/legal-jujitsu-in-california-same-sex-marriage-upheld, accessed May 2, 2010.

58   http://laist.com/2008/08/18/nbc_blogger_prop_8_hate_repeat.php, accessed May 2, 2010.

59   http://townhall.com/columnists/DennisPrager/2008/12/09/a_response_to_marcshaiman%e2%80%99s_musical_against_prop_8, accessed May 2, 2010.

60   As Caleb H. Price asked (in light of the sometimes ugly protests that followed the passage of Prop 8), "So what's going on here? Since when does constitutionally exercising one's religious views at the ballot box on an important issue like marriage call for the vicious reaction we're seeing? What ever happened to the marketplace of ideas, tolerance of differing viewpoints and basic American decency?" Dec. 16, 2008, http://www.citizenlink.org/clcommentary/A000008894.cfm, accessed May 2, 2010.

61   This is the case of Patrick Stuebing and Susan Karolewski. As a young boy, he was separated from his family, not learning that he had a sister, Susan, until he was twenty-three, at which point they met and then fell in love, starting a family together, despite government intervention and a prison sentence for incest. See, e.g, http://news.bbc.co.uk/2/hi/6424937.stm and http://www.spiegel.de/international/germany/0,1518,540831,00.html, both accessed May 2, 2010. See further, below, Chapter Fifteen, for other recent examples of incestuous adult relationship.

62   For the question of the potential health risks of gay (male) sex, see below, Chapters Eleven and Thirteen.

63   Important books opposing same-sex marriage (and/or, emphasizing the importance of male-female marriage) include: Frank Turek, *Correct, Not Politically Correct: How Same-Sex Marriage Hurts Everyone* (Charlotte: CrossExamined, 2008); David Blankenhorn, *The Future of Marriage* (New York: Encounter Books, 2007); Dale O'Leary, *One Man, One Woman: A Catholic's Guide to Defending Marriage* (Manchester, NH: Sophia Institute Press, 2007); Robert P. George and Jean Bethke Elshtain, eds., *The Meaning of Marriage: Family, State, Market, and Morals* (Dallas: Spence Publishing, 2006); Glenn T. Stanton and Dr. Bill Maier, *Marriage on Trial: The Case Against Same-Sex Marriage and Parenting* (Downers Grove, IL: InterVarsity, 2004); Matthew D. Staver, *Same-Sex Marriage: Putting Every Household at Risk* (Nashville: Broadman & Holman, 2004); John Stott, *Same-Sex Partnerships?* (Grand Rapids: Fleming H. Revell, 1998); more broadly, Douglas Farrow, *Nation of Bastards: Essays on the End of Marriage* (Toronto: BPS Books, 2007; note that Farrow's book is focused on Canada); Alan C. Carlson and Paul T. Mero, *The Natural Family: A Manifesto* (Dallas: Spence Publishing, 2007); Carle E. Zimmerman, *Family and Civilization* (ed. by James Kurth, with an introduction by Allan C. Carlson; Wilmington, DE: ISI Books, 2008; the original edition was published in 1947). Important books favoring same-sex marriage include: William N. Eskridge, Jr. and Darren R. Spedale, *Gay Marriage: For Better or Worse? What We've Learned from the Evidence* (Oxford: Oxford University Press, 2006); Mark D. Jordan, *Blessing Same-Sex Unions: The Perils of Queer Romance and the Confusions of Christian Marriage* (Chicago: University of Chicago Press, 2005); Evan Wolfson, *Why Marriage Matters: America, Equality, and Gay People's Right to Marry* (New York: Simon & Schuster, 2004); George Chauncey, *Why Marriage? The History Shaping Today's Debate Over Gay Equality* (New York: Basic Books, 2004); Davina Kolutski, Ph.D., *Why You Should Give a Damn About Gay Marriage* (Los Angeles: Advocate Books, 2004); Jonathan Rauch, *Gay Marriage: Why It Is Good for Gays, Good for Straights, and Good for America* (New York: Henry Holt, 2004). For differing views presented in one volume, see, e.g., Douglas Laycock, Anthony R. Picarello, Jr., and Robin Fretwell Wilson, eds., *Same-Sex Marriage and Religious Liberty: Emerging Conflicts* (Lanham, MD: Rowman & Littlefield, 2008); Andrew Sullivan, ed., *Same-Sex Marriage: Pro and Con* (updated

edition, New York: Vintage, 2004). For discussion of some of the larger issues confronting marriage in America today, see, e.g., Andrew J. Cherlin, *Marriage-Go-Round: The State of Marriage and the Family in America Today* (New York: Alfred A. Knopf, 2009); and Paul R. Amato, Alan Booth, David R. Johnson, and Stacy J. Rogers, *Alone Together: How Marriage in America Is Changing* (Cambridge, MA: Harvard University Press, 2007). For an enlightening exchange of articles see Sherif Girgis, Robert P. George, and Ryan T. Anderson, "What Is Marriage?", *Harvard Journal of Law and Public Policy*, 34 (2010), 245-287 (available online at http://papers.ssrn.com/sol3/papers.cfm?abstract_id=1722155); a response by Kenji Yoshino, "The Best Argument Against Gay Marriage. And why it fails," http://www.slate.com/id/2277781/ (Yoshino is a professor at the New York University School of Law); a response to Yoshino by George, Girgis, and Anderson, "The Argument Against Gay Marriage: And Why it Doesn't Fail," http://www.thepublicdiscourse.com/2010/12/2217, all accessed December 19, 2010.

64 I received an email from a colleague who was present at the Sacramento rally and documented this information; none of the gay activists with whom I shared the email denied the report. For a sustained (and, quite frankly, laughable) attempt to justify the "Taliban" and "jihadist" rhetoric, see Markos Moulitsas, *American Taliban: How War, Sex, Sin, and Power Bind Jihadists and the Radical Right* (Sausalito, CA: PoliPointPress, 2010).

65 Dobson, *Marriage Under Fire*, 70-71, observed, "If there is hate existent in this debate over homosexuality, it appears to be coming from the other side. During the conflict over the Amendment 2 initiative, I was the target of great venom. . . . During that period, our buildings were spray-painted with bigoted slogans. We received death threats and telephone bomb warnings. Bloody animal parts were brought to the front of the headquarters building, and a mock funeral found its way onto our property. . . . These are the tactics, mind you, of the folks who accuse Christians of being hate-filled and intolerant."

66 In an unusually candid admission by a gay writer, James Kirchick noted that "the rage" that Perez Hilton expressed towards Miss California, Carrie Prejean, after the 2009 Miss America pageant "was hardly an isolated incident; it was characteristic of the tenor of many gay writers and activists in the aftermath of Proposition 8's passage. The vitriolic rhetoric expressed then and still today toward those who supported the measure is an issue that many gay people would rather not confront, and it's to our detriment that this nasty tone is slowly taking over the movement. When you portray anyone who disagrees with you as a 'hater' -- and what other conclusion can be drawn from a campaign that adopted 'No H8' as a slogan -- it becomes much easier to demonize one's opposition. Anything goes when the person opposing you is a 'bigot' a la the Ku Klux Klan. In this way many gays mimic the behavior of their worst enemies, who for decades have tried to portray us as sick and depraved threats to society." Interestingly, Kirchick believes that men like Jerry Falwell and Pat Robertson were true haters, and that there is no real substance to the arguments of those who oppose same-sex marriage, yet he notes that "there are many people who voted for Proposition 8 who did so not because of an irrational fear or hatred of homosexuals." Even more interestingly, the article closes with, "James Kirchick, an Advocate contributing writer, is an assistant editor of The New Republic. This article is representative of the author's views and not those of Advocate.com." Was this article a little too candid? See "The Truth About Perez Hilton," July 8, 2009, http://www.advocate.com/exclusive_detail_ektid96838.asp, accessed May 2, 2010.

67 http://www.queerty.com/nom-to-new-jersey-were-coming-for-you-garden-state-gays-20091109/, accessed May 2, 2010.

68 http://www.politico.com/news/stories/1210/46327.html#ixzz18V8NSJxI, accessed December 19, 2010.

69 http://psimo.blogspot.com/2006/08/adam-kautz-white-gay-racist.html, accessed May 2, 2010. The man who wrote this was Adam Kautz; see ibid. for more information on him. Foster notes, "After I sent the emails to yahoo abuse department, I called the Olympia PD and my local police. Not, that I'm frightened of Adam, he just needs help and maybe some punishment for his really bad behavior."

70 http://townhall.com/columnists/MikeAdams/2009/07/15/subsidized_by_hate, accessed May 2, 2010.

71 Archived at http://www.icnministries.org/revolution/hateButton.htm; see now Matthew J. Franck, "On gay marriage, stop playing the hate card," in the *Washington Post*, December 19, 2010, http://www.washingtonpost.com/wp-dyn/content/article/2010/12/17/AR2010121707043.html, both accessed December 22, 2010. Franck opens his editorial by stating, "In the debates over gay marriage, 'hate' is the ultimate conversation-stopper." In closing, however, he notes, "But the charge of 'hate' is not a contribution to argument; it's the recourse of people who would rather not have an argument at all. That is no way to conduct public business on momentous questions in a free democracy. 'Hate' cannot be permitted to be the conversation stopper in the same-sex marriage debate. The American people, a tolerant bunch who have acted to protect marriage in three-fifths of the states, just aren't buying it. And they still won't buy it even if the judges do."

Chapter 3

1   http://www.glsen.org/binary-data/GLSEN_ATTACHMENTS/file/444-1.pdf, 3, accessed May 3, 2010.

2   See, e.g., *Bullycide in America: Moms Speak Out About the Bullying/Suicide Connection*, compiled by Brenda High (Darlington, MD: JBS Publishing, 2007). For moving personal stories, see Mitchell Gold, ed., with Mindy Drucker, *Crisis: 40 Stories Revealing the Personal, Social, and Religious Pain and Trauma of Growing Up Gay in America* (Austin, TX: Greenleaf Book Group Press, 2008). Matt Comer, one of the contributors to this volume and the local gay editor whom I mentioned in the previous chapter, kindly presented me with a copy of this book shortly after its release. The book does a great job of getting the straight reader into the shoes of gays and lesbians.

3   Dan Woog, *School's Out: the Impact of Gay and Lesbian Issues on America's Schools*, (Boston: Alyson Publications, 1995), 373. My appreciation to my former student Kasia Mysliwiec for this quote. In a paper entitled "Exposing and Confronting the Homosexual Agenda in Education," she wrote: "Teachers College in New York City affiliated with Columbia University is a leading graduate institution of education in our nation. In the years 1994-1998, it was rated the number one graduate school of education by U.S. News and World Report. . . . What kind of values does this institution promote and endorse that shape the curricula across the nation? While working at the Teachers College library, I often processed new titles of books that came from our acquisition department. This experience inspired my paper. In the course of my work, I discovered how readily the library is acquiring books that deal with the subject of both homosexual educators and education. Further survey of its collection showed a significant number of aggressively pro-gay books. The picture is clear: the Teachers College is a strong proponent of the homosexual agenda in education, starting as early as elementary school. Their stand clearly reflects the overall picture of the homosexual agenda in our public schools. It is alarming."

4   http://www.glsen.org/cgi-bin/iowa/all/news/record/1810.html, accessed May 3, 2010.

5   All references are to the second edition of the Lunchbox, referenced in n. 4, immediately above.

6   Larry Kramer, *The Tragedy of Today's Gays* (New York: Jerry P. Tarcher/Penguin, 2005), 20, wrote, "Because Abraham Lincoln and George Washington (to name but two) were gay, the history of our country was changed." Focusing on Lincoln, Kramer notes that "for the past several years, I had worked very hard indeed – and against repulsive, odious opposition – to help bring to publication *The Intimate World of Abraham Lincoln* by C. A. Tripp [New York: Free Press, 2005], the first book to present Lincoln as an active homosexual from his youth until his death" (19-20). Actually, Tripp's book makes mountains out of molehills of evidence, molehills that are, to be candid, quite specious at that, offering nothing new by way of facts, often leaving out important, contradictory information, and reading things into the extant evidence that would only "prove" things to the eyes of a gay reader. Preeminent Lincoln biographers have been duly unimpressed with Tripp's work and there remains no strong reason to doubt his heterosexuality, let alone doubt Washington's. Tripp's book even comes with an Afterword by Lincoln historian Michael Burlingame (226-238) in which he expresses his respectful dissent to Tripp's thesis. More forcefully, see the verdict of seven top Lincoln scholars dismissing Tripp's claims, some quite strongly: http://www.claremont.org/publications/crb/id.1099/article_detail.asp. That being said, I agree that Lincoln and others on the GLSEN list must be evaluated along many lines, not exclusively along lines of "sexual orientation." That is to say, all those on the GLSEN list accomplished what they did regardless of whether they were heterosexual or homosexual, and those accomplishments speak for themselves. See further, below, Chapter Seven, n. 57.

7   Cited in http://www.theinterim.com/2002/sept/02study.html, accessed May 3, 2010.

8   http://www.nambla.org/history.htm, accessed May 5, 2010.

9   http://www.nambla.org/famousmen.htm, accessed May 5, 2010. For further details, see Keith Stern, *Queers in History* (Dallas: Benbella Books, 2009); specifically, for Alexander the Great, see 10-11 ("Alexander's relationships with his youthful aides would not have seemed unusual in ancient Greece, particularly among soldiers."); for Leonardo Da Vinci, see 275-277 ("When he was thirty-eight, Leonardo adopted a ten-year-old boy. . . . Their relationship was anything but typical of a father and son, and Leonardo is recognized today as a man with a taste for 'rough trade.'. . . he remained Leonardo's 'kept boy' for the next twenty-five years."); for Michelangelo, see 321-322 ("Michelangelo had numerous gay lovers throughout his long life, especially among the young men who were the models for his work . . . [One of them, named Cecchino dei] Bracci was thirteen when Michelangelo [then sixty-six] fell in love with him."); for Oscar Wilde, see 489-490 ("Although happily married and a doting father, Wilde was perhaps not the ideal husband. He found himself sexually attracted to young men, especially working-class 'rough trade.'") For more on Wilde, see below, Chapter Seven. More broadly, see Martin Duberman, Martha Vicinius, and George Chauncey, Jr., eds., *Hidden from History: Reclaiming the Gay and Lesbian Past* (New York: Meridian, 1989), in particular, David M. Halperin, "Sex Before Sexuality:

Pederasty, Politics, and Power in Classical Athens," 37-53.

10 "The GLSEN Lunchbox: Trainer's Manual," 37.

11 http://www.syrculturalworkers.com/catalog/catalogIndex/CatGender.html#books, accessed August 29, 2006, but since removed, as the book is no longer carried by that vendor. The Product Description on Amazon is somewhat more tame: http://www.amazon.com/Girls-Will-Be-Boys-Coloring/dp/193236062X/ref=sr_1_1?ie=UTF8&s=books&qid=1272932903&sr=8-1, accessed May 3, 2010. The book itself is everything the blurb said it was.

12 http://syracuseculturalworkers.com/poster-things-you-can-do-eradicate-gender-or-multiply-it-exponentially, accessed May 3, 2010. GLSEN has pointed people to this website, where teachers can download signs with inverted, rainbow-colored triangles proclaiming "Safe Zone" to put on their classroom door. They can also print off discussion kits on how to organize gender education sessions and start conversations about homosexuality with the children.

13 For more on Mollie Biewald's background, see below, Chapter Fifteen.

14 The expanded definition also notes, "About 1/7% of the population can be defined as intersexuals born with biological aspects of both sexes to varying degrees. So, in actuality, there are more than two sexes." ("Trainer's Manual," 44)

15 The expanded definition states, "This is what we call ourselves. Such labels include 'lesbian,' 'gay,' 'bisexual,' 'bi,' 'pansexual,' 'pomosexual,' 'queer,' 'questioning,' 'undecided,' 'undetermined,' 'heterosexual,' 'straight,' 'asexual,' and others. . . . Our sexual behavior and how we define ourselves (identity) can be chosen. Though some people claim their sexual orientation is also a choice, for others this does not seem to be the case" (ibid.). Cf. also, "**Gender Identity:** Refers to a person's internal, deeply felt sense of being either male, female, boy or girl or something other. Everyone has a gender identity." See http://www.healthiersf.org/LGBTQ/InTheClassroom/docs/4.4%20Common%20Vocabulary.pdf, accessed May 4, 2010.

16 See, e.g., http://www.boston.com/yourlife/health/other/articles/2006/12/02/supporting_boys_or_girls_when_the_line_isnt_clear/, accessed May 3, 2010.

17 Ibid.

18 http://www.wnd.com/index.php?pageId=63978, accessed November 9, 2010.

19 As cited in n. 16, ibid.

20 Ibid.

21 Ibid, my emphasis.

22 http://www.narth.com/docs/crossdressing.html, accessed May 3, 2010. The links in this article no longer work, very possibly having been disabled due to controversy.

23 http://www.boston.com/bostonglobe/ideas/articles/2008/03/30/qa_with_norman_spack/?page=full, accessed May 3, 2010.

24 March 30, 2008, Pagan Kennedy, "Q & A with Dr. Norman Spack," http://www.transactiveonline.org/documents/health/DocLib-Q%20&%20A%20With%20Norman%20Spack.pdf, accessed May 3, 2010.

25 Ibid.

26 Ibid.

27 According to Kasia Mysliwiec in her paper (cited above, n. 3), "The overall gay agenda [as seen in the educational system] is rooted in the Social Construction Theory (also called social constructionism). This postmodern concept creates and defines identities (or any reality) arbitrarily, as products of the existing culture. The constructionists believe "there are no essential, inborn, and ageless criteria for identity, but that certain values assume importance as a result of society's temporal needs or dictates," citing Arthur Lipkin, "The Case for a Gay and Lesbian Curriculum," in Donovan R. Walling, ed., *Open Lives, Safe Schools*, (Bloomington, IN: Phi Delta Kappa Educational Foundation, 1996), 62.

28 As of this writing, it is believed that Kim Petras (formerly Tim) was the youngest person in the world to have sex change surgery, at the tender age of sixteen. According to Tim/Kim's bio: "Kim Petras was born Tim Petras. She is a German teenager who began her sex change treatments *at the young age of twelve*. She was diagnosed as a transsexual three years ago [meaning, at age thirteen], and when she claimed to be 'in the wrong body,' doctors and psychiatrists agreed upon the sex change. They artificially halted male puberty with a series of potent hormone injections, later administering female hormones to start the development of her breasts. Kim Petras is now 16 years old, and has long blonde hair and blue eyes [after "gender reassignment surgery"]." See, e.g., http://www.rightcelebrity.com/?p=4357, accessed May 3, 2010, my emphasis. How many other lifelong, unalterable decisions would we allow a sixteen-year-old to make?

29 Start watching here: http://www.youtube.com/watch?v=2mYvj6bEpQM&feature=related, accessed May 3, 2010.

30 Dr. Kenneth J. Zucker is widely recognized as one of the foremost authorities on children suffering with

GID, and his book, co-authored with Dr. Susan J. Bradley, *Gender Identity Disorder and Psychosexual Problems in Children and Adolescents* (New York: Guilford Press, 1995), is a standard in the field. And, in his view, if a child with GID ends up content and well-adjusted living as an adult gay or lesbian person, that is considered by him to be a positive outcome (in other words, it would be hard to describe him as homophobic). Zucker is currently the chairman of the The Sexual and Gender Identity Disorders Work Group for the APA committee working on the DSM-V (see below, Chapter Thirteen, for further context and background), thus putting him in a highly influential, not to mention highly respected position. For some of his reflections on the current state of GID research, see http://wthrockmorton.com/2008/06/05/gender-identity-disorder-research-q-a-with-kenneth-zucker/ and http://wthrockmorton.com/tag/ken-zucker/, both accessed May 3, 2010. For the current status of the DSM V and its viewpoint on GID through the eyes of GID reformers, see http://www.gidreform. org/dsm5.html, accessed December 12, 2010. For a pro-transgender attack on the current classification of GID as a mental disorder, see Kelley Winters, Ph.D., *Gender Madness in American Psychiatry: Essays from the Struggle for Dignity* (Dillon, CO: GID Reform Advocates, 2008).

31   For my approach to the bullying issue, see "Gay Is Good or Bullying Is Bad? A Teachable Moment," http://townhall.com/columnists/MichaelBrown/2010/10/25/gay_is_good_or_bullying_is_bad_a_ teachable_moment.

32   http://montgomerypublicschools.blogspot.com/2007/06/response-to-allan-lichtmans-op-ed-in.html, accessed May 3, 2010.

33   The teacher in question was actually a student in our ministry school in Concord, NC, and she and her husband are well-known to our community.

34   For further thoughts on these gender issues from a strongly Christian perspective, see the Citizen Link interview with Randy Thomas at: http://www.citizenlink.org/CLtopstories/A000006818.cfm?eafref=1.

35   http://www.glsen.org/binary-data/GLSEN_ATTACHMENTS/file/000/000/294-6.PDF, 12, accessed December 3, 2010.

36   Ibid., 10.

37   Ibid., 12.

38   For the scope of GLSEN's vision for the distribution of the Safe School Kit, see https://safespace. glsen.org/about.cfm: "GLSEN strives to ensure that every school in America is safe for all students, regardless of sexual orientation or gender identity/expression. We want a Safe Space Kit to be used in the more than 100,000 middle and high schools across America to provide all students a safe place to learn." For Hollywood support of GLSEN's goals (all under the rubric of anti-bullying campaigns), see, e.g., where the stars of TV's "The Closer" strongly advocate this GLSEN initiative – with a threat to the bullies at the end of the video for good measure: http://www.youtube.com/watch?v=Izl7-YCmsqE&feature=player_embedded, both accessed December 3, 2010.

39   Available for download, respectively, at http://www.nyacyouth.org/docs/Bending%20the%20Mold-final.pdf and http://www.nyacyouth.org/docs/Bending%20the%20Mold-final.pdf, among other sites; both accessed December 22, 2010.

40   See, e.g., http://americansfortruth.com/news/letting-your-son-wear-a-dress-nyt-helps-mainstream-gender-confusion-in-children.html, accessed December 12, 2010.

41   See, e.g., http://www.transgenderlaw.org/college/sfusdpolicy.htm , accessed December 12, 2010. For more on the concept of the "gender assigned at birth," see below, Chapter Nine.

42   Although this account was passed on to me by a reliable source, I have not located a news story for it online.

43   On April 17, 2008, it was widely reported that in Australian news that, "Teachers are being urged to stop using terms such as husband and wife when addressing students or families under a major anti-homophobia push in schools. The terms boyfriend, girlfriend and spouse are also on the banned list - to be replaced by the generic "partner" - in changes sought by the gay lobby aimed at reducing discrimination in classrooms." See, e.g., http://www.generationq.net/news/australia/newspaper-causes-homophobic-backlash-170408.shtml. These reports, however, have been both disputed and flatly denied. See http://www.abc.net.au/mediawatch/transcripts/s2223389.htm, both accessed May 5, 2010. What is not in dispute is that the Director-General of the NSW [New South Wales] Education Department, Michael Coutts-Trotter, opened a one-day conference in Sydney last Wednesday [April 16, 2008] aimed at combating homophobia in schools" (cited in ibid.), and, as we know all too well, "combating homophobia" can be quite broad in its scope.

44   See, e.g., http://www.capitolresource.org/blog.php?blog_id=65&frompage=latestblog, accessed October

6, 2010.

45   Ibid.

46   For the actual text of the bill, see http://info.sen.ca.gov/pub/07-08/bill/sen/sb_0751-0800/sb_777_
bill_20070510_amended_sen_v97.html, accessed May 5, 2010. The relevant text reads, "No textbook
or other instructional materials shall be adopted by the state board or by any governing board for use
in the public schools that contains any matter reflecting adversely upon persons reflects or promotes
a discriminatory bias against any person because of a characteristic listed in Section 220." The text
that is struck through represents language that was changed in the final draft, but this only blunts
the effect of the bill since, as we have seen, simply the lack of affirmation of homosexuality can be
viewed as discriminatory, while referring to Moms and Dads can be taken as discriminatory against
same-sex households. Section 220 reads, "disability, gender, nationality, race or ethnicity, religion, sexual
orientation, or any other characteristic that is contained in the definition of hate crimes set forth in
Section 422.55 of the Penal Code in any program or activity conducted by an educational institution
that receives, or benefits from, state financial assistance or enrolls pupils who receive state student
financial aid."

47   See http://www.wnd.com/news/article.asp?ARTICLE_ID=58130, accessed May 5, 2010.

48   http://americansfortruth.com/news/theyre-baacckk-california-gay-brainwashing-bills-sb-777.html,
accessed May 5, 2010.

49   http://findarticles.com/p/articles/mi_m1571/is_1_18/ai_82013574/, accessed May 5, 2010. For
reaction to this same questionnaire when it was used in Port Washington, Milwaukee, see http://www3.
jsonline.com/story/index.aspx?id=424003, accessed September 14, 2010.

50   http://www.boston.com/news/local/massachusetts/articles/2005/04/29/arrested_father_had_point_to_
make/, accessed May 5, 2010. The Parker's son brought the books home in January, 2005.

51   Ibid.

52   From Judge Wolf's decision, Case 1:06-cv-10751-MLW Document 36, http://www.massresistance.
org/docs/parker_lawsuit/motion_to_dismiss_2007/order_motion_to_dismiss_022307.pdf (accessed
May 5, 2010), 4, 29-30 (my emphasis).

53   In October 2008, the Supreme Court refused to hear the case, http://www.boston.com/news/
education/k_12/articles/2008/10/09/us_supreme_court_refuses_lexington_case/ (one of 2,000 it
declined to hear in its opening session), accessed May 5, 2010.

54   http://www.massresistance.org/docs/gen/08b/ash_exchange_040308.html, accessed May 5, 2010.

55   Cited above, Chapter One, with references in n. 82.

56   See, conveniently, http://www.narth.com/docs/details.html; for the full article in *Time*, begin here:
http://www.time.com/time/magazine/article/0,9171,1112856,00.html (both accessed May 5, 2010).

57   http://groundspark.org/our-films-and-campaigns/elementary/ie_calltoaction, accessed August 14,
2010.

58   As cited in the *Time* article, referenced above, n. 56.

59   Lanham, Boulder, New York, Oxford: Rowman & Littlefield Publishers, 1999. I purchased this book
June 28, 2005 at which time it was a volume primarily known to the educational community, and it
was at that time that I decided to incorporate some of the material from that book into this present
one, which was just being formed at that time. However, in 2009, when President Obama appointed
Kevin Jennings (then Executive Director of GLSEN) to be his Safe School Czar, there was a national
focus on this book, since Jennings wrote the Foreword to it. See, e.g., http://townhall.com/columnists/
KevinMcCullough/2009/06/07/why_obamas_elementary_queering_must_be_stopped, accessed May
3, 2010. For that reason, I'm glad to see the book has become better known.

60   All these quotes are taken from the back cover and opening (unnumbered) page.

61   The "Pestalozzi" in question is Johann Heinrich Pestalozzi (1747-1827), "a Swiss educationalist
concerned with 'race regeneration' and education for the masses." (See *Queering Elementary Education*,
28)

62   *Understanding Homosexuality, Changing Schools: A Text for Teachers, Counselors, and Administrators*
(Boulder, CO: Westview Press, 1999). The chapter praising "The Massachusetts Model" is found on
263-287.

63   *Queer Theory in Education* (Mahwah, NJ: Lawrence Erlbaum Associates, 1998).

64   http://www.amazon.com/Oh-Things-Mommies-Do-Better/dp/0578027593/ref=pd_bxgy_b_text_b,
accessed Sept. 5, 2010.

65   For more on this story, see http://www.narth.com/docs/penguins.html, accessed Sept. 5, 2010.

66   See, e.g., Dr. Ronnie W. Floyd, *The Gay Agenda: It's Dividing the Family, the Church, and a Nation* (Green
Forest, AZ: New Leaf Press, 2004), 14.

67   Michael Willhoite (writer and illustrator), *Daddy's Roommate* (Los Angeles: Alyson Wonderland, 1990,

2000; the 2000 printing commemorates the book's tenth anniversary).

68 Lesléa Newman (author) and Diana Souza (illustrator), *Heather Has Two Mommies* (Los Angeles: Alyson Wonderland, 1989, 2000).

69 http://www.glsen.org/cgi-bin/iowa/all/booklink/record/1559.html, accessed May 4, 2010.

70 http://www.worldnetdaily.com/index.php?pageId=63978, accessed May 4, 2010.

71 http://groups.myspace.com/index.cfm?fuseaction=groups.groupProfile&groupID=107324790&Mytok en=C5542335-A7B4-4DA4-93848D2AA9E8D6CF403761475, accessed May 4, 2010.

72 Ibid.

73 http://www.massresistance.org/docs/downloads/glsen_2008/GLSEN_Conf_Program.pdf, 5, accessed May 4, 2010.

74 Ibid., 6.

75 Ibid., 8.

76 http://www.massresistance.org/docs/gen/08b/glsen_conf_0329/bisexuality.html, accessed May 4, 2010.

77 For external verification of this on college campuses in 2004, see "Girls kissing girls a new campus trend," published by the University Wire, April 15, 2004, http://www.encyclopedia.com/doc/1P1-93493814. html. According to the article, this phenomenon is known as the "bisexual chic trend" or "lipstick lesbians," it also being noted there that many of the women involved are not actually bisexual. For clinical verification, see the April 3, 2010 article in *Psychology Today* by Dr. Leonard Sax, "Why are so many girls lesbian or bisexual?," http://www.psychologytoday.com/blog/sax-sex/201004/why-are-so-many-girls-lesbian-or-bisexual?page=2, accessed May 4, 2010. In line with this would be popular songs like Katy Perry's hit, "I Kissed a Girl and I Liked It," and the profusion of women kissing women in movies, for which see below, Chapter Five. On March 29, 2007, Bill O'Reilly devoted a segment of his show to the subject of TV scenes with women kissing.

78 This incident was shared with me by a personal friend of the teacher.

79 http://www.foxnews.com/us/2010/10/15/sex-survey-dc-school-sparks-controversy/?test=latestnews, accessed October 15, 2010.

80 See http://borngay.procon.org/sourcefiles/ccv-handbook.pdf, accessed October 18, 2010. This paper was published by the Cincinnati-based Citizens for Community Values.

81 http://www.exgaywatch.com/wp/2010/09/atlanta-megachurch-bishop-accused-of-male-sexual-abuse/, accessed September 26, 2010, my emphasis.

82 See, concisely, Dr. Neill Whitehead, "The Changeability of Adolescent Same-Sex Attraction," http://www.jonahweb.org/article.print.php?secId=294, accessed September 26, 2010, with reference to further academic studies. Whitehead noted that, "The quoted work of Remafedi looked at 12 year-olds who would be expected to be even more unstable than adolescents. An estimate that 85% changed orientation, or perhaps more accurately attractions, is inherently reasonable.
"The most detailed study to date is a very large longitudinal study by (Savin-Williams & Ream, 2007) who found changes in attraction so great even between ages 16 and 17 that they queried whether the concept of sexual orientation had any meaning for those with same-sex attractions. In considerable contrast those with opposite sex attractions overwhelmingly retained them from year to year. From ages 17-21 those with some initial same sex attraction (this includes those with concurrent opposite-sex attraction) 75% changed to opposite sex attraction only. This is within error the same as the 85% figure which is the current object of debate."

83 See, e.g., http://www.onenewsnow.com/Education/Default.aspx?id=603580, accessed July 25, 2010.

84 http://www.onenewsnow.com/Education/Default.aspx?id=1088280, accessed July 25, 2010.

85 For a list of all NEA caucuses, see http://www.nea.org/assets/docs/nea-handbook-recognized-caucuses. pdf. In the midst of much controversy, there is also an Ex-Gay Educators Caucus, whose stated purpose is, "'Working to eliminate intolerance and discrimination against ex-gay students, teachers, and their supporters." See http://nea-exgay.org/about/, accessed July 25, 2010.

86 http://www.neaexposed.com/blog/?p=476, accessed July 30, 2010. Prof. Konrath was kind enough to respond to a personal email from me, inquiring as to the nature and purpose of the caucus's scholarship. He explained on August 12, 2010 that "The scholarship is for a LGBT public school senior going to college. It's $2,000 with $1,000 awarded the first semester and the second $1,000 if they maintain a B average first semester. The application and requirements will be online at ricfest.org by the middle of August. The site is up, but the national scholarship application isn't totally on yet."

87 See http://www.academia.org/the-nea-vs-teachers/, accessed July 25, 2010. Also influential in this regard is the Southern Poverty Law Center's (SPLC) educational wing, "Teaching Tolerance." As family activist and former school teacher Laurie Higgins pointed out to me in an email of June 18, 2010, "Many teachers subscribe to their free email and use their resources, the newest of which is: https://secure.splcenter.org/donations/donate/overview?ondntsrc=MBS100570BTT" (advertising a film and

study guide "showing viewers that anti-gay bullying is wrong – morally and legally"). See further the following articles by Higgins on the Illinois Family Institute website: http://www.illinoisfamily.org/dsa/contentview.asp?c=34254; http://www.illinoisfamily.org/dsa/contentview.asp?c=34056; http://www.illinoisfamily.org/dsa/contentview.asp?c=34233; http://www.illinoisfamily.org/informed/contentview.asp?c=34138, all accessed December 22, 2010. For the degree to which the SPLC has recently discredited itself, see below, Chapter Fourteen.

88   See http://www.truetolerance.org/curricula.pdf, accessed October 18, 2010. It is found in the GLSEN Lunchbox Trainer's Manual (rev. ed.) on 35, with explanations of each attitude. Thus, "Tolerance" means, "Being different is just a phase of development that most people grow out of," while "Acceptance" means, "One needs to make accommodations for another's differences; another identity does not have the same value as one's own." The manual references Dorothy Riddle, *Alone No More: Developing a School Support System for Gay, Lesbian and Bisexual Youth*, with no further publication details except for year of release (1994). It is interesting that there is no mention of "transgender youth" in the title, perhaps reflecting the date it was published, when the "t" word was not receiving as much attention.

89   Robert Weissberg, *Pernicious Intolerance: How Teaching to "Accept Differences" Undermines Civil Society* (New Brunswick, NJ: Transaction Publishers, 2008), 142.

90   http://www.dayofsilence.org/, accessed April 10, 2008; on May 4, 2010, the home page read, "On the National Day of Silence hundreds of thousands of students nationwide take a vow of silence to bring attention to anti-LGBT name-calling, bullying and harassment in their schools."

91   Previously, the stated purpose of the Day of Silence was "to draw attention to the widespread oppression and persecution of gays and lesbians." See, e.g., Andrew Roth, writing on the Queer Day blog April 22, 2005, and echoing the official language then used by GLSEN; http://www.queerday.com/2005/apr/22/andrew_roth_day_of_silence_day_of_truth.html, accessed April 10, 2008.

92   In response to this, in 2005, the Alliance Defense Fund launched its Day of Truth, held on the day following (or, preceding) the Day of Silence, the purpose being "to affirm every student's constitutional right to free speech and to provide an opportunity to have an honest conversation about sexuality." See http://dayoftruth.org/ (Exodus International actively sponsored the Day of Truth in 2010, after which it was adopted by Focus on the Family with the new name "Day of Dialogue"; see http://www.dayofdialogue.com/). The Illinois Family Institute, together with a coalition of conservative Christian groups launched the Day of Silence Walkout, believing that this would send a message to the schools as well as protect children from unwanted influences; see http://www.illinoisfamily.org/doswalkout/. Prof. Warren Throckmorton has advocated a different strategy, called the Golden Rule Pledge, saying to school kids, "Don't walkout, walk along side and be a hero. Don't preach at gay kids and call it conversation. Instead, walk along side and listen." See http://goldenrulepledge.com/. Those helping to facilitate the Day of Truth (now, Day of Dialogue) would state that they are doing anything but preaching at gay kids, while those helping to facilitate the Day of Silence Walkout would state that the kids have the rest of the school year to show their love and concern for their gay and lesbian friends and that walking out on a day of gay activist propaganda is a responsible (and Christian) thing to do.

93   See, e.g., http://www.cspinet.org/new/201012151.html, accessed December 19, 2010, my emphasis.

94   As reported by Mass Resistance at http://www.massresistance.org/docs/gen/10d/coming_out_assembly/index.html (with an insightful reaction from one protesting parent); for the original news report, see http://www.carlislemosquito.org/2010/2010-10-29/index.html, both accessed December 16, 2010.

95   Ibid., my emphasis.

96   Ibid., emphasis in the original.

97   As stated to me privately by an evangelical Christian attorney, "By university level, it [referring to gay activist values] is required dogma, and the failure to participate results in expulsion from programs, denial of licenses, and removal from professions."

Chapter 4

1   Shane L. Windmeyer, ed., *The Advocate College Guide for LGBT Students* (New York: Alyson Books, 2006). The book is dedicated to "the first generation of 'out' college students: The time is now." Windmeyer's book is one of several devoted to this subject, although his survey fits a particular niche. For a study published by Princeton Review, famous for its college-related books, see *The Gay and Lesbian Guide to College Life* (New York: Princeton Review, 2007).

2   Note that American University is described as a "Private university. Methodist religious affiliation."

3   http://townhall.com/columnists/MattBarber/2007/12/26/a_"gay_man"_trapped_in_a_woman's_body_and_other_nonsense, accessed May 12, 2010.

4   Ibid., my emphasis.

5   http://web.uvic.ca/~ahdevor/HowMany/HowMany.html, accessed November 29, 2010. Cf. also Holly Devor, *Gender Blending: Confronting the Limits of Duality* (Indianapolis and Bloomington: Indiana University Press, 1989), and note that Aaron H. Devor was originally Holly Devor. For the issue of chromosomal abnormalities, discussed in *Gender Blending*, 7-10, see below, Chapter Nine, n. 46.

6   Bonnie Bullough, Vern L. Bullough, and James Elias, eds., *Gender Blending: Transvestism (Cross-Dressing), Gender Heresy, Androgyny, Religion & the Cross-Dresser, Transgender Healthcare, Free Expression, Sex Change Surgery* (Amherst, NY: Prometheus Books, 1997).

7   Cotton Mather, *Magnolia Christi: The Great Works of Christ in America* (Carlisle, PA: Banner of Truth, 1979), 25; for this text (and much more) online, see http://boldhearts.com/massachusetts.htm, accessed May 12, 2010.

8   Mather, *Magnolia Christi*, ibid.; also online at http://boldhearts.com/massachusetts.htm. Contrast this 1642 Harvard requirement with today's college scene: "[students] shall be slow to speak, and eschew not only oathes, Lies, and uncertain Rumours, but likewise all idle, foolish, bitter scoffing, frothy wanton words and offensive gestures" (ibid., in both book and website).

9   Cf. Ben Shapiro, *Brainwashed: How Universities Indoctrinate America's Youth* (Nashville: Thomas Nelson, 2004); see also idem, *Porn Generation: How Social Liberalism is Corrupting our Future* (Washington, DC: Regnery, 2005).

10 Cited at http://www.opinionjournal.com/best/?id=110004916, accessed May 12, 2010, with reference to http://www.thecrimson.com/today/article358622.html/, which is no longer available but was my original source for this information.

11 For the online application, see http://inq.applyyourself.com/?id=hbs&pid=6; cf. also http://www.wdc-media.com/newsArticle.php?ID=1526, both accessed May 12, 2010.

12 See http://boldhearts.com/massachusetts.htm, accessed May 12, 2010. Under Rev. John Leverett, president of Harvard from 1708-1724, standards temporarily declined and there were complaints of "profane swearing," "riotous Actions," and "bringing Cards into the College." Can you imagine such actions creating a stir on our campuses today, especially "bringing Cards into the College"?

13 See http://etcweb.princeton.edu/CampusWWW/Companion/princeton_university_seal.html, accessed May 12, 2010.

14 See http://etcweb.princeton.edu/CampusWWW/Companion/founding_princeton.html, accessed May 12, 2010.

15 See http://www.columbia.edu/about_columbia/history.html, accessed May 12, 2010.

16 See *A History of Columbia University, 1754-1904: Published in Commemoration of the One Hundred and Fiftieth Anniversary of the Founding of King's College (1904)* (Ithaca, NY: Cornell University Library, 2010), 443-44.

17 See, e.g., http://www.bu.edu/sth/admissions/discernment-questions/why-choose-bu/, accessed May 12, 2010, and note the text of this 2004 speech by David Hempton, a professor at Boston University's School of Theology: "What I have tried to parse out in anniversary time has a spatial representation at the heart of the BU campus. The next time you walk across Marsh Plaza, I want you to notice three things. Look at the University's coat of arms, taken from its Methodist foundation: Learning, Virtue, and Piety. Think about what those words might mean for teachers and students: that knowledge and ethics should not be separated; that learning and mentoring are both essential to what we do. Look at the memorial to Martin Luther King, and think about how learning, virtue, and piety in his case were harnessed to fight mediocrity, oppression, and injustice. Look also at Marsh Chapel and let your aspirations soar as ambitiously as those great gothic arches, pointing to something greater than our own self-interest" (ibid.).

18 See http://www.archives.upenn.edu/histy/features/vis_obj/heraldry/guide.html, accessed May 12, 2010.

19 See, e.g., http://audiolatinproverbs.blogspot.com/2007/04/leges-sine-moribus-vanae.html, accessed June 13, 2010.

20 See http://ruweb.rutgers.edu/inauguration/media-color.html, accessed May 12, 2010.

21 See http://catalogue.nla.gov.au/Record/3377105, accessed May 12, 2010.

22 This summarizes the findings of William C. Ringenberg, *The Christian College: A History of Protestant Higher Education in America* (Grand Rapids: Eerdmans, 1984), as noted on the back cover.

23 http://97.74.65.51/readArticle.aspx?ARTID=15628, accessed April 26, 2010. The lecture took place at Oberlin College, of which we will have more to say later in this chapter.

24 Ibid. For a sampling of some of the faculty debate on this subject, see http://www.oberlin.edu/stupub/ocreview/archives/1998.10.02/news/bdsm.html, accessed May 12, 2010. According to the article (from October 2, 1998), Professor of Politics and Law Ronald Kahn "pointed out that a common argument against the charter's approval was one that pointed out the dangers of some BDSM practices. 'That line of reasoning can be used to stop sports at the college: field hockey, football and even worse, gymnastics

because that has a higher level of risk,' he said. Kahn conceded the point that public approval of the BDSM charter might reduce donations to Financial Aid made by wealthy benefactors. He added that, should it be proposed, he would support the establishment of a Hitler youth club or any other group, so long as it only wished to exercise its right to free speech. [Physics Professor John] Scofield strongly opposed Kahn on BDSM. He said the ratification of their charter may alienate alumni and prospective students. 'In particular, it will make it more difficult to recruit Christian students, athletes, science students and African American students, many of whom place a high value on Church and family,' he said. 'Sadomasochism is violent and degrading, and it is totally alien to the Christian ideals that I espouse and upon which this institution was founded long ago,' Scofield said." For more on the Christian foundations of Oberlin, see below. For Scofield's insightful comment on "diversity," see below, Chapter Eight. The student representative for the BDSM club was careful to point out the "difference between such practices as torture and auto-erotic asphyxiation and those of BDSM. 'When someone strangles himself while masturbating and dies, that's not BDSM, that's suicide,' she said." (Yes, this was a serious, on-campus debate. In fact, the photograph accompanying the article was captioned, "Enraptured," with this comment, "Students and faculty packed King 306 Thursday to discuss the chartering of the BDSM club. Students were divided as to whether the school should charter the group." Enrapturing, indeed. For a student editorial critiquing the General Faculty's opposition to the charter (April 21, 2000), see http://www.oberlin.edu/stupub/ocreview/archives/2000.04.21/perspectives/editorials.html, accessed May 12, 2010.

25   My appreciation to Truls Liland, a FIRE School of Ministry graduate, for locating this quote for me and pointing out that it came from Dwight's Baccalaureate Discourse of 1814.

26   See Mortimer Adler, ed., *The Annals of America* (Chicago: Encyclopedia Britannica, 1968), 1:464; for the quote online, with additional information about the early American education, see Dave Miller, Ph.D., "The Purpose of Education," http://www.apologeticspress.com/articles/3392, accessed June 13, 2010.

27   I owe this information about compulsory chapel attendance to John McCandlish Phillips (see Chapter Two, n. 4), who has been involved in Ivy League campus ministry for several decades.

28   Accessed from http://www.yale.edu/lesbiangay/ website January 15, 2006, but since removed; it was found March 27, 2010 at http://jclarkmedia.com/gaybooks/websiteofthemonth.html, with reference to the aforementioned link. The new LGBT link at Yale (http://www.yale.edu/lgbts/) has removed much of this material as of March 27, 2010.

29   Significantly, the "smattering of events in Yale's queer history" offered in support of this statement begins in 1913, with the graduation of musician and composer Cole Porter. Although he became known as a bisexual later in life (in the 1930's, he and his wife separated over this), it is certain that he was *not* known as "queer" while studying at Yale! The next date on the list is 1946, when "Modernist lesbian genius Gertrude Stein bequeaths her papers to Yale," although Stein herself did not study at Yale. One would think that if there had been *any* "prominent queer scholars, activists, and artists" in Yale's first two and a half centuries, this web page would have been only to proud to announce them. It can safely be said that the statement regarding Yale's LGBT activism in the last fifty years is as true as the claim regarding Yale's 300 year "queer" history is false. (To be technical, however, it should be pointed out that it was not until 1969 that "LGBT students found[ed] the first gay organization at Yale," and it is this date that really inaugurates Yale's gay activism.) According to Larry Kramer, who graduated from Yale in 1957, and with whom we shall interact shortly, the college was a very friendly place, "if you weren't gay. If you had the awful, dark secrets in your life, it was a terrifying place." See http://www.sodomylaws.org/usa/connecticut/ctnews03.htm, accessed May 10, 2010. Today, Kramer describes the atmosphere at Yale as "phenomenal," stating, "It's a testament to all of us. It's been hard work on everyone's part. It gives you faith. It gives you faith in the human race" (ibid.)

30   http://www.yale.edu/lgbts/lgbts_history.html, accessed May 12, 2010. Note that the "S" in LGBTS stands for "Studies."

31   PRISM is an acronym for Programs for Research for Smokers with Mental Illness.

32   See above, n. 28.

33   Ibid.

34   For the text online, with the title, "Why Campus Revivals Spark Missionary Advance," see http://www.watchword.org/index.php?option=com_content&task=view&id=163&Itemid=6, accessed May 12, 2010. Orr recounts the absolutely remarkable turnaround as follows: "It began in the early 1800s at schools like Amherst, Dartmouth, Princeton, Williams and Yale where up to half the students turned to Christ. By 1835, 1,500 students had committed their lives to Christ in 36 colleges. Impressive statistics--especially when you realize that in those days student bodies numbered only 100-250. Similar results continued to be seen from one generation of students to the next. In 1853, 11 New England colleges with a total enrollment of 2,163 reported that there were 745 active Christians on campus. Of this

number, 343 planned to go into the ministry. Then in the 1880's, an unprecedented missionary enterprise, known as the Student Volunteer Movement, came into being. 'The Evangelization of the World in This Generation' became its rallying cry. This spirit was evidenced in the movement's results--more than 20,000 serving in overseas mission fields in half a century. College students set the pace in this era of spiritual advance." More broadly, see, e.g., J. Edwin Orr, *Campus Aflame: A History of Evangelical Awakenings in Collegiate Communities*, ed. by Richard Owen Roberts (rev. ed.; Wheaton: International Awakening Press, 1994); Michael F. Gleason, *When God Walked on Campus* (Kitchener, Ontario: Joshua Press, 2002).

35 Nick Pappis, "Campus Revivals of the Past," http://www.sermonindex.net/modules/newbb/viewtopic. php?viewmode=flat&order=0&topic_id=18739&forum=40&post_id=, accessed May 12, 2010.

36 Ibid.

37 http://townhall.com/columnists/AllenHunt/2009/07/20/yales_coveted_title_the_gay_ivy, accessed May 12, 2010.

38 See http://www.yale.edu/lgbts/lgbts_history.html, accessed May 12, 2010: "The five-year-long Initiative was a tremendous success. It brought greater visibility and enduring institutional support to LGBTS at Yale and helped pave the way for continuing growth."

39 http://www.yale.edu/lesbiangay/Pages/Academic/Faculty.html, accessed January 15, 2006, but since relocated.

40 Ibid.

41 http://www.yale.edu/lgbts/faculty.html, accessed May 12, 2010. The website lists twenty-three faculty members involved in teaching classes connected to LGBT Studies in the 2009-2010 school year.

42 http://www.yalealumnimagazine.com/issues/03_04/kramer.html, accessed April 26, 2010. According to the *New York Times*, July 9, 1997, Kramer's terms were: "Yale is to use this money solely for 1) the study of and/or instruction in gay male literature, by which I mean courses to study gay male writers throughout history or the teaching to gay male students of writing about their heritage and their experience. To ensure for the continuity of courses in either or both of these areas tenured positions should be established; and/or 2) the establishment of a gay student center at Yale. . . ," to which Yale replied, "'Although we cannot accept the specific structure you have proposed, I hope that in our meeting we can talk about other ways of directing your generosity, thereby benefiting gay studies and, perhaps, other endeavors here at Yale." See http://www.nytimes.com/1997/07/09/nyregion/writing-own-script-yale-refuses-kramer-s-millions-for-gay-studies.html, accessed April 26, 2010. See further http://www.nytimes.com/2001/04/02/nyregion/gay-writer-and-yale-finally-agree-on-donation.html, where it was reported on April 2, 2001, that Kramer had "agreed to leave his literary papers and political papers chronicling the birth of the groups Gay Men's Health Crisis and Act Up, and other seminal events in the AIDS movement, to Yale's Beinecke Library."

43 This speech was put into written form as *The Tragedy of Today's Gays* (cited above, Chapter Two, n. 37), with a Foreword by Naomi Wolf and an Afterword by Rodger McFarlane. It was held at NYU's Cooper Union and organized by Michael Brown, obviously not the same person as the author of this book.

44 It is impossible to know from this speech whether Kramer was actually referring to an underage boy or if he simply referred to a much younger man (perhaps college age?) in boylike terms. The former case, of course, would have been all the more sickening. For Kramer's positive views on some aspects of man-boy sex, see immediately below, and note also Chapter Eleven, below.

45 Concerning American colleges and universities, Kramer claimed, "But they will not let gay history be taught in schools and universities. And we seem unable to teach ourselves. My own college, Yale, with $1 million of my own brother's money to do just this, will not teach what I call gay history, unencumbered with the prissy incomprehensible gobbledygook of gender studies and queer theory. Abraham Lincoln did not talk that language." (Ibid.)

46 Beth Potier, reporting in the *Harvard Gazette*, http://www.news.harvard.edu/gazette/2003/10.02/15-kramer.html, accessed May 12, 2010. Cf. also Erik Holland, *The Nature of Homosexuality: Vindication for Homosexual Activists and the Religious Right* (New York: iUniverse, 2004), 507-509, for further inflammatory quotes from Kramer and others, including this one (507), "I think the time for violence has now arrived. I don't personally think I'm the guy with the guns to do it, but I'd like to see an AIDS terrorist army, like the Irgun which led to the state of Israel," from the *Wall Street Journal*, May 8, 1990. Holland credits *The American Guardian* for the original collection of quotes that he cites here.

47 Larry Kramer, *Reports from the Holocaust* (New York: St. Martin's Press, 1991), cited in http://www. nambla.org/kramer.htm, accessed April 3, 2010. For a further selection of relevant quotes, see http:// www.qrd.org/qrd/orgs/NAMBLA/quotes, accessed December 15, 2010. Dr. Gunter Schmidt actually cites studies that back Kramer's claim in his article in the *Archives of Sexual Behavior* 31 (2002), entitled "The Dilemma of the Male Pedophile," discussed further, below, Chapter Eight. He notes (476), "There

are now more than 100 studies comparing adults who experienced sexual abuse as children (from exhibitionism to violent sex, inside and outside the family context, in this degree of breadth and generalization) with adults who have not had such experiences. Meta-analysis, for example, shows that fully half of all men and a quarter of all women surveyed describe their experience as neutral or positive (Rind, Tromovitch, & Bauserman, 1998). With respect to the many and varied psychological symptoms and problems experienced during adulthood (alcoholism, depression, anxiety, compulsive behavior, eating disorders, suicide attempts, sexual disorders, etc.), the differences between the index and control groups were statistically significant, although the unbiased effect size estimate . . . was consistently low (0.10-0.20). While these studies do not by any means rule out severe or devastating effects of sexual experiences with adults, the only explanation for the small effect size is that many experiences covered by the broad definition of 'sexual abuse' are neither experienced as negative nor represent sexual trauma. Thus, we should recognize the need to bring our assessment of the impact of sexual acts involving children back into balance in order to do justice to the realities of the children themselves."

48   For an example of another prominent school offering gay and lesbian study emphases, see http://www. colorado.edu/ArtsSciences/LGBTStudies/ (the University of Colorado at Boulder), with courses including the following: Introduction to Lesbian, Bisexual, and Gay Literature; Introduction to Lesbian, Gay, Bisexual, and Transgender Studies; Queer Theory; Queer Film; Queer Modernism; Twentieth-century Anglo-American Lesbian Literature and Theory; African American Literature and Queer Theory; Queer Ethnic Studies; Sex, Gender, and Society; Seminar in American Theatre: Lesbians and Gays; Topics in Writing: Queer Rhetorics – all of which are undergraduate courses. See http://www.colorado.edu/ArtsSciences/LGBTStudies/courses.html, accessed December 12, 2010. Cf. also Alan Sears and Craig Osten, *The Homosexual Agenda: Exposing The Principle Threat to Religious Freedom Today* (Nashville: Broadman & Holman, 2003), 76-92.

49   Cited by Laurie Higgins, "Gustavus Adolphus College Promotes Perversion to Freshmen," http://www.illinoisfamily.org/news/contentview.asp?c=35043. For the national story that broke the reports discussed in Higgins' article, see Bob Unruh's October 6, 2010 article, http://www.wnd.com/index.php?fa=PAGE.view&pageId=212213, both accessed October 12, 2010. Unruh notes that a student at the college, Phil Cleary on his Gustavus.campusreform.org website, "posted several videos captured at the 2010 orientation for freshman in the class of 2014." Both articles just cited link to the videos, which call for viewer discretion.

50   Higgins, ibid.

51   Ibid.

52   For an interesting article on the lasting transformation of Rochester, NY through Finney's ministry there in 1829-30, see John S. Tompkins, "Our Kindest City," in the July, 1994 issue of *Reader's Digest*. This contributed to Rochester becoming an escape route for slaves in the years that followed.

53   C. G. Finney, *Charles G. Finney, An Autobiography* (digital version, Albany, OR: Ages Software, 1997), 409-410.

54   See, conveniently, http://www.gospeltruth.net/oe/OEmainindex.htm, accessed December 19, 2010.

55   See http://www.gospeltruth.net/1862OE/620326_morl_dpravit_pt2.htm, accessed December 19, 2010, my emphasis.

56   Jane Pearce, "Radical Activist U: Oberlin College," FrontPageMagazine.com, November 5, 2003; http://www.frontpagemag.com/Articles/ReadArticle.asp?ID=10633, May 12, 2010.

57   http://oberwiki.net/Sexual_Information_Center, accessed December 19, 2010.

58   In the 2006 edition of The Princeton Review's *The Best 361 Colleges: The Smart Student's Guide to Colleges* (New York: Princeton Review, 2006), 388, Oberlin received an extremely high academic rating of 95 (comparable to Harvard's 96 and Yale's 97).

59   According to quotes cited in *The Best 361 Colleges*, ibid., "The student body of Oberlin 'is made up of kids who really have the urge to speak out and contribute, where it is directly through environmental or volunteer work or indirectly through the arts or humanities. [These] well-intentioned, genuinely nice, out-of-the-box-smart, tree-hugging vegans who are to save the world from corporate corruption, industrial pollution, world hunger, and Republicans' describe themselves as 'intense, irreverent, intellectual, and a little zany. . . . Obies tell us, 'It's a wonderful school for queer people.' Some feel that 'if Oberlin could attract more conventional students as well as ultra-hippy kids, there would be greater diversity on the campus." Note that the quote about "queer people" is not common in the comments regarding other campuses.

60   Linnea Butterfield, "Trans Awareness Week Transcends," *Oberlin Review*, Vol. 129/20, April 13, 2001, http://www.oberlin.edu/stupub/ocreview/archives/2001.04.13/news/article02.htm, accessed December 19, 2010.

61   Ibid.

62   According to Pastor J. Grant Swank Jr., Harvard's 2002 Gay Pride Week, sponsored by the Bisexual, Gay, Lesbian, Transgender and Supporters Alliance, included a showing of "'Toilet Training,' a documentary about 'discrimination linked to gender-segregated bathrooms' [according to a report from Harvard's campus paper, *The Crimson*]. . . . The BGLTSAs 'thorough investigation' of Harvard buildings over the past few months shows the school could be more accommodating for transgendered students by creating more gender-neutral bathrooms, the Crimson said. 'For transgendered people, going to a specific bathroom can be a very stigmatizing experience,' said BGLTSA publicity chairman Adam P. Schneider, who also is a Crimson editor. Schneider said creation of gender-neutral bathrooms would be 'an easy thing to keep under consideration' as Harvard makes plans to construct a new campus." One can presumably expect many more gender-neutral campus bathrooms in the coming days or, as it was termed at the University of Massachussets at Amherst, a "Restroom Revolution" (yes!). See Alyson Ward, "Transcending Gender," *Dallas Star-Telegram*, posted August 24, 2005, http://www.dfw.com/mld/dfw/12461845.htm and accessed October 15, 2005, but no longer available online.
63   http://www.transgenderlawcenter.org/pdf/PIP%20Resource%20Guide.pdf, accessed October 6, 2010.
64   http://www.oberlin.edu/stupub/ocreview/archives/2002.04.19/perspectives/article11.htm. Sears and Osten, *The Homosexual Agenda*, 80, note that, "At Wesleyan College, students no longer have to identify themselves as male or female on their health forms. Instead, they are told to describe their 'gender identity history.'"
65   http://www.oberlin.edu/news-info/02sep/spotlight_on_mrc.html (still showing the September 17, 2002 article), accessed December 19, 2010.
66   Originally accessed on the www.oberlin.edu site on August 25, 2005, but no longer available online.
67   Ibid.
68   http://www.oberlin.edu/newserv/stories/kevin_jennings_release.html, accessed August 25, 2005, but no longer available.
69   http://www.oberlin.edu/regist/spring05schedule.html#anchor54432, accessed August 25, 2004, but no longer available. This week was not chosen because of its extreme nature but rather as a representative sampling when I searched the Oberlin site in 2004.
70   For the syllabi for Prof. Raimondo's classes, see http://www.oberlin.edu/CAS/Syllabus/2004-2005/LGBTQ%20identities%20spring%202005%20syllabus1.pdf and http://www.oberlin.edu/CAS/Syllabus/2004-2005/CAS%20321%20spring%202005%20syllabus1.pdf, accessed August 25, 2005, but no longer available.
71   http://www.oberlin.edu/CAS/Syllabus/2004-2005/MeredithCAS401F04.pdf, accessed August 25, 2005, but no longer available.
72   No longer available on the Oberlin website.
73   To put queer studies in the larger context of shifts in academic emphases on our campuses, cf. Patrick J. Deneen, "Science and the Decline of the Liberal Arts, who noted that, "The scandalous state of the modern university can be attributed to various corruptions that have taken root in the disciplines of the humanities. The university was once the locus of humanistic education in the great books; today, one is more likely to find there indoctrination in multiculturalism, disability studies, queer studies, postcolonial studies, a host of other victimization studies, and the usual insistence on the centrality of the categories of race, gender, and class. The humanities today seem to be waning in presence and power in the modern university in large part because of their solipsistic irrelevance, which has predictably increased students' uninterest in them." See http://www.thenewatlantis.com/publications/science-and-the-decline-of-the-liberal-arts, accessed October 26, 2010.
74   http://www.oberlin.edu/sociology/Syllabi/Syllabi%202002-2003/SOCI236.pdf, accessed October 30, 2005, but no longer available.
75   http://www.smith.edu/swg/queerstudies.html, accessed April 26, 2010.
76   http://www.law.ucla.edu/williamsinstitute/home.html, accessed October 6, 2010.
77   http://www.law.ucla.edu/williamsinstitute/about/index.html, accessed October 6, 2010.
78   http://www.nytimes.com/2009/06/04/education/04harvard.html?_r=2&scp=2&sq=harvard%20gay%20lesbian%20caucus&st=cse, accessed April 26, 2010.
79   See http://www.transgenderwarrior.org/pdf/vitae.pdf, accessed May 7, 2010; according to her CV, through she had spoken at Agnes Scott, Amherst College, University of Arizona, Bard College, Bates College, Bentley College, Bowden, Bowling Green State University, Brown University, University of California at San Diego, Carleton College, Chatham College, University of Cincinnati, Colby College, Colombia School of Public Health, University of Connecticut, Cornell, Dartmouth, Denison University, DePauw University, Drew College, Evergreen State College, University of Florida, George Mason University, Hamilton College, Hampshire College, Harvard University, University of Illinois/Champagne-Urbana, University of Illinois/Chicago, James Madison University, Johns Hopkins, University of

Kansas, University of Maine, University of Massachusetts, University of Memphis, Metro State College of Denver, University of Michigan, Michigan State University, University of Minnesota/Minneapolis, University of Minnesota/Duluth, University of Missouri, Montclair State College, University of Nebraska, University of New Hampshire, New Jersey City University, New York University, University of North Carolina-Chapel Hill, Northwestern University, SUNY New Paltz, Oberlin College, University of Oklahoma, University of Oregon, Penn State University, University of Pennsylvania, Phoenix College, Princeton, Pullman, Reed College, University of Rochester, Rutgers University, University at Stony Brook, St. Cloud University, Simmons College, Skidmore, Swarthmore College, University of Toledo Law School, Trinity College, Tufts University, Vassar College, University of Vermont, University of Washington, Washington State University, Wellesley College, William Patterson College, Williams College, University of Wisconsin, Yale University.

80   See http://www.transgenderwarrior.org/, with photo gallery (quite striking, to say the least), background information, and samplings of her writings. Her novels include *Stone Butch Blues*, *Trans Liberation*, and *Drag King Dreams*. A picture of Ms. Feinberg, after treatment for a serious illness, is dedicated to her grandson Simon and signed, "Your Grampy Leslie." http://www.flickr.com/photos/transgenderwarrior/sets/72157623761231822/, both accessed October 25, 2010.

81   Teresa Theophano, http://www.glbtq.com/literature/feinberg_l.html, accessed May 7, 2010. For more on this linguistic gobbledygook, see Chapter Nine.

82   http://www.oberlin.edu/stupub/ocreview/archives/2001.04.13/news/article02.htm, accessed April 27, 2010.

83   Sears and Osten, *The Homosexual Agenda*, 80, with reference to Gene Edward Veith, "Identity Crisis," *World*, March 27, 2004, 27. They also note (ibid.): "Smith College students (all female) voted to eliminate female pronouns from the student constitution because 'she' and 'her' were 'insensitive' to transgendered students."

Chapter 5

1   David Eisenbach, *Gay Power*, 258, citing Tom Shales, "The First Archie Bunker Award," *The Washington Post*, July 31, 1977.

2   *Gay Power*, 255. There is, however, more to the story about gay influence on Hollywood prior to 1970, for which see William J. Mann, *Behind the Screen: How Gays and Lesbians Shaped Hollywood 1910-1969* (New York: Viking, 2001).

3   *Gay Power*, 257-58.

4   Ibid., 258, and vii. For a more detailed and wide-ranging account, see Kathryn C. Montgomery, *Target: Prime Time: Advocacy Groups and the Struggle Over Entertainment Television* (New York: Oxford University Press, 1989), passim (see the Index under "gay rights"; this book also book gay advocacy groups into the larger context of other advocacy groups, thereby making it possible to compare and contrast gay advocacy strategies and techniques with those of other groups.

5   Ibid., v. For a listing of Major League Baseball teams that feature special "gay community" nights current through 2008, and listing the Washington Nationals, the San Diego Padres, the San Francisco Giants, the Chicago Cubs, and the Philadelphia Phillies, see http://www.gaybaseballdays.com/, accessed May 17, 2010.

6   Ibid.

7   *Gay Power*, vi.

8   http://www.breakfastwithscotmovie.com/, accessed May 17, 2010. The movie first appeared in Canada in November, 2007, not opening in America until October, 2008.

9   http://www.usatoday.com/life/movies/reviews/2010-07-09-kidsareallright09_ST_N.htm, accessed August 5, 2010.

10   Ibid.

11   For an important 2010 study, see http://familyscholars.org/my-daddys-name-is-donor-2/, accessed August 5, 2010.

12   http://abcnews.go.com/Entertainment/wireStory?id=11121781

13   For an overview from the 1950's to early 2000, see Stephen Tropiano, *The Prime Time Closet: A History of Gays and Lesbians on TV* (New York: Applause Theater & Cinema Books, 2002). He writes, "Many of my older gay male friends have described how the negative stereotypes of gays and lesbians in Hollywood films of the 1940s, 1950s, and 1960s served as their first Introduction to the subject of homosexuality. As a member of the post-Kennedy generation, I consider myself fortunate to have grown up (and come out) in an era when some television programs...and made-for-TV movies were beginning to tackle the subject of homosexuality in a sensitive, intelligent manner." (Ibid., vii.)

14   In 2009, Out.com's third annual Power 50 listed Anderson Cooper as the third most influential gay

or lesbian person in America, with one website also providing a reader poll to vote on whether or not they believed he was gay; see http://www.zimbio.com/Barney+Frank/articles/21/Barney+Frank+Ander son+Cooper+Top+Gay+Power; in their 2010 list, he moved up to number 2; see http://out.com/detail. asp?page=1&id=22394, both accessed October 14, 2010.

15   According to Mary A. Fischer, "Why Women Are Leaving Men for Other Women," *O Magazine*, April, 2009, more and more women are leaving men for other women, and this is being reflected (and, I would suggest, stoked) by the media: "Lately, a new kind of sisterly love seems to be in the air. In the past few years, Sex and the City's Cynthia Nixon left a boyfriend after a decade and a half and started dating a woman (and talked openly about it). Actress Lindsay Lohan and DJ Samantha Ronson flaunted their relationship from New York to Dubai. Katy Perry's song 'I Kissed a Girl' topped the charts. The L Word, Work Out, and Top Chef are featuring gay women on TV, and there's even talk of a lesbian reality show in the works. Certainly nothing is new about women having sex with women, but we've arrived at a moment in the popular culture when it all suddenly seems almost fashionable--or at least, acceptable." To read online, see, e.g., http://www.cnn.com/2009/LIVING/personal/04/23/o.women.leave.menfor. women/, accessed May 17, 2010.

16   http://www.drudge.com/archive/101797/military-reduces-gay-discharges, accessed May 17, 2010.

17   Ibid.

18   Ibid. This quote was widely repeated on the Internet.

19   In their official brief in the landmark Lawrence v. Texas Supreme Court decision, a major coalition of thirty-one gay and pro-gay organizations used the figures of 2.8% of the male population and 1.4% of the female population as identifying themselves as gay, lesbian, or bisexual (see p. 16, n. 42 of the brief, folliwing the the National Health and Social Life Survey). For a representative discussion of gay population on a gay website and a conservative Christian website, see http://gaylife.about.com/ od/comingout/a/population.htm; http://www.traditionalvalues.org/urban/two.php, both accessed December 19, 2010. It is widely recognized today that Alfred Kinsey's (in)famous sex survey, which provided the basis for the "one in ten is gay" myth, cannot be relied on here. For other, more searing criticisms of Kinsey's work, including charges of child abuse, see Judith A. Reisman, Ph.D., *Kinsey: Crimes and Consequences* (Arlington, VA: The Institute for Media Education, 1998); idem, *Sexual Sabotage: How One Mad Scientist Unleashed a Plague of Corruption and Contagion on America* (Nashville: WND Books, 2010). For a definitive (937 p.) study of Kinsey, see James H. Jones, *Alfred C. Kinsey: A Public/Private Life* (New York: W. W. Norton & Co., 1997).

20   See, e.g., http://www.barna.org/barna-update/article/13-culture/111-survey-explores-who-qualifies-as-an-evangelical?q=evangelical, accessed October 14, 2000 (the article is from January 18, 2007), where it is noted, "Asking people if they consider themselves to be evangelicals produces a comparatively large number: 38% of the population accepts that label." Based on pollster George Barna's criteria, however, those who actually meet the definition of "evangelical Christian" make up a substantially lower percentage, but one that, nonetheless, still dwarfs the number of self-professed gays and lesbians.

21   "How 25 Years of Gay Activism in Hollywood Has Paid Off," http://townhall.com/columnists/ RobertKnight/2008/10/08/how_25_years_of_gay_activism_in_hollywood_has_paid_off?page=full, accessed May 17, 2010.

22   My appreciation to Prof. Dick Carpenter for these references. For a much more comprehensive listing, frequently updated, see http://en.wikipedia.org/wiki/Category:LGBT-related_television_programs, accessed May 17, 2010, and cited with standard caveats regarding the accuracy of Wikipedia.

23   For this statistic, see above, n. 19.

24   http://www.silive.com/entertainment/tvfilm/index.ssf/2009/07/hbo_leads_tv_in_gay_characters.html, accessed May 17, 2010.

25   See, e.g., http://www.foxnews.com/entertainment/2010/10/26/sesame-street-tweet-sparks-rumors-bert-closet/, accessed October 31, 2010. See also this article for the assertion that the Sesame Street puppet Bert, of Bert and Ernie fame, is secretly gay, allegedly hinted at in a June 11 tweet. According to Ellen Lewis, however, spokeswoman for Sesame Street, "Bert and Ernie don't have a sexuality – 'they're puppets'– and they were created to teach kids to get along with people who are different" (cited in ibid.)

26   http://www.glaad.org/eye/tv_listings.php, accessed July 30, 2009 but since removed. The sampling of shows listed at http://www.glaad.org/tvgayed as of May 17, 2010, was no less enlightening.

27   Commenting on the beginning of the 2008-2009 TV season, GLAAD noted, "At the launch of the 2008-2009 television season, GLAAD estimates that lesbian, gay, bisexual and transgender (LGBT) scripted characters represent 2.6% of all scripted series regular characters on the five broadcast networks: ABC, CBS, Fox, NBC, and The CW. This is nearly double last year, with 16 series regular characters identified as LGBT." See http://www.glaad.org/tvreport08-09, accessed May 17, 2010. On the one hand, this figure of 2.6% would represent a close approximation to the national GLBT population,

but here is where the statistics can be misleading: 1) Many gays and lesbians are not "out," and so their presence is not felt in the same way in the workplace and community as it is on TV; 2) Many gay-themed scripts are extremely slanted in their presentations (as we will see below); 3) Many TV characters are not involved in any sexual contexts, yet since they are not overtly gay, they would automatically be listed as heterosexual, further skewing the numbers; 4) As a point of contrast, what percentage of the TV characters are conservative Christians? (See the Medved quote at the beginning of the chapter.)

28 David Ehrenstein, "More Than Friends," *Los Angeles Magazine*, May, 1996, reprinted in Larry Gross and James P. Woods, *The Columbia Reader on Lesbians & Gay Men in Media, Society, and Politics* (New York: Columbia University Press, 1999), 335-340, here citing 336. Those familiar with TV sitcoms would immediately think of highly-acclaimed shows like *Modern Family*, *Glee*, and *Ugly Betty*, just to name a few.

29 http://www.tv.com/law-and-order-special-victims-unit/bad-blood/episode/12336recaphtml?tag=episo de_recap;recap, accessed May 17, 2010.

30 http://www.episodelist.com/site/index.php?go=seasons.view&season_id=448, accessed May 17, 2010.

31 Ibid. A full online version of the Exodus news release is available at: http://www.exodus-international. org/news_2003_1112.shtml, accessed July 30, 2009.

32 See http://www.democraticunderground.com/discuss/duboard.php?az=showmesg&forum=389&topic_ id=229310&mesg_id=229570; originally posted at http://boston-legal.org/forum/topic.asp?TOPIC_ ID=1315&whichpage=4. For the video, see http://www.youtube.com/watch?v=hBe57dDRp5g&featu re=PlayList&p=487A906CEC70A205&playnext_from=PL&index=0&playnext=1, all accessed July 2, 2010.

33 "How 25 Years of Gay Activism in Hollywood Has Paid Off." The fact that GLAAD is given scripts to vet for potential, gay-offensive content is commonly known; see, e.g., http://www.deadline. com/2010/10/universal-under-pressure-changing-gay-trailer-for-ron-howard-vince-vaughn-pic-the-dilemma/, accessed October 9, 2010. According to the article, GLAAD President Jarrett Barrios was quoted as saying, "Last month, Universal shared a link to the trailer for the film *The Dilemma* with GLAAD. After reviewing, GLAAD called on Universal to remove the scene where the word 'gay' was used as a pejorative from the trailer. Today, after Anderson Cooper also spoke out against the scene, Universal confirmed to GLAAD that the offensive joke will be removed from promotional campaigns from this point forward, including in the trailer currently playing in movie theatres. The use of the word 'gay' in this trailer as a slur is unnecessary and does nothing more than send a message of intolerance about our community to viewers."

34 http://tv.msn.com/tv/year-in-review/gayest-year-ever/, accessed May 17, 2010.

35 http://tv.msn.com/tv/year-in-review/gayest-year-ever/?photoidx=9, accessed May 17, 2010.

36 Other animated TV series or movies featuring gay or transgender characters include *King of the Hill*, *Family Guy*, *X-Men*, and *Lilo and Stich* (where the main alien character Pleakley is a male who dresses in women's clothes and wears makeup).

37 "The Gayest Year Ever" (cited above, n. 34). "We applaud ABC for highlighting Kevin and Scotty's declaration of commitment to each other in the presence of their family and friends," said GLAAD President Neil G. Giuliano about the historic event. "Kevin and Scotty's ceremony reflects 'Brothers & Sisters' and ABC's ongoing commitment to making visible the multi-dimensional lives of gay characters." See http://www.buddytv.com/articles/brothers-and-sisters/glaad-applauds-brothers-sister-19172.aspx, accessed May 17, 2010.

38 http://tv.msn.com/tv/year-in-review/gayest-year-ever/?photoidx=13, accessed May 17, 2010.

39 http://popwatch.ew.com/popwatch/2008/12/boston-legal--1.html, accessed May 17, 2010.

40 http://www.insidesocal.com/outinhollywood/2008/12/the-surprise-same-sex-marriage.html, accessed May 17, 2010.

41 For a vigorous response to this episode, coupled with a picture of the banner ad posted on SLDN, Servicemembers Legal Defense Network, see http://americansfortruth.com/news/whos-got-the-power-abcs-boston-legal-shills-for-homosexuals-in-the-military.html#more-1584, accessed May 17, 2010.

42 http://www.restoringamerica.org/ignored_and_discounted.htm, accessed May 17, 2010 (originally posted April 14, 2006).

43 As noted on PlanetOut.com, "They have been lampooned on *Will and Grace*, ridiculed throughout the gay community, and condemned by virtually all mainstream mental health organizations. But for thousands of 'ex-gays,' turning away from homosexuality is very serious business." Originally posted at http://www.planetout.com/people/features/2000/06/exgay/, but accessed May 17, 2010, at http://www. exodusinternational.org/content/view/435/37/.

44 This is printed frequently on GLAAD's web pages; see, e.g., http://www.glaad.org/Page.aspx?pid=1373,

accessed May 17, 2010; for their Mission Statement, see http://www.glaad.org/mission; for GLAAD's history, see http://www.glaad.org/history.

45   For the Montel Williams ex-gay-bashing show in 2008, see http://www.narth.com/docs/montel2.html; http://www.drthrockmorton.com/article.asp?id=201; http://wthrockmorton.com/2007/10/23/exodus-files-ethics-complaint-against-alicia-salzer-over-montel-show-comments/; http://wthrockmorton.com/2007/03/10/montel-williams-revisits-sexual-reorientation/. For John Stossel's highly-biased report on 20/20 wherein he contested the existence of ex-gays, see The Accuracy in Media report, "John Stossel Sells Out," http://www.aim.org/media-monitor/john-stossel-sells-out/, all accessed May 17, 2010. His basic response to the claim that gays could change was, "Give me a break." Cf. further John Stossel, *Myths, Lies, and Downright Stupidity: Get Out the Shovel–Why Everything You Know is Wrong* (New York: Hyperion, 2007).

46   See above, Chapter One.

47   http://www.cultureandmediainstitute.org/articles/2007/20070425174144.aspx, accessed November 29, 2010.

48   Ibid; my emphasis.

49   http://www.glaad.org/tellcnn, accessed January 11, 2011, my emphasis.

50   http://www.claremont.org/publications/pubid.313/pub_detail.asp; for perspectives on the impact of Ellen Degeneres' coming out, see www.afterellen.com, both accessed May 17, 2010.

51   I understand, of course, that many gay viewers have felt greatly helped by various TV shows and movies, finding a place of identification, among other things. See, e.g., Gross and Woods, *The Columbia Reader on Lesbian and Gay Men in Media, Society, and Politics*, idem and idem, "Introduction: Being Gay in American Media and Society," 3, where a number of touching letters are cited with the explanation following that these letters, "culled from more than two thousand received by the heterosexual actor Ryan Philippe, seem to make a common appeal: Tell me I'm not alone. The writers who composed them have all reached out to a potential role model – in this case playing the fictional gay teenager Billy Douglas on the daytime drama *One Life to Live* in the summer of 1992 – for guidance on how to view themselves, how to function in society. Many claim to have no other friends in whom they can confide . . . . At least one writer speculates that that, for some viewers, Billy Douglas 'may be their only friend.'"

52   "The Battle Over Gay Teens," October 10, 2005; http://www.time.com/time/magazine/article/0,9171,1112856-1,00.html; for NARTH's letter to the editor raising concerns about Cloud's article, in particular, his failure to mention "the serious emotional, mental and physical illnesses associated with the homosexual lifestyle," see http://www.narth.com/docs/details.html. For an example of just how biased Cloud actually is, see his December 18, 2008 *Time* article, "The Problem for Gay with Rick Warren – and Obama," http://www.time.com/time/politics/article/0,8599,1867664,00.html, all accessed September 10, 2010. See further Ritch C. Savin-Williams, *The New Gay Teenager* (Boston: Harvard University Press, 2006).

53   It is also important to remember that teenagers often experience a certain degree of confusion about their sexual orientation, as indicated by the type of Q&A on teen websites, like this gay-friendly one: http://www.teengrowth.com/index.cfm?action=info_article&ID_article=1400&category=sex&catdesc=Sex&subdesc=Homosexuality; see further, above, Chapter Three, n. 81. For more on TV's impact on gay youth, see the CNN report, "Too Gay for TV?", http://www.cnn.com/video/#/video/showbiz/2010/09/09/sbt.too.gay.for.tv.hln?hpt=C2, both accessed September 10, 2010.

54   According to a 2001 report on MediaFamily.org (marking MTV's 20th birthday), "MTV globally reaches 350 million households (PBS On-Line, 2001); . . . 82% of MTV viewers are 12 to 34 years old, with 39% under the age of eighteen (Nielson Media Research, 2000); Music videos are designed for teenagers between 12 and 19 years of age (Rich, 1998); MTV is watched by 73% of boys and 78% of girls in the 12 to 19 years of age group. Boys watch for an average of 6.6 hours per week and girls watch for an average of 6.2 hours per week (Rich, 1998); MTV is the most recognized network among young adults ages 12 to 34 (Nielson Media Research, 2000)." See www.mediafamily.org/facts/facts_mtv.shtml (cached version of this page accessed December 23, 2008).

55   "The Battle Over Gay Teens." Cf. also http://www.afterelton.com/TV/2009/1/prayersforbobby, and note this quote from Signourey Weaver, "I know a very religious family, and they do think that homosexuality is an abomination," says star Sigourney Weaver. *"I'm hoping that this film will begin to open their eyes — if not the older generation, then perhaps the younger one"* (my emphasis). This 2009 movie fictionalizes the real life story of Mary Griffith, with this plot: "a conservative Christian woman refuses to accept her gay teenage son, hounding him to 'change' to the point where he commits suicide. But then, overcome by the realization of what she has done, the woman educates herself, renounces her previous anti-gay beliefs, and becomes a crusader for GLBT youth and gay rights." (Griffith's daughter committed suicide in real life.) For a response to the repeated airing of this movie on Lifetime the weekend of January 23, 2009,

cf. COMMENTS TO LIFETIME TV FROM A JONAH MOM (JANUARY 26, 2009) – JONAH emailing, Jan. 26, 2009.

56 Ironically, the founder of Ironically, the founder of *YGA Magazine*, Michael Glatze, is now an ex-gay, declaring clearly that he has left his homosexuality behind. See, e.g., http://michaelglatze.blogspot.com/, accessed November 29, 2010.

57 See Locksley Hall's article on "'The OC's' Gay Legacy," http://www.afterelton.com/TV/2007/4/theoc. She notes that the show, "showcased — and mocked — the homophobic attitudes of conservative Orange County by putting those attitudes in the mouths of shallow socialites and dim-witted high school students who the main characters can't stand."

58 http://www.vh1.com/shows/dyn/vh1_news_presents/107212/episode_about.jhtml, accessed November 29, 2010.

59 George Chauncey, *Why Marriage? The History Shaping Today's Debate Over Gay Equality* (New York: Basic Books, 2004), 5, emphasis in the original.

60 See, e.g., http://www.godlikeproductions.com/forum1/message510564/pg1, accessed November 29, 2010. Among a number of books written on the Hays Code and censorship in Hollywood, see, e.g., Gregory D. Black, *Hollywood Censored: Morality Codes, Catholics, and the Movies* (Cambridge Studies in the History of Mass Communication; Cambridge: Cambridge University Press, 1994).

61 For a refutation of the argument that "gay is the new black," see below, Chapter Six.

62 http://westwing.bewarne.com/second/25letter.html, accessed November 29, 2010.

63 I was surprised to find this email referenced positively in the otherwise very good, thought-provoking book by Gary Willis, *What Jesus Meant* (New York: Penguin, 2006), although at times he loses sight of the Jewishness and Torah-loyalty of Jesus.

64 The simple answer to the questions posed sarcastically to Dr. Laura is that in the Bible, there were actions universally prohibited (meaning, for all people for all time), such as bestiality, incest, and homosexual practice (within the Torah, see Leviticus 18, with special reference to 18:1-3, 24-30, where God expresses His displeasure with pagan nations that commit these acts – hence, indicating that they are wrong for all people, not just Israel – in contrast with other actions that were specifically prohibited to Israel, such as eating shellfish; see, e.g., Leviticus 11:8, "they [meaning specific animals] are unclean *for you*"). For important works dealing with the Bible and homosexual practice, see below, Chapter Ten, and note my relevant lectures, available online, http://coalitionofconscience.askdrbrown.org/resources/2007_lecture_monday.html (I discuss the letter to Dr. Laura at some length here); and http://coalitionofconscience.askdrbrown.org/resources/2008_lecture_monday.html.

65 According to *Entertainment Weekly*, cited at http://westwing.bewarne.com/second/25letter.html, "Refreshingly candid exec producer Aaron Sorkin admits he lifted the diatribe from a much forwarded anonymous email.... Sorkin, who hoped to give credit, says they "cast a fairly wide net, but we didn't find the author."' (Accessed November 29, 2010.)

66 According to the Media Research Center, this was one of the Top Ten Left Wing scenes in the history of West Wing, which ended in 2006. http://www.mrc.org/Profiles/westwing/welcome.asp, accessed November 29, 2010. The dialogue ended with one further, off color rebuke from the "president," but it is not germane to our topic.

67 http://www.stopdrlaura.com/. As of November 29, 2010, the site was still accessible.

68 For further background, see Tammy Bruce, *The New Thought Police: Inside the Left's Assault on Free Speech and Free Minds* (New York: Three Rivers Press, 2001), 59-68. For Dr. Laura's more recent stances on homosexuality, see now http://transcripts.cnn.com/TRANSCRIPTS/0904/08/lkl.01.html, accessed December 12, 2010.

69 http://www.washingtonpost.com/wp-dyn/content/article/2010/12/17/AR2010121707043.html. For the episode online, see, e.g., http://www.bing.com/videos/watch/video/homophobia/17udoswpi, both accessed December 22, 2010.

70 For the complete transcript, see http://www.antijen.org/ER/, accessed November 29, 2010.

71 For Oprah's September 28, 2007 show on this, see http://www.oprah.com/community/thread/3144 (for comments), accessed November 29, 2010; a blurb states, "Guests who say they were born in the wrong body share their stories on facing the world transgendered. What would you do if your 7-year-old daughter said, 'Mom, I really should be a boy?'" There are hundreds of other relevant sites which can easily be found by searching for "Oprah" together with "born in the wrong body."

72 http://www.cbsnews.com/stories/2006/03/09/60minutes/main1385230.shtml, accessed November 29, 2010.

73 http://abcnews.go.com/2020/Story?id=3072518&page=1, accessed November 29, 2010; note that Grant is a pseudonym used in the story to protect the family's privacy.

74 For an interesting follow-up to the *Sixty Minutes* segment, called "The Science of Sexual Orientation,"

see Prof. Warren Throckmorton's report at: http://wthrockmorton.com/2008/05/14/60-minutes-science-of-sexual-orientation-an-update-from-the-mother-of-twins/, accessed November 29, 2010.

75 See below, Chapter Thirteen, for more on this.

76 See the discussion at: http://rebeccaaugephd.blogspot.com/2007_09_25_archive.html, accessed November 29, 2010. For reflections from four transgender-identifed college students, see the 2005 documentary *TransGeneration.*

77 See http://sugarandmedicine.wordpress.com/2009/03/28/cruel-unusual-documentary-ontransgender-women-in-mens-prisons-across-the-us/; http://www.cruelandunusualfilm.com/, both accessed November 29, 2010.

78 http://www.youtube.com/watch?v=d8jfCWlnOZw (click to expand on the text below the video); accessed November 29, 2010, my emphasis.

79 For further reflections, see Chapter Fifteen, below.

80 http://wnd.com/index.php?fa=PAGE.view&pageId=55892, accessed November 29, 2010. In the CNN interview, Pearson cites that American Pediatric Association to buttress her claim that children have their true gender identity formed between the ages of three and five. She states, "A child, by the time they're five years old, they understand what their gender is, and they're very clear on what gender they are." Check for APA source? Interact? Although Pearson is part of TransYouth Family Advocates, she was not identified as such on the CNN segment.

81 The interview can be watched at: http://www.youtube.com/watch?v=zvuZNS-Wgck, accessed November 29, 2010.

82 A segment from the original TV report on this (KUSA in Denver) was also aired, quoting from a school administrator and then briefly from a concerned father, and nothing more.

83 See, e.g., http://www.thefreelibrary.com/The+Advocate+(The+national+gay+%26+lesbian+newsmagazine)/2006/February/28-p518, accessed November 29, 2010.

84 http://www.glaad.org/media/release_detail.php?id=3865, accessed February 5, 2007, but no longer available.

85 http://www.q-notes.com/editorial/editorsnote_031106.html, accessed November 29, 2010.

86 For the record, *Brokeback Mountain* won three awards: Best Director, Best Adapted Screenplay and Best Original Score. According to GLAAD, "Two other gay-inclusive films also picked up statuettes: Capote star Philip Seymour Hoffman won the Best Actor Oscar for his portrayal of Truman Capote, and Rachel Weisz won Best Supporting Actress for The Constant Gardener. Transamerica was also nominated for two Academy Awards."

87 http://tv.msn.com/tv/year-in-review/gayest-year-ever/, accessed November 29, 2010.

88 These remarks were widely cited; see the report of Dr. Ted Baehr, http://movieguide.org/news/3/228. See http://www.youtube.com/watch?v=9HFRjamyua0, accessed July 2, 2010.

89 Ibid. For the powerful influence of *Milk,* cf. Martha C. Nussbaum, *From Disgust to Humanity: Sexual Orientation and Constitutional Law* (New York: Oxford University Press, 2010), 204-209.

90 For a positive assessment of his comments, see http://gayrights.change.org/blog/view/mark_ruffalo_on_kicking_and_screaming_anti-gay_bigots, accessed August 5, 2010.

91 http://blogs.nypost.com/movies/archives/2008/11/oscar_watch_wea_1.html, accessed November 29, 2010. Baehr, ibid., also notes, "Earlier in the evening, actress Marisa Tomei, who plays a stripper in THE WRESTLER, was applauded for showing that 'a stripper doesn't have to lose her dignity when taking off her clothes.'"

92 A short list includes *Under the Tuscan Sun; DodgeBall; The Birdcage; My Best Friend's Wedding; Wedding Crashers; Bring It On (All or Nothing); The Rocky Horror Picture Show.*

93 http://www.jewishworldreview.com/cols/medved122005.asp, accessed November 29, 2010.

94 And note that some researchers are upset with Hollywood when it promotes "heteronormativity!" Cf. Kathleen Gilbert, "Team of Researchers Blames Children's Films for Perpetuating 'Heteronormativity'," http://www.lifesitenews.com/ldn/2009/jun/09062404.html, accessed November 29, 2010.

Chapter 6

1 http://www.advocate.com/exclusive_detail_ektid65744.asp?page=3, accessed December 14, 2010. Campbell is actually quite careful in pressing the "gay = black" analogy, pointing out significant differences between the two.

2 Ibid.

3 http://www.councilforresponsiblegenetics.org/GeneWatch/GeneWatchPage.aspx?pageId=262, accessed August 31, 2010.a

4 Lori L. Lake, reviewing Toby Johnson's *Gay Spirituality: The Role of Gay Identity in the Transformation of Human Consciousness* (repr., Maple Shade, NJ: Lethe Press, 2004).

5 For details on violent and deadly attacks on gays outside of America, along with a listing of countries that still has the death penalty for homosexual acts, see Louis-Georges Tin, *The Dictionary of Homophobia: A Global History of Gay and Lesbian Experience* (Eng. trans., Marek Redburn; Vancouver, BC: Arsenal Pulp Press, 2008). See also Max Strasser, "The Global Gay Rights Battlefields," December 20, 2010, in *Foreign Policy*, http://www.foreignpolicy.com/articles/2010/12/20/the_global_gay_rights_battlefields?page=full), accessed December 29, 2010.

6 "Love, War – and Gay Marriage," http://bighollywood.breitbart.com/cwinecoff/2009/03/19/love-war-and-gay-marriage/, accessed May 23, 2010.

7 http://www.apa.org/helpcenter/sexual-orientation.aspx, accessed December 14, 2010.

8 http://www.healthyminds.org/More-Info-For/GayLesbianBisexuals.aspx, accessed December 14, 2010. This statement, used by the APA in 2000, is still current today, as cited on this APA website.

9 Regarding Dr. Dean Hamer's paper detailing the alleged discovery of a gay gene, Prof. Gerard van den Aardweg, notes that "'The whole thing was, after all, a storm in a tea cup. Subsequent analysis and research vindicated the verdict by the famous French authority in the field, Jerome Lejeune, that the methodological defects of the investigation were so serious that 'were it not for the fact that this study is about homosexuality, it would probably never have been accepted for publication.'" See Gerard van den Aardweg, "Homosexuality And Biological Factors: Real Evidence -- None; Misleading Interpretations: Plenty," in the *NARTH Bulletin*, 13 (Winter 2005), 19-28, citing a private communication from Lejeune, who discovered a gene that causes Downs syndrome; reprinted https://jonahweb.org/article.php?secId=124, accessed December 14, 2010.

10 http://www.mygenes.co.nz/summary.htm, accessed December 14, 2010.

11 "Myths and Misconceptions: About Behavioral Genetics and Homosexuality," available online at http://www.narth.com/docs/080307Abbott_NARTH_article.pdf, accessed December 14, 2010.

12 "Interview with John D'Emilio; LGBT liberation: Build a broad movement," *International Socialist Review*, Issue 65, May-June 2009 (www.isreview.org/issues/65/featdemilio. shtml), n.p.

13 See also Jonathan Sorum, "Civil Rights & Homosexual Rights - A Flawed Analogy," printed online in *Liberty Magazine*, http://www.libertymagazine.org/index.php?id=1480, accessed October 19, 2010. Just for the record, I am not inferring from my just-used analogy that homosexuality should be illegal.

14 http://www.latimes.com/news/nationworld/nation/la-na-exgay18jun18,0,4259057.story?coll=la-home-center. According to a July 17, 2001 article published in the *Advocate*, "In a Gallup Poll conducted in May [2001], half of those surveyed said they believe homosexuality is genetic, and half said it is environmental. In a 1977 Gallup Poll, respondents pointed to the environment over genetics by more than a 4-to-1 ratio. The poll calls this shift in perception 'one of the more significant changes in American public opinion on gay and lesbian issues.' It is clearly accompanied by increasing tolerance toward gays and lesbians. In May, 52% of Gallup respondents said homosexuality is an 'acceptable alternative lifestyle,' compared with 38% in 1977. And a majority, 54%, agreed that 'homosexual relations between consenting adults should be legal,' compared with 43% in 1977."

15 For exaggerated media reports, see "The Gay Gene?", by Jeffrey Satinover, M.D., http://www.narth.com/docs/istheregene.html, accessed December 19, 2010.

16 Marshall Kirk and Hunter Madsen, *After the Ball: How America Will Conquer Its Fear and Hatred of Gays in the 90's* (New York: Penguin, 1989), 184, my emphasis. For further (and, different) perspectives see Vera Whisman, *Queer by Choice: Lesbians, Gay Men, and the Politics of Identity* (New York: Routledge, 1996); note that Whisman, now a professor at Ithaca College, is a lesbian.

17 Posted on April 10, 2009, at 04:57:08 PM PDT, http://www.dailykos.com/story/2009/4/10/718806/-Gays-Out,-Conservatives-Inthe-Closet.-, accessed April 11, 2009. Similar examples could be multiplied almost ad infinitum. Charles Winecoff points out the fallacious thinking behind such equations: "Two people of the same sex being denied the opportunity to marry is not the same as two people of opposite sexes and different colors being denied that same opportunity. Interracial couples who couldn't marry because of anti-miscegenation laws were still men and women - trying to do what millions of other men and women were already doing: joining together in holy matrimony, usually to raise a family." See "Love, War – and Gay Marriage," cited above, n. 5.

18 Citing C. Mann, "Genes and Behavior," *Science*, 264 (1994), 1686-1689.

19 "Homosexuality: Some Neglected Considerations," *Journal of American Physicians and Surgeons* 10/3 (Fall, 2005), 2.

20 Christl Ruth Vonholdt, "Homosexuality - Expression of an Unresolved Gender Identity Conflict," http://www.ojc.de/dijg/index.php?art_id=74&categ=12&expand=12&file=view_article.tp; for the German original, see http://www.ojc.de/dijg/index.php?art_id=40&categ=7&expand=7&file=view_article.tp#Top, both accessed November 10, 2009.

21 Citing D. H. Hamer, et al., "A linkage between DNA Markers on the X Chromosome and Male Sexual

Orientation," *Science*, 261 (July 16, 1993), 321-327. See further Dean H. Hamer, *Living with Our Genes* (Doubleday, New York, 1998).

22 Citing S. Le Vay, "A Difference in Hypothalamic Structures Between Heterosexuals and Homosexual Men," *Science*, 253 (August 30, 1991), 1036.

23 Citing G. Dörner, "Neuroendocrine response to estrogen and brain differentiation in heterosexuals, homosexuals and transsexuals," *Archives of Sexual Behaviour*, 17 (1998), 57-75.

24 Citing W. Byne et al., "Human Sexual Orientation: The Biological Theories Reappraised," *Archives of General Psychiatry* 50/3 (March, 1993), 227-239; W. Byne, "Homosexualität: ein komplexes Phänomen," *Spektrum der Wissenschaft* (Juli 7, 1994), 43-51; C. R. Vonholdt, "Naturwissenschaftliche Erkenntnisse zur Homosexualität," in *Homosexualität und christliche Seelsorge, Dokumentation eines ökumenischen Symposiums* (Aussaat: Verlag GmbH, Neukirchen-Vluyn, 1995).

25 Citing M. Dannecker, "Sexualwissenschaftliches Gutachten zur Homosexualität," in Jürgen Basedow et al., *Die Rechtstellung gleichgeschlechtlicher Lebensgemeinschaften*, (Tübingen: Mohr–Siebeck, 2000), 339.

26 Louis Berman, *The Puzzle: Exploring the Evolutionary Puzzle of Male Homosexuality* (Wilmette, IL: Godot Press, 2003), 250.

27 "Empowering Parents of Gender Discordant and Same-Sex Attracted Children," 1, with documentation; to download, see http://www.americancollegeofpediatricians.org/Download-document/8-Empowering-Parents-of-Gender-Discordant-and-Same-Sex-Attracted-Children.html, accessed December 14, 2010.

28 *Reinventing the Male Homosexual: The Rhetoric and Power of the Gay Gene* (Bloomington & Indianapolis: Indiana University Press, 2002), 7, n. 1, with reference to J. Gallagher, "Gay for the Thrill of It," *The Advocate*, February 17, 1998, 32-37.

29 Mark A. Yarhouse, *Homosexuality and the Christian: A Guide for Parents, Pastors, and Friends* (Minneapolis: Bethany House, 2010), 80.

30 Cf. http://www.narth.com/docs/trumpeted.html, accessed December 14, 2010, for some critical remarks.

31 http://www.boston.com/news/globe/magazine/articles/2005/08/14/what_makes_people_gay/, accessed April 10, 2009. Swidey's article focuses on the moving story of identical twins boys, one of whom is all boy and other of whom is all girl (in terms of desires and interests). "What makes the case of Patrick and Thomas so fascinating is that it calls into question both of the dominant theories in the long-running debate over what makes people gay: nature or nurture, genes or learned behavior. As identical twins, Patrick and Thomas began as genetic clones. From the moment they came out of their mother's womb, their environment was about as close to identical as possible - being fed, changed, and plopped into their car seats the same way, having similar relationships with the same nurturing father and mother. Yet before either boy could talk, one showed highly feminine traits while the other appeared to be 'all boy,' as the moms at the playgrounds say with apologetic shrugs.

"'That my sons were different the second they were born, there is no question about it,' says the twins' mother.'

"So what happened between their identical genetic starting point and their births? They spent nine months in utero. In the hunt for what causes people to be gay or straight, that's now the most interesting and potentially enlightening frontier."

32 From a traditional Christian perspective, all human beings, while created in the image of God, are born with a fallen nature and thus a predisposition to sin; from a traditional Jewish perspective, all human beings have both a good inclination and an evil inclination. Thus, both religious traditions recognize that all human beings are flawed and must battle to overcome sinful or fleshly desires, and neither tradition accepts the notion that "the devil (or, my fleshly nature) made me do it." For further reflections, cf. Paul Copan, "Original Sin and Christian Philosophy," *Philosophia Christi*, Series 2, 5/2 (2003): 519-541 (online at) http://www.paulcopan.com/articles/pdf/original-sin-christian-philosophy.pdf; and see the relevant chapters Moshe Chaim Luzatto, *The Way of God: Derech Hashem* (Torah Classics Library; Eng. trans. Aryeh Kaplan; Brooklyn: Philip Feldheim, 1996). Note that these references are provided to give just a small hint of the relevant issues involved, the study of which would require hundreds of books, articles, and biblical commentaries. For an insightful lesson, one can compare traditional Jewish and Christian commentaries to Genesis 4:7.

33 "A therapist's guide to the genetics of human sexual orientation," *Sexual and Relationship Therapy* 18 (2003), 429-436; the quote is from 432. In more detail, see A. S. Greenberg and J. M. Bailey, "Do biological explanations of homosexuality have moral, legal, or policy implications?", *Journal of Sex Research* 30 (2003), 245-251.

34 See, e.g., http://www.nature.com/news/2008/080404/full/news.2008.738.html, accessed December 14, 2010.

35   Ibid.

36   The sarcastic comments left by many posters on the article's website underscore the point we're making here.

37   http://www.reuters.com/article/healthNews/idUSN1444872420080714, accessed December 14, 2010.

38   Cf., e.g., http://www.ncbi.nlm.nih.gov/pmc/articles/PMC1458834/, accessed December 14, 2010, on violent behavior and potential genetic predisposition.

39   The article is now available with a different title at http://rbeansrblades.blogspot.com/2008/09/its-all-in-genes.html, accessed December 14, 2010.

40   Ibid.

41   Ibid.

42   Ibid.

43   Ibid.

44   http://findarticles.com/p/articles/mi_qn4161/is_20041212/ai_n12914622/, accessed May 15, 2010.

45   Ibid.

46   http://well.blogs.nytimes.com/2010/05/10/tracking-the-science-of-commitment/?8dpc, accessed May 16, 2010.

47   http://kristof.blogs.nytimes.com/2009/06/23/do-we-have-a-rape-gene/, accessed December 14, 2010.

48   http://www.nbcsandiego.com/news/weird/Scientists-May-Have-IDd-Liberal-Gene-105917218.html, accessed October 29, 2010.

49   http://www.newscientist.com/article/dn9002-common-genetic-change-linked-to-obesity.html, accessed October 29, 2010.

50   See, e.g., the useful summary at http://www.simpalife.com/new-study-shows-obese-kids-get-bullied-more/, accessed December 14, 2010. The post states that "physical traits are the number 1 reason why kids get bullied in school," with obesity at the top of the list.

51   Just for the record, I should note that there is an organization called the National Association to Advance Fat Acceptance (naafa); see http://www.naafaonline.com/dev2/, accessed December 14, 2010. Their "About Us" blurb states, "Founded in 1969, the National Association to Advance Fat Acceptance (NAAFA) is a non-profit, all volunteer, civil rights organization dedicated to protecting the rights and improving the quality of life for fat people. NAAFA works to eliminate discrimination based on body size and provide fat people with the tools for self-empowerment through advocacy, public education, and support."

52   As cited above, n. 49.

53   According to studies I have seen, many children diagnosed with GID end up identifying as gay rather than wanting to identify as the opposite sex once they come into adolescence, while others (a smaller percentage) end up leading normal, heterosexual lives; for perspectives on the upbringing of children with GID, see, e.g., Kenneth J. Zucker, "Gender Identity Development and Issues," *Child and Adolescent Psychiatric Clinics of North America*, 13 (2004) 551-568. For other perspectives, see Marc S. Dillworth, Ph.D., "The Treatment of Childhood Gender Identity Disorder (GID)," reprinted from NARTH Conference Papers 2002, and available online at http://www.narth.com/docs/treatment.pdf, accessed December 14, 2010.

54   http://rex.nci.nih.gov/RESEARCH/basic/biochem/hamer.htm, accessed June 23, 2009.

55   Ibid., current as of December 14, 2010.

56   As cited in n. 31, above; for LeVay's most recent statement, see Simon LeVay, *Gay, Straight, and the Reason Why: The Science of Sexual Orientation* (New York: Oxford University Press, 2011). He argues that, "Sexual orientation is an aspect of gender that emerges from the prenatal sexual differentiation of the brain. Whether a person ends up gay or straight depends in large part on how this process of biological differentation goes forward, with the lead actors being genes, sex hormones, and the brain systems that are influenced by them" (271).

57   Cf., respectively, http://www.mygenes.co.nz/download.htm, especially Chapter Ten ("Twin Studies: the strongest evidence"); and Nicholas D. Kristof, "Gay at Birth?", October 25, 2003, the *New York Times*, http://query.nytimes.com/gst/fullpage.html?res=9904e7d91231f936a15753c1a9659c8b63, both accessed December 14, 2010. All my research convinces me that Whitehead is far closer to the mark.

58   http://www.drthrockmorton.com/article.asp?id=8, accessed December 14, 2010, and also critiquing Kristof's article, cited immediately above, n. 51.

59   http://narth.com/docs/nothardwired.html, accessed December 14, 2010. Note further: ". . . Dr. Collins succinctly reviewed the research on homosexuality and offers the following: "An area of particularly strong public interest is the genetic basis of homosexuality. Evidence from twin studies does in fact support the conclusion that heritable factors play a role in male homosexuality. However, the likelihood that the identical twin of a homosexual male will also be gay is about 20% (compared with 2-4 percent of males

in the general population), indicating that sexual orientation is genetically influenced but not hardwired by DNA, and that whatever genes are involved represent predispositions, not predeterminations."

60   See, e.g., the discussions in Laurence Tancredi, *Hardwired Behavior: What Neuroscience Reveals about Morality* (New York: Cambridge University Press, 2005); Michael S. Gazzaniga, *The Ethical Brain* (New York/ Washington, DC: Dana Press, 2005).

61   http://www.365gay.com/newscon05/05/052605prejudice.htm, accessed August 26, 2005, but no longer available there.

62   Ibid.

63   http://www.nacoa.net/pdfs/addicted.pdf, 1, accessed December 14, 2010; this is just a sampling of the statistics cited.

64   As to the question of whether it is possible for a person to change his or her sexual orientation, see below, Chapter Twelve and Thirteen.

65   Dr. Patrick Chapman has raised several objections to any analogy being made between alcoholism and sexual orientation, following the line of reasoning raised by Prof. Jeffrey Siker, namely, that a person does not know that he or she has propensities towards alcohol until having their first drink, in contrast with homosexual desires and attractions, which are discovered without external provocation. See Patrick M. Chapman, *"Thou Shalt not Love": What Evangelicals Really Say to Gays* (New York: Haiduk Press, 2008), 44-45; Chapman also follows Andrew Sullivan and others in arguing that homosexual acts, in and of themselves, are not immoral and can be contrasted with the "disease" of alcoholism. In response to "the first" drink argument, isn't there something of the "first drink" experience as well for many gays and lesbians who claim that they too had no idea about their same-sex attractions until they either fell in love with someone of the same sex, had a physical encounter with someone of the same sex, or simply felt attracted to someone of the same sex? If there were no people of the same-sex to be attracted to, how would the homosexual person know they had these feelings? Furthermore, in the case of children of alcoholics, the deck is already stacked against them, and so, before they have done anything or had their "first drink," the odds of them becoming alcoholics are very high. For interesting reflections on the alcoholism comparison from the angle of the potential of change, see A. A. Howsepian, "Sexual Modification Therapies: Ethical Controversies, Philosophical Disputes, and Theological Reflections," *Christian Bioethics* 10 (2004): 117-135. (Howsepian is Assistant Clinical Professor of Psychiatry at the University of California San Francisco, a Staff Psychiatrist in the VA Mental Health Clinic, and Director of the Electroconvulsive Therapy Program.)

66   For the most recent, comprehensive studies on health risks experienced by homosexuals, see below, Chapters Eleven and Thirteen.

67   Former lesbian Melissa Fryrear notes that, "Many women were sexually abused yet never became lesbian; many women were never abused yet *did* become lesbian." She continues, however: "In the interviews Anne Paulk conducted for *Restoring Sexual Identity: Hope for Women with Same-Sex Attraction*, 66 percent of the women struggling with same-sex attraction interviewed experienced sexual abuse. Dr. Stanton Jones, provost of Wheaton College and author of the book *Homosexuality: The Use of Scientific Research in the Church's Moral Debate*, adds, 'Experience of sexual abuse as a child . . . more than tripled the likelihood of later reporting homosexual orientation.' And drawing from my own experience, I'll say that in the decade I was on staff with one of Exodus International's largest ministries, I never met one woman struggling with lesbianism who had not been sexually threatened or violated." See Melissa Fryrear, "Counseling Women Who Struggle with Lesbianism," in Joe Dallas and Nancy Heche, eds., *The Complete Christian Guide to Understanding Homosexuality: A Biblical and Compassionate Response to Same-Sex Attraction* (Eugene, OR: Harvest House, 2010), 256; the entire chapter runs from 247-275. Numerous counselors have related similar anecdotal evidence to me.

68   Richard A. Isay, M.D., *Becoming Gay: The Journey into Self-Acceptance* (New York: Henry Holt and Company, 1996).

69   David F. Greenberg, *The Construction of Homosexuality* (Chicago: University of Chicago Press, 1988), 481.

70   Jeffrey Satinover, M.D., *Homosexuality and the Politics of Truth* (Grand Rapids: Baker, 1996), 81.

71   Satinover, *Politics*, 129, citing "Confusing the Actor with the Act: Muddled Notions about Homosexuality," *Archives of Sexual Behavior*, 20 (1990), 421-423.

72   Martin Rovers and Ray A. Seutter, "Emotionally Absent Fathers: Furthering the Understanding of Homosexuality," *Journal of Psychology and Theology*, 32 (2004), 43-49; see the summary of the article at http://www.narth.com/docs/weakfather.html, accessed December 15, 2010.

73   This is the classic "erotic becomes exotic" theory (put forth especially by Daryl Bem), certainly true in many cases of homosexual development. For a recent statement on this, see Joseph J. Nicolosi, Ph.D., *Shame and Attachment Loss: The Practical Work of Reparative Therapy* (Downers Grove, IL: IVP Academic,

2009), which includes discussion of this perspective.

74 *A Separate Creation*, 271.
75 Ibid.
76 Ibid.
77 Ibid., 272.
78 Ibid., 272-273.
79 Ibid., 293-308.
80 See the reflections by Dr. David Botstein on Lewontin's views in ibid., 273-276.
81 According to Dr. Timothy Murphy, "The benefits of genetic explanations for sexual identities do, however, come with a cost. An identified biogenetic trait for homosexuality might open the door to testing and treatment for adults, adolescents, children, and fetuses alike. In the worst case scenarios, some women might abort fetuses they believed likely to become homosexual children, and some adults and adolescents might be subjected to involuntary testing and treatment. When publishing their 1994 linkage study of male homosexuality, geneticist Dean Hamer and his colleagues took the highly unusual step of directly addressing these kinds of downstream effects of their work. At the end of their report in the journal *Science*, these researchers said: "We believe that it would be fundamentally unethical to use such information [about genetic linkages] to try to assess or alter a person's current or future sexual orientation, either heterosexual or homosexual, or other normal attributes of human behavior. Rather, scientists, educators, policy-makers, and the public should work together to ensure that such research is used to benefit all members of society." See Timothy F. Murphy, "The Meaning of Genetics for Gay and Lesbian Identities," http://www.councilforresponsiblegenetics.org/GeneWatch/GeneWatchPage.aspx?pageId=262, accessed December 15, 2010.
82 http://www.albertmohler.com/2009/07/16/then-again-maybe-not-the-gay-gene-theory-takes-a-hit/, accessed December 14, 2010.
83 A synopsis of the book *Crisis* (see, below, Chapter Fifteen, n. 1), states, "A Mental Health Crisis Faces American Teens Right Now - and it is one we can solve. Hundreds of thousands of gay teens face traumatic depression, fear, rejection, persecution, and isolation-usually alone. Studies show they are 190 percent more likely to use drugs or alcohol and four times more likely to attempt suicide. Homophobia and discrimination are at the heart of their pain. Love, support, and acceptance-all within our power to give-can save them." Given this backdrop, it is often noted that no one would choose to be gay in such a hostile environment.
84 http://www.reuters.com/article/newsOne/idUSTRE5764NI20090807, accessed December 14, 2010.
85 Ibid.
86 Dean Hamer and Peter Copeland, *The Science of Desire: The Gay Gene and the Biology of Behavior* (NewYork: Simon & Schuster, 1994), 214.
87 Ibid. (n. 77).
88 See, conveniently, http://www.mygenes.co.nz/PDFs/Ch8.pdf ("Are Brains Gay?"), accessed December 14, 2010.
89 For a listing of useful resources on this, see http://coalitionofconscience.askdrbrown.org/resources/same_sex_marriage_resources.html, and note in particular the statement from the American College of Pediatricians, http://www.acpeds.org/pdf/Homosexual-Parenting-Is-It-Time-For-Change.pdf; and Robert Lerner, Ph.D., and Althea K. Nagai, Ph.D., *No Basis: What the Studies Don't Tell Us About Same-Sex Parenting* (downloadable e-book; Washington, DC: Marriage Law Project, 2001), http://www.homosexinfo.org/uploads/Origin.Support/nobasis.pdf; see further the resources listed at http://www.dawnstefanowicz.com/resources.htm (by subject); all accessed December 14, 2010. See futher below, Chapter Fifteen, with nn. 102-110.
90 See below, Chapters Eleven and Thirteen.

Chapter 7

1 Rabbi Shmuley Boteach, my good friend and frequent debating opponent, claimed that I equated pedophilia and homosexuality in our November 2, 2010 debate, stating in his editorial in the *Washington Post* "On Faith" blog, "The point of no return was when Dr. Brown said that in terms of sinfulness homosexuality was the same as bestiality, incest, and pedophilia. I should have been thrilled at the comparison. Dr. Brown spends most of his time trying to convert Jews to Christianity and I should have welcomed this act of self-immolation. Instead, because he is a friend and, amid our profound disagreements, a refined gentleman, I pleaded with him to come back from the brink. I repeated over and over again that this debate was being recorded for posterity and he would irreversibly damage his credibility with thinking people everywhere if he made the insane comparison. But rather than relent, he instead asked the audience members to raise their hands if they agreed he had come across as an

extremist. Amid hundreds of people, only three hands went up. My heart sank." See http://onfaith. washingtonpost.com/onfaith/guestvoices/2010/11/how_evangelicals_lost_political_credibility.html. While I am aware that this was Rabbi Shmuley's genuine impression of what took place, the reality was that I (and others in the audience) explained that all of our sins were ugly in God's sight, and that my past sins (which included stealing money from my own father as a teenage drug user) were as bad as if not worse than homosexuality. Regarding pedophilia, I repeatedly explained to my friend Rabbi Shmuley that I was speaking only of consensual acts committed between, say, a grown man and a twelve year-old or a fourteen-year old, and my only reason for raising this issue was to say, "If you would not discourage two gay men in a committed relationship from committing homosexual acts, since you believe their desires were innate and immutable, what would you tell a man who was only attracted to boys? Would you give him the same counsel if the acts were consensual?" For my response to Shmuley's editorial in the same blog, see http://onfaith.washingtonpost.com/onfaith/guestvoices/2010/11/what_the_rabbi_doesnt_get.html. To view the actual debate (which should set the record straight in terms of where I stand on the issue), go to http://askdrbrown.org/about-dr-brown/itinerary/shmuley-vs-brown-debate-is-homosexual-activism-americas-greatest-moral-crisis. Cf. also above, Chapter Two, n. 18. And note the even more wide-ranging charge in a gay newspaper that I compare "LGBT people to child rapists and pedophiles, adulterers, murderers"; see http://goqnotes.com/9437/naughty-or-nice-the-heroes-villains-and-foes-of-2010/, all accessed December 15, 2010.

2   John Money, Introduction to Theo Sandfort, *Boys on Their Contacts with Men: A Study of Sexually Expressed Friendships* (Elmhurst, NY: Global Academic Publishers, 1987), n.p. in the online edition (I did not have access to the original).

3   Ibid.

4   Peter J. Fagan, Thomas N. Wise, Chester W. Schmidt, and Fred S. Berlin, "Pedophilia," *Journal of the American Medical Association*, 288 (2002), 2458-2465, cited frequently online, including on the Pedophiliaphobia (!) website, "http://pedophileophobia.com/what_is_a_pedophile.htm, accessed December 15, 2010. The purpose of this site is "to combat the ever growing hysteria over pedophilia."

5   Fred Berlin, M.D., Ph.D., "Pedophilia: When Is a Difference a Disorder?", *Archives of Sexual Behavior* 31 (2002), 479-480. Also available online at http://www.paraphilias.com/publications/pdfs/Peer%20Comment.pdf, accessed May 9, 2010.

6   http://www.nambla.org/pederasty.htm, accessed May 9, 2010. Note that Thorstad, along with being a cofounder of the notorious NAMBLA, was also a former president of New York's Gay Activists Alliance and a cofounder of New York's Coalition for Lesbian and Gay Rights. This is a reminder of how deeply entrenched "man-boy lovers" like Thorstad were at the forefront of the early gay rights movement, as also reflected in some of his comments, quoted here in the main text.

7   Ibid.

8   Ibid.

9   Ibid.

10   Ibid.

11   Ibid.

12   Ibid.

13   Ibid.

14   See, for example, some of the examples cited in the Wikipedia entry under "Same-Sex Marriage," http://en.wikipedia.org/wiki/Same-sex_marriage#History, accessed May 9, 2010. For a scholarly analysis of homosexual behavior across cultures, including pederasty, see Stephen O. Murray, *Homosexualities* (Chicago: University of Chicago Press, 2000).

15   Gunter Schmidt, "The Dilemma of the Male Pedophile," *Archives of Sexual Behavior*, 31 (2002), 476-477.

16   Cited in Ellen Barry, "Despite Therapies, Pedophilia Eludes Cure," *Boston Globe*, Feb. 14, 2002, A1, http://www.jknirp.com/barry.htm,. For a convenient sampling of opinions regarding a potential "cure" for pedophilia, see http://newgon.com/wiki/Research:_A_"cure"_for_pedophilia%3F, both accessed May 9, 2010.

17   Fred S. Berlin, "Treatments to Change Sexual Orientation," *American Journal of Psychiatry*, 157 (2000), 838.

18   Michael Seto, "Pedophilia," *Annual Review of Clinical Psychology*, 5 (2009), 391-407, quoting from the abstract (see http://www.ncbi.nlm.nih.gov/pubmed/19327034), accessed May 9, 2010.

19   Currently available at http://www.jknirp.com/barry.htm, accessed May 9, 2010.

20   See, e.g., the summary of the evidence by gay academic activist Dr. Simon Levay at http://www.simonlevay.com/the-biology-of-sexual-orientation, accessed May 9, 2010. Note in particular, M. L. Lalumiere, R. Blanchard, and K. J. Zucker, "Sexual orientation and handedness in men and women: a

meta-analysis," *Psychological Bulletin*, 126 (2000), 575-592; B. S Mustanski, J. M Bailey, and S. Kaspar, "Dermatoglyphics, handedness, sex, and sexual orientation," *Archives of Sexual Behavior*, 31 (2002), 113-132; R. A. Lippa, "Are 2D:4D finger-length ratios related to sexual orientation? Yes for men, no for women," *Journal of Personality and Social Psychology*, 85 (2003) 179-188; and idem, "Handedness, sexual orientation, and gender-related personality traits in men and women," *Archives of Sexual Behavior*, 32 (2003), 103-114.

21   http://www.canada.com/national/nationalpost/news/bodyandhealth/story.html?id=e6aa33fd-9395-4ec7-a0dc-d9983f946378&p=1, accessed May 9, 2010.

22   Ibid.

23   Ibid.

24   See already Francis Mark Mondimore, *A Natural History of Homosexuality* (Baltimore: Johns Hopkins University Press, 1996), 132: "There is so much evidence linking the effects of prenatal hormone levels to adult sexual orientation that one cannot help but be curious as to the nature of the links." For a recent analysis, see http://www.mygenes.co.nz/PDFs/Ch7.pdf (dealing with "Prenatal hormones? Stress? Immune Attack?"), accessed December 14, 2010.

25   Note, however, the treatment in the online Encyclopedia of Mental Disorders, which points to the ongoing debate over nature vs. nurture: "A variety of different theories exist as to the causes of pedophilia. A few researchers attribute pedophilia along with the other paraphilias to biology. They hold that testosterone, one of the male sex hormones, predisposes men to develop deviant sexual behaviors. As far as genetic factors are concerned, as of 2002 no researchers have claimed to have discovered or mapped a gene for pedophilia. Most experts regard pedophilia as resulting from psychosocial factors rather than biological characteristics. Some think that pedophilia is the result of having been sexually abused as a child. Still others think that it derives from the person's interactions with parents during their early years of life. Some researchers attribute pedophilia to arrested emotional development; that is, the pedophile is attracted to children because he or she has never matured psychologically. Some regard pedophilia as the result of a distorted need to dominate a sexual partner. Since children are smaller and usually weaker than adults, they may be regarded as nonthreatening potential partners. This drive for domination is sometimes thought to explain why most pedophiles are males." See http://www.minddisorders.com/Ob-Ps/Pedophilia.html, accessed December 15, 2010. Interestingly, while it seems that discussion concerning the potential non-biological causes of pedophilia are welcomed in many scientific circles today, they are often met with scorn when the focus is on the causes of homosexuality.

26   http://narth.com/docs/frenchpol.html, accessed December 15, 2010.

27   See http://www2.hu-berlin.de/sexology/BIB/pedophilia.htm, accessed November 8, 2010; this is Richard Green's article, "Is pedophilia a mental disorder?", published in *Archives of Sexual Behavior*, 31 (2002), 467-471.

28   Some of the major books on same-sex behavior among animals include Bruce Bagemihl, Ph.D., *Biological Exuberance: Animal Homosexuality and Natural Diversity* (New York: St. Martin's Press, 1999); note that this volume was hailed as one of the 25 "Books to Remember" for 1999 by the New York Public Library; and Volker Summer and Paul L. Vasey, eds., *Homosexual Behaviour in Animals: An Evolutionary Perspective* (Cambridge: Cambridge University Press, 2006); for a critical analysis of such studies as a justification for homosexual practice being "natural," see, e.g., http://www.narth.com/docs/animalmyth.html, where it is also pointed out that many of the so-called homosexual behaviors among certain species seem to be more social than sexual (meaning, e.g., acts of dominance). Note the similar critique by Erik Holland, posting a review on Amazon: "Bagemihl groups sexual behavior in terms of five broad categories: courtship, affection, interactions involving mounting and genital contact, pair-bonding, and parenting activities. Such broad categorization risks confounding social interactions with sexual behavior, possibly leading one to mistakenly assume that a preference for specific social partners is a sexual preference for these partners." (See http://www.amazon.com/review/R2MRMEL0MKJZYL/ref=cm_cr_rdp_perm.) For the problems with justifying human behavior based on animal behavior, this oft-quoted dictum says it well, "Pigs don't date, ducks don't frequent stripper bars, and horses don't get married." See Dean Hamer and Peter Copeland, *The Science of Desire: The Gay Gene and the Biology of Behavior* (New York: Simon & Schuster, 1994), 213. Preceding this quote, the authors opined, "The fact of the matter is that there is no good animal model of human *heterosexuality*, let alone homosexuality" (their emphasis). Following the quote, they continued, "Anyway, since when are animals good role models? The praying mantis devours her mate while they are still copulating. Male dogs will mount their daughters. Animals don't speak, write love songs, build churches, or do a lot of other things that we consider most worthwhile." For discussion of a Norwegian museum's display about alleged homosexual behavior among animals (by a philosophy professor who questions the applicability of the animal's behavior to human behavior), see http://www.mercatornet.com/articles/view/a_gay_old_time_in_the_

animal_kingdom/). All accessed December 22, 2010.
29   As cited in n. 27, above.
30   Ibid.
31   Ibid.
32   Ibid.
33   http://www.lifesitenews.com/ldn/2009/aug/09081407.html, accessed November 8, 2010.
34   Ibid.
35   Ibid.
36   Ibid.
37   Berman, *The Puzzle*, 208. Speaking of child-sex in Thailand, Christopher P. Baker wrote, "Many Western sex tourists are convinced that, in indulging their fantasies, they are helping the young girls at the same time. 'The Asian boys who sleep with tourists are markedly more exuberant, happy and healthy than the hundreds of millions of poor children who are slowly withering away or being crippled by back-breaking labor,' writes a Dutch observer, Edward Brongersma." This view is then roundly refuted: "'To try and solve the terrible dilemma of Third World poverty by suggesting that a few children will be happier as temporary sex objects for wealthy foreigners is the kind of flippant solution which makes a mockery of human suffering,' replies Ron O'Grady, who claims that tourists almost always end up with a distorted view of the reality under which a majority of child prostitutes live." See Christopher P. Baker, "Child Chattel Lure Tourists for Sex beneath the Palms," *Insight on the News*, Vol. 11, March 13, 1995.
38   David Thorstad, quoting Benedict Friedländer, http://www.nambla.org/pederasty.htm. As of November, 2010, there was a Facebook group focused on "The Origins of the Modern Pederasty Movement: Pre-Nazi Germany and the Homosexual Rift," with reference to Friedländer. See http://www.facebook.com/group.php?gid=129333163958&v=wall, accessed November 8, 2010. (Note that by December 12, 2010, the name had been changed to "Gemeinschaft der Eigenen (The Classic COMMUNITY of LOVE)."
39   See n. 27, above.
40   Bruce Rind, "The Problem with Consensus Morality," in "Peer Commentaries on Green (2002) and Schmidt (2002), *Archives of Sexual Behavior* 31 (2002), 497. Rind provides these studies to "dispute [Gunter] Schmidt's claim that there can never be sexual consensus between prepubescents and adults." For online access, see http://www.paraphilias.com/publications/pdfs/Peer%20Comment.pdf (cited above, n. 5).
41   See also P. Okami, "Self-reports of "positive" childhood and adolescent sexual contacts with older persons: An exploratory study," *Archives of Sexual Behavior*, 20 (1991), 437-457.
42   See n. 26, above.
43   Ibid. He explained: "In the first edition of DSM-I (American Psychiatric Association, 1952), pedophilia was listed as one of the 'sexual deviations.' Pedophilia was labeled 'sociopathic' because of its conflict with societal mores. In DSM-II (American Psychiatric Association, 1968), pedophilia remained a 'sexual deviation,' but 'sociopathy' was gone and pedophilia fell into a group of 'nonpsychotic mental disorders.' Then, in DSM-III (American Psychiatric Association, 1980), pedophilia was included in the group of paraphilias. It was diagnosed for sexual activity or fantasy of sex by an adult with a prepubescent child. The acts needed to range from 'repeatedly preferred' to the 'exclusive method of achieving sexual excitement' (p. 272). But 'isolated sexual acts with children [did] not warrant the diagnosis' (p. 271). In DSM-III-R (American Psychiatric Association, 1987), the requirement was scuttled that sex with children needed to be 'repeatedly preferred.' Pedophilia was diagnosable in persons who also had a sexual interest in adult-adult sex. . . ." For an update on pedophilia in the DSM-IV and in the (forthcoming) DSM-V, see http://www.health.harvard.edu/newsletters/Harvard_Mental_Health_Letter/2010/July/pessimism-about-pedophilia, accessed December 12, 2010.
44   G. D. Wilson and D. N. Cox, *The Child-Lovers: A Study of Paedophiles in Society* (London: Peter Owen, 1983), 57, cited in Green, ibid.
45   D. Howitt, *Pedophiles and Sexual Offences Against Children* (Chichester, England: Wiley, 1998), 44, cited in Green, ibid.
46   Frans Gieles, reporting on the discussion in *Archives of Sexual Behavior* surrounding Green's article; see http://www.ipce.info/library_2/files/asb.htm, accessed November 7, 2010.
47   Green, "Is pedophilia a mental disorder?"
48   http://www.medterms.com/script/main/art.asp?articlekey=4767, accessed November 8, 2010.
49   For the recent claim that polyamorists are entitled to special legal protection, see http://papers.ssrn.com/sol3/papers.cfm?abstract_id=1632653, accessed November 8, 2010.
50   Spitzer's comment has been cited often; see, e.g., http://www.faqs.org/periodicals/201001/1983229151.html, accessed November 8, 2010.

51   http://www.anglicancommunion.org/listening/book_resources/docs/Dreshcher%20Sexual%20
      Conversion%20Therapies.pdf, accessed November 8, 2010.
52   Note the oft-quoted comment of Dr. Fred Berlin, in "Peer commentaries on Green (2002) and Schmidt
      (2002), Pedophilia: When Is a Difference a Disorder?," *Archives of Sexual Behavior* (December 1, 2002):
      "In our society, to have a pedophilic sexual orientation can create both psychological burdens and
      impairments. Thus, it seems reasonable to view pedophilia as a disorder." Online at http://business.
      highbeam.com/435395/article-1G1-94690098/peer-commentaries-green, accessed December 15,
      2010. Couldn't we currently use the same argument about homosexuality?
53   See his paper, with Peggy J. Kleinplatz, "DSM-IV-TR and the Paraphilias: An Argument for Removal,"
      delivered at May 2003 American Psychiatric Conference; see http://home.netcom.com/~docx2/
      mk.html. According to Robert Spitzer, "there is no such thing as pathological sexual behavior," as cited
      by Linda Ames Nicolosi, http://www.narth.com/docs/symposium.html, both accessed December 15,
      2010.
54   Cf. also *Archives of Sexual Behavior*, December 2002: F. E. J. Gieles, "Is pedophilia a mental disorder?"
      Discussion in Archives of Sexual Behavior, in IPCE Newsletter E15, March 2003; see https://www.ipce.
      info/, accessed December 15, 2010.
55   Moser and Kleinplatz, as cited by Linda Nicolosi (above, n. 53). Anecdotally, cf. the wishful quotes from
      NAMBLA members recorded in Bob Hamer, *The Last Undercover: The True Story of an FBI Agent's
      Dangerous Dance with Evil* (New York: Center Street, 2008).
56   See, conveniently (but with highlighting) http://www.article8.org/docs/gay_strategies/overhauling.htm,
      accessed December 15, 2010.
57   See above, Chapter Three, n. 6, for the claim advanced by C. A. Tripp that Lincoln was "predominantly
      homosexual," and note further what leading Lincoln scholars have said in reply to Tripp's main lines of
      argument: "If this is not preposterous, then the word should be declared extinct" (Alan C. Guelzo); "It
      is possible, by Tripp's method of carefully selecting Lincoln's words and behavior, to portray him as an
      avowed racist who cared nothing for blacks, or a ruthless president who disdained the Constitution and
      civil liberties, and so on. Rather than follow the data wherever it may lead him, Tripp follows some of the
      data to where he wants it to lead him" (Edward Steers, Jr.); ". . . not only is Tripp's conclusion flawed, but
      his entire approach to the question is an example of the man who has only one tool, a hammer, and so
      makes every problem into a nail" (Joan L. Flinspach); "In contrast to many of the scholars he condemns,
      Tripp ignores and misreads evidence and ultimately impoverishes the scholarly and public dialogue on
      Lincoln's life and legacy" (Daniel R. Stowell); "Given the paucity of hard evidence adduced by Tripp,
      and given the abundance of contrary evidence indicating that Lincoln was drawn romantically and
      sexually to some women, it is highly unlikely that Abraham Lincoln was 'predominantly homosexual.'"
      (Michael Burlingame). See http://www.claremont.org/publications/crb/id.1099/article_detail.asp,
      accessed November 9, 2010. Note also Guelzo's insightful comment (ibid.), helping snap the "Lincoln
      was gay" theorists back to reality, namely that "The whole proposition ought to collapse under the weight
      of one question: if Lincoln was a homosexual, why haven't we heard of this before? Surely Lincoln was
      so public a figure, and homosexuality so leprous an accusation in Victorian America, that not even P.T.
      Barnum, the Cardiff Giant, and the Feejee Mermaid could have distracted attention from a president
      who committed sodomy with the captain of his guard." See further the review of Tripp's book by Dr.
      Louis Berman in the *NARTH Bulletin* Vol. 13/2 (August, 2005), 28-30; http://www.narth.com/menus/
      NARTHBulletinAugust2005.pdf; the Wikipedia article seems to provide a fair critique of Tripp's thesis
      as well; see http://en.wikipedia.org/wiki/Sexuality_of_Abraham_Lincoln, both accessed November 9,
      2010.
58   See above, Chapter Three.
59   http://www.phrases.org.uk/meanings/364900.html, accessed December 15, 2010. According to this
      article, "Lord Alfred Douglas coined the phrase in his poem Two Loves, which was printed in the
      Chameleon in 1896: 'I am the Love that dare not speak its name.' Of course Douglas and Wilde had
      good reason to be cautious about how they described their relationship - homosexuality was a criminal
      offense in England in the 19th century."
60   The NAMBLA website notes that, "He once bragged to a friend of having had love affairs with five
      different boys in a single night. . . . [He said] 'They were all dirty and appealed to me just for that reason.'
      Wilde claimed to prefer lower-class boys because 'their passion was all body and no soul.'" See http://
      www.nambla.org/famousmen.htm Wilde's poem Panthea, in successive stanzas, spoke of "This hot hard
      flame with which our bodies burn" and "The boy's first kiss."
61   See above, Chapter Three, with reference to some of GLSEN's school materials.
62   See http://www.nambla.org/famousmen.htm, where NAMBLA lists "Fifteen Famous Men Who Had
      Boy Lovers," including: Alexander the Great; Hadrian; Leonardo Da Vinci; Michelangelo; Horatio

Alger; for NAMBLA's claim that Walt Whitman was a pederast, see http://www.nambla.org/whitman.
htm. Both accessed December 15, 2010.

63   http://www.nambla.org/ginsberg.htm, accessed December 15, 2010.

64   See Jeff Johnston, "The Life and Times of Harvey Milk," http://www.citizenlink.com/2010/06/got-milk/, accessed November 8, 2010, citing Randy Shilts, *The Mayor of Castro Street: The Life and Times of Harvey Milk* (New York: St. Martin's Press, 1982).

65   This took place in 1986. See Harry Hay with Will Roscoe, ed., *Radically Gay: Gay Liberation in the Words of its Founder* (Boston: Beacon Press, 1996), 355; cf. also Michael Bronski, "The Real Harry Hay," *The Phoenix*, Nov. 7, 2002, online at http://www.bostonphoenix.com/boston/news_features/other_stories/documents/02511115.htm, accessed May 9, 2010. Cf. also Jeffrey Lloyd's article, "When Nancy Met Harry" (speaking of Nancy Pelosi), cited in the opening quotes at the beginning of this chapter, and available online at http://spectator.org/archives/2006/10/05/when-nancy-met-harry, accessed May 9, 2010.

66   Ibid., 319.

67   See 319-320.

68   Brongersma ultimately cut a tragic figure: see http://en.wikipedia.org/wiki/Edward_Brongersma#Death, with reference to Dutch articles, accessed December 15, 2010.

69   Ibid., 321.

70   *Loving Boys*, 40, cited in ibid., 321.

71   *Boys on Their Contacts with Men*, n.p. (see above, n. 2).

72   Ibid., Introduction, n.p. (see above, n. 2).

73   Ibid.

74   Ibid.

75   See above, Chapter Two.

76   Richard A. Gardner, M.D., *True and False Accusations of Child Sex Abuse* (Cresskill, NJ: Creative Therapeutics, 1992), cited in Kelly Boggs, "Pedophilia: Legalizing the Unthinkable," Baptist Press, September, 2007, http://www.eastwallingfordbaptist.com/pedophilia.htm, accessed May 9, 2010. Gardner dedicates the book, "To all who have taught me about adult-child sexual encounters – Both truly and falsely alleged." Note that the almost 750 page book should not be judged in its entirety based on the very troubling quote cited here.

77   Boggs, "Legalizing the Unthinkable."

78   Gardner, *True and False Accusations*, cited in Boggs, "Legalizing the Unthinkable."

79   Boggs concludes his article with this warning: "If you don't think pedophilia might one day be embraced as a normal part of life in America, you are naïve. You only have to examine how homosexuals have turned society on its head regarding a behavior that was once viewed as immoral and perverse. The exact same arguments that homosexual activists have used to gain sympathy and acceptance for their behavior are the same arguments that will be used to justify pedophilia as natural, normal and healthy."
"Two things stand in the way of pedophilia being accepted in American society. One is that normal, decent people still view it as gross perversion — in the same way homosexuality once was viewed. The other is that age of consent laws make it illegal for an adult to take advantage of a child sexually. If and when society accepts pedophilia as normal, the age of consent laws will quickly fall. And it will only be a matter of time until our nation will follow suit."

80   http://www.exgaywatch.com/wp/2008/02/pedophilia-hedonism-impending-confusion-revisiting-the-anti-gay-rhetoric-of-michael-brown/, accessed May 9, 2010.

81   Ibid.

82   Ibid.; emphasis in the original.

83   On a broader note, it is relevant that, before 1973, homosexuality was included in the standard list of "paraphilias"; for a current list of these sexual disorders, see, e.g., http://www.medterms.com/script/main/art.asp?articlekey=4767, accessed December 15, 2010.

84   "On Pedophilia, Hedonism & Impending Confusion," ibid.

85   See, e.g., Michael L. Brown, *How Saved Are We?* (Shippensburg, PA: Destiny Image, 1990), 59-66; more broadly, see Jean M. Twenge, Ph.D., with W. Keith Campbell, Ph.D., *The Narcissism Epidemic: Living in the Age of Entitlement* (New York: Free Press, 2009); Neil Postman, *Amusing Ourselves to Death: Public Discourse in the Age of Show Business* (20th anniversary edition, with an Introduction by Andrew Postman; New York: Penguin, 2005).

86   "On Pedophilia, Hedonism & Impending Confusion," ibid.

87   See below, Chapter Eleven, especially notes 25, 26, and 35, for concerns some have raised regarding the heavily sexualized nature of many gay male relationships along with the dissimilarities between straight and gay relationships, thereby bringing into question whether homosexual love and heterosexual love

are truly equivalent. Others, of course, would affirm that love is love, be it straight or gay. Even if that is true, however, the feeling of love between two people does not necessarily justify their sexual or romantic union (think, for example of the love felt by an adulterous couple or by an adult incestuous couple; both would be considered illicit, the first morally and the second legally and morally). That is to say, the common gay mantra that "I should have the right to marry the one I love," surely cannot be argued universally and without exception, as even the vast majority of GLBT people would, presumably, have to acknowledge. Thus, gay couples need a better argument than, "But we're in love," to justify the propriety of same-sex relationships. See further John M. Finnis, "Law, Morality, and 'Sexual Orientation,'" *Notre Dame Law Review*, 69 (1994), 1049-1076; with additions, *Notre Dame Journal of Law, Ethics, and Public Policy*, 9 (1995), 11–39; Robert E. Rodes, Jr., "On Love and Metaphysics," *Homiletic and Pastoral Review*, May, 2003, 8-17. Also noteworthy (but not easily accessible) is Alexander Pruss, "Love and Sex: Philosophical Reflections," St. Paul Center, Pittsburgh, PA, December 2006. More broadly, cf. C. S. Lewis, *The Four Loves* (repr., New York: Houghton Mifflin Harcourt, 1991).

88   http://www.nambla.org/boys.htm, accessed May 9, 2010.

89   For similar "testimonies" in pedophile books, see Sandfort, *Boys on Their Contacts with Men*.

90   http://www.nambla.org/dublin.htm (accessed November 12, 2009); from *The NAMBLA Bulletin*, Vol. 6, No. 9 (Nov., 1985), 2. The NAMBLA website also listed these resolutions: We would like to insist that the organizers of the Third International Gay Youth Congress spend as large a time as possible, and make positive discrimination in order to encourage more female delegates, non-white delegates, and younger delegates to attend this congress. Only when this is achieved will the congress be representative of all ..."; and, "We, the Second International Gay Youth Congress, urge the Northern Ireland Gay Rights Association and Cara Friend to withdraw their dismissive attitudes towards gay youth and to campaign strongly for an equal age of consent with their heterosexual counterparts, while ages of consent still exist."

91   See John Corvino, "Homosexuality and the PIB Argument," *Ethics* 115 (April 2005), 501-534, available online at http://wrightjj1.people.cofc.edu/teaching/PHIL3000/corvino%20homosexuality%20and%20 the%20PIB%20arg.pdf. Writing in UCLA's *Legal Affairs*, and addressing the slippery slope argument in general, Prof. Eugene Volokh and David Newman state that "the realities of the political and judicial processes can make the slippery slope—or, more precisely, several different kinds of mechanisms lurking behind the label 'slippery slope'—a real concern." See http://www.law.ucla.edu/volokh/slipperymag.pdf, 1. For Volokh's position in greatly expanded form, see http://papers.ssrn.com/sol3/papers.cfm?abstract_ id=343640 (abstract; for the pre-publication draft, see http://www.law.ucla.edu/volokh/slippery.htm); with respect to same-sex issues, Volokh, who supports same-sex marriage, recognizes the validity of the slippery slope argument as well; see http://blog.beliefnet.com/crunchycon/2009/04/volokh-on-gay-marriage-slipper.html, where he is quoted extensively, along with http://volokh.com/posts/1238948132. shtml. All accessed December 15, 2010.

92   Cf. Hamer, *The Last Undercover*.

93   http://www.foxnews.com/us/2010/11/10/consumers-boycott-amazon-pedophileguide/?test=latestne ws; http://news.blogs.cnn.com/2010/11/10/amazon-com-book-defending-pedophilia-sparks-boycott-call/?hpt=T2, both accessed November 10, 2010.

94   http://www.amazon.com/Pedophiles-Guide-Love-Pleasure-ebook/product-reviews/B0049U4CF6/ ref=cm_cr_pr_helpful?ie=UTF8&showViewpoints=0, accessed November 10, 2010.

95   http://www.huffingtonpost.com/2010/06/22/mike-huckabee-ick-factor_n_621284.html, accessed December 22, 2010.

96   See above, Chapter Three.

97   According to a study in *Archives of Sexual Behavior*, released in November, 2010, "adolescents reared in lesbian families are less likely than their peers to be victimized by a parent or other care giver [which would make sense, since most sexual abuse of children is done by males], and that daughters of lesbian mothers are more likely to engage in same-sex behavior and to identify as bisexual [which would also make sense, since their role models were lesbian]." Although the sampling was fairly small, it included males and females and was longitudinal. See Nanette K. Gartrell, Henny M. W. Bos, and Naomi G. Goldberg, "Adolescents of the U.S. National Longitudinal Lesbian Family Study: Sexual Orientation, Sexual Behavior, and Sexual Risk Exposure," available online at http://www.springerlink.com/content/ d967883qp3255733/fulltext.pdf, and accessed November 10, 2010.

98   http://topnews.co.uk/213743-hiv-infection-gays-increasing-alarming-rate, accessed November 10, 2010; see further, below, Chapters Eleven and Thirteen.

99   Private email, received November 3, 2010; the sender wishes to remain anonymous.

100   http://www.fda.gov/BiologicsBloodVaccines/BloodBloodProducts/QuestionsaboutBlood/ucm108186. htm, accessed November 10, 2010; see below, Chapter Thirteen, for further details. The web page

reporting this was last updated June 18, 2009.

Chapter 8

1   See, e.g., http://www.nytimes.com/marketing/jobmarket/diversity/starbucks.html, accessed December 20, 2010.

2   http://www.starbucks.com/responsibility/diversity/suppliers, accessed December 20, 2010.

3   For details, see below. This, of course, is not something Starbucks would deny; rather, it is proud to be a sponsor of what it certainly considers to be "gay civil rights."

4   For this definition, see http://www.wordiq.com/definition/Doublespeak, accessed December 20, 2010; for further discussion of semantic issues, see Chapter Nine. For the broader issue of "diversity" in contemporary culture, see Peter Wood, *Diversity: The Invention of a Concept* (New York: Encounter Books, 2004); for an interesting theological reflection, see Andreas J. Köstenberger and Michael J. Kruger, *The Heresy of Orthodoxy: How Contemporary Culture's Fascination with Diversity Has Reshaped Our Understanding of Early Christianity* (Wheaton: Crossway Books, 2010).

5   See, conveniently, http://www.newspeakdictionary.com/ns-prin.html, accessed December 20, 2010.

6   See further Chapter Six, above, for discussion of whether gay is "the new black" in terms of civil rights issues.

7   See, e.g., http://www.glsen.org/cgi-bin/iowa/all/news/record/1848.html, accessed December 20, 2010, for a news story relevant to this group.

8   For a lawsuit in 2003 regarding a "Diversity Week" program in a high school, see http://www.wnd. com/?pageId=22172, accessed December 20, 2010.

9   http://www.du.edu/orgs/pride/, emphasis in the original (where "diversity" is linked to "Diversity Statement" from the Office of the Chancellor, http://www.du.edu/chancellor/diversityStatement.html), both accessed December 20, 2010.

10   www.maryannhorton.com/MaryAnnHorton-div.doc, accessed December 20, 2010.

11   In the "Diversity" section of Bank of America's "Career" division on its website, it lists its current "Affinity Groups," stating, "Bank of America recognizes several affinity groups, that is, groups of associates with a common interest and those who support them. Currently, there are groups organized for Asian Americans, Black and African Americans, people with disabilities, Hispanic/Latino associates, Lesbian/Gay/Bisexual/Transgender associates, parents, and women." http://www.bankofamerica.com/careers/index.cfm?template=diversity.

12   Major Glenville Lindsay, of the Royal Artillery, speaking to the BBC news, as quoted in http://news. bbc.co.uk/1/hi/england/manchester/4189634.stm, accessed December 20, 2010. The photograph accompanying the story shows a gay man wearing only underwear and angel's wings walking next to a soldier in uniform.

13   http://www.fcmchurchtoledo.org/, accessed December 28, 2010, my emphasis.

14   http://www.dailymail.co.uk/news/article-1311228/Taxpayer-funds-council-adventures-Sindia-Lesbianandgayland.html, accessed September 12, 2010.

15   http://www.hunton.com/files/tbl_s47Details/FileUpload265/2644/LGBT_Brochure.pdf, accessed December 20, 2010.

16   See Terrence E. Maltbia and Anne T. Power, *A Leader's Guide to Leveraging Diversity: Strategic Learning Capabilities for Breakthrough Performances* (Burlington, MA: Butterworth Heinemann, 2009), 28.

17   See Don Hellriegel and John W. Slocum, Jr., *Organizational Behavior* (11th ed.; Mason, OH: Thomson South-western, 2007), 15.

18   http://www-306.ibm.com/employment/us/diverse/50/exectask.shtml, accessed December 20, 2010.

19   Jeremy Quittner, July 22, 2003, http://findarticles.com/p/articles/mi_m1589/is_2003_July_22/ai_109270124, my emphasis; accessed September 15, 2005, but no longer available at this site (although cited elsewhere online).

20   http://www.fanniemae.com/aboutfm/procurement/supplierdiversity.jhtml;jsessionid=5JGNVGNWJ PJJZJ2FECISFGQ?p=About+Fannie+Mae&s=Corporate+Procurement&t=Supplier+Diversity, my emphasis. See also http://www.fanniemae.com/aboutfm/procurement/whoqualifies.jhtml;jsessionid=V LKC2R3Z30KXHJ2FQSHSFGQ?p=About+Fannie+Mae&s=Corporate+Procurement&t=Supplier+Diversity&q=Who+Qualifies+as+a+Diverse+Supplier?, both accessed August 5, 2010

21   http://www.cultureandfamily.org/articledisplay.asp?id=618&department=CFI&categoryid=cfreport, my emphasis, accessed August 5, 2010.

22   Cited in Joe Kovacs, "Corporate America snuggles up to 'gays'," http://www.wnd.com/?pageId=32440, my emphasis, accessed December 20, 2010.

23   Cited in ibid., my emphasis.

24   See http://www.kodak.com/global/en/corp/diversity/index.jhtml, accessed December 20, 2010, my

emphasis.

25   See ibid. In 2005, ExxonMobil received one of the lowest scores (14%), since, according to the HRC, it had "the dubious distinction of being the only U.S. company to roll back both benefits eligibility for its employees' domestic partners and a sexual orientation non-discrimination policy" (cited in http://www.wnd.com/index.php?fa=PAGE.printable&pageId=32440, accessed December 20, 2010).

26   http://blogs.citypages.com/blotter/2010/08/human_rights_ca.php, accessed September 7, 2010.

27   http://www.brandweek.com/bw/content_display/news-and-features/direct/e3i70ba82a0840c6bbf6596 a26035616cbe, accessed September 7, 2010.

28   From his website, cited, e.g., at http://www.cbsnews.com/8301-503544_162-20011983-503544.html, accessed September 7, 2010.

29   http://www.christianpost.com/article/20100731/target-best-buy-criticized-for-donation-to-tom-emmer-supporter/index.html, accessed September 7, 2010.

30   Cited in the CBS News article above, n. 27.

31   http://www.cbsnews.com/8301-503544_162-20011983-503544.html, accessed September 12, 2010.

32   As cited in the Christian Post article, n. 35, above.

33   http://blogs.citypages.com/blotter/2010/08/target_ceo_greg_1.php, accessed September 7, 2010.

34   Most recently available at http://genderevolve.blogspot.com/2006/02/transgender-employment-solutions.html, accessed December 20, 2010.

35   See http://www.hrc.org/documents/HRC_Corporate_Equality_Index_2010.pdf, accessed August 5, 2010. It appears that one Verizon's biggest failings was in the category of "Prohibits Discrimination Based on Gender Identity or Expression."

36   http://www.wnd.com/?pageId=114315, accessed August 5, 2010.

37   See http://www.hrc.org/issues/4783.htm, accessed October 28, 2010.

38   http://www.hrc.org/Content/NavigationMenu/Work_Life/Get_Informed2/Corporate_Equality_Index/Complete_Survey/CEISurvey.pdf, accessed and downloaded November 15, 2005, but no longer available online. For a summary of the development of the criteria from 2002-2011, see http://www.hrc.org/issues/workplace/11930.htm, http://www.hrc.org/issues/workplace/cei_criteria.htm, and http://www.hrc.org/issues/workplace/cei_criteria.htm, all accessed October 28, 2010.

39   http://www.hrc.org/about_us/what_we_do.asp, accessed October 28, 2010.

40   See the survey section, "Marketing and Advertising / Philanthropy / Sponsorship," which contains questions such as: "During the past year, has your company engaged in marketing or advertising to the LGBT community?" "During the past year, has your company sponsored a LGBT health, educational, political or community event?" The survey ended with: "Please include any other information that would illustrate how your company views lesbian, gay, bisexual or transgender employees, consumers or investors. (This could include information on innovative business practices that affect the gay community, further description of employee benefits, innovative products or services adapted for the gay community, etc.)."

41   See Chapter Fourteen, below.

42   Concerned business owners have shown me emails they have received from major, national companies, making clear to them that they must demonstrate a pattern of hiring gays and lesbians if business transactions are to continue between them. Out of concern for negative consequences, they requested that I not make these emails public, at least at present.

43   See, conveniently, http://www.wnd.com/index.php?fa=PAGE.view&pageId=114304, accessed August 5, 2010. For details, see http://www.hrc.org/documents/HRC_Corporate_Equality_Index_2010.pdf.

44   I certainly believe that it is sometimes appropriate to boycott a company because of personal convictions (as was common during the Civil Rights movement), and I also believe that boycotting can sometimes send an important message to companies (this too was an effective tool in the Civil Rights movement). That being said, it is foolish to think that those offended by gay activism could effectively boycott all the companies just listed. (And remember: This was not a comprehensive list.)

45   This information was found in the program guide for the event, "Fire & Ice: The 2006 HRC Carolinas Gala," Saturday, February 25, 2006, given to me by one of the attendees. Note that the *Charlotte Observer* did not continue its sponsorship after 2006. Presenting Sponsors of the events were Bank of America and Wachovia; IBM was a Platinum Sponsor; Gold Sponsors were Audi, Tall Tale Productions, Sir Speedy Press, and Duke Energy, the local power company (how does one boycott the power company?); the most notable of the Bronze Sponsors was Food Lion, a local grocery chain.

46   See http://www.hrc.org/about_us/what_we_do.asp, accessed October 28, 2010.

47   See http://www.thetaskforce.org/events/creating_change, accessed October 28, 2010.

48   http://www.lambdalegal.org/about-us/sponsors/, accessed October 28, 2010.

49   In all candor, the Charlotte Pride event was much more tame than other gay pride events; my reason for

singling this out in my dealing with Starbucks was simply because I live in the Charlotte area and these things were taking place in a centrally located, city park.

50   http://articles.sfgate.com/2005-06-22/bay-area/17378486_1_boot-parking-lot-leather-alley, accessed October 28, 2010.

51   http://www.edmontonsun.com/news/edmonton/2009/06/22/9884061-sun.html, accessed October 28, 2010.

52   Ibid.

53   http://www.edmontonjournal.com/story_print.html?id=1725034&sponsor=, accessed October 28, 2010.

54   Allyson Smith, "Nudity, Crassness, Perversion on Display as San Francisco Celebrates Legal Sodomy," July 2, 2003, http://www.cwfa.org/articles/4221/CFI/cfreport/, accessed September 15, 2006, but since moved.

55   Ibid.

56   Ibid.

57   From his private email, August 26, 2010. Holmberg is the producer of a forthcoming video, "Is Gay OK?"

58   http://www.baptistpress.com/bpnews.asp?id=28074, accessed December 19, 2010, my emphasis. The featured celebration of the Stonewall Riots of 1969, replete with footage of rioters.

59   Cited August 31, 2005, on WorldNetDaily.com; see http://www.wnd.com/news/article.asp?ARTICLE_ID=46076, accessed September 1, 2005.

60   Case No. 37-2007-00073878-CU-CR-CTL, quoting specifically from par. 15 (p. 4) and pars. 53-54 (p. 10).

61   http://www.massresistance.org/docs/gen/10c/pride_week/general.html, accessed October 26, 2010.

62   http://americansfortruth.com/news/tolerance-gone-wild-in-san-francisco-as-cops-stand-by-amidst-folsom-street-fairs-public-perversions-and-widespread-nudity.html (note that the photographs included in this article, despite being partially covered, are disturbingly graphic), accessed October 25, 2010.

63   http://americansfortruth.com/news/san-francisco-mayor-gavin-newsom-puts-friendly-welcome-letter-in-super-raunchy-folsom-street-fair-program.html, my emphasis, accessed October 25, 2010.

64   For some revealing (and related) anecdotes from a Catholic culture warrior, see William A. Donohue, *Secular Sabotage: How Liberals Are Destroying Religion and Culture in America* (New York: FaithWords, 2009), esp. 56-58.

65   In the words of David Steffen, 37, a pharmaceutical scientist who participated in the Stonewall Festival in Miami in 2004, Stonewall is a way to remind everyone, "We're here, we exist, that we're not all queens and leather guys. We're just regular folks." Cited by Ashley Fantz, "Parade accents pride, politics," *Miami Herald*, http://www.aegis.com/news/mh/2004/MH040609.html, accessed October 28, 2010.

66   See, e.g., http://www.apa.org/pi/lgbt/resources/language.aspx, "Avoiding Heterosexual Bias in Language," published by the American Psychological Association back in 1991, accessed December 20, 2010, and cf. the references to GLAAD, above, Chapter One.

67   Marshall Kirk and Hunter Madsen, *After the Ball: How America Will Conquer Its Fear and Hatred of Gays in the 90's* (New York: Penguin, 1989), are acutely aware of this objection, stating, "The effect of presenting a bigot with an extreme instance of his stereotypic picture/label pair is to augment the strength of the bigotry" (145; see, in detail, 144-147). They conclude: "What it boils down to is that this community isn't the personal turf of drag queens and pederasts. . . . The actions of gay pride marchers don't take place in a vacuum, and, as long as their disastrous tactics drag us down with them, we have a just cause for complaint" (147). As part of their "Self-Policing Social Code," Kirk and Madsen suggest the pledge, "If I'm a Pederast or a Sadmasochist, I'll Keep It Under Wraps, and Out of Gay Pride Marches" (needless to say, the very need to propose such a pledge says a lot). Although much of their strategy in other areas has been adopted by gay leaders (or, at the least, is shared by gay leaders; see above, Chapter One, n. 28), their calls for moderation in this area were not heeded (unless one points to the "taming" of many gay pride events in America in recent years, something, however, that one gay author told me privately was due to the increased role taken by lesbians, with many of the more radical, gay male leaders no longer around). In this regard, Kirk and Madsen show far more sensitivity and political savvy than does corporate America! For an interesting comparison of the strategies of Kirk and Madsen (primarily based on sound marketing principles) and other "conservative" gay leaders, see Paul Robinson, *Queer Wars: The New Gay Right and Its Critics* (Chicago: University of Chicago Press, 2005); cf. also Richard Goldstein, *Homocons: The Rise of the Gay Right* (London: Verso, 2002).

68   Tammy Bruce, *The New Thought Police: Inside the Left's Assault on Free Speech and Free Minds* (New York: Three Rivers Press, 2001), 64.

69   I am *not* making the claim that heterosexuals, by and large, are moral while homosexuals, by and large, are immoral, nor am I stating that heterosexual marriages are, for the most part, healthy and good. I am simply pointing out that gay pride events are *marked* by extreme, highly-offensive sexual displays, whereas men's events such as Promise Keepers, or youth events, such as The Call DC on September 2, 2000, which drew more than 250,000 Christian young people, or the Nation of Islam's Million Man March, are marked by the *absence* of such displays. Contrast this with the overtly sexual nature of the gay pride march on Washington in 1987.

70   http://townhall.com/columnists/MichaelMedved/2010/12/08/the_national_portrait_gallery_and_the_nature_of_gay_pride, my emphasis, accessed December 22, 2010.

71   The specific reason for excluding me in the name of inclusion was that I was working on this event (and the past, similar event) with another Christian leader in the city whom they rejected, hence their refusal to be a sponsor. In point of fact, this leader, although a friend and colleague, had no involvement in our 2006 event and no involvement in the event we were discussing in 2008. When I informed them of these facts, suggesting that this removed the one obstacle to their sponsoring the event, they did not respond. What do you know!

72   See their undated document, "Submitting Donation of Sponsorship Proposals to Starbucks."

73   See the article of Alyson Smith, cited above, n. 53.

74   See Ashley Fantz, cited above, n. 64.

75   http://www.csmonitor.com/From-the-news-wires/2010/0627/Gay-pride-parade-in-San-Francisco-turns-40-thousands-to-march-today, accessed August 26, 2010.

76   http://www.massresistance.org/docs/gen/10c/pride_week/general.html, accessed October 26, 2010.

77   In this letter, I also raised the aforementioned issue of the strongly political content of the 2005 gay pride event in Charlotte, noting that, "The May 7ᵗʰ, 2005 Charlotte Pride event in Marshall Park was overtly political, with many of the invited speakers stressing political themes – such as voting for same-sex marriage – while other speakers strongly encouraged the attendees to visit one particular booth in the park, a booth that was entirely political in content. The attendees were urged to register to vote and get behind gay political issues."

78   http://www.starbucks.com/retail/thewayiseeit_default.asp

79   The Starbucks website states: "Maupin is best-known for his six books in the *Tales of the City* series, which richly documented San Francisco's gay community in the 1970s and '80s." See http://www.starbucks.com/retail/thewayiseeit_contributorscorner.asp, sub Armistead Maupin.

80   For a report on some of the controversy surrounding these cups, see http://www.wnd.com/?pageId=41531, accessed October 28, 2010.

81   See, e.g., http://www.skeptictank.org/nohate/nohate18.htm, accessed December 20, 2010, my emphasis.

82   Ibid., my emphasis.

83   See http://www.oberlin.edu/stupub/ocreview/archives/1998.10.02/news/bdsm.html, accessed December 20, 2010. The article by Douglas Gillison was entitled, "BDSM whips up debate on campus."

84   http://en.wikipedia.org/wiki/Party_for_Neighbourly_Love,_Freedom,_and_Diversity, accessed Nov. 23, 2009. "The PNVD seeks to have the legal age-of-consent lowered to 12, and, in the long run, completely eliminated (except in dependent or intrafamilial relationships.) They reason that only 'coerced' or 'dangerous' sexual activity should be punished. They also aim to equalize the legal age where one can perform in pornography with the legal age-of-consent. Prostitution would be legal at the age of 16."

85   Ibid.

86   See, e.g., http://www.rense.com/general71/legal.htm, accessed December 20, 2010.

87   Ibid.

88   Ibid.

89   For the error of equating skin color or ethnicity with sexual orientation, see above, Chapter Six.

Chapter 9

1   Originally found at http://www.cnn.com/2003/US/11/05/offbeat.queer.evolution.ap/index.html, and accessed August 26, 2005, but now available elsewhere online.

2   Ibid.

3   Ibid.

4   As noted at http://www.thefreedictionary.com/queerness (accessed December 20, 2010), "A reclaimed word is a word that was formerly used solely as a slur but that has been semantically overturned by members of the maligned group, who use it as a term of defiant pride. *Queer* is an example of a word undergoing this process. For decades *queer* was used solely as a derogatory adjective for gays and lesbians,

but in the 1980s the term began to be used by gay and lesbian activists as a term of self-identification. Eventually, it came to be used as an umbrella term that included gay men, lesbians, bisexuals, and transgendered people. Nevertheless, a sizable percentage of people to whom this term might apply still hold *queer* to be a hateful insult, and its use by heterosexuals is often considered offensive. Similarly, other reclaimed words are usually offensive to the in-group when used by outsiders, so extreme caution must be taken concerning their use when one is not a member of the group."

5   See, e.g., http://www.wordnik.com/words/queer, accessed December 20, 2010.

6   See Chapters Three, Four, Five, and Ten for further details.

7   See Marshall Kirk and Hunter Madsen, *After the Ball: How America Will Conquer Its Fear and Hatred of Gays in the 90's* (New York: Penguin, 1989), 147-157. For discussion of the influence of this book (alleged or otherwise), see above, Chapter One, n. 28.

8   Cf. Paul E. Rondeau, "Selling Homosexuality To America," published in the *Regent University Law Review* 14 (2002), 443-485, and available online at http://www.lifeissues.net/writers/rond/shta/shta_01sellinghomosexuality3.html, accessed May 6, 2010. Rondeau has a sales and marketing background. For provocative thoughts on the power of media propaganda from the perspective of a black American advertising leader, see Tom Burrell, *Brainwashed: Challenging the Myth of Black Inferiority* (New York: Smiley Books, 2010). More broadly, see S.I. Hayakawa and Alan R. Hayakawa, *Language in Thought and Action* (Fifth Edition; San Diego: Harcourt, 1990).

9   *After the Ball*, 149.

10 From their article, "The Overhauling of Straight America." For publication details, see above, Chapter One, n. 24.

11 *After the Ball*, 150-152.

12 *After the Ball*, 189.

13 *After the Ball*, 153-154.

14 Ibid., 153.

15 Ibid., 154.

16 See above, Chapter Four.

17 http://gaylife.about.com/cs/gaylifeglossary/a/queer.htm, accessed May 6, 2010.

18 Lewis Carroll, *Through the Looking-Glass* (Raleigh, NC: Hayes Barton Press, 1872), 72.

19 Note that most modern dictionaries now put *that* definition first – "Of, relating to, or having a sexual orientation to persons of the same sex" – while the older, historic definitions are now second and third – "Showing or characterized by cheerfulness and lighthearted excitement; merry" and "Bright or lively, especially in color." As noted in the article cited above, n. 1. Caitlyn Ryan, "a clinical social worker at San Francisco State University who is conducting a long-term survey of gay, lesbian and bisexual youth and their families," observed "that it took years for mainstream newspapers to use the word 'gay' in place of 'homosexual,' a term many people now see as cold and clinical."

20 Cf. the reference to Riddle Homophobia Scale in Chapter Three, above.

21 For an extremely insightful article on the use of the word "homophobia," see Gary Colwell, "Turning the Tables with 'Homophobia,'" *Journal of Applied Philosophy*, Vol. 16, No. 3 (1999), 207-222; Dr. Colwell is Professor Emeritus of Philosophy, Concordia University College of Alberta. He correctly notes that, "Logical argument justifying the widespread use of the charge of 'homophobia,' is exceedingly rare, so rare in fact that, at least in my experience, it does not occur" (ibid., 209).

22 http://phobialist.com/#A-, accessed May 6, 2010.

23 Cited above, Chapter Two.

24 "Turning the Tables with 'Homophobia,'" 210. For a similar shift taking place with regard to the recently coined term "Islamophobia," see, e.g., www.islamophobia.org, where the word is defined as "an irrational fear of prejudice towards Islam and Muslims." Accessed October 26, 2010.

25 This word has now become so common that it has already morphed from non-gay to nongay.

26 See Chapter Five, n. 20.

27 See, e.g., Chapter Two, above.

28 See above, Chapter Eight.

29 See below, Chapter Fourteen.

30 See, e.g., http://polyamory.wikia.com/wiki/Definition, accessed December 22, 2010.

31 See http://www.sfgate.com/cgi-bin/article.cgi?file=/c/a/2004/04/20/BAGIG67LNQ1.DTL, accessed May 6, 2010.

32 http://www.newsweek.com/id/209164, accessed May 6, 2010. The *New York Times* ran an article on polyamory by Alex Williams entitled, "Hopelessly Devoted to You, You and You," see http://www.nytimes.com/2008/10/05/fashion/05polyamory.html, accessed October 26, 2010. The article states that, "Within the past year, books like "Open," by Jenny Block, and "Opening Up," by the sex columnist

Tristan Taormino, have argued for polyamory. Celebrities like Tilda Swinton and Carla Sarkozy, the first lady of France, have expressed support for open relationships."

33 *Newsweek*, ibid.

34 For an abstract of a forthcoming article by Ann E. Tweedy of the Michigan State University College of Law, entitled "Polyamory as a Sexual Orientation," see http://papers.ssrn.com/sol3/papers.cfm?abstract_id=1632653, accessed October 26, 2010. The article will be published in the University of Cincinnati Law Review.

35 See, e.g., http://polyinthemedia.blogspot.com/2009/02/morning-shock-jocks-do-stinker.html, accessed December 22, 2010.

36 See further, above, Chapter Seven.

37 http://members.fortunecity.com/husom/Fikralar/Violence.html, accessed September 19, 2007, but no longer available there.

38 The home page is http://www.amikejo.org/koinose0.html, accessed May 6, 2010, replete with magazine covers picturing smiling boys, allegedly teenaged.

39 http://www.amikejo.org/koin25e.html; according to the magazine's official description, "Koinos is published by the **Amikejo Foundation,** which has as its objective the promotion of humane morals laws in all countries, based upon the right to self-determination. Koinos intends to capture in words and pictures the beauty of boys from the beginning of their puberty until they become adults, and seeks to articulate what makes them special and valuable to others, with all they outwardly manifest and inwardly possess. Koinos intends to reveal the possibilities they have for self-development, but also the ways in which they can be hindered in this by social circumstances. Koinos intends to argue in an unbiased manner for a society in which boys in this phase of their lives are valued, and in which without the obstruction of prejudices they can have the possibility of experiencing intimate relationships and sexual contacts with other persons, including adults, on the basis of mutual respect." See http://www.amikejo.org/koinose1.html, both accessed May 6, 2010.

40 See http://www.wordiq.com/definition/Biphobia; http://en.wikipedia.org/wiki/Transphobia. The word "transphobia" has now become so entrenched that the Gay-Straight Alliance Network uses as its very motto, "Empowering Youth Activists to Fight Homophobia and Transphobia." See http://gsanetwork. org/files/news/Sample%20Activist%20Online%20E-Newsletter.pdf, all accessed December 22, 2010.

41 http://www.wordspy.com/words/pomosexual.asp, accessed May 6, 2010. I have been told that the word is short for PostModernSexual.

42 http://www.thefreedictionary.com/pansexuality, accessed May 6, 2010.

43 http://www.wordspy.com/words/heteroflexible.asp, accessed May 6, 2010.

44 http://www.glbtq.com/social-sciences/genderqueer.html, accessed December 28, 2010.

45 See further below, Chapter Fifteen.

46 I realize, of course, that there are people born with indistinct, indeterminate, or mixed sexual organs (previously called "hermaphrodite" but now generally classified under the heading of intersex), presenting great difficulties to parents, medical personnel, and, above all, the individuals themselves. By no means do I intend to make light of the challenges they face. See further www.isna.org (Intersex Society of North America), and note that many intersex individuals do not consider themselves part of the GLBTIQ community (despite the "I" in the acronym, which, to be sure, does represent others, who do feel that solidarity). For helping to sensitize me to some of the unique struggles experienced by many intersex and/or transgender people, I am indebted to a Trans-Intersexed individual named Zoe Ellen Brain, a rocket scientist (and Ph.D. Candidate) in Canberra, Australia with a highly unusual chromosomal makeup and biological history. See http://aebrain.blogspot.com/, with many relevant articles and links at http://aebrain.blogspot.com/p/reference-works-on-transsexual-and.html. While Brain and I have clear philosophical and spiritual differences, I am deeply appreciative of Brain's irenic spirit, to the point of defending me at times on GLBT websites and even stating, "He's sincere. Wrong but sincere. I'm trying to educate him on the difference between Trans and Gay.... The point is, Dr B is trying to do the right thing by his own lights. He has integrity, and is open to reasoned argument. He has some axioms we disagree on, but nothing too bad. I can work with that." See http://www.pamshouseblend.com/diary/17711/conflating-gay-and-trans-and-more-religious-right-fear-mongering-about-it, all accessed December 28, 2010. Statements like this are a reminder that no matter how passionately we might disagree with each another's positions and no matter how profound our differences might be, there's no reason we can't have civil dialogue. (Despite the rhetoric that can fly on both sides of the issues, let's remember that, with the rarest of fanatical exceptions, neither side is calling for physical violence or attacks against the other.) Needless to say, this is *not* the typical assessment of my character and motives on GLBT websites! See above, Chapter Two.

47 See http://www.transgenderlaw.org/college/sfusdpolicy.htm, accessed October 26, 2010.

48   *Teaching Gender Equity for All: A Guide to Education and Resources Addressing Gender Identity/Expression in Schools*, 6, published by GLSEN San Francisco-East Bay, http://www.glsen-sfeb.org/gender_equity_color.pdf, their emphasis.

49   For a brief statement to this effect, see http://www.youtube.com/watch?v=SeclIYTHz30, accessed May 6, 2010.

50   GLSEN Lunchbox 2, Trainer's Manual, 44 (see above, Chapter Three, for further details).

51   http://bi_gender.tripod.com/Definitions/definitions.htm, accessed May 6, 2010.

52   http://bi_gender.tripod.com/, accessed May 6, 2010, my emphasis. Note this statement from Heather Corinna on her blog at rhrealitycheck.org in terms of having one's sex determined at birth: "I know: it's totally whack that something that is such a huge deal in our lives and to the world is something determined in but a brief moment by a fleeting glance." See http://www.rhrealitycheck.org/node/13570, accessed May 30, 2010.

53   http://www.huffingtonpost.com/2009/11/19/chaz-bono-gender-is-betwe_n_363508.html,   accessed May 6, 2010.

54   Richard P. Fitzgibbons, "The Desire for a Sex Change," http://narth.com/docs/desiresch.html, accessed May 6, 2010, with reference to Gerianne Alexander, "An Evolutionary Perspective of Sex-Typed Toy Preferences: Pink, Blue, and the Brain," *Archives of Sexual Behavior* 32 (2003), 7-14. Fitzgibbons is discussing the article by Dr. Paul McHugh of John Hopkins University, "Surgical Sex," published in *First Things* 147 (2004), 34-38.

55   GLSEN Lunchbox 2, Trainer's Manual, 7.

56   http://www.sex-lexis.com/Sex-Dictionary/transcengender, accessed December 22, 2010.

57   Ibid., my emphasis.

58   See http://www.sex-lexis.com/Sex-Dictionary/TransLesBiGay, for definitions of all these terms; accessed December 22, 2010.

59   http://www.sex-lexis.com/Sex-Dictionary/transgressively%20gendered; see there for definitions; accessed December 22, 2010.

60   For self-descriptions of some LGBT college students, see above, Chapter Four.

61   http://www.oberlin.edu/mrc/about_the_mrc/about_the_mrc_assorted_files/QueerAtOberlin.pdf, accessed May 7, 2010.

62   An August 10, 2005 Google search for "GLBT" yielded 1,250,000 items. That same search conducted on August 4, 2009, yielded 5,210,000 hits. And a search for "LGBT" on August 4, 2009, yielded 11,100,000 hits.

63   A Google search for that acronym yielded 116,000 results on August, 10, 2005 and 305,000 on August 2, 2009, including the online "encyclopedia of gay, lesbian, bisexual, transgender & queer culture"; see www.glbtq.com; note also that "LGBTQ" yielded 106,000 items on Google August 10, 2005 and 493,000 items in August 2, 2009

64   http://borngay.procon.org/view.answers.php?questionID=000012, accessed December 28, 2010. A Google search for "GLBTQI" yielded more than 500 items August 10, 2005 and 40,900 August 2, 2009. A search for LGBTQI yielded 265,000 hits on August 2, 2009. Google searches for GLBTI and LGBTI yielded 40,200 and 62,700, respectively, August 10, 2005 and 36,900 and 135,000, respectively, August 2, 2009.

65   See above, n. 46. For an example of "intersex" being included as part of gay, bisexual, and transgender solidarity, see, e.g., http://www.aarweb.org/About_AAR/Committees/Status_of_LGBTIQ_Persons_in_the_Profession/default.asphttp://www.pridebrisbane.org.au/, accessed December 28, 2010.

66   http://www.myspace.com/queertoday, accessed May 6, 2010.

67   It was not until 1985 that, "To make clear the commitment to gender parity and lesbian issues, NGTF changes its name to the National Gay and Lesbian Task Force (NGLTF)." See http://www.kintera.org/site/c.aeIILVOrGjF/b.1624147/k.B4D0/Task_Force_History.htm, accessed December 28, 2010.

68   http://www.thetaskforce.org/theissues/issue.cfm?issueID=37, accessed September 29, 2006, but no longer available there. Cf. now www.sbequality.org/Bisexuality.rtf, accessed December 28, 2010.

69   http://www.thetaskforce.org/theissues/issue.cfm?issueID=37,   accessed   September   29,   2006, but no longer available there. Cf. now http://www.thetaskforce.org/downloads/reports/reports/TransgenderEquality.pdf, 1, accessed December 28, 2010.

70

71   See, e.g., http://www.thetaskforce.org/issues/transgender, accessed December 28, 2010.

72   See further, above, Chapter One, for more on the NGLTF.

73   http://narth.com/docs/fluidity.html. I will say yet again that I do not minimize the struggles experienced by many people who identify as transgender. I differ with viewing transgender individuals as making up a distinct category of people to be specially protected by the law, and I differ with embracing and

celebrating transgenderism as opposed for looking for better ways to help transgender people find wholeness. For a lengthy (and, perhaps to many readers, a confusing) discussion of the meaning of transgender, see Susan Stryker, http://www.glbtq.com/social-sciences/transgender.html, both accessed December 22, 2010.

74 For an even more complete list, see below, Chapter Fifteen.

75 The largest gay denomination, the Metropolitan Community Church (MCC), defines the following terms and abbreviations under its "TransGlossary" web page: FTM; Gender; Gender Dysmorphia; Gender Identity (incl. Gender Queer); Gender Role; Gonadal; Hormonal; Intersex; MTF; Sex; Sexuality; SO; SOFFA; TG; Trans; Transgender; Transitioning; Transman (also spelled Trans Man or TransMan); Transsexual; Transwoman (or Trans Woman or TransWoman); accessed at http://www.mccchurch.org/AM/Template.cfm?Section=Transgender2&Template=/CM/HTMLDisplay.cfm&ContentID=1054, August 27, 2007, but no longer available there. (It's important to bear in mind that this is a "church" website; the announcement for the TransGlossary reads: "Know what TG, SO, SOFFA, Gender, Trans, Transman, and Transwoman mean? Find out here!" (Ibid.) For the MCC's "TransEtiquette," see below, Chapter Eleven, and cf. http://www.goodhopemcc.org/resources/gender-diversity/trans-etiquette.html; see further http://www.transfaithonline.org/the_basics/trans_etiquette/, both accessed Decembe 28, 2010.

76 See now http://www.facebook.com/group.php?gid=2209890963, where it is added: "Pansexuals are folks who love all kinds of folks, femmy boys, butch girls, femme girls, tough guys...the list goes on. Join if you're questioning, if you want to learn, if a friend or loved one has taken on the label of 'pansexual' or (of course) if you, yourself identify as pansexual! We do not have sexual labels. We are about sexual Expression. *It's not about sleeping with a man or a woman, it's about sleeping with individuals,*" (my emphasis).

77 "Society Confusion Disorder," posted June 23, 2009, http://richmanramblings.blogspot.com/search?q=transwomen, accessed June 30, 2009.

78 http://www.youtube.com/user/therocpd#p/u/6/PyIj6EpEmkE, accessed May 7, 2010.

79 http://www.glbtq.com/social-sciences/transgender.html, first cited above, n. 73.

80 Revised and updated edition; New York: HarperCollins, 1994

81 Cleveland: Pilgrim Press, 2003.

82 Cleveland: Pilgrim Press, 2001. Her other writings include: *The Divine Feminine: The Biblical Imagery of God As Female* (New York: Crossroad Publishing, 1984); and *Sensuous Spirituality: Out from Fundamentalism* (Revised and expanded version; Cleveland: Pilgrim Press, 2008).

83 http://www.amazon.com/Omnigender-Trans-religious-Virginia-Ramey-Mollenkott/dp/0829817719/ref=sr_1_1?ie=UTF8&qid=1293587390&sr=8-1, accessed December 28, 2010.

84 http://www.facebook.com/group.php?gid=2208449086, accessed August 29, 2010.

85 For serious discussion about this concept, see http://www.glbtq.com/social-sciences/gayspeak.html, accessed December 28, 2010.

86 For gaydar, cf. http://www.urbandictionary.com/define.php?term=gaydar; for Gaypril, cf. http://www.campuspride.org/gaypril.asp, both accessed December 28, 2010.

87 http://www.urbandictionary.com/define.php?term=yestergay, accessed December 28, 2010.

88 http://www.urbandictionary.com/define.php?term=hasbian; for a relevant article, also discussing aspects of "polysexuality," see "Gay Today, Hasbian Tomorrow," http://www.rainbownetwork.com/Features/detail.asp?iData=21550&iCat=105&iChannel=25&nChannel=Features, both accessed December 28, 2010. As a famous "hasbian," the article speaks of Ann Heche: "The Hollywood actress who was once famously hitched to comedienne Ellen Degeneres went from A-List lesbian to 'Hasbian' almost overnight. Ironically she had come out at 20, became caught up in the gay scene at college, and then ten years later found herself coming out all over again!"

89 This acronym was originally coined at the all-women's Smith College, with the S standing for Smith rather than selective. As noted by Dr. Jeffrey B. Satinover, the phenomenon of a decrease in homosexuality after college years "was actually first recognized not by sociologists, epidemiologists, psychiatrists, psychiatrists or any other kind of 'ist,' but by savvy Smith College students who first called themselves SLUGs: Smith Lesbians Until Graduation. Elsewhere, the eponym mutated into Selectively Lesbian Until Graduation." See his important article "The 'Trojan Couch': How the Mental Health Associations Misrepresent Science," http://www.narth.com/docs/TheTrojanCouchSatinover.pdf, here citing 20, n. 34; for a YouTube report on Smith College and "SLUGS," see http://www.youtube.com/watch?v=Ie26-NUaXpU, both accessed December 28, 2010.

90 http://www.cnn.com/2010/LIVING/08/12/equally.wed/index.html?hpt=C1, accessed August 29, 2010.

91 http://www.article8.org/docs/issues/license_renewal/license_renewal.htm, accessed August 29, 2010.

92 http://www.cbst.org/trans.shtml, accessed October 30, 2006, but not longer available. For an updated resource page, see http://www.cbst.org/Community/Transgender/Trans-Intersex-and-Gender-Queer-Resource-Page/Making-Your-Jewish-Congregation-or-Community-More-Transgender-Friendly, accessed August 29, 2010.
93 Ibid. For parallel sensitivies in gay churches, see above, n. 75.
94 For helpful guidelines, see the Gender Expression Toolkit, http://204.12.19.102/wp-content/uploads/ Gender-Expression-Toolkit2009.pdf, accessed October 26, 2010. This, of course, raises issues about freedom of conscience and religious liberties (what if an individual felt it was morally wrong to call a man by a woman's pronoun?); for more on related issues, see below, Chapter Fourteen.
95 http://www.oberlin.edu/stupub/ocreview/archives/2001.04.13/news/article02.htm, accessed May 7, 2010, my emphasis.
96 Cited by Kate Bornstein, *Gender Outlaw: On Men, Women and the Rest of Us* (Rutledge, New York 1994), 52.
97 Brian Moylan, "Watch Your Language," *Washington Blade*, Friday, February 11, 2005, see http://www. washblade.com/2005/2-11/locallife/outindc/linguisitics.cfm, accessed August 15, 2005, but no longer available.
98 http://www.american.edu/cas/anthro/lavenderlanguages/abstractsnew.doc, accessed May 6, 2010. This paper was presented at 12th Annual Lavender Languages Conference, February 11-13, 2005, as listed in the Abstract of Papers. Cf. further Sean Griffin, *Tinker Belles and Evil Queens: The Walt Disney Company from the Inside Out* (New York: New York University Press, 2000).
99 For Dr. Jack Drescher's explicit disagreement with this closing statement ("There is no way that six billion people can be categorized into two groups"), see below, Chapter Fifteen, with n. 51. For an important critique, see Babette Francis, "Is gender a social construct or a biological imperative?," delivered at Family Futures: Issues in Research and Policy, 7th Australian Institute of Family Studies Conference, Sydney, Australia, July 24-26, 2000, posted at http://www.aifs.gov.au/conferences/aifs7/ francis.html, accessed August 29, 2010.

Chapter 10
1 http://www.chaplains.harvard.edu/chaplains/profile.php?id=31 , accessed September 16, 2010.
2 Ibid.
3 I put "gay Christian" in quotes here because it is an oxymoron, based on a sound understanding of the Scriptures. In point of fact, no new discoveries have been made – linguistically, textually, historically, archeologically – that would cause us to change our understanding of what the Bible teaches on the subject. Rather, modern perceptions have been read back into the biblical texts or the authority of the Scriptures has been undermined in order to come to the conclusion that the Bible does not forbid homosexual practice (meaning, same-sex, sexual acts). To date, the best academic book on the subject is Robert A. J. Gagnon, *The Bible and Homosexual Practice: Texts and Hermeneutics* (Nashville: Abingdon, 2001); for Gagnon's many other relevant writings, see www.robgagnon.net; other books reflecting the historic understanding of the Scriptures (namely, that homosexual practice is sinful), include: Donald J. Wold, *Out of Order: Homosexuality in the Bible and the Ancient Near East* (Grand Rapids: Baker, 1998); James B. De Young, *Homosexuality: Contemporary Claims Examined in Light of the Bible and Other Ancient Literature and Law* (Grand Rapids: Kregel, 2000); James R. White and Jeffrey D. Niell, *The Same Sex Controversy* (Minneapolis: Bethany House, 2003); E. Earle Fox and David W. Virtue, *Homosexuality: Good and Right in the Eyes of God?* (Alexandria, VA: Emmaus Ministries, 2003); Thomas E. Schmidt, *Straight and Narrow? Compassion and Clarity in the Homosexuality Debate* (Downers Grove, IL: IVP Academic, 1995); Joe Dallas, *The Gay Gospel? How Pro-Gay Advocates Misread the Bible* (the title of the first edition was *A Strong Delusion*; Eugene, OR: Harvest House, 2007; this volume also recounts Dallas's past involvement in "gay Christian" churches); Richard F. Lovelace, *Homosexuality: How Should Christians Respond* (repr.; Eugene, OR: Wipf and Stock, 2002);.Thomas Hopko, *Christian Faith and Same-Sex Attraction: Eastern Orthodox Reflections* (Ben Lomond, CA: Conciliar Press, 2006); Walter Klein, *God's Word Speaks to Homosexuality* (Enumclaw, WA: Winepress Publishing, 2007); Russell E. Saltzman, ed., *Christian Sexuality: Normative and Pastoral Principles* (Minneapolis: Kirk House Publishers; and Delhi, NY: ALPB Books, 2003); Greg Bahnsen, *Homosexuality: A Biblical View* (Grand Rapids: Baker, 1978); for a specific focus on hermeneutical (i.e., interpretive) issues, see William J. Webb, *Slaves, Women and Homosexuals: Exploring the Hermeneutics of Cultural Analysis* (Downers Grove, IL: InterVarsity, 2001); Willard M. Swartley, *Homosexuality: Biblical Interpretation and Moral Discernment* (Scottdale, PA: Herald Press, 2003); for a modern Orthodox Jewish perspective, see Rabbi Chaim Rapoport, *Judaism and Homosexuality: An Authentic Orthodox View* (London: Vallentine Mitchell, 2004); for a more stringent, traditional Jewish perspective, see Arthur Goldberg, *Light in the*

Closet: Torah, Homosexuality and the Power to Change (Beverly Hills: Red Heifer Press, 2008). For books arguing that homosexual practice is not proscribed by the Bible, or that the Church needs to reevaluate its approach, see, e.g., Daniel Helmeniak, *What the Bible Really Says About Homosexuality* (updated and expanded ed.; New Mexico: Alamo Square Press, 2000); Robin Scroggs, *The New Testament and Homosexuality* (Minneapolis: Augsburg Fortress, 1983); Dale B. Martin, *Sex and the Single Savior* (Louisville: Westminster John Knox Press, 2006); Marti Nissinen, *Homoeroticism in the Biblical World: A Historical Perpsective* (Eng. trans. Kirsi Stjerna; Minneapolis: Fortress, 1998); Letha Dawson Scanzoni and Virginia Mollenkott, *Is the Homosexual My Neighbor: A Positive Christian Response* (revised and updated; New York: HarperCollins, 1994); William Stacy Johnson, *A Time to Embrace: Same-Gender Relationships in Religion, Law, and Politics* (Grand Rapids: Eerdmans, 2006); Jack Rogers, *Jesus, the Bible, and Homosexuality: Explode the Myths, Heal the Church* (rev. and expanded ed.; Louisville: Westminster John Knox, 2009); John Boswell, *Christianity, Social Tolerance and Homosexuality* (Chicago: University of Chicago Press, 1980); Walter Wink, ed., *Homosexuality and Christian Faith: Questions of Conscience for the Churches* (Minneapolis: Fortress Press, 1999); Kathy Rudy, *Sex and the Church: Gender, Homosexuality, and the Transformation of Ethics* (Boston: Beacon Press, 1997); Linda J. Patterson, *Hate Thy Neighbor: How the Bible is Misused to Condemn Homosexuality* (West Conshohocken, PA: Infinity Publishing, 2009); more broadly, Patrick M. Chapman, *"Thou Shalt not Love": What Evangelicals Really Say to Gays* (New York: Haiduk Press, 2008); Pastor R. D. Weekly, *Homosexuality: Letting Truth Win the Devastating War Between Scripture, Faith and Sexual Orientation* (n.p.: Judah First Ministries, 2009); note that some of these volumes have been extensively critiqued on Gagnon's website, cited above, or, if published prior to 2001, dealt with in his book. Note also that other, homosexuality-affirming studies will be cited in the rest of this chapter, along with elsewhere in the book, where relevant. For books attempting to help "gay Christians" defend themselves theologically and spiritually, see, e.g., Rick Brentlinger, *Gay Christian 101: Spiritual Self-Defense for Gay Christians* (Pace, FL: Salient Press, 2007); Candace Chellew-Hodge, *Bulletproof Faith: A Spiritual Survival Guide for Gay and Lesbian Christians* (San Francisco: Jossey-Bass, 2008); Craig Bettendorf, *A Biblical Defense Guide: For Gays, Lesbians and Those Who Love Him* (Victoria, BC: Trafford Publishing, 2005); cf. also Rev. Michael S. Piazza, *Gay by God: How to be Lesbian or Gay and Christian* (Dallas: Sources of Hope Publishing, 2008; this was originally published as *Holy Homosexuals*). For books presenting both sides (although, in some cases, not without a pronounced slant in one direction), see, e.g., Dan O. Via and Robert A. J. Gagnon, *Homosexuality and the Bible: Two Views* (Minneapolis: Fortress Press, 2003); Ted Grimsrud and Mark Thiessen Nation, *Reasoning Together: A Conversation on Homosexuality* (Scottdale, PA: Herald Press, 2008); David Ferguson, Fritz Guy, and David Larson, eds., *Christianity and Homosexuality: Some Seventh Day Adventist Perspectives* (Roseville, CA: Adventist Forum, 2008); Sally B. Geis and Donald E. Messer, eds., *Caught in the Crossfire: Helping Christians Debate Homosexuality* (Nashville: Abingdon, 1994); Timothy Bradshaw, ed., *The Way Forward? Christian Voices on Homosexuality and the Church* (Grand Rapids: Eerdmans, 2004); Jeffrey S. Siker, ed., *Homosexuality in the Church: Both Sides of the Debate* (Louisville: Westminster John Knox, 1994); Choon-Leon Seow, *Homosexuality and Christian Community* (Louisville: Westminster John Knox, 1996); Robert L. Brawley, *Biblical Ethics and Homosexuality: Listening to Scripture* (Louisville: Westminster John Knox, 1996). For an extreme contrast in tone and apprpoach (note the titles!), cf. Dr. Jim Reynolds, *The Lepers Among Us: Homosexuality and the Life of the Church* (n.p.: Xulon Press, 2007; the book calls for compassion and understanding towards Christians struggling with same-sex attractions); and Rod Brannum-Harris, *The Pharisees Amongst Us: How the Anti-Gay Campaign Unmasks the Religious Perpetrators of the Campaign to be Modern Day Pharisees* (n.p; n.p., 2005; the book is a frontal assault on the religious right). For a comprehensive (844 page) treatment of Old Testament sexuality, with relevant discussion on same-sex issues, cf. Richard M. Davidson, *Flame of Yahweh: Sexuality in the Old Testament* (Peabody, MA: Hendrickson, 2007); see also Daniel R. Heimbach, *True Sexual Morality: Recovering Biblical Standards for a Culture in Crisis* (Wheaton: Crossway, 2004).

4 For a relevant story from April 1992, shortly after Rev. Gomes made his announcement, see http://www.forerunner.com/forerunner/X0231_Furor_over_Gomes_con.html, accessed September 16, 2010.

5 Peter J. Gomes, *The Good Book: Reading the Bible with Heart and Mind* (San Francisco: HarperSanFrancisco, 1996), 147; the chapter on the "The Bible and Homosexuality," runs from 144-172.

6 Ibid., 146.

7 Ibid., 166.

8 See, e.g., Mel White's, *Stranger at the Gate: To Be Gay and Christian in America* (New York: Plume, 1995).

9 For a representative resource featuring chapters by Christians who have come out of homosexual practice, calling the Church to greater compassion, Alan Chambers, ed., *God's Grace and the Homosexual Next Door: Reaching the Heart of the Gay Men and Women in Your World* (Eugene, OR: Harvest House, 2006). See further below, Chapter Twelve.

10 Pim Pronk, *Against Nature? Types of Moral Arguments Regarding Homosexuality* (Grand Rapids: Eerdmans, 1993), 279. Pronk, however, rejects the plain verdict of the Scriptures based on "hermeneutics." For a critical review of Pronk's book by Gene B. Chase of Messiah College, see http://home.messiah. edu/~chase/talk2/pronk.htm, accessed September 16, 2010.

11 http://www.glbtq.com/social-sciences/paul,2.html, accessed September 16, 2010. This convenient reference source, simply called *glbtq*, claims to be "the world's largest encyclopedia of gay, lesbian, bisexual, transgender, and queer culture."

12 "Truncated Love: A Response to Andrew Marin's *Love Is an Orientation*, Part 1," 3; see http:// robgagnon.net/articles/homosexMarinLoveIsOrientation.pdf, accessed September 16, 2010.

13 See above, n. 3.

14 See Matthew 7:15-20; 12:33; Luke 6:43-45; see also James 3:12.

15 Cf. also the discussion at the end of the previous chapter, above, with reference in particular to the Gay Men's Issues in Religion Group at the 2004 American Academy of Religion.

16 These comments are featured on the back cover of *Queering Christ*.

17 Ibid.

18 Ibid.

19 These comments are featured on the back cover of *Jesus Acted Up*.

20 Ibid.

21 *Queering Christ*, 3.

22 Ibid., 138

23 Ibid.

24 Ibid., 138-139.

25 Ibid., 138.

26 Ibid.

27 Ibid., 139.

28 Of course, sexual imagery can be used in a metaphorical sense in the Bible – Israel is God's bride, but she is promiscuous and plays the harlot, etc. (see, e.g., Ezekiel 16) – and some spiritual mystics may use similar imagery as well, but *not* in explicitly erotic terms. In other words, the sexual imagery is just that: imagery, rather than sexually erotic fantasy. See my treatment of the relevant texts in Jeremiah (especially Jeremiah 2) in Michael L. Brown, "Jeremiah," Tremper Longman, III and David E. Garland, eds., *The Expositor's Bible Commentary* (rev. ed.; Grand Rapids: Zondervan, 2010). In his book *Angels and Demons* (New York: Pocket Books, 2000), bestselling novelist Dan Brown helped popularize the idea that Bernini's famous sculpture, "The Ecstasy of St. Teresa," based on Teresa of Avila's description of her dream in which an angel repeatedly thrust his spear into her heart, depicted an erotic encounter. To be sure, the sculpture can be understood (along with Teresa's account) in completely non-erotic terms (the Wikipedia article on this seems to be accurate, referencing standard sources; see http://en.wikipedia. org/wiki/Ecstasy_of_Saint_Theresa, accessed October 18, 2010). If understood in erotic terms, however, this would only underscore the point I'm making: As an alleged depiction of a sexual encounter between a nun and an angel, the sculpture was considered by many to be blasphemous, rather than hailed as a pioneering work of spiritual erotica. See the Wikipedia article cited for further details, where Teresa's famous words are quoted: "I saw in his [i.e., the angel's] hand a long spear of gold, and at the iron's point there seemed to be a little fire. He appeared to me to be thrusting it at times into my heart, and to pierce my very entrails; when he drew it out, he seemed to draw them out also, and to leave me all on fire with a great love of God. The pain was so great, that it made me moan; and yet so surpassing was the sweetness of this excessive pain, that I could not wish to be rid of it. The soul is satisfied now with nothing less than God. The pain is not bodily, but spiritual; though the body has its share in it. It is a caressing of love so sweet which now takes place between the soul and God, that I pray God of His goodness to make him experience it who may think that I am lying."

29 Note, e.g., that Goss is both an editor and contributor to the 859 page *Queer Bible Commentary*. See Deryn Guest, Robert E. Goss, Mona West, and Thomas Bohache, eds., *The Queer Bible Commentary* (London: SCM Press, 2006). The bio on Goss (ibid., ix) states that he "serves as Pastor/Theologian of the MCC Church in the Valley in North Hollywood, California" and "is currently working with Justin Tannis [a female-to-male] on an anthology of leather spirituality." For more on the MCC (Metropolitan Community Churches), as well as "leather" preferences, see below, Chapter Eleven, "So It's Not About Sex?"

30 *Queer Bible Commentary*, ix.

31 In my 2008 debate with Harry Knox, Director of Religion and Faith with the Human Rights Campaign, I appealed to him three times to repudiate some of the most vulgar examples of queer theology, but he would not respond, despite the fact that Dr. Ken Stone, editor of a volume containing some truly

blasphemous examples (see below) served as a religion editor for the HRC. For the debate, see http://coalitionofconscience.askdrbrown.org/resources/debate.html.

32 *Jesus Acted Up*, 84-85. To give further context to Goss's quote, he continues: "It is the particularity of Jesus the Christ, his particular identification with the sexually oppressed, that enables us to understand Christ as black, queer, female, Asian, African, a South American peasant, Jewish, transsexual, and so forth. It is the scandal of particularity that is the message of Easter, the particular context of struggle where God's solidarity is practiced. God and the struggle for sexual justice are practical correlation in a queer Christology" (ibid., 85). Without entering into Goss's larger theological argument, may it be asked if "queer" and "transsexual" really belong in this list? Read it again and ask: What's wrong with this picture?

33 Ibid., 166.

34 Ibid., 169.

35 See, e.g., http://welcomingministries.blogspot.com/, accessed October 18, 2010. The website identifies itself as, "A BLOG OF CAMBRIDGE WELCOMING MINISTRIES, AN OPEN AND AFFIRMING, PROGRESSIVE, UNITED METHODIST FAITH COMMUNITY DEDICATED TO PROCLAIMING THE GOOD NEWS OF GOD'S LOVE WITH ALL LESBIAN, GAY, BISEXUAL, TRANSGENDER AND STRAIGHT PERSONS. THE TITLE FOR THE BLOG COMES FROM OUR CONGREGATION'S FIRST BOOK STUDY ON A TEXT BY ELIZABETH STUART ENTITLED 'RELIGION IS A QUEER THING: A GUIDE TO THE CHRISTIAN FAITH FOR LESBIAN, GAY, BISEXUAL AND TRANSGENDERED PERSONS' (PILGRIM PRESS, 1998)." I cite this book as representative of scores of other books and countless articles embracing similar themes; some of the relevant literature, which continues to grow rapidly, is cited in this chapter.

36 *Religion is a Queer Thing*, 77.

37 Ibid., 138.

38 Ibid.

39 Ibid., 139.

40 Ibid., 140.

41 Lucia Chappelle, "Silent Night, Raging Night," in *DeColores MCC Hymnal* (Los Angeles: n.p., 1983), 6, cited in Rev. Nancy Wilson, *Our Tribe: Queer Folks, God, Jesus and the Bible* (New Mexico: Alamo Square Press, 2000), 76.

42 As any fair reading of the text indicates, Jesus was talking to his disciples about joining together to make spiritual pronouncements and to agree together in prayer, "For where two or three gather together as my followers, I am there among them" (Matthew 18:20, NLT). As explained by the respected biblical commentator R. T. France, "[Jesus'] spiritual presence among them is the source of their authority to declare the will of God and to expect God to hear their prayers. And that presence is promised not to a formally convened ecclesiastical council, but to any two or three of his people who meet as his disciples." See R. T. France, *The Gospel of Matthew* (New International Commentary on the New Testament; Grand Rapids: Eerdmans, 2007), 698.

43 Cited by Elizabeth Stuart, "Body Theology," in *Religion is a Queer Thing*, 49; the brackets in this quote are in the original. Rudy's article was printed in the journal *Theology and Sexuality* 4 (March 1996), quoted here from 89-90. When the article was published, she was an associate professor of women's studies and ethics at Duke University.

44 *Religion is a Queer Thing*, 128, emphasis in the original. As of October, 2010, Gorsline was the pastor of the Metropolitan Community Church in Richmond, VA. See www.mccrichmond.org.

45 Ibid., 133.

46 For details, see below.

47 From the conference program guide, originally posted in 2005 on the MCC website, http://ufmcc.com/.

48 Rev. Jeff Miner and John Tyler Connoley *The Children Are Free: Reexamining the Biblical Evidence on Same-sex Relationships* (Indianapolis: Found Pearl Press, 2002), 47. The section is headed, "When Jesus meets a gay person."

49 Ibid., 49.

50 Ibid., 50. One of the "proofs" offered by the authors that the slave, also described as such (using the Greek word *doulos*), was the centurion's male lover was that, according to Luke 7:2, this slave was "valued highly" by his master – and so, he *must* have been his master's male lover. After all, why else would a slave be highly esteemed by his master? (Forgive my sarcasm, but "interpretations" such as this do not merit serious refutation. Yet, remarkably, the authors claim that, "all the textual and circumstantial evidence in the Gospels points in one direction." Ibid., 49.)

51 For questions as to the original textual placement of John 8:1-11, see, e.g., Craig S. Keener, *The Gospel of*

John: A Commentary (Peabody, MA: Hendrickson, 2004).

52   A more serious attempt to put forth these arguments was made by Theodore W. Jennings, Jr. and Tat-Siong Benny Liew, "Mistaken Identities but Model Faith: Rereading the Centurion, the Chap, and the Christ in Matthew 8:5–13," in *Journal of Biblical Literature* 123 (2004), 467–94; for a short but clear exposé of some of the errors in their article, see D. B. Saddington, "The Centurion in Matthew 8:5–13: Consideration of the Proposal of Theodore W. Jennings, Jr., and Tat-Siong Benny Liew," *JBL* 125 (2006), 140-142. See further Robert A. J. Gagnon, "Did Jesus Approve of a Homosexual Couple in the Story of the Centurion at Capernaum?," http://robgagnon.net/articles/homosexCenturionStory.pdf, accessed October 2, 2010.

53   *Study New Testament for Lesbians, Gays, Bi, and Transgender. With Extensive Notes on Greek Word Meaning and Context*, translated with notes by Dr. A. Nyland (n.p.: n.p., 2007). Nyland was a scholar in classics and ancient history, specializing in Greek and Hittite lexicography.

54   These Greek lexicons (and theological encyclopedias), which, for the most part, are *not* the product of conservative Christian scholarship and therefore cannot be subject to the charge that they are biased against homosexuals (which, from a scholarly viewpoint, would still be a baseless charge), include: H. G. Liddell and R. Scott, *A Greek-English Lexicon* (Ninth Edition with a Revised Supplement; Oxford: Clarendon Press, 1996); Walter Bauer, Frederick Danker, et al., *A Greek-English Lexicon of the New Testament and Other Early Christian Literature* (Chicago: University of Chicago Press, 2001); Joseph Thayer, *Thayer's Greek-English Lexicon of the New Testament* (repr., Peabody, MA: Hendrickson, 1996); Gerhard Kittel and Gerhard Friedrich, eds., *Theological Dictionary of the New Testament* (10 vols.; Eng. trans., G. W. Bromiley; Grand Rapids: Eerdmans, 1977); Horst Balz and Gerhard Schneider, eds., *The Exegetical Dictionary of the New Testament* (3 vols.; Eng. transl.; Grand Rapids: Eerdmans, 1990); Colin Brown, ed., *The New International Dictionary of New Testament Theology* (4 vols.; Grand Rapids: Zondervan, 1986). See also Johannes P. Louw and Eugene A. Nida, *Greek-English Lexicon of the New Testament Based on Semantic Domains* (2 vols.; second edition; New York: United Bible Societies, 1989). Note that these lexicons are also consistent in their rendering of key Greek terms identified with homosexuality in important New Testament (or, related ancient Greek) contexts.

55   http://www.nbcdfw.com/news/local-beat/Churchs-Billboards-Affirm-Gay-Love-58116877.html,; see further http://www.whywouldwe.net/site/, both accessed September 30, 2010.

56   http://www.whywouldwe.net/site/jesus-affirmed-a-gay-couple, accessed September 30, 2010.

57   Texts cited to allege that Jonathan and David were gay lovers include 2 Sam 18:3-4, "Jonathan and David made a pact, because Jonathan loved him as himself. Jonathan took off the cloak and tunic he was wearing and gave them to David, together with his sword, bow, and belt," and 1 Sam 20:41 (when David has to flee for his life from King Saul, Jonathan's father), "They kissed each other and wept together; David wept the longer." For a comprehensive refutation of a gay reading of these (and other passages), see Gagnon, *The Bible and Homosexual Practice*, where he demonstrates clearly how such a reading of these texts is unthinkable from an ancient, Hebraic point of view and totally uncalled for in terms of what the biblical text actually says. Regarding the act of kissing (as distinguished from "making out"), note that kissing was a common way of saying hello or goodbye in the ancient Near East, as it is in many cultures to this day. Furthermore, if all the kisses that the Bible recorded were interpreted in sexual terms, then Isaac would have been erotically involved with his own son (see Gen 27:26, "Then his father Isaac said to him, 'Come here, my son, and kiss me.'"), Laban would have been erotically involved with his nephew Jacob (see Gen 29:13, "He embraced him and kissed him and brought him to his home"), Laban would have been erotically involved with his grandchildren and daughters (see Gen 31:55, "Early the next morning Laban kissed his grandchildren and his daughters and blessed them"), Esau would have been erotically involved with his brother Jacob (see Gen 33:4, "But Esau ran to meet Jacob and embraced him; he threw his arms around his neck and kissed him"), Joseph would have been erotically involved with all his brothers (see Gen 45:15, "And he kissed all his brothers and wept over them"), Jacob would have been erotically involved with his grandsons (see Gen 48:10, "So Joseph brought his sons close to him, and his father kissed them and embraced them"), and Joseph would have been erotically involved with his just-deceased father Jacob (see Gen 50:1, "Joseph threw himself upon his father and wept over him and kissed him") – and these are just examples from the first book of the Bible, Genesis! Obviously, all this public kissing was not in the least bit sexual! In the next book of the Bible, Exodus, we see Moses kissing his brother Aaron and his father-in-law Jethro (Exod 4:27; 18:7). For a few examples of non-relatives kissing, see Samuel the prophet kissing Saul (1 Sam 10:1), David kissing Jonathan (1 Sam 20:41), Absalom the prince kissing all who would approach him asking him to adjudicate on their behalf (2 Sam 15:5), David the king kissing the old man Barzillai (2 Sam 19:39), and Joab kissing Amasa (2 Sam 20:9). Kissing as a form of greeting was so customary in New Testament times that Paul and Peter taught the believers to "Greet one another with a holy kiss" (Rom 16:16; see also 1 Cor 16:20;

2 Cor 13:12; 1 Thes 5:26; cf. 1 Pet 5:13), the ancient equivalent of a handshake, and presumably men with men and women with women. Note also that, when the Bible wanted to speak of a sensual kiss, it certainly knew how, as in the bride's words in Song of Solomon 1:2, "Let him kiss me with the kisses of his mouth--for your love is more delightful than wine," or as seen in the context of Prov 7:13 – read the whole chapter!).

58   The text that is cited as alleged proof of their lesbian relationship is Ruth 1:16-17, often used in Christian wedding ceremonies by the bride and groom (as if reverse logic proved that Ruth and her mother-in-law Naomi must have been romantically involved). To the contrary, this is simply the devotion of daughter-in-law to her mother-in-law (including her mother-in-law's religious faith – the one true God, rather than idols – and her people – the people of Israel) after both of their husbands had died: "Intreat me not to leave thee, or to return from following after thee: for whither thou goest, I will go; and where thou lodgest, I will lodge: thy people shall be my people, and thy God my God: Where thou diest, will I die, and there will I be buried: the LORD do so to me, and more also, if ought but death part thee and me" (KJV). I'm quite sure that the "gay Christian" attempt to hijack this verse to sanction same-sex relationships will not detract from its beauty and power.

59   See, e.g., http://jesusinlove.blogspot.com/2010/07/mary-and-martha-sisters-or-lesbian.html, where it is claimed that, "Mary and Martha of Bethany were two of Jesus' closest friends. The Bible calls them "sisters" who lived together, but reading the Bible with queer eyes raises another possibility. Maybe Mary and Martha were a lesbian couple. Mary and Martha formed a nontraditional family at a time when there was huge pressure for heterosexual marriage." The article references prominent "gay Christian" leader Rev. Nancy Wilson, who wrote, "Jesus loved Lazarus, Mary and Martha. What drew Jesus to this very non-traditional family group of a bachelor brother living with two spinster sisters? Two barren women and a eunuch are Jesus' adult family of choice. Are we to assume they were all celibate heterosexuals? What if Mary and Martha were not sisters but called each other 'sister' as did most lesbian couples throughout recorded history?" Accessed October 27, 2010. Interestingly, the respected New Testament scholar Ben Witherington suggested the possibility that Mary, Martha, and Lazarus suffered from leprosy, explaining why they were all unmarried and living together. See Ben Witherington III, *What Have They Done with Jesus? Beyond Strange Theories and Bad History--Why We Can Trust the Bible* (New York: Harper One, 2006), 320-321, n. 158.

60   *Religion Is a Queer Thing*, 136.

61   Pilgrim Press, 2003. Among other books, Jennings has also written, *Jacob's Wound: Homoerotic Narrative in the Literature of Ancient Israel* (New York: Continuum Press, 2005).

62   For a healthy perspective on John's special love for Jesus and Jesus' special love for John, see Jack S. Deere, *Surprised by the Power of the Spirit* (Grand Rapids: Zondervan, 1996), 206-07.

63   See also Toby Johnson, *Gay Spirituality: The Role of Gay Identity in the Transformation of Human Consciousness* (repr.; Maple Shade, NJ: Lethe Press, 2004).

64   Note http://ctr.concordia.ca/2002-03/Nov_7/09-UgradAwards/index.shtml, with reference to "The Donald L. Boisvert Scholarship for Gay & Lesbian Studies, established and inducted by Donald L. Boisvert (BA'75 MA'79), Dean of Students," accessed October 27, 2010.

65   The book was published by Pilgrim Press, Cleveland, Ohio, 2000.

66   *Queer Commentary and the Hebrew Bible*, 175.

67   Ibid., 176-77.

68   Ibid., 177-78.

69   Ibid., 178-180. In Koch's "Cruising" world, Lydia in Acts 16:11-15 becomes "a shrewd lesbian merchant"; Absalom, David's son, becomes "a very quickly advancing young man" (1 Samuel 16:14-23); Dinah becomes "a raped lesbian sister" (Genesis 34:1-17); while Judges 12:4-6 points to "a huge number of slaughtered lispers" (ibid., 180, n. 3.). It should be noted that Koch is not dogmatic in his interpretations (180), but that he can read these texts in these ways at all says more than enough about his twisted interpretive method.

70   Ibid., 106. The article runs from 106-115.

71   Gregg Drinkwater, Joshua Lesser, and David Shneer, *Torah Queeries* (New York: New York University Press, 2009), 112. For further examples of what can only be called twisted readings of the biblical texts, see Andrew Ramer, *Queering the Text: Biblical, Medieval, and Modern Jewish Stories* (Brooklyn: White Crane Books, 2010).

72   See Leviticus 6:9, 12-13; on the concept of the eternal flame (*ner tamid*) in Judaism, see, concisely, http://www.jewishvirtuallibrary.org/jsource/Judaism/ner_tamid.html, accessed December 15, 2010.

73   *Torah Queeries*, 133.

74   Ibid., 137. Kamionkowski cites the first-century Jewish philosopher Philo in support of both the priests being naked and their being taken up by God's passionate fire, adding however, "Philo's reading can be

expanded through a queer reading lens" (ibid., 136-37), which is necessary of course, since there was not the slightest hint of anything homoerotic in Philo's reading of the text. In fact, such an interpretation would have been utterly unthinkable to him.

75   The reviewer is anonymous; see http://www.amazon.com/gp/product/0974638838/ref=pd_dp_1c_1_2/104-3173270-1653534?%5Fencoding=UTF8&v=glance&n=283155, accessed October 27, 2010.

76   Even if these alleged charges were ultimately thought to be false, the author's point is that the activities of Jesus would have *suggested* the reality of the charges.

77   See http://inverte.typepad.com/suspectthoughts/history/, accessed October 27, 2010.

78   Malden, MA: Blackwell Publishing, 2007.

79   See also above, n. 3, for further references.

80   http://www.psr.edu/page.cfm?l=283, accessed February 1, 2005, but no longer available.

81   Ibid. According to http://www.answers.com/topic/pacific-school-of-religion, "The Pacific School of Religion is an ecumenical seminary located in Berkeley, California. It is affiliated with the United Church of Christ and the United Methodist Church, training clergy from twenty-four religious traditions. The school was founded in San Francisco in 1866 as the Pacific Theological Seminary. It moved to Oakland shortly thereafter, then again to Berkeley in 1901." Their motto is "Equipping historic and emerging faith communities for ministries of compassion and justice" (see www.psr.edu); both sites accessed October 27, 2010.

82   http://www.ctschicago.edu/pdf/Convoke_FA_2004_Stone.pdf, accessed January 15, 2005, but no longer available.

83   Ibid.

84   Marcella Althaus-Reid, *Indecent Theology* (New York: Routledge, 2000).

85   The Guadalupana refers to Latin American, Catholic veneration of Mary, known as Our Lady of Guadalupe (in Mexico), also called the Dark Virgin of the Americas.

86   *Queer Commentary*, 36-74. Jennings is teaches Biblical and Constructive Theology at Chicago Theological Seminary.

87   Ibid., 57.

88   Ibid., 61.

89   Ibid., 60-61.

90   Ibid., 75-105.

91   Ibid., 78.

92   Ibid., 105.

Chapter 11

1   Marshall Kirk and Hunter Madsen, *After the Ball: How America Will Conquer Its Fear and Hatred of Gays in the 90's* (New York: Penguin, 1989), 107.

2   David Kupelian, *The Marketing of Evil: How Radicals, Elitists and Pseudo-Experts Sell Us Corruption Disguised as Freedom* (Nashville: WND Books, 2005), 24-25.

3   *What Do Gay Men Want? An Essay on Sex, Risk, and Subjectivity* (Ann Arbor: University of Michigan, 2008), 2, emphasis in the original.

4   Cf., more broadly, John D'Emilio, "Placing Gay in the Sixties," in Alexander Bloom, ed., *Long Time Gone: Sixties America Then and Now* (Oxford: Oxford University Press, 2001), 209-229.

5   See now the important volume by the respected philosopher Martha C. Nussbaum, *From Disgust to Humanity: Sexual Orientation and Constitutional Law* (New York: Oxford University Press, 2010), which makes a closely related argument. For an extended, critical review by a legal scholar, see Mary Anne Case, "A Lot to Ask: Review Essay of Martha Nussbaum's 'From Disgust to Humanity: Sexual Orientation and Constitutional Law'," *Columbia Journal of Gender and Law*, 19 (2010), 89-124 (available for download at http://papers.ssrn.com/sol3/papers.cfm?abstract_id=1639186, accessed December 20, 2010). Case concludes (124), "Demanding of the opponents of homosexuality that they tolerate—indeed, not just tolerate but live in a state that embraces—a vision of gay rights anything close to Nussbaum's is, I think we have to recognize, asking a lot; it is asking of the opponents of gay rights something close to what they are asking of gay rights activists today." For an insightful (and critical) review of an earlier, related title by Nussbaum, *Hiding from Humanity: Disgust, Shame, and the Law* (Princeton: Princeton University Press, 2004), see John Kekes, *Mind*, 114 (2005), 439-444.

6   http://www.rickross.com/reference/mormon/mormon670.html; see now http://mormon-chronicles.blogspot.com/2010/02/dramatic-jump-with-utahns-for-gay.html, both accessed September 18, 2010.

7   Ibid. (article on www.rickross.com, immediately above, n. 6).

8   According to Erik Holland, "People who address the sexual behavior of homosexuals at length may be

accused of being obsessed with gay sexuality, but the most important difference between homosexuals and heterosexuals is one of sexuality, which needs to be addressed in some detail if one is to understand the nature of homosexuality better." See http://www.homosexinfo.org/Sexuality/HomePage, accessed December 15, 2010.

9 *Speaking My Mind: The Radical Evangelical Prophet Tackles the Tough Issues Christians Are Afraid to Face* (Dallas: Word, 2004), 71-72. For a more recent (and perhaps even more strident) statement by Campolo, see http://www.exgaywatch.com/wp/2010/10/tony-campolo-in-canada-gays-ex-gays-rights-and-wrongs, accessed October 26, 2010. In the article, Campolo is quoted as saying, "You know why gays think Christians despise them? Because Christians despise them." Note, however, that Campolo also affirmed a conservative Christian understanding of Scripture with regard to homosexual practice.

10 *A Strong Delusion* (Eugene, OR: Harvest House, 1996), 218, emphasis in the original. Dallas continues (addressing fellow-Christians): "This backfires [for the following reasons]: it discredits the speaker, and skirts the larger issue. Homosexuality is wrong, whether committed 5,000 times a year during sadmasochistic rituals, or once in a 50-year monogamous relationship. It is wrong *in and of itself*" (emphasis in the original).

11 http://www.nytimes.com/2005/05/15/opinion/...?pagewanted=all, accessed September 7, 2010. Cf. Nussbaum, *From Disgust to Humanity*, 3, "When [Paul] Cameron and his associates look at male homosexuality, they are virtually obsessed with the disgusting. Feces, saliva, urine, semen, blood . . . together with frequent references to dangerous disease-bearing germs." (Note that Cameron is probably the most criticized "anti-gay" researcher, so it is no surprise that he is singled out in this book for special criticism.) Nussbaum further notes: "Nor does Cameron offer any support for his contention that semen and urine are particularly 'unsanitary.'" (Ibid., 4.) So, one must prove that urine is "unsanitary," especially in the context of sexual acts?

12 *Stranger at the Gate: To Be Gay and Christian in America* (New York: Plume, 1994), 294. In keeping with this mentality, gay leaders would argue that books like Tim LaHaye's, *The Unhappy Gays: What Everyone Should Know About Homosexuality* (Wheaton: Tyndale, 1978) inaccurately and unfairly caricature them. Cf. the personal account of Michael S. Piazza, pastor of the largest "gay Christian" church in the world, who claimed that reading LaHaye's book negatively influenced him as a young, seeking "gay Christian"; see his *Holy Homosexuals: The Truth About Being Gay or Lesbian and Christian* (rev. ed.; Dallas: Sources of Hope Publishing, 1997), 1-6.

13 *Virtually Normal: An Argument About Homosexuality* (New York: Vintage Books, 1995). Note that the content of Sullivan's book goes far beyond the rather understated title. For some fascinating reflections on Sullivan by a conservative Christian leader, Rev. Dr. Al Mohler, see http://www.albertmohler.com/2005/10/27/gay-culture-and-the-riddle-of-andrew-sullivan/, accessed September 6, 2010.

14 Letha Dawson Scanzoni and Virginia Mollenkott, *Is the Homosexual My Neighbor: A Positive Christian Response* (revised and updated; New York: HarperCollins, 1994); the first edition was published in 1978. For other, more radical publications of Mollenkott, see above, Chapter Nine.

15 The reasons normally given for this are: 1) Gays and lesbians, like other social groups, are more inclined to find strength in numbers and unity, hence their inclination to populate specific areas; 2) there is more opportunity for experimentation and open expression in larger cities vs. rural areas, making it easier for people to "come out." Cf. Robert T. Michael, John H. Gagnon, Edward O. Laumann, and Gina Kolata, *Sex in America: A Definitive Survey* (Boston: Little, Brown and Company, 1994), 169-183; for a full-length study of how gay culture can develop in a large city, see Lillian Faderman and Stuart Timmons, *Gay L.A.: A History of Sexual Outlaws, Power Politics, and Lipstick Lesbians* (New York: Basic Books, 2006).

16 For the claim that gays and lesbians make some of the best business leaders, see Kirk Snyder, *The G Quotient: Why Gay Executives are Excelling as Leaders... And What Every Manager Needs to Know* (San Francisco: Jossey-Bass, 2006).

17 http://www.washblade.com/print.cfm?content_id=5922, accessed June 1, 2006, but no longer available online.

18 *After the Ball*, 107. They actually counseled, "*First* you get in the door, by being as *similar* as possible; then, and only then – when your one little difference [sexual orientation] is finally accepted – can you start dragging in your other peculiarities, one by one. **You hammer in the wedge narrow end first.** As the saying goes, Allow the camel's nose beneath your tent, and his whole body will soon follow." See ibid., 146, their emphasis. Cf. also Paul E. Rondeau, "Selling Homosexuality to America," *Regent University Law Review* 14 (2002), 443-485.

19 *Is It a Choice?*, 158, 153.

20 *Is It a Choice?*, 158, 160, his emphasis.

21 Cf., e.g., Rhoads, *Taking Sex Differences Seriously*, esp. 45-78 (the chapter is entitled "Men Don't Get

Headaches"). As noted by Diamond, *Sexual Fluidity*, 45, "both gay and heterosexual men place more emphasis on sex in relationships than do lesbian and heterosexual women (who, comparatively, place more emphasis on emotional intimacy)," with reference to L. A. Peplau and L. R. Spalding, "The close relationships of lesbians, gay men, and bisexuals," in C. Hendrick and S. S. Hendrick, eds., *Close Relationships: A Sourcebook* (Thousand Oaks, CA; Sage, 2000), 111-123.

22   See again Rhoads, *Taking Sex Differences Seriously*, 45-78.

23   This is part of his point that marriage "**Civilizes men** and focuses them on productive pursuits. Unmarried men cause society much more trouble than married men." See Frank Turek, *Correct, Not Politically Correct; How Same-Sex Marriage Hurts Everyone* (Charlotte, NC: Cross Examined, 2008), 18, his emphasis.

24   See http://www.gaytoday.com/garchive/people/030600pe.htm, accessed September 6, 2010.

25   *The Pleasure Principle: Sex, Backlash, and the Struggle for Gay Freedom* (New York: St. Martins Press, 1998), 9. One colleague who reviewed the manuscript of the book added here: "Many would also argue that female and male sexuality differ in such profound ways that they each have a tempering effect on the other. And so, in broad terms, since males tend to be more physically based in terms of their sexuality while females tend to be more emotionally based, two males together would more likely be hyper-sexual while two females would more likely be hyper-emotional. Males and females, however, gel in such a way as to create a sexual balance between the partners. Of course, it isn't always perfect, nor does it always work out like that, but generally speaking, male-female couples achieve this balance to a workable degree."

26   This has been related to me by several men who formerly identified as gay. The technical term for the basis of this behavior, as used by Dr. Joseph Nicolosi, is "incomplete gender identification." For a brief overview of Nicolosi's views with regard to the "reparative drive" (which relates, in part, to the subject at hand), see http://www.josephnicolosi.com/the-meaning-of-same-sex-attrac/. According to Nicolosi (ibid.), "The concept of reparative drive has been well-established within the psychoanalytic literature; in our application, the person is attempting to 'repair' unmet same-sex affective needs (attention, affection and approval) as well as gender-identification deficits . . . through homoerotic behavior." He writes elsewhere, "The basic premise of reparative therapy is that the majority of clients (approximately 90%, in my experience) suffer from a syndrome of male gender-identity deficit. It is this internal sense of incompleteness in one's own maleness which is the essential foundation for homoerotic attraction." See Joseph Nicolosi, *Healing Homosexuality: Case Stories of Reparative Therapy* (Northvale, NJ: Aronson, 1993), 211, available online at http://www.narth.com/docs/cases.html, both accessed December 30, 2010. See also idem, *Shame and Attachment Loss: The Practical Work of Reparative Therapy* (Downers Grove, IL: IVP Academic, 2009), Chapter 4, "Homosexuality as a Repetition Compulsion." For explicit rejection of these concepts, see Kathleen Y. Ritter and Anthony I. Terndrup, *Handbook of Affirmative Psychotherapy with Lesbians and Gay Men* (New York: The Guilford Press, 2002), 56-57. See also n. 35, below, for further psychological discussion of gay (male) promiscuity.

27   See, e.g., Michael, Laumann and others, *Sex in America*, esp. 88-110.

28   See John R. Diggs, Jr., M.D., "The Health Risks of Gay Sex," http://www.corporateresourcecouncil.org/white_papers/Health_Risks.pdf, i. For trenchant (but not necessarily substantive) criticism of Diggs, see, e.g., http://holybulliesandheadlessmonsters.blogspot.com/2009/02/more-on-phony-expert-john-r.html, both accessed September 7, 2010.

29   Satinover, *Homosexuality and the Politics of Truth*, 55.

30   Cf. Rotello, 62; see also the casual comments of Larry Kramer, cited above in Chapter Four. In contrast, the boasts of the late basketball star Wilt Chamberlain, claiming to have been with 20,000 women in his lifetime, were greeted with skepticism, not to mention shock. See http://static.espn.go.com/nba/news/1999/1012/110836.html, accessed September 20, 2010; for the actual claims, see Wilt Chamberlain, *A View from Above* (New York: Random House, 1991).

31   Rotello, *Sexual Ecology*, 5

32   Ibid., 62-63.

33   Cited in Satinover, *Homosexuality and the Politics of Truth*, 55.

34   Robert Gagnon, "Immorality, Homosexual Unhealth, and Scripture. A Response to Peterson and Hedlund's 'Heterosexism, Homosexual Health, and the Church'; Part II: Science: Causation and Psychopathology, Promiscuity, Pedophilia, and Sexually Transmitted Disease," 7; see http://www.robgagnon.net/articles/homoHeterosexismRespPart2.pdf, accessed September 20, 2010.

35   Satinover, *Homosexuality and the Politics of Truth*, 55. For a critique of the use of this study (and other, older studies) by a gay watchdog group, see http://www.boxturtlebulletin.com/Articles/000,017.htm, accessed September 20, 2010. After treating several hundred homosexual clients, and with reference to this same McWhirter and Mattison study, Dutch psychologist Dr. Gerard van den Aardweg opined

that: "Homosexual restlessness cannot be appeased, much less so by having one partner, because these persons are propelled by an insatiable opining for the unattainable fantasy figure. Essentially, the homosexual is a yearning child, not a satisfied one.

"The term neurotic describes such relationships well. It suggests the ego-centeredness of the relationship; the attention seeking, the continuous tensions, generally stemming from the recurrent complaint, 'You don't love me'; the jealousy, which so often suspects, 'He (she) is more interested in someone else.' *Neurotic*, in short, suggests all kinds of dramas and childish conflicts as well as the basic disinterestedness in the partner, notwithstanding the shallow pretensions of 'love'. Nowhere is there more self-deception in the homosexual than in his representation of himself as a lover. One partner is important to the other only insofar as he satisfies that others needs. Real, unselfish love for a desired partner would, in fact, end up destroying homosexual 'love'! Homosexual 'unions' are clinging relationships of two essentially self-absorbed 'poor me's'." See Gerard J. M. van den Aardweg, *The Battle for Normality: A Guide for (Self) Therapy for Homosexuality* (San Francisco: Ignatius Press, 1997), 62-63. I'm aware, of course, that some will affirm these comments as accurate while others with read them with outrage, as representing the height of offensiveness. I am simply citing the perspective of one psychologist, just as I have cited the perspectives of many gay-affirming psychologists throughout this book. Of related interest is the comment of Kenneth Lewes in the *Archives of Sexual Behavior*, 31 (2002), 380-383, reviewing Dr. Jack Drescher's volume, *Psychoanalytic Therapy and the Gay Man* (New York: Routledge, 2001), in which Lewes notes that Drescher does not address issues such as gay clients' "amazing search for sexual variety and frequency, the importance to them of fantasy and sado-masochistic scenarios, the abuse of drugs to heighten sexual experience, their apparently adolescent narcissistic physical display....Therapists working with gay men hear about these behaviors frequently" (383), cited in http://www.narth.com/docs/promiscuity.html, accessed December 20, 2010. Note that both Lewes and Drescher are openly gay as well as advocates for gay issues.

36   Cf. Gagnon, *The Bible and Homosexual Practice*, 453-460, and see further, below.

37   Friday, August 23, 2003, originally located at http://www.washblade.com/2003/8-22/news/national/nonmonog.cfm but now available at http://www.aegis.com/News/WB/2003/WB030811.html, accessed September 20, 2010. Note the comments from a man name Paul who emailed our organization on May 6, 2009: "I live in the UK and became aware of Dr. Brown's ministry through the internet. I lived a 'Gay lifestyle' for years. I was an Evangelical Christian who left the Church and gave in to my desires and pursued a life of wild sexual abandon and with multiple failed relationships. Sadly liberal Christians encouraged me to 'accept myself', which further encouraged me to sin....*I have never met a monogomous [sic] homosexual couple who have been together beyond the 'first stages of romantic and sexual attraction'. The relationships that last have accommodations that include promiscuity of some sort*" (my emphasis).

38   As related by gay psychotherapist Joe Kort, "Are Gay Male Couples Monogamous Ever After?", September 16, 2008, http://www.psychologytoday.com/node/1811, accessed August 5, 2010. Kort seeks to apply the same principles of redefined monogamy to both homosexual and heterosexual couples. For a comparison of studies confirming this trend with studies claiming greater sexual faithfulness among gay couples, see Harold Miller, "Making sense (trying to!) of varying statistics on gay monogamy," http://www.corningmennonite.org/gaymatter/monog.htm, accessed September 20, 2010.

39   *The Gay Agenda*, 78.

40   Michael Warner, *The Trouble with Normal: Sex, Politics, and the Ethics of Queer Life* (Cambridge, MA: Harvard University Press, 1999), vii. For a recent statement by gay activists who *oppose* same-sex marriage, see now Ryan Conrad, ed., *Against Equality: Queer Critiques of Gay Marriage* (Oakland, CA: Against Equality Press, 2010), and cf. http://dailycaller.com/2011/01/04/not-all-gay-activists-suppor-out-against-gay-marriage/#ixzz1A7cPOlrB, quotiong Yasmin Nair, one of the book's contributors: "Yeah, I don't get why a community of people who have historically been f....d over by their families and the state now consists of people who want those exact same institutions to validate their existence."

41   http://www.towleroad.com/2009/06/camille-paglia-gay-activists-childish-for-demanding-rights.html, accessed December 3, 2009. For the record, many of the LGBT comments responding to this video were quite critical of Paglia's statements; see ibid.

42   *After the Ball*, 330.

43   The actor who related this to me is a personal friend who preferred to remain anonymous. The comment is reminiscent of the painful words of Andrew Sullivan, who, after learning that he had contracted the HIV virus, explained to an old high-school friend that he didn't know from whom he had been infected, since he had slept with so many men: "Too many, God knows. Too many for meaning and dignity to be given to every one; too many for love to be present at each; too many for sex to be very often more than a temporary but powerful release from debilitating fear and loneliness." Cited above, by Al Mohler, n. 10.

44   See also Halperin, *What Do Gay Men Want?*

45   Cf., however, the remarks of Timothy Kincaid, cited below, n. 50.
46   As summarized by Dr. Neil Whitehead, http://www.mygenes.co.nz/partner_rates.htm. See further C. H. Mercer, G. J. Hart, A. M. Johnson, and J. A. Cassell, "Behaviourally bisexual men as a bridge population for HIV and sexually transmitted infections?", *International Journal of STD and AIDS*, 20 (2009), 87-94. Whitehead's simplified summary statement is that, "Both gays and lesbians have 3-4 times as many partners as heterosexuals (comparison of medians)." Cf. http://www.mygenes.co.nz/ Misconceptions.pdf, and cf. D. P. Schmitt, "Sexual strategies across sexual orientations: how personality traits and culture relate to sociosexuality among gays, lesbians, bisexuals, and heterosexuals," *Journal of Psychology and Human Sexuality*, 18 (2007), 183-214 (with "sociosexuality" being a code-word for promiscuity). More broadly, see A. Dean Byrd, "Sexual Addiction: A Psycho-Physiological Model for Addressing Obsessive-Compulsive Behaviors," http://www.narth.com/docs/coll-byrd.html, all accessed September 20, 2010.
47   Whitehead, http://www.mygenes.co.nz/partner_rates.htm, comments, "A stereotype of gay sexual behaviour is that it is wildly promiscuous, and the anti-gay literature contains figures which suggest gays may have thousands of times as many sexual partners as straights. Conversely the stereotype is that lesbians have relatively few partners, even compared to straights. The current update suggests neither stereotype is accurate, and that SSA people in general have about 4 times as many partners as OSA people (heterosexuals)."
48   *Is It a Choice?*, 160; his answer on sex clubs continues on 161.
49   For further discussion of the bathhouses, see Rotello, *Sexual Ecology*, esp. 58-63.
50   See, e.g., http://www.answers.com/topic/monogamy, accessed September 20, 2010.
51   See the article on Monogamy in the online Encyclopedia of AIDS, which distinguishes between the more common gay couples' custom of emotional monogamy as opposed to a relationship of sexual exclusivity. See http://www.thebody.com/encyclo/monogamy.html, accessed September 20, 2010, where it is noted that "In gay male relationships, a policy of sexual exclusivity is rarer than an agreement of 'emotional monogamy' in which partners have sanction, sometimes with certain limitations, to have sex outside the relationship provided the extra-relational contact does not threaten the emotional integrity of the partnership." The article also claims that there is a large amount of heterosexual infidelity among married couples.
52   Michelangelo Signorile, *Life Outside* (New York: HarperCollins, 1997), 213, cited by Timothy J. Dailey, Ph.D., "Comparing the Lifestyles of Homosexual Couples to Married Couples," July 21, 2006, http:// www.frc.org/get.cfm?i=IS04C02&v=PRINT#edn54, accessed September 20, 2010.
53   http://www.nytimes.com/2010/01/29/us/29sfmetro.html; for a strong rejection of the conclusions of this report by gay blogger Timothy Kincaid, see http://www.boxturtlebulletin.com/2010/02/10/20202. Kincaid argues that, "If there is any story here, it would be that a study of San Francisco bay area gay male couples, a sample which was highly skewed to include many participants who are less likely to value monogamy and which defined 'couples' to include those who have been dating as little as three months, still found that half of them set monogamy as the agreement for their relationship." He further states that "those who delight in denouncing the hedonistic sex-driven homosexuals and their non-monogamous marriages share a problem with those gays who may champion the abandonment of the heteronormative demands of conformity and spearhead the evolution of marriage: **this study tells us nothing whatsoever about gay marriage** and little about monogamy within gay relationships as a whole." See http://www.boxturtlebulletin.com/tag/monogamy, his emphasis; all articles accessed September 20, 2010. To date, I am not aware of any credible studies that support the idea that same sex "marriage" has decreased gay male promiscuity, nor am I aware of serious anecdotal evidence that would support this idea. Some gay men with whom I have discussed these issues believe that those who wanted to be in more committed relationships made that choice before same-sex "marriage" was legal in any states, while those who choose not to be primarily committed to one partner continue to be more promiscuous regardless of changes in law.
54   James correctly states that, "Open relationships are not exclusively a gay domain, of course." But as noted above, in the vast majority of cases, "With straight people, it's called affairs or cheating." That in itself says a lot.
55   See http://www.simonlevay.com/essay, accessed December 15, 2010. He begins by saying, "It's good to be similar to your partner—but not too similar. So don't expect typical gay partnerships to be simply same-sex versions of straight ones." Among his more salient points are: "Gay partners, being of the same sex, may sometimes be *too* similar to each other for their relationships to be stable. They experience a kind of 'anti-homophily.'" Thus, "Besides gender-based differences, many gay couples are characterized by other kinds of difference, such as disparities in age, race, and cultural background—the very factors that, according to the homophily literature, are supposed to militate against the formation and stability

of relationships.... A common phenomenon, for example, is a couple consisting of an older, professional white man and a younger Asian or Hispanic man—perhaps an immigrant with a very different cultural perspective. Age-disparate homosexual relationships have been a recognized tradition in numerous cultures, from ancient Greece to Afghanistan under the Taliban.... Some degree of difference between partners is probably necessary for the establishment and maintenance of loving sexual relationships. With a man and a woman, this essential difference is supplied automatically by the very fact that the union crosses the sex divide.... In same-sex relationships, on the other hand, where there is no automatic provision of gender-based differences, couples may actually seek out and benefit from dissimilarity, whether in gender-related behaviour traits or any number of other personality or demographic variables." Coming from a man of LeVay's stature in the gay community, these are significant remarks.

56   *Is It a Choice?*, 157.

57   See further Seanna Sugrue, "Soft Depotism and Same-Sex Marriage," in George and Elshtain, eds., *The Meaning of Marriage*, 18-0-86; more broadly, see Zimmerman, *Family and Civilization* and Carlson and Mero, *The Natural Family*.

58   *After the Ball*, 47-48. They still feel, however, that "outsiders have often exaggerated the extent of gay promiscuity far beyond what is known from sex research."

59   For more recent statistics – equally shocking and saddening – see further, below.

60   *After the Ball*, 48.

61   As to the anonymous nature of some gay sex, going as far as sexual encounters through a hole in the wall of a lavatory cubicle in a public bathroom, see, e.g., Don Bapst, "Glory Holes and the Men who use Them," *Journal of Homosexuality* 41 (2001), 89–102; Kirk and Madsen, *After the Ball*, 308-312 (with revealing and damning anecdotes).

62   For the notorious "Fistgate" scandal, see http://www.massresistance.org/docs/issues/fistgate/index.html, accessed August 5, 2010. The article cites this shocking quote, "Fisting ... often gets a bad rap....[It's] an experience of letting somebody into your body that you want to be that close and intimate with...[and] to put you into an exploratory mode," explaining that, "The above quotation comes from Massachusetts Department of Education employees describing the pleasures of homosexual sex to a group of high school students at a state-sponsored workshop on during GLSEN's 'Teach-Out' Conference on March 25, 2000 held at Tufts University. Approximately 200 young teens and 300 adults attended the day-long event. Kids were bussed in from high schools across Massachusetts."

63   See now Amian Ghazani and Thomas D. Cook, Ph.D., "Reducing HIV Infections at Circuit Parties: From Description to Explanation and Principles of Intervention Design," *Journal of the International Association of Physicians In AIDS Care*, 4/2 (2005), 32-46. Cf. also http://www.narth.com/docs/circuit.html, accessed September 20, 2010.

64   "Why many ex-gays go to ex-gay ministries," http://www.boxturtlebulletin.com, August 2, 2010, accessed August 5, 2010.

65   *After the Ball*, 49.

66   Ibid.

67   Ibid.

68   Ibid., 302-303. Dr. Gerard J. M. van den Aardweg makes the claim that, "The life of most committed homosexuals revolves around one thing: homosexuality. In their self-centeredness they are often unaware of the suffering they inflict on their environment." See his review of Dawn Stefanowicz's *Out from Under* (for which see further, below, Chapter Fifteen), in the *Empirical Journal of Same-Sex Sexual Behavior*, 1 (2007), 3.

69   See, e.g., *After the Ball*, 288, where they make sarcastic reference to "that extraordinary epidemic, unremarked by the Centers for Disease Control, of 'liver cancer' (and related factitious ailments), that, since, 1983 or so, has more than decimated the ranks of young, unmarried interior decorators and ballet dancers, at least in the greater metropolitan area of the City of New York," speaking, of course, of AIDS, which they note was rarely featured in the obituary columns as a cause of death. Note also their discussion of "Larry Kramer vs. AIDS vs. the Gay Press: Kill the Messenger," 354, where they cite Kramer's prescient observation that, "gays were going to have to change their lives 'before you f--- your[selves] to death.'"

70   Repr.; Boston: Beacon Press, 2004.

71   http://www.amazon.com/Beyond-Shame-Reclaiming-Abandoned-Sexuality/dp/080707957X/ref=sr_1_1?s=gateway&ie=UTF8&qid=1284950040&sr=8-1#reader_080707957X, accessed September 19, 2010.

72   According to Sabin Russel in a February 11, 2004 article in the *San Francisco Chronicle*, "From 1998 to 2003, the number of syphilis cases reported in San Francisco rose from 40 to more than 600 a year, raising concern because the disease is spread by the same kinds of unprotected sex that transmit the AIDS virus."

At the time of the article, however, it was hoped that things had plateaued and were even beginning to decline. Russell notes, "HIV infections in San Francisco had steadily declined since the mid-1980s but ominously began to climb again after antiviral drugs began to show their effectiveness and safer sexual practices began to fall by the wayside." Dr. Willi McFarland, chief AIDS epidemiologist for the San Francisco Department of Public Health "raised the alarm four years ago that the city's declining rate of HIV infection had reversed and that the number of newly infected -- always an estimate -- was growing to 900 per year from 500 throughout much of the 1990s." This also reflected nationwide patterns that, as of 2004, McFarland hoped were beginning to reverse. See "No HIV spike to mirror syphilis rise Surprising find in S.F. study of gay men," http://www.sfgate.com/cgi-bin/article.cgi?file=/chronicle/archive/2004/02/11/BAGCM4U0TC1.DTL, accessed September 19, 2010.

73   Bill Roundy, "STD Rates on the Rise," *New York Blade News* (15 December, 2000), 1, cited in *Dark Obsession*, 82. More recently, cf. the observations in the January 3, 2011 article by Anemona Hartocollis, "City's Graphic Ad on the Dangers of H.I.V. Is Dividing Activists," accessed January 6, 2011.

74   Toby McDonald and Judy Duffy, "Syphilis rates soar among gay men in Scotland," in the *Sunday Herald*, http://www.sundayherald.com/51288, accessed August 29, 2005, but no longer available at that address.

75   Cited in *Dark Obsession*, 87, emphasis in the original. Cf. http://www.cdc.gov/mmwr/preview/mmwrhtml/00056314.htm, accessed November 4, 2010.

76   Ibid. See further http://www.cdc.gov/mmwr/preview/mmwrhtml/mm5205a2.htm ("HIV/STD Risks in Young Men Who Have Sex with Men Who Do Not Disclose Their Sexual Orientation --- Six U.S. Cities, 1994—2000"), and http://www.cdc.gov/mmwr/preview/mmwrhtml/mm5042a3.htm ("*Shigella sonnei* Outbreak Among Men Who Have Sex with Men --- San Francisco, California, 2000—2001"), both accessed November 4, 2010.

77   Cf. again Rotello, *Sexual Ecology*, for a sober analysis of the problem with an articulate plea for a change in sexual behavior, but all within a homosexual context. For a contrast in gay approaches to the problem of STD's and other pressing, gay men's issues, see Paul Robinson, *Queer Wars: The New Gay Right and Its Critics* (Chicago: University of Chicago Press, 2005).

78   http://topnews.co.uk/213743-hiv-infection-gays-increasing-alarming-rate, accessed November 4, 2010. The article, by Rasik Sharma, began, "With the increase in the rate of HIV infection among the gay and bisexual community, as reported by the study conducted by Centers for Disease Control and Prevention (CDC), it has become the need of the hour to address the issue with grave concern."

79   See Barry D. Adam, Winston Husbands, James Murray, and John Maxwell, "AIDS Optimism, Condom Fatigue, or Self-Esteem? Explaining Unsafe Sex Among Gay and Bisexual Men," *The Journal of Sex Research* 42 (2005), 238-248. See also the discussion in http://www.narth.com/docs/circuit.html.

80   See, e.g., Diggs, "Health Risks," 4.

81   Matt Comer, "Fessing Up: Promiscuity & Unsafe Sex," http://www.interstateq.com/archives/3584/, accessed September 19, 2010.

82   *The Tragedy of Today's Gays*, 35-36.

83   Ibid., 87.

84   Ibid., 42, 44, emphasis in the original.

85   The NGLTF pointed to the removal of sodomy laws nationwide after the landmark 2003 decision; cf. http://www.thetaskforce.org/downloads/reports/issue_maps/sodomymap0603.pdf with http://www.thetaskforce.org/downloads/reports/issue_maps/sodomymap.pdf, both accessed September 19, 2010.

86   See, e.g., 1972 Gay Rights Platform; 1987 March on Washington (both cited in Chapter One, above).

87   See now Lisa M. Diamond, *Sexual Fluidity: Understanding Women's Love and Desire* (Cambridge, MA: Harvard University Press, 2009).

88   The quote has been cited in several different articles; see, e.g., http://www.umd.edu/lgbt/development.html, accessed September 19, 2010.

89   http://lesbianlife.about.com/od/lesbiansinsports/a/Swoopes.htm, accessed September 19, 2010.

90   http://www.advocate.com/Arts_and_Entertainment/People/The_Great_de_Rossi/, accessed September 19, 2010. *The Advocate*, August 21, 2008, notes: "Mark Pasetsky's **Cover Awards** calls the moment 'historic.' He writes, "='When you see this cover of *People* magazine hitting newsstands on Wed, take a second to let it sink in. It's Ellen DeGeneres getting married to Portia de Rossi on the cover of *People*. Who would have ever thought that we would see this day? For all the lesbian and gay partners in the United States, this is more than a magazine cover. It's another sign that this country is finally getting its act together and treating all people as equal.' He ends his piece by praising *People* editor Larry Hackett." See http://www.advocate.com/Arts_and_Entertainment/Entertainment_News/Many,_Many_Points_for_Us/, accessed September 19, 2010.

91   See http://www.newsweek.com/2008/12/05/our-mutual-joy.html; for a solid refutation, see Prof. Robert Gagnon's "More than 'Mutual Joy': Lisa Miller of Newsweek against Scripture and Jesus,"

http://www.robgagnon.net/NewsweekMillerHomosexResp.htm, both accessed September 19, 2010.

92   http://www.thetaskforce.org/downloads/creating_change/cc10/cc10_program_book.pdf, 1, accessed September, 19, 2010.

93   Ibid., 9.

94   Ibid., 17.

95   Ibid.

96   Ibid., 28.

97   Ibid., 47.

98   Ibid., 88. For the 2009 Leather Award to Graylin Thornton, according to Americans for Truth About Homosexuality, a purveyor of gay, S & M porn videos. see http://americansfortruth.com/news/national-gay-and-lesbian-task-force-talks-of-moral-leadership-while-honoring-homosexual-sm-pornographer.html. accessed September 19, 2010.

99   Ibid. (n. 88), 25.

100   Ibid., 36

101   For more on this, see Chapter Ten.

102   Wittman's *Manifesto* has been published many times in many different collections; see, conveniently, http://library.gayhomeland.org/0006/EN/A_Gay_Manifesto.htm, accessed September 19, 2010.

103   For a wide-ranging collection, see Mary Ann Caws, ed., *Manifesto: A Century of Isms* (Lincoln, NE: University of Nebraska Press, 2000); of more specific historical relevance, cf. *Rebellious Generation.*

104   http://www.gaytoday.com/about.asp, current as of September 19, 2010.

105   See, e.g., http://www.gaytoday.com/sextalk/archives.asp, accessed September 19, 2010.

106   It is also enlightening to look at the some of the annual book awards given by the Gay, Lesbian, Bisexual, and Transgendered Round Table of the American Library Association (GLBTRT), formed in 1970 and, according to its website, the oldest GLBT professional organization in America. One of the two 2006 award winners was Abha Dawesar's *Babyji*, described as "the coming of age story of Anamika Sharma, a brilliant, spirited, and sexually adventurous New Delhi, India, [lesbian] teenager." Receiving honorable mention, among others, were *Queer London: Perils and Pleasures in the Sexual Metropolis, 1918-1957*, by Matt Houlbrook; *The Secret Life of Oscar Wilde*, by Neil McKenn, and *The Wild Creatures: Collected Stories of Sam D'Allesandro*, edited by Kevin Killian, described, in part, on the publisher's (Suspect Thoughts) website as exploring "a strange terrain of urban legend, the power of sexual obsession, and the thin line where the too-cool becomes the too-hot." (A brief perusal of the book's contents indicates that it is sexually graphic in the extreme.) See http://www.suspectthoughts.com/presswild.htm; for the GLBTRT awards, see http://www.ala.org/Template.cfm?Section=pressrelea ses&template=/contentmanagement/contentdisplay.cfm&ContentID=114246, accessed September 19, 2010. Don't these book awards also reflect an obsession with sexual issues?

107   One of the leading gay sex manuals, *The Joy of Gay Sex*, by Dr. Charles Silverstein and Felice Picano (third, expanded edition; New York: Harper Collins, 2003) speaks in non-condemning terms about bestiality; see pp. 250-252 ("Sex with Animals").

108   See, http://www.nambla.org/ginsberg.htm; cf. also http://www.qrd.org/qrd/orgs/NAMBLA/quotes; for discussion of some of the extreme vulgarity of Ginsberg's poems, see http://arts.hurryupharry.org/2008/11/15/allen-ginsberg-%E2%80%93-a-degenerate/, which ends with the question, "Was Ginsberg a poetic genius and someone whose work is deserved of study and criticism by in the English departments of the worlds great universities, or is he someone that deserves no better than to be forgotten and his books of poetry to remain gathering dust in library bookshelves, only to be used by doctoral students in sociology departments researching an obscure subject such as twentieth century literary perverts?", all accessed September 19, 2010. (Readers offended by profanity should avoid the last reference cited; note also that typos in this quote are in the original.)

109   http://www.narth.com/docs/arguecase.html, accessed September 19, 2010.

110   http://cbst.org/twentythirty.shtml, accessed August 30, 2005, but no longer available.

111   From the conference program guide, and posted in 2005 on the MCC website, http://ufmcc.com/, but no longer accessible there.

112   Ibid.

113   http://www.glbtq.com/social-sciences/leather_culture.html; for the question of how much the leather (and BDSM) culture is accepted in the general LGBT community, see http://goqnotes.com/9023/leather-bdsm-lifestyle-provides-security-stability/, both accessed November 7, 2010.

114   http://www.glbtq.com/social-sciences/bear_movement.html, accessed November 7, 2010.

115   Mark Thompson, *Leatherfolk* (Boston: Alyson, 1991).

116   Cited on http://www.pfox.org/Rev_Troy_Perry_leather_queen.html, accessed December 12, 2010.

117 See n. 107, above. Gay activist Wayne Besen ridicules any connection between same-sex marriages and polygamy, writing, "in the one state that has gay marriage and in the other nations that also have it - there has been no push for polygamy. *Experience* teaches us that this is nothing more than a perverse fantasy in the minds of sexually repressed conservatives. In the real world, they are the only creeps who ever talk about polygamy." Really? See http://www.waynebesen.com/2006/02/nj-court-hears-marriage-case.html, accessed October 25, 2010.

118 Bob Davies stated, "I wish pro-gay religious leaders would admit that their endorsement and promotion of monogamous homosexual relationships is a facade. Many–probably most–men and women involved in long-term partnerships are not sexually monogamous, but gay churches don't discipline members for committing 'adultery' outside their 'gay marriage.' Neither do they discipline gays or lesbians who have sex before entering into a "holy union" with their partner." See "Seven Things I Wish Pro-Gay People Would Admit," http://www.evergreeninternational.org/7_things.htm, accessed September 20, 2010.

119 See n. 107, above.

120 http://mccla.org/pdf/Queer_Theology_Dissertation_of_Reverend_Dr_Neil_G_Thomas.pdf, accessed September 20, 2010.

121 Ibid., 108-09.

122 See in particular 1 Corinthians 11:23-34.

123 Reported by Accuracy in Academia, http://www.academia.org/fastfind/?query=homosexuality&type=simple&results=20&searchType=1&page=1, accessed January 15, 2006, but no longer available.

124 My emphasis; cited in http://gatewaypundit.firstthings.com/2009/12/breaking-obamas-safe-schools-czar-is-promoting-porn-in-the-classroom-kevin-jennings-and-the-glsen-reading-list/, accessed September 20, 2010.

125 Cited in ibid.

126 Cited in ibid.

127 For the controversy surrounding this, see, e.g., http://www.wnd.com/?pageId=119428, with reference to other, relevant articles; accessed September 20, 2010.

128 Cited in ibid.

129 My appreciation to Prof. Robert Gagnon for drawing attention to these papers on his website; see http://www.robgagnon.net/AARGayMen'sGroup.htm, accessed September 20, 2010, where additional information, along with Gagnon's incisive comments, are included. The actual call for papers for this section stated: "The Gay Men's Issues in Religion Group explores the intersections between the gay male experience and forms of religious discourse and practice. This year, we are particularly interested in receiving proposals for papers and panels on the following topics: transgenderism, its construction and religious dimensions; queer theory and its relevance to the religious/spiritual lives of gay men; queer latino/a theologies and spiritualities; S/M, submission, and the spiritual dimensions of power. We also seek proposals on topics not listed here, and from all religious traditions. Submissions by Latin American scholars are especially encouraged." See http://www.aarweb.org/annualmeet/2004/call/listcall.asp?PUNum=AARPU025, also referenced in Gagnon, ibid., but no longer available.

130 See further Chapter Seven. Is it fair to ask why it is gay men who are the editors of pedophile publications (such as *Paidika*) and who run organizations like NAMBLA, or why it was the *Journal of Homosexuality* that originally published *Male Intergenerational Intimacy*?

131 In the 2005 annual conference of the American Academy of Religion, a theme for discussion in the Gay Men's Issues in Religion Group was, "Sacred Tops, Manly Bottoms: Readings of Ron Long's *Men, Homosexuality, and the Gods*," with panelists including Robert Goss, who will be featured in the next chapter. I obtained an abstract of the theme on October 30, 2005, at http://www.aarweb.org/annualmeet/2005/pbook/abstract.asp?ANum=&KeyWord=bottoms&B1=Submit, but it no longer available.

Chapter 12

1 Throughout this chapter, the terms "reorientation therapy" and "reparative therapy" are used almost interchangeably, although critics tend to use the latter term. The former term is also known as "sexual reorientation therapy," or SRT.

2 This, of course, is my paraphrase of the common gay and gay-allied response, represented by books such as Rev. Sylvia Pennington's *Ex-gays? There Are None! What It Means To Be a New Creature in Christ* (Hawthorne, CA: Lambda Christian Fellowship, 1986; Pennington was a self-described straight grandmother); or websites such as www.homonomo.com, telling Peterson Toscano's story of, "How I Survived the Ex-gay Movement"; see further the abstract of his paper presented at the 12th Lavender Language Conference in 2005, "Talking trash at the Homo-No-Mo Halfway House: Looking at language and life in the ex-gay movement," at http://www1.american.edu/anthro/lavenderlanguages/

previous/2005abstracts.pdf, accessed August 30, 2010. See also http://www.hrc.org/documents/missionimpossible.pdf and http://www.hrc.org/documents/finallyfree.pdf.

3   http://www.washblade.com/print.cfm?content_id=5922, accessed June 1, 2006, but no longer available online.

4   Marcus answers the question, "What are some ways in which mental health experts and doctors have tried to 'cure' homosexuals?" in the most lurid, "shocking" (literally!) terms: "Some mental health professionals who believed homosexual people were mentally ill or physically sick tried to 'cure' gay men and lesbians by using a variety of techniques, including electroshock therapy, brain surgery, hormone injections, and even castration." See *Is It a Choice? Answers to 300 of the Most Frequently Asked Questions About Gay and Lesbian People* (San Francisco: HarperSanFrancisco, 1999), 14-15. Apparently, such practices are considered to be the norm, or, they are portrayed as such in order to give a misleading, totally negative impression. Cf. also Kevin Naff, "Lock up the 'ex-gays'" (cited immediately above, n. 3), where he sarcastically makes reference to electro-shock therapy and solitary confinement as supposed Christian therapy options.

5   *Is It a Choice?*, 142.

6   *Speaking My Mind* (Dallas: Word, 2004), 61.

7   Naff, "Lock up the 'ex-gays'."

8   Ibid.

9   http://www.outfront.org/library/exgay/facts, accessed August 30, 2010.

10   *Is It a Choice?*, 14.

11   *Just the Facts* (GLSEN Report), 6. Note GLESN's negative evaluation of "transformational ministries," ibid., 10.

12   http://www.glsen.org/cgi-bin/iowa/all/news/record/278.html, accessed August 30, 2010. For the story of Jallen Rix, a professing "gay evangelical Christian," who also describes the "fall out" from ex-gay groups – specifically, ex-gay ministries, see http://www.ecwr.org/resources/exgay_recovery.html, also accessed August 30, 2010.

13   http://www.exgay.com/exgaycom/exgay3.html, accessed August 30, 2010.

14   http://www.pflagupstatesc.org/reparative_therapy.htm, accessed August 30, 2010.

15   http://gaylife.about.com/library/blgaytherapy.htm, accessed August 30, 2010.

16   Ibid. Joe Kort "received his doctorate (PhD) in clinical sexology from the American Academy of Clinical Sexologists. Now an adjunct professor teaching Gay and Lesbian Studies at Wayne State University's School of Social Work, he is doing more writing and workshops on a national level." See http://www.joekort.com/about_joe.htm. For his explanation of how "so called reparative therapists" receive insurance funding for their work although it is opposed by major national organizations, see http://www.gaytoday.badpuppy.com/kortskorner/, both accessed August 30, 2010.

17   See the painful story recounted by Richard A. Isay, M.D., *Becoming Gay: The Journey to Self-Acceptance* (New York: Henry Holt, 1996), 99-109, one in which sexual morality and faithfulness to marital vows seems to play little or no role.

18   See further Dominic Davies and Charles Neal, eds., *Pink Therapy* (Maidenhead, Berkshire: Open University Press, 1996), and note www. pinktherapy.com.

19   New York: W. & W. Norton, 2008. See the many gay affirming therapies suggested in Kathleen J. Bieschke, Ruperto M. Perez, Kurt A. DeBord, eds., *Handbook of Counseling and Psychotherapy with Lesbian, Gay, and Bisexual Clients* (second ed.; Washington, DC: American Psychological Association, 2006); note that this is a publication of the APA, and it contains only gay-affirming therapies as opposed to gay-changing therapies.

20   See http://www.thetaskforce.org/downloads/reports/reports/CalculatedCompassion.pdf, Executive Summary, emphasis in the original; more fully, see http://www.thetaskforce.org/downloads/resources_and_tools/ChallengingExGay.pdf, both accessed August 30, 2010.

21   http://www.otkenyer.hu/truluck/truth_for_ever_on_the_scaffold.html, accessed August 30, 2010. For a less polemical statement, cf. Tanya Erzen, *Straight to Jesus: Sexual and Christian Conversions in the Ex-Gay Movement* (Berkeley: University of California Press, 2006); see also Michelle Wolkomir, *Be Not Deceived: The Sacred and Sexual Struggles of Gay and Ex-gay Christian Men* (New Brunswick, NJ: Rutgers University Press, 2006).

22   http://chicago.gopride.com/news/article.cfm/articleid/2759956, accessed August 30, 2010. Ironically, the registration fee for the seminar was $60 (or $50 for pre-registration) – hardly "big bucks" for an event of its kind. In contrast, registration fees advertised for the multi-day, 2011 National Gay and Lesbian Task Force annual conference ranged from $256 for pre-registration to $365 at the door, with special pricing for those with limited income at $150, while fees for the one-day Love Won Out conference on Sept. 25, 2010, were listed at $65 for pre-registration, $75 at the door, and $45 for students. So then,

would Ray Hill raise the same charges – or, even more serious charges – against the NGLT? I personally had the opportunity to see the inner workings of the Love Won Out conferences as a speaker in 2008 and 2009, and they were run on a very tight budget, needing to be underwritten by Focus on the Family (which actually devoted less than 3% of its annual budget to homosexual issues), since the conferences were a financial drain rather than a profit making venture. (They were certainly not a profit-making venture for the speakers!) In 2009, the conferences were transferred from Focus on the Family to Exodus International, but the nonsensical accusations of "bringing in the bucks through the ex-gay sham" have not let up; cf. this entry from Wayne Besen on the Truth Wins Out website from April 28, 2010, "It seems that Exodus has trouble finding genuine success stories to share and settles on a recycled cast of slick characters who inevitably have products to sell on the lucrative right wing speaking circuit. One wonders if the conference should be renamed 'Loot Wins Out'." See http://www.truthwinsout.org/pressreleases/2010/04/8443/, accessed September 19, 2010.

23 Wayne R. Besen, *Anything But Straight: Unmasking the Scandals and Lies Behind the Ex-Gay Myth* (New York: Harrington Park Press, 2003), 21, 18. According to Besen, "Focus on the Family is a bigoted hate group. They make money demeaning homosexuals and unsuccessfully trying to turn gay people straight." And, with reference to Focus on the Family being involved in one show on ABC "Extreme Makeover Home Edition," Besen writes, "One wonders if Hitler were alive, would ABC offer to trim his mustache or vacuum his house? ABC ought to drop this show immediately and stop all future cooperation with Focus on the Family." So, Dobson and Focus on the Family are comparable to Hitler! See http://www.waynebesen.com/2005/09/abc-must-dump-big-hair-home-makeover.html, accessed August 30, 2010.

24 *Is It a Choice?*, 142-143, with reference to Leroy Aarons, *Prayers for Bobby: A Mother's Coming to Terms with the Suicide of Her Gay Son* (San Francisco: Harper One, 1996).

25 *Anything But Straight*, 9.

26 http://www.waynebesen.com/2005/07/ex-gay-therapy-gone-awry.html, accessed August 30, 2010.

27 Ibid.

28 Ibid. For an attempt to support a similar perspective on legal grounds, see Karolyn Ann Hicks, "'Reparative'Therapy: Whether Parental Attempts to Change a Child's Sexual Orientation Can Legally Constitute Child Abuse," *American University Law Review* 49 (2000), 505-547, based on the premise that homosexual behavior is not immoral.

29 Speaking of a 2006 NGLTF report on the ex-gay movement's outreach to young people and children, Matt Foreman, then executive director of the NGLTF, said: "It is morally repugnant and downright dangerous the way these extremists demonize young people and prey on the fears of parents through their so-called ex-gay programs. This report exposes the extent to which these zealots will go, including reformulating their ex-gay snake oil at the expense of vulnerable children and young adults." He added, "These programs and conferences are often established in states that are fertile ground for right-wing organizing efforts, notably in states that are considering anti-same-sex marriage ballot measures. It is no wonder that their organizers are viewed as politically motivated." See http://www.thetaskforce.org/press/releases/pr923_030206, and cf. Jason Cianciotto and Sean Cahill, *Youth in the Crosshairs: The Third Wave of Ex-Gay Activism*, http://www.thetaskforce.org/reports_and_research/crosshairs, both accessed August 30, 2010.

30 http://www.waynebesen.com/2005/07/ex-gay-therapy-gone-awry.html, accessed August 30, 2010 (note that many of the posts here are laden with profanity and make for unsavory reading).

31 All the posts cited in the following paragraphs are from this same web page, cited immediately above, n. 30.

32 See, http://archive.frontpagemag.com/readArticle.aspx?ARTID=4944, accessed November 5, 2010. The article also notes, "'It was clear six years ago, and remains clear today,' said Focus on the Family President Don Hodel in December 2004, after NBC had defended Couric's comments, 'that Ms. Couric's tone and manner were not that of an impartial journalist seeking the truth about a tragedy. It was the tone and manner of an advocate intent on repeating an unfounded accusation disguised as a question.'"

33 According to New Testament teaching, to be "born again" or "born from above" (John 3:3, 5) includes receiving a new nature, since human nature itself is considered corrupt and fatally flawed. See, e.g., Ephesians 2:1-9; Romans 6; 2 Corinthians 5:17; Colossians 3:1-14. In keeping with this concept, all kinds of human orientations – including sexual – can be changed through faith in Jesus. Note the statement on the Exodus International website: "We believe and we have seen in thousands of lives that this freedom is possible through the power of God working in our hearts and minds. The bottom line - **you don't have to be gay!** You can lead a life of fulfillment and holiness as God intended, a life far better than what you have experienced so far." This then, would be a somewhat different approach than that of reparative therapy. The website continues, "The journey to wholeness isn't an easy one, but

we will be with you through the process. Our international network of Christian ministries, therapists and churches are devoted to providing the love and care you need as you pursue God, holiness, and healing." See http://www.exodusinternational.org/help/?option=com_content&task=view&id=327&Ite mid=147, accessed August 30, 2010.

34   See Tony Campolo's call for the church to repent for its attitudes towards homosexuals in *Speaking My Mind*, 73-74.

35   Posted on Besen's website, September 7, 2005, "'Ex-gay' Ministry Sued for Sex with Client," http://www.waynebesen.com/2005/09/ex-gay-ministry-sued-for-sex-with.html, accessed August 30, 2010. Ironically, the woman filing the suit, who claims to be a devout Christian, states that through prayer and Bible study, she *has* changed her sexual orientation! It is also interesting that this article referenced by Besen notes that: "A poll conducted in 2003 by the Pew Forum on Religion & Public Life showed that Americans are evenly split on opinions about whether they think gay people could change. The survey of 1,515 adults indicated that 42% said homosexuals could change their orientation, 42% said they couldn't and 16% had no opinion."

36   This is the consistent theme of Besen's more recent website, TruthWinsOut.org; see also the discussions on websites such as ExGayWatch.org and BoxTurtleBulletin.org, which are sometimes more nuanced. Cf. also the four-part series by Mark Benjamin published in Salon Magazine in 2005, see http://www.salon.com/news/feature/2005/07/18/ungay/index_np.html, accessed August 30, 2010.

37   http://www.otkenyer.hu/truluck/truth_for_ever_on_the_scaffold.html (see above, n. 20).

38   For their story in book form, see John and Anne Paulk, *Love Won Out* (Wheaton: Tyndale, 1999). Note that Besen has also questioned whether Anne Paulk was really a lesbian.

39   *Anything But Straight*, 15-16.

40   According to Besen, "The founder of every ex-gay ministry in America has proved to be an extraordinary failure. The two founders of Exodus International divorced their wives to move in together. The founder of Homosexuals Anonymous was accused of illicit behavior by his clients. . . . After seeing a parade of failures, lies, and fraud, why should we believe the guys in this film [called "I Do Exist"]?", as quoted by Natalie Troyer, "Film depicts gay reorientation," *Washington Times*, October 8, 2004, still available at http://www.cwfa.org/articles/6807/CFI/family/index.htm, accessed August 30, 2010. Besen's exaggerated comment reflects the almost invariable claim in gay circles that Bussee and Cooper were the founders of the Exodus International. In actuality, as stated in the main text, Bussee was one of the original board members while Cooper was one of his ministry helpers. The accurate story is as follows, as related by Warren Throckmorton, "Critic Ignores the Whole Truth About Ex-Gays," http://www.drthrockmorton.com/article.asp?id=156 (accessed August 30, 2010), "The original board of Exodus included 5 formerly gay identified people, including Mr. Bussee. The incorporators of the group included Frank Worthen, Ron Dennis and Greg Reid. None of these men have returned to homosexuality and two of the three are still in ex-gay ministry. One other original board member, although still straight, requested his name not be included in this article." There are a number of documentaries that attack the concept of "ex-gay," including *One Nation Under God* (1993); *Abomination: Homosexuality and the Ex-Gay Movement* (2006); and *The Bible Tells Me So* (2008); see also *Fish Don't Fly* (2005). For a response to the claims that ex-gays ministries are failing, see Bob Davies, "Are Exodus Ministries Flakey?", http://www.evergreeninternational.org/are_ministries_flakey.htm, where he notes that out of 147 ex-gay ministries cited in an anti-ex-gay study, ". . . 13 former Exodus ministries dissolved because the director returned to active homosexuality. Five of these 13 ministries collapsed prior to 1979. Only eight Exodus ministries have dissolved in the past 18 years due to a director's return to homosexuality–a gay related failure rate of 5%." Cf. also idem, "The Top Five Myths About Ex-Gay Ministry," http://www.evergreeninternational.org/davies.htm, where he lists as the #1 Myth, "EX-GAY MINISTRIES ARE A FRAUD," both accessed August 30, 2010.

41   *Anything But Straight*, back cover.

42   Actually, the question is not whether sexual orientation is a matter of choice in the first place, but: 1) What does one do with one's sexual orientation?, and 2) Is it possible to change one's sexual orientation?

43   For Besen's attack on Alan Chambers, the President of Exodus International, see http://www.waynebesen.com/2009/07/in-stunning-admission-ex-gay-activist.html, "In Stunning Admission, 'Ex-Gay' Activist Says He Lives In 'Self-Denial'" (accessed August 30, 2010), where Besen misunderstands the Christian concept of "self-denial." Besen is responding to an interview regarding Chambers' book, written with Yvette Schneider, *Leaving Homosexuality: A Practical Guide for Men and Women Looking for a Way Out* (Eugene, OR: Harvest House, 2009).

44   I'm aware that every statement in this sentence would be challenged by some; for further discussion, see below, Chapter Fourteen.

45   Satinover, *The Politics of Truth*, 179-209, notes that Christian, faith-based efforts to help people overcome

unwanted same-sex attractions appear to be more effective than "secular" efforts, to which, however, he also credits success.

46   For some moving examples from the Orthodox Jewish world, see the the HBO documentary *Trembling Before God*. For a strong, religious Jewish critique of the documentary, see Adam Jessel, M.S., "Unsung Heroes," in *Jewish Action*, Spring, 2003, available online at http://www.ou.org/publications/ ja/5763/5763spring/JUSTBETW.PDF. For a realistic assessment of both the challenges and possibilities of genuine change, see Sue Bohlin, "Can Homosexuals Change," http://bible.org/article/ can-homosexuals-change, both accessed January 2, 2011.

47   For one of the best-known contemporary stories, see Mel White, *Stranger at the Gate: To Be Gay and Christian in America* (New York: Plume, 1994).

48   Bruce Bawer, *Stealing Jesus: How Fundamentalism Betrays Christianity* (New York: Three Rivers, 1997), 254-255.

49   See "Seven Things I Wish Pro-Gay People Would Admit," http://www.evergreeninternational.org/7_ things.htm, accessed August 31, 2010.

50   Sometimes ex-gays are accused of becoming "breeders!" Cf. this interesting anecdote from Davies: ". . . back in the 1970s, there were picketers who would attend our seminars and conferences. They would hold up the most outrageous signs. One of my all-time favorites was the accusation that we were a 'fertility cult,' I guess because some of the single guys in our ministry eventually went on to become married and have children!" See http://www.evergreeninternational.org/davies.htm, accessed August 31, 2010.

51   See Rich Wyler "Anything but Straight: A Book Review," *NARTH Bulletin*, April, 2004, originally available at http://www.witnessfortheworld.org/besenbook.html, and downloaded January 10, 2006, but now only available through www.archive.org. At an event held by Grand State Valley University on June 12, 2009, I had the opportunity to ask Besen if he would repudiate these statements. He claimed, quite inaccurately, that he was simply quoting statements made by ex-gays as they had described their own struggles (particularly, when identified as gays). For an academically-based, even-handed review of *Anything But Straight*, see Mark A. Yarhouse, Psy. D., *Archives of Sexual Behavior* 35 (2006), 237-239.

52   Remember: It was this one incident in Paulk's life that proved beyond a doubt to Besen that Paulk never changed his sexual orientation. The possibility of a temporary moral lapse – however small – does not appear to be a possibility in Besen's mind, although it is quite in keeping with human nature. See also http://www.evergreeninternational.org/john_paulk.htm for a fair assessment, accessed August 24, 2010.

53   Rev. Irene Monroe, http://goqnotes.com/oped/oped_022407c.html, accessed August 24, 2010.

54   It would not be an overstatement to say that, just as John Paulk was once the "poster boy" for the ex-gay movement, he has now become the whipping post for all anti-ex-gay sentiments. In fact, it is hard to find an attack on the ex-gay movement that does not mention him directly or indirectly. A quick Internet search would quickly demonstrate this point. See, e.g., Naff, "Lock up the 'ex-gays'," who states, "The 'ex-gays' usually make headlines only when their leaders are caught emerging from a gay bar at 2 a.m. But they are everywhere these days."

55   See http://www.evergreeninternational.org/davies.htm, accessed August 24, 2010.

56   See http://www.citizenlink.com/2010/06/what-do-we-mean-when-we-talk-about-change/, accessed November 5, 2010.

57   See further, below, Chapter Thirteen. For a positive approach with useful guidelines, see the National Association for Research and Therapy of Homosexuality, Task Force on Practice Guidelines for the Treatment of Unwanted Same-Sex Attractions and Behavior, *Practice Guidelines for the Treatment of Unwanted Same-Sex Attractions and Behavior*, *Journal of Human Sexuality*, 2 (2010), 5-65 (with a useful bibliography); from a different perspective, but presenting alternatives to embracing a gay identity, see now http://sitframework.com/, with links. For some caveats to this approach, see A. A. Howsepian, "Treating Homosexuality: a Response to Yarhouse," *Christian Bioethics* 10 (2004), 259-267. For a clear legal defense of the ethics of sexual reorientation therapy, see Erin K. DeBoer, "Sex, Psychology, and the Religious 'Gerrymander': Why the APA's Forthcoming Policy Could Hurt Religious Freedom," *Regent University Law Review* 21 (2009), 407-427, available online at http://www.regent.edu/acad/ schlaw/student_life/studentorgs/lawreview/docs/issues/v21n2/13DeBoervol.21.2r-1%5B1%5D.pdf, both accessed December 15, 2010.

58   For background, see http://wthrockmorton.com/2008/02/15/i-think-aca-violated-its-policies-so-i-complained/; for Prof. Warren Throckmorton's letter of protest, signed by hundreds of professional counselors, see http://wthrockmorton.com/wp-content/uploads/2008/02/aca-complaint.doc. To my knowledge, although Dr. Brian Canfield, president of the ACA, promised to forward to these concerns to the Ethics Committee in April, 2008, there has been no action to date; see http://wthrockmorton. com/2008/04/01/aca-president-canfield-promises-ethics-committee-review/; all accessed August 24,

2010. See also, M. A. Yarhouse and W. Throckmorton, "Ethical issues in attempts to ban reorientation therapies," *Psychotherapy: Theory, Research, Practice, Training*, 39 (2002) 66–75.

59   http://psychology.ucdavis.edu/rainbow/html/facts_changing.html, accessed August 24, 2010.

60   See Douglas C. Haldeman, Ph.D., "The Pseudo-science of Sexual Orientation Conversion Therapy," *Angles: The Policy Journal of the Institute for Gay and Lesbian Strategic Studies* 4 (1999), 1-4 (here citing 2); available online at http://www.drdoughaldeman.com/doc/Pseudo-Science.pdf.

61   It also appears that Herek and Haldeman have failed to consider the pervasive *pro-gay* influences in today's society, encouraging kids in particular to come out as gay (or, at the least to experiment with their sexuality). Perhaps we should suggest to these good doctors that the only reason people choose to be gay is because of positive societal pressure (i.e., "internalized heterophobia")? Would that be any more absurd than the arguments they raise?

62   http://www.waynebesen.com/news/pr101404.htm, accessed August 24, 2010.

63   Ibid. In his September 1, 2005 column, Besen announced: "Right wing group Focus on the Family has lurid new website designed, in-part, to distort gay life. It is sad that a ministry that has the potential to help a lot of familes [sic] thinks that it must destroy gay families to carry out its mission." He was referring to the new troubledwith.com site, with a specific section devoted to homosexuality. I encourage every reader, gay and straight alike, to visit the website and, with a real attempt to be objective, to ask the question: How can this website be called "lurid"? See, in particular http://www.troubledwith.com/LoveandSex/Homosexuality.cfm, accessed August 24, 2010.

64   Based on the testimonials to Besen's speaking engagements posted on his website (see http://www.waynebesen.com/testimonials.htm), his presentation inflames lots of listeners, as indicated by the testimonial comment of Kelley Doherty, President of the Charlotte Business Guild, a gay and lesbian organization, in Charlotte, NC: "Captivating! Compelling! There's no better way to learn about this historically relevant subject than to relive *the perversion* of the ex-gay ministries with Wayne Besen as your guide" (accessed August 24, 2010, my emphasis). Besen is to be commended as an excellent communicator who believes passionately in his cause – anyone who has watched his anti-ex-gay presentation can attest to this – but whose rhetoric goes over the top and whose charges are often exaggerated or unfounded.

65   http://www.waynebesen.com/2005/06/twelve-shows-that-logo-should-consider.html, accessed August 24, 2010.

66   See www.pathinfo.org, under, "We Advocate Compassion and Respect." See also Christopher Doyle, "Equality for All," http://pfox-exgays.blogspot.com/2010/05/equality-for-all.html (May 17, 2010, and accessed on that date.)

67   Jeff Konrad, *You Don't Have to Be Gay: Hope and Freedom for Males Struggling with Homosexuality or for Those Who Know of Someone Who Is* (rev. ed.; Hilo, HI: Pacific Publishing, 1992), n.p.

68   Mike Haley, *101 Frequently Asked Questions about Homosexuality* (Eugene, Oregon: Harvest House, 2004), 15.

69   Ibid., 21.

70   Ibid., 86-87.

71   See Bob Davies statement, "Seven Things I Wish Pro-Gay People Would Admit," posted on http://www.evergreeninternational.org/7_things.htm, accessed August 24, 2010. For excellent examples of a Christian-based approach to ministering to men and women with unwanted homosexual desires, see Joe Dallas and Nancy Heche, eds., *The Complete Christian Guide to Understanding Homosexuality: A Biblical and Compassionate Response to Same-Sex Attraction* (Eugene, OR: Harvest House, 2010), 219-359. See also Alan Chambers, ed., *God's Grace and the Homosexual Next Door* (Eugene, OR: Harvest House, 2006). More broadly, with a focus on both personal and social issues, see Debbie Thurman, *Post-Gay? Post-Christian?: Anatomy of a Cultural and Faith Identity Crisis* (Madison Heights, VA: Cedar House Publishers, 2011).

72   http://peoplecanchange.com/change/possible.php, "Research Shows Change Is Real," accessed December 20, 2010. For Newman's (i.e., Wyler's) insightful critique of Besen's *Anything But Straight*, see above, n. 51.

73   Jessel, "Unsung Heroes," cited above, n. 46, my emphasis. The article claims that, "Jewish men struggling with homosexual attractions must battle on two fronts—their own desires and a culture that devalues their struggle."

74   In an email sent to me January 2, 2011, during the final proofreading of the manuscript. He also supplied me with the Jessel quote.

75   See http://www.youtube.com/watch?v=-2oHXsstW8c; for an impassioned response to this program, see http://www.youtube.com/watch?v=cPI0BXvDGWU, both accessed December 15, 2010.

76   For the full text, see http://www.jonahweb.org/article.php?secId=298, accessed November 24, 2010.

77   http://www.exodusinternational.org/stories, accessed Sept. 1, 2010; for every one of these names, another hundred – or thousand – would add their voices and say, "Listen to my story too!" This is the emphasis of Exodus, from their home page: "Though homosexuality continues to gain cultural acceptance, many who consider themselves gay or experience homosexual tendencies feel puzzled and even apprehensive about their sexuality — *If this is normal, why am I so confused? Do I have a choice in the matter?* Perhaps you've struggled with same-sex attraction, making you wonder if you're gay. Maybe you've even sought to meet your needs for companionship and acceptance through a same-gender relationship. If so, realize that you do have a choice in the matter. You're not simply 'wired that way.' For those with unanswered questions or a desire to change, we offer a compassionate message of transformation and truth." For other online testimonies of individuals mentioned here, along with others not mentioned, see, e.g., http://www.zacchaeus.ca/mario.html; http://www.masteringlife.org/; http://www.witnessfortheworld. org/founder.html; see also Charlene E. Cothran, http://www.venusmagazine.org/cover_story.html; Janet Boynes, http://www.janetboynesministries.com/; Stephen Bennett, http://www.sbministries.org/ members/sbm; all accessed Sept. 1, 2010. Note also that these websites just referenced are all to ex-gays who today are in full-time ministry, hence the prominence of their testimonies online. See also above, n. 76. While it is possible that, ten years from now, not everyone listed here will be walking strongly in an ex-gay identity, bear in mind that: 1) There are thousands of names that could have been listed. This is just a tiny sampling of those whose stories are better known. 2) If only 90% (or, really, only 50%, or even 25%) of those who claimed to come out of homosexuality really did, that would still demonstrate the fact that people can and do change their sexual orientation.

78   Besen, of course, would say yes! "I have long said that there are virtually no longterm 'ex-gays' who are not on the payroll of right wing organizations or working for a ministry." See http://www.waynebesen. com/blog/2005_07_17_archive.html, Thursday, July 21, 2005 (accessed Sept. 2, 2010), with incredibly specious evidence garnered to support this extraordinary claim, which can be refuted anecdotally by hearing the stories of those in churches or synagogues throughout America who came out of homosexuality, who shun the spotlight, and who are on nobody's payroll (my late brother-in-law, David Fenton, would be one of those).

79   Most ex-gay websites contain sections for testimonies; see, e.g., www.jonahweb.org, sub "Our Stories"; www.newdirection.ca, sub "Telling Our Stories"; and see also above, n. 69. For testimony books, see, e.g., Bob Davies and Lela Gilbert, *Portraits of Freedom: 14 People Who Came Out of Homosexuality* (Downers Grove, IL: InterVarsity Press, 2001); Swan, *Closing the Closet*; cf. also Goldberg, *Light in the Closet*, 532-69. Cf. also Perri W. Roberts, *Dying for Love: The Plain Truth About Homosexuality* (Enumclaw, WA: WinePress Publishing, 2003), for a lengthy personal account and an emphasis on spiritual deliverance; see further http://www.gaysavedbyjesus.com/. For a moving account by a man who has chosen to be a celibate Christian because of (as of the writing of his book) unchanged same-sex attractions, see Wesley Hill, *Washed and Waiting: Reflections on Christian Faithfulness and Homosexuality* (Grand Rapids: Zondervan, 2010). For Christian books discussing compassionate outreach to gays and lesbians, see, e.g., W. P. Campbell, *Turning Controversy into Church Ministry: A Christlike Response to Homosexuality* (Grand Rapids: Zondervan, 2010); Dr. Brian Keith Williams, *Ministering Graciously to the Gay and Lesbian Community* (Shippensburg, PA: Destiny Image, 2005); Briar Whitehead, *Craving for Love: Relationship Addiction, Homosexuality, and the God Who Heals* (Grand Rapids: Monarch Books, 2003); for a slightly more controversial approach, challenging some conservative Christians, see Chad W. Thompson, *Loving Homosexuals as Jesus Would: A Fresh Christian Approach* (Grand Rapids: Brazos, 2004). For a comprehensive statement of the method of reparative therapy, see Joseph J. Nicolosi, Ph.D., *Shame and Attachment Loss: The Practical Work of Reparative Therapy* (Downers Grove, IL: IVP Academic, 2009).

80   http://pfox.org/default.html, accessed December 15, 2010.

81   See http://www.jonahweb.org/index.php; the organization was originally named Jews Offering New Alternatives to Healing, but changed their name in 2010. For Wayne Besen's anachronistic claim regarding the changing of the name, see http://www.truthwinsout.org/pressreleases/2010/07/10016/, accessed December 15, 2010. The leadership of JONAH informed me that the name change was planned before the "scandal" of which Besen speaks and, not surprisingly, had nothing to do with him at all.

82   For a convenient listing of these organizations, with links, see http://www.pathinfo.org/, accessed December 15, 2010.

83   See below, Chapter Thirteen, and cf. now Stanton L. Jones and Mark A. Yarhouse, *Ex-Gays: A Longitudinal Study of Religiously Mediated Change in Sexual Orientation* (Downers Grove, IL: IVP Academic, 2007).

84   Note that there are also "ex-gays" who have simply rejected a "gay identity" and are living satisfied

celibate lives, without becoming heterosexual (at least, as of yet), some of whom I know personally.

Chapter 13

1   This was the third edition, commonly known as *DSM-III*. The much-anticipated *DSM-V* is currently in the revision process, with the final version due out in 2013.

2   American Psychiatric Association, *Position Statement on Homosexuality*, December, 1992, cited in "A False Focus on My Family," http://www.soulforce.org/pdf/false_focus.pdf, 4, accessed August 6, 2010.

3   http://www.rainbowhistory.org/apazap.htm, accessed August 6, 2010.

4   Barbara Gittings, "Preface: Show-and-Tell," in Jack Drescher, MD, and Joseph P. Merlino, MD, MPA, eds., *American Psychiatry and Homosexuality: An Oral History* (New York: Harrington Park Press, 2007), xv.

5   Report of the American Psychological Association Task Force on Appropriate Therapeutic Responses to Sexual Orientation (Washington, DC: American Psychological Association, 2009), 54 (and repeated *passim* in the report); my emphasis.

6   Ibid., 119

7   Ibid., 121, my emphasis. According to http://www.rainbowhistory.org/apazap.htm, accessed August 6, 2010, this was a position that gay activists had been advocating since 1965, when the (pioneer gay lib organization) Mattachine Society of Wasthington "was on the record stating that homosexuality and heterosexuality were equally 'normal'.

8   http://mccph.wordpress.com/2008/02/. This is the website of the Metropolitan Community Churches of the Philippines, accessed August 6, 2010. For further quotes supporting these positions, see http://www.soulforce.org/pdf/false_focus.pdf, 5 (see above, n. 2).

9   http://www.rainbowhistory.org/apazap.htm, cited above, n. 3.

10 Quoting Arthur Evans, http://gaytoday.badpuppy.com/garchive/viewpoint/083099vi.htm, accessed August 6, 2010.

11 http://www.rainbowhistory.org/apazap.htm, cited above, n. 3.

12 http://en.wikipedia.org/wiki/John_E._Fryer, accessed December 29, 2010.

13 Ronald Bayer, *Homosexuality and American Psychiatry* (With a new Afterword; Princeton, NJ: Princeton University Press, 1987), 3-4.

14 Ibid., 140-41.

15 Ibid., 141.

16 Ibid.

17 Ibid.

18 A. Dean Byrd, http://www.narth.com/docs/destructive.html, accessed August 6, 2010, summarizing material from Rogers H. Wright and Nicholas A. Cummings, eds., *Destructive Trends in Mental Health: The Well-Intentioned Path to Harm* (New York: Routledge, 2005), 9. For more on this important volume, see below.

19 Bayer, *Homosexuality and American Psychiatry*, 145.

20 Ibid.

21 Ibid., 146.

22 Ibid., 148.

23 Jeffrey Satinover, M.D., *Homosexuality and the Politics of Truth* (Grand Rapids: Baker, 1996), 35.

24 His last book on the subject, which can only be deemed intolerant by the intolerant, was *Homosexuality: A Freedom Too Far* (Phoenix, AZ: Adam Margrave Books, 1995). Note that he dedicated the book, "To my homosexual patients, whose courage and endurance in the search for self-knowledge have made this work possible." For contrasting assessments of Socarides, see http://www.narth.com/docs/socobits.html. For Socarides' account of how the APA depathologized homosexuality, see http://www.narth.com/docs/annals.html, both accessed August 6, 2010.

25 Charles W. Socarides "Sexual Politics and Scientific Logic: The Issue of Homosexuality," *The Journal of Psychohistory*, 10:3 (1992), 315.

26 Bayer, *Homosexuality and American Psychiatry*, 4.

27 *Oral History*, 86; Marmor refers to Bayer's volume as "otherwise excellent," and he blames "'The so-called 'politics' surrounding the decision" on "opponents led by Drs. Irving Bieber and Charles Socarides" (ibid).

28 Cf. http://www.narth.com/menus/future.html, accessed August 6, 2010.

29 http://www.narth.com/menus/mission.html, accessed August 6, 2010.

30 See esp. B. Rind, P. Tromovitch, and R. Bauserman, "A Meta-Analytic Examination of Assumed Properties of Child Sexual Abuse Using College Samples," *Psychological Bulletin* 124 (1998), 22–53. The Wikipedia entry contains a useful review of the controversy and primary documents. See http://en.wikipedia.org/wiki/Rind_et_al._controversy, and cf. http://www.narth.com/docs/whatapa.html,

both accessed August 6, 2010.

31   http://www.narth.com/docs/masquerades.html, accessed August 6, 2010.

32   "In Defense of the Need for Honest Dialogue," http://www.narth.com/docs/indefense.html, accessed August 6, 2010.

33   Wright and Cummings, *Destructive Trends in Mental Health*, xiv. According to family therapist Adam Jessel, "The climate in the mental health community has become so hostile to such treatment that even mentioning it can lead to therapists being ostracized or blacklisted.
      "A case in point: A therapist I know asked members of an online discussion group of mental health professionals for ideas to help a client reduce his SSA. The reaction against him was so virulent that the moderator had to step in and end the discussion (although the offending therapist did get a number of private replies with suggestions and ideas). And yet this was a message board that claimed to be devoted to therapy techniques that 'honor the client's wishes.'" See http://www.ou.org/publications/ja/5763/5763spring/JUSTBETW.PDF (cited above, Chapter Twelve, n. 73).

34   Ibid., xv. Note, however, the outstanding endorsements the book received once published. As noted by Prof. Warren Throckmorton, "Drs. Wright and Cummings cannot be dismissed as disgruntled conservatives. Their deeds validate their claim to be lifelong liberal activists." See conveniently http://www.amazon.com/Destructive-Trends-Mental-Health-Intentioned/dp/0415950864/ref=dp_return_2?ie=UTF8&n=283155&s=books, accessed August 6, 2010.

35   *Destructive Trends in Mental Health*, xvi.

36   Nicholas A. Cummings and William T. O'Donahue, "Psychology's Surrender to Political Correctness," in ibid., 9. The chapter runs from 3-27.

37   http://www.narth.com/docs/cummings.html, accessed August 12, 2010.

38   A. Dean Byrd, http://www.narth.com/docs/destructive.html, accessed August 6, 2010. See J. D. Gartner, "Antireligious prejudice in admissions to doctoral programs in clinical psychology," *Professional Psychology: Research and Practice* 17 (1986), 473-475.

39   Byrd, ibid.

40   Richard E. Redding, "Sociopolitical Diversity in Psychology: The Case for Pluralism," in *Destructive Trends in Mental Health*, 312; the chapter runs from 303-324.

41   Ibid., 318.

42   New York: Routledge, 2008. Cf. also Sally Satel, M.D., "PC, M.D.: How Political Correctness Is Corrupting Medicine," in *American Experiment Quarterly*, Fall 2001, 55-67, available online at http://www.americanexperiment.org/uploaded/files/aeqv4n3satel.pdf, accessed January 2, 2011. More fully, idem, *PC, M.D.: How Political Correctness Is Corrupting Medicine* (New York: Basic Books, 2000). Dr. Satel is currently with the Yale School of Medicine.

43   Nicholas A. Cummings and William T. O'Donohue *Eleven Blunders that Cripple Psychotherapy in America: A Remedial Unblundering* (New York: Routledge, 2008), 213-14.

44   See above, n. 34.

45   *Eleven Blunders*, 211 (with references on 227-228, n. 15).

46   Ibid., 212.

47   See http://www.narth.com/docs/cummings.html, cited in n. 37, above.

48   http://www.narth.com/docs/barring.html, accessed August 12, 2010.

49   Ibid.

50   "Same Office, Different Aspirations," APA *Monitor on Psychology*, December 2001, 20, cited in ibid.

51   http://www.narth.com/docs/barring.html, cited above, n. 48.

52   Ibid.

53   To illustrate the point, when I did a Google search of this list of organizations on August 6, 2010, the first item that came up was a well-known, gay-slanted publication for schools called "Just the Facts About Sexual Orientation." See http://www.naswdc.org/pressroom/media/justthefacts.pdf.

54   See further Jeffrey B. Satinover, "The 'Trojan Couch': How the Mental Health Associations Misrepresent Science," http://www.narth.com/docs/TheTrojanCouchSatinover.pdf, accessed December 28. 2010.

55   Bayer, *Homosexuality and American Psychiatry*, 140.

56   "Gay Rights vs. Sexual Reorientation Therapy," http://thelivingcenter.150m.com/Articles.htm, accessed December 29, 2010.

57   http://www.peoplecanchange.com/stories/rich.php, accessed December 30, 2010.

58   http://www.lifesitenews.com/news/archive/ldn/2009/aug/09081407, accessed December 30, 2010. Cf. also Adam Jessel's comments, "In today's climate, if Bill tells me that he is attracted to his neighbor Fred's young child and he wants to reduce these attractions, I, as a therapist, can try to help him. If Bill has an unwanted attraction to Fred's wife, this too is something I am permitted to help him with. But if Bill has an unwanted attraction to Fred himself, then it's regarded as unethical for me to help." See

http://www.ou.org/publications/ja/5763/5763spring/JUSTBETW.PDF, cited above, n. 33.

59   Cf. further the chapter on "The Politics of Treatment" in Joseph Nicolosi, Ph.D., and Linda Ames Nicolosi, *A Parent's Guide to Preventing Homosexuality* (Downers Grove, IL: InterVarsity Press, 2002), 166-181.

60   Wayne R. Besen, *Anything But Straight: Unmasking the Scandals and Lies Behind the Ex-Gay Myth* (New York: Harrington Park Press, 2003), 241.

61   A. Dean Byrd, "Spitzer Study Critiqued in the Journal of Gay and Lesbian Psychotherapy," http://www.narth.com/docs/spitzer4.html, accessed December 30, 2010.

62   Cited by Byrd, ibid.

63   Deroy Murdock, "Gays Can Go Straight. And Straights Can Go Gay," http://www.nationalreview.com/articles/204921/gays-can-go-straight/deroy-murdock, accessed August 24, 2010.

64   Ariel Shidlo & Michael Schroeder, "Changing Sexual Orientation: A Consumer's Report," *Professional Psychology: Research and Practice* 33 (2002), 249-259.

65   For a useful, short statement on the two studies, see Warren Throckmorton's observations at "Montel Williams, Ted Haggard and the Psychiatrist," http://www.drthrockmorton.com/article.asp?id=201; for a side-by-side comparison of the studies, with reference to relevant further discussion, see http://web.archive.org/web/20041211162352/www.newdirection.ca/research/spitzers-peers.htm, both accessed August 29, 2010.

66   Michael Schroeder and Ariel Shidlo, "Ethical Issues in Sexual Orientation Conversion Therapies: An Empirical Study of Consumers," in idem and idem and Jack Drescher, *Sexual Conversion Therapy: Ethical, Clincial, and Research Perspectives* (Binghamton, NY: Haworth Medical Press, 2002), 131-66.

67   In a fascinating sidebar, Shidlo and Schroeder inadvertently discovered that some gay men did, in fact, have positive results from sexual reorientation therapy, despite the fact that, initially, they were *only* looking for negative reports about gay men's experiences with attempts to change their orientation. See the Throckmorton article cited in n. 65, above.

68   http://www.drthrockmorton.com/article.asp?id=201, cited above, n. 65. To quote this in full, Throckmorton wrote, "Drs. Shidlo and Schroeder interviewed 202 people who had pursued sexual reorientation. When the authors began, the project was titled: 'Homophobic Therapies: Documenting the Damage.' In other words, these researchers looked for people who were harmed and so it is no surprise that the vast majority of their subjects said the therapy did not work. Later in the study, they opened their research up to people who benefited from reorientation because some of these people began to contact them."

69   http://www.narth.com/docs/berman.html, accessed December 30, 2010, emphasis in the original.

70   http://www.narth.com/docs/popmusic.html, accessed December 30, 2010.

71   Ibid.

72   Ibid.

73   Ibid. Links to the video of Povia's performance are embedded in the article; or, go to: http://www.narth.com/videos/povia.html or http://www.youtube.com/watch?v=583GBge-U-c for a studio version; both accessed December 30, 2010.

74   Dr. Joseph Nicolosi, at that time president of NARTH (i.e., in 2007), did, in fact, express his sentiments when the APA task force was formed: "My impression, looking over this list, is amusement - and then anger. First, the amusement: the APA never stops talking about its passion for 'diversity.' Where is the worldview diversity on this list?
"Next, the anger. We offered a strong list of candidates. All were rejected.
"Judging from these members' backgrounds, I do not believe this task force will be fair in its analysis of appropriate therapies. By rejecting any real reorientation therapist for the task force and stacking it with so many gay-affirmative opponents of sexual reorientation, the committee has already pre-determined what it will find.
"I predict that this task force will recommend ruling that reparative therapy is unethical and harmful to individuals and should be banned by the APA.
"Such a conclusion will inevitably violate patient autonomy and self-determination, and will silence intellectual diversity.
"We will fight this effort with all of our resources." See http://www.narth.com/docs/lacks.html. Thankfully, the report was not quite as bad as Nicolosi expected, although his predictions were not far off; for a more popular perspective, see Rich Wyler, "The APA Remains Unconvinced By The Evidence -- So What?", http://people-can-change.blogspot.com/2009/08/apa-remains-unconvinced-by-evidence-so.html; both accessed December 30, 2010.

75   See again http://www.narth.com/docs/lacks.html.

76   See, e.g., http://www.truthwinsout.org/blog/2009/10/4301/, accessed December 30, 2010.

77 New York: Routledge, 2008.

78 See, e.g., "Sexual conversion ('reparative') therapies: A history and update," in B. E. Jones and M. J. Hill, eds., *Mental Health Issues in Lesbian, Gay, Bisexual, and Transgender Communities* (*Review of Psychiatry*, 21:4; Washington, DC: American Psychiatric Press, 2002), 71-91; see also the volume edited by Drescher, Shidlo, and Schroeder, *Sexual Conversion Therapy*, cited above, n. 66.

79 See, e.g., Jack Drescher, "Gold or Lead? Introductory Remarks on Conversions," in idem and Kenneth J. Zucker, eds., *Ex-Gay Research: Analyzing the Spitzer Study and Its Relation to Science, Religion, Politics, and Culture* (New York: Harrington Park Press, 2006), 13-26 (see 16 for a specific example).

80 See further http://www.stjohns.edu/academics/graduate/liberalarts/departments/psychology/faculty/greene/publications.stj, accessed December 30, 2010.

81 Roger L. Worthington, "Heterosexual Identities, Sexual Reorientation Therapies, and Science," in *Ex-Gay Research: Analyzing the Spitzer Study*, 209-215, here quoting 213.

82 Ibid.

83 http://www.boxturtlebulletin.com/2007/05/22/372, accessed August 6, 2010.

84 http://www.apadivision44.org/honors/clarity.php, accessed August 6, 2010.

85 Kathleen Melonakos, M.A., R.N., "Why Isn't Homosexuality Considered A Disorder On The Basis Of Its Medical Consequences?," http://www.leaderu.com/orgs/narth/medconsequences.html, accessed August 6, 2010.

86 http://www.josephnicolosi.com/apa-task-force/, accessed August 6, 2010.

87 This was the official description of the selection process: "Task Force members were selected after an open nominations process. *All nominations were reviewed by the APA Committee on Lesbian, Gay, Bisexual and Transgender Concerns* (CLGBTC) which forwarded the complete list of nominations and a suggested slate of nominees to the APA Board for the Advancement of Psychology in the Public Interest (BAPPI) for review. The CLGBTC and BAPPI recommendations as well as the full list of nominations were then sent to the APA President who made the final appointments to the task force in consultation with the APA Board of Directors" (my emphasis). See http://www.emaxhealth.com/48/12282.html, accessed August 6, 2010. Note that in 2009, at the same convention in which the Task Force report was released, Stanton L. Jones and Mark A. Yarhouse were given the opportunity to discuss the findings of their six-year study of individuals who went through Exodus-related ministries; see their volume *Ex-Gays: A Longitudinal Study of Religiously Mediated Change in Sexual Orientation* (Downers Grove, IL: IVP Academic, 2007).

88 The first headline yielded 366,000 hits on Google on August 22, 2009; the second headline was from a local publication (Salt Lake City) and simply provides a typical example of the way things were reported; the third headline circulated on gay websites, such as: http://www.q-notes.com/3360/apa-exposes-ex-gay-myth/, accessed December 30, 2010.

89 See http://www.usnews.com/blogs/god-and-country/2009/08/21/does-the-american-psychological-association-want-gays-to-switch-churches.html, accessed December 30, 2010.

90 http://www.advocate.com/news_detail_ektid107255.asp; the comment was posted by Alex on August 25, 2009, 1:53 PM, accessed December 30, 2010. For those unfamiliar with Advocate.com, it is the oldest, and still highly influential, gay website.

91 Ibid., posted at 2:20 PM, August 25, 2009.

92 Ariel Shidlo, Ph.D., Michael Schroeder, Psy.D., and Jack Drescher, M.D., eds., *Sexual Conversion Therapy: Ethical, Clinical, and Research Perspectives* (Binghamton, NY: The Haworth Medical Press, 2001), co-published simultaneously as *Journal of Gay and Lesbian Psychotherapy* 5 (Numbers 3-4); the endorsements cited are found on the back cover of the book, from psychology professor Marvin R. Goldfried and research scientist Joyce Hunter, respectively.

93 Not surprisingly, anti-ex-gay activist Wayne Besen (among many other gay leaders) cited the APA report as confirmation that reorientation therapy was harmful; see http://www.waynebesen.com/2009/08/apa-no-evidence-in-support-of-ex-gay.html (notice the Patrick McAlvey video at the beginning of the article); in an animated, cartoon video between a straight Orthodox Jew and a "gay Orthodox Jew," the former is pointing out to the latter the many dangers associated with gay, male sex, as pointed out in the recent CDC report, discussed in this chapter, below (see also above, Chapter Eleven). At one point, the straight Orthodox Jew asks, "Can anyone seriously believe that reparative therapy is more dangerous than a lifestyle that is factually proven to infect one of out five of its members with a deadly, life-threatening disease?"; see http://www.youtube.com/watch?v=lSTCO-5soVE; see also "A Conversation with a Gay Orthodox Jew," http://www.youtube.com/watch?v=jUNYBisUe8E; all accessed December 30, 2010.

94 On a positive note, on August 12, 2010, at the APA annual convention (held in San Diego), a number of NARTH psychologists participated in a symposium which critiqued aspects of the APA's report. It was

entitled, "APA Task Force on Sexual Orientation: Science, Diversity and Ethicality," and was chaired by A. Dean Byrd. For the report, see http://www.narth.com/docs/Symposium2010.pdf, accessed December 30, 2010.

95   See above, n. 5, for references.

96   Compare this 2009 statement with the American Psychological Association's 1998 statement: "There is considerable recent evidence to suggest that biology, including genetic or inborn hormonal factors, play a significant role in a person's sexuality," still available at http://www.apa.org/helpcenter/sexual-orientation.aspx, accessed December 30, 2010.

97   See above, Chapter Six, for further discussion of the "nature vs. nurture" debate.

98   Andrew Marin, *Love Is an Orientation* (Downers Grove, IL: IVP Books, 2009), 42; Marin is quick to note that, "Even though these stories exist, we must be careful not to generalize abuse as an explanation of why GLBT people are the way they are – as research suggests that on average only 7 to 15 percent of the GLBT community was sexually abused in their youth" (ibid.). Since he cites no sources for these figures, it is difficult to evaluate what "research" he is referring to (although, at the time of writing his book, his organization was involved in a major research project); others have suggested much higher figures, especially counselors and therapists who have spoken to me privately, relating their own, anecdotal experiences. For Marin's very poor use of representation of the biblical witness concerning homosexual practice, see above, Chapter Ten, n. 12.

99   http://thesaurus.reference.com/browse/positive, accessed December 30, 2010.

100 http://www.advocate.com/news_detail_ektid105247.asp, accessed December 20, 2010. See also David Fergusson et al., "Is Sexual Orientation Related to Mental Health Problems and Suicidality in Young People?," *Archives of General Psychiatry* 56 (1999), 876-880, and Richard Herrell et al., "Sexual Orientation and Suicidality: Co-twin Control Study in Adult Men," in ibid., 867-874.

101 Ibid. The report was published in *BMC Psychiatry*.

102 James E. Phelan, Neil Whitehead, and Philip M. Sutton, "What Research Shows: NARTH's Response to the APA Claims on Homosexuality," A Report of the Scientific Advisory Committee of the National Association for Research and Therapy of Homosexuality, *Journal of Human Sexuality* 1 (2009), 93.

103 Prof. Douglas Farrow, "The Government of Québec Declares War on a 'homophobic' and 'heterosexist' populace," http://www.ccrl.ca/doc/Farrow%20article%20for%20upload.pdf, 8, accessed December 20, 2010, when the *Québec policy against homophobia* makes reference to high rates of depression and suicide among GLBT's , it "is acknowledged mainly for the purpose of further tarnishing the intolerant. 'The risk of suicidal thoughts or suicide attempts,' we are told, 'is between six and sixteen times greater for young gays and bisexuals than for young heterosexuals. Young lesbians are almost five times more likely to attempt suicide than heterosexual girls.' And who is responsible for that? Over and over again, the culprit is the homophobe: 'Various health problems, especially in the field of mental health, affect *the victims of homophobia*: stress, isolation, psychological distress, suicidal thoughts, etc.'" (Farrow is citing p. 26 of the policy, his emphasis; see also 9, 14, 20, 25, 26-27.) Farrow, ibid., 8, writes, "If everyone can be persuaded not only to tolerate but to celebrate homosexuality, runs the argument, then the reasons why one might not celebrate it – those dark realities of depression and suicide – will disappear and it will turn out to be worth celebrating."

104 http://www.advocate.com/news_detail_ektid30767.asp, cited above, n. 100. The article concludes: "Centers for Disease Control and Prevention researchers say the rising syphilis rates among gay men is partly fueled by HIV complacency. They say that because newer anti-HIV medications are so effective in controlling HIV disease, more gay men are engaging in unprotected sex because they are less worried about serious complications or even death due to AIDS. The CDC plans to work more closely with local health departments and community-based organizations to craft syphilis awareness and testing campaigns targeting sexually active gay and bisexual men." Cf. also http://www.edgeboston.com/index.php?ch=news&sc&sc3&id=110029, accessed December 20, 2010.

105 Matt Comer, http://www.q-notes.com/3314/syphilis-on-the-rise/, accessed December 20, 2010. The article was dealing with the rise of syphilis cases being reported in Mecklenberg County, North Carolina.

106 Originally accessed http://www.sovo.com/2009/8-28/news/localnews/10521.cfm, September 15, 2009, but now available at http://www.boxturtlebulletin.com/category/surveys-statistics/page/2; for a gay reflection on this, see Timothy Kincaid's comments at http://www.boxturtlebulletin.com/2009/08/28/14358; for a conservative Christian perspective, see http://www.lifesitenews.com/ldn/2009/aug/09082609.html, all accessed December 29, 2010.

107 http://www.fda.gov/BiologicsBloodVaccines/BloodBloodProducts/QuestionsaboutBlood/ucm108186.htm, accessed December 29, 2010. The report was dealing with questions about restrictions on blood donations by men who have sex with men, and it had to address the question of discrimination: "FDA's deferral policy is based on the documented increased risk of certain transfusion transmissible infections,

such as HIV, associated with male-to-male sex and is not based on any judgment concerning the donor's sexual orientation."

Men who have sex with men also have an increased risk of having other infections that can be transmitted to others by blood transfusion. For example, infection with the Hepatitis B virus is about 5-6 times more common and Hepatitis C virus infections are about 2 times more common in men who have sex with other men than in the general population. Additionally, men who have sex with men have an increased incidence and prevalence of Human Herpes Virus-8 (HHV-8). HHV-8 causes a cancer called Kaposi's sarcoma in immunocompromised individuals. . . .

Having had a low number of partners is known to decrease the risk of HIV infection. However, to date, no donor eligibility questions have been shown to reliably identify a subset of MSM (e.g., based on monogamy or safe sexual practices) who do not still have a substantially increased rate of HIV infection compared to the general population or currently accepted blood donors. In the future, improved questionnaires may be helpful to better select safe donors, but this cannot be assumed without evidence.

108 See above, Chapter Eleven, for details.

109 I put "monogamous" in quotes because the different definition the word often carries in gay circles, especially among gay men, as discussed in Chapter Eleven, above.

110 http://news.bio-medicine.org/medicine-news-3/Study-shows-that-anal-cytology-predicts-anal-precancer-in-HIV-positive-gay-men-1428-1/; accessed December 29, 2010. I inserted brackets in the quote for clarity, where parentheses seemed to be missing in the original source cited. No additional words, however, have been added.

111 http://www.cdc.gov/nchhstp/Newsroom/msmpressrelease.html, accessed December 29, 2010. The report states that, "Research shows that a range of complex factors contribute to the high rates of HIV and syphilis among gay and bisexual men. These factors include high prevalence of HIV and other STDs among MSM, which increases the risk of disease exposure, and limited access to prevention services. Other factors are complacency about HIV risk, particularly among young gay and bisexual men; difficulty of consistently maintaining safe behaviors with every sexual encounter over the course of a lifetime; and lack of awareness of syphilis symptoms and how it can be transmitted (e.g., oral sex). Additionally, factors such as homophobia and stigma can prevent MSM from seeking prevention, testing, and treatment services." Is anyone surprised that homophobia would also be cited as a factor?

112 As noted by Bob Ellis, August 26, 2009, http://www.dakotavoice.com/2009/08/cdc-official-aids-rate-is-50x-higher-in-homosexual-men/, accessed December 29, 2010: "The dangers of homosexual behavior have been long known to anyone with eyes to see them and ears to hear them, despite the 'mainstream' media's efforts to sweep this information under the rug and pretend it doesn't exist; they are, after all, willing and eager participants in the effort to whitewash homosexuality in the eyes of the public.

"Yet the information keeps popping up in places like the Centers for Disease Control (CDC), the New England Journal of Medicine, the Department of Justice, the American Sociological Review, the Archives of General Psychology, the Washington Blade, the Journal of Sex Research and more. No matter how badly the minions of political correctness want it to stay buried, the truth keeps slipping out."

113 Phelan, Whitehead, and Sutton, "What Research Shows: NARTH's Response to the APA Claims on Homosexuality," *Journal of Human Sexuality* 1 (2009), 87. Note that the entire report is 106 pages long, including a twenty-seven page list of bibliographical references.

114 http://www.narth.com/docs/berman.html, cited above, n. 69.

115 http://open.salon.com/blog/max_the_communist/2009/08/15/bi_health_summit_exposes_critical_health_needs, accessed December 29, 2010.

116 http://americansfortruth.com/news/researcher-74-percent-of-bisexuals-experienced-child-sex-abuse.html#more-3039, accessed December 29, 2010.

117 For a Massachusetts study that pointed to increased health problems among bisexuals, see http://www.mass.gov/Eeohhs2/docs/dph/commissioner/lgbt_health_report.pdf, accessed December 29, 2010.

118 See ibid.

119 "Why Isn't Homosexuality Considered A Disorder On The Basis Of Its Medical Consequences?," cited above, n. 85. Melonakos supplies this endnote reference (n. xxii): "For an extensive survey of the articles promoting the view opposing reorientation therapy, see Diamond, Eugene, et.al, *Homosexuality and Hope*, the results of a two-year study, published by the Catholic Medical Association, p. 14, obtainable at P.O. Box 757, Pewaukee, WI, 53072 or http://www.cathmed.org. . . . See also, 'Psychiatrists Reject Therapy to Alter Gays: Efforts aimed at Turning Homosexuals into Heterosexuals are Harmful, Professional Board Declares, Even for Those Not Being Treated,' *Los Angeles Times*, Dec. 12, 1998."

120 "Why Isn't Homosexuality Considered A Disorder On The Basis Of Its Medical Consequences?" I do

not believe that Melonakos was comparing homosexuality to a lethal illness. If that, however, was her intent, I would take issue with that language.

121 See, e.g, Martin Kantor, *Homophobia: Description, Development, and Dynamics of Gay Bashing* (Westport, CT: Praeger, 1998). According to Cantor, ibid., 3, "Most homophobes tend to be *dereistic*. They live in a world all their own, where reality consists of myths substituted for facts and maintained in the face of evidence to the contrary."

122 From his letter to the *New York Times*, quoted in the NARTH Bulletin, Volume 1, Number 3, July, 1993, 7.

123 For Dr. Scasta's interview on NPR, see http://www.npr.org/templates/story/story.php?storyId=90365869, accessed December 29, 2010. The headline from the staunchly liberal NPR read, "Homosexuality Panel Squelched by Gay Activists."

124 http://www.washingtontimes.com/news/2008/may/02/gay-activists-shut-down-apa-panel/, accessed December 29, 2010.

125 There is currently intense pressure on the APA to depathologize GID, and the battle is hardly being played out on scientific grounds alone; cf., e.g., http://www.transadvocacy.org/?p=54, accessed December 29, 2010, calling for the removal of Dr. Kenneth Zucker from the APA's DSM-V Task Force (for which see above, Chapter Three, n. 30).

Chapter 14

1 The title for this chapter was inspired by the December 17th, 2001 article by John Haskins, "It's 1984 in Massachusetts – And Big Brother Is Gay," currently available at http://www.theinteramerican.org/commentary/157-its-1984-in-massachusetts-and-big-brother-is-gay.html, accessed November 24, 2010.

2 See the NARTH article on this at http://www.narth.com/docs/persecution.html. On his blog, Mullan describes himself as "a humble and harmless professor of history and religious studies at Cape Breton University who is overwhelmed by the insanity of life in the twenty-first century." See http://sleepyoldbear.wordpress.com/about-2/, both accessed November 24, 2010.

3 http://robgagnon.net/articles/homosexHateCrimeFull2.pdf, 5, accessed November 24, 2010.

4 Ibid.

5 Ibid.

6 http://www.msnbc.msn.com/id/16696521/, accessed November 24, 2010.

7 Ibid.

8 Ibid.

9 Ibid.

10 Washington ultimately called foul and fought back: "On July 2, 2007, Washington appeared on Larry King Live on CNN, to present his side of the controversy. According to Washington, he never used the 'F Word' in reference to Knight, but rather blurted it out in an unrelated context in the course of an argument 'provoked' by [fellow-actor Patrick] Dempsey, who, he felt, was treating him like a 'B-word,' a 'P-word,' and the 'F-word,' which Washington said conveyed 'somebody who is being weak.'" See http://en.wikipedia.org/wiki/Isaiah_Washington; for the Larry King transcript, see http://transcripts.cnn.com/TRANSCRIPTS/0707/02/lkl.01.html, both accessed November 24, 2010.

11 *The Tragedy of Today's Gays* (New York: Jerry P. Tarcher/Penguin, 2005), 3.

12 http://www.amazon.com/Thats-Mr-Faggot-You-Further/dp/1555834965/ref=sr_1_3?ie=UTF8&s=books&qid=1262104499&sr=8-3, accessed November 24, 2010.

13 For the video clip, see http://www.youtube.com/watch?v=tR7EPk-f-Lo, accessed November 24, 2010.

14 For Savage's explanation (and attack on Peter LaBarbera of Americans for Truth), see http://slog.thestranger.com/slog/archives/2010/01/11/what-can-you-say-about-peter-labarbera-at-this-point-besides; for LaBarbera on Savage, see http://americansfortruth.com/news/video-nonmonogamy-advocate-dan-savage-uses-adopted-child-to-promote-homosexual-marriage.html, both accessed November 24, 2010.

15 Cf., e.g., Dan Savage's (and Keith Olberman's) attack on some members of the "religious right" at http://www.youtube.com/watch?v=Zg6QKZ2dSb8; Perez Hilton's attacks on Carrie Prejean also come to mind, for which see http://www.wnd.com/?pageId=95743; for Hilton's apology for being part of the "bullying" problem (but without any reference to Carrie Prejean), see now http://www.cultureandmedia.com/articles/2010/20101013174416.aspx, all accessed November 24, 2010.

16 http://politicususa.com/en/Olbermann-Scott-Brown, accessed November 24, 2010.

17 http://www.mediaite.com/tv/keith-olbermann-apologizes-for-attacking-scott-brown-too-lightly/, accessed November 24, 2010. Olbermann stated that there was outrage from the right about his comments whereas, he claimed, the very people attacking him said worse things about President Obama

in their sleep. If this is true – and I'm not saying that it is – it only further illustrates the hyper-sensitivity of which we have been speaking in this chapter. You can say almost anything you want about anyone in politics these days, on the right or on the left, as long as you don't criticize gays or use "the f- word."

18   http://www.encyclopedia.com/doc/1G1-160292367.html, accessed November 24, 2010.

19   Note that Tammy Bruce began her chapter "Pot. Kettle. Black. The Hypocrisy of the Gay Establishment" (in *The New Thought Police: Inside the Left's Assault on Free Speech and Free Minds* [New York: Three Rivers Press, 2001], 57-85), with this citation: "All animals are equal, but some animals are more equal than others," George Orwell, *Animal Farm.*

20   Paulo Freire, *Pedagogy of the Oppressed* (repr., New York: Continuum, 2000), 45. For Freire, ibid., this is the goal: "Because it is a distortion of being more fully human, sooner or later being less human leads the oppressed to struggle against those who made them so. In order for this struggle to have meaning, the oppressed must not in seeking to regain their humanity (which is a way to create it), become in turn oppressors of the oppressors, but rather restorers of the humanity of both."

21   Marvin E. Frankel, *Faith and Freedom: Religious Liberty in America* (New York: Hill and Wang, 1994), 112.

22   Already in 1994, trial lawyer Roger Magnuson could write, "The intolerance is almost entirely one way. Homosexual speakers are not generally shouted down, disinvited, or threatened. But those who do not share their views often remain silent for fear of loss of academic status, personal intimidation, or physical safety. Many voices that need to be heard are not." See his *Informed Answers to Gay Rights Questions* (Sisters, OR: Multnomah, 1994), 17; for relevant examples, see 14-17, 20-21.

23   Charles Winecoff, "Love, War – and Gay Marriage," http://bighollywood.breitbart.com/cwinecoff/2009/03/19/love-war-and-gay-marriage/, accessed May 23, 2010, my emphasis.

24   http://www.washingtonpost.com/wp-dyn/content/article/2009/04/09/AR2009040904063_pf.html, accessed November 24, 2010.

25   Ibid.

26   Ibid.

27   Cited in Maggie Gallagher, "Banned in Boston: The coming conflict between same-sex marriage and religious liberty," *The Weekly Standard*, Volume 11, Issue 33, May 15, 2006, http://www.afa.net/websites/weeklystandard_05_15_2006.htm. For opposition to her appointment by the president, see, e.g., http://americansfortruth.com/news/obama-eeoc-appointee-chai-feldblum-would-turn-christians-and-moral-foes-of-homosexuality-into-second-class-citizens.html, both accessed November 24, 2010.

28   See her article "Moral Conflict and Conflicting Liberties," in Laycock, Picarello, Jr., and Wilson, *Same-Sex Marriage and Religious Liberty*, 123-156, here citing 156.

29   http://www.washingtonpost.com/wp-dyn/content/article/2010/12/17/AR2010121707043.html, accessed December 22, 2010.

30   http://www.change.org/petitions/view/tell_the_apple_itunes_store_to_remove_anti-gay_anti-choice_iphone_application, emphasis in the original, accessed December 22, 2010.

31   http://www.glaad.org/tellapple/. To read the Manhattan Declaration, which cannot rationally be called "hateful" in any sense of the word, see http://www.manhattandeclaration.org/the-declaration/read.aspx, both accessed December 22, 2010.

32   Cited in http://www.wnd.com/index.php?pageId=63459, accessed November 24, 2010.

33   See http://americansfortruth.com/news/civil-wrongs-in-the-name-of-civil-rights-the-crystal-dixon-firing.html, accessed April 27, 2010.

34   For an excellent critique of Dixon's firing along with a defense of the "gay is not equal to black" concept (for which also see Chapter Six, above), see Robert Gagnon, http://www.robgagnon.net/Toledo%20University%20President%20Suspends%20Administrator.htm; for a gay *defense* of the dismissal, see http://www.pamshouseblend.com/showDiary.do?diaryId=5329; for a "conservative" gay critique, see http://www.gaypatriot.net/2008/05/15/on-crystal-dixon-the-problem-of-enda/. For a follow-up report in the Toledo Free Press from Dec. 5, 2008, see http://www.toledofreepress.com/2008/12/05/crystal-dixon-sues-ut-for-rights-violations/, all accessed November 24, 2010.

35   Witness the title of his book, *Holy Bullies and Headless Monsters: Exposing the Lies of the Anti-Gay Industry* (Bloomington, IN: Xlibris, 2007).

36   Cross-posted at Pam's House Blend by the black lesbian blogger Pam Spaulding; http://www.pamshouseblend.com/showDiary.do;jsessionid=60BF2A90A45BD95217C3D77C8BD51E9B?diaryId=5329, emphasis in the original, accessed November 24, 2010.

37   Posted by Melsucceeded @ Sat May 10, 2008 at 18:23:54 PM CDT.

38   http://joemygod.blogspot.com/2008/05/university-official-canned-for-anti-gay.html,   accessed November 24, 2010.

39   KatRose @ Fri May 09, 2008 at 20:22:39 PM CDT.

40   Dagon @ Fri May 09, 2008 at 21:08:29 PM CDT.

41   Darnell Sherman, September 20, 2010; http://letters.ocregister.com/2010/09/20/gay-rights-black-struggle-not-the-same/, accessed November 24, 2010.

42   http://www.robgagnon.net/Toledo%20University%20President%20Suspends%20Administrator.htm, accessed November 24, 2010; Gagnon added, "Of course, generally people don't wake up one morning and say, 'I think I'll be a homosexual.' Yet that is different from arguing that homosexual development is always and only something "given" like race and sex. Even the Kinsey Institute has acknowledged that nine out of ten persons who have experienced same-sex attractions have experienced at least one shift on the Kinsey spectrum from 0 to 6 during their life; six out of ten experienced two or more shifts. The intensity of impulses, and sometimes even their direction, can and often do change over time." His whole letter should be read carefully.

43   http://www.wnd.com/index.php?pageId=63459, accessed November 24, 2010.

44   http://www.utoledo.edu/studentaffairs/lgbt/resources.html, accessed November 24, 2010.

45   Ibid.; see more fully http://www.spectrumut.org/home.html; when I accessed the home page at 12:42AM, December 31, 2009, the pop-up ad asked, "Is your wardrobe gay enough?"

46   Downloaded as a Microsoft Word document from the Spectrum home page, December 31, 2009.

47   As of this writing, Dixon is suing for reinstatement based on a violation of her civil rights.

48   http://americansfortruth.com/news/prof-gagnons-open-letter-to-u-of-toledo-re-suspension-of-crystal-dixon.html, accessed November 24, 2010.

49   http://www.splcenter.org/get-informed/intelligence-report/browse-all-issues/2010/winter/10-myths. Evelyn Schlatter is a professor at Columbia State Community College; see http://eschlatter. columbiastate.edu/. One of her previous articles was, "Drag's a Life: Women, Gender, and Cross-Dressing in the Nineteenth-Century West." See http://eschlatter.columbiastate.edu/Office_Hours. htm. For other articles by Robert Steinback, see http://www.awarela.org/author/robert-steinback/; all accessed November 26, 2010.

50   http://splcenter.org/get-informed/intelligence-report/browse-all-issues/2010/winter/the-hard-liners, accessed November 26, 2010, my emphasis.

51   "10 Anti-Gay Myths Debunked," cited above, n. 49.

52   Among the other "anti-gay myths" listed is, "Gay people can choose to leave homosexuality," despite substantial scientific and anecdotal evidence that some people can, in fact, leave homosexuality (see above, Chapters Twelve and Thirteen). Another is, "Allowing homosexuals to serve openly would damage the armed forces," which would mean that leaders in our American military that support "Don't Ask Don't Tell," along with many congressional leaders, would all be guilty of propagating a demonizing myth. Amazing! Another alleged myth is, "Hate crime laws will lead to the jailing of pastors who criticize homosexuality and the legalization of practices like bestiality and necrophilia," whereas pastors have already been jailed for this (see the examples cited in this chapter), while some groups have argued for the legalizing of bestiality based on principles of "diversity" (see above, Chapter Eight). Still another alleged myth is that, "Homosexuals are more prone to be mentally ill and to abuse drugs and alcohol," yet the SPLC report acknowledges that these things exist among gays and lesbians yet blames these conditions on homophobia! (For more on this question, see above, Chapter Thirteen.) See further my article, "The Southern Poverty Law Center Debunks Itself," http://voiceofrevolution.askdrbrown. org/2010/11/29/the-southern-poverty-law-center-debunks-itself/; for other strident criticisms of the SPLC's latest list, cf., e.g., http://www.cnsnews.com/news/article/meese-southern-poverty-law-center-despic (where former Attorney General Ed Meese called the list "despicable"; http://www.coralridge. org/partnercentral/ministrynewsdetail.aspx?id=261; all accessed December 22, 2010. Note also that Franck, cited above, n. 29, refers to the SPLC as "a once-respected civil rights organization."

53   Quoted in George Archibald, "Changing minds: Former gays meet resistance at NEA convention," *The Washington Times*, July 27, 2004, p. A2; cf. http://goliath.ecnext.com/coms2/gi_0199-534617/ Changing-minds-Former-gays-meet.html. In September, 2009, Rep. Steve King led an unsuccessful attempt to have Jennings removed from his post, stating, "Despite serving as the 'safe schools' czar, Jennings has no experience keeping students safe or keeping our schools drug free. Jennings is committed to the 'safety' of only a narrow portion of American students, while expressing disdain for religion and traditional values. President Obama should fire Kevin Jennings immediately." See http://cnsnews.com/ news/article/fiscal-commission-calls-elimination-safe, where on November 10, 2010, it was reported that, "A draft report by the president's National Commission on Fiscal Responsibility and Reform calls for, among other items, eliminating a division of the Education Department run by one of the most controversial appointees in the Obama administration: Kevin Jennings, the safe schools czar." Both web addresses accessed November 10, 2010.

54   http://www.wnd.com/index.php?fa=PAGE.view&pageId=114779, accessed November 10, 2010.

55 http://www.youtube.com/watch?v=BWxOKOcf3zQ&feature=player_embedded, accessed November 10, 2010.
56 http://www.boxturtlebulletin.com/2009/11/07/16442, accessed November 10, 2010.
57 For the argument that "hate crimes" against gays are really "thought crimes," see, e.g., http://www.wnd.com/index.php?fa=PAGE.view&pageId=89786, accessed November 24, 2010.
58 Ibid.
59 See Chris Kempling, Psy.D., R.C.C., "Against The Current: The Cost Of Speaking Out For Orientation Change," in the *NARTH Bulletin*, Vol. 13/2 (August, 2005), 30 (with some details of his own case as well); http://www.narth.com/menus/NARTHBulletinAugust2005.pdf, accessed November 9, 2010.
60 http://www.robgagnon.net/homosexHateCrimePart3.htm; according to the complaint lodged against Whatcott, "The material referred to gay people as sodomites and said that gay, lesbian and transgendered people were sick and predatory." See http://www.shrc.gov.sk.ca/pdfs/SHRC2005ARnew.pdf, 18, both accessed November 9, 2010.
61 http://www.stephenboissoin.com/letter.html, accessed May 30, 2010, but no longer available at that site.
62 Ibid.
63 Ibid.
64 http://www.slapupsidethehead.com/2007/12/free-speech-hate-speech/, accessed November 24, 2010.
65 Cited at http://stephenboissoin.com/downloads/scan013_20091203_180444[1].pdf, 2, accessed May 30, 2010, but no longer available at that site.
66 This was widely reported in conservative Christian circles; see, e.g., WND's article, "Government to pastor: Renounce your faith!", http://www.wnd.com/index.php?fa=PAGE.view&pageId=66704, accessed November 24, 2010.
67 http://www.huffingtonpost.com/eugene-volokh/stop-all-disparaging-rema_b_106360.html; for more on Prof. Volokh, see http://www.law.ucla.edu/volokh/. Both accessed May 16, 2010.
68 http://joemygod.blogspot.com/search?q=boisson, accessed November 24, 2010.
69 http://www.slapupsidethehead.com/2009/12/hateful-letter-cleared-as-free-speech/; see further http://www.cbc.ca/canada/calgary/story/2009/12/04/calgary-court-gay-human-rights-ruling.html, both accessed November 24, 2010.
70 http://www.wnd.com/?pageId=17314, accessed November 24, 2010. See further Rory Leishman, *Against Judicial Activism: The Decline of Freedom and Democracy in Canada* (Montreal: McGill-Queen's University Press, 2006).
71 http://www.culturalrenewal.ca/qry/page.taf?id=146; http://www.cardus.ca/comment/article/339/, accessed November 24, 2010.
72 http://www.justice.gouv.qc.ca/english/ministere/dossiers/homophobie/homophobie-a.htm, my emphasis, accessed November 24, 2010.
73 http://www.justice.gouv.qc.ca/english/publications/rapports/pdf/homophobie-a.pdf, 7, accessed November 24, 2010.
74 http://www.justice.gouv.qc.ca/english/publications/rapports/pdf/homophobie-br-a.pdf; in detail, see http://www.justice.gouv.qc.ca/english/publications/rapports/pdf/homophobie-a.pdf. For the policy's definition of homophobia, see ibid., 11.
75 See Douglas Farrow, "The Government of Québec Declares War on a 'homophobic' and 'heterosexist' populace," http://www.ccrl.ca/doc/Farrow%20article%20for%20upload.pdf, 3, accessed November 24, 2010. Farrow observes that, "Of all the words bent with Orwellian cynicism into blunt ideological instruments, 'homophobia' is currently the prime example. It is time for a moratorium on its use in any discourse aspiring to intelligent debate on human sexuality." See ibid., 3-4, for a further, important discussion of the term "homophobia"; see also Colwell, "Turning the Tables with 'Homophobia,'"; Rabbi Steven Pruzansky, "Homophobia-Phobia," http://rabbipruzansky.com/2010/07/30/homophobia-phobia/, both accessed November 24, 2010. On p. 12 of the bill, it is explained that homophobia refers to "all negative attitudes leading to the rejection of and direct or indirect discrimination against gays, lesbians, bisexuals, transsexuals and transgenders, or against persons whose appearance or behaviour does not conform to masculine or feminine stereotypes." In response, Farrow, ibid., 5, exclaims, "Not much wiggle room there!"
76 "Québec Policy Against Homophobia," (see above, n. 64), 14.
77 Quoting Attorney General Weil, ibid., 7.
78 Farrow, "The Government of Québec Declares War," 12. For related thoughts, see also Douglas Farrow, *A Nation of Bastards*.
79 Farrow, "The Government of Québec Declares War," 2, citing p. 19 of the bill. Farrow, ibid., 3, is careful to point out that not everyone in the GLBT community is happy with the tenor of the bill: "They do not wish to find themselves in a society where it is not possible to enquire openly about the causes and

consequences of sexual behaviour, or to make moral claims about sexual behaviour that do not suit the people in power."

80   Page 23 of the bill, cited in Farrow, ibid., 18.

81   http://www.billmuehlenberg.com/2010/02/08/heterosexuality-a-new-hate-crime/, accessed November 24, 2010.

82   http://www.justice.gouv.qc.ca/english/publications/rapports/pdf/homophobie-a.pdf, 5.

83   Ibid., 1, n. 1. Farrow boldly calls for the bill to be retracted and repudiated ("The Government of Québec Declares War," 18); see also ibid., 4, where Farrow, a professor of Christian Thought at McGill University noted, "Consider the fate of two of my McGill colleagues, whose only crime was to answer the government's call for an expert opinion on the history and social merits of reserving the category of marriage for stable heterosexual unions. Their email systems were jammed by a risible petition circulated by something called Project Interaction: The Gay, Lesbian, Bisexual and Two-Spirit Initiative of the McGill School of Social Work (a quite unofficial body, I hasten to add, which presumably wishes to see the definition of marriage expanded to include communities of three or more). Neither their academic work nor their personal views would support a charge of homophobia, on any definition, against these scholars. Yet the petition boldly asserts that it is 'unacceptable and unethical' for the university even to employ such obvious enemies of the people. So much for civil discourse."

84   http://www.alliancedefensefund.org/news/story.aspx?cid=4899, accessed April 27, 2010.

85   Ibid.

86   Ibid.

87   Ibid.

88   Ibid.

89   As reported in http://www.wnd.com/index.php?fa=PAGE.view&pageId=144881; the case has been widely reported online. For a weak attempt to defend the university, see http://studentactivism. net/2009/05/02/julea-ward-and-client-referral/#more-2082. Pastor Joe Coffman was not overstating things when he entitled his editorial about this case, "When conscience is criminalized." See http:// www.onenewsnow.com/Perspectives/Default.aspx?id=529674, all sites accessed April 27, 2010.

90   http://www.foxnews.com/us/2010/07/28/court-university-expel-student-opposes-homosexuality/, accessed July 28, 2010.

91   For discussion of the larger issue of counseling ethics and freedom of religion and conscience, see, e.g., http://www.alliancedefensefund.org/Home/ADFContent?cid=4395 and http://wthrockmorton.com/ tag/american-counseling-association/, both with further links; see also http://wthrockmorton.com/apa-resolution-on-religious-religion-based-andor-religion-derived-prejudice/, all accessed November 24, 2010.

92   http://www.adftruthandtriumph.org/200805/emily.html, accessed July 12, 2010.

93   Ibid.

94   Ibid.

95   Ibid. Ultimately, the entire department in question was shut down after the university's internal investigation.

96   http://www.israelnationalnews.com/News/News.aspx/138437, accessed July 12, 2010.

97   Ibid.

98   See http://www.huffingtonpost.com/2010/07/06/yeruham-leavitt-ben-gurio_n_636927.html, accessed July 12, 2010.

99   Ibid.

100 http://m.news-gazette.com/news/university-illinois/2010-07-09/instructor-catholicism-ui-claims-loss-job-violates-academic-free, accessed July 12, 2010.

101 Ibid.

102 See, e.g., Roger Kimball, *Tenured Radicals: How Politics Has Corrupted Our Higher Education* (3rd ed;, Lanham, MD: Ivan Dee, 2008); Alan Charles Kors and Harvey A. Silvergate, *The Shadow University: The Betrayal of Liberty on America's Campuses* (New York: Free Press, 1999); Dinesh D'Souza, *Illiberal Education: The Politics of Race and Sex on Campus* (New York: Free Press, 1998); David Horowitz, *Reforming Our Universities: The Campaign for an Academic Bill of Rights* (Washington, DC: Regnery, 2010).

103 See, e.g., http://www.ledger-enquirer.com/2010/07/29/1211810_professor-fired-for-remark-on.html, accessed August 5, 2010.

104 http://www.billmuehlenberg.com/2010/02/08/heterosexuality-a-new-hate-crime/, accessed November 24, 2010.

105 http://www.christian.org.uk/wp-content/downloads/marginchristians.pdf,   http://www. billmuehlenberg.com/2010/02/08/heterosexuality-a-new-hate-crime/, accessed November 24, 2010.

The report totals 84 pages and deals with many other examples unrelated to homosexuality.
106 *Marginalising Christians*, 13.
107 Ibid.
108 Ibid., 34.
109 Ibid., See Sunday program, BBC Radio 4, 23 August 2009. For additional instances, see *Marginalising Christians*, 39-40.
110 Ibid., 36, my emphasis.
111 For another situation in which Summerskill responded with less grace, see above, Chapter One.
112 *Marginalising Christians*, 36.
113 Ibid., 37.
114 Ibid., 38.
115 Ibid., 39-40; see further http://www.melaniephillips.com/diary/archives/001518.html, accessed May 16, 2010.
116 The story has been widely reported; see, e.g., http://www.worldmag.com/articles/10257; https://www.christianpost.com/article/20050217/philly-five-freed-from-undue-charges/; for a video of the arrest, see http://www.youtube.com/watch?v=K1m90cBzIN8&feature=related, all accessed November 26, 2010. There were originally eleven people arrested, but charges against only five of the group remained until the judge dismissed them in 2005.
117 *Marginalising Christians*, 40.
118 For similar instances of this, see the description of the San Francisco gay pride event, Chapter Eight, above.
119 *Marginalising Christians*, 47; for the very similar experience of San Diego firemen who were forced to participate in the San Diego gay pride event, see above, Chapter Eight.
120 *Marginalising Christians*, 48.
121 Ibid.
122 Ibid., 68-69.
123 The March 11, 2006 headline in the *Boston Globe* read, "Catholic Charities stuns state, ends adoptions." See http://www.boston.com/news/local/articles/2006/03/11/catholic_charities_stuns_state ends_adoptions/, accessed November 24, 2010. For further background, including the fact that the organization had previously placed thirteen children into same-sex households ("a legal accommodation in the name of a greater social good") before reversing this policy, see http://www.catholic.org/featured/headline.php?ID=3136; for enlightening interaction on this on a gay watchdog website, see http://www.boxturtlebulletin.com/2010/08/17/25493 (note in particular the comments), all accessed November 24, 2010.
124 *Marginalising Christians*, 61-62.
125 http://gay.brighton.co.uk/, my emphasis; accessed April 29, 2010.
126 See http://news.bbc.co.uk/2/hi/uk_news/england/southern_counties/4546976.stm, accessed April 29, 2010.
127 *Marginalising Christians*, 62.
128 http://www.telegraph.co.uk/news/newstopics/religion/7668448/Christian-preacher-arrested-for-saying-homosexuality-is-a-sin.html, accessed May 2, 2010.
129 Ibid.
130 http://www.topix.com/forum/news/gay/T49S6RPRB87E47II6#comments, accessed May 2, 2010. A number of other comments were moderate and fair, such as, "As the paper has a Tory slant, wonder how accurate the story is. If it is true, it is most definitely a case of suppression of speech, but the UK is not a country guaranteeing freedom of speech."
131 http://www.thisislondon.co.uk/standard/article-23893013-christian-couple-in-fostering-fight.do, accessed November 1, 2010.
132 Ibid.
133 Cf., e.g., David Limbaugh, *Persecution: How Liberals Are Waging War Against Christianity* (Washington, DC: 2003), see Index under "homosexual agenda" and "homosexuality"; among books previously cited, see, e.g., Wildmon, *Speechless: Silencing the Christians*; Folger, *The Criminalization of Christianity*; Sears and Osten, *The Homosexual Agenda*; Bruce, *The New Thought Police*, esp. 57-85. It is common for those who claim that gay activism is not a threat to religious liberties and freedoms of conscience to attempt to refute the accuracy of some of the many examples cited in these books, most all of which, however, have been carefully documented, to my knowledge. Nonetheless, even if some of the examples could be dismissed (and I'm not personally aware of any cited in these books that can be dismissed), the cumulative evidence of accurately reported cases is overwhelming and undeniable.
134 Among the many examples provided on the Citizens for Community Values site are: "Police

psychologist Dr. Michael Campio was discriminated against and fired under Minneapolis' [MN] 'sexual orientation' law because he supported a pro-family group which believes homosexual behavior is wrong"; "Ann Arbor [MI] police detective Richard Stern, president of the local police officers union, was fired for violating the city's 'sexual orientation' ordinance by asking a candidate for Police Chief at a public forum if she supported the 'gay rights' agenda." See http://www.ccv.org/wp-content/uploads/2010/10/Religious-Persecution-homosexual-agenda.pdf, accessed November 24, 2010.

135   http://www.cultureandfamily.org/articledisplay.asp?id=448&department=CFI&categoryid=cfreport, accessed April 28, 2010.

136   Ibid. According to the report, "Despite the 'Cootie Shots' program's appeal to 'diversity,' the play is little more than a cover to promote homosexuality. It was developed by the theatrical group 'Fringe Benefits,' which calls itself a 'coalition of theater activists dedicated to building bridges between gay, lesbian, bisexual and transgender (GLBT) youth and their straight peers, teachers and parents.' The Gay, Lesbian and Straight Education Network (GLSEN), which also created a classroom activity guide, has endorsed the course."

137   http://www.billmuehlenberg.com/2010/04/17/when-the-thought-police-come-knocking-on-your-door/, accessed April 28, 2010. The law intersects directly with the material covered in this chapter but is much broader. For discussion of how the bill relates to homosexual issues, see the comments following the article.

138   Ibid.

Chapter 15

1   Mitchell Gold, ed., with Mindy Drucker, *Crisis: 40 Stories Revealing the Personal, Social, and Religious Pain and Trauma of Growing Up Gay in America* (Austin, TX: Greenleaf Book Group Press, 2008).

2   "While We're At It," *First Things*, August, 2001, 87.

3   http://www.suspectthoughtspress.com/califia.html, accessed September 1, 2009.

4   http://www.villagevoice.com/2000-06-20/news/family-values/, accessed October 31, 2010.

5   New York: Plume, 2000.

6   Mel White, *Religion Gone Bad: The Hidden Dangers of the Christian Right* (New York: Jeremy P. Tarcher/Penguin, 2006), 1, note *.

7   Dr. Christl Ruth Vonholdt, "The Deconstruction of Marriage and Family," http://www.narth.com/docs/deconstruction.pdf, accessed November 23, 2010.

8   Noelle Howey, in Meredith Maran, ed., with Angela Watrous, *50 Ways to Support Gay and Lesbian Equality* (Maui, Hawaii; San Francisco: Inner Ocean Publishing, 2005), 27.

9   Ibid., 28.

10   See, e.g., http://www.cathedralofhope.com/documents/sermons/20070304-9a.pdf, accessed November 23, 2010.

11   Theologians would be quick to point out that God transcends gender and that He is neither male nor female. Rather, He combines the spiritual and personal qualities of each gender, which is why Genesis states that God created human beings "in His image and according to His likeness .... Male and female He created them" (see Genesis 1:27). Titles such as "Father," then, are meant to convey deep spiritual lessons (see, e.g., Floyd McClung, *The Father Heart of God: Experiencing the Depths of His Love for You* [Eugene, OR: Harvest House, 2004]), rather than to promote sexism, and it is these lessons that are lost in the gay change of "Father" to "Creator."

12   For details, see Arthur Goldberg, *Light in the Closet: Torah, Homosexuality and the Power to Change* (Beverly Hills: Red Heifer Press, 2008), 283-284. Goldberg explains (ibid., n. 27), "The first 'blessing' is apparently meant to be recited before initiating hormone treatments preparatory to surgery,' the second, upon commencement of surgery, and the third, upon completion of surgery. This may rightly strike the reader as bizarre."

13   Ben Harris, in http://www.somethingjewish.co.uk/articles/2819_gay_prayer_slammed.htm, accessed October 31, 2010.

14   Ibid.

15   Making this all the more distasteful is the fact that the prayer is based on the patriarch Jacob's encounter with God (through His angelic messenger) in Genesis 32. For a wide-ranging, homiletical treatment, see F. B. Meyer, *Jacob: Wrestling With God* (repr., Chattanooga TN: AMG Publishers, 2001).

16   Ibid. For the inclusion of gays in the new Conservative Jewish prayer book, see http://www.advocate.com/News/Daily_News/2010/09/17/Gays_in_Updated_Jewish_Prayer_Book/, accessed September 19, 2010.

17   See, e.g., http://www.foxnews.com/story/0,2933,267543,00.html, accessed October 31, 2010.

18   Joan Nestle, Riki Wilchins, and Clare Howell, eds., *GenderQueer: Voices From Beyond the Sexual Binary*

(Los Angeles: Alyson Publications, 2002).

19   Mollie, it may be remembered, authored the "How to Eradicate Gender or Multiply It Exponentially" card/poster, referred to in Chapter Three, above.

20   Ibid., 33. If ever people needed to be reminded that there are many troubled souls in the GLBT community, many with tragic family backgrounds, this book serves as a reminder. While readers may well want to skip over much of the very profane, openly sexual content (as I did), the painful, personal stories are quite telling. See, e.g., the chapter by Sylvia Rivera, "Queens in Exile, the Forgotten Ones," 67-85.

21   See, e.g., http://usjf.net/2010/10/court-brief-prop-8-judge-plain-wrong/, accessed October 31, 2010. These were the words of Judge Marvin Baxter.

22   For a pro-gay perspective on this, see http://www.gaylesbiantimes.com/?id=14043, accessed October 31, 2010.

23   See, e.g., http://www.foxnews.com/story/0,2933,445865,00.html, accessed October 31, 2010.

24   Julia Reischel, "Queer in the Crib," *Village Voice*, June 19th, 2007, http://www.villagevoice.com/nyclife/0725,reischel,76971,15.html, accessed October 21, 2010.

25   Ibid.

26   Quoting Whei Wong, the district spokesperson for the Douglas County School District in Castle Rock, Colorado. See "8-year-old boy returning to class *as girl*," http://www.worldnetdaily.com/index.php?fa=PAGE.view&pageId=55892. The same father quoted earlier, identified as "Dave M.," aptly observed, "I just find it ironic that they can dictate the dress style of children to make sure they don't wear inappropriate clothing, but they have no controls in place for someone wearing transgender clothing."

27   http://www.youtube.com/watch?v=Qk8LkkZMpe8&feature=related, accessed November 23, 2010.

28   http://www.youtube.com/watch?v=1jRJV8rvosA, accessed November 23, 2010.

29   "The Ontario Court of Appeals issued a decision on 2003-JUN-10 requiring the province of Ontario to provide marriage licenses to, and to register the marriages of, same-sex couples. However 73 pieces of existing legislation in the province violated this court ruling by referring to wife, husband, widow, widower, and similar sex-related terms. In order to bring the legislation in synchronism with the court decision which legalized SSM, each of these laws had to be amended to include gender-neutral language." See http://www.religioustolerance.org/hom_marb44.htm, accessed November 23, 2010.

30   http://www.foxnews.com/politics/2011/01/07/passport-applications-soon-gender-neutral/, accessed January 7, 2011. The article added: "Only in the topsy-turvy world of left-wing political correctness could it be considered an 'improvement' for a birth-related document to provide less information about the circumstances of that birth," Family Research Council president Tony Perkins wrote in a statement to Fox News Radio. "This is clearly designed to advance the causes of same-sex 'marriage' and homosexual parenting without statutory authority, and violates the spirit if not the letter of the Defense of Marriage Act." Robert Jeffress, pastor of the First Baptist Church in Dallas, agreed. "It's part of an overall attempt at political correctness to diminish the distinction between men and women and to somehow suggest you don't need both a father and a mother to raise a child successfully," said Jeffress. "(This decision) was made to make homosexual couples feel more comfortable in rearing children."

31   http://www.philly.com/philly/wires/ap/news/nation/20110108apstatedeptstepsbackongenderneutralparentage.html, accessed January 11, 2011. According to the report, "Gay and lesbian groups had applauded the initial change, which was announced with little fanfare in late December. But conservative groups criticized it as an attack on traditional marriage and family values."

32   http://www.nytimes.com/2006/11/07/nyregion/07gender.html, accessed November 23, 2010.

33   http://www.worldnetdaily.com/news/article.asp?ARTICLE_ID=52667, accessed November 23, 2010.

34   Ibid.

35   Ibid.

36   http://www.massresistance.org/docs/gen/08b/tranny_parade/part1/index.html, accessed November 23, 2010.

37   http://health.discovery.com/tv/pregnant-man/pregnant-man.html; the first part of the quote, cited in the text, above, can be found at http://www.google.com/search?sourceid=chrome&ie=UTF-8&q=%22pregnant+man%22, under "Pregnant Man: Discovery Health," both accessed November 23, 2010.

38   A Google search for "Pregnant Man" on December 13, 2008, yielded 764,000 hits.

39   *Workplace Gender Transition Guidelines: For Transgender Employees, Managers and Human Resource Professionals*, originally published by the Human Rights Campaign in 2007.

40   http://www.hrc.org/documents/HRC_CEI_2010_Survey_NOT_FOR_SUBMISSION.pdf, 11, accessed November 23, 2010.

41 The bill includes the categories of sexual orientation and "gender identity" as protected classes in employment and public accommodations See, e.g., http://hr.cch.com/news/employment/061908a.asp, accessed November 23, 2010.

42 See, e.g., http://action.afa.net/Detail.aspx?id=2147483698, accessed November 23, 2010.

43 See above, Chapter Eight, with reference to the HRC and Target; similar examples can easily be multiplied.

44 Reprinted in Karla Jay and Allen Young, eds., *Out of the Closets: Voices of Gay Liberation* (New York: Douglas Book Corporation, 1972), 344.

45 *Social Work*, July 1, 2007. For a summary, see "Lesbian Professor Urges Deconstruction Of Gender" at http://www.narth.com/docs/deconstruction.html, accessed November 23, 2010.

46 Ibid. (at www.narth.com).

47 http://www.nytimes.com/2006/11/07/nyregion/07gender.html?pagewanted=print, accessed November 23, 2010.

48 Originally accessed at http://www.advocate.com/currentstory1_w.asp?id=28281 but now available at http://musingsonlifelawandgender.typepad.com/life_law_gender/2006/04/life_in_the_t_z.html and elsewhere; accessed November 23, 2010.

49 http://www.exgaywatch.com/wp/2006/03/youth-in-the-ex/, accessed November 23, 2010.

50 http://www.huffingtonpost.com/2010/03/18/norrie-may-welby-the-worl_n_502851.html, accessed May 13, 2010.

51 Ibid.

52 http://www.pinknews.co.uk/2010/03/19/australian-government-withdraws-non-specified-gender-status/, accessed May 13, 2010, my emphasis. For more on the "ze" and "hir" terminology, see above, Chapter Four; cf. also Chapter Nine. Unfortunately for May-Welby, the government quickly had a change of heart, saying that it had made a mistake and was revoking the non-gender status, as reported in the article cited here.

53 http://www.newsweek.com/2010/08/16/life-without-gender.html, accessed December 28, 2010.

54 Blurb on back cover. Not surprisingly, the back cover also carries an endorsement from Patrick Califia, discussed earlier in this chapter.

55 Nestle, Wilchins, and Howell, *Genderqueer*, 250.

56 In 1956, the Russian-born, Harvard Sociology professor Pitirim Sorokin wrote, "Divorce, desertion and scandal have ceased to be punished by public ostracism. *Many a divorced professor is teaching in our colleges*; some of them are even regarded as authorities in the fields of marriage, sexual adjustment and family," my emphasis. See *The American Sex Revolution* (Boston: Porter Sargent, 1956), 44. How many among us can even imagine the day when a professor at Harvard University would rue the number of *divorced professors* on our campuses? And would Sorokin have possibly believed that the day would come when major universities would have Queer Studies programs, and openly gay and lesbian professors – not to mentioned transgendered professors?

57 In its typical style, the *New York Post* article on this situation was entitled "YE-SHE-VA: UNIVERSITY IS RATTLED BY TRANSGENDER PROF; see http://www.nypost.com/p/news/regional/item_aYZ0rKq8eDhUrHe6My3s3O, accessed December 15, 2010.

58 http://abcnews.go.com/US/transgender-golfer-lana-lawless-sues-lpga-compete/story?id=11881508; http://www.csmonitor.com/The-Culture/Sports/2010/1202/Lana-Lawless-gets-chance-to-compete-on-LPGA-Tour-with-gender-requirement-change; http://bl102w.blu102.mail.live.com/default.aspx?wa=wsignin1.0, all accessed December 2, 2010.

59 http://www.nytimes.com/2007/02/01/garden/01renee.html?pagewanted=all, accessed December 2, 2010.

60 Renée Richards and John Ames, *No Way Renée: The Second Half of My Notorious Life* (New York: Simon & Schuster, 2007).

61 As cited in n. 59.

62 Ibid.

63 Goldberg, *Light in the Closet*, 284, notes that, "The most obvious danger [with sex-change surgery] is that after the operation the person will change his/her mind and discover him- or herself irretrievably and vitally maimed," with reference in n. 28 to this same *New York Times* article on Renée Richards, along with Lynn Conway, "A Warning for Those Considering MtF SRS," (March 16, 2007), http://ai.eecs.umich.edu/people/conway/TS/Warning.html. Conway's article mentions the unfortunate predicament of Sandra (Ian) MacDougal: "The former member of the Scots Guards says she has suffered verbal and physical abuse since her sex swap operation almost four years ago, and wishes it could be reversed. But MacDougall now finds herself trapped in a woman's body after she consulted doctors and was told the operation could never be reversed." For a clinical study, see Anne M. Lawrence, "Sexuality before and

684

after Male-to-Female Sex Reassignment Surgery," *Archives of Sexual Behavior* 34 (2005), 325-330.
64 To be clear: We are not dealing with cases in which children have ambiguous (or, dual) sexual organs, for which see above, Chapter Nine, n. 46.
65 http://ai.eecs.umich.edu/people/conway/TS/Warning.html, accessed November 23, 2010. For a transgender perspective that downplays as minimal the possibility of regret for sex-change surgery, see Joanne Herman, *Transgender Explained: For Those Who Are Not* (Bloomington, IN: Author House, 2009), 65-68.
66 Colleen Raezler, "When Dad Becomes a Woman, Things Aren't 'Perfectly Fine,'" July 22, 2009, http://www.cultureandmediainstitute.org/articles/2009/20090722161441.aspx, accessed November 23, 2010.
67 Ibid.
68 Ibid.
69 The dialogue was held at the Blumenthal Performing Arts Center in Charlotte, North Carolina.
70 See http://www.youtube.com/watch?v=ZgPAP1tQa9A&feature=player_embedded, accessed December 15, 2010. (This video clip is from MSNBC, March 23, 2007.)
71 http://articles.latimes.com/2007/dec/17/nation/na-gaydad17, accessed November 24, 2010.
72 Ibid.
73 To view my dialog with Harry Knox online, see http://coalitionofconscience.askdrbrown.org/resources/debate.html.
74 See, e.g., http://celebgalz.com/tim-petras-kim-petras-before-after-sex-change-pictures/, accessed December 15, 2010.
75 http://www.firstthings.com/ftissues/ft0411/articles/mchugh.htm, accessed November 23, 2010.
76 Ibid.
77 Ibid.
78 Ibid.
79 Ibid.
80 *Journal of Law, Medicine and Ethics*, 32 (2004), 148-158, available for download at http://papers.ssrn.com/sol3/papers.cfm?abstract_id=1006644, accessed December 15, 2010.
81 By Richard J. Wassersug, Ph.D., Sari A. Zelenietz, B.S., and G. Farrell Squire, B.S., in *Archives of Sexual Behavior*, 33 (2004), 433–442, available online at http://www.springerlink.com/content/hr8n121051x2t45n/fulltext.pdf, accessed December 15, 2010.
82 As cited in n. 75.
83 September 28, 2009, "Our Sexual Identity Crisis," http://www.americanthinker.com/2009/09/our_sexual_identity_crisis.html, accessed December 15, 2010.
84 Cited at http://biid-info.org/The_Right_to_Define_Oneself_-_How_Far_Should_it_Go%3F_source, accessed December 15, 2010. Those rightly shocked by such statements can find more information at the BIID (Body Identity Integrity Disorder) website. While we do well to have sympathy for people who struggle with this, we must not forget that the condition is rightly classified as a disorder.
85 http://www.stuff.co.nz/national/709154, accessed December 15, 2010.
86 See Anne A. Lawrence, M.D., Ph.D. (a male-to-female psychologist), "Clinical and Theoretical Parallels Between Desire for Limb Amputation and Gender Identity Disorder," *Archives of Sexual Behavior* (35), 263-278, available online at http://www.annelawrence.com/publications/amputation-GID.pdf, accessed December 15, 2010. The abstract begins by saying, "Desire for amputation of a healthy limb has usually been regarded as a paraphilia (*apotemnophilia*), but some researchers propose that it may be a disorder of identity, similar to Gender Identity Disorder or transsexualism." Cf. further Duke, "Our Sexual Identity Crisis," who makes reference to gender dysphoria, "which is the persistent feeling that one is a member of one sex trapped in the body of the other" and what is now called "body dysphoria," defined as the "persistent feeling that a certain body part, such as an arm or leg (or multiple body parts), doesn't belong on one's body."
87 *The Atlantic Monthly* 283:6 (December 2000), 72-84; see http://www.theatlantic.com/magazine/archive/2000/12/a-new-way-to-be-mad/4671/, accessed December 15, 2010.
88 http://www.narth.com/docs/define.html, accessed December 15, 2010.
89 Ibid. In a May 19, 2001 article for *World Magazine*, "The real me: Self-obsessed madness is becoming more extreme," Janie B. Cheaney writes, "Since professional documentation is scarce, many psychiatrists and psychologists have never heard of apotemnophilia, but the Internet provides plenty of anecdotal evidence. In various websites and chat rooms, apotemnophiles (informally known as 'wannabes') sell photographs of amputees, review books and movies on the subject, share recollections and stories and deep longings—chiefly for the kind of 'completeness' to be found only by severing." See http://www.worldmag.com/articles/5005.
90 Elliot, as cited in n. 87, specifically http://www.theatlantic.com/magazine/archive/2000/12/a-new-way-

to-be-mad/4671/4/.

91 Ibid. Elliot further notes: "But gender-identity disorder is far more complicated than the 'trapped in the wrong body' summary would suggest. For some patients seeking sex-reassignment surgery, the wish to live as a member of the opposite sex is itself a sexual desire. Ray Blanchard, a psychologist at the University of Toronto's Clarke Institute of Psychiatry, studied more than 200 men who were evaluated for sex- reassignment surgery. He found an intriguing difference between two groups: men who were homosexual and men who were heterosexual, bisexual, or asexual. The 'woman trapped in a man's body' tag fit the homosexual group relatively well. As a rule, these men had no sexual fantasies about being a woman; only 15 percent said they were sexually excited by cross-dressing, for example. Their main sexual attraction was to other men.
"Not so for the men in the other group: almost all were excited by fantasies of being a woman. Three quarters of them were sexually excited by cross-dressing. Blanchard coined the term 'autogynephilia'- 'the propensity to be sexually aroused by the thought or image of oneself as a woman'-as a way of designating this group. Note the suffix -philia. Blanchard thought that a man might be sexually excited by the fantasy of being a woman in more or less the same way that people with paraphilias are sexually excited by fantasies of wigs, shoes, handkerchiefs, or amputees. But here sexual desire is all about sexual identity-the sexual fantasy is not about someone or something else but about yourself. Anne Lawrence, a transsexual physician and a champion of Blanchard's work, calls this group 'men trapped in men's bodies.'"

92 As cited in n. 75, above; note also the comments of Duke, "Our Sexual Identity Crisis," who notes that, "we've all heard that old stereotype of a lunatic, the guy in an asylum who thinks he is Napoleon. Now the asylums have largely been emptied, and I think I know why: we've turned the outside world into an asylum. What was once only acceptable to a small group within the scariest of walls -- detachment from reality -- has now been mainstreamed. You can be a man who thinks he is a woman, yet no straitjacket is slapped on you. It is slapped on the mouths of those who dare say self-image isn't reality.
"And that is the point: there is something called reality. When feelings tell one he is, or should be, something he is not or shouldn't be -- a girl, a legless man or Napoleon -- the sane conclusion is that you're confronted with a psychological problem, not a physical one. It may be intractable, and it is certainly easier to mutilate the body than cure the mind. But you cannot mutilate reality, only obscure it."

93 With reference to his appearance on the Dr. Phil show on January 13, 2009, Dr. Joseph Nicolosi commented, "No one on the Dr. Phil Show mentioned the implications of taking the opposite approach--actively preparing a boy for future sex-change surgery. Surgery can never truly change a person's sex. Doctors can remove the male genitals and form an imitation of the female sex organs, but they cannot make the simulated organs reproductively functional--nor can they change the DNA which exists in every cell of the boy's body to indicate that he is, and always will be, biologically a male." Email report sent out by JONAH, January 18, 2009.

94 As cited above, n. 45. From Sweden, Arvid Börtz raises these ominous concerns, "The feminist conclusion: people do not consist of two biologically different categories; they are categorized by existing norms into men and women. This was a PhD thesis at the University of Stockholm, which is like all other universities in Sweden: funded by the state to serve the latter.
The state wants this kind of research for one purpose only: to crank out 'evidence' that proves that there are no differences between men and women biologically. They say that the very concept of sex is completely made up by old cultural and social evil conservative norms, which have [the] sole purpose of suppressing all women in society.
Once the 'science is in place, these norms must be crushed without hesitation. There is no way the 'homophobes' and 'xenophobes' can oppose them.
Sweden's racial biology of the 1920s and the 21st century's science of gender are strikingly similar. Both institution[s] were founded by state to prove a scientific basis for their version of political correctness. Both were used to legitimize an extreme; one wanting to prove all differences and the other [wanting] to prove that there were no differences.
And I have disturbing fear that the science of gender will meet the same terrible destiny as racial biology. I just don't know how." See his article "Subverting Science to Ideology," originally posted January 6, 2008, at http://www.americanthinker.com/2008/01/subverting_science_to_ideology.html, but now available at http://pcwatch.blogspot.com/2008/01/americas-nazi-police-again-for-more.html, accessed December 28, 2010.

95 Not surprisingly, Scalia's comments regarding state laws against masturbation raised some eyebrows and were the object of ridicule; see, e.g., http://www.davidchess.com/words/log.20030627.html, and cf. this related news article at http://www.digitaljournal.com/article/280303, both accessed December 20, 2010. One should think twice, however, before dismissing his strongly worded and insightful dissenting

opinion over his stance on this particular issue.

96   http://www.time.com/time/nation/article/0,8599,1607322,00.html, accessed December 20, 2010, my emphasis.

97   See http://www.beyondmarriage.org; for the impressive list of signatories, see http://www. beyondmarriage.org/signatories.html; for a critique, cf. Robert George, http://www.firstthings.com/ onthesquare/?p=373. Coming from a different, deconstructionist viewpoint, see Robert Epstein, "Same-Sex Marriage Is Too Limiting," *Los Angeles Times*, December 4, 2008, reprinted at http:// theskepticalpsychologist.com/?p=50, all accessed December 20, 2010.

98   See, e.g., Dale O'Leary, *One Man, One Woman: A Catholic's Guide to Defending Marriage* (Manchester, NH: Sophia Institute Press, 2007), 193-222, and note especially the section, "The Problem with Donor Dads," with reference to John Bowe's *New York Times Magazine* article, "Gay Donor or Gay Dad?" (November 19, 2006), for which see http://www.nytimes.com/2006/11/19/magazine/19fathering. html?_r=1, accessed December 20, 2010.

99   "Roberta" was happily married to another woman (his second marriage, this one lasting more than twenty-five years) and claimed to be committed to the total infallibility of the Bible and, politically, to the right of Rush Limbaugh.

100   See above, Chapter Six, n. 82, for references. For a recent gay attempt to deny this, cf. Rob Tisinai, "A Good Man Tries and Fails," December 16, 2010, at http://www.boxturtlebulletin.com/2010/12/16/28553, critiquing the *First Things* article by left-wing evangelical leader Ron Sider, "Bearing Better Witness," at http://www.firstthings.com/article/2010/11/bearing-better-witness. Tisinai argues that "Children, yes, generally do better with their biological parents than in single-parent homes or in homes with a step-parent. However ... children often do even better than that with *adoptive* parents, as the expert witness *for* Prop 8 testified...." (his emphasis). So then, is Tisinai claiming that there are longitudinal studies with a sufficiently large database that look at all aspects of a child's development (including sexual orientation) and that indicate that a child raised by two mothers or two fathers will do just as well as an adoptive child raised by a mother and father? Putting this dubious claim aside, note the illogicality of Tisinai's argument: 1) Yes, children generally do better with their biological parents; but 2) Children of adoptive parents often do even better; therefore, 3) Children raised by gay parents should be compared to those raised by adoptive parents, and since they often do better than those raised by their biological parents, children raised in same-sex households should do better than those raised by their biological mother and father. Can he really mean this? For a conservative Christian review of the literature on adoption, see now http://www.frc.org/researchsynthesis/adoption-works-well-a-synthesis-of-the-literature, all accessed December 20, 2010. For the oft-cited affidavit of the late Professor Steven Nock, critiquing the methodology of earlier literature supporting same-sex parenting, see "Affidavit of Steven Lowell Nock, Halpern v. Toronto, [2003] 65 O.R. (3d) 161 (No. 684/00)", previously available at http://marriagelaw.cua.edu/Law/ cases/Canada/ontario/halpern/aff_nock.pdf.

101   Note carefully that I said "transcends" not "contradicts"!

102   Dawn Stefanowicz, *Out from Under: The Impact of Homosexual Parenting* (Enumclaw WA: Annotation Press, 2007), 230

103   Gerard J.M. van den Aardweg, book review of *Out from Under*, in the "Empirical Journal of Same-Sex Sexual Behavior," 1 (2007), 4.

104   Cited in van den Aardweg, ibid.

105   http://www.help4families.com/crisis.htm, accessed December 20, 2010.

106   Ibid.; see further Denise Shick and Jerry Gramckow, *My Daddy's Secret* (n.p.: Xulon, 2008).

107   David L. Tubbs, *Freedom's Orphans: Contemporary Liberalism and the Fate of American Children* (Princeton, NJ: Princeton University Press, 2007), 73; Okin's book was published in 1989 by Basic Books in New York.

108   For controversy regarding Prof. Walter Schumm's research that gay parents were far more likely to raise gay kids, see, e.g., http://www.aolnews.com/2010/10/17/study-gay-parents-more-likely-to-have-gay-kids/; http://www.boxturtlebulletin.com/2010/10/28/27609, both accessed December 15, 2010. More broadly, see nn. 109-110, immediately below. See further Patricia M. Morgan, *Children As Trophies: Examining the Evidence on Same-Sex Parenting* (Newcastle upon Tyne: The Christian Institute, 2002); Robert Lerner, Ph.D., and Althea K. Nagai, Ph.D., *No Basis: What the Studies Don't Tell Us About Same-Sex Parenting* (downloadable e-book; Washington, DC: Marriage Law Project, 2001).

109   A. Dean Byrd, "When Activism Masquerades as Science: Potential Consequences of Recent APA Resolutions," http://www.narth.com/docs/masquerades.html, citing Judith Stacey and Timothy J. Biblarz, "(How) Does the Sexual Orientation of Parents Matter," *American Sociological Review*, 66 (2001), 171 (the entire article, which analyzed twenty earlier studies, runs from 159-183). Cf. also A. Dean Byrd, "New Lesbian Parenting Study Makes Claims Unsupported by the Evidence," http://www.

narth.com/docs/makesclaims.html, both accessed December 15, 2010.

110 O'Leary, *One Man, One Woman*, 227, with reference to the *The Los Angeles Times* are "Professors Take Issue With Gay-Parenting Research," April 27, 2001, and "Report: Kids of Gays More Empathetic," by David Crary, National Writer, Associated Press. For the American Pediatric Association's statement, and the protest letter from doctors within the APA, see above, Chapter Six, n. 89. For a 2010 article in USA Today that cites a more recent Stacey-Bilbarz study, see http://www.usatoday.com/news/health/2010-01-21-parentgender21_ST_N.htm?csp=usat.me. The article cites "fatherhood expert Michael Lamb, a psychology professor at the University of Cambridge in Cambridge, England," who says "he has changed his views about gender roles based on more recent research." Lamb states, "It is well-established that children do not need parents of each gender to adjust healthily." Really?

111 For an insightful study on gender distinctions, see Steven E. Rhoads, *Taking Sex Differences Seriously* (San Francisco: Encounter Books, 2004); cf. also Simon Baron-Cohen, *The Essential Difference* (New York: Penguin, 2004). For other, related studies (not without controversy), of which there are many, see, e.g., Ann Moir and David Jessel, *Brain Sex: The Real Difference Between Men and Women* (New York: Delta, 1992); Deborah Blum, *Sex on the Brain: The Biological Differences Between Men and Women* (New York: Penguin, 1998). For a recent challenge to some of this thinking, see Rebecca M. Jordan-Young, *Brain Storm: The Flaws in the Science of Sex Differences* (Boston: Harvard University Press, 2010).

112 My appreciation to Caleb H. Price for this list.

113 Someone might protest, "What about people who are intersexed, born with ambiguous or dual genitalia, or people with chromosomes that don't conform to the normal patterns?" That actually supports the point I'm making, since such people suffer from a congenital biological and/or chromosomal abnormality, hardly the basis for challenging the male-female pattern, a pattern without which none of us would exist today. And so, we recognize this terribly difficult and stigmatizing condition for what it is – an anomaly, an abnormality – and we do our best to help these people find a way to live healthy, fulfilled and productive lives. But we don't redefine gender or sexual orientation based on a physical (or, in non-intersex cases, an emotional or psychological or even chromosomal) abnormality, any more than we tell schoolchildren that they must all use sign-language rather than talk because of the presence of a deaf child in their class. See further, above, Chapter Nine, n. 46. For the larger question of sickness, disease, physical abnormalities, and divine intent, see Michael L. Brown, *Israel's Divine Healer* (Studies in Old Testament Biblical Theology; Grand Rapids: Zondervan, 1995).

114 http://www.digitaldreamdoor.com/pages/lyrics/wedding_song.html; for different renditions of the song by Stookey, older and more recent, see, e.g., http://www.youtube.com/watch?v=L6tlo0aVII0 and http://www.youtube.com/watch?v=A1v84WKC6Pg&feature=related, all accessed November 29, 2010. This is not to say that there is not love between same-sex couples but rather that the divine intent for marriage in all its fullness is only seen in the male-female union.

115 I recognize, of course, that many children are raised in single parent homes, and that many of those children grow up to be exemplary human beings. That being said, I know very few people who would argue that a single parent home represents the *ideal* setting for a child to be raised.

116 http://www.lifesitenews.com/news/archive/ldn/2010/nov/10110901, LifeSiteNews.Com, November 9, 2011.

117 http://news.sky.com/skynews/Home/World-News/Incestuous-Grandmother-Pearl-Carter-Having-Baby-With-Grandson-Phil-Bailey-In-Indiana-USA/Article/201004415623115, accessed November 21, 2010.

118 For the biblical support for this statement, see Leviticus 18:6-18; for relevant discussion, see Richard M. Davidson, *Flame of Yahweh: Sexuality in the Old Testament* (Peabody, MA: Hendrickson, 2007), 425-446 ("Intimacy versus Incest"); Donald J. Wold, *Out of Order: Homosexuality in the Bible and the Ancient Near East* (Grand Rapids: Baker, 1998), 201-205 (dealing specifically with the incestuous situation addressed in 1 Corinthians; see elsewhere in his book for ancient Near Eastern background).

119 Ibid.

120 http://abcnews.go.com/Health/switzerland-considers-legalizing-consensual-incest-columbia-professor-accused/story?id=12395499. And notice the full headline: Professor Accused of Incest With Daughter. Teacher Says Sex Was Consensual, as Switzerland Considers Lifting Incest Ban Between Adults," and see further http://www.illinoisfamily.org/news/contentview.asp?c=35107, both accessed December 16, 2010.

121 http://www.rushlimbaugh.com/home/daily/site_121410/content/01125104.guest.html, accessed December 15, 2010.

122 http://blog.beliefnet.com/flirtingwithfaith/2010/12/are-we-on-the-road-to-legalizing-incest-the-rise-and-fall-of-taboos-in-a-changing-society.html, accessed December 27, 2010. As of this same date, a small, online debate featured on http://debates.juggle.com/should-incest-between-consenting-

adults-be-legal showed 39% saying "Yes" and 61% saying "No" to the question, "Should incest between consenting adults be legal?" Comments like this from the "Yes" side were typical: "Like any legal sexual activity, incest between two consenting ADULTS shouldn't be given a second thought."

123   http://www.youtube.com/watch?v=DA43DS2c12c, accessed November 21, 2010.

124   For comments on the documentary *Whole*, dealing with people suffering from Body Identity Integrity Disorder, see http://www.illinoisfamily.org/news/contentview.asp?c=35104, accessed December 15, 2010.

So as to provide both an extensive index and a full bibliography without adding many more pages to the print version of this book, an online index and bibliography have been provided at **www.aqueerthing.com**. Please visit there and click on Bibliography for both resources.